Linda Bailey

Fodor's 2014
LONDON

D0103642

WELCOME TO LONDON

History and tradition greet you at every turn in London; it's also one of the coolest, most modern cities in the world. If London contained only landmarks such as Westminster Abbey and Buckingham Palace, it would still rank as one of the world's great destinations, but Britain's capital is much more. People come to glimpse the royals and stop by hot galleries; to take in theater and trendy shops; to sample tea and scones or cutting-edge cuisine. When you need a break from the action, pop into a pub, relax in a park—or take a walk and make London your own.

TOP REASONS TO GO

★ **Architectural Icons:** The Tower of London and Big Ben are quintessential London.

★ **Art Museums:** From the National Gallery to the Tate Modern, a visual feast awaits.

★ **Top Theater:** Whether it's Shakespeare or avant-garde drama, the play's the thing.

★ **City of Villages:** Unique neighborhoods from Mayfair to the East End invite discovery.

★ **Shopping:** Fun markets, famous flagship department stores, chic boutiques.

★ **Parks and Squares:** Distinctive green spaces large and small are civilized retreats.

Fodor's LONDON 2014

Publisher: Amanda D'Acierno, *Senior Vice President*

Editorial: Arabella Bowen, *Executive Editorial Director*; Linda Cabasin, *Editorial Director*

Design: Fabrizio La Rocca, *Vice President, Creative Director*; Tina Malaney, *Associate Art Director*; Chie Ushio, *Senior Designer*; Ann McBride, *Production Designer*

Photography: Melanie Marin, *Associate Director of Photography*; Jessica Parkhill and Jennifer Romains, *Researchers*

Maps: Rebecca Baer, *Map Editor*; Mark Stroud, Moon Street Cartography, and David Lindroth, *Cartographers*

Production: Linda Schmidt, *Managing Editor*; Evangelos Vasilakis, *Associate Managing Editor*; Angela L. McLean, *Senior Production Manager*

Sales: Jacqueline Lebow, *Sales Director*

Marketing & Publicity: Heather Dalton, *Marketing Director*; Katherine Fleming, *Senior Publicist*

Business & Operations: Susan Livingston, *Vice President, Strategic Business Planning*; Sue Daulton, *Vice President, Operations*

Fodors.com: Megan Bell, *Executive Director, Revenue & Business Development*; Yasmin Marinaro, *Senior Director, Marketing & Partnerships*

Copyright © 2014 by Fodor's Travel, a division of Random House, Inc.

Writers: Julius Honnor, Kate Hughes, Jack Jewers, James O'Neill, Ellin Stein, Alex Wijeratna

Editors: Stephen Brewer, Robert I. C. Fisher, Jess Moss, Caroline Trefler

Production Editor: Elyse Rozelle

ISBN 978-0-7704-3215-7

ISSN 0149-631X

SPECIAL SALES

This book is available at special discounts for bulk purchases for sales promotions or premiums. For more information, e-mail specialmarkets@randomhouse.com

PRINTED IN COLOMBIA

10 9 8 7 6 5 4 3 2 1

CONTENTS

MAPS

ABOUT
THIS GUIDE

Fodor's Ratings

Everything in this guide is worth doing—we don't cover what isn't—but exceptional sights, hotels, and restaurants are recognized with additional accolades. **Fodor's**Choice ★ indicates our top recommendations, and **Best Bets** call attention to notable hotels and restaurants in various categories. Care to nominate a new place? Visit Fodors.com/contact-us.

Trip Costs

We list prices wherever possible to help you budget well. Hotel and restaurant price categories from $ to $$$$ are noted alongside each recommendation. For hotels, we include the lowest cost of a standard double room in high season. For restaurants, we cite the average price of a main course at dinner or, if dinner isn't served, at lunch. For attractions, we always list adult admission fees; discounts are usually available for children, students, and senior citizens.

Hotels

Our local writers vet every hotel to recommend the best overnights in each price category, from budget to expensive. Unless otherwise specified, you can expect private bath, phone, and TV in your room. For expanded hotel reviews, facilities, and deals visit Fodors.com.

Restaurants

Unless we state otherwise, restaurants are open for lunch and dinner daily. We mention dress code only when there's a specific requirement and reservations only when they're essential or not accepted. To make restaurant reservations, visit Fodors.com.

Credit Cards

The hotels and restaurants in this guide typically accept credit cards. If not, we'll say so.

Top Picks	Hotels &
★ **Fodor's**Choice	**Restaurants**
	▦ Hotel
Listings	↵ Number of
✉ Address	rooms
✉ Branch address	⁑⃝⁑ Meal plans
☎ Telephone	✕ Restaurant
🖷 Fax	⌕ Reservations
⊕ Website	🏛 Dress code
✍ E-mail	▭ No credit cards
▱ Admission fee	$ Price
⊙ Open/closed	
times	**Other**
Ⓜ Subway	⇨ See also
⊹ Directions or	☞ Take note
Map coordinates	⅃ Golf facilities

EXPERIENCE
LONDON

LONDON TODAY

"London," so a local saying goes "will be nice when it's finished." You'll soon get the joke— it's hard to turn a corner in the city center without finding some work-in-progress crater so vast you can only imagine what was there before. This latest wave of development started in the 1990s and was accelerated by the 2012 Olympics. Meanwhile, new neighborhoods are brought into the limelight— currently, a visit to Hoxton or Shoreditch should provide you with your quotient of London hipness—and the creative fervor that has always swirled through London like fog shows up in art galleries, designer boutiques, and theaters.

Ask any time-pressed, phlegmatic, but savvy local and they'll tell you that . . .

Today's London . . .

. . . is heading skyward.

London seized upon the occasion of the 2012 Olympics to showcase some sparkling new architecture. With the exceptions of Canary Wharf, the Swiss Re Headquarters ("the Gherkin"), the Lloyd's of London building, and the London Eye, London's skyline has traditionally been low-key, with little of the brash swagger of, say, Shanghai or Manhattan. But a spectacular crop of new architecture—the 945-foot "Helter-Skelter" Bishopsgate Tower, 740-foot Leadenhall Building "Cheese Grater," and 1,020-foot Shard—is injecting fresh adrenaline into London's otherwise staid streetscapes and revitalizing its skyline.

Some new skyscrapers, such as "The Quill" in Southwark, and the funky "Walkie-Talkie" and the "Cheese Grater" in The City, have gotten very mixed reviews. The verdict is still out on the Shard at London Bridge—designed by Enzo Piano, this irregular triangle of glass (how can such a tall building look so squat and graceless?) is the tallest building in Europe. Whatever critics and those who must look at these structures every day may say, London will never be quite the same again.

. . . is more global.

The nationalities *keep* on coming, and London now swipes the crown as one of *the* most cosmopolitan cities on earth. White Britons are in the minority for the first time (according to the 2011 Census), representing 45% of London's burgeoning 8.2 million population, while Asians make up 18%, Black Londoners 13%, European "White Others" 13%, and with a growing 5% of mixed-race residents

WHAT'S NEW

We really shouldn't begrudge it, but some of London's top cultural attractions seem to be in a Cold War upgrade arms race and are now investing heavily in new galleries, exhibits, refurbs, expansions, and assorted shiny new bells and whistles.

Look, then, for the new first-floor gallery at the Natural History Museum, where you'll find treasures like the 14th-century skull of a Barbary lion (a relic from the Tower of London's royal menagerie) to a 147-million-year-old archae-

opteryx fossil, plus moon rocks from the last Apollo mission.

Similarly, Shakespeare's Globe has constructed a new back-to-the-future, candlelit, 340-seat, Jacobean *indoor* theater—the Sam Wanamaker

adding spice to the pot, too. Now that the British Empire has come home to roost, large factions of former subjects have relocated to London, and the presence of so many international influences is changing the very essence of what it is to be British.

...is more happening.

Have you picked up a free *Evening Standard* or *Time Out London* arts-listing magazine recently? They're stuffed with an ever-groovy, bleeding-edge, and endlessly delectable smorgasbord of world-class London shows, plays, performances, recitals, readings, concerts, fashion follies, happenings, poetry slams, talks, debates, auctions, cabaret, burlesque, and esoteric or blockbuster art exhibitions. Whether it's contemporary *art* at the Frieze London art fair or experimental performances at Yellow Lounge classical music "club nights" at the Old Vic Tunnels in Waterloo, London is one of the more happening places on the planet.

...is better connected

Finally, while you buzz around town, you'll notice that the public transportation has gotten better, more frequent, more reliable, and generally more integrated—thanks, in large part, to the 2012 Olympics. Remember that although London's traffic can often seem more chaotic than New York City's, the Congestion Charge—the £10-per-day fee imposed on vehicles entering central London—has reduced both traffic and pollution.

Massive tunneling and investment continue apace on building London's flagship, high-speed, east–west Cross Rail underground railway line, which includes new interchanges at Paddington, Tottenham Court Road, and Farringdon stations, with all slated to open in 2018. In the meantime, don't miss out on a ride on one of London's smash-hit and distinctive sky-blue hire bikes—known formally as Barclay's Cycle Hire scheme—and locally as "Boris Bikes," after Boris Johnson, the mayor of London. With 8,333 bikes available at 587 docking stations around town—which now extends from East India DLR in Blackwall in the east to Shepherd's Bush in the west—you'll find (after laying out £45 for an annual pass) that the first half hour is free, an hour's a pound, and two hours is only £6.

Theatre—to exhaustively accurate historical designs.

And Tate Modern on the South Bank has invested £90 million (out of a £215 million expansion plan) to open up two new vast, underground, former oil tanks—known as The Tanks—to create a huge, spooky, and already-popular new subterranean video and performance-art space (not to mention one of London's most fashionable party venues).

WHAT'S WHERE

The following numbers refer to chapters.

2 **Westminster, St. James's,** and Royal London. This is the place to embrace the "gran turismo" label. Snap pictures of the mounted Horse Guards, watch kids clambering onto the lions in Trafalgar Square, and visit stacks of art in the fantastic national galleries. Do brave the crowds to peruse historic Westminster Abbey and its ancient narrative in stone.

3 **Mayfair and Marylebone.** You might not have the wallet for London's most prestigious shops, but remember window-shopping in Mayfair is free. Meanwhile boutique shops in Marylebone are a refreshing change from gaudy Oxford Street a few blocks south.

4 **Soho and Covent Garden.** More sophisticated than seedy these days, the heart of London puts Theaterland, strip joints, Chinatown, burger boîtes, and the trendiest of film studios side by side. Nearby Charing Cross Road is a bibliophile's bookfest. And hold tight amongst the hectic hordes in Leicester Square, London's crowd-packed answer to Times Square. Covent Garden's historic piazza is one of the busiest, most raffishly enjoyable parts of the city.

5 **Bloomsbury and Holborn.** Once the bluestocking and intellectual center of London, elegant Bloomsbury is now also a mixed business district—albeit with the mother lode of museums at its heart. The British Museum has enough amazing artifacts to keep you busy for a month of Sundays; otherwise, offerings are limited, though the Law Courts, University of London, and Lamb's Conduit Street are worth a gander.

6 **The City.** London's Wall Street might be the oldest part of the capital, but thanks to futuristic skyscrapers and a sleek blade-of-light Millennium Bridge, it looks like the newest. History fans won't be short-changed, however: head for the baroque dome of St. Paul's Cathedral; the Victorian iconography of Tower Bridge; and the grisly medieval terrors of the Tower of London.

7 **The East End.** Once famed for the noxious 19th-century slums immortalized by Charles Dickens and Jack the Ripper, today the area's become a fulcrum of London's contemporary art scene and a trendy youthquake party zone. For spit-and-sawdust sensations of market London on the weekend, dive headfirst into the wares at Spitalfields, Brick Lane (popular for curry houses and 24-hour bagel bakeries),

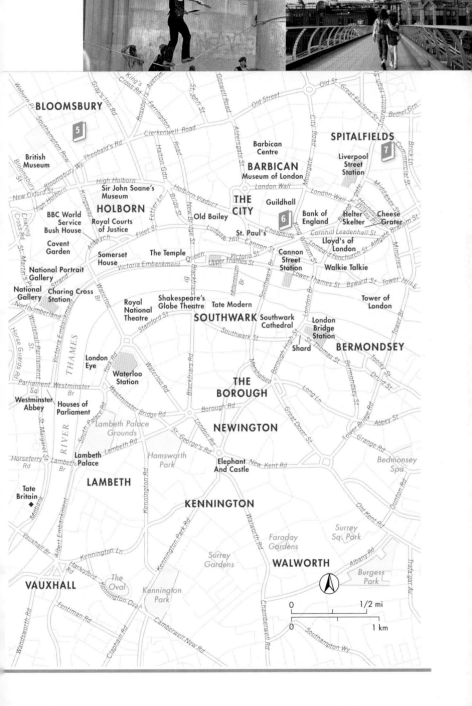

WHAT'S WHERE

and Columbia Road's much-loved flower market.

8 South of the Thames.
Die-hard culture vultures could spend a lifetime here. The Southbank Centre—including the National Theatre and Royal Festival Hall, the Haywood Gallery, Shakespeare's Globe, and Tate Modern—showcases the capital's crowning artistic glories. Or put it all in aerial perspective from high up on the London Eye.

9 Kensington, Chelsea, and Knightsbridge. Although the many boutiques of the King's Road have lost much of their heady '60s swagger, the free museums are as awe-inspiring as ever. Kensington High Street (or "High Street Ken" to locals) is slightly more affordable than the King's Road; otherwise, flash your cash at London's snazziest department stores, Harrods and Harvey Nichols.

10 Notting Hill and Bayswater. For that effortlessly hip west London demeanor, hang out in its coolest residential postal code: Notting Hill, north of Kensington. Around Portobello Road, Notting Hill Gate is a trendsetting square mile of multi-ethnicity, galleries, bijou shops, and see-and-be-seen-in restaurants. Nearby, Bayswater mixes eclectic ethnic fashions,

fresh-food shops, and Chinese restaurants.

11 Regent's Park and Hampstead. Surrounded by the supremely elegant "terraces"—in truth, mansions as big as palaces—designed by 19th-century architect John Nash, Regent's Park is a Regency extravaganza, and the nearby hilltop "villages" of Hampstead and Primrose Hill attract residents like Kate Moss and Gwyneth Paltrow.

12 Greenwich. The Royal Observatory, Christopher Wren architecture, the Old Royal Naval College, *Cutty Sark,* and the Greenwich Meridian Line all add up to one of the best excursions beyond the cut-and-thrust of central London.

13 The Thames Upstream. As an idyllic retreat from the city, stroll around London's historic gardens and enjoy the stately homes of Kew, Richmond, and Putney. Better yet, take a river cruise and fetch up at the famous maze of Hampton Court Palace.

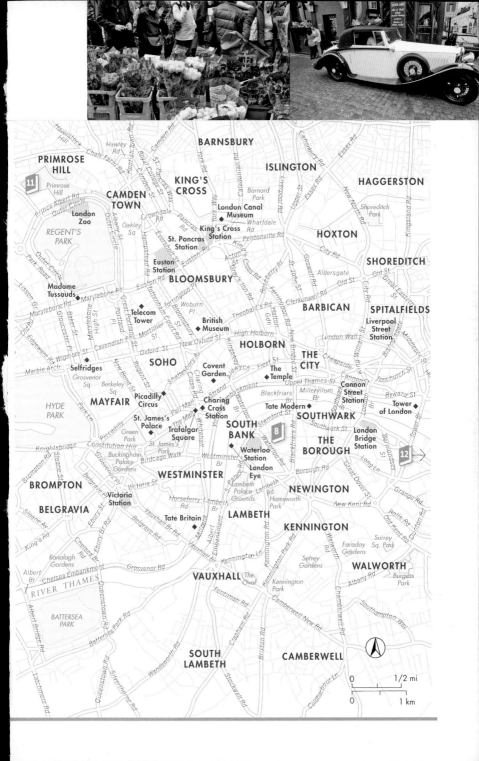

LONDON PLANNER

When to Go

The heaviest tourist season runs mid-April through mid-September, with another peak around Christmas—though the tide never really ebbs. Late spring is the time to see the countryside and the Royal parks and gardens at their freshest; fall brings autumnal beauty and fewer people. Summer gives the best chance of good weather, although the crowds are most intense. Winter can be dismal—the sun sets at 4 and it's dark by 5—but all the theaters, concerts, and exhibitions go full-speed ahead, and Christmas lights bring a touch of festive magic to the busy streets. For a schedule of festivals, check ⊕ *www.visitbritain. com.*

When Not to Go

The October "half-term," when schools in the capital take a break for a week, results in most attractions being overrun by children. The start of August can be a very busy time, and hot weather makes Tube travel a sweaty nightmare. Air-conditioning is far from the norm in London, even in hotels; so although it rarely tops 90°F, it can feel much hotter. And shopping in central London just before Christmas borders on the insane.

Addresses

Central London and its surrounding districts are divided into 32 boroughs—33, counting The City of London. More useful for navigating, however, are the subdivisions of London into postal districts. Throughout the guide we've given the abbreviated postal code for most listings. The first one or two letters give the location: N means north, NW means northwest, and so on. Don't expect the numbering to be logical, however. (You won't, for example, find W2 next to W3.) The general rule is that the lower numbers, such as W1 or SW1, are closest to the city center.

Getting Around

London is, above all, a walker's city, and will repay every moment you spend exploring on foot. But if you're in a rush, there are other options. By far the easiest and most practical way to get around is on the Underground, or "Tube." Trains run daily from early morning to late at night.

Buses crisscross London and often have their own lanes, which only buses and taxis can use. They are a great way to see London, but routes are more complicated than the Tube's; scan the route posted at the bus stop and check the number and destination on the front of the bus.

Buy an Oyster Card for £5, which will allow you to use London's transport—including bus, Tube, tram, DLR, London Overground, and most National Rail services in London—at a lower cost than using paper tickets. The plastic card can be topped up as often as you want, and your £5 deposit will be reimbursed when you hand the card back. Alternatively, buy a Travelcard pass (from £7.30 per day in the central zones 1 and 2), which offers unlimited use of the Tube, buses, and the commuter rail. Check ⊕ *www.tfl. gov.uk* for details on ongoing Tube renovations.

For further details on transport around London, see the Travel Smart section at the end of this book.

London Hours

The usual shop hours are Monday–Saturday 9–6 and Sunday 11–5. Around Oxford Street, Kensington High Street, and Knightsbridge, hours are 9:30–6, with late-night hours (until 7:30 or 8) on Wednesday or Thursday.

Many businesses are closed on Sunday and national ("bank") holidays, except in the center, where most open 10–4. Banks are open weekdays 9:30–4:30; offices are generally open 9–6.

The major national museums and galleries are open daily, mainly 10–6, and often they're open late one night a week.

Deal or No Deal?

There's no getting around it: London can be as expensive as—or even *more* expensive than—New York, Paris, or any other large global city. So it's much better to accept this fact in advance and factor it into your vacation planning, tailoring outings and trips that will reflect your interests—and your budget.

Often, booking in advance, harnessing low-season deals, and taking advantage of Internet specials for flights and hotel rooms can cut down on costs. London is also great at offering things for free (particularly the museums), and the quality of the culture, entertainment, relaxation, and general fun to be had in the city means that if you target your spending wisely, you'll go home penny-pinched but deeply satisfied.

How's the Weather?

It's a long-standing joke that Londoners—and the English in general—chat obsessively about the weather. The London drizzle generates a fatalism that kicks off any conversation with a long-suffering nod to the heavens. Winter is usually dreary, cold, and wet (with occasional snow), spring is colorful and fair, June to August can be anything from a total washout to a long, hot summer and anything in between, while autumn can be "Indian-summer" warm, cool, or mild—or all three. Come prepared for anything: layers and a brolly are your best friends. One thing is sure: it's virtually impossible to forecast London weather, but you can be fairly certain that it will *not* be what you expect.

The following are the average daily maximum and minimum temperatures for London.

WHAT IT COSTS		
	In London	**In New York**
Pair of theater tickets	£40–£90	$70–$250
Museum admission	Usually free; sometimes £4–£16	Usually $5–$25; rarely free
Fast-food value meal	£5	$6
Tall latte	£3.40	$4
Pint of beer in a pub	£3.80 and up	$6 and up
1-mile taxi ride before tip	£6	$5
Subway ride within city center	£4.50 without Oyster or Travelcard	$2.50

AVERAGE LONDON
TEMPERATURES

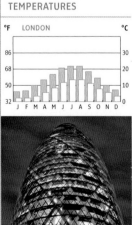

LONDON
TOP ATTRACTIONS

Westminster Abbey

(A) Steeped in history and tradition, the pillars of this great early–English Gothic edifice stand around the tombs of the great men and women who built Britain. Not only an iconic monument, the Abbey continues to play a preeminent role in the spiritual life of the nation, from the coronation of sovereigns to royal weddings and state funerals.

Buckingham Palace

(B) Not the largest or prettiest royal residence, the palace at the heart of London is nonetheless a must-see for the glimpse it affords into the life of the Royal Family. The opulence of the 19 State Rooms open to the public are jaw-dropping, and don't forget the collection of old masters and gilded state carriages at the Queen's Gallery and Royal Mews stables next door.

Tower of London

(C) The Tower is London at its majestic, historic, gory best. This is truly the heart of the kingdom—with foundations dating back nine centuries, every brick tells a grisly story, and the ax-blows and fortunes that have risen and fallen within this 20-towered mini-city provide an inexhaustible supply of intrigue.

St. Paul's Cathedral

(D) No matter how many times you've been here before, Sir Christopher Wren's masterpiece never fails to take the breath away. Climb the enormous dome, one of the world's largest, to experience the freaky acoustics of the Whispering Gallery, and higher still to the Golden Gallery for far-reaching views across London.

British Museum

(E) "Mankind's Attic" has been wowing visitors to London since 1753. Its unrivalled 8 million-strong collection spans virtually all recorded history, including

the Elgin Marbles, the Rosetta Stone, and the warrior treasures of Sutton Hoo.

Shakespeare's Globe

(F) You can catch a Shakespeare play almost every night of the year in London. But standing in the "pit" or yard with the "groundlings" on a floor of sawdust in a scrupulously re-created oak version of the original thatched Tudor theater for which Shakespeare wrote is a genuine thrill.

Tate Modern

(G) The world's most visited modern art gallery, and housed in the *ginormous* 1940s former Bankside Power Station, Tate Modern is a hip and hugely successful feature of London's artistic landscape. Passing judgment on the latest controversial exhibit inside the giant sloping Turbine Hall has become almost a civic duty among art-loving Londoners.

London's Central Parks

(H) A whopping 25% of London is parkland, so it is mighty hard to choose between St. James's Park (those fairy-tale views), Kensington Gardens (the beloved Peter Pan statue), Hyde Park (pedelos on the Serpentine Lido), and Regent's Park's rose gardens.

Hampton Court Palace

(I) Henry VIII's palace has a Tudor-turreted charm, augmented by Wren's touch, and a picturesque location, all of which make for a great day out—not even dour republican Oliver Cromwell, who moved here in 1653, could resist its charms.

National Gallery

(J) There are enough amazing world-class paintings here to have the most casual art enthusiast drooling with admiration. Note the raised front entrance and its great photo op: Big Ben and Nelson's Column framed by a pedestrianized Trafalgar Square.

LONDON
ROYAL LEGACY

Don't know your House of Tudor from your Houses of Parliament? Here's the lowdown on the most famous kings and queens who have influenced London, and where you can still see their mark.

Queen Mary I
(A) "Bloody Mary" (r. 1553–58, House of Tudor), the Roman Catholic daughter of Henry VIII and his first wife, Catherine of Aragon, persecuted Protestants in an attempt to reverse the Reformation and return England to Catholicism. She imprisoned her half sister, Elizabeth—daughter of Anne Boleyn—in the Tower, suspecting her of a plot against her, but there was no evidence and Elizabeth came to the throne after her death.

Edward the Confessor
(B) Edward (r. 1042–66) came to the throne in 1042 and ordered the construction of the original Westminster Abbey, which was consecrated in 1065, just a week before he died.

William the Conqueror
(C) The Battle of 1066 was won by William (r. 1066–87, House of Normandy) when he shot the then-king Harold through the eye with an arrow at the battle of Hastings. He is credited with starting the building of the White Tower in the Tower of London, though it wasn't completed until after his death.

Queen Elizabeth I
(D) The "Virgin Queen" (r. 1558–1603, House of Tudor) never married—perhaps because she thought that any man would try to wrest control from her (though she did move Robert Dudley, Earl of Leicester, into rooms close to her own at Hampton Court). She oversaw and supported a golden age of playwriting and poetry and famously inspired her troops as they prepared to battle the Spanish Armada.

Henry VIII

(E) A true Renaissance man, Henry (r. 1509–47, House of Tudor) was keen to bring new ideas to the Royal Court. All of Henry's six wives lived at Hampton Court Palace. Henry was desperate for a male heir—the main reason for having two of his wives executed: Anne Boleyn and Catherine Howard.

George III

(F) His frequent bouts of irrational behavior led to the nickname "The Mad One," but George (r. 1760–1820, House of Hanover) is now thought to have suffered from an inherited metabolic illness and often secluded himself at Kew Palace. With the Declaration of Independence in 1776, he lost the American colonies. One of the most cultured monarchs, George donated 65,000 of his books to the British Museum.

Duke and Duchess of Cambridge

(G) It's exciting to catch the Windsors and heir Prince William on a royal walkabout—so go to ⊕ *www.royal.gov.uk* and search for "Future engagements" under "the Royal Diary" section to catch the prince and his wife Catherine at a public event.

Charles I

(H) "The Martyr" (r. 1625–49, House of Stuart) is famous for losing the English Civil War, and was beheaded at Banqueting House—a twist of fate, as Charles had commissioned the palace to be decorated with paintings showing a monarch being received into heaven.

Queen Victoria

(I) Famous for the longest reign so far in British history, 63 years, Victoria (r. 1837–1901, House of Hanover) was born in, and spent her childhood at, Kensington Palace, where she learned she would become queen.

GIVE THE SPORTS SCENE A GO

London may well have hosted possibly the *best ever* summer Olympic Games in 2012, but don't expect to see many residents practicing their long jumps in Hyde Park or going for a synchronized swim across the Thames. Sport in the capital comes into its own when it's watched, rather than participated in.

If you're lucky enough to score a ticket for a big Premier League football match, you'll experience a seething, jeering mass of mockery and rude chants, especially if the opposition happens to be a rival London team. Amid all the aggression you might also catch a glimpse of why the fervor of English football (refer to it as "soccer" at your peril) makes it world sport's hottest media property.

Rugby, tennis, racing, and cricket impinge on Londoners' sporting horizons at crucial times of the year, too, but you're unlikely to see grown men crying at the outcome of finals at Wimbledon, or beating each other up about the Ashes.

Football

The English may not be the world's best when it comes to football (they last won the World Cup in 1966), but they invented the modern game, and the sport is *the* national obsession.

London's top teams—Chelsea, Arsenal, Tottenham Hotspur—are world-class (especially the first two) and often progress in the European Champions League.

It's unlikely you'll be able to get tickets for anything except the least popular Premier League games during the August–May season, despite absurdly high ticket prices—as much as £41 for a standard, walk-up, match-day seat at Chelsea, and a whopping £126 for the dearest match-day tickets at Arsenal!

You'll have a better chance of seeing a game if you avoid the top-tier teams—try Queens Park Rangers in Shepherd's Bush in west London, nearby Fulham on the Thames, or West Ham in the East End.

Arsenal. Arsenal (aka the Gunners) is historically London's most successful club. Under the managerial reign of Arsene Wenger they have shed their boring image to become proponents of tippy-tappy, attractive, free-flowing football—while hardly ever employing any English players. ✉ *Emirates Stadium, 75 Drayton Park* ☎ *020/7619–5000* ⊕ *www.arsenal.com* Ⓜ *Arsenal.*

Chelsea. Chief rivals of Manchester United in the Premier League, Champions League winners in 2012, and Premier League title and FA Cup winners in 2009 and 2010, Chelsea (aka the Blues) is owned by one of Russia's richest oligarchs, Roman Abramovich. In recent years the team has been forged into a formidable and ruthless footballing machine. ✉ *Stamford Bridge, Fulham Rd., Fulham* ☎ *0871/984–1905* ⊕ *www.chelseafc.com* Ⓜ *Fulham Broadway.*

Tottenham Hotspur. Tottenham Hotspur (aka Spurs)—bitter North London rivals of Arsenal—has underperformed for decades but there are strong hints of a revival with a bevy of England national team regulars. ✉ *White Hart Lane, 748 High Rd.* ☎ *0844/499–5000* ⊕ *www.tottenhamhotspur.com* Ⓜ *National Rail: White Hart Lane.*

West Ham. Known as "The Hammers," West Ham, despite the name, is the team of the East End. After a long period of failing to match their former glories, the Hammers have created a more consistent team, but one unlikely to claim many trophies. ✉ *Boleyn Ground, Green St.,*

Upton Park ☎ *0871/222–2700* ⊕ *www. whufc.com* Ⓜ *Upton Park.*

Cricket

At its best, Test cricket can be a slow-build of smoldering tension and unexpected excitement. At its worst, it can be too slow for the casual observer, as five-day games crawl toward a draw, or as the English weather interferes and rain stops play. Try to visit the resplendent Lord's—the home of cricket—for at least one day of a big Test match to see the upper echelons of the English class system on full public display.

Lord's. Lord's—the home of Marylebone Cricket Club (MCC)—has been hallowed cricketing turf since 1814 and MCC rules codified the game. Tickets for major Test matches are hard to come by: obtain an application form and enter the ballot (lottery) to purchase them. Forms are sent out in early December or apply online. Test Match tickets cost between £28 and £95. Much cheaper county matches (Middlesex plays here) can usually be seen by standing in line on match day. ✉ *Marylebone Cricket Club, Lord's Cricket Ground, St. John's Wood Rd., St. John's Wood* ☎ *020/7432–1000* ⊕ *www. lords.org* Ⓜ *St. John's Wood.*

Horse Racing

Derby Day. Derby Day, a flat horse race usually held in early June on Epsom Downs in Surrey, is the second-biggest social event of the flat racing calendar. Drawing crowds of 130,000—from the Queen to ruffian gypsy travelers—it's also one of the world's greatest horse races, first run in 1780. Tickets are between £20 and £110. ✉ *The Grandstand, Epsom Downs, Surrey* ☎ *0844/579–3003* ⊕ *www.epsomderby.co.uk.*

Royal Ascot. The Queen attends Royal Ascot in mid-June, driving from Windsor in an open carriage for a procession before the assembled plebs. Grandstand tickets, which go on sale in November, cost £55–£75, although some tickets can usually be bought on the day of the race (generally on Tuesday or Wednesday) for around £20. The real spectacle is the glamorous and be-hatted crowd itself, and those who arrive dressed inappropriately (jeans, shorts, sneakers) will be turned away from their grandstand seats. ✉ *Ascot Race Course, Ascot, Berkshire* ☎ *0844/346–3000* ⊕ *www.ascot.co.uk.*

Tennis

Wimbledon Lawn Tennis Championships. The Wimbledon Lawn Tennis Championships are famous for the green grass of Centre Court, Andy Murray never quite winning the Men's Final, and an old-school insistence on players wearing white.

Rain, a perennial hazard even in the last-week-of-June–first-week-of-July timing, has been banished on Centre Court by the addition of a retractable roof.

Whether you can get Centre Court tickets is literally down to the luck of the draw, because there's a ballot system (lottery) for advance purchase. For more information, see their Web site. You can also buy entry to roam matches on the outside courts, where even the top-seeded players compete early on.

Five hundred show court tickets are also sold daily, but these usually go to those prepared to stand in line all night. ✉ *The All England Lawn Tennis Club, Church Rd.* ☎ *020/8944–1066* ⊕ *www. wimbledon.com.*

FREE (AND ALMOST FREE) THINGS TO DO

The exchange rate may vary a bit, but there is one conversion that will never change: £0 = $0. Here are our picks for the top free things to do in London.

MUSEUMS AND GALLERIES

Many of London's biggest and best cultural attractions are free to enter, and the number of museums offering free entry is staggering. Donations are often more than welcome, and special exhibits usually cost extra.

Major Museums
British Museum
Imperial War Museum London
Museum of London
National Gallery
National Maritime Museum, Queen's House, and Royal Observatory
National Portrait Gallery
Natural History Museum
Science Museum
Tate Britain
Tate Modern
Victoria & Albert Museum

Smaller Museums and Galleries
Courtauld Institute Gallery (free on Monday 10–2)
Geffrye Museum
Hogarth's House
Horniman Museum
Houses of Parliament
Institute of Contemporary Arts (ICA) Gallery
Museum of London Docklands
Saatchi Gallery
Serpentine Gallery
Sir John Soane's Museum
V&A Museum of Childhood
Wallace Collection

CONCERTS

St. Martin-in-the-Fields, St. Stephen Walbrook, and St. James's Church have regular free lunchtime concerts, as does St. George Bloomsbury on Sunday, Hyde Park Chapel on Thursday, and St. Giles-in-the-Fields on Friday. There are regular organ recitals at Westminster Abbey.

Of the music colleges, the Royal Academy of Music, the Royal College of Music, the Guildhall, the Trinity College of Music, and the Royal Opera House have regular free recitals.

For contemporary ears, the area outside the National Theatre on the South Bank (known as the Djanogly Concert Pitch) reverberates to an eclectic range of music weekdays at 5:45 pm, Saturday at 1 pm and 5:45 pm, and Sunday at 1 pm. St. Olave's Church in The City (✉ 8 Hart St.) has lunchtime recitals on Wednesday and Thursday at 1 pm. You can often catch some pretty good musicians busking on the Tube—they're licensed and have to pass an audition first.

Free jazz and classical evenings (sometimes there's a charge) are held Thursday to Saturday (plus two Sundays per month) at the excellent Dysart Arms (☎ 0208/940–8005 ⊕ www.thedysartarms.co.uk) in Richmond. Live jazz also comes to the central and ancient Lamb and Flag (✉ 33 Rose St. ☎ 0207/497–9504) on one Sunday a month, from 7:30 pm. For regular doses of free blues, down a drink at the Ain't Nothing But Blues Bar (✉ 20 Kingly St. ☎ 020/7287–0514). One of Camden's most celebrated pubs, the Dublin Castle (✉ 94 Parkway ☎ 020/7485–1773) has long been one of the best places in London to catch big and soon-to-be-big indie acts for about the price of two beers.

FILM, THEATER, AND OPERA

If all seats have been sold, the National Theatre sells standing tickets for £5 each. Check at the box office.

Standing-only tickets with slightly obstructed views at the Royal Opera House are between £4 and £15.

"Groundling," standing-only tickets for £5, are a traditional way to experience Shakespeare's Globe theater.

Sloane Square's Royal Court Theatre, one of the United Kingdoms's best venues for new playwriting, has four restricted-view, standing-room-only tickets at the down-stairs Jerwood Theatre for 10 pence (yes, 10p), available one hour before the per-formance; otherwise *all* tickets in the Jer-wood are £10 on Monday.

Under 30? Becoming an "Access all Arias" member of the English National Opera is free, and allows you to buy tick-ets for £10.

OFFBEAT EXPERIENCES

Take a walk down the Greenwich Foot Tunnel. Claustrophobics steer clear, but for those looking for a quirky journey, take the old lift or the spiral stairs down and stroll under the Thames from the Isle of Dogs to the *Cutty Sark* tea clipper in Greenwich.

There are free spectacles throughout the year, but one of the most warmly enjoyed is Guy Fawkes' Night (November 5), when parks throughout the country hold spectacular fireworks displays. On New Year's Eve thousands of revelers descend the South Bank to watch free fireworks near the London Eye. The Underground usually runs for free well into the small hours.

Barclays Cycle Hire. The popular Barclays Cycle Hire (☎ 0845/026–3630 ⊕ *www.tfl. gov.uk*) scheme has 587 docking stations housing 8,300 bicycles—known locally as "Boris Bikes," after the Mayor of Lon-don, Boris Johnson—around Central Lon-don. The first 30 minutes is free, but then it's £1 for the first hour and £6 for up to 120 minutes; the catch is that you need a £45 yearly membership to get a card (you can also pay for casual use by credit card at most docking stations).

SIGHTSEEING ON THE CHEAP

Join a ragtag group of real Londoners on the top deck of a double-decker bus for a ride through some of the most scenic parts of the city. Routes 9 and 15 also operate shortened Heritage routes on the traditional Routemaster buses. You can use your Oyster card or buy tickets from machines at the bus stops for the follow-ing routes:

Bus 11: King's Road, Sloane Square, Vic-toria station, Westminster Abbey, Houses of Parliament and Big Ben, Whitehall, Trafalgar Square, the Strand, the Royal Courts of Justice, Fleet Street, and St. Paul's Cathedral.

Bus 19: Sloane Square, Knightsbridge, Hyde Park Corner, Green Park, Piccadilly Circus, Shaftsbury Avenue, Oxford Street, Bloomsbury, Angel Islington.

Bus 88: Oxford Circus, Conduit Street, Piccadilly Circus, Haymarket, Trafalgar Square, Whitehall, Horse Guards Parade, Westminster station, Westminster Abbey, Horseferry Road, Tate Britain.

A LONDON HISTORIC PUB CRAWL

A brilliant, beery, and *traditional* way to see London and its medieval backstreets is on a "pub crawl." This walk takes you through some of the city's most historically textured neighborhoods. Settle back with a pint and drink in all the history.

The South Bank

Like Chaucer's *Canterbury Tales* pilgrims, we start in Southwark near London Bridge. Head down Borough High Street to the **George Inn**, a long black-and-white affair with wonky galleries, warped beams, open fires, and smoothed wooden stairs. First chronicled in 1542, the pub is mentioned in Charles Dickens's *Little Dorrit*. Cross Borough High Street and take the Bedale Street entrance to **Borough Market**; walk along until it turns into Cathedral Street, with the striking **Southwark Cathedral** on your right. At the fork head left to Sir Francis Drake's **Golden Hinde** replica galleon and walk past Pickfords Wharf to reach the **Anchor Bankside**. This old tavern was originally built in 1615 and was frequented by Shakespeare and other actors from the nearby Globe, Swan, and Rose theaters. Head up to the roof terrace for sweeping views of the River Thames and **St. Paul's.**

Across the Thames

Cross Southwark Bridge to The City. On the corner of Bow Lane, **Ye Olde Watling** was originally built before the Great Fire, and promptly torched. Rebuilt around 1668, again in 1901, and again after the Blitz, it's named after Watling Street, the Roman road on which it sits.

Head west along Watling Street to St. Paul's Cathedral and take a left down Creed Lane from Ludgate Hill. Wind your way down to Queen Victoria Street and turn right to **Blackfriar** at No 174.

The spectacular interior is all marble and brass bas-reliefs of Dominican friars interspersed with aphorisms and quotes.

Head north up New Bridge Street and turn left onto Fleet Street to the 1667 **Ye Olde Cheshire Cheese** at No. 145. Dr. Samuel Johnson, author of the first dictionary, used to drink here, as did Dickens, Voltaire, Mark Twain, Oscar Wilde, and Teddy Roosevelt.

Bloomsbury

Wander west along Fleet Street, then walk north up Fetter Lane to the hidden-away **Ye Olde Mitre** at 1 Ely Court, which has served up brews since 1546. Look for the old maypole–cherry-tree trunk (in the front bar) that Elizabeth I supposedly once danced around.

For the final stretch, walk north up Gray's Inn Road, then left onto Theobald's Road before turning right onto quaint Lamb's Conduit Street, to find **The Lamb**, notable for its 1720s wooden horseshoe bar with etched-glass "snob screens" to shield the well-to-do when drinking with women of dubious distinction. Head west along Great Ormond Street to the far side of Queen Square and **The Queens Larder**, where Queen Charlotte reputedly rented out a cellar to keep special foods for her sick husband, George III. Just north is Russell Square Tube station, or you can continue southwest to the British Museum, which is opposite the **Museum Tavern**, where Karl Marx would take time off from researching *Das Kapital*.

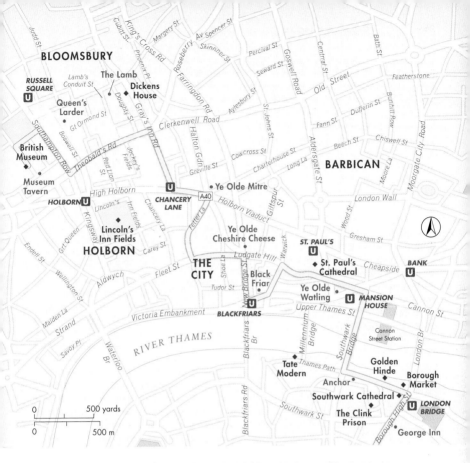

Where to Start:	On the South Bank at the London Bridge Tube/rail station.
Length:	4 miles (about 1½ hours without stopping). Just part of this walk will give you a taste of the oldest bits of London.
Where to Stop:	Russell Square Tube station or Tottenham Court Road.
Best Time to Go:	Weekday afternoons (most pubs open late in the morning).
Worst Time to Go:	Busy summer weekends may be too crowded.
Eating and Drinking:	All the pubs will serve food at lunchtime. Stop when you're hungry or pick up some tasty grub in Borough Market and stop in either Gray's Inn Fields or Lincoln's Inn Fields for a picnic.
Diversions:	From the Anchor, consider continuing along the riverside to the Tate Modern, before crossing over the River Thames to ferret out Ye Olde Watling or The Blackfriar.
Pub Highlights:	The Anchor, The Blackfriar, George Inn, The Lamb, Ye Olde Cheshire Cheese, Ye Olde Watling, Ye Olde Mitre.

IN PURSUIT OF THE EAST END ART SCENE

From the atmospheric period streets of Whitechapel and Spitalfields to the warehouses-turned-galleries of Hackney, a tour of the East End's art spaces presents the area in all its rich variety.

Whitechapel and Bethnal Green

To start your tour, tube it to the Aldgate East station, then walk east along Whitechapel High Street to the **Whitechapel Gallery**, a center for exciting exhibitions since its founding in 1901. Head back towards the Tube, then turn left into Commercial Street, go north past, then right, at the Ten Bells pub into Fournier Street, with its handsome, 18th-century, former silk workshops. Turn left into Brick Lane, then right into Cheshire Street, known for quirky shops like the Duke of Uke (for all your ukulele needs). The shops give way to a railway line as Cheshire Street turns into Dunbridge Street and then Three Colts Lane, as you walk directly east, until you come to industrial Herald Street, where you'll turn left. At No. 21 is the **Maureen Paley Gallery**, founded by an American expat who is now a doyenne of the East End art scene.

Hackney

Turn right onto Witan Street and then left onto Cambridge Heath Road. The **V&A Museum of Childhood** is just past Bethnal Green Tube station. Continue heading north (take Bus 106 or 254 if you're flagging) to just past Hackney Road. A few yards on the right is **Vyner Street**, not quite as sizzling as it used to be, but still a gallery hot spot. Cross back over Cambridge Heath Road and head west along Andrews Street, paralleling the Regent's Canal with its residential houseboats. Here you can either turn right to visit **Broadway Market** or left, going straight until you reach Hackney Road. Turn right and then take your first left at the Ion Square Gardens. Bear right onto **Columbia Road** (helpfully signed for Shoreditch), site of London's best flower market on Sundays.

Shoreditch

A short way past where the shops of Columbia Road end, you'll see another sign for Shoreditch on the left at Virginia Road. Turn left here, bear right, and then turn left again at Hocker Street. This brings you to **Arnold Circus**, an Arts and Crafts housing development. From the southern end of the Circus, take the first right off Club Row, Old Nichol Street. Here you'll find the **Kate MacGarry Gallery**, known for its cutting-edge conceptual and video art. Turn left into Boundary Road at the end of the street and stop for a restorative coffee or bite at the **Albion Café** at the end of Boundary Road. At this point you can either turn left around the corner to explore more fun boutiques on **Redchurch Street**, or right, which will bring you almost immediately to Shoreditch High Street and the huge Tea Building to the left. It houses **Rocket**, a gallery specializing in color photography (Martin Parr shows here) and minimalist painting and sculpture. Turn left onto Bethnal Green Road, where you'll find the Shoreditch High Street Overground station just past the Boxpark pop-up mall.

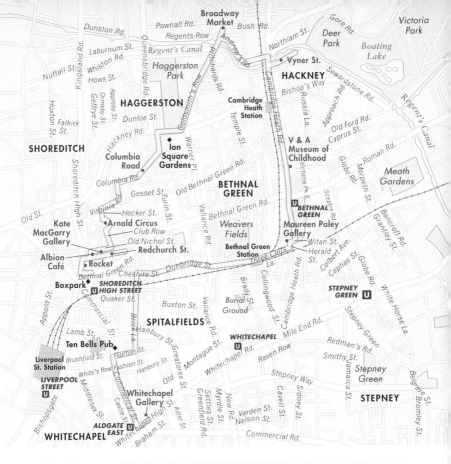

Where to Start:	At Aldgate East Tube station in Whitechapel.
Length:	3½ miles (about 2 hours without stopping).
Where to Stop:	Shoreditch High Street Overground station.
Best Time to Go:	Weekdays for galleries, weekends for markets.
Worst Time to Go:	Busy summer weekends may be too crowded.
Eating and Drinking:	Wine and small plates of charcuterie at Brawn on Columbia Road; excellent modern British food upstairs at the Ten Bells on Commercial Street; coffee and light meals at Terence Conran's Albion Café on Boundary Road.
Diversions:	Consider crossing to the west side of Shoreditch High Street to explore London's new media hub near the Old Street (aka "Silicon") roundabout. The digerati gather at the Book Club on Leonard Street for coffee by day and drinks by night.
Gallery Highlights:	Maureen Paley Gallery, Whitechapel Gallery, V&A Museum of Childhood, Kate MacGarry Gallery, Rocket Gallery, Vyner Street Gallery.

AFTERNOON TEA

So, what is Afternoon Tea, exactly? Well, it means real tea—Earl Grey, English Breakfast, Ceylon, Darjeeling, or Assam—brewed in a china pot, and served with china cups and saucers, milk, or lemon, and preferably with silver spoons, taken between noon and 6 pm.

For the full monty there should be elegant finger foods on a three-tiered cake stand: crustless sandwiches on the bottom; fruit scones with Devonshire clotted cream and strawberry preserves in the middle; and rich fruit cakes, shortbread, patisseries, macaroons, and delicate fancies on top.

Tea goers dress smartly (though not ostentatiously), and conversation by tradition should avoid politics and religion. Here are some top places in town to head:

Hands down, the super-glamorous Savoy hotel, on the Strand, offers the most beautiful setting for tea: the Thames Foyer, a symphony of grays and golds centered around a "winter garden" wrought-iron gazebo, just the place for the house pianist to accompany you as you enjoy the award-winning house teas along with finger sandwiches, homemade scones, and *yumptious* pastries. Don't forget to stop in the adjacent Chinoiserie Vestibule—a gloriously chic, black-and-white chintz-covered room—to make some purchases in the Savoy Tea Boutique.

Setting the standard in its English Tea Room for some of London's best-known traditional teas, Brown's Hotel, at 33 Albermarle Street—charmingly set in a classic Mayfair town house—offers a great Afternoon Tea for £35 or, if you wish to really splash out, a Champagne Tea for £45.

If you want timeless chic, the sumptuous dining room at the Wolseley hotel, at 160 Piccadilly, has barely changed since the 1920s, and it remains as fashionable a hangout as it was in its roaring heyday. The teas here—Afternoon Tea is £21 and Champagne Tea £30—are among the best in all England.

The hallowed tradition is given a sophisticated, contemporary twist at Claridge's, on Brook Street in Mayfair, where your teatime companions are more likely to be film stars and supermodels than aristocrats. Afternoon Tea is £38 and Champagne Tea is £49.

At the fabled Dorchester hotel at 53 Park Lane, tea in the Promenade is best taken on comfy sofas and to the sound of the resident pianist amid a maze of marble and gold leaf. Afternoon Tea is £38.50, Champagne Tea is £46.50. Book well ahead.

For frilly grandeur, few can compete with the tea at the Ritz hotel, at 150 Piccadilly, served in the impressive Palm Court, replete with marble tables, Louis XIV chaises, gigantic bouquets, and musical accompaniment: a true taste of "Edwardian London" in the 21st century. Afternoon Tea is £52 and Champagne Tea £54. Reserve two to three months ahead and remember to wear a jacket and tie.

For more information on the above places, see our Where to Stay chapter for the hotels and our Shopping chapter for the shops.

LONDON WITH KIDS

Education Without Yawns

London Dungeon. Gore galore (did you ever see a medieval disembowelment?) plunges you into murky depths of London history, with gruesome rides and special effects scary enough to frighten the coolest of kids.

London Zoo. City? *What* city? Disappear into the animal kingdom among the enclosures, complete with sessions for kids about all kinds of spiders (even bird-eating ones!), in this popular animal retreat set in Regent's Park.

Kew Gardens. If the sun penetrates the London clouds, Kew Gardens is great for kids, with family activities, the "climbers and creepers" play zone, treetops sky walk, zip wires, scramble slides, and children's trails; it's free for children.

Natural History Museum. It doesn't get much more awe-inspiring than bloodsucking bats, fake earthquakes, and a life-size blue whale. Just make sure you know your diplodocus from your dodo.

Science Museum. Special effects, virtual space voyages, interactive galleries, puzzles, and mysteries from the world of science can keep kids effortlessly amused all day.

Tower of London. Perfect for playing prince and princesses in front of the crown jewels. Not so perfect for imagining what becomes of the fairy tale—watch your royal necks.

Performances

Applaud street performers. You can't beat the gaggle of jugglers, fire-eaters, unicyclists, and the human statues tantalizing crowds at Covent Garden piazza.

Enjoy Regent's Park Open Air Theatre. Welcome to the land of fairy dust and magic. Don't miss an evening performance under the stars of *A Midsummer Night's Dream* in summer.

Activities

Ride the London Eye. Europe's biggest observation wheel looks like a giant fairground ride, and you can see across what seems like half of London from the top.

Pose with a Queen's Guard. There's always an erect soldier, dressed in full traditional uniform, standing watch (or on horseback) by the entrance to Horse Guards on the Trafalgar Square end of Whitehall. They don't mind you posing for pictures, but they're not allowed to smile . . . which some kids see as a *challenge.*

Ice-skating at the Natural History Museum. Send your kids whizzing, arms whirling, across ice from November to January at this fantastic ice rink right outside the museum.

Night at the Museum. Find out what the dinosaurs really do when the lights go out at the monthly Dino Snores sleepover (minimum of one adult and five kids per group).

Paddle on the Serpentine. Pack a picnic and take a pedelo out into the middle of Hyde Park's famed lake; settle back and tuck in to lunch.

Lose your kids at Hampton Court. The topiary might be more than 300 years old, but the quest to reach the middle of Hampton Court's world-famous hedge maze remains as challenging as ever.

West End musicals. Foot-stompingly good West End musicals and shows like *Les Misérables, Billy Elliot, Matilda, Mamma Mia!, War Horse. Oliver!, Grease,* and *The Phantom of the Opera* will mesmerize over-sevens.

Millennium Bridge and St. Paul's Cathedral.

THE BUILDING OF LONDON

The past is knit into the very fabric of the lives of Londoners: they live in Regency townhouses, worship in Baroque churches, and chill out in Edwardian-era parks. Unfolding like a gigantic historical pop-up book, London reveals—building by building—the pageant of a nation's history. To make sense of it all, here's a quick architectural tour through time.

Despite invading tribes, an epic fire, and 20th-century bombing, London has always survived, and a surprising amount of yesterday remains visible in its streets today. Starting with remnants of Londinium, the early Roman city contained by a defensive wall some 2,000 years ago, you can trace the city's beginnings. Only pieces of the wall remain, but the name of each entrance to the city has been preserved: Aldgate, Newgate, Bishopsgate, Cripplegate, Aldersgate, and Ludgate.

As commerce grew the city over the centuries, London expanded between two centers of power, Westminster in the west and the Tower in the east. Following both the Great Fire and World War II destruction, the need to rebuild outweighed the desire for sensible street layouts, and often any aesthetic considerations. In fact, London as a whole has rarely been planned, and the financial center is still roughly in the shape of that original Roman wall. London's haphazard streets and alleys are filled with diverse architectural styles side-by-side, each representing a piece of the city's history.

| 56, 64 BC Julius Caesar arrives on Britain's shores | 43 AD–410 AD Roman rule | 61 AD Boudicca attacks and destroys Londinium | | 600s Anglo-Saxon Lundenwic settlement in Covent Garden area |

| 0 | 250 | 500 | 750 |

(top left) Statue of the Roman Emperor Trajan (r. AD 98-117) outside the largest remaining section of the Roman wall at Tower Hill. (right) Tower of London; (left) Carausius coin struck circa 288-290 AD at the Londinium mint.

Roman Londinium

Pre–410

As the Roman Empire expanded, Britain was conquered and the first city where London now stands began to develop along the Thames. Among many building projects, the Romans enclosed Londinium with a wall to protect against invading tribes after the Celtic warrior queen Boudicca razed the city. Today chunks of the ancient barrier remain in the City, and at the Guildhall art gallery you can see a partial Roman amphitheatre from this time.

■ Visit: Guildhall (Ch. 6), London Wall at Tower Hill Tube station (Ch. 6), Museum of London (Ch. 5)

Saxon and Medieval London

410–1485

Little is known of the 250 years after the Romans left London. Following these "Dark Ages," most medieval houses and bridges were built of timber or wattle and daub and the perishable materials didn't last in the changing city.

England's royalty began building heavily in the capital as a sign of strength and power, focusing on defensive structures. In 1042, the Saxon King Edward the Confessor moved his court and began a church on the site of the current Westminster Abbey, where almost all the monarchs of England have been crowned since. From

across the English Channel, William the Conqueror brought Norman architectural styles with him. William built the White Tower; later expanded, the solid castle became the heart of the Tower of London complex. His son and heir William II saw the construction of Westminster Hall, the oldest part of the Palace of Westminster (today's Houses of Parliament). St. Bartholomew's Hospital, founded in 1123, and the Guildhall, a center of commerce from the early 15th century, are among the few buildings that survived the later Great Fire.

■ Visit: Guildhall (Ch. 6), St. Bartholomew's Hospital (Ch. 6), Tower of London (Ch. 6)

1066 William the Conqueror becomes King of England	1240 Parliament sits at Westminster for the first time	1348 The Black Death	1605 Guy Fawkes's Gunpowder Plot uncovered 1534 Dissolution of the Monasteries	1642–51 Civil War 1666 Great Fire
1000	1250		1500	1750

1

IN FOCUS THE BUILDING OF LONDON

(top left) Painted ceiling of Banqueting House by Peter Paul Rubens; (top right) *The Great Fire of London, with Ludgate and old St Paul's*; (bottom right) St. Paul's Cathedral, built 1675–1708, designed by Christopher Wren

Tudor and Stuart London

1485–1700

As London grew, the Tudor royals influenced the architecture of London not only by creating, but also by destroying. Henry VII continued the expansion of Westminster Abbey and his successor, Henry VIII, resided at Hampton Court. The arts flourished under Elizabeth I, and the original Globe Theatre was built in 1599. Yet many fine medieval churches were torn down as England separated from the Roman Catholic Church.

Architects brought continental ideas to London, notably the influential Italian Palladian style introduced by Inigo Jones. You can see this classical style with it's mathematical proportions and balanced lines at the Queen's House in Greenwich and at Banqueting House, where Charles I was executed following the civil war. Eleven years later, Charles II was restored to the throne, returning from exile in France.

The Great Fire of 1666 destroyed five-sixths of London, but it also wiped out the plague that had ravaged the impoverished and overcrowded population the year before. Sir Christopher Wren was given the Herculean charge of rebuilding London. He wanted to map out a more organized grid for the city, but it was rebuilt on the old haphazard lines. It took Wren 35 years to build his baroque masterpiece, St. Paul's Cathedral. Wren also designed 50 other churches (only 23 still stand, including St. Bride's and St. Stephen Walbrook) and Monument to commemorate the fire. Nicholas Hawksmoor assisted Wren and designed his own highly original churches including the splendid Christ Church in Spitalfields.

■ Visit: Banqueting House (Ch. 2), Christ Church, Spitalfields (Ch. 7), Shakespeare's Globe Theatre (Ch. 8), Queen's House, Greenwich (Ch. 12), St. Bride's (Ch. 6), St. Paul's Cathedral (Ch. 6), St. Stephen Walbrook (Ch. 6), Hampton Court (Ch. 13)

(top left) Courtyard of Neo-classical Somerset House, built for George III. (right) The Rotunda of the Victoria and Albert (V&A) Museum with modern Chihuly sculpture; (bottom left) St Martin-in-the-Fields on Trafalgar Square.

Georgian Era

1700–1836

By the beginning of the 18th century, London was the biggest city in Europe and a center of world trade. This growth led to changes in politics, as power moved to a parliamentary system. Increased wealth led to an explosion of art and architecture.

Many different styles flourished—rococo, neo-classical, regency, and gothic revival. The predominant neo-classical, based on the styles of ancient Greece, can be seen in many stately homes. You can admire the elegant Regency terraces around John Nash's Regent's Park.

■ Visit: Regent's Park (Ch. 11), Somerset House (Ch. 4), St. Martin-in-the-Fields (Ch. 2)

Victorian Age

1837–1901

Queen Victoria ruled the British Empire for 63 years. London experienced the growth of wealth, industrialization, and philanthropy; this was also a period of desperate poverty, as depicted in Charles Dickens's novels. At the start of the 19th century the population of the city was over a million; by the end of Victoria's reign it was six million.

This rapid growth required many building programs, from worker housing to even bigger projects such as the bridges, government buildings, and the first subway system in the world. Businessmen, artists, and architects helped create many institutions that still exist today from the Tate Britain to the Ragged Schools and Foundling hospitals.

The clean, classical lines of the previous era gave way to more elaborate styles—which were considered more "English"—such as the Gothic Revival Houses of Parliament. Other Victorian projects included covered markets, canal locks, arcades, palaces, memorials, museums, theaters, and parks. So much building took place during this period that it's hard to miss the style: look for elaborate, highly decorated architecture.

■ Visit: Burlington Arcade (Ch. 3), Houses of Parliament (Ch. 2), Leadenhall Market in The City (Ch. 6), V&A and Natural History Museum (Ch. 9)

1851 Great Exhibition held in Hyde Park
1863 Underground opens
1901 Death of Queen Victoria
1939–1945 WWII
1914–1918 WWI
1951 Festival of Britain

1870   1900   1930   1960

1

IN FOCUS THE BUILDING OF LONDON

(left) Theatregoers at The National Theatre on the South Bank of the Thames River; (right) Tower block at Barbican Centre, a 1980s complex of art venues and apartments.

20th-century building

1901–1979

The turn of the 20th century saw wealthy Westminster widening its streets to accommodate the arrival of motor cars and department stores. Even after the First World War, a "live for today" attitude continued among the upper classes, while the poorest Londoners suffered increasing prices and low wages. While modernism—a cultural movement embracing the future and rejecting anything associated with the past—was gathering pace in 1920s Europe, conservative British architecture continued to hark back to traditional influences of ancient Greece and the middle ages.

The WWII devastation of the Blitz bombings changed this and an enormous amount of post-war building was needed quickly. Émigrés such as Hungarian Ernö Goldfinger and Russian-born Berthold Lubetkin brought the modernist architectural movement to London with their high-rise buildings—a solution to the desperate housing shortage. One of the most exciting post-war projects was the 1951 Festival of Britain, celebrating the great inventions of the century. Out of a host of new architecture at the South Bank for this event, only the Royal Festival Hall remains.

Mass-produced concrete, steel, and glass ushered in the brutalist style in the '60s. This outgrowth of modernism can be seen in the Hayward Gallery and National Theatre. It was not a popular style, partly because the use of raw concrete—pioneered in the sunny south of France—looked gray, ugly, and even sinister against the backdrop of wet and windy London.

London's powers-that-be haven't always embraced modernist architecture, and many examples have been torn down. Today some iconic buildings are protected and the massive concrete Barbican Centre finally brought modernism right into the conservative City.

■ Visit: The Barbican Centre (Ch. 6), Hayward Gallery (Ch. 8), National Theatre (Ch. 8), Royal Festival Hall (Ch. 8)

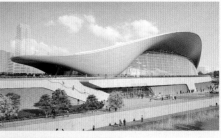

(left) Lloyd's of London by the Richard Rogers Pertnership, completed in 1986. (top right) Current design of the London Aquatics Centre by Zaha Hadid. (bottom right) The 2000 Great Court at the British Museum by Sir Norman Foster.

1980–Present

Modern and Millennium London

While the sun may have set on the British empire, London remains a global city, perhaps more now than ever before. The '80s saw changes in economic policy and ambitious building projects, including the Jubilee Line extension to the Underground system. Great business and banking centers reached higher into the sky as London's importance in financial markets increased. London's disused Docklands area got a revitalizing boost with the Canary Wharf development and the DLR (Docklands Light Railway).

Internationally-known architects began to make their mark on the city with creative projects. Known as Tower 42, the NatWest Tower opened in 1980 as the tallest skyscraper in the city—for a great view, head to its bar on the 42nd floor. The Richard Rogers Partnership designed the fabulous 1986 Lloyd's of London building. Sir Norman Foster and his associates have designed the Sackler Galleries at the Royal Academy of Arts, the British Museum's Great Court, City Hall, and the Swiss Re Headquarters (known as the Gherkin).

Building projects to celebrate the Millennium are now so beloved it's hard to imagine London without the pedestrian-only Millennium Bridge and the London Eye.

The stunning structures keep on coming. There's Zaha Hadid's curvaceous Aquatics Center, built for the Olympics but currently undergoing modification for opening to the public in 2014; the Bishopsgate Tower (aka, "Helter Skelter") whose construction is well under way; and the Richard Rogers Partnership's "Cheese Grater", also due for completion in 2014. But dwarfing them all is "The Shard", a 1,016-foot skyscraper designed by Italian Renzo Piano which, when it opens in 2013, will be the tallest building in the EU. As London is finding out—the sky's the limit.

■ Visit: Canary Wharf (Ch. 12), Lloyd's of London (Ch. 6), Shard (Ch. 8), Swiss Re (Ch. 6)

WESTMINSTER, ST. JAMES'S, AND ROYAL LONDON

GETTING ORIENTED

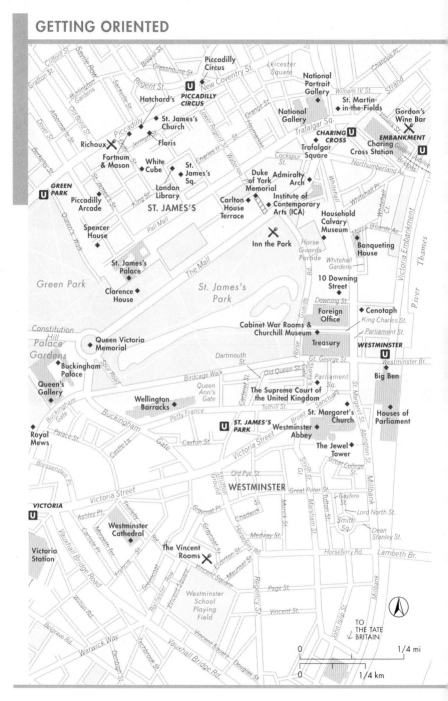

TOP REASONS TO GO

Time-Burnished Westminster Abbey: This sublime Gothic church was not only the site of Prince William's 2011 marriage but has also seen 38 hallowed coronations, starting with William the Conqueror in 1066.

Calling on Buckingham Palace: Even if you miss the palace's summer opening, keep pace with the marching soldiers and bands as they enact the time-honored ceremony of the "Changing the Guard" in front of the residence of Her Majesty.

Masterpieces Theater: Leonardo, Raphael, Van Eyck, Rembrandt, and many other artistic greats are shown off in the splendor of gorgeously renovated rooms at the National Gallery.

Relive Britain's "Finest Hour" in the Churchill War Rooms: Listen to Churchill's radio addresses to the British people as you explore this cavernous underground wartime hideout.

Hear Big Ben's chimes: As the Eiffel Tower is to Paris, so is Big Ben to London—just follow your ears from Trafalgar Square to catch sight of the 320-foot-high Clock Tower.

FEELING PECKISH?

Gordon's Wine Bar. The oldest wine bar in London (1890), Gordon's is certainly the most atmospheric, hidden below ground among vaulted brick arches and bathed in candlelight. Reasonably priced, it also serves an excellent buffet of meat, pies, and cheeses. ⊠ *47 Villiers St., Trafalgar Sq.* ☏ *020/7930–1408* ⊕ *www.gordonswinebar.com* Ⓜ *Embankment, Charing Cross.*

Inn the Park. Great food, drink, and location—what more could you want? Inn the Park is the perfect place to while away an hour or three, especially on the terrace in the summer. ⊠ *St. James's Park, St. James's* ☏ *020/7747–5942* ⊕ *www.innthepark.com* Ⓜ *St. James's Park.*

GETTING THERE

Trafalgar Square is easy to access and smack-dab in the center of the action. Take the Tube to Embankment (Northern, Bakerloo, District, and Circle lines) and walk north until you cross the Strand, or alight at the Charing Cross (Bakerloo and Northern lines) Northumberland Avenue exit. Buses are another great option, as almost all roads lead to Trafalgar Square.

Two tube stations are right in the heart of St. James's: Piccadilly Circus (Piccadilly or Bakerloo lines), and Green Park (Piccadilly, Victoria, or Jubilee lines).

MAKING THE MOST OF YOUR TIME

A lifetime of exploring may still be insufficient to cover this historically rich part of London. But don't fret: two to three days can take in the highlights.

For royal pageantry begin with Buckingham Palace, Westminster Abbey, and the Guards Museum. For more constitutional sightseeing, there are the Houses of Parliament. For art, the National Gallery, the Tate Britain, and the Queen's Gallery head anyone's list.

NEAREST PUBLIC RESTROOMS

If you get caught short in Westminster Abbey, paid loos (£1.50) are across the street at the bottom of Victoria Street. Banqueting House and the Queen's Gallery have very elegant restrooms.

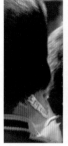

Sightseeing
★★★★★

Nightlife
★★

Dining
★★★

Lodging
★

Shopping
★★

This is postcard London at its best. Crammed with historic churches, grand state buildings, and major art collections, Royal London and Westminster unite politics, high culture, and religion. (Oh, and the Queen lives here, too.) The places you'll want to explore are grouped into four distinct areas—Trafalgar Square, Whitehall, St. James's, and Buckingham Palace—each nudging a corner of triangular St. James's Park. Happily, there is as much history in these few acres as in many whole cities, so pace yourself—this is concentrated sightseeing.

WESTMINSTER

Updated by
James O'Neill

Erstwhile home to London's most photogenic pigeons, **Trafalgar Square** is not only the official center of the district known as **Westminster,** it is the official center of London. What will bring you here are the two magnificent museums on the northern edge of the square, the **National Gallery** and the **National Portrait Gallery.** From the square two boulevards lead to the seats of different ideas of governance. The avenue called **Whitehall** drops south to the neo-Gothic **Houses of Parliament,** where members of both Houses (Commons and Lords) hold debates and vote on pending legislation, and, just opposite, **Westminster Abbey,** a monument to the nation's history and for centuries the scene of daily worship, coronations, and royal weddings—the latter gives this area its official name of **Westminster.** Poets, political leaders, and 17 monarchs are buried in this world-famous, 13th-century Gothic building. Halfway down Whitehall, **No. 10 Downing Street** is both the residence and the office of the prime minister. One of the most celebrated occupants, Winston Churchill, is commemorated in the **Churchill War Rooms,** his underground wartime headquarters off Whitehall. Just down the road is the **Cenotaph,** which acts as a focal point for the annual remembrance of those lost in war.

The **Mall,** a wide, elegant avenue beyond the stone curtain of **Admiralty Arch,** heads southwest from Trafalgar Square toward the **Queen Victoria Memorial** and **Buckingham Palace,** the sovereign's official residence. The building is open to the public only in summer, but you can see much of the royal art collection in the Queen's Gallery and spectacular ceremonial coaches in the **Royal Mews,** both open all year. Farther south toward Pimlico, **Tate Britain** focuses on prominent British artists from 1500 to today.

Geographically speaking, Westminster runs from Trafalgar Square to Westminster Abbey (east to west) and from Buckingham Palace and the Mall (north) to the Thames (south).

This area can be considered "Royal London" partly because it is neatly bounded by the triangle of streets that make up the route that Queen Elizabeth II usually takes when processing from Buckingham Palace to Westminster Abbey or to the Houses of Parliament on state occasions, and also because it contains so much that is historic and magnificent in British history. Naturally, in an area that regularly sees the pomp and pageantry of royal occasions, the streets are wide and the vistas long. There is a feeling here of timeless dignity—long avenues of ancient trees framing classically proportioned buildings, constant glimpses of pinnacles and towers over the treetops, the distant throb of military bands on the march, the statues of resolute kings, queens, and statesmen standing guard at every corner, the deep tones of Big Ben counting off the hours. The main drawback to sightseeing here is that half the world is doing it at the same time as you. So, remember that for a large part of the year a lot of Royal London is floodlit at night (when there's more elbow-room), adding to the theatricality of the experience.

TOP ATTRACTIONS

FAMILY **Churchill War Rooms.** It was from this small warren of underground rooms—beneath the vast government buildings of the Treasury—that Winston Churchill and his team directed troops in World War II. Designed to be bombproof, the whole complex has been preserved almost exactly as it was when the last light was turned off at the end of the war. Every clock shows almost 5 pm, and the furniture, fittings, and paraphernalia of a busy, round-the-clock war office are in situ, down to the colored map pins.

During air raids, the leading government ministers met here, and the Cabinet Room is still arranged as if a meeting were about to convene. In the Map Room, the Allied campaign is charted on wall-to-wall maps with a rash of pinholes showing the movements of convoys. It really is the stuff out of *Boy's Own* stories. In the hub of the room, a bank of different-color phones known as the "Beauty Chorus" linked the War Rooms to control rooms around the nation. The Prime Minister's Room holds the desk from which Churchill made his morale-boosting broadcasts; the Telephone Room (a converted broom cupboard) has his hotline to FDR. You can also see the restored suite of rooms that the PM used for dining and sleeping. Telephonists and clerks who worked 16-hour shifts slept in lesser quarters in unenviable conditions; it would

A BRIEF HISTORY OF WESTMINSTER

The Romans may have gunned for The City, but England's royals went for Westminster. London's future home of democracy started out as Edward the Confessor's palace, when he moved his cramped court west in the 11th century. He founded Westminster Abbey in 1050, where every British monarch since then has been crowned. Under the Normans, the palace of Westminster was an elaborate and French-speaking affair. The politicos finally got their hands on it in 1529 (when Henry VII and his court shifted up to the roomier Whitehall Palace), but nearly lost it forever with the Gunpowder Plot of 1605, when Catholic militants attempted to blow the prototypical Parliament to smithereens.

Inigo Jones's magnificent Banqueting House is the only surviving building of Whitehall Palace, and was the setting for the 1649 beheading of Charles I. The Westminster we see today took shape during the Georgian and Victorian periods, as Britain reached the zenith of its imperial power. Grand architecture sprang up, and Buckingham Palace became the principal royal residence in 1837, when Victoria acceded to the throne. Trafalgar Square and Nelson's Column were built in 1843, to commemorate Britain's most famous naval victory, and the Houses of Parliament were rebuilt in 1858 in the trendy neo-Gothic style of the time. The illustrious Clarence House, built in 1825 for the Duke of Clarence (later William IV), is now the home of Prince Charles and Camilla, Duchess of Cornwall.

not have been unusual for a secretary in pajamas to scurry past a field marshal en route to a meeting.

A great addition to the War Rooms is the Churchill Museum, a tribute to the stirring politician and defiant wartime icon himself. Different zones explore his life and achievements—and failures, too—through objects and documents, many of which, such as his personal papers, had never previously been made public. Most popular with children is the 50-foot long interactive Lifeline, which explores the man and his times in an informative but fun way. ⊠ *Clive Steps, King Charles St., Westminster* ☎ *020/7930–6961* ⊕ *www.iwm.org.uk* ✉ *£17 (includes audio guide)* ⊙ *Daily 9:30–6; last admission 5; disabled access* Ⓜ *Westminster.*

Downing Street. Looking like an unassuming alley but for the iron gates at both its Whitehall and Horse Guards Road approaches, this is the location of the famous **No. 10,** London's modest equivalent of the White House. The Georgian entrance is deceptive, though, since the old house now leads to a large mansion behind it, overlooking the Horse Guards Parade. Only three houses remain of the terrace built circa 1680 by Sir George Downing, who spent enough of his youth in America to graduate from Harvard—the second man ever to do so. **No. 11** is traditionally the residence of the chancellor of the exchequer (secretary of the treasury), and **No. 12** is the party whips' office. No. 10 has officially housed the prime minister since 1732. Just south of Downing Street, in the middle of Whitehall, you'll see the **Cenotaph,** a stark white monolith designed in 1920 by Sir Edwin Lutyens to commemorate the 1918 armistice. On Remembrance Day (the Sunday nearest November 11, Armistice Day) it's strewn with red poppy wreaths to honor the dead of both world wars and all British and Commonwealth soldiers killed in action since; the first wreath is laid by the Queen or the senior member of the Royal Family present, and there's a march-past by war veterans, who salute their fallen comrades. ⊠ *Whitehall* Ⓜ *Westminster.*

FAMILY **Horse Guards Parade.** Following its brief transformation into the beach volleyball arena for the 2012 Olympics, the Horse Guards Parade is most known for the annual Trooping the Colour ceremony, in which the Queen takes the salute, her official birthday tribute, on the second Saturday in June. (Like Paddington Bear, the Queen has two birthdays; her real one is on April 21.) In what was once the tiltyard for jousting tournaments, there is still pageantry galore, with marching bands and throngs of onlookers, and the ceremony is televised. Throughout the rest of the year the changing of two mounted sentries known as the **Queen's Life Guard** at the Whitehall facade of Horse Guards provides what may be London's most popular photo opportunity. The ceremony last about half an hour. ⊠ *Whitehall* ☎ *020/7930–4832* ⊙ *Changing of the Queen's Life Guard at 11 am Mon.–Sat. and 10 am Sun.; inspection of the Queen's Life Guard daily at 4 pm* Ⓜ *Westminster.*

Houses of Parliament.
See the highlighted listing in this chapter.

FAMILY **National Gallery.**
Fodor'sChoice
★ *See the highlighted listing in this chapter.*

QUICK
BITES **Notes Music and Coffee.** Next door to the London Coliseum (home of the English National Opera), this hip café serves some of the best sandwiches, salads, and coffee in town. Keep an eye out for their popular jazz nights. ⊠ *31 St. Martin's La., Westminster* ☎ *020/7240–0424* ⊕ *www.notes-uk. co.uk* Ⓜ *Charing Cross.*

FAMILY **National Portrait Gallery.** Tucked around the corner from the National
Fodor'sChoice
★ Gallery, the National Portrait Gallery was founded in 1856 with a single aim: to gather together portraits of famous (and infamous) British men and women. More than 150 years and 160,000 portraits later, it is an essential stop for all history and literature buffs. The spacious galleries make it a pleasant place to visit, and you can choose to take in a little or a lot. Need to rest those legs? Then use the Portrait Explorer in the Digital Space on the ground-floor mezzanine for interactive, computer-aided exploration of the gallery's extensive collection. If you visit with little ones, ask at the desk about the excellent Family Trails, which make exploring the galleries with children much more fun. On the top floor, the Portrait Restaurant (check website for details) will delight skyline aficionados. ■ TIP➜ The restaurant vista will reveal stately London at its finest: a panoramic view of Nelson's Column and the backdrop along White-hall to the Houses of Parliament.

Galleries are arranged clearly and chronologically, from Tudor times to contemporary Britain. In the Tudor Gallery—a modern update on a

HOUSES OF PARLIAMENT

✉ St. Stephen's Entrance, St. Margaret St., Westminster ☎ 020/7219–4272 Information, 0844/847–1672 Public Tours ⊕ www.parliament.uk/ visiting 🎫 Free; tours £15 (must book ahead) ⊘ Tours: Aug., Mon., Tues., Fri., and Sat. 9:15–4:30, Wed. and Thurs. 1:15–4:30; Sept., Mon., Fri., and Sat. 9:15–4:30, Tues., Wed., and Thurs. 1:15–4:30. Call to confirm hrs for Visitors Galleries Ⓜ Westminster.

TIPS

■ The only guided tour non-residents can go on is the paid-for (£15) tour offered on Saturday, or Monday to Saturday during August and September (book throughw-www.ticketmaster.co.uk).

■ Nonresidents are able to watch debates when Parliament is in session if they wait in line for tickets. Embassies and High Commissions often have a quota of debate tickets available to their citizens, which can help you avoid long lines.

■ If you're pressed for time, lines for the House of Lords are often shorter than for the House of Commons. The easiest time to get into the Commons is during an evening session—Parliament is still sitting if the top of the Clock Tower is illuminated.

■ The most romantic view of the Houses is from the opposite (south) bank, across Lambeth Bridge. It is especially dramatic at night when floodlighted green and gold.

If you want to understand some of the centuries-old traditions and arcane idiosyncrasies that make up constitutionless British parliamentary democracy, the Palace of Westminster, as the complex is still properly called, is the place to come. The architecture in this 1,100-room labyrinth impresses, but the real excitement lies in stalking the corridors of power. A palace was first established on this site by Edward the Confessor in the 11th century. William II started building a new palace in 1087, and this gradually became the seat of English administrative power. However, fire destroyed most of the palace in 1834, and the current complex dates largely from the middle of the 19th century.

Highlights

Visitors aren't allowed to snoop too much, but the **Visitors' Galleries** of the House of Commons do afford a view of democracy in process when the banks of green-leather benches are filled by opposing MPs (members of Parliament). When they speak, it's not directly to each other but through the Speaker, who also decides who will get time on the floor. Elaborate procedures notwithstanding, debate is often drowned out by raucous jeers. When MPs vote, they exit by the "Aye" or the "No" corridor, thus being counted by the party "tellers." There are also Visitors Galleries for The House of Lords, which does not have the power to generate legislation, although it plays a role in scrutiny.

Westminster Hall, with its remarkable hammer-beam roof, was the work of William the Conqueror's son William Rufus. It's one of the largest remaining Norman halls in Europe.

After the 1834 fire, the Clock Tower—renamed the **Elizabeth Tower** in 2012, in honor of the Queen's Diamond Jubilee—was completed in 1858, and contains the 13-ton bell known as **Big Ben.**

Tudor long hall—is a Holbein cartoon of Henry VIII. Joshua Reynolds's self-portrait hangs in the refurbished 17th-century rooms. Portraits of notables, including Shakespeare, the Brontë sisters, Jane Austen, and the Queen are always on display. Other faces are more obscure because the portraits outlasted their sitters' fame—not so surprising when the portraitists are such greats as Reynolds, Gainsborough, Lawrence, and Hockney. Look for the four Andy Warhol *Queen Elizabeth II* silkscreens from 1985 and Maggi Hambling's surreal self-portrait. Contemporary portraits range from the iconic (*Julian with T-shirt*—an LCD screen on a continuous loop—by Julian Opie) to the creepy (Marc Quinn's *Self*, a realization of the artist's head in frozen blood) and the eccentric (Tim Noble's ghoulish *Head of Isabella Blow*). Temporary exhibitions can be explored in the ground-floor Wolfson and Porter galleries. ⊠ *St. Martin's Pl., Westminster* ☏ *020/7312–2463, 020/730–0555 recorded switchboard information* ⊕ *www.npg.org.uk* ☞ *Free; charge for special exhibitions; audiovisual guide £3* ⊙ *Mon.–Wed. and weekends 10–6, Thurs. and Fri. 10–9; last admission 1 hr before closing* Ⓜ *Charing Cross, Leicester Sq.*

FAMILY **St. Martin-in-the-Fields.** One of London's best-loved and most welcoming of churches is more than just a place of worship. Named after the saint who helped beggars, St Martin's has long been a welcome sight for the homeless, who have sought soup and shelter at the church since 1914. The church is also a haven for music lovers; the internationally known Academy of St. Martin-in-the-Fields was founded here, and a popular program of concerts continues today. (Although the interior is a wonderful setting for a recital, beware the hard wooden benches!) The crypt is a hive of activity, with a popular café and shop, plus the **London Brass-Rubbing Centre,** where you can make your own life-size souvenir knight, lady, or monarch from replica tomb brasses, with metallic waxes, paper, and instructions from about £5. Also watch out for a new alfresco café set to open in summer 2013.

St. Martin's is often called the royal parish church, partly because Charles II was christened here. Originally a small medieval chapel (probably used by the monks of Westminster Abbey), the 18th-century saw the church get a major revamp: completed in 1726, James Gibbs's classical temple-with-spire design also became a familiar pattern for churches in early colonial America. Though it has to compete for attention with Trafalgar Square's many prominent structures, St. Martin-in-the-Fields manages to do just fine. ⊠ *Trafalgar Sq., Westminster* ☏ *020/7766–1100, 020/7839–8362 brass rubbings, 020/7766–1122 evening-concert credit-card bookings* ⊕ *www.smitf.org* ☞ *Free; concerts £7–£30* ⊙ *Open all day for worship; sightseeing: Mon., Tues., and Fri. 8:30–1 and 2–6; Wed. 8:30–1:15 and 2–5; Thurs. 8:30–1.15 and 2–6; Sat. 9:30–6; Sun. 9:30–5* Ⓜ *Charing Cross, Leicester Sq.*

QUICK
BITES

The atmospheric St. Martin's Café in the Crypt, with its magnificent high-arched brick vault and gravestone floor, serves full English and continental breakfasts, sandwiches, salads, snacks, afternoon tea, and wine. Lunch and dinner options include vegetarian meals and the setting, at the heart of London, is superb.

NATIONAL GALLERY

✉ *Trafalgar Sq., Westminster*
☏ *020/7747–2885* ⊕ *www.nationalgallery.org.uk* ⌛ *Free; charge for special exhibitions; audio guide £3.50*
◷ *Sun.–Thurs. 10–6, Fri. 10–9*
Ⓜ *Charing Cross, Embankment, Leicester Sq.*

TIPS

■ Color coding throughout the galleries helps you keep track of the period in which you're immersed.

■ Begin at an "Art Start" terminal in the Sainsbury Wing or East Wing Espresso Bar. The interactive screens give you access to information on all of the museum's holdings; you can choose your favorites, and print out a free personal tour map.

■ Try a free weekday lunchtime lecture, or Ten Minute Talk, which illuminates the story behind a key work of art. One-hour free, guided tours start at the Sainsbury Wing daily at 11:30 and 2:30 (also Friday at 7 pm).

■ If you are eager for even more insight into the art, pick up a themed audio guide, which takes in about 20 paintings.

■ If you visit with children, don't miss special programs for young visitors, including free Family Sundays (every Sunday) with special talks for children and their parents.

Standing proudly on the north side of Trafalgar Square, this is truly one of the world's supreme art collections, with more than 2,300 masterpieces on show. Picasso, van Gogh, Michelangelo, Leonardo, Monet, Turner, and more—all for free. Watch out for special temporary exhibitions, too.

Highlights

This brief selection is your jumping-off point, but there are hundreds of other paintings to see, enough to fill a full day. In chronological order: (1) **Van Eyck** (circa 1395–1441), *The Arnolfini Portrait*—a solemn couple holds hands, the fish-eye mirror behind them mysteriously illuminating what can't be seen from the front view. (2) **Holbein** (1497–1543), *The Ambassadors*—two wealthy visitors from France stand surrounded by what were considered luxury goods at the time. Note the elongated skull at the bottom of the painting, which takes shape when viewed from an angle. (3) **Leonardo da Vinci** (1452–1519), *The Virgin and Child*—this exquisite black-chalk "Burlington Cartoon" depicts the master's most haunting Mary. (4) **Velazquez** (1599–1660), *Christ in the House of Martha and Mary*—in this enigmatic masterpiece the Spaniard plays with perspective and the role of the viewer. (5) **Turner** (1775–1851), *Rain, Steam and Speed: The Great Western Railway*, the whirl of rain, mist, steam, and locomotion is nothing short of astonishing (spot the hare). (6) **Caravaggio** (1573–1610), *The Supper at Emmaus*—a freshly resurrected Christ blesses bread in an astonishingly domestic vision from the master of chiaroscuro. (7) **Van Gogh** (1853–90), *Sunflowers*—painted during his sojourn with Gauguin in Arles, this is quintessential Van Gogh. (8) **Seurat** (1859–91), *Bathers at Asnières*—this summer day's idyll is one of the pointillist extraordinaire's best-known works.

FAMILY
Fodor's Choice
★
Tate Britain. The stately neoclassical institution may not be as ambitious as its sibling Tate Modern on the South Bank, but Tate Britain's bright galleries lure only a fraction of the Modern's crowds and are a great place to explore British art from 1500 to the present. First opened in 1897, funded by the sugar magnate Sir Henry Tate, the museum includes the Linbury Galleries on the lower floors, which stage temporary exhibitions, whereas the upper floors show the permanent collection. From early

> ### ST. MARTIN'S CONCERTS
>
> Classical concerts (some by candlelight) are held every Thursday to Saturday (and some Tuesdays) at 7:30 pm with evening jazz concerts in the crypt every Wednesday at 8 pm. Tickets are available from the box office in the crypt. Free (donation appreciated) lunchtime concerts take place Monday, Tuesday, and Friday, 1–2 pm.

2014, much more of the Tate's collection will be on permanent display as part of a major re-development of the galleries. So you'll have no excuse not to pop in and view classic works by John Constable, Thomas Gainsborough, David Wilkie, Francis Bacon, Duncan Grant, Barbara Hepworth, and Ben Nicholson and an outstanding display from J.M.W. Turner in the Clore Gallery, including many later vaporous and light-infused works such as *Sunrise with Sea Monsters*. Sumptuous Pre-Raphaelite pieces are a major drawcard while the Contemporary British Art galleries bring you face to face with Damien Hirst's *Away from the Flock* and other recent conceptions. The Tate Britain also hosts the annual Turner Prize exhibition, with its accompanying furor over the state of contemporary art, from about October to January each year. Details of activities for families are on the website.

■ TIP➔ Craving more art? Head down the river on the Tate to Tate (£5.50 one way) to the Tate Modern, running between the two museums every 40 minutes. A River Roamer ticket (£13.60) permits a day's travel, with stops including the London Eye and the Tower of London. ⊠ *Millbank, Westminster* ☎ *020/7887–8888* ⊕ *www.tate.org.uk/britain* ✇ *Free, special exhibitions £9–£15* ☉ *Sat.–Thurs. 10–6 (last entry at 5:15), Fri. 10–10 (last entry at 9:15)* Ⓜ *Pimlico.*

QUICK BITES
Rex Whistler Restaurant. Due to re-open in mid-2013 following a major refurbishment, this restaurant, in the Tate Britain, is almost a destination in itself, with its celebrated Rex Whistler murals and a daily fixed-price three-course lunch menu (under £25) as well as à la carte choices. Ingredients celebrate British produce, such as Cornish crab, Welsh lamb, Scottish smoked salmon, and Stilton cheese. It also offers a legendary wine list. Open for lunch and afternoon tea daily; breakfast is served on weekends from 10 to 11:30. ⊠ *Tate Britain, Millbank, Westminster* ☎ *020/7887–8825.*

Manton Café at Tate Britain. Drinks, sandwiches, and cakes are available daily from 10 am to 5 pm. ⊠ *Tate Britain, Millbank, Westminster* ☎ *020/7887–8825.*

The Tate Britain showcases British art from the last 500 years, including contemporary works.

Trafalgar Square. This is literally the center of London: a plaque on the corner of the Strand and Charing Cross Road marks the spot from which distances on U.K. signposts are measured. **Nelson's Column** stands at the heart of the square (which is named after the great admiral's most important victory), guarded by haughty lions designed by Sir Edwin Landseer and flanked by **statues of Charles Napier and Henry Havelock,** two generals who helped establish the British Empire in India. The fourth plinth is given over to rotating works by contemporary artists. The square is a magnet for national celebrations and protests—V.E. Day, New Year's Eve, sporting triumphs, political demonstrations—and is, thankfully, more pleasant to visit since the pedestrianization of its northern side. Although Chinese tourists know it as Pigeon Square, feeding the birds is now banned and the gray flocks have flown.

In the 13th century, the site housed birds of a different kind: the royal hawks and falcons. Come 1530, those buildings had been replaced by the "Great Mews" (the royal stables) which in turn were demolished in 1830 as part of John Nash's Charing Cross Improvement Scheme. Nash envisioned the square as a cultural public space and exploited its natural north–south incline to create a succession of high points from which to look down upon the Thames, the Houses of Parliament, and Buckingham Palace. Upon Nash's death, the work continued under Sir Charles Barry and then Sir Edwin Lutyens, with the square finally completed in 1850.

At the southern point of the square, en route to Whitehall, is the **equestrian statue of Charles I.** After the Civil War and the king's execution, Oliver Cromwell, the anti-Royalist leader, commissioned a scrap dealer, brazier John Rivett, to melt the statue. The story goes that Rivett buried it in his garden and made a fortune peddling knickknacks wrought, he claimed, from its metal, only to produce the statue miraculously unscathed after the restoration of the monarchy—and to make more cash reselling it to the authorities. In 1667 Charles II had it placed where it stands today, near the spot where his father was executed in 1649. Each year, on January 30, the day of the king's death, the Royal Stuart Society lays a wreath at the foot of the statue. ⊠ *Westminster* Ⓜ *Charing Cross.*

Fodor's Choice **Westminster Abbey.**

★ *See the highlighted listing in this chapter.*

WORTH NOTING

Admiralty Arch. This stately gateway to the Mall (rhymes with 'shall') is one of London's finest set pieces. On the southwest corner of Trafalgar Square, the arch, named after the adjacent Royal Navy headquarters, was designed by Sir Aston Webb and completed in 1912 as a memorial to Queen Victoria. Actually comprised of five arches—two for pedestrians, two for traffic, and the central arch, which is opened only for state occasions—it's a suitably grand, impressive way to approach Buckingham Palace.

A quirky feature of the arch is its curious "nose": About 7 feet up, on the inside wall of the most northerly arch is a nose-sized and -shaped protrusion; many thought it based on the schnozzle of Wellington himself, until it turned out to be the work of guerilla artist, Rick Buckley, in 1997. ⊠ *The Mall, Cockspur St., and Trafalgar Sq., Westminster* Ⓜ *Charing Cross.*

Banqueting House. James I commissioned Inigo Jones, one of England's great architects, to undertake a grand building on the site of the original Tudor Palace of Whitehall, which was (according to one foreign visitor) "ill-built, and nothing but a heap of houses." Jones's Banqueting House, finished in 1622 and the first building in England to be completed in the neo-classical style, bears all the hallmarks of the Palladian sophistication and purity which so influenced Jones during his sojourn in Italy. James's son, Charles I, enhanced the interior by employing the Flemish painter Peter Paul Rubens—enticed to England by the promise of a knighthood—to glorify his father and himself (naturally) in a series of vibrant painted ceiling panels called "The Apotheosis of James I." As it turned out, these allegorical paintings, depicting a wise monarch being received into heaven, were the last thing Charles saw before stepped through the open first floor window onto the scaffold, which had been erected directly outside for his execution by Cromwell's Parliamentarians in 1649. Yet 20 years later his son, Charles II, would celebrate the restoration of the monarchy in the exact same place. ⊠ *Whitehall, Westminster* ☎ *020/3166–6154, 020/3166–6155, 020/3166–6153 concert information* ⊕ *www.hrp.org.uk* 🎫 *£5, includes audio guide* ⊙ *Mon.– Sat. 10–5, last admission 4:15. Closed Christmas wk. Liable to close at short notice for events so calling first is advisable* Ⓜ *Charing Cross, Embankment, Westminster.*

Carlton House Terrace. Architect John Nash designed Carlton House, a glorious example of the Regency style, between 1812 and 1830, under the patronage of George IV (Prince Regent until George III's death in 1820). Nash was the architect of the grand scheme for Regent Street, which started here and ended with the sweep of neoclassical houses encircling Regent's Park, where the Prince Regent, who lived at Carlton House, had plans to build a country villa. Even though Carlton House was considered a most extravagant building for its time, it was demolished after the prince's accession to the throne, and Nash built Carlton House Terrace, no less imposing, with white-stucco facades and massive Corinthian columns, in its place. Carlton Terrace was a smart address and one that prime ministers Gladstone (1856) and Palmerston (1857–75) enjoyed. Today Carlton House Terrace houses the Royal College of Pathologists (No. 2), the Royal Society (Nos. 6–9), whose members have included Isaac Newton and Charles Darwin, and the Turf Club (No. 5). ⊠ *The Mall, St. James's* Ⓜ *Charing Cross.*

FAMILY **Household Cavalry Museum.** Horse lovers can see working horses belonging to the British Army's two senior regiments, the Life Guards and the Blues and Royals, being tended to in their stable block behind a glass wall. Located in the cavalry's original 17th-century stables, the museum has displays of uniforms and weapons going back to 1661 as well as interactive exhibits on the regiments' current operational roles. In the tack room you can handle saddles and bridles, and try on a trooper's uniform, including its distinctive brass helmet with horsehair plume. ⊠ *Horse Guards, Whitehall* ☎ *020/7930–3070* ⊕ *www. householdcavalrymuseum.org.uk* ⊠ *£6* ⊗ *Mar.–Sept., daily 10–6; Oct.– Feb., daily 10–5* Ⓜ *Charing Cross, Westminster.*

St. Margaret's Church. Dwarfed by its neighbor, Westminster Abbey, St. Margaret's was founded in the 11th century and rebuilt between 1488 and 1523. As the unofficial parish church of the House of Commons, St. Margaret's is available for weddings and memorial services for MPs and Lord Mayors—Winston Churchill tied the knot here in 1908. Samuel Pepys, Chaucer, and John Milton worshipped here, and since 1681, a pew off the south aisle has been set aside for the Speaker of the House (look for the carved portcullis). The stained glass in the north windows is classically Victorian, facing abstract glass from John Piper in the south, replacing the originals, which were ruined in World War II. ⊠ *St. Margaret's St., Parliament Sq., Westminster* ☎ *020/7654–4840* ⊕ *www.westminster-abbey.org/st-margarets* ⊗ *Weekdays 9:30–3:30, Sat. 9–1:30, Sun. 2–5 (entry via east door). Church may close on short notice for services, so call ahead* Ⓜ *Westminster.*

The Supreme Court. The highest court of appeal in the U.K. is housed in the carefully restored Middlesex Guildhall. Visitors are welcome to pop in (for free) and look at the three courtrooms, including the impressive Court Room 1, on the second floor, with its magnificent carved wood ceiling. There is a café downstairs. ⊠ *Parliament Sq., Westminster* ☎ *020/7960–1500, 020/7960–1900* ⊕ *www.supremecourt.gov.uk* ⊠ *Free* ⊗ *Weekdays 9:30–4:30* Ⓜ *Westminster (take Exit 6 for Whitehall west).*

Continued on page 60

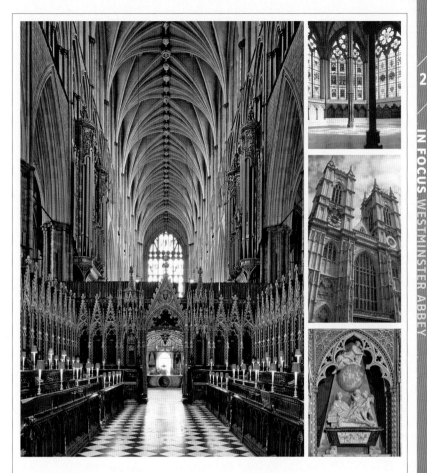

WESTMINSTER ABBEY

A monument to the rich—and often bloody and scandalous—history of Great Britain, Westminster Abbey rises on the Thames skyline as one of the most iconic sites in London.

The mysterious gloom of the lofty medieval interior is home to more than 600 monuments and memorial statues. About 3,300 people, from kings to composers to wordsmiths, are buried in the abbey. It has been the scene of 14 royal weddings and no less than 38 coronations—the first in 1066, when William the Conqueror was made king here.

TOURING THE ABBEY

There's only one way around the abbey, and as there will almost certainly be a long stream of shuffling tourists at your heels, you'll need to be alert to catch the highlights. Enter by the north door.

When you enter the church, turn around and look up to see the ❶ **painted-glass rose window**, the largest of its kind.

The ❷ **Coronation Chair**, at the foot of the Henry VII Chapel, has been briefly graced by nearly every regal posterior since Edward I ordered it in 1301. Look for the graffiti on the back of the Coronation chair. It's the work of 18th- and 19th-century visitors and Westminster schoolboys who carved their names there.

The ❸ **Henry VII's Lady Chapel** contains the tombs of Henry VII and his queen, Elizabeth of York. Close by are monuments to the young daughters of James I, and an urn purported to hold the remains of the so-called Princes in the Tower—Edward V and Richard. Interestingly, arch enemies Elizabeth I and her half-sister Mary Tudor share a tomb here. Begun in 1503, the chapel is famed for its ceiling—a dazzling fan-vaulted roof with carved pendants—and the heraldic banners of living knights that hang above its oak stalls.

In front of the ❹ **High Altar**, which was used for the funerals of Princess Diana and the Queen Mother, is a black-and-white marble pavement laid in 1268. The intricate Italian Cosmati work contains three Latin inscriptions, one of which states that the world will last for 19,683 years.

The ❺ **Shrine of St. Edward the Confessor** contains the shrine to the pre-Norman king. Because of its great age, you must join a tour with the verger to be admitted to the chapel. (Details are available at the admission desk; there is a small extra charge.)

Geoffrey Chaucer was the first poet to be buried in ❻ **Poets' Corner** in 1400. Other memorials include: William Shakespeare, William Blake, John Milton, Jane Austen, Samuel Taylor Coleridge, William Wordsworth, and Charles Dickens.

A door from the south transept and south choir aisle leads to the calm of the ❼ **Great Cloisters.**

West Entrance

College Hall

Dean's Court

Deanery

Choir

Site of Refectory

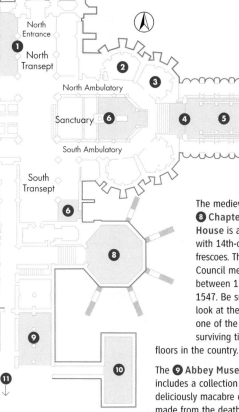

and actual clothing of Charles II and Admiral Lord Nelson (complete with eye patch).

The ❿ **Little Cloister** is a quiet haven, and just beyond, the ⓫ **College Garden** is a delightful diversion. Filled with medicinal herbs, it has been tended by monks for more than 900 years.

The ⓬ **Dean's Yard** is the best spot for a fine view of the massive flying buttresses above.

The medieval ❽ **Chapter House** is adorned with 14th-century frescoes. The King's Council met here between 1257 and 1547. Be sure to look at the floor, one of the finest surviving tiled floors in the country.

The ❾ **Abbey Museum** includes a collection of deliciously macabre effigies made from the death masks

In the choir screen, north of the entrance to the choir, is a marble ⓭ **monument to Sir Isaac Newton.**

⓮ **A plaque to Franklin D. Roosevelt** is one of the Abbey's very few tributes to a foreigner.

The ⓯ **Grave of the Unknown Warrior,** in memory of the soldiers who lost their lives in both world wars, is near the exit of the abbey.

QUIRKY LONDON

Near the Henry VII chapel, keep an eye open for St. Wilgefortis, who was so concerned to protect her chastity that she prayed to God for help and woke up one morning with a full growth of beard.

A BRIEF HISTORY

960 AD Benedictine monastery founded on the site by King Edward and King Dunstan.

1045–65 King Edward the Confessor enlarges the original monastery, erecting a stone church in honor of St. Paul the Apostle. Named "west minster" to distinguish from "east minster" (St. Paul's Cathedral).

1065 The church is consecrated on December 28. Edward doesn't live to see the ceremony.

1161 Following Edward's canonization, his body is moved by Henry III to a more elaborate resting place behind the High Altar. Other medieval kings are later buried around his tomb.

1245–54 Henry III pulls down the abbey and starts again with a new Gothic style influenced by his travels in France. Master mason Henry de Reyns ("of Rheims") constructs the transepts, north front, and rose windows, as well as part of the cloisters and Chapter House.

1269 The new abbey is consecrated and the choir is completed.

1350s Richard II resumes Henry III's plan to rebuild the monastery. Henry V and Henry VII continue as benefactors.

1503 The Lady Chapel is demolished and the foundation stone of Henry VII's Chapel is laid on the site.

1540 The abbey ceases to be used as a monastery.

1560 Elizabeth I refounds the abbey as a Collegiate Church. From this point on it is a "Royal Peculiar," exempt from the jurisdiction of bishops.

1745 The western towers, left unfinished from medieval times, are finally completed, based on a design by Sir Christopher Wren.

1995 Following a 25-year restoration program, saints and allegorical figures are added to the niches on the western towers and around the Great West Door.

PLANNING YOUR DAY

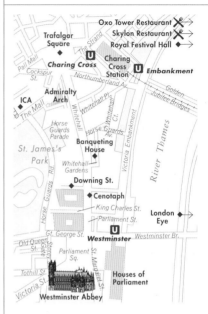

GETTING HERE: The closest Tube stop is Westminster. When you exit the station, walk west along Great George Street, away from the river. Turn left on St. Margaret Street.

CONTACT INFO: ✉ Broad Sanctuary, Westminster SW1 P3PA ☎ 020/7222-5152 ⊕ www.westminster-abbey.org.

ADMISSION: Adults: Abbey and museum £6. **Family tickets:** 2 adults and 2 children, £38. **Children under 11:** free.

HOURS: The abbey is a house of worship. Services may cause changes to the visiting hours on any given day, so be sure to call ahead.
Abbey: Weekdays 9:30–3:30; Sat. 9:30–2:30; (last admission 1:30); Sun, worship only.
Museum: Mon.–Sat. 10:30–4.
Cloisters: Daily 8–6
College Garden: Apr.–Sept.: Tues.–Thurs. 10–6; Oct.–Mar.: Tues.–Thurs. 10–4.
Chapter House: Mon.–Sat. 10–4

WHAT'S NEARBY: To make the most of your day, arrive at the abbey early (doors open at 9:30), then make an afternoon visit to the Parliament buildings and finish with a sunset ride on the **London Eye**. Post-flight, take a walk along the fairy-lit South Bank and have dinner (or a drink in the bar) with a view, at the **Oxo Tower Restaurant** (☎ 020/7803–3888) or the Royal Festival Hall's **Skylon Restaurant** (☎ 020/7654–7800).

Please note that overseas visitors can no longer visit the **Houses of Parliament** during session. However, tours of the buildings are available in August and September. For more information and booking call ☎ 0844/847–1672. Also, it's advisable to prebook tickets for the London Eye. Do this online at www.londoneye.com, or call 0871/781–3000.

IN A HURRY?

If you're pressed for time, concentrate on the following four highlights: the Coronation Chair; Chapter House; Poets' Corner; and Grave of the Unknown Warrior.

THINGS TO KNOW

■ Photography and filming are not permitted anywhere in the abbey.

■ In winter the interior of the abbey can get quite cold; dress accordingly.

■ For an animated history of the Abbey, join one of the verger-led tours (90 minutes) that depart from the North Door: Apr.–Sept.: Mon.–Fri. 10, 10:30, 11, 2, 2:30, Sat. 10, 10:30, 11; Oct.–Mar.: Mon.–Fri. 10:30, 11, 2, 2:30, Sat. 10:30, 11. Ask at information desk, £3 per person (in addition to entrance charge).

■ Touring the abbey can take half a day, especially in summer, when lines are long.

■ To avoid the crowds, make sure you arrive early. If you're first in line you can enjoy parts of the abbey in relative calm before the mad rush descends.

■ If you want to study up before you go, visit www.westminster-abbey.org, which includes an in-depth history and self-guided tour of the abbey. Otherwise pick up a free leaflet from the information desk.

■ On Sundays the abbey is not open to visitors. Join a service instead. Check the Web site for service times, as well as details of concerts, organ recitals, and special events.

FAMILY **Wellington Barracks.** These are the headquarters of the Guards Division, the Queen's five regiments of elite foot guards (Grenadier, Coldstream, Scots, Irish, and Welsh) who protect the sovereign and, dressed in tunics of gold-purled scarlet and tall bearskin caps, patrol her palaces. Guardsmen alternate these ceremonial postings with serving in current conflicts, for which they wear more practical uniforms. If you want to learn more about the guards, visit the **Guards Museum,** which has displays on all aspects of a guardsman's life in conflicts dating back to 1642; the entrance is next to the Guards Chapel. Next door is the **Guards Toy Soldier Centre,** a great place for a souvenir. ✉ *Birdcage Walk, Westminster* ☎ *020/7414–3428* ⊕ *www.theguardsmuseum.com* 🎫 *£5* ⊙ *Daily 10–4; last admission 3:30* Ⓜ *St. James's Park, Green Park.*

Westminster Cathedral. Amid the concrete jungle of Victoria Street lies this remarkable neo-Byzantine gem, seat of the Archbishop of Westminster, head of the Roman Catholic Church in England and Wales (often, the archbishop is also a cardinal, although that currently isn't the case). Faced with having Westminster Abbey as a neighbor, architect John Francis Bentley looked to the east for inspiration, to the basilicas of St. Mark's in Venice and the Hagia Sofia in Istanbul. The asymmetrical redbrick edifice, dating from 1903, is banded with stripes of Portland stone and abutted by a 273-foot-high bell tower (containing Big Edward) at the northwest corner, ascendable by elevator for sterling views. The interior remains incomplete but the unfinished overhead brickwork of the ceiling lends the church a dark, brooding intensity. Several side chapels, such as the Chapel of the Blessed Sacrament and the Holy Souls Chapel, are beautifully finished in glittering mosaics. The Lady Chapel—dedicated to the Virgin Mary—is also sumptuously decorated. Look out for the Stations of the Cross, a meditative representation of the *Via Dolorosa* found in all Catholic churches (by Eric Gill), and the striking baldachin—the enormous stone canopy standing over the altar with a giant cross suspended in front of it. The nave, the widest in the country, is constructed in green marble, which also has a Byzantine connection—it was cut from the same place as that used in the Hagia Sofia, and was almost confiscated by warring Turks as it traveled west. All told, more than 200 different types of marble can be found within the cathedral's interior. Just inside the main entrance is the tomb of Cardinal Basil Hume, head of the Catholic Church in England and Wales for more than 25 years. There's a café in the crypt. ✉ *Ashley Pl., Westminster* ☎ *020/7798–9055* ⊕ *www.westminstercathedral.org. uk* 🎫 *Bell Tower and viewing gallery £5; Treasures of the Cathedral exhibition £5; joint ticket for Bell Tower and exhibition £8* ⊙ *Weekdays*

ROYALTY WATCHING

You've seen Big Ben, the Tower, and Westminster Abbey. But somehow you feel something is missing: a close encounter with Britain's most famous attraction—Her actual Majesty, Elizabeth II. The Queen and the Royal Family attend hundreds of functions a year, and if you want to know what they are doing on any given date, turn to the Court Circular, printed in the major London dailies, or check out the Royal Family website, ⊕ *www.royal.gov.uk*, for the latest events on the Royal Diary. Trooping the Colour is usually held on the second Saturday in June, to celebrate the Queen's official birthday. This spectacular parade begins when she leaves Buckingham Palace in her carriage and rides down the Mall to arrive at Horse Guards Parade at 11 exactly. To watch, just line up along the Mall with your binoculars!

Another time you can catch the Queen in all her regalia is when she and the Duke of Edinburgh ride in state to open the Houses of Parliament. The famous black and gilt-trimmed Irish State Coach travels from Buckingham Palace—on a clear day, it's to be hoped, for this ceremony takes place in late October or early November. The Gold State Coach, an icon of fairy-tale glamour, is used for coronations and jubilees only.

But perhaps the most relaxed, least formal time to see the Queen is during Royal Ascot, held at the racetrack near Windsor Castle—a short train ride out of London—usually during the third week of June (Tuesday–Friday). The Queen and members of the Royal Family are driven down the track to the Royal Box in an open carriage, giving spectators a chance to see them. After several races, the famously horse-loving Queen invariably walks down to the paddock, greeting race goers as she proceeds. If you meet her, remember to address her as "Your Majesty."

7–6, weekends 8–7; Treasures of the Cathedral exhibition weekdays 9:30–5, weekends 9:30–6 Ⓜ *Victoria.*

ST. JAMES'S

As a fitting coda to all of Westminster's pomp and circumstance, St. James's—packed with old-money galleries, restaurants, and gentlemen's clubs that embody the history and privilege of traditional London—is found to the south of the gaudy avenue called Piccadilly and north of the Mall.

When Whitehall Palace burned down in 1698, all of London turned its attention to St. James's Palace, the new royal residence. In the 18th and 19th centuries, the area around the palace became the place to live, and many of the estates surrounding the palace disappeared in a building frenzy, as mansions were built and streets laid out. Most of the homes here are privately owned and so closed to visitors, but there are some treasure houses that you can explore (such as Spencer House), as well as a bevy of fancy shops that have catered to the great and good for centuries.

Today, St. James's remains a rather masculine enclave, containing most of the capitol's celebrated gentle-men's clubs (especially the classic Atheneum), long-established men's outfitters and clothiers, and some interesting art galleries and antiques shops. In one corner is St. James's Park, a fitting prelude to the biggest monument in the area: Buckingham

Palace, home to Her Majesty. Impressive St. James's Palace is where much of the office work for the House of Windsor gets done; nearby is Clarence House, London abode of Prince Charles and his Camilla.

TOP ATTRACTIONS

Fodor's Choice
★

Buckingham Palace.

See the highlighted listing in this chapter.

The Mall. This stately, 115-foot-wide processional route sweeping from Admiralty Arch to the Queen Victoria Memorial at Buckingham Pal-ace is an updated 1904 version of a promenade laid out around 1660 for the game of *paille-maille* (a type of croquet crossed with golf), which also gave the parallel road Pall Mall its name. The **Duke of York Memorial** up the steps toward Carlton House Terrace is a towering column dedicated to George III's second son, further immortalized in the English nursery rhyme "The Grand old Duke of York." Sadly, the internal spiral steps are inaccessible. ■TIP➔ Be sure to stroll along The Mall on Sunday when the road is closed to traffic, or catch the bands and troops of the Household Division on their way from St. James's Palace to Buckingham Palace for the Changing the Guard. ⊠ *St. James's* Ⓜ *Charing Cross, Green Park.*

Piccadilly Circus. The origins of the name "Piccadilly" relate to a humble 17th-century tailor from the Strand named Robert Baker who sold picadils—a stiff ruffled collar all the rage in courtly circles—and built a house with the proceeds. Snobs dubbed his new-money mansion Pic-cadilly Hall, and the name stuck.

Pride of place in the circus—a circular junction until the construction of Shaftesbury Avenue in 1886— belongs to London's favorite statue, Eros (actually, the 1893 work is a representation of Eros's brother Anteros, the Greek God of requited love). The creation of young sculp-tor Alfred Gilbert is a memorial to the selflessness of the philanthropic Earl of Shaftesbury (the god's bow and arrow are an allusion to the earl's name). Gilbert cast the statue in the then-novel medium of alu-minum. Unfortunately, he spent most of his £8,000 fee ensuring the bronze fountain beneath was cast to his specifications. Already in debt, Gilbert eventually went bankrupt and fled to the continent (although, years later, he'd return and receive a knighthood). Beneath the modern bank of neon advertisements surrounding the circus are some of the most elegant Edwardian-era buildings in London. ⊠ *St. James's* Ⓜ *Pic-cadilly Circus.*

A classic photo op: cavalry from the Queen's Life Guard at Buckingham Palace.

The Queen's Gallery. Twenty years after it was destroyed in an air raid in 1940, this former chapel at the south side of Buckingham Palace was redeveloped, at the say-so of the Queen, into a gallery fit to house the Royal Collection—and what a collection it is! Technically speaking, the sovereign doesn't "own" these rare and exquisite works of art, she merely holds them in trust for the nation. Only a selection from the Royal Collection is on view at any one time, presented in themed exhibitions. Let the excellent audio guide take you through the elegant galleries filled with some of the world's greatest art works.

A rough timeline of the major royal collectors starts with Charles I (who also commissioned Rubens to paint the Banqueting House ceiling). An avid art enthusiast, Charles established the basis of the Royal Collection, purchasing works by Raphael, Titian, Caravaggio, and Dürer. During the Civil War and in the aftermath of Charles's execution, many masterpieces were sold abroad and subsequently repatriated by Charles II. George III, who bought Buckingham House, scooped up a notable collection of Venetian (including Canaletto), Renaissance (Bellini and Raphael), and Dutch (Vermeer) art, and a large number of baroque drawings, in addition to patronizing English contemporary artists such as Gainsborough and Beechey. He also took a liking to American artist Benjamin West. The Prince Regent, later George IV, transformed his father's house into a palace, filling it with fine art from paintings to porcelain; he had a particularly good eye for Rembrandt, equestrian works by Stubbs, and lavish portraits by Lawrence. Queen Victoria had a penchant for Landseer animals and landscapes, and Frith's contemporary scenes. Later, Edward VII indulged Queen Alexandra's love

BUCKINGHAM PALACE

✉ *Buckingham Palace Rd.,
St. James's* ☎ *020/7766–7300*
⊕ *www.royalcollection.org.uk/
visit* 💷 *£19 (includes audio
tour)* ⊙ *Open Aug., daily
9:30–7 (last admission 4:45);
Sept., daily 9:30–6:30 (last
admission 3:45). Times subject
to change; check website*
Ⓜ *Victoria, St. James's Park,
Green Park.*

TIPS

■ If bought directly from the palace ticket office, tickets are valid for a repeat visit over the course of 12 months from the first visit.

■ Admission is by timed ticket with entry every 15 minutes throughout the day. Allow up to two hours.

■ A Royal Day Out ticket, available only in August and September, gives you the regal triple whammy of the Royal Mews, the Queen's Gallery, and the State Rooms, and is valid throughout the day. Tickets cost £33.25. Allow four hours.

■ Get there by 10:30 to grab a spot in the best viewing section for the Changing the Guard (www.changing-the-guard.com), daily at 11:30 from May until the end of July (varies according to troop deployment requirements) and on alternate days for the rest of the year, weather permitting.

It's rare to get a chance to see how the other half—well, other minute fraction—lives and works. But when the Queen heads off to Scotland on her annual summer holiday (you can tell because the Union Jack flies above the palace instead of the Royal Standard), the palace's 19 State Rooms open up to visitors, although the north wing's private apartments remain behind closed doors. With fabulous gilt moldings and walls adorned with masterpieces by Rembrandt, Rubens, and other old masters, the State Rooms are the grandest of the palace's 775 rooms.

Highlights

The **Grand Hall,** followed by the **Grand Staircase** and **Guard Room,** give a taste of the marble, gold leaf galore, and massive, twinkling chandeliers that embellish the palace. Don't miss the theatrical **Throne Room,** with the original 1953 coronation throne, or the sword in **the Ballroom,** used by the Queen to bestow knighthoods and other honors. Royal portraits line the **State Dining Room,** and the **Blue Drawing Room** is splendor in overdrive. The bow-shaped **Music Room** features lapis lazuli columns between arched floor-to-ceiling windows, and the alabaster-and-gold plasterwork of the **White Drawing Room** is a dramatic crescendo. Spend some time ambling around the splendid gardens, a gorgeous epilogue to the visit.

The **Changing the Guard,** also known as **Guard Mounting,** remains one of London's best free shows and culminates in front of the palace. Marching to live bands, the old guard proceeds up the Mall from St. James's Palace to Buckingham Palace. Shortly afterward, the new guard approaches from Wellington Barracks. Then within the forecourt, the captains of the old and new guards symbolically transfer the keys to the palace.

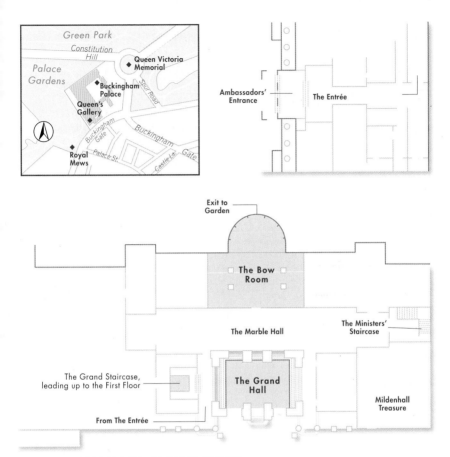

BUCKINGHAM PALACE: GROUND FLOOR

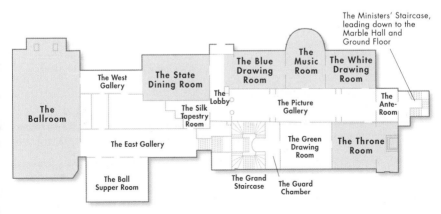

BUCKINGHAM PALACE: FIRST FLOOR

of Fabergé, and many royal tours around the empire produced gifts of gorgeous caliber, such as the Cullinan diamond from South Africa and an emerald-studded belt from India.

More than 3,000 other objects from the Royal Collection reside in museums and galleries in the United Kingdom and abroad: check out the National Gallery, the Victoria & Albert Museum, the Museum of London, and the British Museum. ■■TIP➜ The E-gallery provides an interactive electronic version of the collection, allowing the user to open lockets, remove a sword from its scabbard, or take apart the tulip vases. It's probably the closest you could get to eyeing practically every diamond in the sovereign's glittering diadem. ✉ *Buckingham Palace, Buckingham Palace Rd., St. James's* ☎ *020/7766–7301* ⊕ *www.royalcollection. org.uk* 🎧 *£9.50 with free audio guide; joint ticket with Royal Mews £15.75* ☉ *Daily 10–5:30; last admission 4:30* Ⓜ *Victoria, St. James's Park, Green Park.*

> **BEARSKIN, NOT BUSBY**
>
> While on duty, guardsmen take their job very, very seriously. They don't speak, don't acknowledge anyone (even those tourists trying in vain to make them laugh), don't even swat away troublesome flies from their noses. Worse: they're not even allowed to keel over under the weight of their enormous, sauna-like hats. Called "bearskins," the headdress was originally worn by the French Imperial Guard defeated in the Battle of Waterloo in 1815.

FAMILY **Royal Mews.** Fairy-tale gold-and-glass coaches and sleek Rolls-Royce state cars emanate from the Royal Mews, next door to the Queen's Gallery. The John Nash–designed Mews serve as the headquarters for Her Majesty's travel department (so beware of closures for state visits), complete with the Queen's own special breed of horses, ridden by wigged postilions decked in red-and-gold regalia. Between the stables and riding school arena are exhibits of polished saddlery and riding tack. The highlight of the Mews is the splendid Gold State Coach, like a piece of art on wheels, with its sculpted tritons and sea gods. Mews were originally falcons' quarters (the name comes from their "mewing," or feather shedding), but nowadays the horses rule the roost. There are activities for children, and guided tours are available March to October; call for details. ✉ *Buckingham Palace Rd., St. James's* ☎ *020/7766–7302* ⊕ *www.royalcollection.org.uk* 🎧 *£8.25 (includes audio tour); joint ticket with Queen's Gallery £15.75* ☉ *Mar.–Oct., Mon.–Sat. 10–5 (last admission 4:15); Nov.–Feb., Mon.–Sat. 10–4 (last admission 3:15)* Ⓜ *Victoria, St. James's Park.*

St. James's Palace. Commissioned by Henry VIII, this Tudor brick palace was the residence of kings and queens for more than 300 years; indeed, it remains the official residence of the Sovereign even though since Queen Victoria's day all monarchs have lived up the road in the more expansive Buckingham Palace. Today it contains various royal apartments and offices, including the working office of Charles, Prince of Wales (although the front door opens right onto the street, His Royal Highness always uses a back entrance). It's not open to the public but matters to ponder as you peer past the solitary sentry on duty: an

Gentlemen's shops in St. James's specialize in high-quality, handmade goods.

11th-century hospital for lepers once stood on the site; Charles I spent his last night here before execution; foreign ambassadors to Britain are still accredited to the Court of St. James's; and after the death of a monarch, the accession of the new sovereign is announced by the Garter King of Arms from the Proclamation Gallery overlooking Friary Court. Friary Court out front is a splendid setting for Trooping the Colour, part of the Queen's official birthday celebrations. Everyone loves to take a snapshot of the scarlet-coated guardsman standing sentry outside the imposing Tudor gateway. Note that the Changing the Guard ceremony at St. James's Palace occurs only on days when the guard at Buckingham Palace is changed. ⇨ *See entry for Buckingham Palace for details.* ✉ *Friary Ct., St. James's* ⊕ *www.royal.gov.uk* Ⓜ *Green Park.*

FAMILY **St. James's Park.** In a city of royal parks, this one—bordered by three palFodor's Choice aces (the Palace of Westminster, the Tudor **St. James's Palace,** and Buck-★ ingham Palace)—is the most regal of them all. It's not only London's oldest park, but also its smallest and most ornate. Once marshy meadows, the land was acquired by Henry VIII in 1532 as royal deer-hunting grounds (with dueling and sword fights strictly forbidden). Later, James I drained the land and installed an aviary and zoo (complete with crocodiles, camels, and an elephant). When Charles II returned from exile in France, where he had been hugely impressed by the splendor of the gardens at the Palace of Versailles, he transformed the park into formal gardens, with avenues, fruit orchards, and a canal. Lawns were grazed by goats, sheep, and deer, but in the 18th century the park became a different kind of hunting ground, for wealthy lotharios looking to pick up nighttime escorts. A century later, John Nash redesigned the landscape in a more naturalistic, romantic style, and if you gaze down the lake toward Buckingham Palace, you could believe yourself to be on a country estate.

A large population of waterfowl—including pelicans, geese, ducks, and swans (which belong to the Queen)—breed on and around Duck Island at the east end of the lake. From April to September, the deck chairs (charge levied) come out, crammed with office workers at midday, lunching while being serenaded by music from the bandstands. One of the best times to stroll the leafy walkways is after dark, with Westminster Abbey and the Houses of Parliament rising above the floodlighted lake. The popular Inn the Park restaurant is a wood-and-glass pavilion with a turf roof that blends in beautifully with the surrounding landscape; it's an excellent stopping place for a meal or a snack on a nice day. ⊠ *The Mall or Horse Guards approach or Birdcage Walk, St. James's* ⊕ *www.royalparks.gov.uk* ⊗ *Daily 5 am–midnight* Ⓜ *St. James's Park, Westminster.*

WORTH NOTING

Clarence House. The London home of Queen Elizabeth the Queen Mother for nearly 50 years, Clarence House is now the residence of the Prince of Wales, Camilla, Duchess of Cornwall, and Prince Harry. The Regency mansion was built by John Nash for the Duke of Clarence (later to become William IV) who considered next-door St. James's Palace to be too cramped for his liking, although post-War renovation work means that little remains of Nash's original. Since then it has remained a royal home for princesses, dukes, and duchesses, including the present monarch, Queen Elizabeth, as a newlywed before her coronation. The rooms have been sensitively preserved to reflect the Queen Mother's taste, with the addition of many works of art from the Royal Collection, including works by Winterhalter, Augustus John, and Sickert. You'll find it less palace and more home, with informal family pictures and comfortable sofas. The tour (by timed ticket entry only) is of the ground-floor rooms and includes the Lancaster Room, so called because of the marble chimneypiece presented by Lancaster County to the newly married Princess Elizabeth and the Duke of Edinburgh. Clarence House is usually open only for the month of August and tickets must be booked in advance. ⊠ *St. James's Palace, The Mall, St. James's* ☎ *020/7766–7303* ⊕ *www.royalcollection.org.uk* ⊒ *£9* ⊗ *Aug. 1.–Sept. 1, Mon.–Fri. 10–4 (last admission 3), weekends 10–5:30 (last admission 4:30)* Ⓜ *Green Park.*

Institute of Contemporary Arts (ICA). You would never suspect that behind the stately white-stucco facade in the heart of Establishment London is to be found that champion of the avant-garde, the ICA. Since 1947, the ICA has been pushing boundaries in the visual arts, performance, theater, dance, and music. There are two movie theaters, a performance theater, three galleries, a highbrow bookstore, a reading room, a café, and a hip bar. ⊠ *The Mall, St. James's* ☎ *020/7930–3647* ⊕ *www.ica. org.uk* ⊒ *Free; £10 for screenings* ⊗ *Tues.–Sun. 11–11 (galleries, open during exhibitions only, may have shorter hours)* Ⓜ *Charing Cross, Piccadilly Circus.*

ICA Café Bar. Overlooking The Mall, this café and bar offers a tasty, reasonably priced lunch and dinner menu, with coffees and snacks available throughout the day. Like the venue itself, it's open Tuesday–Sunday 11–11. ⊠ *The Mall, St. James's* ☎ *020/7930–8619* ⊕ *www.ica.org.uk.*

Spencer House. Ancestral abode of the Spencers—Diana, Princess of Wales's family—this is perhaps the finest example of an elegant 18th-century town house extant in London. Reflecting his passion for the Grand Tour and classical antiquities, the first Earl Spencer commissioned architect John Vardy to adapt designs from ancient Rome for a magnificent private palace. Vardy was responsible for the external elevation, including the gorgeous west-facing Palladian facade, its pediment adorned with classical statues, and the ground-floor interiors, notably the lavish Palm Room, which boasts a spectacular screen of columns covered in gilded carvings that resemble gold palm trees. The purpose of the bling-tastic style was not only to attest to Spencer's power and wealth but also to celebrate his marriage, a love match then rare in aristocratic circles (the palms are a symbol of marital fertility). Midway through construction—the house was built between 1756 and 1766—Spencer changed architects and hired James "Athenian" Stuart, whose designs were based on a classical Greek aesthetic, to decorate the gilded State Rooms on the first floor. These include the Painted Room, the first completely neoclassical room in Europe. In recent years the house was superlatively restored by Lord Rothschild (to impress close friend, Princess Diana, but in 2010 the Spencer family scandalously decided to sell off all the house's best furnishings and paintings at Christie's so that today's viewers see a decidedly denuded house. The garden, of Henry Holland design, has also been replanted in the 18th- and 19th-century fashion. The house is open only for one-hour guided tours. The garden is open some Sundays in summer. Check the website for details. ⊠ *27 St. James's Pl., St. James's* ☎ *020/7499–8620 recorded information, 020/7514–1958 tour reservations* ⊕ *www.spencerhouse. co.uk* ☑ *£12* ⊙ *Sept.–Dec. and Feb.–July, Sun. 10:30–5:45 (last tour 4:45)* Ⓜ *Green Park.*

St. James's Church. Blitzed by the German Luftwaffe in 1940 and not restored until 1954, this was one of the last of Sir Christopher Wren's London churches—and his favorite. Completed in 1684, it envelops one of Grinling Gibbon's finest works, an ornate limewood reredos (the screen behind the altar), and the organ was brought here in 1691 from Whitehall Palace. The church is a lively place, with all manner of lectures and concerts (some are free). A café enjoys a fine location right alongside the church, while a small, sedate garden is tucked away at the

PHOTO OP

The best place for a photo opportunity alongside one of the Queen's guardsmen is at St. James's Palace, or try to keep up alongside them during the morning Changing the Guard. They leave St. James's at about 10:50 am, for Buckingham Palace. Failing that, shuffle up to the mounted horse guards on the Whitehall side, there until 4 pm.

2

rear. The market out front is full of surprises, hosting antiques on Tuesday, and arts and crafts from Wednesday to Saturday. ✉ *197 Piccadilly, St. James's* ☎ *020/7734–4511, 020/7381–0441 concert program and tickets* ⊕ *www.st-james-piccadilly.org* Ⓜ *Piccadilly Circus, Green Park*.

St. James's Square. One of London's oldest and leafiest squares was also the most snobbish address of all when it was laid out around 1670, with 14 resident dukes and earls installed by 1720. Since 1841, No. 14—one of the several 18th-century residences spared by World War II bombs—has housed the **London Library** (⊕ *www.londonlibrary.co.uk*), founded by Thomas Carlyle. With its million or so volumes, this is the world's largest independent lending library and is also considered the best private humanities library in the land. The workplace of literary luminaries from T.S. Eliot to Bruce Chatwin, Kingsley Amis, Winston Churchill, John Betjeman, and Charles Dickens, the library invites you to read famous authors' complaints in the comments book—but you'll need a day (£15) or week (£50) membership to peruse the collection (bring ID and proof of a U.K. address), although these have to be applied for online in advance. Other notable institutions around the square include the East India Club at No. 16, the Naval and Military Club (known as the "In and Out" after the signage on its gateposts) at No. 4, as well as Chatham House, a think tank on international affairs. A small epitaph to WPC Yvonne Fletcher—shot by a Libyan gunman—can be found on the sidewalk around the square. ✉ *St. James's* Ⓜ *Piccadilly Circus*.

3

MAYFAIR AND MARYLEBONE

GETTING ORIENTED

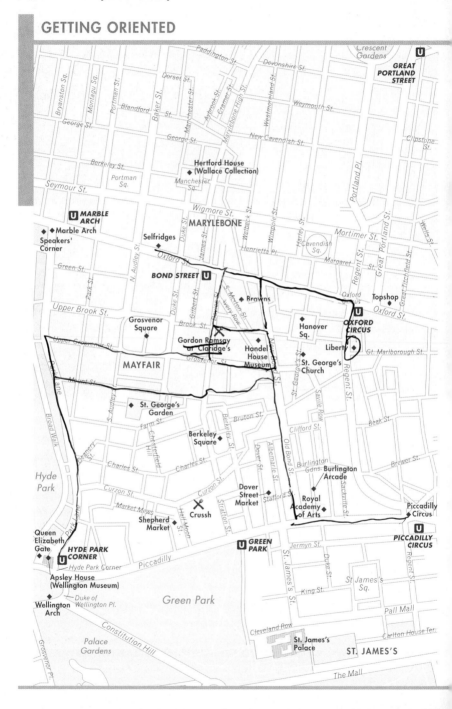

TOP REASONS TO GO

At home with the Duke of Wellington: His Apsley House—known as No. 1, London—is filled with splendid salons lined with grand old-master paintings.

Get a passion for fashion: The shopping on Bond and Mount streets will keep your credit card occupied at McQueen and McCartney, but don't forget stylish, gigantic Selfridges.

London's most charming shopping arcade: Built for Lord Cavendish in 1819, the beautiful Burlington Arcade is right out of a Victorian daguerreotype.

The Wallace Collection: Savor room after room of magnificent furniture, porcelain, silver, and top old-master paintings, in the former residence of the marquesses of Hertford.

Dress to impress at Claridge's: Afternoon tea at this sumptuous art deco gem is the perfect end to a shopping spree in Mayfair.

FEELING PECKISH?

Crussh. Delicious juices, smoothies, and soups are top choices here, as well as sandwiches, salads, and wraps. Take them to nearby Green Park, where—if you're lucky!—you can grab one of the deck chairs. ⊠ *1 Curzon St., Mayfair* ☎ *020/7629–2554* ⊕ *www.crussh.com* Ⓜ *Green Park.*

Gordon Ramsay at Claridge's. Fine dining is elevated to exquisite heights of elegance here; it's the perfect marriage of art deco beauty and culinary genius from one of England's most celebrated chefs. ⊠ *55 Brook St., Mayfair* ☎ *020/7499–0099* ⊕ *www.gordonramsay.com/claridges* Ⓜ *Bond St., Oxford Circus.*

Richoux. Since 1909, Richoux has been an affordable refuge from busy Piccadilly. Simple but well-executed French bistro food is served all day, as well as scrumptious afternoon tea. ⊠ *172 Piccadilly, Mayfair* ☎ *020/7493–2204* ⊕ *www.richoux. co.uk* Ⓜ *Green Park, Piccadilly Circus.*

GETTING THERE

Three Tube stations on the Central line will leave you smack in the center of these neighborhoods: Marble Arch, Bond Street (also on the Jubilee line), and Oxford Circus (also on the Victoria and Bakerloo lines).

You can also take the Piccadilly or Bakerloo line to the Piccadilly Circus Tube station, the Piccadilly line to the Hyde Park Corner station, or the Piccadilly, Victoria, or Jubilee line to the Green Park station.

The best buses are the 8, which takes in Green Park, Berkeley Square, and New Bond Street, and the 9—one of the few routes that still use the traditional double-decker Routemaster model—which runs along Piccadilly.

MAKING THE MOST OF YOUR TIME

Reserve at least a day to experience Mayfair and Marylebone. Leave enough time for shopping and also to wander casually through the streets and squares.

The only areas to avoid are the Tube stations at rush hour, and Oxford Street if you don't like crowds. At all costs, stay away from Oxford Circus around 5 pm, when the commuter rush can, at times, resemble an East African wildebeest migration—but without the charm.

The area becomes as quiet at night—so plan to party elsewhere.

Sightseeing
★★★★
Nightlife
★
Dining
★★★★
Lodging
★★★★
Shopping
★★★★

Mayfair forms the core of London's West End, the city's smartest central area. This neighborhood epitomizes the stately flavor that is peculiarly London's—the sense of being in a great, rich, powerful city is almost palpable as you wander along the posh and polished streets. Scoot across the district's one exception to all this elegance—Oxford Street—and you'll discover the pleasant streets of Marylebone, the most central of London's many "villages."

MAYFAIR

Updated by
James O'Neill

Ultra-ritzy Mayfair, lined with beautiful 18th-century mansions (along with Edwardian apartment buildings faced with deep-red brick) is the address of choice for many of London's wealthiest residents. Once you note the sheer number of Rolls-Royces, Bentleys, and Jaguars, you may become acutely aware of how poor you are. Even the delivery vans hereabouts all seem to bear some royal coat of arms, proclaiming them to be purveyors of fine goodies for as long as anyone can remember.

The district can't claim to be stuffed with must-sees—but that is part of its appeal. There is no shortage of history and gorgeous architecture; the streets here are custom-built for window-shopping, expansive strolling, and getting a peek into the lifestyles of London's rich and famous, past and present. Mayfair is primarily residential, so its homes are off-limits except for one satisfyingly grand house: Apsley House, the Duke of Wellington's home, built by Robert Adam in 1771, and once known as No. 1, London.

Despite being bounded by four of the busiest streets in London—bustling budget-shopping mecca Oxford Street to the north, traffic artery Park Lane with Hyde Park beyond to the west, and elegant boulevards Regent Street and Piccadilly to the east and south, respectively—Mayfair itself is remarkably traffic-free and a delight to explore. Starting at **Selfridges** on Oxford Street, a southward stroll will take you through quiet residential streets lined with Georgian town houses (the area was largely developed in the 17th and 18th centuries) and, with a bit of artful navigating, to four lovely greenswards: **Grosvenor Square, Berkeley Square, Hanover Square,** with its splendid **St. George's Church** where Handel worshipped, and the quiet St. George's Gardens, bounded by a maze of atmospheric streets and mews. Mayfair is also London's most exclusive shopping destination, with such enclaves as **Mount Street, Bruton Street, Savile Row,** and the **Burlington Arcade.** At the western end of Mayfair at Hyde Park corner are two memorials to England's great hero the Duke of Wellington: **Wellington Arch** and the duke's restored London residence, **Apsley House.**

> ### A BRIEF HISTORY
>
> The name Mayfair derives from the 15-day May fair that was once held in the charming warren of small streets known as Shepherd Market. But in the 18th century, the residents of this now-fashionable neighborhood felt the fair was lowering the tone and so put a stop to it.

The **Royal Academy of Arts** is at the southern fringe of Mayfair on Piccadilly, and just across the road begins more sedate St. James's, with its old-money galleries, restaurants, and gentlemen's clubs that embody the history and privilege of traditional London. You'll get the best sense of the neighborhood just to the south on **St. James's Square** and **Pall Mall,** with its private clubs tucked away in 18th- and 19th-century patrician buildings.

TOP ATTRACTIONS

Fodor's Choice
★

Apsley House (Wellington Museum). The mansion built by Robert Adam and presented to the Duke of Wellington in thanks for his victory over Napoléon at the Battle of Waterloo in 1815 was long celebrated as the best address in town. Once popularly known as Number 1, London, because it was the first and grandest house at the old tollgate from Knightsbridge village, the mansion was the residence of the Duke of Wellington from 1817 until his death in 1852. The years of war against the French made the "Iron Duke"—born in Ireland as Arthur Wellesley—the greatest soldier and statesman in the land, so much so that the house's location at Hyde Park Corner was soon nicknamed "hero's corner" (in the nearby subway, beneath the turmoil of traffic, the Duke of Wellington's heroic exploits are retold in murals). Opposite the house is the 1828 **Wellington Arch** ⇨ *See below*, designed by Decimus Burton, with the four-horse chariot of peace at its pinnacle (open to the public as an exhibition area and viewing platform); the **Achilles** statue (legendarily naked and cast from captured French guns) points the way with thrusting shield to the ducal mansion from the edge of Hyde Park, entered through an elaborate gateway designed and built by Burton at the same time as the arch.

The duke's former residence shows off his uniforms, weapons, a fine collection of paintings (partially looted from his war campaigns), and his porcelain and plate collections acquired as a result of his military success, such as a Sèvres dessert service commissioned by Napoléon for his empress, Josephine. Wellington's extensive art collection, much of it

Old Bond Street is great for window-shopping—it has some of the most exclusive stores in London.

presented to him by admirers, includes works by Brueghel, Van Dyck, and Rubens, as well as the famous Velázquez portrait of Pope Innocent X and a portrait of the duke on horseback by Goya. A gigantic Canova statue of a nude (fig-leafed) Napoléon presides over the grand staircase that leads to the many elegant reception rooms. The sculptor chose to present his subject, at the time the most powerful man in Europe, as Mars the Peacemaker, depicting the short and stocky emperor as a classical god more than 11 feet tall with a perfect physique. Napoléon wasn't happy with the nudity or the athleticism of Canova's approach and ordered the marble statue to be hidden behind a screen.

The free audio guide highlights the most significant works and the superb interior, most notably the stunning Waterloo Gallery, where an annual banquet for officers who fought beside Wellington was held beneath the sculpted and gilded ceiling and old-master paintings on red damask walls. Special events take place on the annual Waterloo weekend and occasionally on Waterloo Day (June 18) itself, in addition to other special events throughout the year. Call or check the website for details. Limited disabled access. ✉ *149 Piccadilly, Hyde Park Corner, Mayfair* ☎ *020/7499–5676* ⊕ *www.english-heritage.org.uk* 🎟 *£6.50 (includes audio tour); joint ticket with Wellington Arch £8.20* ☉ *Mar.– Oct., Wed.–Sun. and bank holiday Mon. 11–5; Nov.–Feb., Sat.–Sun. 10–4* Ⓜ *Hyde Park Corner.*

Bond Street. This world-class shopping haunt is divided into northern "New" (1710) and southern "Old" (1690) halves. You can spot the juncture by a bronzed bench on which Franklin D. Roosevelt sits companionably next to Winston Churchill. On New Bond Street you'll find **Sotheby's,** the world-famous auction house, at No. 35, as well as upscale retailers like Asprey's, Burberry, Louis Vuitton, Georg Jensen, and Church's. You'll find even more opportunities to flirt with financial ruin on Old Bond Street: flagship boutiques of top-end designers like Chanel, Gucci, and Yves St. Laurent; an array of fine jewelers including Tiffany; and art dealers Colnaghi, Spink Leger, and Agnew's. **Cork Street,** which parallels the top half of Old Bond Street, is where London's foremost dealers in contemporary art have their galleries. ⊠ *Mayfair* Ⓜ *Bond St., Green Park.*

Fodor'sChoice **Burlington Arcade.** With ceilings and ★ lights now restored to how they would have looked when it was built in 1819, Burlington Arcade is the finest of Mayfair's enchant-ing covered shopping alleys. Originally built for Lord Cavendish, it was meant to stop hoi polloi from flinging rubbish into his garden at next-door Burlington House. Top-hatted watchmen called Beadles—the world's smallest private police force—still patrol, preserving decorum by preventing you from singing, running, or carrying an open umbrella. The arcade is also the main link between the Royal Academy of Arts and its extended galleries at 6 Burlington Gardens. ⊠ *Piccadilly, Mayfair* ☎ *020/7493–1764* ⊕ *www.burlington-arcade.co.uk* ⊙ *Weekdays 8–8, Sat. 9–8, Sun. 11–6; opening times of shops within the arcade vary* Ⓜ *Green Park, Piccadilly Circus.*

ROYALTY IN AISLE 9

Shoppers and historians alike will enjoy **Fortnum & Mason** at 181 Piccadilly. This old-fashioned fine-foods store seems to have been lifted from another century, with ornate murals decorating the walls, glass cabinets, and brass fixtures casting a dazzling glow all around. The store is especially famous for its loose-leaf tea and luxury picnic hampers (a wise purchase with St. James's Square just a stone's throw away). Built in 1788, Fortnum & Mason sent hams to the Duke of Wellington's army and baskets of treats to Florence Nightingale in the Crimea. (It also happens to be the Queen's grocery store.)

QUICK BITES

Several of London's most storied and stylish hotels are in Mayfair. Even if you're not staying at one, sample the high life by popping into their glamor-ous bars for a cocktail or some afternoon tea. **Claridge's Bar** takes its cue from art deco, as do the Ritz's intimate **Rivoli Bar** and the eponymous **Connaught Bar**; the bar at **Brown's Hotel** is modernist.

Marble Arch. John Nash's 1827 arch, moved here from Buckingham Palace in 1851, stands amid the traffic whirlpool where Bayswater Road segues into Oxford Street, at the top of Park Lane. The arch actually contains three small chambers, which served as a police station until the mid-20th century. Search the sidewalk on the traffic island opposite the movie theater for the stone plaque recalling the Tyburn Tree, an elaborately designed gallows that stood here for 400 years, until 1783. The condemned would be conveyed here in their finest clothes from Newgate Prison in The City, and were expected to affect a casual indifference or face a merciless heckling from the crowds. Towering

Marble Arch was originally a gateway to Buckingham Palace before it was moved to the corner of Hyde Park.

across the grass from the arch toward Tyburn Way is a vast patina-green statue of a horse's head called *Horse at Water,* by sculptor Nic Fiddian-Green. Cross over (or under) to the northeastern corner of Hyde Park for Speakers' Corner, a parcel of land long-dedicated to the principle of free speech, and where every Sunday people of all views—or none at all—come to pontificate, listen, and debate about anything and everything under the sun. ⊠ *Park La., Mayfair* Ⓜ *Marble Arch*.

Fodor's Choice **Royal Academy of Arts.** Burlington House was built in 1664, with later
★ Palladian additions for the 3rd Earl of Burlington in 1720. The piazza in front is a later conception from 1873, when the Renaissance-style buildings around the courtyard were designed by Banks and Barry to house a gaggle of noble scientific societies, including the Royal Society of Chemistry, the Linnean Society of London, and the Royal Astronomical Society.

The house itself is home to the draw-card tenant, the Royal Academy of Arts. The statue of the academy's first president, Sir Joshua Reynolds, palette in hand, is prominent in the piazza of light stone with fountains by Sir Phillip King. Within the house and up the stairs are statues of creative giants J.W.M. Turner and Thomas Gainsborough. Free tours show off part of the RA collection, some of it housed in the John Madejski Fine Rooms, and the RA hosts excellent temporary exhibitions. Every June for the past 240 years, the RA has put on its Summer Exhibition, a huge and always surprising collection of art by living Royal Academicians and a plethora of other contemporary artists. ⊠ *Burlington House, Piccadilly, Mayfair* ☎ *020/7300–8000, 0207/300–5839 lectures, 0207/300–5995 family programs* ⊕ *www.royalacademy.org*.

uk ✉ *Prices vary with exhibition £7–£15* ⊘ *Sat.–Thurs. 10–6, Fri. 10–10; tours Tues. 1, Wed.–Fri. 1 and 3, Sat. 11:30* Ⓜ *Piccadilly Circus, Green Park.*

QUICK
BITES

Restaurant at the Royal Academy of Arts. With its walls covered in Gilbert Spencer murals, the restaurant at the Royal Academy is almost as beautiful as the art hanging in the galleries. The accent is on flexibility: you can linger over a three-course meal, order tapas-style, or just pop in for a quick, delicious bite. Open daily 10–6, except Friday 10 am–11 pm. ✉ *Burlington House, Piccadilly, Mayfair* ☏ *020/7300–5608* ⊕ *www.royalacademy.org.uk* Ⓜ *Piccadilly Circus, Green Park.*

Wellington Arch. Opposite the Duke of Wellington's mansion, Apsley House, this majestic stone arch surveys the traffic rushing around Hyde Park Corner. Designed by Decimus Burton and built in 1828, it was created as a grand entrance to the west side of London and echoes the design of that other landmark gate, Marble Arch ⇨ *See above.* Both were triumphal arches commemorating Britain's victory against France in the Napoleonic Wars. The exterior of the arch was intended to be much more ornate but King George IV was going vastly over budget with his refurbishment of Buckingham Palace and cutbacks had to be made elsewhere. Atop the building, the Angel of Peace descends on the quadriga, or four-horse chariot of war. This replaced the Duke of Wellington on his horse, which was considered too large and moved to an army barracks in Aldershot. Inside the arch, three floors of permanent and temporary exhibits reveal the monument's history and explore the world's other great arches. Don't miss the platform at the top of the arch, where you can enjoy a panoramic view over Hyde Park and peer into the private gardens of Buckingham Palace. ✉ *Hyde Park Corner, Mayfair* ☏ *020/7930–2726* ⊕ *www.english-heritage.org.uk* ✉ *£4* ⊘ *Sun.–Wed. 10–5, but platform sometimes closed for exhibition installations; check website* Ⓜ *Hyde Park Corner.*

WORTH NOTING

Grosvenor Square. Pronounced *Grove*-na, this leafy square was laid out in 1725–31 and is as desirable an address today as it was then. Americans have certainly always thought so—from John Adams, the second president, who as ambassador lived at No. 38, to Dwight D. Eisenhower, whose wartime headquarters was at No. 20. Now the massive 1960s block of the U.S. Embassy occupies the entire west side (although a new one is being built south of the river), and a British memorial to Franklin D. Roosevelt stands in the center. There is also a classically styled memorial to those who died in New York on September 11, 2001. Grosvenor Chapel, completed in 1730 and used by Eisenhower's men during World War II, stands a couple of blocks south of the square on

Regent Street, home to Liberty department store and Hamleys toy shop, decorated for the holidays

South Audley Street, with the entrance to pretty **St. George's Gardens** to its left. Across the gardens is the headquarters of the English Jesuits as well as the society-wedding favorite, the mid-19th-century Church of the Immaculate Conception, known as Farm Street Church because of its location. Barclays Cycle Hire docking stations can be found on the southern and northeastern stretches of the square. ✉ *Mayfair* Ⓜ *Bond St.*

Handel House Museum. The former home of the composer, where he lived for more than 30 years until his death in 1759, is a celebration of his genius. It's the first museum in London solely dedicated to one composer. In rooms decorated in fine Georgian style you can linger over original manuscripts (there are more to be seen in the British Library) and gaze at portraits—accompanied by live music if the adjoining music rooms are being used by musicians in rehearsal. Some of the composer's most famous pieces were created here, including *Messiah* and *Music for the Royal Fireworks*. To hear a live concert here is to imagine the atmosphere of rehearsals and "salon" music in its day (check the website for details of recitals and events). Handel House makes a perfect cultural pit stop after shopping on nearby Bond and Oxford streets, and, if you come on a weekend, there is free admission for kids. The museum occupies both No. 25 and the adjoining house, No. 23, where another musical star, Jimi Hendrix, lived for a brief time in the 1960s, as a blue plaque outside the house indicates. Tours of Hendrix's flat, currently the administrative offices of the museum and not usually open to the public, are offered during London's "Open House" weekend every September. Phone or check the website for details. ✉ *25 Brook St., entrance* *in Lancashire Court, Mayfair ☎ 020/7495–1685 ⊕ www.handelhouse. org ⬚£6 ⊙ Tues., Wed., Fri., and Sat. 10–6, Thurs. 10–8, Sun. noon–6 (last admission half hour before closing)* Ⓜ *Bond St.*

MARYLEBONE

A favorite of newspaper style sections everywhere, Marylebone High Street forms the heart of Marylebone (pronounced "Marr-le-bone") Village, a vibrant, upscale neighborhood that encompasses the squares and streets around High Street and nearby Marylebone Lane. The district took its name from a church dedicated to St. Mary and the bourne (another word for "stream") that ran through the original village. Its development, by various members of the aristocracy, began in the early 18th century. Today, it's hard to believe that you're just a few blocks north of gaudy Oxford Street as you wander in and out of Marylebone's small shops and boutiques, the best of which include La Fromagerie (2–6 Moxon Street), an excellent cheese shop; Daunt Books (Nos. 83–84), a travel bookshop; "Cabbages and Frocks" market on the grounds of the St. Marylebone Parish Church, held Saturday 11–5, which purveys specialty foods and vintage clothing; and on Sunday 10–2, a large farmers' and artisanal-food market in a parking lot on Cramer Street, just behind the High Street. But some memorable sights await, too, including that best remnant of ancien régime France in London, the fabled Wallace Collection. The best metro stop for the area is Bond Street.

TOP ATTRACTIONS

FAMILY **Wallace Collection.** This exquisite labyrinth of an art gallery is housed in
Fodor's Choice Hertford House, an 18th-century mansion that was bequeathed to the
★ nation, along with its contents, by the widow of Sir Richard Wallace (1818–90). Wallace was the last in a line of wealthy aristocrats who voraciously scoured Europe in search of beautiful art. His father, the 4th Marquess of Hartford, was a particularly shrewd dealer. After the French Revolution he took a house in Paris, where he went about snapping up paintings by what were then dangerously unpopular artists, for a song. Frans Hals's *Laughing Cavalier* is probably the most famous painting here, or perhaps Jean-Honoré Fragonard's *The Swing*, which perfectly encapsulates the frilly Rococo decadence and playful eroticism of pre-revolutionary French art. The full list of painters in the collection reads like a roll call of classical European masters, from Rubens, Rembrandt, and Van Dyck to Canaletto, Titian, and Velázquez. English works include paintings by Gainsborough and Turner, plus a dozen by Joshua Reynolds. There are also fine collections of furniture, porcelain, Renaissance gold, and maiolica (15th- and 16th-century Italian tin-glazed pottery). As if the holdings aren't incentive enough to visit, the conditions of the bequest mean that no part of the collection can leave the building, so this is literally the only place in the world you'll ever see these works. Stay for lunch at the restaurant, which is elegantly sited in a glass-roofed courtyard. ⊠ *Hertford House, Manchester Sq., Marylebone* ☎ *020/7563–9500* ⊕ *www.wallacecollection.org* ⬚*Free* ⊙ *Daily 10–5* Ⓜ *Bond St.*

WORTH NOTING

FAMILY **Ripley's Believe It Or Not!.** Six floors of the weird, the wacky, and the downright bizarre (life-size knitted Ferrari, anyone?) to astonish and delight even the most tired and jaded among us. Inspired by the legendary American traveller/cartoonist/curator Robert Ripley, nothing is considered too unusual or outlandish to take its place among the 700-plus authentic artifacts. From dinosaur eggs to an albino alligator, from a maze of mirrors to a sculpture of the Beatles made entirely from chewing gum (yes, chewing gum!), from Ecudorian shrunken heads to pieces of the Berlin Wall, there is so much to see, with interactive exhibits aplenty. ✉ *The London Pavilion, 1 Piccadilly Circus, Mayfair* 🖀 *020/3238–0022* ⊕ *www.ripleyslondon.com* 🎟 *£26.95* ⊗ *Daily 10 am–midnight (last admission 10:30 pm)* Ⓜ *Piccadilly Circus (use exit 4 to Coventry St.).*

SOHO AND COVENT GARDEN

GETTING ORIENTED

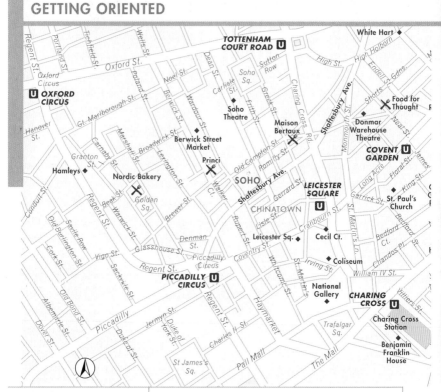

GETTING THERE

Almost all Tube lines cross the Covent Garden and Soho areas, so it's easy to hop off for a dinner or show in the hippest area of London. For Soho, take any train to Piccadilly Circus, or Leicester Square, Oxford Circus, or Tottenham Court Road. For Covent Garden, get off at the Covent Garden station on the Piccadilly line. It might be easier to exit the Tube at Leicester Square or Holborn and walk. Thirty buses connect to the Covent Garden area from all over London; check out the area's website, ⊕ *www.coventgarden. uk.com.*

TOP REASONS TO GO

Find tomorrow's look in the Newburgh Quarter: Head to this adorable warren of cobblestone streets for an ultrahip array of specialist boutiques, edgy stores, and young indie upstarts.

Indulge yourself in Gourmet Country: London has fallen in love with its tummy, and Soho is home to many of the most talked-about restaurants in town.

Covent Garden Piazza: Eliza Doolittle's former backyard has been taken over by fun boutiques and street performers (who play to the crowds at night).

Royal Opera House: Even if you're not going to the opera or ballet, take in the beautiful architecture and sense of history.

See a West End hit in Theatreland: Shaftesbury Avenue is the heart of London's theater district, where more than 40 West End theaters pull in the crowds with a mix of extravagant musicals and Shakespeare.

MAKING THE MOST OF YOUR TIME

You can comfortably tour all the sights around Soho and Covent Garden in a day. Visit the small but perfect Courtauld Gallery on Monday before 2 pm, when entry is free. That leaves plenty of time to watch street entertainment or shop at the stalls around Covent Garden Piazza or in the fashion boutiques of Soho. Save some energy for a night on the town in Soho.

FEELING PECKISH?

The coffee shops and snack bars on Covent Garden Piazza can be overpriced and of poor quality. Head north for Neal Street or west for Soho when the munchies strike.

Food for Thought. This place is always crowded, with hungry customers lining up outside for a delicious range of vegetarian dishes. ✉ *31 Neal St., Covent Garden* ☎ *020/7836–9072* Ⓜ *Covent Garden, Leicester Sq.*

Nordic Bakery. On quiet Golden Square, this is an immaculately designed Scandinavian café that serves dark breads and the city's best cinnamon rolls, large enough to sink a small ship. ✉ *14A Golden Sq., Soho* ☎ *020/3230–1077* ⊕ *www.nordicbakery.com* Ⓜ *Piccadilly Circus.*

Princi. This chic Italian bakery and café fills up around lunchtime with office workers who come for the richly colorful salads, oozingly fresh lasagna, and warm-from-the-oven cakes and pastries. ✉ *135–137 Wardour St., Soho* ☎ *020/7478–8888* ⊕ *princi.co.uk* Ⓜ *Tottenham Court Rd., Piccadilly Circus.*

GAY LONDON

Old Compton Street in Soho is the epicenter of London's affluent, stylish gay scene. There are some smart nightclubs in the area, with crowds forming in Soho Square, south of Oxford Street.

Madame Jojo's. This club has been drawing the crowds for nearly 50 years. It's **Kitsch Cabaret,** performed every Saturday eveninq, is so popular (with straights as well as gays) that it's usually booked weeks in advance. ✉ *8–10 Brewer St., Soho* ☎ *020/7734–3040* ⊕ *www.madamejojos.com* Ⓜ *Piccadilly Circus.*

Sightseeing
★★★

Nightlife
★★★★

Dining
★★★★

Lodging
★★

Shopping
★★★

Once a red-light district, today's Soho is more stylish than seedy and offers some of London's best nightclubs, live music venues, restaurants, and theaters. By day, this hotbed of media production reverts to the business side of its late-night scene. If Soho is all about showbiz, neighboring Covent is devoted to culture. Both districts offer an abundance of narrow streets packed with one-of-a-kind shops and lots of antique character.

SOHO

Updated by
Julius Honnor

Soho, which, along with Covent Garden is loosely known as "the West End," has long been known as the entertainment and arts quarter of London's center. Bordered to the north by Oxford Street, Regent Street to the west, and Chinatown and Leicester Square to the south, the narrow, winding streets of Soho are unabashedly devoted to pleasure. Wardour Street bisects the neighborhood, with lots of interesting boutiques and some of London's best-value restaurants to the west (especially around Foubert's Place and on Brewer and Lexington streets). Nightlife central lies to the east—including London's gay mecca, Old Compton Street—and beyond that is the city's densest collection of theaters, on Shaftesbury Avenue. London's compact Chinatown is wedged between Soho and **Leicester Square**. A bit of erudition surfaces to the east of the square on Charing Cross Road, famous for its secondhand bookshops, and on tiny **Cecil Court**, a pedestrianized passage lined with small antiquarian booksellers.

TOP ATTRACTIONS

Fodor's Choice
★

Newburgh Quarter. Want to see the hip style of today's London? Find it just one block east of Carnaby Street—where the look of the '60s "Swinging London" was born—in an adorable warren of cobblestone streets now lined with specialty boutiques, edgy stores, and young indy upstarts. Here, not far from roaring Regent Street, the future of

DID YOU KNOW

Covent Garden was a convent garden for 300 years before it was Britain's first planned public square with a fruit and vegetable market. The greengrocers are gone but the 1840 market building and the courtyard still teem with shoppers.

COVENT
GARDEN
MARKET
aftershock
POLLOCK'S
TOY THEATRES
Ag
REGENT gifts

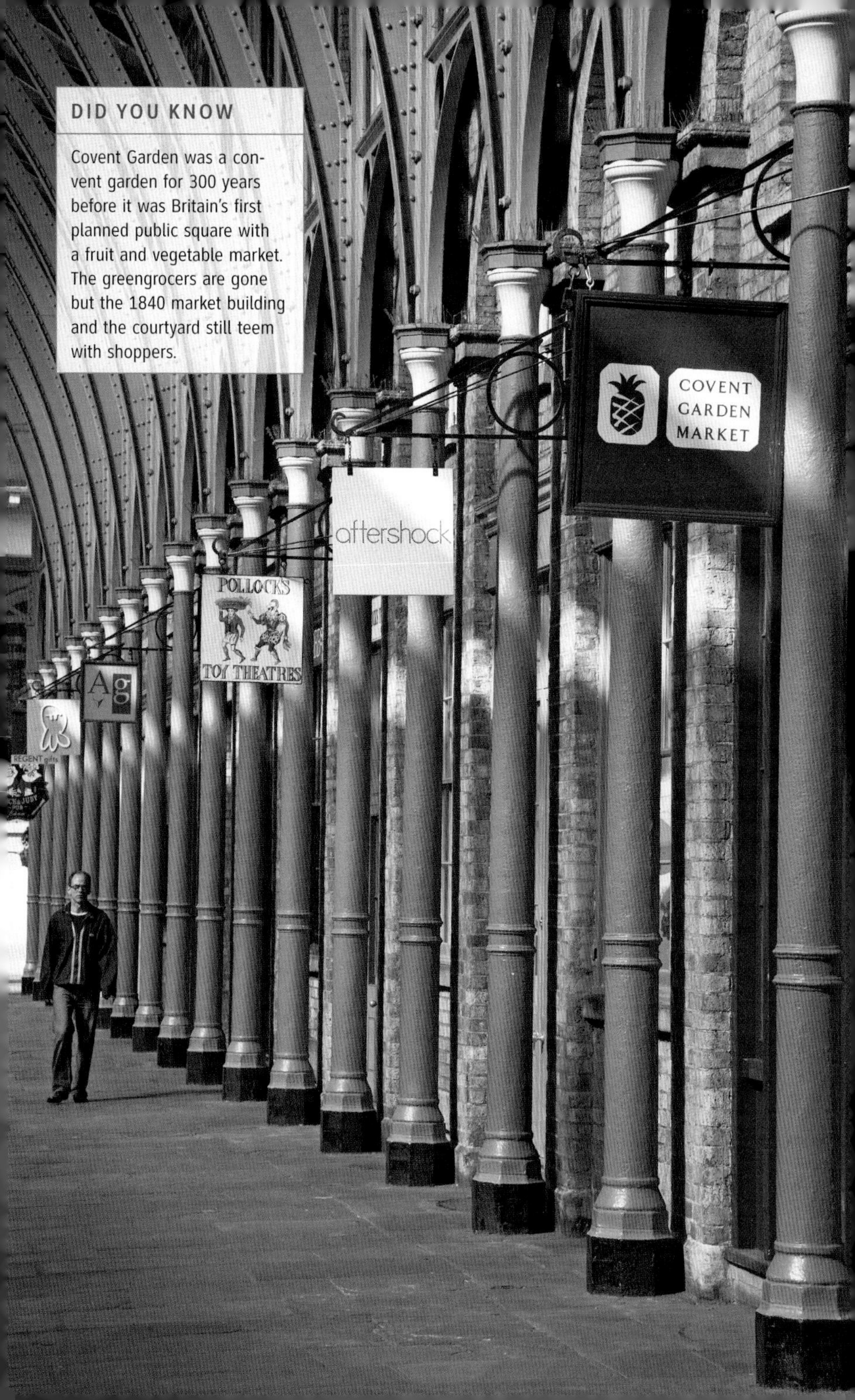

You can't miss the buskers performing in the streets of Soho and Covent Garden.

England's fashion is being incubated in stores like Lucy in Disguise and Sweaty Betty. A check of the ingredients reveals one part '60s London, one part Futuristic Fetishism, one part Dickensian charm, and one part British street swagger. The Nouveau Boho look best flourishes in shops like Peckham Rye, a tiny boutique crowded with rockers and fashion plates who adore its grunge-meets-*Brideshead Revisted* vibe. Or continue down Newburgh Street to Beyond the Valley, an art-school showcase whose designers have successfully paired graphic art–prints with kitschy outfits. ⊠ *Newburgh St., Foubert's Pl., Ganton St., and Carnaby St., Soho* ⊕ *carnaby.co.uk.*

COVENT GARDEN

To the east of Charing Cross Road lies Covent Garden, the famous marketplace turned shopping mall. Although boutiques and haute fashion shops line the surrounding streets, many Londoners come to Covent Garden for its two outposts of culture: the **Royal Opera House** and the **Donmar Warehouse,** one of London's best and most innovative theaters. The area becomes more sedate just to the north, at the end of Wellington Street, where semicircular Aldwych is lined with grand buildings, and from there the Strand leads to the huge, stately piazza of **Somerset House,** a vibrant center of contemporary arts and home to the many masterpieces on view at the **Courtauld Institute Gallery.** You'll get a sense of old-fashioned London just behind the Strand, where small lanes are little changed since the 18th century. On the way to the verdant **Embankment Gardens** bordering the Thames, you may pass the **Adam Houses, the**

A BRIEF HISTORY

Almost as soon as a 17th-century housing development covered what had been a royal park and hunting ground, Soho earned a reputation for entertainment, bohemianism, and cosmopolitan tolerance. When the authorities introduced zero tolerance of soliciting in 1991 (the most recent of several attempts to end Soho's sex trade), they cracked down on an old neighborhood tradition that still resurfaces from time to time.

Successive waves of refugees—French Huguenots in the 1680s, followed by Germans, Russians, Poles, Greeks, Italians, and Chinese—settled and brought their ethnic cuisines with them. So when dining out became fashionable after World War I, Soho was the natural place for restaurants to flourish (as they continue to do today).

In the 1950s and '60s, Soho was London's artists' quarter and the place to find the top jazz clubs and art galleries. Among the luminaries who have made their home here are landscape painter John Constable; Casanova, the famous lothario; Canaletto, the great painter of Venice; poet William Blake; and the revolutionary Karl Marx.

Present-day Covent Garden took shape in the 1630s, when Inigo Jones turned what had been agricultural land into Britain's first planned public square. After the Great Fire of 1666, it became the site of England's largest fruit-and-vegetable market (the flower market arrived in the 19th century). This, along with the district's many theaters and taverns, gave the area a somewhat dubious reputation, and after the produce market relocated in 1973, the surviving buildings were scheduled for demolition. A local campaign saved them, and the restored market opened in 1980.

4

remnants of a grand 18th-century riverside housing development, and the Benjamin Franklin House, where the noted statesman lived in the years leading up to the American Revolution.

Covent joins Soho as an arts and entertainment center in the city, popularly referred to as "the West End." The neighborhood centers on the Piazza, site of the original Covent Garden market. High Holborn to the north, Kingsway to the east, and the Strand to the south form its other boundaries.

TOP ATTRACTIONS

Courtauld Institute Gallery. One of London's most beloved art collections, the Courtauld is to your right as you pass through the archway into the grounds of the beautifully restored, grand 18th-century neoclassical Somerset House. Founded in 1931 by the textile magnate Samuel Courtauld to house his remarkable private collection, this is one of the world's finest Impressionist and post-Impressionist galleries, with artists ranging from Bonnard to van Gogh. A déjà-vu moment with Cézanne, Degas, Seurat, or Monet awaits on every wall (Manet's *Bar at the Folies-Bergère* and *Le Déjeuner sur L'Herbe* are two of the stars). Botticelli, Brueghel, Tiepolo, and Rubens are also represented, thanks to the exquisite bequest of Count Antoine Seilern's Princes Gate collection. German Renaissance paintings, bequeathed in 1947, include the colorful and delightfully wicked *Adam and Eve* by Lucas Cranach the Elder. The second floor has a more provocative, experimental feel, with masterpieces such as Modigliani's iconic *Female Nude*. Don't miss the little café downstairs—a perfect place for a spot of tea. ✉ *Somerset House, Strand, Covent Garden* ☎ *020/7848-2526* ⊕ *www.courtauld.ac.uk* 🖃 *£6, free Mon. 10–2, except bank holidays* ☉ *Daily 10–6; last admission 5:30* Ⓜ *Temple, Covent Garden.*

WORD OF MOUTH

"If you accept the consensus that Mayfair and Soho aren't 'real' neighborhoods, you're mostly left with tourist ghettoes like Bloomsbury, Earl's Court, Gloucester Rd, Covent Garden, Bayswater, and Victoria, where hotelization and foreigners' London pads have driven full-time residents out."

—Flanneruk

Covent Garden Piazza. Once home to London's main flower market, where *My Fair Lady*'s Eliza Doolittle peddled her blooms, the square around which Covent Garden pivots is known as the Piazza. In the center, the fine old market building now houses stalls and shops selling higher-class clothing, plus several restaurants and cafés and knickknack stores that are good for gifts. One particular gem is Benjamin Pollock's Toyshop at No. 44 in the market. Established in the 1880s, it sells delightful toy theaters. The superior **Apple Market** has good crafts stalls on most days, too. On the south side of the Piazza, the indoor **Jubilee Market,** with its stalls of clothing, army-surplus gear, and more crafts and knickknacks, has a distinct flea-market feel. In summer it may seem that everyone you see around the Piazza (and the crowds are legion) is a fellow tourist, but there's still plenty of office life in the area. Londoners who shop here tend to head for Neal Street and the area to the north of Covent Garden tube station rather than the market itself. In the Piazza, street performers— from global musicians to jugglers and mimes—play to the crowds, as they have done since the first English Punch and Judy Show, staged here in the 17th century. ✉ *Covent Garden* ⊕ *www.coventgardenlondonuk. com* Ⓜ *Covent Garden.*

FAMILY **London Transport Museum.** Housed in the old flower market at the southeast corner of Covent Garden, this stimulating museum is filled with impressive vehicle, poster, and photograph collections. As you watch the crowds drive a Tube-train simulation and gawk at the horse-drawn trams (and the piles of detritus that remained behind) and steam locomotives, it's unclear who's enjoying it more, children or adults. Best of all, the kid-friendly museum (under 16 admitted free) has a multilevel approach to education, including information for the youngest visitor to the most advanced transit aficionado. Food and drink are available at the Upper Deck café and the shop has lots of good options for gift-buying. ■**TIP**➔ Tickets are valid for unlimited entry for 12 months. ✉ *Covent Garden Piazza, Covent Garden* ☎ *020/7565-7298* ⊕ *www. ltmuseum.co.uk* 🖃 *£13.50* ☉ *Sat.–Thurs. 10–6 (last admission 5:15), Fri. 11–6 (last admission 5:15)* Ⓜ *Covent Garden, Leicester Sq.*

DID YOU KNOW?

Somerset House was lapped by the River Thames before the Victoria Embankment was built in the 19th century. The neoclassical building's grand courtyard is home to ice-skating in winter and dancing fountains in summer.

FAMILY
Fodor's Choice
★

Somerset House. In recent years this huge complex—the work of Sir William Chambers (1726–96), and built during the reign of George III to house offices of the Navy—has completed its transformation from dusty government offices to one of the capital's most buzzing centers of culture and the arts, hosting several interesting exhibitions at any one time. The cobblestone Italianate courtyard, where Admiral Nelson used to walk, makes a great setting for 55 playful fountains and is transformed into a romantic ice rink in winter; the grand space is the venue for music and outdoor movie screenings in summer. The **Courtauld Institute Gallery** (⇨ *See above*) occupies most of the north building, facing the busy Strand. Across the courtyard are the Embankment Galleries, with a vibrant calendar of design, fashion, architecture, and photography exhibitions. Creative activities for children are a regular feature (the website has details). The East Wing has another fine exhibition space and events are sometimes also held in the atmospherically gloomy cellars below the Fountain Court. Tom's Kitchen offers fine dining and the Deli has mouthwatering cakes and pastries. In summer eating and drinking spills out onto the large terrace next to the Thames. ✉ *Strand, Covent Garden* ☎ *020/7845–4600* ⊕ *www.somersethouse.org.uk* 🎟 *Embankment Galleries price varies, Courtauld Gallery £6, other areas free* ⊗ *Daily 10–6; last admission 5:30* Ⓜ *Charing Cross, Waterloo, Blackfriars.*

> ## ICE-SKATING
>
> It's hard to beat the skating experience at Somerset House, where from November through January a rink is set up in the grand courtyard of this central London palace. Check the website for current prices; its popularity is enormous, and if you can't get a ticket, other venues such as Hampton Court, the Tower of London, the London Eye, and the Natural History Museum are following Somerset House's lead in having temporary winter rinks. ☎ *0844/847–1520* ⊕ *www.somersethouse.org.uk/ice-rink.*

WORTH NOTING

The Adam Houses. Only a few structures remain of what was once a regal riverfront row of houses on a 3-acre site, but such is their quality that they are worth a detour off the Strand. The work of 18th-century Scottish architects and interior designers (John, Robert, James, and William Adam, known collectively as the Adam brothers), the original development was damaged in the 19th century during the building of the embankment, and mostly demolished in 1936 to be replaced by an art deco tower. The original houses still standing are protected, and give a glimpse of their former grandeur. Nos. 1–4 Robert Street and Nos. 7 and 10 Adam Street are the best. ✉ *Robert St. and Adam St., off The Strand, Covent Garden* Ⓜ *Charing Cross, Embankment.*

Royal Society of Arts. At the Royal Society of Arts, you can sometimes see a suite of Adam rooms; ring ahead to check. ✉ *8 John Adam St.* ☎ *020/7451–6847* ⊕ *www.thersa.org* 🎟 *Free* Ⓜ *Charing Cross, Embankment*

Benjamin Franklin House. This architecturally significant 1730 house is the only surviving residence of American statesman, scientist, writer,

Leicester Square is home to many cinemas and a half-price theater ticket booth.

and inventor Benjamin Franklin, who lived and worked here for 16 years preceding the American Revolution. The restored Georgian town house has been left unfurnished, the better to show off the original features—18th-century paneling, stoves, beams, bricks, and windows. Visitors are led around the house by the costumed character of Polly Hewson, the daughter of Franklin's landlady. There's also a glass armonica (an instrument which Franklin invented while living here) and a scholarship center with a complete collection of Franklin's papers. On Monday you can take a guided tour focusing on the architectural details of the building. ⊠ *36 Craven St., Covent Garden* ☎ *020/7839–2006, 020/7925–1405 booking line* ⊕ *www.benjaminfranklinhouse. org* ⊠ *Historical experience £7; architectural tour £3.50* ☉ *Historical Experience Wed.–Sun., noon, 1, 2, 3:15, and 4:15; Architectural tour Mon., noon, 1, 2, 3:15, and 4:15.*

Leicester Square. Looking at the neon of the major movie houses, the fast-food outlets, and the disco entrances, you'd never guess that this square (pronounced *Lester*) was a model of formality and refinement when it was first laid out around 1630. By the 19th century the square was already bustling and disreputable, and although it's not a threatening place, you should still be on your guard, especially at night—any space so full of people is bound to attract pickpockets, and Leicester Square certainly does. Although there's a bit of residual glamour (red-carpet film premieres), and Londoners generally tend to avoid the place, it's still worth a visit for its hustle and bustle, its mime artists, and a pleasant green area in its center. In the middle is a statue of a sulking Shakespeare, perhaps remembering the days when the movie houses were live theaters—burlesque houses, but live all the same. Here, too, are figures of Newton, Hogarth, Reynolds, and Charlie Chaplin. On the northeast corner, in Leicester Place, stands the church of **Notre Dame de France,** with a wonderful mural by Jean Cocteau in one of its side chapels. For more in the way of atmosphere, head north and west from here, through Chinatown and the narrow streets of Soho. ⊠ *Covent Garden* Ⓜ *Leicester Sq.*

St. Paul's Church. If you want to commune with the spirits of Vivien Leigh, Noël Coward, Edith Evans, or Charlie Chaplin, this might be just the place. Memorials to them and many other theater greats are found in this 1633 work of the renowned Inigo Jones, who, as the King's Surveyor of Works, designed the whole of Covent Garden Piazza. St. Paul's Church has been known as "the actors' church" since the Restoration, thanks to the neighboring theater district and St. Paul's prominent parishioners. (Well-known actors often read the lessons at services, and the church still hosts concerts and small-scale productions.) Fittingly, the opening scene of Shaw's *Pygmalion* takes place under its Tuscan portico (you might know it better from the musical *My Fair Lady,* starring Audrey Hepburn). The western end of the Piazza is a prime pitch for street entertainers, but if they're not to your liking, you can repair to the serenity of the garden entered from King or Bedford Street. ⊠ *Bedford St., Covent Garden* ⊕ *www.actorschurch.org* Ⓜ *Covent Garden.*

Theatre Royal, Drury Lane. This is London's best-known auditorium and almost its largest. Since World War II, Drury Lane's forte has been musicals (from *My Fair Lady* and *South Pacific* to *Miss Saigon* and *Shrek*)—though David Garrick, who managed the theater from 1747 to 1776, made its name by reviving the works of the by-then-obscure William Shakespeare. Drury Lane enjoys all the romantic accessories of a London theater—a history of fires (it burned down three times), riots (in 1737, when a posse of footmen demanded free admission), attempted regicides (George II in 1716 and his grandson George III in 1800), and even sightings of the most famous phantom of theaterland, the Man in Grey (in the Circle during matinees). One-hour dramatized tours, led by actors, are available. ⊠ *Catherine St., Covent Garden* ☎ *020/7494–5000, 0844/412–2705 Tour reservations* ⊕ *www. reallyuseful.com* ⏎ *Tours £9* ☉ *Through the Stage Door tours: Mon.– Wed. and Fri., 2:15 and 4:15; Thurs. and Sat., 10:15 and 11:45. Sun by arrangement* Ⓜ *Covent Garden.*

CHEAP TICKETS

One landmark certainly worth a visit by theatergoers is the **Society of London Theatre ticket kiosk (TKTS),** on the southwest corner of Leicester Square, which sells half-price tickets for many of that evening's performances. It's open Monday to Saturday from 10 to 7, and Sunday from noon to 3. One window sells matinee tickets and the other sells tickets for evening performances, so make sure you join the correct line. Watch out for illegal ticket touts (scalpers), who target tourists around the square.

BLOOMSBURY
AND HOLBORN

GETTING ORIENTED

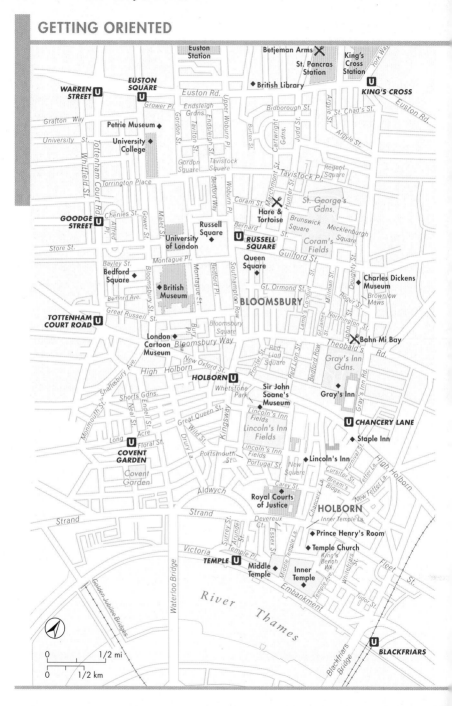

TOP REASONS TO GO

Take a tour of "Mankind's Attic": From the Rosetta Stone to the Elgin Marbles, the British Museum is the golden hoard of booty amassed by centuries of the British Empire.

Stroll through the Inns of Court: The quiet courts, leafy gardens, and magnificent halls that comprise the heart of Holborn are the closest thing to the spirit of Oxford in London.

Time travel at Sir John Soane's Museum: Quirky and fascinating, the former home of the celebrated 19th-century architect is a treasure trove of antiquities and oddities.

View rare treasures at the British Library: In keeping with Bloomsbury's literary traditions, this great repository shows off the Magna Carta, a Gutenberg Bible, Shakespeare's First Folio, and other masterpieces of the written word.

Pay your respects to Charles Dickens: The former residence of the *Oliver Twist author* is now a fascinating museum.

FEELING PECKISH?

The Betjeman Arms. Inside St. Pancras International's wonderfully Victorian station, this is the perfect place to stop for a pint and grab some traditional pub fare. Perched above the tracks of the Eurostar Terminal, the view of the trains and travelers will keep you entertained for hours. ✉ *Unit 53, St. Pancras International Station, Pancras Rd., King's Cross* 🕾 *020/7923–5440* ⊕ *www.geronimoinns.co.uk/thebetjemanarms* Ⓜ *King's Cross St. Pancras.*

The Hare and Tortoise Dumpling & Noodle Bar. This bright café, serving scrumptious Asian fast food from noon to 11 pm, is a favorite with students, and it's easy to see why: ingredients are all natural, the portions are huge, and the price is always reasonable. ✉ *15–17 Brunswick Shopping Centre, Brunswick Sq., opposite the Renoir Cinema, Bloomsbury* 🕾 *020/7278–9799* ⊕ *www.hareandtortoise.co.uk/bloomsbury* Ⓜ *Russell Sq.*

GETTING THERE

The Russell Square Tube stop on the Piccadilly line leaves you right at the corner of Russell Square.

The best Tube stops for the Inns of Court are Holborn on the Central and Piccadilly lines or Chancery Lane on the Central line.

Tottenham Court Road on the Northern and Central lines is best for the British Museum.

Once you're in Bloomsbury, you can easily get around on foot.

MAKING THE MOST OF YOUR TIME

Bloomsbury can be seen in a day, or in half a day, depending on your interests and your time constraints.

If you plan to visit the Inns of Court as well as the British Museum, and you'd also like to get a feel for the neighborhood, then you may wish to devote an entire day to this literary and legal enclave.

An alternative scenario is to set aside a separate day for a visit to the British Museum, which can easily consume as many hours as you have to spare.

It's a pleasure to wander through the quiet, leafy squares at your leisure, examining historic Blue Plaques or relaxing at a street-side café. The many students in the neighborhood add bit of street life.

5

Sightseeing ★★★ Nightlife ★★ Dining ★★ Lodging ★★★★ Shopping ★★	Guarded by the British Library to the north, the British Museum at its heart, and the Inns of Court of the Holborn district (right by the Thames), Bloomsbury might appear all bookish and cerebral—but fear not, it's much more than that. There's a youthfulness about its buzzing thoroughfares—not surprising, given all the nearby universities and colleges, let alone students heading to the British Library. To the southeast, Holborn was once Dickens territory and now is home to legal London.

BLOOMSBURY

Updated by
James O'Neill

Fundamental to the region's spirit of open expression and scholarly debate is the legacy of the Bloomsbury Group, an elite corps of artists and writers who lived in this neighborhood during the first part of the 20th century. **Gordon Square** was at one point home to Virginia Woolf, John Maynard Keynes (both at No. 46), and Lytton Strachey (at No. 51). But perhaps the best-known square in Bloomsbury is the large, centrally located **Russell Square,** with its handsome gardens. Scattered around the **University of London** campus are Woburn Square, Torrington Square, and Tavistock Square. The **British Library,** with its vast treasures, is a few blocks north, across busy Euston Road.

Bloomsbury itself is bordered by Tottenham Court Road on the west, Euston Road on the north, Woburn Place (which becomes Southampton Row) on the east, and New Oxford Street on the south.

The area from Somerset House on the Strand, all the way up Kingsway to the Euston Road, is known as London's **Museum Mile** for the myriad historic houses and museums that dot the area. **Charles Dickens Museum,** where the author wrote *Oliver Twist*, pays homage to the master, and artists' studios and design shops share space with tenants near the majestic **British Museum.** And guaranteed to raise a smile from the most blasé and footsore tourist is **Sir John Soane's Museum**, where the colorful collection reflects the eclectic interests of the namesake founder. Bloomsbury's liveliness extends north to the exciting redevelopment of King's Cross—once the ugly sister of *all* ugly sisters—and, indeed, even farther north to quaint, busy Islington.

TOP ATTRACTIONS

FAMILY **British Library.** This collection of around 18 million volumes, formerly in the British Museum, now has a home in state-of-the-art surroundings. The library's greatest treasures are on view to the general public: the Magna Carta, a Gutenberg Bible, Jane Austen's writings, Shakespeare's First Folio, and musical manuscripts by G.F. Handel as well as Sir Paul McCartney are on display in the Sir John Ritblat Gallery. Also in the gallery are headphones with which you can listen to pieces in the **National Sound Archive** (it's the world's largest collection), such as the voice of Florence Nightingale and an extract from the Beatles' last tour interview. Marvel at the six-story glass tower that holds the 65,000-volume collection of George III, plus a permanent exhibition of rare stamps. On weekends and during school vacations there are hands-on demonstrations of how a book comes together, and the library frequently mounts special exhibitions. If all this wordiness is just too much, you can relax in the library's piazza or restaurant, or take in one of the occasional free concerts in the amphitheater outside. ⊠ *96 Euston Rd., Bloomsbury* ☎ *0843/208–1144* ⊕ *www.bl.uk* 🖃 *Free, donations appreciated; charge for special exhibitions* ⊙ *Mon. and Wed.–Fri. 9:30–6, Tues. 9:30–8, Sat. 9:30–5, Sun. and public holidays 11–5* Ⓜ *Euston, Euston Sq., King's Cross St. Pancras.*

Fodor'sChoice **British Museum.**
★ *See the highlighted listing in this chapter.*

Charles Dickens Museum. This is one of the few London houses Charles Dickens (1812–70) inhabited that is still standing—and is the place where the master wrote *Oliver Twist* and *Nicholas Nickleby* and finished *Pickwick Papers*. The house looks exactly as it would have in Dickens's day, complete with first editions, letters, and a tall clerk's desk (where the master wrote standing up, often while chatting with visiting friends and relatives). Down in the basement is a replica of the Dingley Dell kitchen from *Pickwick Papers*. A program of changing special exhibitions gives insight into the Dickens family and the author's works, with sessions where, for instance, you can try your own hand with a quill pen. Visitors have reported a "presence" upstairs in the Mary Hogarth bedroom, where Dickens's sister-in-law died—see for yourself! Christmas is a memorable time to visit, as the rooms are decorated in traditional style: better than any televised costume drama, this is the real thing (tickets must be pre-booked for December 24–26). Extensively redeveloped as part of the author's bicentenary, the museum also houses a shop and café. ⊠ *48 Doughty St., Bloomsbury* ☎ *020/7405–2127* ⊕ *www.dickensmuseum.com* 🖃 *£8* ⊙ *Daily 10–5 (last admission 4:30)* Ⓜ *Chancery La., Russell Sq.*

Fodor'sChoice **Sir John Soane's Museum.** A wonderful, eccentric jewel of a place, Sir
★ John (1753–1837), architect of the Bank of England, bequeathed his

Continued on page 108

THE BRITISH MUSEUM

Anybody writing about the British Museum had better have a large stack of superlatives close at hand: most, biggest, earliest, finest. This is the golden hoard of nearly three centuries of the Empire, the booty brought from Britain's far-flung colonies.

5

IN FOCUS THE BRITISH MUSEUM

The first major pieces, among them the Rosetta Stone and the Parthenon Sculptures (Elgin Marbles), were "acquired" from the French, who "found" them in Egypt and Greece. The museum has since collected countless goodies of worldwide historical significance: the Black Obelisk, some of the Dead Sea Scrolls, the Lindow Man. And that only begins the list.

The British Museum is a vast space split into 94 galleries, generally divided by continent or period of history, with some areas spanning more than one level. There are marvels wherever you go, and—while we don't like to be pessimistic—it is, yes, impossible to fully appreciate everything in a day. So make the most of the tours, activity trails, and visitors guides that are available.

The following is a highly edited overview of the museum's greatest hits, organized by area. Pick one or two that

whet your appetite, then branch out from there, or spend two straight hours indulging in the company of a single favorite sculpture. There's no wrong way to experience the British Museum, just make sure you do!

✉ Great Russell St., Bloomsbury WC1

☎ 020/7323–8000

🌐 www.britishmuseum.org

🎟 Free; donations encouraged. Tickets for special exhibits vary in price.

🕐 Galleries (and Reading Room exhibition space): Sat.–Thurs. 10–5:30, Fri. 10–8:30. Great Court: Sat.–Thurs. 9–6, Fri. 9–8:30.

Ⓤ Russell Square, Holborn, Tottenham Court Rd.

(left) The Great Court
(top) *Cradle to Grave* by Pharmacopoeia

MUSEUM HIGHLIGHTS

Ancient Civilizations

The Rosetta Stone. Found in 1799 and carved in 196 BC by decree of Ptolemy V in Egyptian hieroglyphics, demotic, and Greek, it was this multilingual inscription that provided French Egyptologist Jean-François Champollion with the key to deciphering hieroglyphics. *Room 4.*

Colossal statue of Ramesses II. A member of the 19th dynasty (ca. 1270 BC), Ramesses II commissioned innumerable statues of himself—more than any other preceding or succeeding king. This one, a 7-ton likeness of his perfectly posed upper half, comes from his mortuary temple, the Ramesseum, in western Thebes. *Room 4.*

(top) Portland vase
(bottom) Colossal statue of Ramesses II

The Parthenon Sculptures. Perhaps these marvelous treasures of Greece shouldn't be here—but while the debate rages on, you can steal your own moment with the Elgin Marbles. Carved in about 440 BC, these graceful decorations are displayed along with an in-depth, high-tech exhibit of the Acropolis; the **handless, footless Dionysus** who used to recline along its east pediment is especially well known. *Room 18.*

Mausoleum of Halikarnassos. All that remains of this, one of the Seven Wonders of the Ancient World, is a fragmented form of the original "mausoleum," the 4th-century tomb of Maussollos, King of Karia. The highlight of this gallery is the marble forepart of the **colossal chariot horse from the** *quadriga. Room 21.*

The Egyptian mummies. Another short flight of stairs takes you to the museum's most popular galleries, especially beloved by children: the Roxie Walker Galleries of Egyptian Funerary Archaeology have a fascinating collection of relics from the Egyptian realm of the dead. In addition to real corpses, wrapped mummies, and mummy cases, there's a menagerie of animal companions and curious items that were buried alongside them. *Rooms 62–63.*

Portland Vase. Made in Italy from cameo glass at the turn of the first century, it is named after the Dukes of Portland, who owned it from 1785 to 1945. It is considered a technical masterpiece—opaque white mythological figures cut by a gem-cutter are set on cobalt-blue background. *Room 70.*

The **Enlightenment Gallery** should be visited purely for the fact that its antiquarian cases hold the contents of the British Museum's first collections—Sir Hans Sloane's natural-history loot, as well as that of Sir Joseph Banks, who acquired specimens of everything from giant shells to fossils to rare plants to exotic beasts during his voyage to the Pacific aboard Captain Cook's *Endeavour.* *Room 1.*

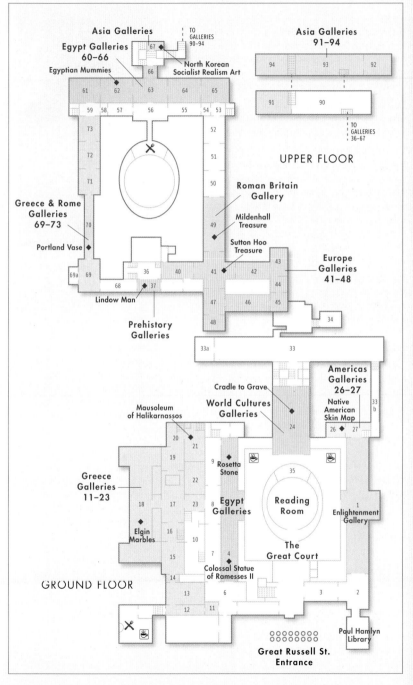

Asia Galleries

Egypt Galleries
60–66

Egyptian Mummies

TO GALLERIES 90–94

67

66

North Korean
Socialist Realism Art

Asia Galleries
91–94

94   93   92

91   90

TO GALLERIES 36–67

UPPER FLOOR

61   62   63   64   65

59 58 57 56 55 54 53

73   52

72   51

71   50

Greece & Rome
Galleries
69–73

70

Portland Vase

Roman Britain
Gallery

49   Mildenhall
Treasure

Sutton Hoo
Treasure

69a 69   36   40   41   42   43

68   37   44

Lindow Man   47   46   45

Prehistory
Galleries   48   34

33a   33

Europe
Galleries
41–48

Americas
Galleries
26–27

Cradle to Grave

World Cultures
Galleries

24

Native
American
Skin Map

33 b

26   27

Mausoleum
of Halikarnassos

20   21

19

9   Rosetta
Stone

35

Greece
Galleries
11–23

22

18   17   23   8   Egypt
Galleries

Reading
Room

1
Enlightenment
Gallery

16   10

Elgin
Marbles

15   7   4   The
Great Court

14

Colossal Statue
of Ramesses II

GROUND FLOOR

13   6   3   2

12   11

Great Russell St.
Entrance

Paul Hamlyn
Library

Asia

The Korea Foundation Gallery. Delve into striking examples of **North Korean Socialist Realism art** from the 1950s to the present and a reconstruction of a **sarangbang,** a traditional scholar's study, complete with hanji paper walls and tea-making equipment. *Room 67.*

The Percival David Collection. More than 1400 pieces of Chinese ceramics (the most comprehensive collection outside China) are on display. *Room 95.*

World Cultures

The JP Morgan Chase North American Gallery. This is one of the largest collections of native culture outside North America, going back to the earliest hunters 10,000 years ago. Here a 1775 **native American skin map** serves as an example of the importance of such documents in the exploration and cartography of North America. Look for the beautifully displayed **native American costumes.** *Room 26.*

The Mexican Gallery. The most alluring pieces sit in this collection side by side: a 15th-century **turquoise mask of Xiuhtecuhtli,** the Mexican Fire God and Turquoise Lord, and a **double-headed serpent** from the same period. *Room 27.*

Britain and Europe

The Mildenhall Treasure. This glittering haul of 4th-century Roman silver tableware was found beneath the sod of a Suffolk field in 1942. *Room 49.*

The Sutton Hoo Treasure. Next door to the loot from Mildenhall—and equally splendid, including brooches, swords, and jewel-encrusted helmets—the treasure was buried at sea with (it is thought) Redwald, one of the first English kings, in the 7th century, and excavated from a Suffolk field in 1938–39. *Room 41.*

Lindow Man. "Pete Marsh"—so named by the archaeologists who unearthed the body from a Cheshire peat marsh—was ritually slain, probably as a human sacrifice, in the 1st century and lay perfectly pickled in his bog until 1984. *Room 50.*

Theme Galleries

Living & Dying. The "Cradle to Grave" installation pays homage to the British nation's wellbeing—or ill-being, as it were. More than 14,000 drugs (the number estimated to be prescribed to every person in the U.K. in his lifetime) are displayed in a colorful tapestry of pills and tablets. *Room 24.*

Colossal chariot horse from the *quadriga* of the Mausoleum at Halikarnassos

LOWER GALLERY

The three rooms that comprise the **Sainsbury African Galleries** are of the main interest here: together they present a staggering 200,000 objects, featuring intricate pieces of old ivory, gold, and wooden masks and carvings—highlighting such ancient kingdoms as the Benin and Asante. The displays include a collection of **55 throwing knives;** ceremonial garments including a dazzling pink and green **woman's coif** (*qufiya*) from Tunisia made of silk, metal, and cotton; and the *Oxford Man, a* 1992 woodcarving by Owen Ndou, depicting a man of ambiguous race clutching his Book of Knowledge.

DID YOU KNOW?

Galleries help divide this sprawling space into manageable sizes for visitors. The Sainsbury African Galleries are just some of the 94 galleries; the British Museum's collection totals more than 7 million objects.

THE NATION'S ATTIC: A HISTORY OF THE MUSEUM

The collection began when Sir Hans Sloane, physician to Queen Anne and George II, bequeathed his personal collection of curiosities and antiquities to the nation. The collection quickly grew, thanks to enthusiastic kleptomaniacs after the Napoleonic Wars—most notoriously the seventh Earl of Elgin, who obtained the marbles from the Parthenon and Erechtheion on the Acropolis in Athens during his term as British ambassador in Constantinople.

Soon thereafter, it seemed everyone had something to donate—George II gave the old Royal Library, Sir William Hamilton gave antique vases, Charles Townley gave sculptures, the Bank of England gave coins. When the first exhibition galleries opened to visitors in 1759, the trustees agreed to admit only small groups guided by curators. The British Museum quickly became one of the most fashionable places to be seen in the capital, and tickets, which had to be booked in advance, were treated like gold dust.

The museum's holdings quickly outgrew their original space in Montague House. After the addition of such major pieces as the Rosetta Stone and other Egyptian antiquities (spoils of the Napoleonic War) and the Parthenon sculptures, Robert Smirke was commissioned to build an appropriately large and monumental building on the same site. It's still a hot ticket: the British Museum now receives more than 5 million visitors every year.

THE GREAT COURT & THE READING ROOM

The museum's classical Greek-style facade features figures representing the progress of civilization, and the focal point is the awesome Great Court, a massive glass-roofed space. Here is the museum's inner courtyard (now the largest covered square in Europe) that, for more than 150 years, had been used for storage.

The 19th-century Reading Room, an impressive 106-foot-high blue-and-gold-domed library, forms the centerpiece of the Great Court. The 104,000 ancient tomes are at the British Library until 2012. H.G. Wells, Thomas Hardy, Lord Tennyson, Oscar Wilde, George Orwell, T.S. Elliot, and Beatrix Potter are just a few writers who have used this space as a literary and academic sanctuary over the past 150 years or so. Temporary exhibitions here now include China's Terracotta Army, Hadrian, and Shah 'Abbas.

(above) Reading Room

PLANNING YOUR VISIT

Tours

The **50 minute eyeOpener tour (free)** by Museum Guides does just what it says; ask for details at the information desk. After this tour, you can then dip back into the collections that most captured your imagination at your leisure.

An excellent **multimedia guide (£5)** is a good way to explore the galleries at your own pace, via a series of differently-themed tours.

Alternatively, the **Visitor's Guide (£3.50)** gives a brief but informative overview of the museum's history and is, again, divided into self-guided themed tours.

Before you go, take a look at the online **COMPASS tour** using the museum's navigation tool (www.thebritishmuseum.org/compass), which allows users to browse past and present exhibits as well as search for specific objects. A children's version can also be found here. Computer stations in the Reading Room offer onsite access to COMPASS.

▦ TIP→ The closest underground station to the British Museum is Russell Square on the Piccadilly line. However, since you will be entering via the back entrance on Montague Place, you will not experience the full impact of the museum's grand facade. To do so, alight at Holborn on the Central and Piccadilly lines or Tottenham Court Road on the Central and Northern lines. The walk from these stations is about 10 minutes.

WITH KIDS

■ Take a look at the "Family Visits" page online for the top 12 objects to see with children.

■ The Families Desk in the Great Court has trails for kids ages 3 to 5 and 6 to 11. The Ford Centre for Young Visitors has free activity backpacks.

■ Art materials are available for free from information points, where you can also find out about workshops, performances, storytelling sessions, and other free events.

■ Around the museum, there are Hands On desks open daily 11–4, which let visitors handle objects from the collections.

WHERE TO REFUEL

The British Museum's self-service **Gallery Café** gets very crowded but serves an acceptable menu beneath a plaster cast of a part of the Parthenon frieze that Lord Elgin didn't remove. It's open daily, but isn't particularly family friendly.

The **café in the Great Court** keeps longer hours and is a great place to people-watch and admire the spectacular glass roof while you eat your salad and sandwich.

If the weather is nice, exit the museum via the back entrance on Montague Place and amble over to **Russell Square,** which has grassy lawns, water fountains, and a glass-fronted café for post-sandwich coffee and ice cream.

5

IN FOCUS THE BRITISH MUSEUM

house to the nation on one condition: that nothing be changed. It's a house full of surprises. In the Picture Room, for instance, two of Hogarth's *Rake's Progress* series are among the paintings on panels that swing away to reveal secret gallery pockets with even more paintings. Everywhere, mirrors and colors play tricks with light and space, and split-level floors worthy of a fairground fun house disorient you. In a basement chamber sits the vast 1300 BC sarcophagus of Seti I, lit by a domed skylight two stories above. (When Sir John acquired this priceless object for £2,000, after it was rejected by the British Museum, he celebrated with a three-day party.) The elegant, tranquil courtyard gardens are also open to the public, and a below-street-level passage joins two of the courtyards to the museum. Because of the small size of the museum, limited numbers are allowed entry at any one time, so you may have a short wait outside—but it's worth it. Hour-long tours are offered (check the website for details), and on the first Tuesday of the month the museum offers a very popular candle-light evening opening, from 6 to 9 pm. ⊠ *13 Lincoln's Inn Fields, Bloomsbury* ☎ *020/7405–2107* ⊕ *www.soane.org* ⌸ *Free; tours £10* ⊗ *Tues.–Sat. 10–5; also 6–9 on 1st Tues. of month* Ⓜ *Holborn.*

> ### KING'S CROSS STATION
>
> Sick of living in the shadow of its sumptuously renovated next-door neighbor, St. Pancras station, King's Cross—and the area behind it—is undergoing a major makeover of its own, with bars, restaurants, shops, and even a stunning fountain display. That said, its chief attraction is still as the departure point for Harry Potter and his fellow aspiring wizards aboard the *Hogwarts Express* from the imaginary platform 9¾. The station has helpfully put up a sign for platform 9¾ if you want to take a picture there—just don't try to run through the wall.

WORTH NOTING

Lincoln's Inn. There's plenty to see at one of the oldest, best preserved, and most attractive of the Inns of Court—from the Chancery Lane Tudor brick gatehouse to the wide-open, tree-lined, atmospheric Lincoln's Inn Fields and the 15th-century chapel remodeled by Inigo Jones in 1620. Visitors are welcome to attend Sunday services in the chapel; otherwise, you must pre-book a place on of the official tours. But be warned: they tend to prefer group bookings of 15 or more, so it's best to check the website or call for details. ⊠ *Chancery La., Bloomsbury* ☎ *020/7405–1393* ⊕ *www.lincolnsinn.org.uk* ⌸ *Free* ⊗ *Gardens and chapel, weekdays noon–2:30; services Sun. at 11:30 during legal term* Ⓜ *Chancery La.*

OFF THE BEATEN PATH

London Canal Museum. This quirky little museum, based in a former ice-house, is dedicated to the rise and fall of London's once-extensive canal network. Children enjoy the activity zone and learning about Henrietta, the museum's horse. Outside, on the Battlebridge Basin, float in the painted narrowboats of modern canal dwellers—a stone's throw and a world away from the crowds of St. Pancras International train station. You can walk to the museum along the towpath from Camden Lock— download a free audio tour from the museum's website to accompany the route. ✉ *12–13 New Wharf Rd., King's Cross* ☎ *020/7713–0836* ⊕ *www.canalmuseum.org. uk* 🎫 *£4* ⊙ *Tues.–Sun. and holiday Mon. 10–4:30; last admission 30 mins before closing. First Thurs. in month open until 7:30. Closed Dec. 24–Jan. 1* Ⓜ *King's Cross.*

WORD OF MOUTH

"Our next stop, the [British] Museum, was more captivating, as we kind of thought it might be. First we had some lunch in their café, which was good. We like the early Greek historic archaeological finds, and took our time going through those rooms.... Stayed there a couple of hours." —BillJ

Royal Courts of Justice. Here is the vast Victorian Gothic pile of 35 million bricks containing the nation's principal law courts, with 1,000-odd rooms running off 3½ miles of corridors. This is where the most important civil law cases—that's everything from divorce to fraud, with libel in between—are heard. You can sit in the viewing gallery to watch any trial you like, for a live version of Court TV. The more dramatic criminal cases are heard at the Old Bailey. Other sights are the 238-foot-long main hall and the compact exhibition of judges' robes. Guided tours must be booked in advance. ✉ *The Strand, Bloomsbury* ☎ *020/7947–6000, 020/7947–7684 tour reservations* ⊕ *www.hmcourts-service.gov.uk (search for "Royal Courts of Justice" in A–Z option)* 🎫 *Free; tours £12* ⊙ *Weekdays 9–4:30* Ⓜ *Temple, Holborn, Chancery La.*

Temple Church. As featured in *The Da Vinci Code* (both book *and* film), this church was built by the Knights Templar in the late 12th century. The Red Knights held their secret initiation rites in the crypt here. Having started poor, holy, and dedicated to the protection of pilgrims, they grew rich from showers of royal gifts until, in the 14th century, they were charged with heresy, blasphemy, and sodomy, thrown into the Tower, and stripped of their wealth. So it goes. Featuring a rare, circular nave, the church isn't quite as thickly atmospheric as you might expect—largely due to the efforts of Victorian and postwar restorers. That said, it remains a fine Gothic-Romanesque church. ✉ *King's Bench Walk, The Temple, Bloomsbury* ☎ *020/7353–8559* ⊕ *www. templechurch.com* 🎫 *£5* ⊙ *Check website for details* Ⓜ *Temple.*

University College London. Founded in 1826 the college is set in a classical edifice designed by the architect of the National Gallery, William Wilkins. Committed to providing higher education without religious exclusion, in 1878 it also became the first British University to accept women on an equal footing with men. The college has within its portals the **Slade School of Fine Art,** which did for many of Britain's artists what the nearby Royal Academy of Dramatic Art (on Gower Street) did for actors. The South Cloisters contain one of London's weirder treasures: the skeleton of one of the university's founders, Jeremy Bentham, who bequeathed himself to the college. Legend has it that students from a rival college, King's College London, once stole Bentham's head and played football with it. Whether or not the story is apocryphal, Bentham's clothed skeleton, stuffed with straw and topped with a wax head, now sits (literally) in the UCL collection. Be sure to take a look at the stunning Gotham-esque Senate House on Malet Street. ⊠ *Malet Pl., Bloomsbury.*

Petrie Museum. If you didn't get your fill of Egyptian artifacts at the British Museum, you can see more in the neighboring Petrie Museum, accessed from the DMS Watson building. The museum houses an outstanding, huge collection of fascinating objects of Egyptian archaeology—jewelry, toys, papyri, and some of the world's oldest garments. ☎ *020/7679–2884* ⊕ *www.petrie.ucl.ac.uk* ▭ *Free, donations appreciated* ☉ *Tues.–Sat. 1–5; closed over Christmas and Easter holidays* Ⓜ *Euston Sq., Goodge St.*

HOLBORN

Southeast of Bloomsbury and west of the City, Holborn may appear to be little more than a buffer zone between the two—but while it may lack the panache and headline must-sees of its neighbors, don't underestimate this varied, fascinating slice of the capital. Home to legal London and the impressive Inns of Court, this is also Charles Dickens territory, with the Old Curiosity Shop and the Dickens museum snug within its borders. Add to that its fair share of ancient churches and quirky places of interest, and you'll soon discover that Holborn can be a rewarding place to while away an hour or three. Holborn's massive Gothic-style **Royal Courts of Justice** ramble all the way to the Strand, and the **Inns of Court—Gray's Inn, Lincoln's Inn, Middle Temple,** and **Inner Temple**—are where most British trial lawyers have offices to this day. Geographically, Holborn's a bit amorphous, but it's probably best geographically defined as: west, Kingsway; north, Theobald's Road; east, Gray's Inn Road (running into High Holborn); south, where the Strand becomes Fleet Street (around where the Royal Courts of Justice are).

WORTH NOTING

Gray's Inn. Although the least architecturally interesting of the four Inns of Court and the one most damaged by German bombs in the 1940s, Gray's still has romantic associations. In 1594 Shakespeare's *Comedy of Errors* was performed for the first time in the hall—which was restored after World War II and has a fine Elizabethan screen of carved oak. You must make advance arrangements to view the hall, but the secluded and spacious gardens, first planted by Francis Bacon in 1606, are open to the public. ⊠ *Gray's Inn Rd., Holborn* ☎ *020/7458–7800* ⊕ *www.graysinn. org.uk* ▭ *Free* ☉ *Weekdays noon–2:30* Ⓜ *Holborn, Chancery La.*

THE CITY

GETTING ORIENTED

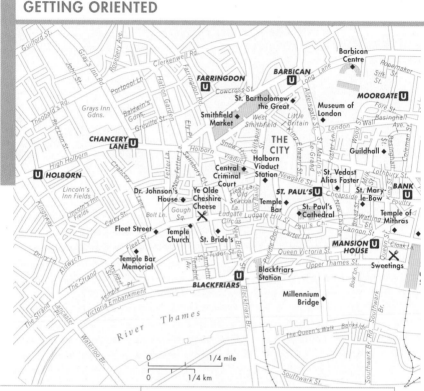

GETTING THERE	TOP REASONS TO GO
The City area is well served by a concentrated selection of Tube stations—St. Paul's and Bank are on the Central line, and Mansion House, Cannon Street, and Monument are on the District and Circle lines. Liverpool Street and Aldgate border The City's eastern edge, while Chancery Lane and Farringdon lie to the west. Barbican and Moorgate provide easy access to the theaters and galleries of the Barbican, and Blackfriars, to the south, leads to Ludgate Circus and Fleet Street.	**St. Paul's Cathedral, the "Symbolic Heart of London":** Now nudged by skyscrapers, St. Paul's still dominates the skyline. Once inside, you'll see the genius of Sir Christopher Wren's 17th-century masterpiece. **Linger on the Millennium Bridge:** Hurtle the centuries with this promenade between the Tate Modern and St. Paul's—and get a great river view, too. **Treachery and Treasures at the Tower:** This minicity of melodramatic towers is stuffed to bursting with heraldry, pageantry, and the stunning Crown Jewels (bring sunglasses). **Channel history at the Museum of London:** From a Roman leather bikini to Queen Victoria's crinoline gowns; from Selfridges' art deco elevators to a diorama of the Great Fire (sound effects! flickering flames!), this gem of a museum's got it all.

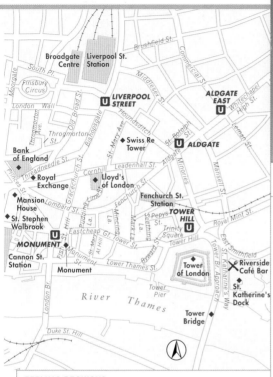

MAKING THE MOST OF YOUR TIME

The "Square Mile" is as compact as the nickname suggests, with little distance between points of interest, making an afternoon stroll a rewarding experience. For full immersion in the Tower of London, however, set aside half a day, especially if seeing the Crown Jewels is a priority. Allow an hour minimum each for the Museum of London, St. Paul's Cathedral, and Tower Bridge. On weekends, without the scurrying suits, The City is nearly deserted, making it hard to find lunch—and yet this is when the major attractions are at their busiest.

A GOOD WALK

Crossing the Millennium Bridge from the Tate Modern to St. Paul's is one of the finest walks in London—with the river to either side and Christopher Wren's iconic dome towering at one end. Dubbed the "blade of light," the shiny aluminum-and-steel span was the result of a collaboration between architect Norman Foster and sculptor Anthony Caro.

FEELING PECKISH?

Riverside Café Bar. This friendly eatery is one of the few places you're sure to find a good cup of hot chocolate and hot and cold meals, with waterside views of the luxurious yachts and gin palaces moored at the docks. Closed in the evenings. ⊠ *St. Katherine's Dock, St. Katherine's Way, The City* ☎ *020/7481–1464* Ⓜ *Tower Hill.*

Sweetings. Here since 1889, Sweetings is not cheap, takes no reservations, is only open weekdays, and it closes at 3 pm—but it serves one of the best fish lunches in London. ⊠ *39 Queen Victoria St., The City* ☎ *020/7248–3062* ⊕ *www. sweetingsrestaurant.com* Ⓜ *Mansion House.*

Ye Olde Cheshire Cheese. When you're finished exploring Fleet Street, head to the fabled Ye Olde Cheshire Cheese for a reviving pint of ale. Parts of the building date from 1667 and the pub's past customers are like a Literary Who's Who: Tennyson, Mark Twain, W. B. Yeats, Sir Arthur Conan Doyle, as well as its most famous regular, Dr. Johnson. Closed Sunday. ⊠ *145 Fleet St., The City* ☎ *020/7353–6170* Ⓜ *St. Paul's.*

DID YOU KNOW?

In The City—the oldest part of London—streets still follow a medieval pattern. Here you can see financial institutions, and notable buildings, like the Bank of England and Lloyd's of London.

Sightseeing
★★★★★
Nightlife
★
Dining
★★★
Lodging
★
Shopping
★★★

The City is the capital's fast-beating financial heart, with a powerful architectural triumvirate at its epicenter: the Bank of England, the Royal Exchange, and Mansion House. The "Square Mile" also has currency as the place where London began, its historic heart. St. Paul's Cathedral has been looking after Londoners' souls for hundreds of years, and the Tower of London—that moat-surrounded royal fortress, prison, and jewel house—has occasionally taken care of their heads.

Updated by
James O'Neill

The City is a dizzying juxtaposition of the old and the new. You'll find yourself immersed in historic London if you begin your explorations on **Fleet Street,** the site of England's first printing press and the undisputed seat of British journalism until the 1980s. Nestled behind Fleet Street is **Dr. Johnson's House,** former home of the author of *Dictionary of the English Language*, who claimed that "when a man is tired of London, he is tired of life." The nearby church of **St. Bride's,** recognizable by its tiered wedding-cake steeple, is a Sir Christopher Wren gem and still the church for journalists, while eastward rises the iconic **St. Paul's Cathedral,** also designed by Wren and the architect's masterpiece. You'll encounter more of traditional London at the **Central Criminal Court** (nicknamed **Old Bailey,** and home to London's most sensational criminal trials) and the 800-year-old **Smithfield Market,** whose Victorian halls are the site of a daily early-morning meat market. Nearby are the ancient church of **St. Bartholomew the Great** and St. Bartholomew Hospital, both begun in 1123; the **Guildhall,** the site of the only Roman amphitheater in London; the church of **St. Mary-le-Bow;** and the maze of charmingly old-fashioned, narrow streets around **Bow Lane.**

You can put all this history into context at the **Museum of London,** where archaeological displays include a portion of the original **Roman Wall** that ringed The City.

A BRIEF HISTORY

Although there is evidence of Celtic inhabitation on the north bank of the Thames, in many ways London begins with the Romans, who established the settlement of Londinium in AD 47 as an outpost of the Empire before those pesky Celts, led by Queen Boudicca, returned and burnt it to the ground 17 years later. The Saxons came and stayed for a while, as did the Vikings, and by the time the Normans turned up in the 11th century, London was already established as the most important city in England. William the Conqueror began building the palace that was to become the Tower of London, which by Tudor times was known as the world's most forbidding prison, and where two of Henry VIII's six wives were executed. During the Middle Ages, powerful guilds that nurtured commerce took root in the capital, followed by the foundation of great trading companies, such as the Honourable East India Company, which started up in 1600.

London's history has often been one of disaster and renewal. The Great Fire of 1666 spared only a few of the cramped, labyrinthine streets upon which the Great Plague had visited such devastation only the previous year. Yet the gutted wastelands ushered in an era of architectural renaissance, led by Sir Christopher Wren. Further punishment would come during the Blitz of World War II, when German bombers destroyed many buildings—but yet again London rebounded. As always.

6

Just beyond rises the modern **Barbican Centre,** a concrete complex of arts venues and apartments that was controversial at the time it was built, but now has become an indispensible part of the London landscape. The sight of some other new structures rising above The City—especially the **Lloyd's of London Building** and the **Swiss Re Tower,** popularly known as "the Gherkin"—may or may not be more reassuring.

The **Monument,** near the banks of the Thames, was built to commemorate the Great Fire of London of 1666. From here, the river leads to one of London's most absorbing and bloody attractions, the **Tower of London. Tower Bridge** is a suitably giddying finale to an exploration of this fascinating part of London.

London's X-factor is that it's full of contradictions, and nowhere are those contradictions more evident than in The City. Here, 12th-century churches nestle in the shadows of 21st-century skyscrapers; its streets, a medieval labyrinth, are thronged with office workers by day but become ghostly quiet at night; financial-industry suits work cheek by jowl with the trendy media-company hipsters of **Clerkenwell**—a place that epitomizes London's genius for reinvention. Once a haven for political radicals, Clerkenwell's many fashionable boutiques and eateries give this western edge of The City a carefree vitality. Ultimately, this is The City's trump card: the ability to harmonize so many opposites. Yes, it's one of the world's premier money centers, but it offers the visitor sights and experiences that no amount of money could buy.

TOP ATTRACTIONS

FAMILY   **Monument.** Commemorating the "dreadful visitation" of the Great Fire of London, in 1666, this is the world's tallest isolated stone column. It is the work of Sir Christopher Wren and Dr. Robert Hooke, who were asked to erect it "on or as neere unto the place where the said Fire soe unhappily began as conveniently may be." And so here it is—at 202 feet, exactly as tall as the distance it stands from Farriner's baking house in Pudding Lane, where the fire started (note the gilded urn of fire at the column's pinnacle). If climbing the 311 steps is enough to put you off your lunch, cheat a little and watch the live views that are relayed from the top. ⊠ *Monument St., The City* ☎ *020/7626–2717* ⊕ *www. themonument.info* ⊒ *£3; combined ticket with Tower Bridge exhibition £9* ⊙ *Daily 9:30–5:30, last admission 5* Ⓜ *Monument.*

FAMILY   **Museum of London.** If there's one place to absorb the history of London, from 450,000 BC to the present day, it's here: Oliver Cromwell's death mask, Queen Victoria's crinoline gowns, Selfridges' art deco elevators, the London's Burning exhibition, fans, guns and jewelry, an original Newgate Prison Door, and the incredible late-18th-century Blackett Dolls House—7,000 objects to wonder at in all. The museum appropriately shelters a section of the 2nd- to 4th-century London wall, which you can view through a window, and permanent displays highlight Pre-Roman, Roman, Medieval, and Tudor London. The Galleries of Modern London are equally enthralling: experience the "Expanding City," "People's City," and "World City," each gallery dealing with a section of London's history from 1666 until the 21st century. Innovative interactive displays abound, and you can even wander around a 19th-century London street with impressively detailed shopfronts and interiors, including a pawnbrokers, a pub, a barber, and a bank manager's office, in case you're running short on holiday money. There's also a fine schedule of temporary exhibitions. ⊠ *London Wall, The City* ☎ *020/7001–9844* ⊕ *www.museumoflondon.org.uk* ⊒ *Free* ⊙ *Mon.– Sun. 10–6; last admission 5:30* Ⓜ *Barbican, St. Paul's.*

Fodor's Choice   **St. Paul's Cathedral.**
★   *See the highlighted listing in this chapter.*

FAMILY   **Tower Bridge.** Despite its medieval, fairy-tale appearance, this is a Vic-
Fodor's Choice   torian youngster. Constructed of steel, then clothed in Portland stone,
★   the Horace Jones masterpiece was deliberately styled in the Gothic persuasion to complement the Tower next door, and it's famous for its enormous bascules—the 1,200-ton "arms" that open to allow large ships to glide beneath. This still happens occasionally (the website has details), but when river traffic was dense, the bascules were raised about five times a day.

The **Tower Bridge Exhibition** is a child-friendly tour where you can discover how one of the world's most famous bridges actually works before heading out onto the walkways for the wonderful city views. First, take in the romance of the panoramas from the east and west walkways between those grand turrets. On the east are the modern superstructures of the Docklands, and on the west is the Tower of London, St. Paul's, the Monument, and the steel-and-glass "futuristic

Continued on page 124

ST. PAUL'S CATHEDRAL

Sir Christopher Wren's maxim "I build for eternity" proves no empty boast.

Sublime, awesome, majestic, and inspirational are just some of the words to describe Wren's masterpiece, St. Paul's Cathedral—and thanks to a painstaking, recently-completed 15-year restoration project, it's now looking better than ever.

This is the spiritual heart of the nation, where people and events are celebrated, mourned, and honored. As you approach the cathedral your eyes are inevitably drawn skyward to the great dome, one of the largest in the world and an amazing piece of engineering. Visit in the late afternoon for evensong, and let the choir's voices transport you to a world of absolute peace in a place of perfect beauty, as pristine as the day it was completed.

TOURING ST. PAUL'S

Enter the cathedral via the main west entrance, and walk straight down the length of the nave to the central Dome Altar. Nobody can resist making a beeline for the dome, so start your tour beneath it, standing dead center on the beautiful sunburst floor, Wren's focal mirror of the magnificent design above. A simple quotation marks the floor "Lector si momentum requiris, circumspice" (Reader if you seek his monument, look around). The dome crowns the center of the cathedral and rises to 364 feet—but save your strength for the "great climb" to get some fantastic views.

THE CATHEDRAL FLOOR

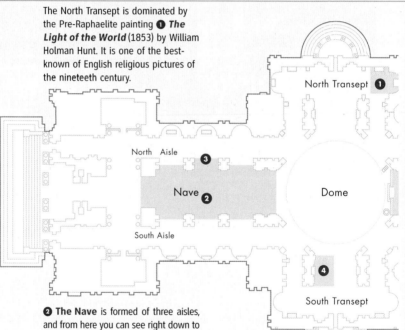

The North Transept is dominated by the Pre-Raphaelite painting ❶ *The Light of the World* (1853) by William Holman Hunt. It is one of the best-known of English religious pictures of the nineteeth century.

North Transept ❶

North Aisle

❸

Nave ❷

South Aisle

Dome

❹

South Transept

❷ **The Nave** is formed of three aisles, and from here you can see right down to the High Altar at the far end of the Choir, more than 100 yards away. Take time to admire the mastery of space and light.

In the north aisle of the Nave is Flaxman's grandiose ❸ **monument to the Duke of Wellington,** who sits astride his faithful charger, Copenhagen, the horse that carried him through the Battle of Waterloo.

The South Transept displays a ❹ **monument to Admiral Lord Nelson,** Britain's favorite naval hero, with an anchor. Other memorials commemorate the explorer Captain Robert Scott and the darling of British landscape painting J.M.W. Turner.

CELEBRITY STATUS

St. Paul's has witnessed many momentous processions along its checkered nave. The somber state funerals of heroes Admiral Lord Nelson and the Duke of Wellington, and of Sir Winston Churchill, drew huge crowds. It was here, also, that the fairy-tale wedding of Prince Charles and Lady Diana Spencer took place, and the jubilees of Queen Victoria, George V, and the present Queen were celebrated.

6

IN FOCUS ST. PAUL'S CATHEDRAL

The North Choir Aisle features the beautiful ❺ **gilded gates** by Jean Tijou, perhaps the most accomplished artist in wrought iron of all time, as well as Henry Moore's sculpture ❻ *Mother and Child,* its simple lines complementing the ornate surroundings.

The Choir contains the ❽ **Bishop's Throne** or cathedra, hence the name cathedral. Look aloft to the fabulous mosaics. Don't miss the exquisite, delicate carvings by Grinling Gibbons, in particular on the case of the ❾ **grand organ,** one of the Cathedral's greatest artifacts. It was designed by Wren and played by such illustrious figures as Handel and Mendelssohn.

❿ **The High Altar,** with its glorious canopy, is a profusion of marble and carved and gilded oak.

Map labels:
❻
North Choir Aisle
❺
Apse
Choir (Quire)
⓾ ⓫
❾
❽ ❺
South Choir Aisle
❼

The South Choir Aisle contains a ❼ **marble effigy of poet John Donne,** who was Dean of old St. Paul's for his final 10 years (he died in 1631). This is the only statue to have survived the Great Fire of London intact. You can see the scorch marks at the base of the statue.

The Apse is home to the ⓫ **American Memorial Chapel,** which honors the more than 28,000 U.S. soldiers who died while stationed in the U.K. during World War II. The lime-wood paneling incorporates a rocket as a tribute to the United States' achievements in space.

MUSICAL FRICTION

The organ, with its cherubs and angels, was not installed without controversy. The mighty instrument proved a tight fit, and the maker, known as Father Schmidt, and Wren nearly came to blows. Wren was reputed to have said he would not adapt his cathedral for a mere "box of whistles."

THE DOME

The dome is the crowning glory of the cathedral, a must for visitors.

At 99 feet, the ❶ **Whispering Gallery** is reached by 259 spiral steps. This is the part of the cathedral with which you bribe children—they will be fascinated by the acoustic phenomenon: whisper something to the wall on one side, and a second later it transmits clearly to the other side, 107 feet away. The only problem is identifying your whisper from the cacophony of everyone else's. Look down onto the nave from here and up to the monochrome frescoes of St. Paul by Sir James Thornhill.

More stamina is required to reach the ❷ **Stone Gallery**, at 173 feet and 378 steps from ground level. It is on the exterior of the cathedral and offers a vista of the city and the River Thames.

For the best views of all—at 280 feet and 530 steps from ground level—make the trek to the small ❸ **Golden Gallery**, the highest point

of the outer dome. A hole in the floor gives a vertiginous view down. You can see the lantern above through a circular opening called the oculus. If you have a head for heights you can walk outside for a spectacular panorama of London.

The top of the dome is crowned with a ❹ **ball and cross**. At 23 feet high and weighing approximately 7 tons, it is the pinnacle of St. Paul's.

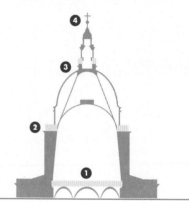

A BRIEF HISTORY

The cathedral is the masterpiece of Sir Christopher Wren (1632–1723), completed in 1710 after 35 years of building and much argument with the Royal Commission. Wren had originally been commissioned to restore Old St. Paul's, the Norman cathedral that had replaced, in its turn, three earlier versions, but the Great Fire left so little of it standing that a new cathedral was deemed necessary.

Wren's first plan, known as the New Model, did not make it past the drawing board; the second, known as the Great Model, got as far as the 20-foot oak rendering you can see here today before it, too, was rejected, whereupon Wren is said to have burst into tears. The third, however, known as the Warrant Design (because it received the royal warrant), was accepted, with the fortunate coda that the architect

be allowed to make changes as he saw fit. Without that, there would be no dome, because the approved design had featured a steeple. Parliament felt that building was proceeding too slowly (in fact, 35 years is lightning speed, as cathedrals go) and withheld half of Wren's pay for the last 13 years of work. He was pushing 80 when Queen Anne finally coughed up the arrears.

▥ **TIP➜ To see Wren's Great Model, you must join a Triforium Tour (Mon. and Tues. at 11:30 and 2, Fri. at 2). These one-hour tours include a visit to the library and a glimpse of the famous Geometric staircase. The visit ends in the Trophy Room, where Wren's Great Model is on display. The tour costs £19.50 per person and includes entry to the cathedral and access to the crypt and galleries. It's best to book in advance by calling 020/7246–8357 or sending an e-mail to visits@stpaulscathedral.org.uk.**

THE CRYPT

A visit to the vast crypt is a time for reflection and contemplation, with some 200 memorials to see. If it all becomes too somber, take solace in the café or shop near the crypt entrance.

Here lies ❶ **Admiral Nelson,** killed at the Battle of Trafalgar in 1805. His body was preserved in alcohol for the journey home, and his pickled remains were buried here beneath Cardinal Wolsey's unused 16th-century sarcophagus.

The ❷ **tomb of the Duke of Wellington** comprises a simple casket made from Cornish granite. He is remembered as a hero of battle, but his name lives on in the form of boots, cigars, beef Wellington, and the capital of New Zealand.

Surrounded by his family and close to a plethora of iconic artists, musicians, and scientists, the ❸ **tomb of Sir Christopher Wren** is a modest simple slab.

The beautiful ❹ **O.B.E. Chapel** (dedicated 1960) is a symbol of the Order of the British Empire, an order of chivalry established in 1917 by George V. The theme of sovereign and Commonwealth is represented in the glass panels.

The vast ❺ **treasury** houses the cathedral's plate, although a good deal has been lost or stolen over the centuries—in particular in a daring robbery of 1810—and much of the display comes from other London churches.

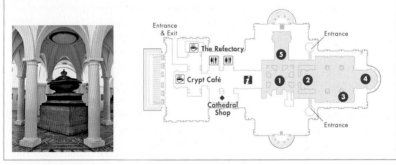

6

PLANNING YOUR DAY

WHAT'S NEARBY: Stroll over the Millennium Bridge (look back for a great view of St. Paul's) and have lunch at Tate Modern. The restaurant at the top of the gallery has spectacular views of London. ■**TIP**➜ To avoid lines visit early in the morning. For a different experience return for Evensong at 5 pm.

CONTACT INFO: ✉ *St. Paul's Churchyard, Ludgate Hill EC4 8AD* ☎ *020/7236-4128* ⊕ *www.stpauls.co.uk* Ⓤ *St. Paul's.*

ADMISSION: Adults: cathedral, crypt, ambulatory, and gallery £15 (includes multimedia guides and guided tours). **Family ticket** (2

adults, 2 children): £36. **Children 6–17:** £6.

TOURS: A guided tour of the cathedral, choir, Geometric staircase, and crypt lasts 1½–2 hours and is included in the price of admission (as are the multimedia guides) . Tours start at 10, 11, 1, and 2.

HOURS: The cathedral is a house of worship. Services may cause changes to the visiting hours on any given day, so be sure to call ahead.

Cathedral: Mon.–Sat. 8:30–4.
Shop: Mon., Tues., Thurs–Sat. 8:30–5, Wed. 9–5, Sun. 10–4:30.
Crypt café: Mon.–Sat. 9–5, Sun. 12–4.

mushroom" that is Greater London Assembly's City Hall. Then it's back down to explore the Victorian engine rooms and discover the inner workings, which you learn about through hands-on displays and films. ☒ *Tower Bridge Rd., The City* ☎ *020/7403–3761* ⊕ *www. towerbridge.org.uk* ☒ *£8* ⊙ *Apr.– Sept., daily 10–6; Oct.–Mar., daily 9:30–5.30; last admission 30 min before closing* Ⓜ *Tower Hill.*

Fodor's Choice   **Tower of London.**
★   *See the highlighted listing in this chapter.*

WORTH NOTING

Bank of England. The country's top vault has been central to the British economy since 1694. Known for the past couple of centuries as "the Old Lady of Threadneedle Street," after the name appeared in a caption to a political cartoon (which can be seen in the museum), the bank manages the national debt and the foreign exchange reserves, issues banknotes, sets interest rates, looks after England's gold, and regulates the country's banking system. Sir John Soane designed the neoclassical hulk in 1788, wrapping it in windowless walls, which are all that survives of his original building. The bank's history is traced in the Bank of England Museum (entrance is around the corner on Bartholomew Lane), where interactive exhibits chart the bank's more recent history and offer the chance to try your hand at controlling inflation. But most visitors still make a beeline for the solid-gold bar that can be stroked and held in the central trading hall (but before you get any ideas, there's security everywhere). ☒ *Threadneedle St., The City* ☎ *020/7601–5545* ⊕ *www. bankofengland.co.uk* ☒ *Free* ⊙ *Weekdays and Lord Mayor's Show day (2nd Sat. in Nov.) 10–5, last admission 4:45* Ⓜ *Bank, Monument.*

Barbican Centre. The Barbican is an enormous 1980s concrete maze that Londoners either love or hate—but the importance of the complex to the cultural life of the capital is beyond dispute. It houses two theaters; the London Symphony Orchestra and its auditorium; the Guildhall School of Music and Drama; a major art gallery for changing exhibitions; two movie theaters; a convention center; an upscale restaurant, cafés, terraces with fountains, and bookshops; and living space in some of the most desirable tower blocks in town. Navigation around the complex is via the yellow lines running, Wizard-of-Oz-like, along the floors, with signs on the walls, although it's still easy to get lost. Actors and audiences alike rate the theater for its excellent acoustics and sightlines. The dance, music, and theater programs have been transformed into a yearlong fest named BITE, which stands for Barbican International Theatre Events, and encompasses dance, puppetry, and music. Emphasis is on presenting tomorrow's names today, although there are performances by established companies and artists as well. ☒ *Silk St., The City* ☎ *020/7638–8891 box office* ⊕ *www.barbican.org.*

Interior of the "Inside-Out" Lloyd's of London building, designed by Richard Rogers Partnership.

uk ✉ *Barbican Centre free, art gallery £6–£12, movies £7.50–£14.50, concerts £6.50–£80, theater £7–£100* ☉ *Barbican Centre Mon.–Sat. 9 am–11 pm, Sun. and holidays noon–11; gallery Thurs. 11–10, Mon., Fri.–Sun. 11–8, Tues.–Wed. 11–6* Ⓜ *Barbican, Moorgate.*

Dr. Johnson's House. This is where Samuel Johnson lived between 1748 and 1759. Built in 1700, the elegant Georgian residence, with its paneled rooms and period furniture, is where the Great Bear (as he was known) compiled his *Dictionary of the English Language* in the attic as his health deteriorated. Two early editions are on view, among other mementos of Johnson and his friend, diarist, and later, his biographer, James Boswell. After soaking up the atmosphere, repair around the corner in Wine Office Court to the famed **Ye Olde Cheshire Cheese** pub, once Johnson and Boswell's favorite watering hole. ✉ *17 Gough Sq., The City* ☎ *020/7353–3745* ⊕ *www.drjohnsonshouse.org* 🖅 *£4.50* ☉ *May–Sept., Mon.–Sat. 11–5:30; Oct.–Apr., Mon.–Sat. 11–5* Ⓜ *Holborn, Chancery Lane, Temple.*

Guildhall. The Corporation of London, which oversees The City, has ceremonially elected and installed its Lord Mayor here for the last 800 years. The Guildhall was built in 1411, and though it failed to avoid either the 1666 or 1940 flames, its core survived. The Great Hall is a psychedelic patchwork of coats of arms and banners of the City Livery Companies, which inherited the mantle of the medieval trade guilds. Tradesmen couldn't even run a shop without kowtowing to these prototypical unions, and their grand banqueting halls, the plushest private dining venues in The City, are testimony to the wealth they amassed. Inside the hall, Gog and Magog, the pair of mythical giants who founded ancient Albion and the city of New Troy, upon which London was said to be built, glower down from their west-gallery grandstand in 9-foot-high painted lime wood. The hall was also the site of famous trials, including that of Lady Jane Grey in 1553, before her execution at the Tower of London. To the right of Guildhall Yard is the **Guildhall Art Gallery,** which includes portraits of the great and the good, cityscapes, famous battles, and a slightly cloying pre-Raphaelite section. The construction of the gallery in the 1980s led to the exciting discovery of London's only **Roman amphitheater,** which had lain underneath Guildhall Yard undisturbed for more than 1,800 years. It was excavated, and now visitors can walk among the remains, although most of the relics can be seen at the Museum of London. ⊠ *Aldermanbury, The City* ☎ *020/7606–3030, 020/7332–3700 gallery* ⊕ *www.cityoflondon. gov.uk* ⊠ *Free (fee for some gallery exhibitions)* ⊗ *Mon.–Sat. 9:30–5; gallery Mon.–Sat. 10–5, Sun. noon–4, last admission 4:30 or 3:30* Ⓜ *St. Paul's, Moorgate, Bank, Mansion House.*

Old Bailey. This is the place to watch the real-life drama of justice in action in one of the 16 courtrooms that are open to the public. Previous trials have included those of Crippen and Christie, two of England's most notorious wife murderers, as well as the controversial trials of Oscar Wilde and the notorious East End gangsters, the Kray twins. The day's hearings are posted on the sign outside, but your best bet is to consult the previous day's tabloid newspapers for an idea of the trials that are making waves. There are security restrictions, and children under 14 are not allowed in; call the information line first. The present-day **Central Criminal Court** is where Newgate Prison stood from the 12th century until the beginning of the 20th century. Called by the novelist Henry Fielding the "prototype of hell," few survived for long in the version pulled down in 1770. The Central Criminal Court replaced Newgate in 1907, and the most famous feature of the solid Edwardian building is the 12-foot gilded statue of Justice perched on top; she was intended to mirror the dome of St. Paul's. ⊠ *Newgate St., The City* ☎ *020/7248–3277 information* ⊕ *www.cityoflondon.gov. uk* ⊗ *Public Gallery weekdays 9.:45–12:45 and 1:45–4 (approx.); line forms at Newgate St. entrance or in Warwick St. Passage; closed bank holidays and day after* Ⓜ *St. Paul's.*

St. Bartholomew the Great. This is one of London's oldest churches. Construction on the church and the hospital nearby was begun in 1123 by Henry I's favorite courtier, Rahere, who, surviving malaria, dedicated his life to serving the saint who had visited him in his fevered dreams. With the dissolution of the monasteries, Henry VIII had most of the place torn down; the Romanesque choir loft is all that survives from the 12th century. In recent times, this ancient church has become a bit of a movie star, having appeared in *The Other Boleyn Girl, Four Weddings and a Funeral,* and *Shakespeare in Love,* to name but a few. ⊠ *Cloth Fair, West Smithfield, The City* ☎ *020/7606–5171* ⊕ *www. greatstbarts.com* ⊠ *Church £4 (free for first hour and for those coming to pray); museum free* ⊗ *Church weekdays 8:30–5 (closes at 4 Nov.– Feb.), Sat. 10:30–4, Sun 8:30–8. Museum Tues.–Fri. 10–4* Ⓜ *Barbican, Farringdon.*

Continued on page 134

THE TOWER OF LONDON

The Tower is a microcosm of the city itself—a sprawling, organic hodgepodge of buildings that inspires reverence and terror in equal measure. See the block on which Anne Boleyn was beheaded, marvel at the Crown Jewels, and pay homage to the ravens who keep the monarchy safe.

An architectural patchwork of time, the oldest building of the complex is the fairytale White Tower, conceived by William the Conqueror in 1078 as both a royal residence and a show of power to the troublesome Anglo-Saxons he had subdued at the Battle of Hastings. Today's Tower has seen everything, as a palace, barracks, a mint for producing coins, an armoury, and the Royal menagerie (home of the country's first elephant). The big draw is the stunning opulence of the Crown Jewels, kept on-site in the heavily fortified Jewel House. Most of all, though, the Tower is known for death: it's been a place of imprisonment, torture, and execution for the realm's most notorious traitors as well as its martyrs. These days, unless you count the killer admission fees, there are far less morbid activities taking place in the Tower, but it still breathes London's history and pageantry from its every brick and offers hours of exploration.

TOURING THE TOWER

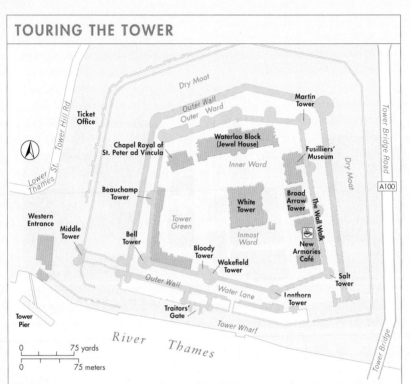

Entry to the Tower is via the **Western Entrance** and the **Middle Tower**, which feed into the outermost ring of the Tower's defenses.

Water Lane leads past the dread-inducing **Traitors' Gate**, the final point of entry for many Tower prisoners.

Toward the end of Water Lane, the **Lanthorn Tower** houses by night the ravens rumored to keep the kingdom safe, and by day a timely high-tech reconstruction of the Catholic Guy Fawkes's plot to blow up the Houses of Parliament in 1605.

The **Bloody Tower** earned its name as the apocryphal site of the murder of two young princes, Edward and Richard, who disappeared from the Tower after being put there in 1483 by their uncle, Richard III. Two little skeletons (now in Westminster Abbey) were found buried close to the White Tower in 1674 and are thought to be theirs.

The **Beauchamp Tower** housed upper-class miscreants: Latin graffiti about Lady Jane Grey can be glimpsed today on its walls.

Like a prize gem set at the head of a royal crown, the **White Tower** is the centerpiece of the complex. Its four towers dominate the Inner

GOLD DIGGER?

Keep your eyes peeled as you tour the Tower: according to one story, Sir John Barkstead, goldsmith and Lieutenant of the Tower under Cromwell, hid £20,000 in gold coins here before his arrest and execution at the Restoration of Charles II.

Ward, a fitting and forbidding reminder of Norman strength at the time of the conquest of England.

Once inside the White Tower, head upstairs for the **Armouries**, where the biggest attraction, quite literally,

Jewel House, Waterloo Barracks

ROYAL BLING

The Crown of Queen Elizabeth, the Queen Mother, from 1937, contains the exotic 105-carat Koh-i-Noor (mountain of light) diamond.

6

IN FOCUS THE TOWER OF LONDON

TIME KILLERS

Some prisoners managed to keep themselves plenty amused: Sir Walter Raleigh grew tobacco on Tower Green, and in 1561 suspected sorcerer Hugh Draper carved an intricate astronomical clock on the walls of his Salt Tower cell.

is the suit of armor worn by a well-endowed Henry VIII. There is a matching outfit for his horse.

Other fascinating exhibits include the set of Samurai armor presented to James I in 1613 by the emperor of Japan, and the tiny set of armor worn by Henry VIII's young son Edward.

The **Jewel House** in Waterloo Block is the Tower's biggest draw, perfect for playing pick-your-favorite-crown from the wrong side of bul-

letproof glass. Not only are these crowns, staffs, and orbs encrusted with heavy-duty gems, they are invested with the authority of monarchical power in England, dating back to the 1300s.

Outside, pause at **Tower Green,** permanent departure point for those of noble birth. The hoi polloi were dispatched at nearby Tower Hill. The Tower's most famous female victims—Anne Boleyn, Margaret Countess of Salisbury, Catherine Howard, and Lady Jane Grey—all went this "priviledged" way.

Behind a well-kept square of grass stands the **Chapel Royal of St. Peter ad Vincula,** a delightful Tudor church and final resting place of six beheaded Tudor bodies. ■ TIP➜ **Visitors are welcome for services and can also enter after 4:30 pm daily.**

The **Salt Tower,** reputedly the most haunted corner of the complex, marks the start of the **Wall Walk,** a bracing promenade along the stone spiral steps and battlements of the Tower that looks down on the trucks, taxis, and shimmering high-rises of modern London.

The Wall Walk ends at the **Martin Tower,** former home of the Crown Jewels and now host to the crowns and diamonds exhibition that explains the art of fashioning royal headwear and tells the story of some of the most famous stones.

On leaving the Tower, browse the gift shop, and wander the wharf that overlooks the Thames, leading to a picture-postcard view of Tower Bridge.

WHO ARE THE BEEFEATERS?

First of all, they're Yeoman Warders, but probably got the nickname "beefeater" from their position as Royal Bodyguards which entitled them to eat as much beef as they liked. Part of the "Yeoman of the Guard," started in the reign of Edmund IV, the warders have formed the Royal Bodyguard as far back as 1509 when Henry VIII left a dozen of the Yeoman of the Guard at the Tower to protect it.

Originally, the Yeoman Warders also served as jailers of the Tower, doubling as torturers when necessary. (So it would have been a Beefeater tightening the thumb screws, or ratchetting the rack another notch on some unfortunate prisoner. Smile nicely.) Today 36 Yeoman Warders (men and women since 2007), along with the Chief Yeoman Warder and the Yeoman Gaoler, live within the walls of the Tower with their families, in accommodations in the Outer Ward. They stand guard over the Tower, conduct tours, and lock up at 9:53 pm every night with the Ceremony of the Keys.

■ TIP→ Free tickets to the Ceremony of the Keys are available by writing several months in advance; check the Tower Web site for details.

HARK THE RAVENS!

Legend has it that should the hulking black ravens ever leave, the White Tower will crumble and the kingdom fall. Charles II, no doubt jumpy after his father's execution and the monarchy's short-term fall from grace, made a royal decree in 1662 that there should be at least six of the carrion-eating nasties present at all times. There have been some close calls. During World War II, numbers dropped to one, echoing the precarious fate of the war-wracked country. In 2005, two (of eight) died over Christmas when Thor—the most intelligent but also the largest bully of the bunch—killed new recruit Gundolf, named after the Tower's 1070 designer. Pneumonia put an end to Bran, leaving lifelong partner Branwen without her mate.

■ DID YOU KNOW? In 1981 a raven named Grog, perhaps seduced by his alcoholic moniker, escaped after 21 years at the Tower. Others have been banished for "conduct unbecoming."

The six that remain, each one identified by a colored band around a claw, are much loved for their fidelity (they mate for life) and their cheek (capable of 440 noises, they are witty and scolding mimics). It's not only the diet

of blood-soaked biscuits, rabbit, and scraps from the mess kitchen that keeps them coming back. Their lifting feathers on one wing are trimmed, meaning they can manage the equivalent of a lop-sided air-bound hobble but not much more. For the first half of 2006 the ravens were moved indoors full-time as a preventive measure against avian flu but have since been allowed out and about again. In situ they are a territorial lot, sticking to Tower Green and the White Tower, and lodging nightly by Wakefield Tower. They've had free front-row seats at all the most grisly moments in Tower history—Anne Boleyn's execution included.

■ TIP→ Don't get too close to the ravens: they are prone to pecking and not particularly fond of humans, unless you are the Tower's Raven Master.

And *WHAT* are they wearing?

A **pike** (or halberd), also known as a partisan, is the Yeoman Warder's weapon of choice. The Chief Warder carries a staff topped with a miniature silver model of the White Tower.

This **Tudor-style ruff** helps date the ceremonial uniform, which was first worn in 1552.

Insignia on a Yeoman Warder's upper right arm denote the rank he carried in the military.

This version of the **royal livery** bears the insignia of the current Queen ("E" for Elizabeth) but originally dates from Tudor times. The first letter changes according to the reigning monarch's Christian name; the second letter is always an "R" for *rex* (king) or *regina* (queen).

The **red lines down the trousers** are a sign of the blood from the swords of the Yeoman Warders in their defense of the realm.

Anyone who refers to this as a costume will be lucky to leave the Tower with head still attached to body: this is the ceremonial uniform of the Yeoman Warders, and it comes at a cool £13,000 a throw.

The black Tudor **bonnet** is made of velvet; the blue undress consists of a felt top hat, with a single Tudor rose in the middle.

The **medals** on a Yeoman Warder's chest are more than mere show: all of the men and women have served for at least 22 years in the armed forces.

Slits in the **tunic** date from the times when Beefeaters were expected to ride a horse.

Red socks and **black patent shoes** are worn on special occasions. Visitors are more likely to see the regular blue undress, introduced in 1858 as the regular working dress of the Yeoman Warders.

(IN)FAMOUS PRISONERS OF THE TOWER

Anne Boleyn   Lady Jane Grey   Sir Walter Raleigh

Sir Thomas More. A Catholic and Henry VIII's friend and chancellor, Sir Thomas refused to attend the coronation of Anne Boleyn (Henry VIII's second wife) or to recognize the multi-marrying king as head of the Church. Sent to the Tower for treason, in 1535 More was beheaded.

Anne Boleyn. The first of Henry VIII's wives to be beheaded, Anne, who failed to provide the king with a son, was accused of sleeping with five men, including her own brother. All six got the chop in 1536. Her severed head was held up to the crowd, and her lips were said to be mouthing prayer.

Margaret, Countess of Salisbury. Not the best-known prisoner in her lifetime, she has a reputation today for haunting the Tower. And no wonder: the elderly 70-year-old was condemned by Henry VIII in 1541 for a potentially treacherous bloodline (she was the last Plantagenet princess) and hacked to death by the executioner after she refused to put her head on the block like a common traitor and attempted to run away.

Queen Catherine Howard. Henry VIII's fifth wife was locked up for high treason and infidelity and beheaded in 1542 at age 20. Ever eager to please, she spent her final night practicing how to lay her head on the block.

Lady Jane Grey. The nine-days-queen lost her head in 1554 at age 16. Her death was the result of sibling rivalry gone seriously wrong, when Protestant Edward VI slighted his Catholic sister Mary in favor of Lady Jane as heir, and Mary decided to have none of it.

Guy Fawkes. The Roman Catholic soldier who tried to blow up the Houses of Parliament and kill the king in the 1605 Gunpowder plot was first incarcerated in the chambers of the Tower, where King James I requested he be tortured in ever-worsening ways. Perhaps unsurprisingly, he confessed. He met his seriously grisly end in the Old Palace Yard at Westminster, where he was hung, drawn, and quartered in 1607.

Sir Walter Raleigh. Once a favorite of Elizabeth I, he offended her by secretly marrying her Maid of Honor and was chucked in the Tower. Later, as a conspirator against James I, he paid with his life. A frequent visitor to the Tower (he spent 13 years there in three stints), he managed to get the Bloody Tower enlarged on account of his wife and growing family. He was finally executed in 1618 in Old Palace Yard, Westminster.

Josef Jakobs. The last man to be executed in the Tower was caught as a spy when parachuting in from Germany and executed by firing squad in 1941. The chair he sat in when he was shot is preserved in the Royal Armouries' artifacts store.

FOR FURTHER EVIDENCE . . .

A trio of buildings in the Inner Ward, the **Bloody Tower, Beauchamp Tower,** and **Queen's House,** all with excellent views of the execution scaffold in Tower Green, are the heart of the Tower's prison accommodations and home to a permanent exhibition about notable inmates.

TACKLING THE TOWER (without losing your head)

✉ H.M. Tower of London, Tower Hill
☎ 0844/482–7777/7799 ⊕ www.hrp.org.uk
🎟 Adult: £19.50, children under 16: £9.75, Family tickets (2 adults, 2 children): £52, children under 5, free. ⏲ Mar.–Oct., Tues.–Sat. 9–5:30, Sun. and Mon. 10–5:30; last admission at 5. Nov.–Feb., Tues.–Sat. 9–4:30, Sun. and Mon. 10–4:30; last admission at 4 Ⓤ Tower Hill

▥ TIP➜ You can buy tickets from automatic kiosks on arrival, or up to seven days in advance at any Tube station. Avoid lines completely by booking by telephone (0844 482 7777/7799 weekdays 9–5), or online.

MAKING THE MOST OF YOUR TIME: Without doubt, the Tower is worth two to three hours. A full hour of that would be well spent by joining one of the Yeoman Warders' tours (included in admission). It's hard to better their insight, vitality, and humor—they are knights of the realm living their very own fairytale castle existence.

The Crown Jewels are worth the wait, the White Tower is essential, and the Medieval Palace and Bloody Tower should at least be breezed through.

▥ TIP➜ It's best to visit on weekdays, when the crowds are smaller.

WITH KIDS: The Tower's centuries-old cobblestones are not exactly stroller-friendly, but strollers are permitted inside most of the buildings. If you do bring one, be prepared to leave it temporarily unsupervised (the stroller, that is—not your child) outside the White Tower, which has no access. There are baby-changing facilities in the Brick Tower restrooms behind the Jewel House. Look for regular free children's events such as the Knight's school where children can have a go at jousting, sword-fighting, and archery.

▥ TIP➜ Tell your child to find one of the Yeoman Warders if he or she should get lost; they will in turn lead him or her to the Byward Tower, which is where you should meet.

IN A HURRY? If you have less than an hour, head down Wall Walk, through a succession of towers, which eventually spit you out at the Martin Tower. The view over modern London is quite a contrast.

TOURS: Tours given by a Yeoman Warder leave from the main entrance near Middle Tower every half-hour from 10–4, and last about an hour. Beefeaters give occasional 30-minute talks in the Lanthorn Tower about their daily lives. Both tours are free. Check website for talks and workshops

St. Bride's. According to legend, the distinctively tiered steeple of this Christopher Wren–designed church gave rise to the shape of the traditional wedding cake. One early couple inspired to marry here were the parents of Virginia Dare, the first European child born in colonial America in 1587. As St. Paul's (in Covent Garden) is the actors' church, so St. Bride's belongs to journalists, many of whom have been buried or memorialized here. By 1664 the crypts were so crowded that diarist Samuel Pepys, who was baptized here, had to bribe the gravedigger to "justle together" some bodies to make room for his deceased brother. Now the crypts house a museum of the church's rich history, and a bit of Roman sidewalk. Guided tours are available on some Tuesday afternoons (check website for dates). ⊠ *Fleet St., The City* ☎ *020/7427–0133* ⊕ *www.stbrides.com* 🖙 *Free; guided tours £6* ☉ *Weekdays 8–6, Sat. call to confirm, Sun. for services only 10–6:30* Ⓜ *St. Paul's, Blackfriars.*

> ### SUMMER FESTIVAL
>
> Every year, for three weeks in June and July, the **City of London Festival** (⊕ *www.colf.org*) features numerous walks, dances, and street art, and you can see concerts that are held in buildings not usually open to the public.

St. Mary-le-Bow. Various versions of this church have stood on the site since the 11th century. In 1284 a local goldsmith took refuge here after committing a murder, only to be killed inside the church by enraged relatives of his victim. The church was abandoned for a time afterward, but started up again, and was rebuilt in its current form after the Great Fire. Wren's 1673 incarnation has a tall steeple (in The City, only St. Bride's is taller) and one of the most famous sets of bells around—a Londoner must be born within the sound of the "Bow Bells" to be a true Cockney. The origin of that idea may have been the curfew rung on the bells during the 14th century, even though "Cockney" only came to mean "Londoner" centuries later, and then it was an insult. The Bow takes its name from the bow-shaped arches in the Norman crypt. The garden contains a statue of local boy Captain John Smith, who founded Virginia in 1606 and was later captured by Native Americans. ⊠ *Cheapside, The City* ☎ *020/7248–5139* ⊕ *www.stmarylebow.co.uk* ☉ *Mon.–Wed. 7:30–6, Thurs. 7:30–6:30, Fri. 7:30–4; closed weekends* Ⓜ *Mansion House, St. Paul's.*

QUICK BITES

Café Below. In St. Mary-le-Bow's Norman crypt, this café is packed with City workers weekdays from 7:30 am until 2:30 pm for a menu covering breakfasts, scrumptious light lunches, and delicious cakes. ⊠ *Cheapside, The City* ☎ *020/7329–0789* ⊕ *www.cafebelow.co.uk* Ⓜ *Mansion House, St. Paul's.*

THE EAST END

GETTING ORIENTED

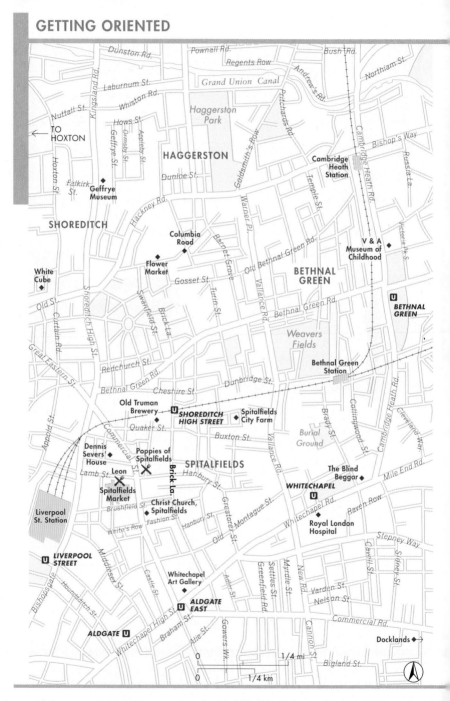

TOP REASONS TO GO

Take a candlelight tour of Dennis Severs' House: This handsome Georgian town house is stage-set to suggest that its 18th- and 19th-century occupants have just stepped out.

Go clubbing: For London's most hedonistic bar or club crawl, head to Hackney and Shoreditch.

Check out London's coolest, hottest art scene: The art scene here is vibrant, and small galleries are interspersed with larger collections.

Trace the footsteps of Jack the Ripper: Track Britain's most infamous serial killer through the former Victorian slum streets of the East End.

Peek into the lives of Londoners at the Geffrye Museum: The magical collection of this museum showcases an array of period rooms rich in antiques, brocades, and crystal.

FEELING PECKISH?

Poppies of Spitalfields. This restaurant strikes a balance between trendy and traditional with retro-diner decor and efficient service. The specialty is fish and chips, but if fish isn't your thing, free-range grilled chicken is also available. ⊠ *6–8 Hanbury St., Spitalfields* ☎ *0207/247–0892* ⊕ *www. poppiesfishandchips.co.uk.*

Sweet & Spicy. There are numerous curry houses on Brick Lane but locals recommend this unpretentious canteen-style place. In three words, it's authentic, cheap, and good. ⊠ *40 Brick La., Spitalfields* ☎ *020/7247–1081* ⊕ *www. sweetandspicylondon.co.uk.*

SAFETY

Around the central hubs of Hoxton, Shoreditch, Spitalfields, and Brick Lane, most streets are safe during daylight hours. Be on your guard at all times if venturing into the mean streets of Whitechapel, Bethnal Green, and Hackney.

GETTING THERE

The London Overground, with stops at Shoreditch High Street, Hoxton, Whitechapel, Dalston Kingsland, and Hackney Central is the easiest way to reach the East End. Alternatively, the best Tube stations to use are Old Street on the Northern Line, Bethnal Green on the Central Line, and Liverpool Street on the Metropolitan and Circle lines.

MAKING THE MOST OF YOUR TIME

To experience the East End at its most lively, make sure you visit on the weekend, when it's possible to shop, eat, drink, and party your way through a whole 72 hours. Spitalfields Market bustles all weekend, while Brick Lane and Columbia Road are best on a Sunday morning. If you're planning to explore the East End art scene, pick up a free art map at the Whitechapel Art Gallery. As for the booming nightlife scene here, there's no time limit.

GUIDED TOURS

Researcher and actor Declan McHugh leads the Ripper-oriented **Blood and Tears Walk: London's Horrible Past** (☎ *07905–746733*), which departs daily from Barbican Tube station. Street Art London (⊕ *streetartlondon.co.uk*) offers two- and four-hour walking tours of East London's street art on Tuesday at 10 am and weekends at 11 am.

7

Sightseeing
★★★

Nightlife
★★★★★

Dining
★★★★

Lodging
★

Shopping
★★★★

Made famous by Dickens and infamous by Jack the Ripper, the East End is one of London's most enduringly evocative neighborhoods, rich in popular history, architectural gems, and artists' studios. Since the early 1990s, hip gallerists, designers, and new-media entrepreneurs have colonized its handsome Georgian buildings and converted industrial lofts. Today, the East End lays claim to being one of London's most trendsetting neighborhoods.

Updated by
Ellin Stein

London's equivalent of Brooklyn, the East End is an eye-popping patchwork of districts now home to struggling artists, ethnic enclaves, sleek professionals, and many of London's card-carrying hipsters. The vast area ranges from gentrified districts like Spitalfields—where bankers and successful artists live in desirable renovated Georgian town houses—to parts of Hackney, where seemingly derelict, graffiti-covered industrial buildings are hives to the art of tomorrow. As with all neighborhoods in transition, it can be a little rough around the edges, so stick to busier streets at night.

At the start of the new millennium, Hoxton, an enclave of Shoreditch, became the glossy hub of London's buzzing contemporary art scene. Crowds had always headed here to discover one of London's quaintest and friendliest flower markets, held every Sunday on Columbia Road. But now fashion plates (wearing sneakers to help with the long treks everywhere here) toting Sotheby's catalogues also make the scene. Today, that scene has spread to encompass the entire area, with numerous stylish boutiques (especially on Redchurch Street), destination restaurants, and new-media companies (along with attendant bars and cafés) pricing out the original bohemian and working-class residents. Some, now world famous, have remained, such as Tracey Emin and Gilbert & George, and they have remade Spitalfields's handsome Georgian terraces into super-stylish town houses.

Of course, where artists go, everyone else follows—including art galleries, many found eastward toward Whitechapel and Bethnal Green, all drawn to East London by the inexpensive industrial spaces that could be cheaply and imaginatively remodeled.

The core district of the East End remains Spitalfields, where most of the East End's important attractions lie, such as that fabulous "time machine" known as **Dennis Severs' House,** transformed two decades ago into a unique "living history museum" that evokes how past generations of a fictional Huguenot family might have lived there. Not far away, Spitalfields Market offers an ever-changing selection of crafts and funky designer stalls located under a glass roof in what was once a Victorian produce market.

At the eastern end of Spitalfields is crowded **Brick Lane,** the heart of the Bangladeshi community and lined with innumerable curry houses, glittering sari shops, and also a Sunday-morning junk market that complements the neighborhood's many vintage-clothing shops. Here you'll also find the **Old Truman Brewery,** an East End landmark converted into a warren of street fashions and pop-up shops. Toward the east, in Bethnal Green—rapidly becoming the "new Spitalfields" in terms of galleries, independent boutiques, and loft conversions—is the quirky **V&A Museum of Childhood** and that connoisseur's favorite, the **Geffrye Museum,** a collection of domestic interiors that occupies a row of early-18th-century almshouses.

Probably the best start to an East End tour is via the London Overground, getting off at the Shoreditch High Street station. Immediately northwest of the station, on the west side of Shoreditch High Street, is the part of the neighborhood aspirationally dubbed the U.K.'s equivalent to Silicon Valley, thanks to the number of Internet start-ups based in its narrow streets. To the northeast is Shoreditch's boutique, gallery, and restaurant zone. The sub-neighborhood of Hoxton is located just above Shoreditch, north of the Old Street roundabout (itself being redeveloped as "Tech City"). To the southeast of the station are the handsome Georgian streets of Spitalfields. Bethnal Green is due east, past lively Brick Lane. Whitechapel, formerly Jack the Ripper's patch, is to the south of Spitalfields.

TOP ATTRACTIONS

Broadway Market. This parade of shops in hipster-centric Hackney (located north of Regent's Canal) is worth visiting for the specialist bookshops, independent boutiques, organic cafés, good neighborhood restaurants, and even a traditional (but now rare) pie-and-mash shop. But wait for Saturdays, when it really comes into its own with a farmers' market and food stalls rivaling those of south London's famed Borough Market. Artisanal breads, cheeses, and chocolates, organic meats, produce, and smoked salmon, ethnic offerings: this is foodie heaven.

If you're prepared for a wait, the Lucky Chip van sells what are reputedly the best burgers in town. There are also stalls selling vintage clothes, hand-made instruments, and more. ✉ *Broadway Market, Hackney* ⊕ *www.broadwaymarket. co.uk* ⊙ *sat. 9–5* Ⓜ *Bethnal Green.*

Fodor'sChoice ★ **Dennis Severs' House.** An extraordinary time-machine of a house, this mansion was the creation of Dennis Severs (1948–99), a performer-

designer-scholar from Escondido, California, who dedicated his life to restoring this Georgian terraced house. More than that, he created "still-life dramas" using sight, sound, and smell to evoke the world of a fictitious family of Hugenot silk weavers, the Jervises, who might have inhabited the house between 1728 and 1914. Each of the 10 rooms has a distinctive, compelling atmosphere that encourages visitors to become lost in another time. The rooms are shadowy set-pieces of rose-laden Victorian wallpaper, Jacobean paneling, Georgian wing chairs, Baroque carved ornaments, "Protestant" colors (upstairs), and "Catholic" shades (downstairs). Don't miss it! ▮TIP→ The "Silent Night" candlelight tours, each Monday and Wednesday evening, are the most theatrical and memorable way to "feel" the house; this is a magical experience relished by both Londoners and out-of-towners. Private individual Silent Night tours are available one night per month, and private group visits can also be arranged. ✉ *18 Folgate St., Spitalfields* ☎ *020/7247–4013* ⊕ *www.dennissevershouse.co.uk* ✆ *£10 Sun., £7 Mon., £14 Mon. and Wed. evenings* ⊙ *Sun. 12–4 (last admission 3:15); 1st and 3rd Mon. noon–2 (last admission 1:15); Mon. and Wed. 6–8 (reservations essential)* Ⓜ *Shoreditch High Street Overground.*

Fodor'sChoice ★ **Geffrye Museum of the Home.** Here's where you can explore the life of London's middle class over the years (in contrast to the lifestyle evoked by the West End's grand aristocratic town houses) thanks to a spectacular array of period rooms. Originally a row of almshouses built in 1714 by Sir Robert Geffrye, a former Lord Mayor of London, this charming museum contains a series of 11 salons that re-create everyday domestic interiors from the Elizabethan period through the 1950s to the present day. One almshouse was restored to its original condition (to visit the almshouse you must go as part of a tour, which is offered at specific times each month). Outside, a series of period gardens charts the evolution of the town garden over the past 400 years, and next to them is a walled herb garden. The museum's extension wing houses the 20th-century galleries, a lovely café overlooking the gardens, and a shop. ✉ *136 Kingsland Rd., Hoxton* ☎ *020/7739–9893* ⊕ *www. geffrye-museum.org.uk* ✆ *Free (charge for special exhibitions); Almshouse £2.50* ⊙ *Tues.–Sat. 10–5, Sun. and bank holiday Mons. noon–5; gardens: Apr. 1–Oct. 31* Ⓜ *Hoxton (London Overground); Old St., then Bus 243; Liverpool St., then Bus 149 or 242.*

DID YOU KNOW?

On Sunday, the Columbia Road Flower Market opens at 8 am. Arrive early to see the photogenic market in full sway and at its best. Victorian shops nearby sell horticultural wares, accessories, and antiques.

EAST END STREET SMARTS

Brick Lane and the narrow streets running off it offer a paradigm of the East End's development. Its population has moved in waves: communities seeking refuge, others moving out in an upwardly mobile direction.

Brick Lane has seen the manufacture of bricks (during the 16th century), beer, and bagels, but nowadays it's primarily known as the heart of Banglatown—Bangladeshis make up one-third of the population in this London borough, and you'll see that the names of the surrounding streets are written in Bengali—where you find many kebab and curry houses along with shops selling videos, colorful saris, and stacks of sticky sweets. On Sunday morning the entire street becomes pedestrianized. Shops and cafés are open, and several stalls are set up, creating a companion market to the one on nearby **Petticoat Lane**.

Fournier Street contains fine examples of the neighborhood's characteristic Georgian terraced houses, many of them built by the richest of the early-18th-century Huguenot silk weavers (note the enlarged windows on the upper floors). Most of those along the north side of Fournier Street have been restored, but some still contain textile sweatshops—only now the workers are Bengali.

Wilkes Street, with more 1720s Huguenot houses, is north of the Christ Church, Spitalfields, and neighboring **Princelet Street** was once important to the East End's Jewish community. Where No. 6 stands now, the first of several thriving Yiddish theaters opened in 1886. **Elder Street,** just off Folgate, is another gem of original 18th-century houses. On the south and east side of Spitalfields Market are yet more time-warp streets that are worth a wander, such as **Gun Street,** where artist Mark Gertler (1891–1939) lived at No. 32.

Spitalfields Market. A gorgeous piece of architecture in itself, this large restored Victorian market hall (covered by a glass canopy) is one part bazaar and one part food court. There's a notable antiques markets on Thursdays and a fashion market on Fridays (plus, on every first and third Friday, a record fair), as well as markets on other days selling goods ranging from vintage clothes to toys, hats, and jewelry. While some of the quality is pedestrian, you can also find interesting clothes, accessories, and leather goods by new designers. The adjoining brick market building houses upscale shops. ■ TIP➔ The nearer the weekend, the busier it all gets. ✉ *65 Brushfield St., Spitalfields* ☎ *020/7247–8556* ⊕ *www.visitspitalfields.com* ⊒ *Free* ⊗ *Shops daily 10–7; market stalls Tues.–Fri. 10–4, Sun. 9–5* Ⓜ *Liverpool St.*

FAMILY
Fodor'sChoice
★
V&A Museum of Childhood. This is a Children-of-all-ages alert! The East End outpost of the Victoria & Albert Museum—in an iron, glass, and brown-brick building transported here from South Kensington in 1868—houses one of the world's biggest toy collections. One highlight (among many) is the large Dolls' Houses collection—a bit like the Geffrye Museum zapped into miniature, with houses from 1673 up to the present—but other favorites range from board games to teddy bears

Blimey, Gov'nor, It's Jack the Ripper!

The spirit of Jack the Ripper, one of the world's most infamous serial killers, haunts the "Jack the Ripper Walk" that takes you to the deserted squares and warehouse alleys where he claimed his unfortunate victims.

No. 90 Whitechapel High Street was once the site of the George Yard Buildings, where the body of the Ripper's first victim, Martha Turner, was discovered in August 1888. His third mutilated victim, "Dark" Annie Chapman, was left on Hanbury Street, behind what was then a seedy lodging house at No. 29. A double homicide followed, and then, after a month's lull, came the death on this street of the Ripper's last victim and the grimmest murder of all. The Ripper had been able to work indoors this time—in a ground-floor apartment today occupied by an Indian restaurant—and left the remains of Mary Kelly, a young widow, strewn around the room. Jack the Ripper's identity has never been proven, although theoretical candidates abound, including, among others, a prominent member of the British aristocracy, the artist Walter Sickert, and Francis Tumblety, an American quack doctor.

Today, many outfitters offer walking tours of the Victorian slums that Jack once stalked: the most popular is run by Original London Walks (⊕ *www.walks.com*) and led by Donald Rumbelow, "the leading authority on Jack the Ripper"; it leaves every night from Tower Hill at 7:30 pm (though Don himself only shows up a few nights a week).

and train sets. The collection is organized into galleries: Moving Toys, which includes everything from rocking horses to Xboxes; Creativity, which encompasses dolls, puppets, chemistry sets, play kitchens, construction toys, and musical instruments; and Childhood, with areas devoted to baby paraphernalia and baby dolls, an exhibit of children's clothes from the mid-1600s to the present, and toys inspired by adult pursuits, such as toy soldiers, toy guns, and toy hospitals. Don't miss the magnificent 18th-century *commedia dell'arte* puppet theater thought to have been made in Venice. ⊠ *Cambridge Heath Rd., Bethnal Green* ☎ *020/8983–5200* ⊕ *www.vam.ac.uk/moc* ⊠ *Free* ☉ *Daily 10–5:45* Ⓜ *Bethnal Green.*

Fodor's Choice **Whitechapel Art Gallery.** Founded in 1901, this gallery has expanded into
★ fabulous new spaces and presents internationally renowned shows that are often on the cutting edge of contemporary art. The American painter Jackson Pollock exhibited here in the 1950s, as did pop artist Robert Rauschenberg in the 1960s; David Hockney had his first solo show here in the 1970s. The gallery also hosts talks, film screenings, workshops, and other events. Pick up a free East End art map to help you with the rest of your gallery hopping. ⊠ *77–82 Whitechapel High St., Whitechapel* ☎ *020/7522–7888* ⊕ *www.whitechapelgallery.org* ⊠ *Free, charge for some special exhibits* ☉ *Tues., Wed., Fri., and Sun. 11–6, Thurs. 11–9* Ⓜ *Aldgate East.*

On Sunday, additional clothing and crafts stalls surround Spitalfields covered market.

WORTH NOTING

Christ Church, Spitalfields. This is the 1729 masterpiece of Sir Christopher Wren's associate Nicholas Hawksmoor, one of his six London churches. It was commissioned as part of Parliament's 1711 "Fifty New Churches" Act, passed in response to the influx of immigrants with the idea of providing for the religious needs of the "godless thousands"— actually, to ensure they joined the Church of England as opposed to such nonconformist denominations as the Protestant Huguenots. (It must have worked; you can still see gravestones with epitaphs in French in the crypt.) As the local silk industry declined, the church fell into disrepair, and by 1958 the structure was crumbling, with the looming prospect of demolition. But after 25 years—longer than it took to build the church—and a huge local fund-raising effort, the structure was completely restored and is a joy to behold, from the colonnaded Doric portico and tall spire to its soaring, heavily ornamented English Baroque plaster ceiling. As a concert venue it truly comes into its own. Tours that take you "backstage" to the many hidden rooms and passages, from the tower to the vaults, are offered by appointment. ▉ TIP➔ Don't miss the chance to attend one of the classical concerts held year round in this atmospheric ecclesiastical venue. ✉ *Commercial St., Spitalfields* ☎ *020/7377–6793* ✇ *Free, tours £6* ☉ *Mon.–Fri. 10–4 (may be closed for event; call for info), Sun. 1–4* Ⓜ *Shoreditch High Street Overground.*

Kate MacGarry Gallery. Located on what was once one of the worst slum streets in London, this achingly contemporary gallery space (MacGarry's third in the East End—she's been here since 2002) has an excellent reputation for its shows of cutting-edge international artists like Chicks

The East End Art Scene

The East End is now one of the world's most exciting districts for contemporary art. But its avant-roots go way back. Shoreditch's cheap industrial units and Georgian–Victorian terraced streets attracted artists since the 1960s, when op-art pioneer Bridget Riley established a service to find affordable studio space for British artists. In the early '90s it gained new notoriety when Young British Artists Sarah Lucas and Tracey Emin began selling their own and their friends' work in The Shop, joining Maureen Paley's influential Bethnal Green gallery, and the long-established Whitechapel Art Gallery, where many leading abstract expressionists and pop artists had their first U.K. shows. Hoxton truly became a destination for well-heeled collectors when Jay Jopling, the most important modern-art dealer in town, set up his White Cube gallery in 2000 (it's now relocated to southeast London), followed by Kate MacGarry's gallery in 2002. Priced out by the growing number of loft-style luxury apartments, boutiques, bars, clubs, and restaurants, the emerging artists themselves have relocated to newer, rougher hoods.

Many artists have, as of 2013, moved north and east to the edgier neighborhoods of Hackney and Dalston, with several trendsetting galleries found clustered around Cambridge Heath Road and Vyner Street. But there are more genteel attractions in these districts as well. Broadway Market on Saturday is a foodie's paradise, offering organic meats and produce, plus artisanal cakes and cheeses. The area is dotted with other innovative restaurants that regularly turn up on lists of critics' favorites. Though heavily urbanized, Hackney has some delightful public parks, notably Victoria Park, just east of Cambridge Heath Road.

Hackney is a huge area, bordered, broadly speaking, on the south by Bethnal Green, by the former Olympic Village on the east, and by The City and Clerkenwell to the west. The galleries of Vyner Street are due north of Bethnal Green, past the Museum of Childhood. From here Broadway Market, also in Hackney, is to the west, following the Regent's Canal. North of Hoxton, Shoreditch High Street becomes funky Kingsland Road in Dalston, known for its variety of ethnic restaurants and railway arches housing everything from auto repairs to artists' studios.

7

on Speed, Luke Rudolf, and Iain Forsythe & Jane Pollard, with a particular emphasis on conceptual works and video. ✉ *27 Old Nichol St., Shoreditch* ☎ *020/7613–0515* ⊕ *www.katemacgarry.com* Ⓜ *Shoreditch High Street Overground.*

Maureen Paley Gallery. Inspired by the DIY punk aesthetic and the funky galleries of New York's Lower East Side, Maureen Paley, started putting on exhibitions in her East End home back in 1984, when it was virtually the only gallery in the area. Since then this American artist and gallerist has shown such respected contemporary artists as Gillian Wearing, Helen Chadwick, Jenny Holzer, Peter Fischli, and Wolfgang Tillmans and, today, is considered the doyenne of East End gallerists. The gallery has been in its current home, a converted warehouse in Bethnal Green, since 1999. ✉ *21 Herald St., Bethnal Green* ☎ *020/7729–4112* ⊕ *www. maureenpaley.com* Ⓜ *Bethnal Green.*

Old Truman Brewery. The last East End brewery still standing—a handsome example of Georgian and 19th-century industrial architecture, and in late Victorian times the largest brewery in the world—has been transformed into a cavernous hipster mall housing galleries, independent shops, fashion-forward boutiques, bars, clubs, and restaurants. The retailers are at street level with offices and studios on the upper floors. Events include fashion shows for both new and established designers, excellent sample sales, art installations, and, on weekends, a food hall and a vintage clothes fair. The Vibe Bar is a hot spot to chill out behind a traditional Georgian facade—it also has a great outdoor space. ✉ *91 Brick La., Spitalfields* ⊕ *www.trumanbrewery.com* Ⓜ *Shoreditch High Street Overground.*

Royal London Hospital Museum. Located in the crypt of Victorian church, the Royal London Hospital Museum uses exhibits of historic medical equipment, surgical instruments, and archives to document the history of this East London institution from its foundation in 1740 to the present day. Highlights include a forensic medicine section with original material on the Jack the Ripper murders and the RLH surgeon who helped investigate them, artifacts and documents relating to Joseph Merrick—better known as "The Elephant Man"—who spent his final years in the hospital, and a set of dentures worn by George Washington. Opening hours are subject to change on short notice, so call before you go. ✉ *Newark St., Whitechapel* ☎ *020/7377–7608* ⊕ *www. bartsandthelondon.nhs.uk/museums* ◷ *Tues.–Fri. 10–4:30.*

FAMILY **Spitalfields City Farm.** An oasis of rural calm in an urban landscape, this little community farm raises a variety of animals, including some rare breeds, to help educate city kids about life in the country. A tiny farm shop sells freshly laid eggs, along with organic seasonal produce. ✉ *Buxton St., Spitalfields* ☎ *020/7247–8762* ⊕ *www.spitalfieldscityfarm.org* ⌨ *Free* ◷ *Tues.–Sun. 10–4:30* Ⓜ *Shoreditch High Street Overground.*

The Ten Bells. Although the number of bells in its name has varied between eight and twelve (depending on many bells were used by neighboring Christ Church Spitalfields), this pub retains its authentic mid-Victorian interior and original tiles, with a tiled frieze depicting the area's weaving tradition on the north wall and particularly fine floral tiling on two others. Legend has it the Ripper's third victim, Annie Chapman, had a drink here before meeting her gory end and the pub is depicted in Alan Moore's acclaimed graphic novel *From Hell.* More recently, the Ten Bells has gained a more positive kind of fame for its outstanding upstairs restaurant. ✉ *84 Commercial St., Spitalfields* ☎ *020/7366–1721* ⊕ *www.tenbells.com* Ⓜ *Shoreditch High Street Overground.*

SOUTH OF THE THAMES

GETTING ORIENTED

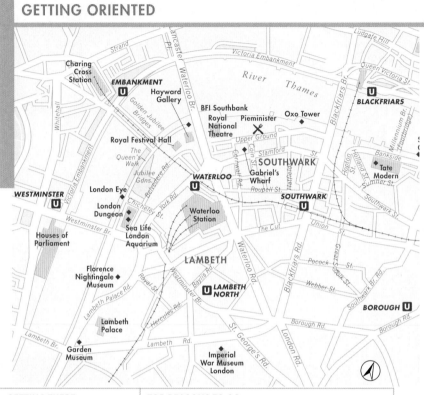

GETTING THERE	TOP REASONS TO GO

GETTING THERE

For the South Bank, use the Embankment on the District, Circle, Northern, and Bakerloo lines and walk across the Golden Jubilee Bridges; or Waterloo on the Northern, Jubilee, and Bakerloo lines, from where it's a 10-minute walk.

London Bridge on the Northern and Jubilee lines is five minutes from Borough Market and Southwark Cathedral. The station also serves Bermondsey Street, though, confusingly, the next stop on the Jubilee line is called Bermondsey. Brixton has its own stop on the Victoria Line.

TOP REASONS TO GO

Join the "groundlings" at Shakespeare's Globe: Get caught up in the Bard's great words from the Elizabethan-style standing-room pit of this celebrated theater.

Marvel at the Tate Modern: One of the world's great shrines of contemporary and modern art, this branch of the Tate is noted for a spectacularly renovated electric turbine hall.

Be a ghoul at the London Dungeon: Did you ever wonder what a disembowelment looks like? That's just one of the torture tableaux on view in this old-fashioned "chamber of horrors." You'll be amazed how many children adore this place.

Take in a sunset on Waterloo Bridge: This is one of London's most romantic views, with St. Paul's to the east and the Houses of Parliament to the west; after, stroll east along a fairy-light embankment toward the Oxo Tower.

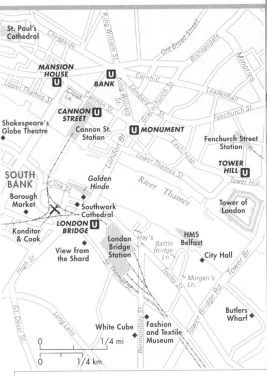

MAKING THE MOST OF YOUR TIME

Don't attempt to explore the area south of the Thames all in one go. Not only will you exhaust yourself, but you will miss out on the varied delights that it has to offer. The Tate Modern alone deserves a whole morning or afternoon, especially if you want to do justice to both the temporary exhibitions and the permanent collection. The Globe requires about two hours for the exhibition theater tour and two to three hours for a performance. Finish with drinks at the Oxo Tower or the Shard, with their spectacular views, or dinner at one of the many restaurants in the Southbank Centre. You can return across the river to central London via Southwark on the Jubilee line from Tate Modern, although it's a good 15-minute walk from the station. Crossing the elegant Millennium Bridge for St. Paul's on the Central line or the Golden Jubilee Bridges to Embankment offer longer but more-scenic alternatives.

FEELING PECKISH?

Konditor & Cook. Known for its exquisite handmade cakes, cookies, and pastries, most baked on-site, this small chain of bijou patisseries also offers daily specials such as chicken paella or vegetarian moussaka. ⊠ *10 Stoney St., Borough* ☎ *020/0844–854–9363* ⊕ *www.konditorandcook. com* ⊘ *Closed Sun.* Ⓜ *London Bridge.*

Pieminister. This branch of Pieminister began life as a Borough Market stall. Have a hot meat pie made with locally sourced ingredients, such as chicken, bacon and tarragon, or stilton and beef (there are also vegetarian options). ⊠ *56 Upper Ground, Gabriel's Wharf, South Bank* ☎ *020/7928–5755* ⊕ *www.pieminister.co.uk* Ⓜ *Waterloo.*

SAFETY

At night, it's best to stick to where the action is at the Butler's Wharf and Bermondsey Street restaurants, the Southbank Centre, and the Cut near the Old Vic.

Sightseeing
★★★★★

Nightlife
★★★★

Dining
★★★

Lodging
★

Shopping
★★

That old, snide North London dig about needing a passport to cross the Thames hasn't been heard for a decade now. Once upon a time, even tourists rarely ventured to south London except to go to Waterloo station. But now the area is home to some of London's grandest attractions: Shakespeare's Globe, the Tate Modern, the London Eye, and the new 1,000-foot-high "Shard" skyscraper. Clearly, south of the Thames—centered around the districts of Southbank and Southwark—has become a dazzling perch for culture vultures.

Updated by
Ellin Stein

It is fitting that so much of London's artistic life should once again be centered here south of the Thames—back in the days of Ye Olde London Towne, Southwark was the city's first "suburb." A borough of the City of London since 1327, it first became well known for its inns (the pilgrims in Chaucer's *A Canterbury Tale* set off from one), prisons, tanneries, and brothels: for four centuries, this was a sort of border town where Londoners went to let their hair down and behave badly. Just outside the City walls and laws, it was therefore the ideal location for the taverns, cock-fighting arenas, and theaters that served as entertainment back then. In truth, the Globe was as likely to stage a few bouts of bearbaiting as the latest interpretations of Shakespeare. Today, at the reconstructed "Wooden O," of course, you can just see the latter.

In fact, now that south London encompasses high-caliber art, music, film, and theater venues as well as an aquarium, a historic warship, two popular food markets, and greatly improved transportation links, this region has become one of the leading destinations in England.

Today, the **Thames Path** along the river embankment in South Bank and Bankside is alive with skateboarders, secondhand book stalls, and street entertainers. At one end the **London Eye**, a millennium project that's a favorite with both Londoners and out-of-towners, rises next

The restaurant at the Tate Modern has some of the best views in London. Here you can St. Paul's Cathedral in the distance.

to the **London Aquarium** and the **Southbank Centre,** home to the recently renovated **Royal Festival Hall**, the **Hayward Gallery**, the **BFI Southbank**, and the **National Theatre.** Farther east you'll come to a reconstruction of Sir Francis Drake's ship the **Golden Hinde; Butlers Wharf,** where some notable restaurants occupy what were once shadowy Dickensian docklands; The Shard, at over 1,000 feet the tallest building in the EU, which offers spectacular views over the city; and, next to **Tower Bridge,** the massive headlight-shaped **City Hall**. Nearby Bermondsey Street (the name derives from "Beormund's Eye," as it was known in Saxon times), home to the bright yellow Fashion Museum, White Cube Gallery, and lots of trendy shops, restaurants, and cafés, is rapidly becoming the center of one of the city's hippest enclaves. Meanwhile, younger visitors will enjoy the **London Dungeon** and **HMS *Belfast*,** a decommissioned Royal Navy cruiser, while food lovers will head for London's oldest food market, **Borough Market,** now reinvented as a gourmet mecca where independent stall-holders provide farm-fresh produce, artisanal bread and cheese, and specialty fish and meat.

Even from high aloft the observation terrace of the "Shard," the south of the Thames area still won't look beautiful but you'll be able to see how this patchwork of neighborhoods fits together. The heart is the South Bank, which extends from the London Eye east to Blackfriars Bridge, with the river to the north and Waterloo station to the south. East of this, between Blackfriars and London bridges, is Bankside, then Borough, with its cobbled streets and former factories now turned into expensive lofts. Next, southeast of Borough, is youthful, urban Bermondsey, while leafy Dulwich, with its renowned gallery and charming period streets, is quite a distance to the south. Upstream (southwest) from the South Bank is Lambeth and then Vauxhall, with the imposing Imperial War Museum, a thriving gay scene, and scary through-traffic routes—a rapidly changing district, thanks to a regeneration spearheaded by the construction of the new U.S. Embassy in adjacent Nine Elms and a slew of upscale riverside residential developments. South of here is Brixton, long the heartland of London's vibrant Afro-Caribbean community—with a lively club scene—and now attracting young families priced out of nearby Clapham.

TOP ATTRACTIONS

FAMILY

Fodor's Choice

★

Dulwich Picture Gallery. Famed for its regal Old Master painting collection, the Dulwich Picture Gallery (pronounced "Dull-ich") was Britain's first purpose-built art museum when it opened in 1811. The permanent collection includes landmark works by Rembrandt, Van Dyck, Rubens, Poussin, and Gainsborough, and it also hosts three major international exhibitions each year. As one British art critic puts it, "we would all travel bravely for a day in Tuscany or Umbria in order to see much less." The gallery also has a lovely café serving meals and drinks, and there's a schedule of family activities (see website for details). Most of the land around here belongs to Dulwich College, a local boys' school, which keeps strict control over development. Consequently, Dulwich Village feels a bit like a time capsule, with old-fashioned street signs and handsome 18th-century houses strung out along its main street. Take a short wander and you'll find a handful of cute clothing and crafts stores and the well-manicured Dulwich Park, with lakeside walks and a fine display of rhododendrons in late May. ⊠ *Gallery Rd., Dulwich* ☎ *020/8693–5254* ⊕ *www.dulwichpicturegallery.org.uk* ✉ *£5–£11. Free guided tours weekends at 3* ⊗ *Tues.–Sun. and bank holiday Mon. 10–5* Ⓜ *National Rail: West Dulwich from Victoria or North Dulwich from London Bridge.*

Fashion and Textile Museum. The bright yellow and pink museum (it's hard to miss) designed by Mexican architect Ricardo Legorreta features changing exhibitions devoted to developments in fashion design, textiles, and jewelry from the end of World War II in 1945 to the present. Founded by designer Zandra Rhodes, an icon of Swinging London, and now owned by Newham College, the FTM is a favorite with fashionistas and offers weekday lectures on aspects of fashion history and fashion-based workshops. The excellent gift shop sells books on fashion and one-of-a-kind pieces by local designers. After your visit, check out the many trendy restaurants, cafés, and boutiques that have bloomed on Bermondsey Street. ⊠ *83 Bermondsey St., Bermondsey* ☎ *020/7407–8664* ⊕ *www.ftmlondon.org* ✉ *£7* ⊗ *Tues.–Sat. 11–6; last admission 5:15* Ⓜ *London Bridge.*

FAMILY

Fodor's Choice

★

The Globe Theatre.

See the highlighted listing in this chapter.

Continued on page 158

SHAKESPEARE AND THE GLOBE THEATRE

At Shakespeare's Globe Theatre, they say the Bard does not belong to the British; he belongs to the world. Not a day has gone by since the Restoration when one of his plays isn't being performed or reinterpreted somewhere. But here, at the site of the original Globe, in a painstaking reconstruction of Shakespeare's own open-air theater, is where seeing one of his plays can take on an ethereal quality.

If you are exceedingly well read and a lover of the Bard, then chances are a pilgrimage to his Globe Theatre is already on your list. But if Shakespeare's works leave you wondering why exactly the play is the thing, then a trip to the Globe—to learn more about his life or to see his words come alive—is a must.

The Globe Theatre in Shakespeare's Day

In the 16th and 17th centuries, a handful of theaters—the Rose, the Swan, the Globe, and others whose names are lost—rose above the higgledy-piggledy jumble of rooftops in London's rowdy Southwark neighborhood. They were round or octagonal open-air playhouses, with galleries for the "quality" members of society, and large, open pits for the raucous mobs. People from all social classes, from royalty down to the hoi polloi, shared the communal experience of drama in these places. Shakespeare's Globe was one.

A fire in 1613 destroyed the first Globe, which was quickly rebuilt; however, Oliver Cromwell and waves of other reformers put an end to all the Southwark playhouses in the 1640s. By the time American actor and director Sam Wanamaker visited in 1949, the only indication that the world's greatest dramatist created popular entertainment here was a plaque on a brewery wall. Wanamaker was shocked to find that all evidence of the playwright's legendary playhouse had vanished into air.

And thereby hangs a tale.

Wanamaker's Dream

Over the next several decades, Wanamaker devoted himself to the Bard. He was director of the New Shakespeare Theatre in Liverpool and, in 1959, joined the Shakespeare Memorial Theatre Company (now the Royal Shakespeare Company) at Stratford-upon-Avon. Finally, in the 1970s he began the project

SHAKESPEARE'S ALL-TIME TOP 10

1. *Romeo and Juliet.* Young love, teenage rebellion, and tragedy are the ingredients of the greatest tearjerker of all time.

2. *Hamlet* (*right*). The very model of a modern antihero and origin of the most quoted line of any play: "To be or not to be…"

3. *A Midsummer Night's Dream.* Spells and potions abound as the gods use humans for playthings; lovers' tiffs are followed by happy endings for all.

4. *Othello.* Jealousy poisons love and destroys a proud man.

5. *The Taming of the Shrew.* The eternal battle of the sexes.

6. *Macbeth.* Ambition, murder, and revenge. Evil gets its just reward.

7. *The Merry Wives of Windsor.* A two-timing rascal gets his comeuppance from a pack of hysterically funny gossips.

8. *Richard III.* One of literature's juiciest villains. The whole audience wants to hiss.

9. *The Tempest.* On a desert island, the concerns of men amaze and amuse the innocent Miranda: "Oh brave new world, that has such people in't."

10. *King Lear.* A tragedy of old age, filial love, and grasping, ungrateful children.

8

that would dominate the rest of his life: reconstructing Shakespeare's theater, as close to the original site as possible.

Today's Globe was re-created using authentic Elizabethan materials and craft techniques—green oak timbers joined only with wooden pegs and mortise-and-tenon joints; plaster made of lime, sand, and goat's hair; and the first thatched roof in London since the Great Fire of 1666. The complex, 200 yards

from the site of the original Globe, includes an exhibition center, cafés, and restaurants. (The shell of a 17th-century-style theater, built adjacent to the Globe to a design by Inigo Jones, awaits further funds for completion.)

FUN FACT: Plays are presented in the open air (and sometimes the rain) to an audience of 1,000 on wooden benches in the bays, and 500 "groundlings," who stand on a carpet of hazelnut shells and cinder, just as they did nearly four centuries ago.

The eventual realization of Wanamaker's dream, a full-scale, accurate replica of the Globe, was the keystone that supported the revitalization of the entire district. The new Globe celebrates Shakespeare, his work, and his times, and as an educational trust it is dedicated to making the Bard continually fresh and accessible for new audiences. Sadly, Wanamaker died before construction was completed, in 1997. In Southwark Cathedral, a few hundred yards west of the Globe, a memorial to him stands beside the statue memorializing Shakespeare himself.

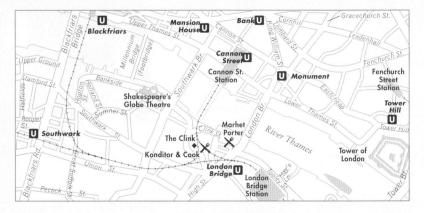

The season of plays is limited to the warmer months, from April 23 (Will's birthday) to the first week in October, with the schedule announced in late January on the theater's website. Tickets go on sale in mid-February. The box office takes phone and mail orders as well as in-person sales, but the most convenient way to buy tickets is online. Book as early as possible.

FUN FACT: "Groundlings"—those with £5 standing-only tickets—are not allowed to sit during the performance. Reserve an actual seat, though, on any one of the theater's three levels, and you can join the "Elizabethan" crowd.

If you do have a seat, you can rent cushions for £1 (or bring your own) to soften the backless wooden benches. A limited number of backrests are also available for rent for £4. The show must go on, rain or shine, warm or chilly—so come prepared for whatever the weather throws at you. Umbrellas are banned, but you can bring a raincoat or buy a cheap Globe rain poncho, which doubles as a great souvenir.

MAKING THE MOST OF YOUR TIME
Give yourself plenty of time: there are several cafés and restaurants, as well as fascinating interactive exhibitions, and theater tours with occasional live demonstrations. Performances can last up to three hours.

WITH CHILDREN
Childsplay, a program for 8- to 11-year-olds, is held every Saturday during the theatre season. While Mom and Dad enjoy the play, children—helped by actors, musicians, and teachers—learn the background and story and become accustomed to Shakespearean language. By the time they are admitted to the theater for the last 20 minutes of the play, the children have become Shakespeare enthusiasts for life. Workshops start at 1:30 pm and tickets are £15.00; book in advance.

Year-Round at Shakespeare's Globe

Shakespeare's Globe Exhibition is a comprehensive display built under the theater (the entry is adjacent) that provides background material about the Elizabethan theater and about the surrounding neighborhood, Bankside. The exhibition describes the process of building the modern Globe and the serious research that went into it.

FUN FACT: In Shakespeare's day, this was a rough part of town. The Bear Gardens, around the corner from the Globe, was where bear baiting, a cruel animal sport, took place. Farther along, the local *gaol* (jail) stood on the site of what is now the Clink Prison Museum..

Daily live demonstrations include Elizabethan dressing, stage fighting, and swordplay, performed by drama students and stage-fighting instructors from the Royal Academy of Dramatic Art (RADA) and the London Academy of Music and Dramatic Art (LAMDA).

FUN FACT: Many performances are done in Elizabethan dress. Costumes for "original practices" productions, which aim to recreate the production techniques of Shakespeare's day, are handmade from period materials—wool, silk, cotton, animal skins, and natural dyes.

Admission also includes a tour of the theater. On matinee days, the tour visits the archaeological site of the nearby (and older) Rose Theatre.

FUN FACT: Shakespeare's casts were all male, with young men and boys playing the female roles. The live demonstration of Elizabethan dressing that forms part of the "Elizabethan Experience" shows how this was done—and how convincing it can be.

Visiting the Globe

✉ 21 New Globe Walk, Bankside, Bankside SE1 9DT

☎ 020/7902–1400 box office, 7401–9919 Globe Exhibition & Tour

🌐 www.shakespeares-globe.org

🎟 Exhibition & tour £13.50, family ticket (2 adults, 3 children) £36; ticket prices for plays vary (£5–£39)

🕐 Exhibition daily 9–5; plays Apr. 23–early Oct., call for performance schedule.

Ⓤ London Bridge; Mansion House, then cross Southwark Bridge; St. Paul's, then cross the Millennium Bridge.

Borough Market brings hungry shoppers to the London Bridge area every Friday and Saturday.

QUICK
BITES

Gabriel's Wharf. This is a cluster of small shops specializing in jewelry, art, clothing, and ceramics by designer-manufacturers interspersed with informal restaurants. A project of the Coin Street Community Builders, a social enterprise group, it bustles with activity. The same group converted the nearby Oxo Tower Wharf, an art deco warehouse with three levels of designer studios that also serve as retail outlets. The Oxo Tower Restaurant, Bar and Brasserie, a pricey restaurant operated by the swish department store Harvey Nichols, occupies the top floor, and you can see the same spectacular views from an adjacent free public viewing area (open daily). ⊠ *56 Upper Ground, South Bank* ☎ *020/7021–1686* ⊕ *www. coinstreet.org* ▱ *Free* ⊙ *Shops and studios Tues.–Sun. 11–6* Ⓜ *Blackfriars, Waterloo.*

FAMILY **Golden Hinde.** Famed Elizabethan explorer Sir Francis Drake circumnavigated the globe in a little galleon just like this one. Launched in 1973, this exact replica made two round-the-world voyages and called in at ports—many along the Pacific and Atlantic coasts of the United States—to do duty as a maritime museum. Now berthed at the St. Mary Overie Dock, the ship continues its educational purpose, complete with "crew" in period costumes and five decks of artifacts. Call for information on guided tours. ⊠ *St. Mary Overie Dock, Cathedral St., Bankside* ☎ *020/7403–0123* ⊕ *www.goldenhinde.com* ▱ *£6* ⊙ *Daily 10–5:30* Ⓜ *London Bridge.*

FAMILY
Fodor's Choice
★

London Dungeon. Here's the goriest, grisliest, most gruesome attraction in town, where unfortunate prisoners (or at least realistic waxworks) are subjected in graphic detail to all the historical horrors that the Tower of London merely describes. Perhaps most shocking are the crowds of children roaring to get in—kids absolutely adore this place, although those with more a sensitive disposition may find it too frightening (that goes for adults as well). Since moving to new quarters next to the London Aquarium in March 2013, this attraction has eschewed its former penny-dreadful aesthetic in favor of a more "theatrical, history-based" approach. But rest assured; there are still plenty of tableaux depicting the bloody demise of famous figures alongside the torture, murder, and ritual slaughter of lesser-known victims, all to a soundtrack of screaming, wailing, and agonized moaning. There are displays on the Great Plague, Henry VIII, and Jack the Ripper, and, to add to the fear and fun, costumed characters leap out of the gloom to bring the exhibits to life. If you ever wondered what a disembowelment looked like, here's your chance to find out. Be sure to get the souvenir booklet to impress all your friends back home. ▓TIP→ Expect long lines on weekends and during school holidays. Savings are available for online booking. ⊠ *County Hall, Westminster Bridge Rd., South Bank* ☎ *020/7403–7221* ⊕ *www. thedungeons.com* 🎫 *From £16* ⊙ *Mar.–July, Fri.–Wed. 10–6, Thurs. 11–6; Aug., Fri.–Wed. 10–7, Thurs. 11–7; Sept.–Feb., Fri.–Wed. 10–5, Thurs. 11–5; phone or check website to confirm times* Ⓜ *Waterloo.*

FAMILY

London Eye. To mark the start of the new millennium, architects David Marks and Julia Barfield conceived a beautiful and celebratory structure that would allow people to see this great city from a completely new perspective. They came up with a giant Ferris wheel, which, as well as representing the turn of the century, would also be a symbol of regeneration. The London Eye is the largest cantilevered observation wheel ever built and among the tallest structures in London. The 25-minute slow-motion ride inside one of the enclosed passenger capsules is so smooth you'd hardly know you were suspended over the Thames. On a clear day you can see for up to 25 miles, with a bird's-eye view over London's most famous landmarks as you circle through 360 degrees. If you're looking for a special place to celebrate, champagne and canapés can be arranged ahead of time. ▓TIP→ Buy your ticket online to avoid the long lines and get a 10% discount. For an extra £10, you can save even more time with a Fast Track flight for which you check in 15 minutes before your "departure." You can buy a combination ticket for the Eye and other London attractions—check online for details—and board the London Eye River Cruise here for a 40-minute sightseeing voyage on the Thames. ⊠ *Westminster Bridge Rd., Riverside Bldg., County Hall, South Bank* ☎ *0870/990–8883* ⊕ *www.londoneye.com* 🎫 *£18.90; cruise £12.50* ⊙ *June and Sept., daily 10 9; July and Aug., daily 10–9:30; Oct.–Mar., daily 10–8:30* Ⓜ *Waterloo.*

Southbank Centre. The public has never really warmed to the Southbank Centre's hulking concrete buildings, products of the Brutalist style popular when the Centre was built in the 1950s and '60s, but they flock to its concerts, recitals, festivals, and exhibitions. The **Royal Festival Hall** is truly a People's Palace, with seats for 2,900, and a schedule that

8

ranges from major symphony orchestras to pop stars (catch the annual summer Meltdown Festival, where "curators" like David Bowie, Patti Smith, or Jarvis Cocker put together a personal selection of concerts by favorite performers); the smaller **Queen Elizabeth Hall** is more strictly classically oriented. It contains the smaller **Purcell Room,** which hosts lectures and chamber performances. For art, head to the **Hayward Gallery,** which hosts shows on top contemporary artists such as Anthony Gormley and Cy Twombly (the terrace here is home to some exciting restaurants). Not officially part of the Southbank Centre but moments away on the east side of Waterloo Bridge, the **National Theatre** is home to some of the best productions in London (several, such as *War Horse* and *The History Boys,* have become movies) at prices well below the West End. Meanwhile, film buffs will appreciate the **BFI Southbank** (formerly the National Film Theatre), which has a schedule that true connoisseurs of the cinema will relish. The Centre's riverside street level has been overhauled and now offers a terrific assortment of restaurants and bars. The BFI's Benugo bar and the Wahaca restaurant at Queen Elizabeth Hall are particularly attractive. ■**TIP**→ Hear leading actors, directors, and writers discuss their work at the National Theatre's Platforms, a series of inexpensive afternoon and early evening talks. ⊠ *Belvedere Rd., South Bank* 🕾 *020/7960–4200* ⊕ *www.southbankcentre.co.uk* 🎫 *Varies; check website* ⊗ *Varies according to venue; check website* Ⓜ *Waterloo, Embankment.*

FAMILY **Tate Modern.**

Fodor's Choice *See the highlighted listing in this chapter.*
★

WORTH NOTING

Florence Nightingale Museum. Compact, highly visual, and engaging, this museum is dedicated to Florence Nightingale, who founded the first school of nursing and played a major role in establishing modern standards of health care. Exhibit are divided into three areas: one focuses on Nightingale's Victorian childhood, while the other two cover her work tending soldiers during the Crimean War (1854–56) and her subsequent health-care reforms. The museum is creative and accessible, incorporating photographs and personal items (including Nightingale's own books and famous lamp), as well as interactive displays of medical instruments and medicinal herbs. ⊠ *2 Lambeth Palace Rd., Lambeth* 🕾 *020/7620–0374* ⊕ *www.florence-nightingale.co.uk* 🎫 *£5.80* ⊗ *Daily 10–5* Ⓜ *Waterloo, Westminster, Lambeth North.*

The Garden Museum. This rather unassuming museum was created in the mid-1970s after two gardening enthusiasts came upon a medieval church which, they were horrified to discover, was about to be bulldozed. The churchyard contained the tombs of two adventurous 17th-century plant collectors, a father and son both called John Tradescant, who introduced many new species to England. Inspired to action, the gardeners rescued the church and opened this museum. With the support of a dedicated team of volunteers, it has subsequently acquired one of the largest collections of historic garden tools, artifacts, and curiosities in Britain, in addition to creating beautiful walled gardens that are maintained year-round with seasonal plants. One section

TATE MODERN

✉ *Bankside* ☎ *020/7887–8888* ⊕ *www.tate.org.uk/modern* ✂ *Free, charge for special exhibitions* ◷ *Sun.–Thurs. 10–6, Fri. and Sat. 10–10 (last admission to exhibitions 45 min before close)* Ⓜ *Southwark, Mansion House, St. Paul's.*

TIPS

■ Join one of the free, 45-minute guided tours. Each one covers a different gallery: Poetry and Dream at 11, Transformed Visions at noon, Structure and Clarity at 2, and Energy and Process at 3. No need to book; just show up in the appropriate room.

■ Levels 2 and 3 include temporary exhibitions, for which there's usually a charge of around £15. Bypass these if you're just here to see the main collection, which is free. Look for the ever-changing video installations scattered throughout the building, often in semi-hidden alcoves and side rooms.

■ Make it a two-for-one art day by taking advantage of the Tate to Tate Boat, which takes visitors back and forth between Tate Britain and Tate Modern every 40 minutes.

■ Private "Tate Tours for Two" can be booked online from £100 to £120, with an afternoon tea for an additional £20 or a champagne dinner for an additional £90.

This spectacular renovation of a mid-20th-century power station is one of the most-visited museums of modern art in the world. Its great permanent collection, which starts in 1900 and ranges from Modern masters like Matisse to the most cutting-edge contemporary artists, is arranged thematically—Landscape, Still Life, and the Nude. Its blockbuster temporary exhibitions showcase the work of individual artists like Gaugin, Roy Lichtenstein, and Gerhard Richter.

Highlights

The vast **Turbine Hall** is a dramatic entrance point used to showcase big, audacious installations that tend to generate a lot of publicity. Past highlights include Olafur Eliasson's massive glowing sun and Carsten Holler's huge metal slides.

The **Material Gestures** galleries on Level 3 feature an impressive offering of post–World War II painting and sculpture. Room 7 contains a breathtaking collection of Rothkos and Monets; there are also paintings by Matisse, Pollock, and Picasso, and newer works from the likes of the sculptor Anish Kapoor.

Head to the Restaurant on Level 7 or the Espresso Bar on Level 3 for stunning vistas of the Thames. The view of St. Paul's from the Espresso Bar's balcony is one of the best in London.

An extension to the front of the building is not ony ambitious but also controversial—you won't be alone if you don't care for it.

8

contains a perfect replica of a 17th-century knot garden, built around the Tradescants' tombs; another is devoted entirely to wildflowers. It's also worth visiting the church itself, which contains the tombs of William Bligh, captain of the *Bounty*, several members of the Boleyn family, and quite a few Archbish-

ops of Canterbury. As well, there's a green-thumb gift shop and the **Garden Café** serving vegetarian lunches and home-baked cakes—the toffee-apple variety is a must! ⊠ *5 Lambeth Palace Rd., Lambeth* ☎ *020/7401–8865* ⊕ *www.gardenmuseum.org.uk* ⊠*£6 (includes garden and all exhibitions)* ☉ *Sun.–Fri. 10:30–5, Sat. 10:30–4; closed 1st Mon. of month* Ⓜ *Lambeth North, Vauxhall.*

FAMILY **HMS Belfast.** At 613½ feet, this is one of the last remaining big-gun armored warships from World War II, in which it played an important role in protecting the Arctic convoys and supporting the D-Day landings in Normandy; the ship later saw action during the Korean War. The *Belfast* has been moored in the Thames as a maritime branch of the **Imperial War Museum** since 1971. A tour of all nine decks—which include the Admiral's quarters, mess decks, bakery, punishment cells, operations room, engine room, and more—gives a vivid picture of life on board the ship, while the riveting interactive gun turret experience puts you in the middle of a World War II naval battle. ⊠ *Morgan's La., Tooley St., Borough* ☎ *020/7940–6300* ⊕ *www.iwm.org.uk* ⊠*£14.50* ☉ *Mar.–Oct., daily 10–6; Nov.–Feb., daily 10–5; last admission 1 hr before closing* Ⓜ *London Bridge.*

Imperial War Museum. Despite its title, this museum of 20th-century warfare does not glorify bloodshed but emphasizes understanding through evoking what life was like for citizens and soldiers alike through the two world wars and beyond. Closed to the public for many years and finally reopening its doors in July 2013 after an enormous renovation, this museum will be even more spectacular than before. A redesigned atrium will tower over six storeys, and this dramatic space will hold some of the collection's top items. The renovation's heart, however, will be the new First World War Galleries, noted for using sights, sounds, and smells to re-create the very uncomfortable Trench Experience of this most carnage-filled war. Also new will be shops and a café overlooking Harmsworth Park. Before the renovation, an impressive amount of hardware greeted the viewer at the main entrance, including a Battle of Britain Spitfire, a German V2 rocket, tanks, guns, and submarines. The Blitz Experience in the World War II gallery gives you a 10-minute taste of an air raid in a street of acrid smoke with sirens blaring and searchlights glaring. There are two galleries of war art (by Henry Moore, John Singer Sargent, Stanley Spencer, and William Orpen, to name a few), a permanent Holocaust exhibition, and a Crimes Against Humanity exhibition, which is not suitable for younger children. James Bond fans won't want to miss the intriguing Secret War Gallery, which charts the history of agents' intrepid work in the wars and the inception

London City Hall, with the almost finished "Shard" building towering in the background.

of MI5 and MI6, the government's secret services. Note: service info below was collected before museum reopened. ✉ *Lambeth Rd., South Bank* ☎ *020/7416–5000* ⊕ *www.iwm.org.uk* ✉ *Free (charge for special exhibitions)* ◷ *Daily 10–6* Ⓜ *Lambeth North.*

FAMILY **Sea Life London Aquarium.** The curved, colonnaded, neoclassic former County Hall that once housed London's local government administration is now home to a superb three-level aquarium full of sharks and stingrays, along with many other aquatic species, both common and rare. There are also feeding and hands-on displays, including a tank full of shellfish that you can touch. It's not the biggest aquarium you've ever seen, but the educational exhibits are particularly well arranged, with areas for different oceans, water environments, and climate zones ranging from a stunning coral reef to a rain forest. Regular feeding times and free talks are offered throughout the day, behind-the-scenes tours are available, and look out for new additions to the tanks from the conservation breeding program. ✉ *County Hall, Westminster Bridge Rd., South Bank* ☎ *0871/663–1678* ⊕ *www.sealife.co.uk* ✉ *£20.50* ◷ *Mon.–Thurs. 10–6, Fri.–Sun. 10–7, last admission 1 hr before closing* Ⓜ *Westminster, Waterloo.*

The View from the Shard. At 1,016 feet, this 2012 addition to the London skyline is currently the tallest building in Western Europe and, as a design of noted architect Renzo Piano, has attracted both admiration and opprobrium. While the building itself is generally highly regarded—although there are those who wonder how such a tall building can appear so squat and graceless—many feel it would be better sited in Canary Wharf (or, indeed, Dubai) as it spoils views of St. Paul's

Cathedral from traditional vantage points such as Hampstead's Parliament Hill. No matter how you feel about the building, there's no denying that it offers a spectacular 360-degree view *over* London (extending to 40 miles on a clear day) from viewing platforms on floors 68, 69, and 72—almost twice as high as any other vantage point in the city. Digital telescopes provide information about 200 points of interest. ■TIP➜ If you find the price as eye-wateringly high as the viewing platforms, there's a less dramatic but still very impressive—and free—view from the multi-floor bars on floors 31 to 33. ✉ *32 London Bridge St., Borough* ☎ *0844/499–7111* ⊕ *www.theviewfromtheshard.com* 🎫 *£24.95* ☉ *Daily 9 am–10 pm, last admission 8:30* Ⓜ *London Bridge.*

BEDLAM

The Imperial War Museum is in an elegant domed and colonnaded building, erected in the early 19th century to house the Bethlehem Hospital for the Insane, better known as the infamous Bedlam. By 1816, when the patients were moved here, they were no longer kept in cages to be taunted by tourists (see the final scene of Hogarth's *Rake's Progress* at Sir John Soane's Museum for a sense of how horrific it was), since reformers—and George III's madness—had effected more humane standards. Bedlam moved to Surrey in 1930.

White Cube Gallery. When the United Kingdom's highest-profile commercial gallery moved to this converted '70s-era warehouse on Bermondsey Street, it sealed Hoxton's reputation as a rising art-scene hot spot. This is the home gallery of Young Turks–turned–pillars of the Britart establishment: Damien Hirst, Gilbert and George, Tracey Emin, Gary Hume, Anthony Gormley, Sam Taylor-Wood, and many other trailblazers who have gone on to become internationally renowned. Alas, while this gallery became the epicenter of East End fashionableness, the gallery relocated to Mason's Yard in the posh West End in 2012 (not enough big collectors were as enchanted with East End bohemia as the press). Today, this branch of the gallery hosts smaller exhibitions, which fill the principal galleries here, along with a central cuboid gallery—the "white cube," also called "9 x 9 x 9" (meaning, 9 meters, or about 29 feet, on each side). There is also a bookshop and auditorium. ✉ *144–152 Bermondsey St., Bermondsey* ☎ *0207/930–5373* ⊕ *www.whitecube.com* ☉ *Tues.–Sat. 10–6, Sun. noon–6* Ⓜ *London Bridge.*

KENSINGTON, CHELSEA, KNIGHTSBRIDGE, AND BELGRAVIA

GETTING ORIENTED

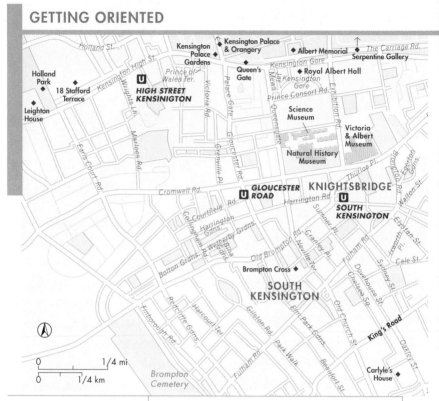

GETTING THERE	TOP REASONS TO GO
There are several useful Tube stations nearby: Sloane Square and High Street Kensington on the District and Circle lines; Knightsbridge and Hyde Park Corner on the Piccadilly line; Earl's Court, South Kensington, and Gloucester Road on the District, Circle, and Piccadilly lines; Holland Park on the Central line; and Victoria on the District, Circle, and Victoria lines.	**Treasure-hunt the V&A Museum:** The Victoria & Albert Museum is the greatest museum of decorative arts in the world—even Edwardians got "interactive" by sketching in the Sculpture Court (stools are still provided today).
	Those Fearsome Dinosaurs at the Natural History Museum: Watch children catch on that the museum's animatronic *T. rex* has noticed *them*—and is licking its dinosaur chops. Then see some of those fearsome teeth for real in the dinosaur room.
	Get a peek of royal lifestyles at Kensington Palace: Home to royal personages including Queen Victoria, Princess Diana, and current residents the Duke and Duchess of Cambridge (William and Kate).
SAFETY	
This is one of London's safest districts, but beware of pickpockets in shopping areas.	**Go Wilde at 18 Stafford Terrace:** Filled with Victorian and Edwardian antiques and art, the charming Linley Sambourne House could be the perfect setting for *The Importance of Being Earnest*.

MAKING THE MOST OF YOUR TIME

You could fill three or four days in this borough: A shopping stroll along the length of the King's Road is easily half a day. Give yourself a half day, at least, for the Victoria & Albert Museum and a half day for either the Science or Natural History Museum.

A GRAZER'S PARADISE

Duke of York Square Food Market. West London's answer to Borough Market, this Saturday open-air market is in a pedestrianized plaza off Duke of York Square, a chic shopping precinct. It hosts 40 stalls purveying artisinal and locally produced meat, game, fish, breads, cakes, cupcakes, honey, pasta, cheese, and chocolate from more than 150 small specialty food producers. Like Borough Market, this is a grazer's paradise, offering the chance to sample fresh oysters and cooked sausages as well as yummy hot snacks from around the world. ⊠ *Duke of York Sq., Chelsea* ☎ *020/7823–5577* ⊕ *www.dukeofyorksquare.com* ⊙ *Sat. 10–4* Ⓜ *Sloane Sq.*

FEELING PECKISH?

The Café at the V&A. Breakfast, light snacks, tea, and full meals are served throughout the day (10–5:15), all in a grand room at modest prices. You can eat in the courtyard if the weather's good, or have a buffet supper on Friday late nights (until 9:30 pm). Stop by just to see the original Arts and Crafts part of the café, one of William Morris's earliest commissions, with stained-glass panels by Edward Burne-Jones. ⊠ *Victoria & Albert Museum, Cromwell Rd., South Kensington* ☎ *020/7942–2000* Ⓜ *South Kensington.*

NEAREST PUBLIC RESTROOMS

Most old-style public restrooms have been replaced by futuristic "autoloos"—podlike booths on street corners that usually cost £1 to use. If you're not brave enough to trust the push-button locks, try the free and clean restrooms at department stores Peter Jones or Harvey Nichols. Or ask for the "loo" in a pub, but be prepared for "sorry" if you're not a paying customer.

Sightseeing
★★★★
Nightlife
★★
Dining
★★★★
Lodging
★★★★
Shopping
★★★★★

In the Royal Borough of Kensington & Chelsea (or "K&C" as the locals call it) you'll find London at its richest, and not just in the moneyed sense. In South Kensington you'll come upon a concentration of great museums near Cromwell Road, and, within Hyde Park, is historic Kensington Palace. Once-bohemian Chelsea is where the Pre-Raphaelites painted and Mick Jagger partied. Knightsbridge has become a playground for the international wealthy, with shopping to match their tastes.

KENSINGTON

Updated by
Ellin Stein

Kensington incorporates the area along the southern edge of Hyde Park from Exhibition Road (where the big museum complex is) and the area to the west of the park bordered by leafy Holland Park Avenue on the north and traffic-heavy Cromwell Road on the south. This more westerly zone includes the satellite neighborhood of Holland Park, with its serenely grand villas and charming park, as well as local shopping mecca Kensington High Street and the antiques shops on Kensington Church Street.

Kensington's first royal connection was created when King William III, fed up with the dampness arising from the Thames, bought a country place there in 1689 and converted it into **Kensington Palace.** Queen Victoria's consort, Prince Albert, added the jewel in the borough's crown when he turned the profits of the Great Exhibition of 1851 into South Kensington's metropolis of museums: The **Victoria & Albert Museum (V&A),** the **Science Museum,** and the **Natural History Museum.** His namesakes in the area include the **Royal Albert Hall,** with bas-reliefs that make it resemble a giant, redbrick Wedgwood pot, and the lavish **Albert Memorial.**

Turn into Derry Street or Young Street and enter **Kensington Square,** one of the most complete 17th-century residential squares in London.

Holland Park is about ¾ mile farther west; both **Leighton House** and **18 Stafford Terrace**—two of London's most gorgeously decorated Victorian-era houses (the lavish use of Islamic tiles, inlaid mosaics, gilded ceilings, and marble columns make the former into an Arabian Nights fantasy)—are nearby as well.

TOP ATTRACTIONS

Albert Memorial. This gleaming, neo-Gothic shrine to Prince Albert created by Sir Gilbert Scott epitomizes the Victorian era. After Albert's early death from typhoid in 1861, his grieving widow, Queen Victoria, had this elaborate confection erected to the west of where the Great Exhibition had been held a decade before. A 14-foot bronze gilt statue of the prince—depicted thumbing through a catalogue for his Great Exhibition—rests on a 15-foot-high pedestal, along with other statues representing his passions and interests. ⊠ *Kensington Gardens, Hyde Park, Kensington* Ⓜ *South Kensington, High Street Kensington.*

Fodor's Choice
★

18 Stafford Terrace. The home of *Punch* cartoonist Edward Linley Sambourne in the 1870s is filled with delightful Victorian and Edwardian antiques, fabrics, and paintings (as well as several samples of Linley Sambourne's work for *Punch*) and is one of the most charming 19th-century London houses extant—small wonder that it was used in Merchant Ivory's *A Room with a View.* The Italianate house was the scene for society parties when Anne Messel was in residence in the 1940s. This being Kensington, there's inevitably a royal connection: Messel's son, Antony Armstrong-Jones, was married to the late Princess Margaret, and their son has preserved the connection by taking the title Viscount Linley. Admission is by guided tour only, and the afternoon tours on weekends are given by costumed actors. ⊠ *18 Stafford Terr., Kensington* ☎ *0207/602–3316* ⊕ *www.rbkc.gov.uk (under Leisure and Libraries)* 🎟 *£8* ⊙ *Guided tours Wed. 11:15, 2:15, weekends 11:15, 1, 2:15, 3:30. Closed mid-June–mid-Sept.* Ⓜ *High Street Kensington.*

Kensington Palace.
See the highlighted listing in this chapter.

Leighton House Museum. Leading Victorian artist Frederic, Lord Leighton lived and worked in this building on the edge of Holland Park, spending 30 years (and quite a bit of money) transforming it into an opulent "private palace of art" infused with an orientalist aesthetic sensibility. The interior is a sumptuous Arabian Nights fantasy, with walls lined in peacock blue tiles designed by Leighton's friend, the ceramic artist William de Morgan, and beautiful mosaic wall panels and floors, marble pillars, and gilded ceilings. The centerpiece is the Arab Hall, its marble walls adorned with even more intricate murals made from 16th- and 17th-century ceramic tiles imported from Syria, Turkey, and Iran, surmounted by a domed ceiling covered in gold leaf with a gold mosaic frieze running underneath. You can also visit Leighton's studio, with its huge north window and dome, and the house is filled with several of his paintings along with works by other Pre-Raphaelites. There are free tours of the house on Wednesday and Sunday at 3. ⊠ *12 Holland Park Rd., Holland Park* ☎ *020/7332–3316* ⊕ *www.rbkc.gov.uk*

9

KENSINGTON PALACE

⊠ *The Broad Walk, Kensington Gardens, Kensington* ☎ *0844/482-7799 advance booking, 0844/482-7777 information, 0203/166-6000 from outside U.K.* ⊕ *www.hrp.org.uk* ⌨ *£14.50 (subject to change)* ⊙ *Mar.–Sept., daily 10–6; Oct.–Feb., daily 10–5; last admission 1 hr before closing* Ⓜ *Queensway, High Street Kensington.*

TIPS

■ The palace now has a wheelchair-accessible elevator, and Kensington Gardens has electric buggies for mobility-impaired visitors.

■ If you also plan to visit the Tower of London, Hampton Court Palace, Banqueting House, or Kew Palace, become a member of Historic Royal Palaces. It costs £43 per person, or £83 for a family, and gives you free entry to all five sites for a year.

■ Picnicking is allowed on the benches in the palace grounds. (You can also picnic anywhere in the adjoining Kensington Gardens.)

■ There's a delightful café in the Orangery, near the Sunken Garden. Built for Queen Anne, it's a great place for formal afternoon tea, although it gets busy during peak hours.

Neither as imposing as Buckingham Palace nor as charming as Hampton Court, Kensington Palace is something of a Royal Family commune, with various close relatives of the Queen occupying large apartments in the private part of the palace. Bought in 1689 by Queen Mary and King William III, it was converted into a palace by Sir Christopher Wren and Nicholas Hawksmoor, and Royals have been in residence ever since. Its most famous resident, Princess Diana, lived here with her sons after her divorce, and this is where Prince William now lives with his wife, Catherine, Duchess of Cambridge.

The State Apartments, however, are open to the public, and galleries showcase three permanent exhibitions that delve into palace history: Queen Victoria (with the theme "love, duty, and loss"); William and Mary and Queen Anne ("the private life of the Queen"); and George II ("the curious world of the court"). There is also a changing temporary exhibition during the summer months.

Highlights

Look for the King's Staircase, with its panoramic trompe l'oeil painting, and the King's Gallery, with royal artworks in a jewelbox setting of rich red damask walls, intricate gilding, and a beautiful painted ceiling. Outside, the grounds are almost as lovely as the palace itself.

(under Leisure and Libraries) 🖾 *£5 (includes free return visit within 12 months)* ⊘ *Wed.–Mon. 10–5:30* Ⓜ *Holland Park, South Kensington.*

FAMILY **Natural History Museum.**

Fodor's Choice *See the highlighted listing in this chapter.*
★

FAMILY **Victoria & Albert Museum.**

Fodor's Choice *See the highlighted listing in this chapter.*
★

WORTH NOTING

FAMILY **Holland Park.** Formerly the grounds of an aristocrat's house and open to the public only since 1952, Holland Park is an often-overlooked gem and possibly London's most romantic park. The nothern "Wilderness" end offers woodland walks among native and exotic trees first planted in the early 18th century. Foxes, rabbits, and hedgehogs are among the residents The central part of the park is given over to the manicured lawns—still stalked by raucous peacocks—one would expect at a stately home, although Holland House itself, originally built by James I's chancellor and later the site of a 19th-century salon frequented by Byron, Dickens, and Disraeli, was largely destroyed by incendiary bombs in 1940. The east wing was reconstructed and has been incorporated into a youth hostel, while the remains of the front terrace provide an atmospheric backdrop for the open-air performances of the April–September **Holland Park Opera Festival** (☎ *0300/999–1000 box office* ⊕ *www.operahollandpark.com*). The glass-walled Garden Ballroom (every home should have one) is now the **Orangery,** which hosts art exhibitions and other public events, as does the **Ice House,** while an adjoining former granary has become the upscale Belvedere restaurant. In spring and summer the air is fragrant with aromas from a rose garden, great banks of rhododendrons, and an azalea walk. Garden enthusiasts will also not want to miss the tranquil, traditional **Kyoto Garden,** a legacy of London's 1991 Japan Festival. The southern part of the park is given over to sport and play: cricket and football (soccer) pitches; a golf practice area; tennis courts; a well-supervised children's Adventure Playground; and a giant outdoor chess set. ⊠ *Holland Park* ⊕ *www.rbkc.gov.uk (under Leisure and Libraries)* ⊘ *Daily 7:30–30 min. before dusk* Ⓜ *Holland Park, High Street Kensington.*

Science Museum. This, one of the three great South Kensington museums, stands next to the Natural History Museum in a far plainer building. It has lots of hands-on painlessly educational exhibits, with entire schools of children apparently decanted inside to interact with them, but don't dismiss the Science Museum as just for kids. Highlights include the Launch Pad gallery, which demonstrates basic laws of physics; *Puffing Billy,* the oldest steam locomotive in the world; and the actual *Apollo 10* capsule. The six floors are devoted to subjects as diverse as the history of flight, space exploration, steam power, medicine, and a sublime exhibition on science in the 18th century. Overshadowed by a three-story blue-glass wall, the Wellcome Wing is an annex to the rear of the museum, devoted to contemporary science and technology. It contains a 450-seat IMAX theater and the Legend of Apollo—an advanced motion

Ice-skaters outside the Natural History Museum in South Kensington.

simulator that combines seat vibration with other technical gizmos to re-create the experience of a moon landing. **TIP→** If you're a family of at least five, you might be able to get a place on one of the popular new Science Night sleepovers by booking well in advance. Aimed at kids 8–11 years old, these nighttime science workshops offer the chance to camp out in one of the galleries, and include a free IMAX show the next morning. Check the website for details. ⊠ *Exhibition Rd., South Kensington* ☎ *0870/870–4868* ⊕ *www.sciencemuseum.org.uk* ⊠ *Free; charge for special exhibitions, cinema shows and simulator rides* ☉ *Daily 10–6, 10–7 during school holidays (check website)* Ⓜ *South Kensington.*

Serpentine Gallery. Overlooking the large stream that winds its way through Hyde Park and from which the gallery takes its name, this small brick building set in Kensington Gardens is one of London's foremost showcases for contemporary art, and has featured exhibitions by lumiaries such as Damien Hirst, Louise Bourgeois, John Currin, Gabriel Orozco, and Gerhard Richter. A permanent work on the gallery's grounds, consisting of eight benches and a carved stone circle, commemorates its former patron, Princess Diana. A new extension, the Serpentine Sackler Gallery, is set to open in the fall of 2013. If you're in town between May and September, check out the annual Serpentine pavillion, which each year is commissioned from a leading architect who is given free rein to interpret the brief—leading to imaginative results. Past designers have included Frank Gehry, Daniel Liebeskind, and Jean Nouvel. ⊠ *Kensington Gardens, Kensington* ☎ *0207/402–6075* ⊕ *www.serpentinegallery.org* ⊠ *Free* ☉ *Daily 10–6* Ⓜ *Lancaster Gate, Knightsbridge, South Kensington.*

NATURAL HISTORY MUSEUM

✉ *Cromwell Rd., South Kensington* ☏ *0207/942–5000* ⊕ *www.nhm.ac.uk* ✉ *Free (some fees for special exhibitions)* ☉ *Daily 10–5:50, last admission at 5:30* Ⓜ *South Kensington.*

TIPS

■ "Nature Live" is a program of free, informal talks given by scientists, covering a wildly eclectic range of subjects, usually at 2:30 (and on some days, at 12:30) in the David Attenborough Studio in the Darwin Centre.

■ The museum has an outdoor ice-skating rink from November to January, and a popular Christmas fair.

■ Free, daily behind-the-scenes Spirit collection tours of the museum can be booked on the day, but space is limited so come early; recommended for children over eight years old.

■ Got kids under seven with you? Check out the museum's free "Explorer Backpacks." They contain a range of activity materials to keep the little ones amused, including a pair of binoculars and an explorer's hat.

The ornate terra-cotta facade of this enormous Victorian museum is strewn with relief panels depicting living creatures to the left of the entrance and extinct ones to the right (although some species have subsequently changed categories). It's an appropriate design, for within these walls lie more than 70 million different specimens. Only a small percentage is on public display, but you could still spend a day here and not come close to seeing everything. The museum is full of cutting-edge exhibits, with all the wow-power and interactives necessary to secure interest from younger visitors.

Highlights

A giant diplodocus skeleton dominates the vaulted, cathedral-like entrance hall, affording you perhaps the most irresistible photo opportunity in the building. It's just a cast, but the **Dinosaur Gallery** (Gallery 21) contains plenty of real-life dino bones, fossils, and some extremely long teeth.

You'll also come face to face with a giant animatronic Tyrannosaurus rex—who is programmed to sense when human prey is near and "respond" in character. When he does, you can hear the shrieks of fear and delight all the way across the room.

A dizzyingly tall escalator takes you into a giant globe in the **Earth Galleries,** where there's a choice of levels— and Earth surfaces—to explore. Don't leave without checking out the earthquake simulation in Gallery 61.

The **Darwin Centre** houses some of the (literally) millions of items the Museum itself doesn't have room to display, including "Archie," a 28.3-foot giant squid. The Centre's new **Cocoon Experience** allows you to see specimens from plant and insect collections previously in storage, such as huge tarantulas and historic items dating back 400 years.

9

VICTORIA & ALBERT MUSEUM

✉ *Cromwell Rd., South Kensington* ☎ *020/7942–2000* ⊕ *www.vam.ac.uk* ✆ *Free; charge for some special exhibitions (from £5)* ◷ *Sat.–Thurs. 10–5:45, Fri. 10–10* Ⓜ *South Kensington.*

TIPS

■ The V&A is a tricky building to navigate, so be sure to use the free map.

■ As a whirlwind introduction, you could take a free one-hour tour (10:30, 11:30, 12:30, 1:30, 2:30, or 3:30). There are also tours devoted just to the British Galleries at 12:30 and 2:30. Occasional public lectures during the week are delivered by visiting bigwigs from the art and fashion worlds (prices vary). There are free lectures throughout the week given by museum staff, who also give an Introductory tour of the collection on Friday nights at 7.

■ Whatever time you visit, the spectacular sculpture hall will be filled with artists, both amateur and professional, sketching the myriad of artworks on display there. Don't be shy; bring a pad and join in.

■ Although the permanent collection is free—and there's enough there to keep you busy for a week—the V&A also hosts high-profile special exhibitions that run for several months.

Known to all as the V&A, this huge museum is devoted to the applied arts of all disciplines, all periods, and all nationalities. Full of innovation, it's a wonderful, generous place in which to to get lost. First opened as the South Kensington Museum in 1857, it was renamed in 1899 in honor of Queen Victoria's late husband and has since grown to become one of the country's best-loved cultural institutions.

Many collections at the V&A are presented not by period but by category—textiles, sculpture, jewelry, and so on. Nowhere is the benefit of this more apparent than in the **Fashion Gallery** (Room 40), where formal 18th-century court dresses are displayed alongside the haute couture styles of contemporary designers, creating an arresting sense of visual continuity.

The **British Galleries** (rooms 52–58 and 118–125), devoted to British art and design from 1500 to 1900, are full of beautiful diversions—among them the Great Bed of Ware (immortalized in Shakespeare's *Twelfth Night*). Here, a series of actual rooms have been painstakingly reconstructed piece by piece after being rescued from historic buildings. These include an ornate music room and the Henrietta St. Room, a breathtakingly serene parlor dating from 1722.

The **Asian Galleries** (rooms 44–47) are full of treasures, but among the most striking items on display is a remarkable collection of ornate samurai armor in the **Japanese Gallery** (Room 44). There are also galleries devoted to China, Korea, and the Islamic Middle East. More recently installed areas include the Buddhist Sculpture gallery, the Ceramics gallery, and the Medieval and Renaissance galleries, which have the largest collection of works from the period outside of Italy.

Historic Plaque Hunt

As you wander around London, you'll see lots of small blue, circular plaques on the sides and facades of buildings, describing which famous, infamous, or obscure but brilliant person once lived there. The first was placed outside Lord Byron's birthplace (now no more) by the Royal Society of Arts. There are about 700 blue plaques, erected by different bodies—you may even find some green ones that originated from Westminster City Council—but English Heritage now maintains the responsibility, and if you want to find out the latest, check the website ⊕ *www.english-heritage.org.uk. Below are some of the highlights:*

James Barrie (⊠ 100 Bayswater Rd., Bayswater); **Frederic Chopin** (⊠ 4 St. James's Pl., St. James's); **Sir Winston Churchill** (⊠ 28 Hyde Park Gate, Kensington Gore); **Captain James Cook** (⊠ 88 Mile End Rd., Tower Hamlets); **T.S. Eliot** (⊠ 3 Kensington Court Gardens, Kensington); **Benjamin Franklin** (⊠ 36 Craven St., Westminster); **Mahatma Gandhi** (⊠ 20 Baron's Court Rd., West Kensington); **George Frederic Handel** and **Jimi Hendrix** (⊠ 23 Brook St., Mayfair); **Alfred Hitchcock** (⊠ 153 Cromwell Rd., Earl's Court); **Karl Marx** (⊠ 28 Dean St., Soho); **Wolfgang Amadeus Mozart** (⊠ 180 Ebury St., Pimlico); **Horatio Nelson** (⊠ 103 New Bond St., Mayfair); **Sir Isaac Newton** (⊠ 87 Jermyn St., St. James's); **Florence Nightingale** (⊠ 10 South St., Mayfair); **George Bernard Shaw** (⊠ 29 Fitzroy Sq., Fitzrovia); **Percy Bysshe Shelley** (⊠ 15 Poland St., Soho); **Mark Twain** (⊠ 23 Tedworth Sq., Chelsea); **H.G. Wells** (⊠ 13 Hanover Terr., Regent's Park); **Oscar Wilde** (⊠ 34 Tite St., Chelsea); **William Butler Yeats** (⊠ 23 Fitzroy Rd., Primrose Hill).

CHELSEA

Chelsea was settled before the Domesday Book was compiled and already fashionable when two of Henry VIII's wives lived there. On the banks of the Thames are the vast grounds of the **Royal Hospital,** designed by Christopher Wren. A walk along the riverside embankment will take you to **Cheyne Walk,** a lovely street dating back to the 18th century. Several of its more notable residents—who range from J.M.W. Turner and Henry James to Laurence Olivier and Keith Richards—are commemorated by blue plaques on their former houses.

The **Albert Bridge,** a candy-color Victorian confection of a suspension bridge, provides one of London's great romantic views, especially at night. Nearby is one of London's most exciting shopping streets, the **King's Road** (once Charles II's private way from St. James's to Fulham). Leave time to explore the tiny Georgian lanes of pastel-color houses that veer off the King's Road to the north—especially **Jubilee Place** and

WORD OF MOUTH

"We went to the Chelsea Flower Show last year—it was one of the greatest memories from our trip. There was no problem ordering the tickets on-line and having them delivered. It was just a wonderful day with my Mom! I can't recommend it enough if you love gardening." —willowjane

Burnsall Street, leading to the hidden "village square" of Chelsea Green. On Saturday there's an excellent farmers' market up from the Saatchi Gallery selling artisanal cheese and chocolates, local oysters, and organic meats, plus stalls serving international food.

Residential Chelsea extends along the river from the Chelsea Bridge west to the Battersea Bridge and north as far as the Old Brompton Road.

TOP ATTRACTIONS

Royal Hospital Chelsea. Charles II founded this hospice for elderly and infirm soldiers in 1682 to reward the troops who had fought for him in the civil wars of 1642–46 and 1648. Charles wisely appointed the great architect Sir Christopher Wren to design this small village of brick and Portland stone set in manicured gardens (which you can visit) surrounding the Figure Court—the figure being a 1682 gilded bronze statue of Charles II dressed as a Roman general—the Great Hall (dining room), and a chapel. The chapel is enhanced by choir stalls created by Grinling Gibbons (who made the statue of Charles as well), the Great Hall by Antonio Verrio's vast oil painting of Charles on horseback, and both are open to the public at certain times during the day. There is a small museum devoted to the history of the resident "Chelsea Pensioners," but the real attraction, along with the building, is the pensioners themselves. Recognizable by their traditional scarlet frock coats with gold buttons, medals, and tricorne hats, they are all actual veterans, who wear the uniform, and the history it conveys, with a great deal of pride. They celebrate Founder's Day—the closest Thursday to May 29, Charles II's birthday—by draping oak leaves on his statue and parading in front of it, a tribute to a historic hollow oak tree that expedited the king's escape from the Civil War's final conflict, the 1651 Battle of Worcester, leaving him free to fight another day. ⊠ *Royal Hospital Rd., Chelsea* ☎ *020/7881–5298* ⊕ *www.chelsea-pensioners.org.uk* ⊠ *Free* ☉ *Grounds, Chapel, Courts, and Great Hall open Mon.–Sat. 10–noon and 2–4. Museum open weekdays 10–noon and 2–4. Closed holidays and for special events.*

Chelsea Flower Show. Also in May (usually the third week), the Chelsea Flower Show, the year's highlight for thousands of garden-obsessed Brits, is held here. Run by the Royal Horticultural Society, this mammoth event takes up vast acreage, and the surrounding streets throng with visitors. ⊠ *Chelsea* ☎ *0844/338–7506 in U.K., 121/767–4063 from outside U.K.* ⊕ *www.rhs.org.uk* Ⓜ *Sloane Sq.*

Saatchi Gallery. Charles Saatchi, who made his fortune building an advertising empire that successfully "rebranded" Margaret Thatcher's

ARTISTIC CHELSEA

Artists and writers flocked to the area in the 19th century, establishing a creative colony in Cheyne Walk; at one time Turner, Whistler, John Singer Sargent, Dante Gabriel Rossetti, and Oscar Wilde were residents. In the 1960s it was the turn of Mick Jagger and Keith Richards; in the 1970s Bob Marley wrote "I Shot the Sheriff" in a flat off Cheyne Walk. It's now one of London's most expensive streets, completely unaffordable for latter-day Bob Marleys.

World-famous Harrods has been attracting shoppers since 1834.

Conservative Party, is Britain's most highly regarded collector of contemporary art. The museum's home—its third in 10 years—is at the former Duke of York's HQ, just off the King's Road. Built in 1803, its suitably grand period exterior belies its imaginatively restored modern interior, which was transformed into 14 gallery exhibition spaces of varying size and shape. Unlike Tate Modern, there is no permanent collection beyond an ongoing site-specific installation; instead, at any one time the galleries are given over to between one and three exhibitions that normally run for up to six months, such as a highly successful exhibition that showcased contemporary Chinese art. There's also an excellent café, which is open late. ⊠ *Duke of York's HQ Bldg., King's Rd., Chelsea* ☎ *020/7811–3085* ⊕ *www.saatchigallery.com* ✉ *Free* ◷ *Daily 10–6* Ⓜ *Sloane Sq.*

KNIGHTSBRIDGE

There's no getting away from it. London's wealthiest enclave (not many other neighborhoods are plagued with street racers in Maseratis) is shop-'til-you-drop territory of the highest order. With two world-famous department stores, **Harrods** and **Harvey Nichols**, a few hundred yards apart, and every bit of space between and around taken up with designer boutiques, international luxury chains, and eye-wateringly expensive jewelers, it's hard to imagine why anyone who doesn't like shopping would even think of coming here.

Nearby Sloane Street is lined with top-end designer boutiques such as Prada, Dior, and Tods. If the bling factor becomes too much, **Beauchamp**

Place (pronounced "Beecham") is a good tonic. It's lined with equally chic and expensive boutiques, but they tend to be smaller, more personal, and less hectic.

Posh Knightsbridge is located to the east of Kensington, bordered by Hyde Park on the north and Pont Street just past Harrods on the south.

BELGRAVIA

A good way to find serenity is on a divinely peaceful stroll in fashionable Belgravia, one of the most gorgeous set-pieces of urban 19th-century planning, and found just to the west of Kensington and Chelsea. Street after street is lined with grand white terraces of aristocratic town houses, still part of the Grosvenor estate owned by the Dukes of Westminster. Many are leased to embassies, but a remarkable number around **Lowndes Square, Belgrave Square,** and **Eaton Square** remain homes of the discreet independently wealthy and outright super-rich. Some people consider the area near **Elizabeth Street** southern Belgravia, others Pimlico–Victoria. Either way, now that you've had a break, it's time to shop again, though the stores here are smaller and more unique, specializing in baked goods, wine, gifts, and stationery rather than fashion. You'll have to look hard for these shops, though: most Belgravia blocks are strictly residential, and we do mean strictly.

TOP ATTRACTIONS

Belgrave Square. This is the heart of Belgravia, once the epicenter of posh London though now mostly occupied by organizations, embassies, and the international rich. The square and the streets leading off it share a remarkably consistent stately yet elegant architectural style thanks to all being part of a Regency redevelopment scheme commissioned by the Duke of Westminster and designed by Thomas Cubitt with George Basevi. The grand, porticoed mansions were snapped up by aristocrats and politicians due to their proximity to Buckingham Palace just around the corner, and still command record prices on the rare occasion when they come onto the market. The private garden in the center is open to the public once a year (⊕ *www.opensquares.org*). Walk down Belgrave Place toward Eaton Place and you pass two of Belgravia's most beautiful mews: Eaton Mews North and Eccleston Mews, both fronted by grand rusticated entrances right out of a 19th-century engraving. ⚠ Traffic can really whip around Belgrave Square, so be careful. ⊠ *Belgrave Sq., Belgravia* Ⓜ *Hyde Park Corner.*

NOTTING HILL
AND BAYSWATER

GETTING ORIENTED

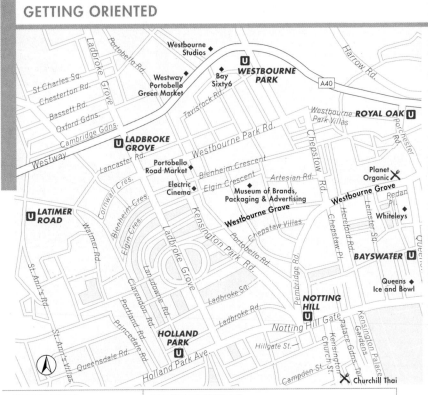

GETTING THERE

For Portobello Market and environs, the best Tube stops are Ladbroke Grove and Westbourne Park (Hammersmith and City lines); ask for directions when you emerge. The Notting Hill stop on the District, Circle, and Central lines enables you to walk the length of Portobello Road on a downhill gradient.

A GOOD WALK

To gape at Notting Hill's grandest houses, stroll over to Lansdowne Road, Lansdowne Crescent, and Lansdowne Square—two blocks west of Kensington Park Row.

TOP REASONS TO GO

Find a bargain on Portobello Road: Seek and ye shall find; go early-morning antique hunting at London's best and most famous market on Saturday, or come during the week for a leisurely browse.

Shop for vintage clothing: In addition to the Portobello market, you can search for vintage designer pieces at Notting Hill's numerous secondhand and retro clothing stores.

See and be seen on Westbourne Grove: Watch the locals stroll the streets as if they were one big catwalk, then drop in for lunch at one of the Grove's colorful ethnic restaurants.

Catch a film at the Electric Cinema: Recline on a two-seater leather sofa, beer and bar snacks in hand, at this restored early-20th-century theater—then splurge for dinner at its fantastic Electric Brasserie.

MAKING THE MOST OF YOUR TIME

Saturday is Notting Hill and Portobello Road's most fun and frenetic day. You could easily spend the whole day shopping, eating, and drinking here.

The market can get crowded by noon in warm weather so come early if you are serious about shopping.

You may prefer to start at the north end of Portobello Road and work your way south, using the parks for relaxation after your shopping exertions. Do the same on Friday if you're a flea-market fan.

On Sunday, the Hyde Park and Kensington Gardens railings all along Bayswater Road are lined with artists peddling their (often dubious) work, which may slow your progress.

This is also the day when the well-heeled locals are out in force, filling the pubs at lunch-time or hitting the parks with their kids if it's sunny.

10

FEELING PECKISH?

The Churchill Arms. This eccentric, traditional pub, swamped in Churchill memorabilia, has a peculiar selling point: the attached Thai Kitchen, which is so popular that they've been known to give diners an hour in which to finish their meal. Not only is the food delicious, at around £7 per dish, it's a real bargain for this part of town. ⊠ *119 Kensington Church St., Notting Hill* ☎ *020/7727–4242* ⊕ *www. churchillarmskensington.co.uk* Ⓜ *Notting Hill Gate.*

Planet Organic. A haven for the health conscious, this spot serves upscale vegetarian meals at nongourmet prices, with a wide selection of specials to take out. ⊠ *42 Westbourne Grove, Bayswater* ☎ *020/7727–2227* ⊕ *www.planetorganic. com* Ⓜ *Bayswater.*

SAFETY

At night, be wary of straying too far off the main streets, as it gets "edgier" toward Ladbroke Grove's high-rise estates and surrounding areas.

Sightseeing
★★
Nightlife
★★★
Dining
★★★
Lodging
★★★
Shopping
★★★★

Notting Hill is a trendsetting square mile full of multiethnicity, music, magnificent street markets, bars, restaurants, and chic shops. The area is studded with some of London's most handsome old crescents and terraces, now home to those well-dressed residents—musicians, novelists, and fashionistas—who the style-watching London media has dubbed the "Notting Hillbillies." Every weekend, hordes descend on Portobello Road to go bargain-hunting at one of the world's great antiques markets. Who knows what treasures they'll find among the acres of bric-a-brac and curios.

NOTTING HILL

Updated by
Jack Jewers

Notting Hill, as we know it, was born in the 1840s when the wealthy Ladbroke family laid out a small suburb to the west of London. Before then the area had been far less glamorously known as "the Potteries and the Piggeries," in honor of its two industries: ceramics and pig farming.

During the 1980s, Notting Hill was quickly transforming from poverty-stricken backwater to super-trendy enclave. By the early 2000s the neighborhood was clearly established as chic—helped massively by the hit movie that bore its name. For the Notting Hill of the silver screen, head straight for **Westbourne Grove,** replete with quirky boutiques and charity shops laden with the castoffs from wealthy residents. This is also where you'll find a smattering of boutique art

NOTTING HILL CARNIVAL

Loud, colorful, and very crowded, the annual Carnival (⊕ *www.nottinghillcarnival.biz*) was started by Afro-Caribbean immigrants in the 1960s. Held the last weekend in August, it attracts hundreds of thousands of visitors, mostly young and raucous. Very high crime rates make this a no-no for families—even on "family day." Be careful.

galleries, such as **England and Co.,** which welcome browsers as much as serious collectors.

The whole area has mushroomed around the **Portobello Road**, with the beautifully restored early-20th-century **Electric Cinema** at No. 191. The famous Saturday antiques market and shops are at the southern end; **Westway Portobello Green Market**, under the Westway overpass, is occupied by bric-a-brac, secondhand threads, and clothes and accessories by young, up-and-coming designers.

Technically part of Kensington, Notting Hill has no official boundaries, but is generally accepted to cover the area from the northwestern edge of Hyde Park to the far end of Ladbroke Grove (its main thoroughfare), where it becomes the more down-at-heel Kensal Rise. The "heart" of the neighborhood is the famous Portobello Road, which runs the length of the district from north to south.

TOP ATTRACTIONS

FAMILY **Hyde Park and Kensington Gardens.**

See the highlighted listing in this chapter.

Museum of Brands, Packaging and Advertising. This extraordinary little museum does exactly what it says on the package. The massive collection of toys, fashion, food wrappers, advertising, and the assorted detritus of everyday life is from all corners of the globe and presents a fascinating and eccentric chronicle of how consumer culture has developed since the Victorian age. ⊠ *2 Colville Mews, Lonsdale Rd., Notting Hill* ☎ *020/7908–0880* ⊕ *www.museumofbrands.com* ✎ *£6.50* ⊙ *Tues.–Sat. 10–6, Sun. 11–5; last entry 45 min before closing. Closed during Notting Hill Carnival* Ⓜ *Notting Hill.*

Portobello Road. Tempted by tassels, looking for a 19th-century snuff spoon, on the hunt for a Georgian *objet d'art?* Fancy an original sixties minidress, or a dashingly deco party frock? Then head to Portobello Road, world famous for its Saturday antiques market. Arrive at about 9 am to find the real treasures-in-the-trash; after 10, the crowds pack in wall-to-wall. Actually, the Portobello Market is three markets: antiques, "fruit and veg," and a flea market. Portobello Road begins at Notting Hill Gate, though the antiques stalls start a couple of blocks north, around Chepstow Villas. Lining the sloping street are also dozens of antiques shops and indoor markets, open most days—in fact, serious collectors will want to do Portobello on a weekday, when they can explore the 90-some antiques and art stores in relative peace. Where the road levels off, around Elgin Crescent, youth culture and a vibrant neighborhood life kicks in, with all manner of interesting small stores and restaurants interspersed with the fruit and vegetable market. This continues to the Westway overpass ("flyover" in British), where on

10

Continued on page 190

HYDE PARK AND KENSINGTON GARDENS

Every year millions of visitors descend on the royal parks of Hyde Park and Kensington Gardens, which sit side by side and roll out over 625 acres of grassy expanses that provide much-craved-for respite from London's frenetic pace. The two parks incorporate formal gardens, fountains, sports fields, great picnic spots, shady clusters of ancient trees, and even an outdoor swimming pool.

Although it's probably been centuries since any major royal had a casual stroll here—you're more likely to bump into Chris Martin and Gwyneth Paltrow than Her Royal Highness these days—the parks remain the property of the Crown, which saved them from being devoured by the city's late-18th-century growth spurt.

Today the luxury of such wide open spaces continues to be appreciated by the Londoners who steal into the parks before work for a session of tai chi, say, or on weekends when the sun is shining. Simply sitting back in a hired deck chair or strolling through the varied terrain is one of the most enjoyable ways to spend time here.

KENSINGTON GARDENS

At the end of the 17th century, William III moved his court to the impeccably kept green space that is now **Kensington Gardens**. He was attracted to the location for its clean air and tranquillity and subsequently commissioned Sir Christopher Wren to overhaul the original redbrick building, resulting in the splendid **Kensington Palace**.

To the north of the palace complex is the early-20th-century **Sunken Garden**, complete with a living tunnel of lime trees (i.e., linden trees) and golden laburnum.

On western side of the **Long Water** is George Frampton's 1912 *Peter Pan*, a bronze of the boy who lived on an island in the Serpentine and never grew up and whose creator, J.M. Barrie, lived at 100 Bayswater Road, not 500 yards from here.

Back toward Kensington Palace, at the intersection of several paths, is George Frederick Watts's 1904 bronze of a muscle-bound horse and rider, entitled **Physical Energy.** The **Round Pond** is a magnet for model-boat enthusiasts and duck feeders.

Near the Broad Walk, toward Black Lion Gate, is the **Diana Princess of Wales**

- - - - - *Diana Memorial Walk*

LANCASTER GATE

LANCASTER GATE

Italian Gardens

QUEENSWAY Bayswater Rd.

NOTTING HILL GATE BLACK LION GATE

The Fountains

Diana Princess of Wales Memorial Playground

Kensington Gardens

Peter Pan

The Long Water

Elfin Oak

(RESTRICTED AREA)

Orangery

Physical Energy

Kensington Palace Gardens

Sunken Garden

The Round Pond

Broad Walk

Kensington Palace

Serpentine Gallery

The Serpentine

Afternoon tea taken at the Orangery, a short walk from the Sunken Garden on the palace grounds, is a quintessentially English experience.

Flower Walk

Kensington Rd. QUEEN'S GATE

Albert Memorial Kensington ALEXANDRA GATE

Memorial Playground, an enclosed space with specially designed structures and areas on the theme of Barrie's Neverland. Hook's ship, crocodiles, "jungles" of foliage, and islands of sand provide a fantasy land for kids—more than 70,000 visit every year. Just outside its bounds is Ivor Innes's *Elfin Oak,* the remains of a tree carved with scores of tiny woodland creatures.

One of the park's most striking monuments is the **Albert Memorial.** This Victorian high-Gothic celebration of Prince Albert is

adorned with marble statues representing his interests and amusements.

Diminutive as it may be, the **Serpentine Gallery** has not been afraid of courting controversy with its temporary exhibitions of challenging contemporary works.

Hyde Park was once the hunting ground of King Henry VIII. This stout, bawdy royal more or less stole Hyde Park, along with the smaller St. James's and Green parks, from the monks of Westminster in 1536. The public wasn't to be granted access

HYDE PARK

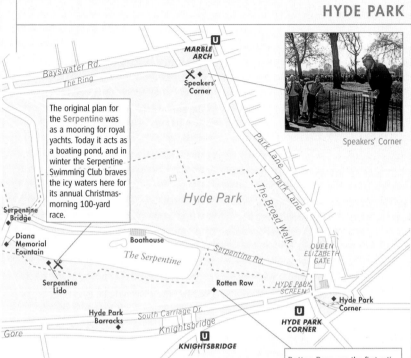

The original plan for the **Serpentine** was as a mooring for royal yachts. Today it acts as a boating pond, and in winter the Serpentine Swimming Club braves the icy waters here for its annual Christmas-morning 100-yard race.

Speakers' Corner

Hyde Park

MARBLE ARCH

Speakers' Corner

Bayswater Rd.

The Ring

Park Lane

Park Lane

The Broad Walk

Serpentine Bridge

Diana Memorial Fountain

Boathouse

The Serpentine

Serpentine Rd.

QUEEN ELIZABETH GATE

HYDE PARK SCREEN

Serpentine Lido

Rotten Row

Hyde Park Corner

Hyde Park Barracks

South Carriage Dr.

Knightsbridge

HYDE PARK CORNER

Gore

KNIGHTSBRIDGE

10

to Hyde Park's delights until James I came to the throne and opened up limited parts to "respectably dressed" plebeians.

It was Charles I, in the 1700s, however, who was to shape the Hyde Park that visitors see today. Once he had created **the Ring** (North Carriage Drive), which forms a curve north of the **Serpentine** and boathouses, Charles allowed the general public to roam free. During the Great Plague of 1665, East Enders and City dwellers fled to the park, seeking refuge from the black bilious disease.

The **Serpentine Bridge**, built in 1826 by George Rennie, marks the boundary between Hyde Park and Kensington Gardens. **Rotten Row**, a corruption of the French *route de roi* (king's road), runs along the southeastern edge of Hyde Park and is still used by the Household Cavalry, who live at the **Hyde Park Barracks**—a high-rise and a long, low, red block—to the left. This is where the brigade that mounts the guard at Buckingham Palace resides; you can see them at about 10:30 am, as they leave to perform their duty in full regalia, or await the return of the guard about noon.

Rotten Row was the first artificially lit highway in Britain. In the late 17th century, William III was concerned that his walk to from Kensington Palace to St. James's Park was too dangerous, so he ordered 300 lamps to be placed along the route.

On the south side of the 1930s **Serpentine Lido** (open to swimmers from June to September) is the £3.6 million oval **Diana Memorial Fountain**.

Ever since the 1827 legislation of public assembly, **Speakers' Corner** near Marble Arch has provided an outlet for political debate: on Sundays, it's a spectacle of vehement, sometimes comical, and always entertaining orators.

ENJOYING THE PARKS

Ride. **Hyde Park Riding Stables** keeps horses for hacking the sand tracks. Group lessons (usually just a few people) are £64 per person per hour. Private lessons are £89 Tuesday–Friday, £99 on weekends. ⊠ 63 Bathurst Mews, Bayswater W2 ☎ 020/7723–2813 ⊕ www. hydeparkstables.com Ⓤ Lancaster Gate.

Row. **The Serpentine** has paddleboats and rowboats for £10 per person per hour, kids £5, April through October from 10 am to dusk, later in good weather in summer. ☎ 020/7262–1330.

Run. You can run a **4-mi route** around the perimeter of Hyde Park and Kensington Gardens or a **2½-mi route** in Hyde Park alone if you start at Hyde Park Corner or Marble Arch and encircle the Serpentine.

Skate. On Friday, skaters of intermediate ability and upward meet at 8 pm at the Duke of Wellington Arch, Hyde Park Corner, for the **Friday Night Skate,** an enthusiastic two-hour mass skating session, complete with music and whistles. If you're a bit unsure on your wheels, arrive at 6:30 pm for the free lesson on how to break and turn. The **Sunday Rollerstroll,** a more laid-back version of the same thing, runs on Sunday afternoons; meet at 2 pm on the east side of Serpentine Road ⊕ www.thefns. com Ⓤ Hyde Park Corner.

Swim. **Serpentine Lido** is technically a beach on a lake, but a hot day in Hyde Park is surreally reminiscent of the seaside. There are changing facilities, and the swimming section is chlorinated. There is also a paddling pool, sandpit, and kids' entertainer in the afternoons. It's open daily from June through September (and weekends in May), 10–6; admission £4, ☎ 020/7706–3422 ⊕ www.royalparks.org.uk Ⓤ Knightsbridge.

WHERE TO REFUEL

✗ The **Lido Café,** near the Diana Memorial Fountain, has plenty of seating with views across the Serpentine Lake.

✗ **Serpentine Bar and Kitchen** on the eastern side of the lake, is a good pit stop for tasty snacks, salads, and sandwiches.

✗ The **Broadwalk Café & Playcafe** next to the Diana Memorial Playground has a children's menu.

✗ The **Orangery** beside Kensington Palace is a distinctly more grown-up affair for tea and cakes.

SPEAKERS' CORNER

Once the site of public executions and the Tyburn hanging trees, the corner of Hyde Park at Cumberland Gate and Park Lane now harbors one of London's most public spectacles: Speakers' Corner. This has been a place of assembly and vitriolic outpourings and debates since the mid-19th century. The pageant of free speech takes place every Sunday afternoon.

Anyone is welcome to mount a soapbox and declaim upon any topic, which makes for an irresistible showcase of eccentricity—one such being the (now-deceased) Protein Man. Wearing his publicity board, the Protein Man proclaimed that the eating of meat, cheese, and peanuts led to uncontrollable acts of passion that would destroy Western civilization. The pamphlets he sold for four decades are now collector's items. Other more strait-laced campaigns have been launched here by the Chartists, the Reform League, the May Day demonstrators, and the Suffragettes.

PRACTICAL INFO

ADMISSION: Free for both parks

HOURS: Kensington Gardens 6 am–dusk; Hyde Park 5 am–midnight

CONTACT INFO: ☎ 030/0061–2000, ⊕ www.royalparks.gov.uk

GETTING HERE: Ⓤ **Kensington Gardens:** Kensington High Street, Queensway, Lancaster Gate, South Kensington. **Hyde Park:** Hyde Park Corner, Knightsbridge, Lancaster Gate, Marble Arch

EVENTS: Major events, such as rock concerts and festivals, road races, and talks, are regular features of the parks' calendar; check online for what's on during your visit.

Each summer, a different modern architect designs an outdoor pavilion for the contemporary Serpentine Gallery, the venue for outdoor film screenings, readings, and other such cultural soirees.

Every June or July, Hyde Park hosts The Wireless, one of the U.K.'s biggest music festivals. It's held over a weekend, on several stages, and attracts some of the biggest global names in pop, indie, and rock.

(left) Horseback riding, Hyde Park

(top) The Fountains, Kensington Gardens

(bottom) Both parks are lovely year-round, but spring blooms are spectacular.

TOURS: There are **themed guided walks** about once a month, usually on Thursday or Friday afternoons. They are free but must be booked in advance. Check online or call the park offices for dates and details.

A 45-minute tour (£6) of the **Albert Memorial** is available. It's held at 2 and 3 pm on the first Sunday of the month from March to December. For information call ☎ 020/7495–0916.

Kensington Palace is open daily from 10 am to 6 pm, March to September, and 10 am to 5 pm from October to February. Tickets are £14.50; kids with an adult go free. For information call ☎ 0844/482–7799 or visit ⊕ www.hrp.org.uk.

Friday and Saturday you'll find London's best flea market—a ragtag of high-class, vintage, antique, and second-hand clothing, together with jewelry and assorted junk. There's a strong West Indian flavor to Notting Hill, with a Trinidad-style Carnival centered along Portobello Road on the August bank-holiday weekend. *For more on Portobello Road, see* ⇨ *Shopping, Chapter 18.* ⊠ *Notting Hill* ⊕ *www.portobelloroad. co.uk* Ⓜ *Notting Hill Gate, Ladbroke Grove.*

BAYSWATER

Next to Notting Hill is the district of Bayswater. It separates the south side of Notting Hill from Paddington, and is a hub for cheap tourist hotels.

The main thoroughfare of this district is **Queensway,** a rather peculiar, cosmopolitan street of late-night cafés and restaurants, multiethnic food shops, and the **Whiteleys** shopping-and-movie mall. Nearby **Paddington station,** one of London's most handsome rail terminal, is the namesake for the world's most famous marmalade fan: Paddington Bear.

REGENT'S PARK
AND HAMPSTEAD

GETTING ORIENTED

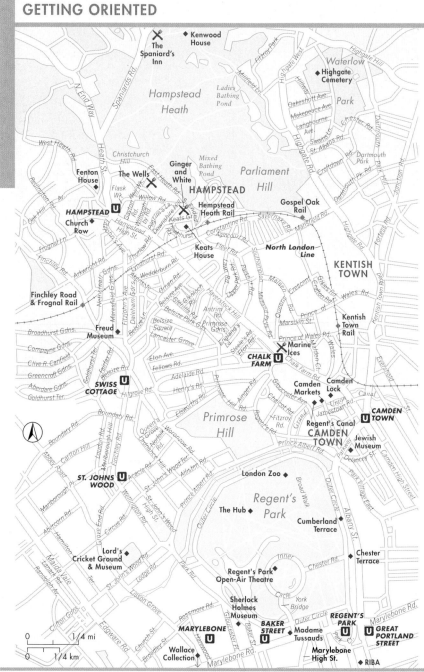

TOP REASONS TO GO

Ramble across Hampstead Heath: Londoners adore the Heath for its wild, unkempt beauty—and the unparalleled views across the city.

Find your inner muse at Keats House: Stroll through the very garden where the great Romantic sat while writing "Ode to a Nightingale."

Marvel at London's grandest Regency terraces: With their Wedgwood-blue pediments, snow-white statuary, and porticos of Ionic columns, Nash's 18th-century mansions make a splendid backdrop for Regent's Park.

Strawberry Beatles Forever!: For countless Beatlemaniacs and baby boomers, a visit to No. 3 Abbey Road is an unforgettable experience.

Speak Parseltongue at the London Zoo: Harry Potter fans may recognize the snakes in the reptile house, but the zoo's waddling penguins steal the animal spotlight here.

FEELING PECKISH?

Ginger and White. This is a delightful fusion of continental-style café and traditional British coffee shop. ⊠ *4 Perrins Ct., Hampstead* ☎ *020/7431–9098* ⊕ *www.gingerandwhite. com* Ⓜ *Hampstead.*

Marine Ices. This place has some of London's best ice cream, while the indoor Italian restaurant section lures diners. ⊠ *8 Haverstock Hill, Camden Town* ☎ *020/7482–9003* ⊕ *www. marineices.co.uk* Ⓜ *Chalk Farm.*

SAFETY

It's best to stay out of Hampstead Heath and Regent's Park proper at night unless there's an event taking place; both are perfectly safe during the day. Also to be avoided after dark: the canal towpath in Camden.

GETTING THERE

Reaching Hampstead by Tube is as easy as it looks: Simply take the Edgware branch of the Northern line to Hampstead station, or the overground North London line to Hampstead Heath. The south side of Hampstead Heath can also be reached by the Gospel Oak station on the North London line. To get to Regent's Park, take the Bakerloo line to Regent's Park Tube station or, for Primrose Hill, the Chalk Farm stop on the Northern line.

MAKING THE MOST OF YOUR TIME

Depending on your pace and inclination, Regent's Park and Hampstead can realistically be covered in a day. It might be best to spend the morning in Hampstead, with at least a brief foray onto the Heath, then head south to Regent's Park in the afternoon so that you're closer to central London come nightfall, if that is where your hotel is located. If you have time, you may want to return to Hampstead another day for a longer walk across the Heath.

A GOOD WALK

These are two of the most walkable districts in London. Everything from Hampstead "village" to Regent's Park (and its outlying terraced streets) is best explored on foot—even Hampstead Heath has marked footpaths.

Sightseeing
★★★★
Nightlife
★★★
Dining
★★
Lodging
★★
Shopping
★★★

As civilized as a Gainsborough landscape, Regent's Park and Hampstead contain some of the prettiest and most aristocratic architecture that London has to offer. The city becomes noticeably calmer and greener as you head north from Oxford Street, past the newly chic shopping streets of Marylebone and immensely regal mansions that encircle Regent's Park, up to the well-tended lawns of Primrose Hill and the handsome Georgian streets of Hampstead. All in all, this area will provide a taste of how laid-back (moneyed) Londoners can be.

REGENT'S PARK

Updated by
Jack Jewers

Regent's Park, the youngest of London's great parks, was laid out in 1812 by John Nash, working, as ever, for his patron, the Prince Regent (hence the name), who was crowned George IV in 1820. Framed by gloriously stylish Regency mansions, the park is home to many attractions, including the London Zoo and the summer display of prize roses in Queen Mary's Gardens.

The well-worn, but entirely accurate cliché about the enclaves north of Regent's Park (Primrose Hill and Hampstead) is that several of the residents claim to be artists—and yet the cost of a coffee at a café along Regent's Park Road will run you as much as, if not more than, one in central London. In the last decade, real estate prices here have skyrocketed, and the elephants of London Zoo now count some of the best-dressed folks in town (Gwyneth Paltrow, Madonna) as their neighbors.

A livelier, cooler vibe prevails at **Camden Market,** a magnet for dedicated followers of fashion. The southeastern exit of the park is just around the corner from two of London's most traditional tourist destinations, the **Sherlock Holmes Museum** and **Madame Tussauds.**

A BRIEF HISTORY

When John Nash, the great architect of Regency style, laid out Regent's Park in 1812, the idea was to re-create the feel of a grand country residence close to the center of town. No genuine palace was built but almost something far grander: a series of magnificent white-stucco terrace "houses," many combined under one extra-ornamental pediment, as if part of a gigantic Grecian temple. As you walk "the Outer Circle," you'll see how success-fully Nash's plans were carried out, especially as you walk past the most famous of his Regent's Park creations, Cumberland Terrace, replete with a central block of Ionic columns surmounted by a triangular Wedgewood-blue pediment and giant statuary personifying Britannia and her empire. Nearby is Chester Terrace, an entire street designed by Nash and the ultimate in architec-tural good breeding.

In the early 18th century, the com-mercial development of the mineral springs in Hampstead led to its success as a spa; people traveled from miles around to drink the pure waters from Hampstead Wells, and small cottages were hastily built to accommodate the influx. Though the spa phenomenon was short-lived, Hampstead remained a favorite place for many artistic figures whose legacies still mark the landscape as much as they permeate the culture.

The 410-acre expanse of Regent's Park loosely connects several London districts—most of which are shadowed, like contrasts on a Monopoly board, by less salubrious versions of themselves. To the west of the park, Paddington (famous for a station, a bear, and not much else) is rather grimy and run-down; but nearby Little Venice is a bohemian oasis of undiscovered beauty and character. To the north of the park lies leafy Primrose Hill, one of the city's most upscale districts; and cool-by-day, dodgy-after-dark Camden. Also northwards is gorgeous Hampstead, the ultimate London "village," with its wild Heath and lolloping hills, which segue alarmingly soon into Kilburn, an unloved residential district good for little but passing through quickly. Farther north of Hampstead are two London curiosities: Highgate, another upscale 'hood famous for its magnificent Gothic cemetery, and Golder's Green, the closest the city gets to a proper Jewish quarter.

TOP ATTRACTIONS

FAMILY

Fodor's Choice

★

London Zoo. Owned by the Zoological Society of London (a charity), the zoo opened in 1828. A recent modernization program has seen the introduction of several big attractions, with a focus on wildlife conservation, education, and the breeding of endangered species. The huge **BUGS** pavilion (Biodiversity Underpinning Global Survival) is a self-sustaining, contained ecosystem with 140 species of exotic plants, animals, and creepy-crawlies. At **Gorilla Kingdom** you can watch the four residents—Effie, Kesho, Jookie, and Zaire—at close range. **Rain-forest Life** is a recreated nighttime rainforest environment, home to tiny marmosets and other rain-forest-dwelling creatures, including bats. The new **Children's Zoo** allows kids to see a host of unusual creatures up close, including aardvarks and mongooses. It also contains play areas and a petting zoo. The state-of-the-art **Penguin Beach** is the most popular place in the zoo at 11:30, when the penguins receive their main feed—or you could try and nab one of the six VIP tickets for 2 pm that allow guided access to the enclosure, where you get close enough to actually stroke the placid creatures; tickets are £25 week-days, £40 weekend and demand is high. Other zoo highlights include the **Butterfly Paradise**; the **Blackburn Pavilion**, with its hundreds of tropical bird species; and the **Big Cats** enclosure, home to a pack of lions and a pair of beautiful Sumatran tigers. ■ TIP→ Check the website or the information board out front for free events, including creature close encounters and "ask the keeper" sessions. ⊠ *Outer Circle, Regent's Park* 🕾 *020/7722–3333* ⊕ *www.zsl.org* ⊠ *£20* ⊙ *Mid-Nov.–Feb., daily 10–4; Mar.–early Sept., daily 10–6; early-Sept.–Oct., daily 10–5:30; early-mid-Nov., daily 10–4:30; last admission 1 hr before closing* Ⓜ *Camden Town, then Bus 274.*

FAMILY **Regent's Park.**
See the highlighted listing in this chapter.

Sherlock Holmes Museum. Outside Baker Street station, by the Maryle-bone Road exit, is a 9-foot-high bronze statue of the celebrated detective. Nearby is number 221B Baker Street—the address of Arthur Conan Doyle's fictional detective. Inside, Mrs. Hudson, "Holmes's housekeeper," conducts you into a series of Victorian rooms full of Sherlock-abilia. There are more than enough photo ops, and it's all carried off with such genuine enthusiasm that you almost believe that the fictional detective really lived here. ⊠ *221B Baker St., Regent's Park* 🕾 *020/7224–3688* ⊕ *www.sherlock-holmes.co.uk* ⊠ *£6* ⊙ *Daily 9:30–6* Ⓜ *Baker St.*

WORTH NOTING

Camden Market. What started as a small group of clothing stalls in the 1970s has since grown into one of London's biggest (and most crowded) tourist attractions. Centered on the Grand Union Canal, this isn't actually a single market, but a vast honeycomb of them that sell crafts, clothing (vintage, ethnic, and young designer), antiques, and just about everything in between. Here, especially on weekends, the crowds are dense, young, and relentless, with as many as 100,000 visitors on the busiest days. **Camden Lock Market** specializes in crafts; **Camden Stables Market** is popular with Goth kids and aspiring rock stars. ■ TIP→ Print out the (appropriately psychedelic) map of Camden Market from the website before coming; it's super helpful for first-time visitors. ⊠ *Camden High St., Camden Town* ⊕ *www.camdenmarkets.org* ⊙ *Daily 10–6 (some stalls close 5:30)* Ⓜ *Camden Town, Chalk Farm.*

Electric Ballroom. A nightclub that doubles as a retro/designer fashion and music market on weekends, the Electric Ballroom has been a scuzzy, dilapidated, wild, and wonderful Camden institution for decades. On a half dozen or so dates per year it also plays host to the busy **Camden Film Fair,** beloved of collectors and old-school cult movie enthusiasts. ⊠ *184 Camden High St., Camden Town* 🕾 *020/7485–9006* ⊕ *www. electricballroom.co.uk.*

REGENT'S PARK

11

✉ *Marylebone Rd., Regent's Park* ☎ *0300/061–2000*
⊕ *www.royalparks.gov.uk*
🎫 *Free* ⊙ *5 am–dusk.*

TIPS

■ Soccer, rugby, tennis, field hockey, and softball are played on the park's many sports grounds. Head up to the area around the Hub (☎ 0300/061–2323)—a state-of-the-art sports pavilion—to watch some action. You'll have to book in advance if you want to join in, but you're just as likely to find an informal soccer match anywhere in the park.

■ At the Garden Café (Elnner Circle, Regent's Park ☎ 020/7935–5729), enjoy breakfast, lunch, or supper on a patio next to the rose gardens, or take away some smoked-salmon bagels for a picnic. Stop by Cow and Coffee Bean (The Boardwalk; ☎ 020/7224-3872) for a coffee or some delicious, organic Cornish ice cream.

■ Check the Regent's Park Open-Air Theatre schedule—they have been mounting summer Shakespeare productions here since 1932 (☎ 0844/826–4242 ⊕ www.openairtheatre.org). Don't leave without exploring the London Zoo—it's at the very edge of the park on the northeastern side.

Cultivated and formal, compared with the relative wildness of Hampstead Heath, Regent's Park was laid out in 1812 by John Nash in honor of the Prince Regent, who was later crowned George IV. The idea was to re-create the feel of a grand country residence close to the center of town. Most of Nash's plans were carried out successfully, although the focus of it all—a palace for the prince—was never built. Now the park is a favorite destination for sporty types and dog owners. Not for nothing did Dodie Smith set her novel *A Hundred and One Dalmatians* in an Outer Circle house. (Nearby, along East Heath Road, is the Gothic manse that inspired Cruella DeVil's Hell Hall.)

Highlights

The most famous and impressive of Nash's white-stucco terraces facing the park, **Cumberland Terrace** has a central block of Ionic columns surmounted by a triangular Wedgwood-blue pediment that looks like a giant cameo. The noted architectural historian Sir John Summerson described it as "easily the most breathtaking architectural panorama in London."

The **Broad Walk** is a good vantage point from which to glimpse the minaret and the golden dome of the **London Central Mosque** on the far west side of the park. As in all London parks, planting here is planned with the aim of having something in bloom in all seasons, but if you hit the park in summer, head first to the Inner Circle. Your nostrils should lead you to **Queen Mary's Gardens**, a fragrant 17-acre circle that riots with 400 different varieties of roses in summer.

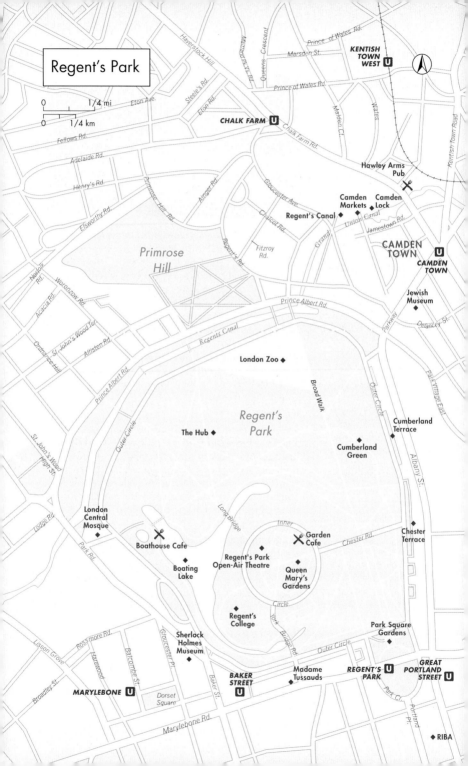

Regent's Park

0   1/4 mi
0   1/4 km

KENTISH TOWN WEST Ⓤ

Prince of Wates Rd.
Marsden St.

Haverstock Hill
Mansfield Rd.
Queens Crescent
Prince of Wales Rd.

CHALK FARM Ⓤ

Eton Ave.
Steele's Rd.
Eton Rd.
Chalk Farm Rd.
Marsden Ct.
Wates
Kentish Town Road

Fellows Rd.

Hawley Arms Pub 🍴

Adelaide Rd.

Gloucester Ave.

Camden Markets
Camden Lock
Regent's Canal ◆
Union Canal
Jamestown Rd.

CAMDEN TOWN
Ⓤ
CAMDEN TOWN

Henry's Rd.
Elsworthy Rd.
Primrose Hill Rd.
Arnger Rd.
Chalcot Rd.
Regent's Rd.
Fitzroy Rd.
Grand

Primrose Hill

Narfolk Rd.
Acacia Rd.
Woronzow Rd.
St. John's Wood Ter.
Ordnance Hill
Allisten Rd.

Prince Albert Rd.

Jewish Museum ◆
Parkway
Delancey St.

Prince Albert Rd.

Regents Canal

London Zoo ◆

Broad Walk

Regent's Park

Outer Circle
Park Village East
Albany St.

Cumberland Terrace ◆

The Hub ◆

Cumberland Green ◆

St. John's Wood High St.
Outer Circle

Lodge Rd.

London Central Mosque ◆

Long Bridge

Inner

Garden Cafe 🍴

Chester Rd.

Chester Terrace ◆

Park Rd.

Boathouse Cafe 🍴

Boating Lake ◆

Regent's Park Open-Air Theatre ◆

Queen Mary's Gardens ◆

Circle

York Bridge Rd.

Regent's College ◆

Park Square Gardens ◆

Lisson Grove
Rossmore Rd.
Harewood
Gloucester Pl.
Balcombe St.
Baker St.

Sherlock Holmes Museum ◆

Circle

Outer Circle

REGENT'S PARK Ⓤ

GREAT PORTLAND STREET Ⓤ

Broadley St.

MARYLEBONE Ⓤ

Dorset Square

BAKER STREET Ⓤ

Madame Tussauds ◆

Park Cr.

Portland Pl.

Marylebone Rd.

◆ RIBA

221B Baker Street and "Holmes" himself.

Hawley Arms Pub. Just around the corner, the Hawley Arms Pub gained fame as a hangout for celebrities such as Kate Moss and the late Amy Winehouse. It's a good spot for an inexpensive pub lunch. ⊠ *2 Castlehaven Rd., Camden Town* ☎ *020/7428–5979* ⊕ *www. thehawleyarms.co.uk.*

QUICK BITES

You will not go hungry in Camden Town, with its countless cafés, bars, and pubs, plus appealing restaurants at all price points on Parkway. Within the market at Camden Lock there are various stalls selling the usual hot dogs and burgers, but you can also find good value at the stalls selling ethnic food if you don't mind standing as you eat outdoors, or perching on a canal-side bench.

Jewish Museum. This fascinating museum on the history of the Jewish people in British contains precious little from before the 17th century—and with good reason. Judaism was outlawed in England for almost four centuries, until the Jews were finally allowed to settle once more in 1656. "History: A British Story" provides a general overview of this and other facets of the Jewish story in Britain over the centuries, through a mix of rare artifacts and interactive displays. The Holocaust Gallery features the incredible story of Leon Greenman (1910–2008), a British Jew who survived six concentration camps, including Auschwitz, to become a prominent anti-racism campaigner. Other highlights include a recreation of a street from the Victorian-era Jewish quarter of London's East End. ▮▮TIP➜ There's a free overview of the collection on the ground floor, including a medieval mikveh (ritual bath), excavated a few miles from here in 2001. ⊠ *Raymond Burton House, 129–131 Albert St., Camden Town* 🕾 *020/7284–7384* ⊕ *www.jewishmuseum.org.uk* 🖾 *£7.50* ☉ *Sun.–Thurs. 10–5, Fri. 10–2; last admission 30 min before closing. Closed on major Jewish festivals* Ⓜ *Camden Town.*

Lord's Cricket Ground & Museum. If you can't manage to lay your hands on tickets for a cricket match, the next best thing is to take a tour of the spiritual home of this most English of games. Founded by Thomas Lord, the headquarters of the MCC (Marylebone Cricket Club) opens its "behind the scenes" areas to visitors. You can see the Long Room with cricketing art on display; the players' dressing rooms; and the world's oldest sporting museum, where the progress from gentlemanly village-green game to worldwide sport over 400 years is charted. Don't miss the prize exhibit: the urn containing the sport's most iconic trophy, the Ashes—the remains of a cricket bail (part of the wicket assembly) presented to the English captain in 1883, a jokey allusion to a newspaper's premature obituary for the death of English cricket published after the home team's defeat by Australia. The two nations still play for possession of the Ashes every two years, though only a replica actually changes hands these days. Tours are not available during major matches (it's offered during smaller "county" matches), but the museum remains open to match ticket holders. ⊠ *St. John's Wood Rd., St. John's Wood* 🕾 *020/7616–8595* ⊕ *www.lords.org* 🖾 *£15. Museum only, £7.50 match days* ☉ *Museum Mon.–Fri. 10–5 (hours vary on match days, call to confirm). Tours Apr.–Oct., daily 10–5, except during major matches; Nov.–Mar., weekdays 10, 11, noon, and 2 (no 10 am tour, Jan.–Mar.), weekends 10, 11, noon, 1, and 2.* Ⓜ *St. John's Wood.*

FAMILY **Madame Tussauds.** One of London's busiest tourist attractions, this is nothing less—but also nothing more—than the world's most famous exhibition of lifelike waxwork models of celebrities. Madame T. learned her craft while making death masks of French Revolution victims, and in 1835 she set up her first show of the famous ones near this spot. Top billing still goes to the murderers in the Chamber of Horrors, who stare glassy-eyed at visitors—one from an electric chair, one sitting next to the tin bath where he dissolved several wives in quicklime. What, aside from ghoulish prurience, makes people stand in line to invest in one of London's most expensive museum tickets? It must be the thrill of all those photo opportunities with royalty, Hollywood stars, and world leaders—all in a single day. ■**TIP**➔ Beat the crowds by booking timed entry tickets in advance. You can also buy non-dated, "priority access" tickets via the website (at a premium). ⊠ *Marylebone Rd., Regent's Park* 🕾 *0870/400–3000 for timed entry tickets* ⊕ *www.madame-tussauds. com* 🖾 *£15–£35 according to time; call or check website. Combination ticket with London Eye, London Dungeons, and London Aquarium £35–£57.* ☉ *Early Apr. and mid-July–Aug., daily 9–7; Sept.–Mar. and mid-Apr.–mid-July, weekdays 9–5:30 (last admission), weekends 9:30–6 (last admission)* Ⓜ *Baker St.*

Regent's Park Open-Air Theatre. The theater has mounted productions of Shakespeare every summer since 1932; everyone from Vivien Leigh to Jeremy Irons has performed here. Today it also hosts other plays,

A match being played at Lord's Cricket Ground.

musicals, concerts, and comedy shows. However, *A Midsummer Night's Dream* is the one to catch, if it's on—never is that enchanted Greek wood more lifelike than it is here, enhanced by genuine birdsong and a rising moon. You can buy light suppers or choose from a (somewhat limited) barbecue selection in the evening, or prebook a picnic lunch for matinees. The park can get chilly, so bring a blanket; only very heavy rain stops the plays, in which case you can exchange your ticket (umbrellas aren't allowed during performances). ✉ *Inner Circle, Regent's Park* ☎ *0844/826–4242 tickets, 0844/375–3460 enquiries* ⊕ *www.openairtheatre.org* ✎ *£15–£45* ◷ *June–mid-Sept., evening performances at 8, matinees at 2:30* Ⓜ *Baker St., Regent's Park.*

HAMPSTEAD

John Keats (1795–1821) lived in **Hampstead** as a virtual pauper; you'll find **Keats House**, where the poet wrote his most famous work, among the homes of artistic types who these days are more likely to be millionaire film stars or musicians. However, this neighborhood still retains a gorgeously bohemian vibe, which all but shimmers through the moneyed haze of swank boutiques and artisanal food stores. Perhaps it's something to do with the high concentration of wonderful, atmospheric pubs. Also hidden among Hampstead's winding streets are **Fenton House**, a Georgian town house with a lovely walled garden, and **Kenwood House**, with its remarkable art collection.

Overlooking it all is **Hampstead Heath** (known locally as just "The Heath"), a huge, wild urban park with great views across

PUBS WITH A PAST

Hampstead has some of the most storied pubs in London—although a few have distinctly shady pasts.

Holly Bush. Tucked away down the lolloping hills and leafy sideroads of old Hampstead is this gorgeously unspoiled old pub, built in 1807. The dim, cozy interior has an open fireplace and wooden booths. The classic British food is excellent; take it in the bar with a pint, or in the rather swankier dining room. ⊠ *22 Holly Mount, Hampstead* ☎ *020/7435–2892* ⊕ *hollybushhampstead.co.uk* Ⓜ *Hampstead.*

Magdala. Meanwhile, a much sadder tale is associated with the Magdala, the site of a notorious murder in 1955 for which Ruth Ellis was the last woman in Britain to be hanged. It's a sedate place these days (though weekly events include comedy, quiz, and poetry nights), but the famous bullet holes near the door have been left untouched. ⊠ *2A South Hill Park, Hampstead* ☎ *020/7435–2503* ⊕ *the-magdala. com* Ⓜ *Hampstead Heath.*

Spaniard's Inn. The legendary highwayman Dick Turpin is said to have been born at the Spaniard's Inn, which was once frequented by the likes of Dickens, Shelley, and Stoker. The owners will happily tell you how the latter borrowed one of their many resident ghost stories to furnish the plot of *Dracula*. After a few hours in this atmospheric spot, you might even believe it. ⊠ *Spaniards Rd., Hampstead* ☎ *020/8731–8406* ⊕ *www.thespaniardshampstead.co.uk* Ⓜ *Golders Green, then Bus 210, 268 to Whitestone Pond.*

Wells. A plaque outside this Georgian pub delicately informs visitors that it was originally built to provide "facilities for the celebration of unpremeditated and clandestine marriages." These days the spot is far better known as one of the finest gastropubs in the area. ⊠ *30 Well Walk, Hampstead* ☎ *020/7794–3785* ⊕ *www.thewellshampstead.co.uk* Ⓜ *Hampstead.*

London—although **Primrose Hill** has perhaps the most spectacular view you can find without getting onto the London Eye.

TOP ATTRACTIONS

FAMILY
Fodor's Choice
★

Hampstead Heath. For an escape from the ordered prettiness of Hampstead, head to the Heath—a unique remnant of London's pre-industrial countryside, with habitats ranging from wide grasslands to ancient woodlands spread over some 791 acres. **Parliament Hill**, one of the highest points in London, offers a stunning panorama over the city. There are signposted paths, but these can be confusing, so pick up a map at ⇨ *Kenwood House*, or the Education Centre near the Lido off Gordon House Road, where you can also get details about the history of the Heath and the flora and fauna growing there. An excellent café near the Athletics Field offers light refreshment under the trees. ⊠ *Hampstead* ☎ *020/7482–7073 Heath Education Centre* ⊕ *www.cityoflondon. gov.uk/hampstead* 🖼 *Free* Ⓜ *Gospel Oak, Hampstead Heath for south of Heath; Hampstead for east of Heath; Golders Green, then Bus 210, 268 to Whitestone Pond for north and west of Heath.*

11

Highgate Cemetery. Highgate is not the oldest cemetery in London, but it is probably the best known. After it was consecrated in 1839, Victorians came from miles around to appreciate the ornate headstones, the impressive tombs, and the view. Such was its popularity that 19 acres on the other side of the road were acquired in 1850, and this additional East Cemetery contains what may be the most visited grave—of Karl Marx (1818–83)—and those of a host of other famous names, including George Eliot (1819–80) and Malcolm McLaren (1946–2010). At the summit is the **Circle of Lebanon**, a ring of vaults built around an ancient cypress tree—a legacy of 17th-century gardens that occupied the site. Leading from the circle is the **Egyptian Avenue,** a subterranean stone tunnel lined with catacombs, itself approached by a dramatic colonnade that screens the main cemetery from the road. Both sides are impressive, with a grand (locked) iron gate leading to a sweeping courtyard built for the approach of horses and carriages. By the 1970s the cemetery had become unkempt and neglected until a group of volunteers, the Friends of Highgate Cemetery, undertook the huge upkeep. Tours are arranged by the Friends, and they will show you the most notable graves among the huge variety of statues and memorials once hidden by overgrowth. East side tours are limited to 15 and tickets are sold on a first-come, first-served basis. The west side is accessible only by tour, though these can be booked ahead. You're expected to dress respectfully, though in practice this just means erring on the conservative side. ■**TIP**➜ Children under eight are not admitted; nor are dogs, tripods, or video cameras. ⊠ *Swains La., Highgate* ☎ *020/8340–1834* ⊕ *www.highgate-cemetery. org* ⊠ *East Cemetery £3, tours £7; West Cemetery tours £7. No credit cards* ⊙ *Daily; usually Apr.–Oct. 10–5, Nov.–Mar. 10–3:30, but call ahead as hrs vary according to whether a funeral service is scheduled. East Cemetery tours, Sat. 2. West Cemetery tours, Mar.–Nov., weekdays 1:45, weekends hourly 11–3* Ⓜ *Archway, then Bus 210, 271, or 143 to Highgate Village.*

Keats House. It was in February 1820 that John Keats (1795–1821) coughed blood up into his handkerchief and exclaimed, "That drop of blood is my death warrant. I must die." He duly left his beloved home in Hampstead and moved to Rome, where he died of consumption, at just 25. Here you can see the plum tree under which the young Romantic poet composed *Ode to a Nightingale*; many of his original manuscripts; his library; and other possessions he managed to acquire in his short life. There are frequent guided tours and special events, such as poetry readings. The house has been restored to its original Regency style of decoration, and the design of the gardens is inspired by elements of Keats' poetry, such as "autumn" and "nightingale." The ticket gives you entry for a full year, so you can come back as often as you like. ■**TIP**➜ Picnics can be taken into the grounds during the summer. ⊠ *Wentworth Pl., Keats Grove, Hampstead* ☎ *020/7332–3868* ⊕ *www.keatshouse.cityoflondon.gov.uk* ⊠ *£5* ⊙ *Apr.–Oct., Tues.–Sun. 1–5; Nov.–Mar., Fri.–Sun. 1–5; closed Good Friday and Christmas wk* Ⓜ *Hampstead; North London Line overground: Hampstead Heath from Highbury & Islington.*

The fabled cover of the Beatles *Abbey Road* album, with the world's most famous traffic crossing.

FAMILY **Kenwood House.** This gracious Georgian villa was first built in 1616 and remodeled by Robert Adam between 1764 and 1779. Adam refaced most of the exterior and added the splendid library, which, with its curved painted ceiling and gilded detail, is the highlight of the house for lovers of the decorative arts and interior design. Kenwood is also home to the **Iveagh Bequest,** an extraordinary collection of paintings that the Earl of Iveagh gave the nation in 1927, including a wonderful self-portrait by Rembrandt and works by Reynolds, Van Dyck, Hals, Gainsborough, and Turner. Most iconic amongst them is Vermeer's *Guitar Player,* considered by many to be among the most beautiful paintings in the world. In front of the house, a graceful lawn slopes down to a little lake crossed by a trompe-l'oeil bridge—all in perfect 18th-century upper-class taste. The grounds are skirted by Hampstead Heath. ▥TIP➔ In summer the grounds host a series of popular and classical concerts, culminating in fireworks on the last night. The Brew House café, occupying part of the old coach house, has outdoor tables in the courtyard and terraced garden. ✉ *Hampstead La., Hampstead* ☎ *020/8348–1286* ⊕ *www.english-heritage.org.uk* ⊠ *Free* ⊗ *House daily 11:30–4. Gardens daily dawn–dusk* Ⓜ *Golders Green, then Bus 210.*

WORTH NOTING

Burgh House. One of Hampstead's oldest buildings, Burgh House was built in 1704 to take advantage of the natural spa waters of the then-fashionable Hampstead Wells. A private house until World War II, Burgh was saved from near-dereliction in the 1970s by local residents, who have been restoring and maintaining it ever since. The building is a fine example of the gentle elegance common to the Queen Anne period,

A TRIP TO ABBEY ROAD

11

For countless Beatlemaniacs and baby boomers, No. 3 Abbey Road is one of the most beloved spots in London. Here, outside the legendary Abbey Road Studios, is the most famous zebra crossing in the world, immortalized on the Beatles' 1969 *Abbey Road* album. This footpath became a mod monument when, on August 8 of that year, John, Paul, George, and Ringo posed for photographer Iain Macmillan's famous cover shot. The recording facility's Studio 2 is where the Beatles recorded their entire output, from "Love Me Do" onward, including *Sgt. Pepper's Lonely Hearts Club Band* (early 1967).

Meanwhile, there's never any shortage of tourists re-creating "the photo" outside. ▥ TIP➡ Be very careful if you're going to attempt this. Abbey Road is a dangerous intersection. One of the best—and safer—ways Beatle lovers can enjoy the history of the group is to take one of the excellent walking tours offered by **Original London Walks** (☎ 020/7624-3978 ⊕ www.walks. com), including **The Beatles In-My-Life Walk** (11:20 am outside Marylebone Underground on Saturday and Tuesday) and **The Beatles Magical Mystery Tour** (Wednesday at 2 pm, February to November, and Thursday and Sunday at 11 am, year-round, at Underground Exit 3, Tottenham Court Road), which cover nostalgic landmark Beatles spots in the city.

Abbey Road is in the elegant neighborhood of St. John's Wood, a 10-minute ride on the Tube from central London. Take the Jubilee line to the St. John's Wood Tube stop, head southwest three blocks down Grove End Road, and be prepared for a view right out of Memory Lane.

with its redbrick box frontage, oak panelled rooms, and terraced garden (originally designed by Gertrude Jekyll). Today the house contains a small but diverting museum on the history of the area, and also hosts regular talks, concerts, and recitals. The secluded garden courtyard of the café is a lovely spot for lunch, tea, or glass of wine on a summer's afternoon. Call ahead if you're visiting the on a weekend, however, as the house is often hired out as a wedding venue on Saturdays. ⊠ *New End Square, Hampstead* ☎ *020/7431–0144* ⊕ *www.burghhouse.org. uk* ⊠ *Free* ۩ *Wed.–Sun. noon–5* Ⓜ *Hampstead.*

Fenton House. Hampstead's oldest surviving house, a National Trust property, shows off a fine collections of porcelain and Georgian furniture and has a superb walled garden, complete with an apple orchard that dates back to the 17th century. Baroque music enthusiasts can join a tour of the important collection of keyboard instruments, and there's a summer series of concerts on these very same instruments on Thursday evenings. Check the website for details. ⊠ *Hampstead Grove, Hampstead* ☎ *020/7435–3471* ⊕ *www.nationaltrust.org.uk* ⊠ *£7, garden only £2* ۩ *Mar.–Nov., Wed.–Sun. 11–5; Dec., weekends 11–4* Ⓜ *Hampstead.*

Freud Museum. The father of psychoanalysis lived here for a year, between his escape from Nazi persecution in his native Vienna in 1938 and his death in 1939. Many of his possessions emigrated with him and were set up by his daughter, Anna (herself a pioneer of child psychoanalysis), as a shrine to her father's life and work. Shortly after Anna's death in 1982 the house was opened as a museum. It replicates Freud's famous consulting rooms, particularly through the presence of *the* couch. You'll find Freud-related books, lectures, and study groups here, too. ■ TIP→ Looking for a unique souvenir for the person who has everything? The gift shop here sells "Freudean Slippers." ⊠ *20 Maresfield Gardens, Hampstead* ☎ *020/7435–2002* ⊕ *www.freud.org.uk* ⌂ *£6* ⊘ *Wed.–Sun. noon–5* Ⓜ *Swiss Cottage, Finchley Rd.*

GREENWICH

GETTING ORIENTED

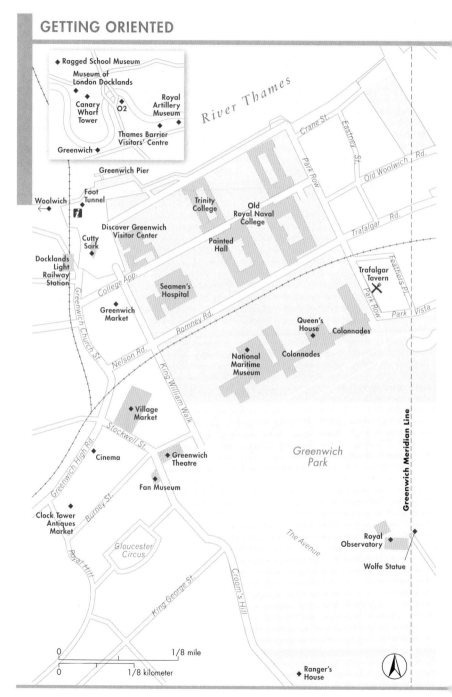

TOP REASONS TO GO

Stand astride the Greenwich Meridian Line: At the Royal Observatory—where the world's time is set—you can be in the eastern and western hemispheres simultaneously.

Sir Inigo Jones's Queen's House: This 17th-century building was massively influential in its day as the first in England to embrace the styles of the Italian Renaissance. See what all the fuss was about.

Old Royal Naval College: Come to the chapel at lunchtime to catch a free concert by one of Britain's most prestigious music schools.

Discover Britain's seafaring past at the **National Maritime Museum:** See how Britannia ruled the waves and helped shape the modern world.

Step aboard the *Cutty Sark*: Take a stroll along the deck of the last surviving 19th-century tea clipper, newly shipshape after years of renovation.

FEELING PECKISH?

The Honest Sausage. Right next to the Maritime Museum, this delightful little café is a great pit stop for a traditional lunchtime snack. It specializes in straight-down-the-line, traditional sausage or bacon sandwiches, all sourced from an organic, free-range farm in Gloucester. And if a porcine snack doesn't curl your tail, you can opt for cake or coffee instead. ⊠ *Pavillion Tea House, Blackheath Ave., Greenwich Park, Greenwich* ☎ *020/8858–9695* ⊕ *www.companyofcooks.com.*

Trafalgar Tavern. With its excellent vista of the Thames, there is no more handsomely situated pub in Greenwich than the Trafalgar Tavern. Featured in Charles Dickens's *Our Mutual Friend*, it's still as grand a place to have a pint and some (upscale) pub grub as it ever was. ⊠ *Park Row, Greenwich* ☎ *020/8858–2909* ⊕ *www.trafalgartavern.co.uk.*

GETTING THERE

Docklands Light Railway (DLR) is a zippy way to get to Cutty Sark station, from Canary Wharf and Bank Tube stations in The City. Or take the DLR to Island Gardens and walk the old Victorian Foot Tunnel under the river. (Sitting at the front of a train can be disconcerting, as you watch the controls in the fully automated driver's cab move about, as if a ghost were at the helm.) The best way to arrive, however—time and weather permitting—is like a sea captain of old: by water (though this way takes an hour from central London; *for more on cruising the Thames, see Chapter 13*).

MAKING THE MOST OF YOUR TIME

Set apart from the rest of London, Greenwich is worth a day to itself—those who love maritime history will want to spend at least two—to make the most of walks in the rolling parklands and to immerse yourself in the richness of Greenwich's history, science, and architecture. The boat trip takes about an hour from Westminster Pier (next to Big Ben), or 25 minutes from the Tower of London, so factor in enough time for the round-trip.

NEAREST PUBLIC RESTROOMS

Duck into the tourist information center (near the Old Royal Naval College), where loos are free.

Sightseeing
★★★★
Nightlife
★
Dining
★★
Lodging
★
Shopping
★★★

About 8 miles downstream—which means seaward, to the east—from central London lies a destination you'd think had been conceived to provide the perfect day out. The small borough of Greenwich is only small in size: it actually looms large in the world. It is not only home to the Old Royal Observatory, which measures time for our entire planet, but also the Greenwich Meridian, which divides the world into two (you can stand astride it with one foot in either hemisphere).

Updated by
Jack Jewers

Bear in mind that the journey to Greenwich is an event in itself. In a rush, you can take the driverless DLR train—but many opt for arriving by boat along the Thames. This way, you glide past famous sights on the London skyline (there's a guaranteed spine chill on passing the Tower) and ever-changing docklands, and there's usually a cockney navigator enlivening the journey with his fun commentary.

A visit to Greenwich feels like a trip to a rather elegant seaside town—albeit one with more than its fair share of historic sites. The grandiose **Old Royal Naval Hospital,** designed by Christopher Wren, was originally a home for veteran sailors. Today it's a popular visitor attraction, with a more glamorous second life as one of the most widely used movie locations in Britain.

Greenwich was originally home to one of England's finest Tudor palaces, and the birthplace of Henry VIII, Elizabeth I, and Mary I. Inigo Jones built what is considered the first "classical" building in England in 1616—the **Queen's House,** which now houses a collection of fine art. Right next door, the excellent **National Maritime Museum** details the history of the glorious seafaring past of Britain, this island kingdom. Its prize exhibits include the coat worn by Admiral Lord Nelson (1758–1805) in his final battle—bullet hole and all. The 19th-century tea clipper **_Cutty Sark_** was nearly destroyed by fire in 2007, but reopened in 2012 after a painstaking restoration. Now it's more pristine than ever, complete with an impressive new visitor center.

Greenwich Park, London's oldest royal park, is still home to fallow red deer, just as it has been since they were first introduced here for hunting by Henry VIII. The **Ranger's House** now houses a private art collection, next door to a beautifully manicured rose garden. Above it all is the **Royal Observatory**, where you can be in two hemispheres at once by standing along the **Greenwich Meridian Line**, before seeing a high-tech planetarium show.

In town, opposite the Greenwich Theatre, the **Fan Museum** is home to 4,000 fans dating as far back as the 11th century. The **Clock Tower Antiques Market** and the lively **Greenwich Market** keep bargain-hunters busy on weekends.

Toward north Greenwich, the hopelessly ambitious Millennium Dome has been successfully reborn as the O2 and now hosts major concerts and stand-up comedy gigs. In the opposite direction, downstream in Woolwich, lies the modern engineering marvel of the **Thames Flood Barrier**. And just a couple of miles south of the borough is the shamefully underappreciated **Eltham Palace**; once a favorite of Henry VIII, parts of the mansion were transformed into an art deco masterpiece during the 1930s.

TOP ATTRACTIONS

Fodor's Choice ★ **Cutty Sark.** This sleek, romantic clipper was built in 1869, one among fleets and fleets of tall-masted wooden ships that plied the oceanic highways of the 19th century, trading in exotic commodities—in this case, tea. *Cutty Sark* (named after an old Scottish term for women's undergarments) was the fastest, sailing the London–China route in 1871 in only 107 days. The clipper has been preserved in dry docks as a museum ship since the 1950s, but was severely damaged in a devastating fire in 2007. As luck would have it, however, roughly half the ship had been dismantled and taken away for cleaning at the time. The ship re-opened in 2012, with hugely improved visitor facilities; not only can you tour the painstakingly restored ship in its entirety, but the glittering new visitor center (above which the ship now rests, in an enormous gold mount) allows you to view the hull from below. A veritable museum of seafaring life, this boat was never too comfortable for the 28-strong crew (as you'll see). And don't forget to take in the very amusing collection of figureheads. ⊠ *King William Walk, Greenwich* ☎ *020/8858–4422* ⊕ *www.rmg.co.uk* ⊡*£12* ☉ *Daily 10–5; last admission 4* Ⓜ *DLR: Cutty Sark.*

Discover Greenwich. Intended as a kind of anchor point for Greenwich's big three attractions—the Old Royal Naval College, *Cutty Sark,* and National Maritime Museum—this excellent, state-of-the-art visitor center includes interactive exhibitions on the history of Greenwich, plus an assortment of local treasures and artifacts. Most intriguing among them is a 17th-century "witch bottle," once used to ward off evil spirits.

ROYAL OBSERVATORY

✉ *Romney Rd., Greenwich* ☎ *020/8858–4422* ⊕ *www. rog.nmm.ac.uk* 🖾 *Astronomy Galleries free; Flamsteed house and Meridian Line courtyard £7; planetarium shows £6.50; combined ticket £11.50* ⊙ *Daily 10–5 (May–Aug., Meridian court-yard until 6); last entry 30 min before closing; last planetarium show 4* Ⓜ *DLR: Greenwich.*

TIPS

■ A brass line laid among the cobblestones here marks the meridian, one side being the Eastern, one the Western hemisphere. As darkness falls, a funky green laser shoots out across London for several miles, following exactly the path of the meridian line.

■ The Time Ball atop Flamsteed House is one of the world's earliest time signals. Each day at 12:55, it rises halfway up its mast. At 12:58 it rises all the way to the top, and at 1 exactly, the ball falls.

■ The steep hill that is home to the observatory gives fantastic views across London, topped off with £1-a-slot telescopes to scour the skyline. Time a walk to catch the golden glow of late-afternoon sun on Canary Wharf Tower and head back into Greenwich via the rose garden behind Ranger's House. Youngsters under five are not usually allowed into the auditorium. Tickets can be purchased ahead online.

Greenwich is on the prime meridian at 0° longitude, and the ultimate standard for time around the world has been set here since 1884, when Britain was the world's largest and most important maritime power.

Highlights

The observatory is actually split into two sites, a short walk apart—one devoted to astronomy, the other to the study of time. The enchanting **Peter Harrison Planetarium** is London's only planetarium, its bronze-clad turret poking out of the ground like a crashed UFO. Shows on black holes and how to interpret the night sky are enthralling and enlightening. Even better for kids are the high-technology rooms of the **Astronomy Galleries,** where cutting-edge touch screens and interactive programs give young explorers the chance to run their own space missions to Ganymede, one of Jupiter's moons.

Across the way is **Flamsteed House,** designed by Christopher Wren in 1675 for John Flamsteed, the first Royal Astronomer. A climb to the top of the house reveals the **28-inch telescope,** built in 1893 and now housed inside an onion-shaped fiberglass dome. It doesn't compare with the range of modern optical telescopes, but it's still the largest in the U.K. Regular viewing evenings reveal startlingly detailed views of the lunar surface. In the **Time Galleries,** linger over the superb workmanship of John Harrison (1693–1776), whose famous **Maritime Clocks** won him the Longitude Prize for solving the problem of accurate timekeeping at sea and greatly improved navigation.

Rome 12° ... E
Istanbul 28° ... E

Beijing 116° ... E

Athens 23° ... E
Seoul 127° ... E
Tokyo 139° ... E
Tehran 51° ... E

New York 75° ... W
Madrid 3° ... W
Washington 77° ... W
Albany 45° ... W

Los Angeles 118° ... W
Guadalajara 2° ... W
Dallas 96° ... W
Portsmouth 44° ... W

Jerusalem ...
Cairo 31° ...

Bahamas 78° ... W

Riyadh ...

Hong ...
Han ...

Havana 821° ... W
Nashville 1571° ... W
Mexico City 89° ... W

Kingston 761° ... W

Rangoon 96° ... E

... 39° ... W

DID YOU KNOW?

Once sailors could deter-mine their distance from the Greenwich meridian (longi-tude), maritime navigation was greatly improved. Look for the brass line marking the two hemispheres throughout the cobblestone streets.

Modern x-rays have revealed it to contain a mixture of human hair, fingernails, and urine. ✉ *Pepys Bldg., King William Walk, Greenwich* ☎ *020/8269–4799* ⊕ *www.ornc.org* ✈ *Free* ☉ *Daily 10–5* Ⓜ *DLR: Greenwich.*

Fodor's Choice ★ **Eltham Palace.** Once a favorite getaway for Henry VIII (who liked to spend Christmas here), Eltham Palace has been drastically remodeled twice in its lifetime; once during the 15th and 16th centuries, and again during the 1930s, when a grand mansion was annexed onto the Tudor great hall by the superwealthy Coulthard family. Today it's an extraordinary combination of late medieval grandeur and Art Deco masterpiece, laced with an eccentric whimsy—the Coulthards even built an entire room as the personal quarters of their beloved pet

> ## GREENWICH FOOT TUNNEL
>
> In a brilliant piece of foresight in 1849, Greenwich Hospital bought Island Gardens, on the other side of the Thames, to guard against industrial sprawl and preserve one of the most beautiful views in London. Take the stone spiral steps down into Greenwich Foot Tunnel and head under the Thames (enjoying the magnificently creepy echo) to Island Gardens, at the southern tip of the Isle of Dogs. Then look back over the river for a magnificent vista: the Old Royal Naval College and Queen's House in all their glory, framed by the verdant green borders of the park.

lemur. The house and its extensive gardens were fully restored when the palace finally entered public ownership in the late 1990s. ✉ *Court Rd., Eltham* ☎ *020/8294–2548* ⊕ *www.english-heritage.org.uk* ✈ *£9.60* ☉ *Apr.–Oct., and late Feb. school holiday Sun.–Wed. 10–5; Nov.–Feb., Sun. 10–6* Ⓜ *Eltham.*

Greenwich Market. Established as a fruit-and-vegetable market in 1700, and granted a royal charter in 1849, the covered market now offers mixed stalls of art and crafts on Wednesday, Saturday, and Sunday; antiques, and collectibles on Tuesday, Thursday, and Friday. You can get food-to-go on each market day, although the offerings are usually best on weekends. Shopping for handicrafts is a pleasure here, as in most cases you're buying directly from the artist. ✉ *College Approach, Greenwich* ☎ *020/8269–5093* ⊕ *www.shopgreenwich.co.uk* ☉ *Tues.– Sun. 10–5:30* Ⓜ *DLR: Cutty Sark.*

Museum of London Docklands. This wonderful old warehouse building, on a quaint cobbled quayside, beside the tower of Canary Wharf, is alone worth a visit. With uneven wood floors, beams, and pillars, the museum used to be a storehouse for coffee, tea, sugar, and rum from the West Indies—hence the name West India Quay. The fascinating story of the old port and the river is told using films, together with interactive displays and reconstructions; a permanent exhibition, London, Sugar and Slavery, highlights the capital's involvement in the slave trade. The museum runs a highlights tour (free) on Wednesday and Sunday at 3 pm. There are also a few special themed tours per season; call or see the website for details. ■ TIP→ On the second Friday of every month the museum hosts the Docklands Cinema Club, which shows rare and classic films, together with talks, inside the old warehouse. ✉ *No. 1 Warehouse,*

Without a central support, the Tulip Stair spirals up to the Great Hall of Queen's House.

West India Quay, Canary Wharf, Canary Wharf ☎ *020/7001–9844* ⊕ *www.museumindocklands.org.uk* ✉ *Free* ☉ *Daily 10–6; last admission at 5:40* Ⓜ *Canary Wharf; DLR: West India Quay.*

Fodor's Choice ★ **National Maritime Museum.** From the time of Henry VIII until the 1940s Britain was the world's preeminent naval power, and the collections here trace half a millennia of that seafaring history. The story is as much about trade as it is warfare; the "Atlantic Worlds" gallery explores how trade in goods—and people—helped shape the New World, while "Voyagers: Britons and the Sea" focuses on stories of the ordinary people who took to the waves over the centuries. One gallery is devoted to Admiral Lord Nelson, Britain's most famous naval commander, and among the exhibits is the uniform he was wearing, complete with bloodstains, when he died at the Battle of Trafalgar in 1805. Temporary exhibitions here are usually fascinating; those in recent years have included the Arctic convoys of World War II and the history of piracy. ▓ TIP➜ The museum has a good café with views over Greenwich Park. The adjacent **Queen's House** is home to the museum's art collection, the largest collection of maritime art in the world, including works by William Hogarth, Canaletto, and Joshua Reynolds. Permission for its construction was granted by Queen Anne only on condition that the river vista from the house be preserved, and there are few more majestic views in London than Inigo Jones's awe-inspiring symmetry. Completed around 1638, the Tulip Stair, named for the fleur-de-lis-style pattern on the balustrade, is especially fine, spiraling up without a central support to the Great Hall. The Great Hall itself is a perfect cube, exactly 40 feet in all three dimensions, decorated with paintings of the Muses

DID YOU KNOW?

The Docklands Light Railway (DLR) connects former warehouses that have been converted to museums and malls, such as Hay's and Butler's wharves, and the gleaming office buildings of Canary Wharf shown here.

THE DOCKLANDS RENAISSANCE

For centuries the Thames was a fevered hub of activity. Great palaces were built along the river, most long gone (such as Whitehall, which dwarfed even Versailles in splendor). Dock warehouses sprang up to the east of London in the 18th century to cater to the burgeoning trade in luxury goods, from tea, coffee, and spices to silks and exotic pets. By the 1950s, however, this trade had all but disappeared—partly due to the devastation of World War II, but also because trading vessels had simply gotten too big to fit along the river. The area all but died away until a massive regeneration scheme known as Docklands was completed in the 1980s. It brought renewal in the form of cutting-edge architecture, galleries, restaurants, and bars. Many of the old warehouses were restored and are now used as museums or shopping malls, such as Hay's and Butler's Wharves. The best way to explore is on the **Docklands Light Railway (DLR)**, an elevated track that appears to skim over the water past the swanky glass buildings. If you explore on foot, the Thames Path has helpful plaques along the way, with nuggets of historical information.

12

and the Virtues. ⊠ *Romney Rd., Greenwich* ☎ *020/8858–4422* ⊕ *www. rmg.co.uk* ⊠ *Free* ☉ *Daily 10–5; last admission 30 min before closing* Ⓜ *DLR: Greenwich.*

Old Royal Naval College. Begun by Christopher Wren in 1694 as a rest home for ancient mariners, the college became instead a school for young ones in 1873. Today the University of Greenwich and Trinity College of Music have classes here. Architecturally, you'll notice how the structures part to reveal the **Queen's House** across the central lawns. Behind the college are two more buildings you can visit: the **Painted Hall,** the college's dining hall, derives its name from the baroque murals of William and Mary (reigned 1689–95; William alone 1695–1702) and assorted allegorical figures. James Thornhill's frescoes, depicting scenes of naval grandeur with a suitably pro-British note of propaganda, were painstakingly done over installments in 1708–12 and 1718–26, and were good enough to earn him a knighthood. In the opposite building stands the **College Chapel,** which was rebuilt after a fire in 1779 in an altogether more restrained, neo-Grecian style. ▇ TIP→ Check the website for special events. Trinity College of Music holds free classical music concerts in the chapel every Tuesday lunchtime during the school year. ⊠ *Old Royal Naval College, King William Walk, Greenwich* ☎ *020/8269–4747* ⊕ *www.ornc.org* ⊠ *Free, guided tours £6* ☉ *Painted Hall and chapel daily 10–5 (Sun. chapel from 12:30); grounds 8–6* Ⓜ *DLR: Greenwich.*

Royal Observatory.
See the highlighted listing in this chapter.

WORTH NOTING

Clock Tower Antiques Market. The weekend Clock Tower Antiques Market on Greenwich High Road has vintage shopping, and browsing among the "small collectibles" makes for a good half-hour diversion. ⊠ *166 Greenwich High Rd., Greenwich* ⊕ *www.clocktowermarket.co.uk* ⊙ *Weekends 10–5* Ⓜ *Greenwich Rail.*

Fan Museum. An arcane but frequently alluring marriage between art and function, the simple fan is more than a mere fashion accessory; historically, fans can tell as much about craftsmanship and social mores as they can about fashion. There are 2,000 of them here, dating from the 17th century onward, often exquisitely crafted from ivory, mother-of-pearl, and tortoiseshell. It was the personal vision of Helene Alexander that brought this enchanting museum into being, and the workshop and conservation–study center that she has also set up ensure that this art form continues to have a future. If your interest is really piqued, you can attend 3-hour fan-making workshops on the first Saturday of every month (£20 for the afternoon, and you have to bring your own paper. Call ahead or visit the website for booking details.). ▇ TIP➜ Afternoon tea is served in the café on Tuesday and Sunday at 2:45 and 3:45 pm—a great value at £6. ⊠ *12 Crooms Hill, Greenwich* ☎ *020/8305–1441* ⊕ *www. fan-museum.org* ⌂ *£4; £5 with tour* ⊙ *Tues.–Sat. 11–5, Sun. noon–5* Ⓜ *DLR: Cutty Sark.*

FAMILY **Ragged School Museum.** In its time, the Ragged School Museum was the largest school in London and a place where impoverished children could get free education and a good meal. The museum re-creates a classroom dating from the 1880s. It's an eye-opener for adults, and fun for kids, who get the chance to work just like Victorian children did in one of the many organized workshops. ▇ TIP➜ If you really want to get into the spirit, visitors of all ages can attend a Victorian-style lesson (first Sunday of every month, 2:15–3:30), complete with a fully costumed schoolmistress who tests your slate-writing technique—and might give you a dunce hat if you're naughty. ⊠ *46–50 Copperfield Rd., Mile End* ☎ *020/8980–6405* ⊕ *www.raggedschoolmuseum.org.uk* ⌂ *Free; £2 donation requested for Victorian lessons* ⊙ *Wed. and Thurs. 10–5, 1st Sun. of month 2–5* Ⓜ *Mile End; DLR: Limehouse.*

THE THAMES UPSTREAM

GETTING ORIENTED

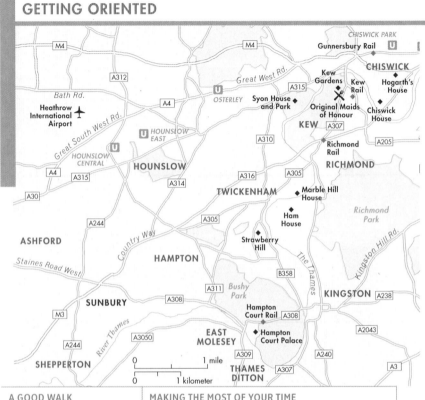

A GOOD WALK	MAKING THE MOST OF YOUR TIME
From Chiswick House, follow Burlington Lane and take a left onto Hogarth Lane—which, in reality, is anything but a lane—to reach Hogarth's House. Chiswick's Church Street (reached by a rather unappealing underpass from Hogarth's House) is the nearest thing to a sleepy country village street you're likely to find in London. Follow it down to the Thames and turn left at the bottom to reach the 18th-century riverfront houses of Chiswick Mall, referred to by locals as "Millionaire's Row." There are several pretty riverside pubs near Hammersmith Bridge.	Hampton Court Palace requires at least half a day to fully experience its magic, although you could make do with a couple of hours for any of the other attractions. Because of the distance between the sights, too much traveling eats into your day. Best to concentrate on one principal sight, add in a stately home or village stroll, then a riverside promenade before a pint at a pub.

FEELING PECKISH?

The Original Maids of Honour. This most traditional of Old English tearooms, is named for a type of jam tart invented here and still baked by hand on the premises. Legend has it that Henry VIII loved them so much he had the recipe kept under guard. Tea is served daily 2:30–6, lunch in two sittings at 12:30 and 1:30. Or opt for take-out to picnic at Kew Gardens or on Kew Green. ⊠ 288 Kew Rd., Kew ☎ 020/8940–2752 ⊕ www.theoriginalmaidsofhonour.co.uk.

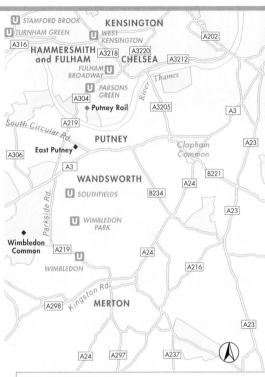

13

GETTING THERE

The District line is the best of the Tube options, stopping at Turnham Green (in the heart of Chiswick but a fair walk from the houses), Gunnersbury (for Syon Park), Kew Gardens, and Richmond. For Hampton Court, overland train is your quickest option: South West trains run from Waterloo twice an hour, with most requiring a change at Surbiton. There are also regular, direct trains from Waterloo to Chiswick station (best for Chiswick House), Kew Bridge, Richmond (for Ham House), and St. Margaret's (best for Marble Hill House). London overground trains also stop at Gunnersbury, Kew Gardens, and Richmond.

A pleasant, if slow, way to go is by river. Boats depart upriver from Westminster Pier, by Big Ben, for Kew (1½ hours), Richmond (2 hours), and Hampton Court (3 hours). The boat trip is worth taking only if you make it an integral part of your day out, and be aware that it can get very breezy on the water. The round-trip costs around £23; for more details contact **Transport For London** (☎ *0843/222–1234* ⊕ *www.tfl.co.uk*).

TOP REASONS TO GO

Explore Hampton Court Palace: Go ghost hunting or just admire the beautiful Tudor architecture at Henry VIII's beloved home, then lose yourself in the maze as dusk begins to fall.

Go "Goth" at Strawberry Hill: The 19th-century birthplace of connoisseur Horace Walpole's "Gothick" style, this mock-castle is a joyous riot of color and invention.

Escape to magical Kew Gardens: See the earth from above by visiting Kew's treetop walkway at the famous Royal Botanic Gardens.

Pay your respects to Father Thames: Enjoy a pint from the creaking balcony of a centuries-old riverside pub as you watch the boats row by on the loveliest stretch of England's greatest river.

NEAREST PUBLIC RESTROOMS

Richmond Park, Kew Gardens, and all the stately homes have public restrooms.

Sightseeing
★★★★
Nightlife
★★
Dining
★★★
Lodging
★★
Shopping
★★

The upper stretch of the Thames links a string of fashionable districts—Chiswick, Kew, Richmond, and Putney—with winding old streets, horticultural delights, cozy riverside pubs, and Henry VIII's Hampton Court Palace. The neighborhoods along the way are as proud of their villagey feel as of their stately history, witnessed by such handsome estates as Strawberry Hill and Syon House. After the sensory overload of the West End, it's easy to forget you're in a capital city at all.

CHISWICK

Updated by
Jack Jewers

On the banks of the Thames just west of central London, far enough out to escape the crush and crowds you've probably just started to get used to, Chiswick is a low-key, upscale district, content with its run of restaurants, stylish shops, and film-star residents. No doubt its most famous son wouldn't approve of all the conspicuous wealth, though; Chiswick was home to one of Britain's best-loved painters, William Hogarth, who tore the fabric of the 18th-century nation to shreds with his slew of satirical engravings. **Hogarth's House** has been restored to its former glory. Incongruously stranded among Chiswick's row houses are a number of fine 18th-century buildings, which are now some of the most desirable suburban houses in London. By far the grandest of all is **Chiswick House,** a unique Palladian-style mansion born from the 3rd Earl of Burlington's love of classical and Renaissance architecture—a radical style at the time.

TOP ATTRACTIONS

Chiswick House. Completed in 1729 by the 3rd Earl of Burlington (also known for Burlington House—home of the Royal Academy—and Burlington Arcade on Piccadilly), this extraordinary Palladian mansion was envisaged as a kind of temple to the arts. Burlington was fascinated by the architecture he saw in Italy while on the Grand Tour as a young man. When his country home was destroyed by fire in 1725, he seized the chance to rebuild it in homage to those classical and Renaissance styles. The building is loosely modeled on the Villa Capra near Vicenza, while the colonnaded frontage is a partial replica of the Pantheon in Rome (which also inspired the domed roof).

The sumptuous interiors were the work of William Kent (1685–1748), his most extraordinary achievement being the Blue Velvet Room, with its gilded decoration and intricate painted ceiling. The design of Chiswick House sparked a great deal of interest—such ideas were radical in England at the time—and you'll see its influence reflected in numerous later buildings. The rambling gardens are one of the hidden gems of West London. Italianate in style (of course), they are filled with classical temples, statues, and obelisks. Also on the grounds are a café and a children's play area. ⊠ *Burlington La., Chiswick* ☎ *020/8995–0508* ⊕ *www.chgt.org.uk* 🎫 *£5.70* ⏱ *Grounds daily 7 am–dusk; house Apr.–Oct., Sun.–Wed. 10–5* Ⓜ *Turnham Green, Chiswick. National Rail: Chiswick.*

Hogarth's House. Besieged by a roaring highway that somewhat spoils the atmosphere, the home of the satirist and painter William Hogarth (1697–1764) is still worth a visit by fans of his amusing, moralistic engravings (such as *The Rake's Progress* and *Marriage à la Mode*). Sadly the house has had an unlucky few years; initially closed by a fire in 2008, restoration work was halted by a second fire the following year. However, now fully restored, the house contains new exhibition spaces devoted to Hogarth and his work. Look out for the 300-year-old mulberry tree in the garden—a vain attempt to get silkworms to breed in England. Hogarth's tomb can be found in the cemetery of St. Nicholas's church on nearby Chiswick Mall. ⊠ *Hogarth La., Great West Rd. (A4), Chiswick* ☎ *020/8994–6757* ⊕ *www.hounslow.info/arts/hogarthshouse* 🎫 *Free* ⏱ *Tues.–Sun. noon–5* Ⓜ *Turnham Green. National Rail: Chiswick.*

QUICK BITES

Some of the loveliest pubs in London sit beside the Thames at Chiswick, dotted along the northern bank of the river as far as Hammersmith Mall—the last remaining fragment of what was once a pretty old village, now all but replaced by urban sprawl.

Blue Anchor. Briefly famous in the late 1990s, thanks to the movie *Sliding Doors,* the Blue Anchor is a cozy 18th-century watering hole on the Thames, with rowing memorabilia lining the walls. ⊠ *13 Lower Mall, Hammersmith* ☎ *020/8748–5774* ⊕ *www.blueanchorlondon.com.*

City Barge. Opposite a tiny island in the middle of the Thames, the City Barge has a lovely riverside terrace and honest pub grub. ⊠ *27 Strand-on-the-Green, Chiswick* ☎ *020/8994–2148* Ⓜ *Gunnersbury. National Rail: Kew Bridge.*

Dove Inn. Retaining the charm of its 300-plus-year heritage, the Dove has a tiny terrace that's a tranquil place to watch the river flow by. The food is good here, too (especially Sunday lunch). ⊠ *19 Upper Mall, Hammersmith* ☎ *020/8748–9474* ⊕ *www.dovehammersmith.co.uk* Ⓜ *Ravenscourt Park, Hammersmith.*

KEW

A mile or so beyond Chiswick is Kew, a leafy suburb with little to see other than its two big attractions: the lovely **Kew Palace** and the **Royal Botanic Gardens**—anchored in the landscape for several miles around by a towering, mock-Chinese pagoda.

TOP ATTRACTIONS

FAMILY **Kew Gardens.**
See the highlighted listing in this chapter.

Fodor's Choice ★ **Kew Palace and Queen Charlotte's Cottage.** The elegant redbrick exterior of the smallest of Britain's royal palaces seems almost humble when compared with the grandeur of, say, Buckingham or Kensington palaces. Yet inside is a fascinating glimpse into life at the uppermost end of society from the 17th to 19th century. This is actually the third of several palaces that stood here; once known as Dutch House, it was one of the havens to which George III retired when insanity forced him to withdraw from public life. Queen Charlotte had an *orné*—a rustic-style cottage retreat—added in the late 18th century. In a marvelously regal flight of fancy, she kept kangaroos in the paddock outside. The main house and gardens are maintained in the 18th-century style. There are extended tours of the palace on a few Sunday evenings each summer that cover areas not usually on show, such as the Tudor undercroft. Check the website for details. The palace is within the grounds of Kew Gardens so you have to buy a ticket to the gardens *in addition to* the palace if you want to enter. ⊠ *Kew Gardens, Kew Rd. at Lichfield Rd., Kew* ☎ *0844/482–7777 (only in U.K.), 020/3166–6000* ⊕ *www.hrp. org.uk* ⌂ *£6, in addition to ticket for Kew Gardens* ☉ *Apr.–Sept., daily 10–5:15; Oct., Thurs.–Sun. 11–4; also daily during school holidays, late Oct. and late Feb. (call to confirm times)* Ⓜ *Kew Gardens.*

RICHMOND

Named after the (long-vanished) palace Henry VII started here in 1500, Richmond is still a welcoming suburb with a small-town feel, marred only by choking levels of traffic. Duck away from the main streets to find many handsome Georgian and Victorian houses, antiques shops,

KEW GARDENS

✉ *Kew Rd. at Lichfield Rd., for Victoria Gate entrance, Kew* ☎ *020/8332–5655* ⊕ *www. kew.org* 🎫 *£16* ⊗ *Mid-Feb.– mid-Mar., daily 9:30–5:30; mid-Mar.–Aug., weekdays 9:30–6:30, weekends 9:30– 7:30; Sept. and Oct., daily 9:30–6; Nov.–mid-Feb., daily 9:30–4:15. Glasshouses and galleries close 5:30 (3:45 Nov.– mid-Feb., 5 mid-Feb.–late Mar.) Palm House closes 2 on Tues.* Ⓜ *Kew Gardens. National Rail: Kew Gardens, Kew Bridge.*

TIPS

■ Free guided tours, run by volunteers, are held daily at 11 am and 1:30 pm.

■ The Kew Explorer bus runs on a 40-minute, hop-on, hop-off route around the gardens every hour from 11 am. Tickets cost £4.

■ Discovery Tours are specially adapted and fully accessible, aimed at disabled visitors. Options include walking tours designed for deaf or blind visitors, or bus tours for those with mobility problems. Walking tours are £5 per group, bus tours £30 per group. They're usually available on Tuesdays and Thursdays only, and it's a good idea to book.

■ Treat your taste buds to a light tea at the Victoria Terrace Café or a meal at the far more elegant Orangery, or dine outside at White Peaks.

■ You can download the official Kew Gardens app for free on the website.

Enter the Royal Botanic Gardens, as Kew Gardens are also known, and you are enveloped by blazes of color, extraordinary blooms, hidden trails, and lovely old follies. Beautiful though it all is, Kew's charms are secondary to its true purpose as a major center for serious research. Academics are hard at work on more than 300 scientific projects across as many acres, analyzing everything from the cacti of eastern Brazil to the yams of Madagascar. First opened to the public in 1840, Kew has been supported by royalty and nurtured by landscapers, botanists, and architects since the 1720s. Today the gardens, now a Unesco World Heritage site, hold more than 30,000 species of plants, from every corner of the globe.

Although the plant houses make Kew worth visiting even in the depths of winter (there's also a seasonal garden), the flowerbeds are, of course, best enjoyed in the fullness of spring and summer.

Highlights

Two great 19th-century greenhouses—the **Palm House** and the **Temperate House**—are filled with exotic blooms, and many of the plants have been there since the final glass panel was fixed into place. The enormous Temperate House contains the largest greenhouse plant in the world, a Chilean wine palm rooted in 1846. (It's so big that you have to climb the spiral staircase to the roof to get a proper view of it). Architect Sir William Chambers built a series of temples and follies, of which the crazy 10-story **Pagoda,** visible for miles around, is the star turn. The Princess of Wales conservatory houses 10 climate zones, and the Rhizotron and Xstrata Treetop Walkway takes you 59 feet up into the air.

13

a Victorian theater, a grand stately home—and, best of all, the largest of London's royal parks.

TOP ATTRACTIONS

Ham House. To the west of Richmond Park, overlooking the Thames and nearly opposite the memorably named Eel Pie Island, Ham House was built in 1610 and remodelled 50 years later. It's one of the most complete examples in Europe of a lavish 17th-century house, together with a restored formal garden that has become an influential source for other European palaces and grand villas. The original decorations in the Great Hall, Round Gallery, and Great Staircase have been replicated, and all the furniture and fittings are on permanent loan from the Victoria & Albert Museum. A tranquil and scenic way to reach the house is on foot, which takes about 30 minutes, along the eastern riverbank south from Richmond Bridge. ⊠ *Ham St., Richmond* ☎ *020/8940–1950* ⊕ *www. nationaltrust.org.uk* ⊠ *House, gardens, and outbuildings £10.90; gardens only £3.65* ⊙ *House mid-Feb.–Mar., Sat.–Mon. 11:30–3:30; Apr.– Sept., Sat.–Wed. noon–4; Oct.–Nov., Sat.–Tues. 11:30–3. Gardens Nov.–mid-Feb., daily 11–4; mid-Feb.–Oct., daily 11–5* Ⓜ *Richmond, then Bus 65 or 371.*

Fodor's Choice
★
Hampton Court Palace.
See the highlighted listing in this chapter.

Marble Hill House. This handsome Palladian mansion is set in 66 acres of parkland on the northern bank of the Thames, almost opposite Ham House. It was built in the 1720s by George II for his mistress, the "exceedingly respectable and respected" Henrietta Howard. Later the house was occupied by Mrs. Fitzherbert, who was secretly married to the Prince Regent (later George IV) in 1785. The house was restored in 1901 and opened to the public two years later, looking very much like it did in Georgian times, with extravagant gilded rooms in which Ms. Howard entertained the literary superstars of the age, including Pope, Gay, and Swift. A ferry service from Ham House operates during the summer; access on foot is a half-hour walk south along the west bank of the Thames from Richmond Bridge. Entry is by guided tour only, but the tour info given in review text differs from that given in Open Hours box. The actual hours should only appear in the service info anyway, so please check which is correct and amend as necessary. ⊠ *Richmond Rd., Twickenham* ☎ *020/8892–5115* ⊕ *www.english-heritage. org.uk* ⊠ *£5.50 (guided tour only)* ⊙ *Apr.–Oct., Sat. 10–2, Sun. and bank holidays 10–5; Tours start at 10:30 and noon on weekends, with additional tours at 2:15 and 3:30 on Sunday* Ⓜ *Richmond. National Rail: St Margarets.*

FAMILY **Richmond Park.** This enormous park was enclosed in 1637 for use as a royal hunting ground—like practically all other London parks. Unlike the others, however, Richmond Park still has wild red and fallow deer roaming its 2,360 acres (that's three times the size of New York's

WORD OF MOUTH

"If you go to Kew…you can have tea at the Maids of Honour tearoom across from the main entrance. It is delightful and supposed to have been in business since Henry VIII." —carolyn

HAMPTON COURT PALACE

⊠ *Hampton Court Rd., East Molesley, Surrey*
☎ *0844/482–7799 tickets, 0844/482–7777 information (24 hr)* ⊕ *www.hrp.org.uk/ hamptoncourtpalace* ⊐ *Palace, maze, and gardens £17; maze only £3.85; gardens only £5.50 (free Oct.-Mar.)*
⊙ *Late Mar.–Oct., daily 10–6; Nov.–late Mar., daily 10–4:30; last admission one hr before closing; last entry to maze 45 min before closing); check website before visiting*
Ⓜ *Richmond, then Bus R68; National Rail: Hampton Court Station, 35 min from Waterloo (most trains require change at Surbiton).*

TIPS

■ Family tickets offer huge savings, with £44 covering two adults and up to six children (£36 if you buy them in advance online).

■ Choose which parts of the palace to explore based on a number of self-guided audio walking tours. Come Christmas time, there's ice-skating on a rink before the West Front of the palace.

■ Are you brave enough to explore the Haunted Gallery by candlelight? Evening ghost tours (£25 per person) are held throughout the year. Not only are they entertainingly spooky, but they're a great way to see the older parts of the palace without the crowds. Call or go online to check dates.

The beloved seat of Henry VIII's court, sprawled elegantly beside the languid waters of the Thames, this beautiful palace really gives you two for the price of one: the magnificent Tudor redbrick mansion, begun in 1514 by Cardinal Wolsey to curry favor with the young Henry, and the larger 17th-century baroque building, which was partly designed by Christopher Wren (of St. Paul's fame).

Highlights

Wander through the **State Apartments,** decorated in the Tudor style, complete with priceless paintings, and on to the wood-beamed magnificence of **Henry's Great Hall,** before taking in the strikingly azure ceiling of the **Chapel Royal.** Well-handled reconstructions of Tudor life take place all year, from live appearances by "Henry VIII" and his elaborately costumed court, to a small retinue of cook-historians preparing authentic Tudor feasts in the 15th-century **Henry's Kitchens.**

Feel a chill in the air? Watch out for the ghost of Henry VIII's doomed fifth wife, Catherine Howard, who literally lost her head yet is said to scream her way along the **Haunted Gallery.** Weirdly, the ambient temperature really is prone to drop noticeably and nobody knows why. Latter-day masters of the palace, the joint rulers William and Mary (reigned 1689–1702), were responsible for the beautiful **King's and Queen's Apartments** and the elaborate baroque of the **Georgian Rooms.**

Don't miss the famous **maze** (the oldest hedge maze in the world), its half mile of pathways among clipped hedgerows still fiendish to negotiate.

The **Lower Orangery Exotic Garden** shows off thousands of exotic species that William and Mary, avid plant collectors, gathered from around the globe.

Central Park) of grassland and heath. Its ancient oaks are among the last remnants of huge forests that once encroached on London in medieval times. The Isabella Plantation (near the Ham Gate entrance) is an enchanting and colorful woodland garden, first laid out in 1831. ▥ TIP➡ There's a splendid, protected view of St. Paul's Cathedral from King Henry VIII's Mound, the highest point in the park. Find it and you have a piece of magic in your sights. The park is also home to White Lodge, a 1727 hunting lodge that now houses the Royal Ballet School. ✉ *Richmond* ☎ *020/8948–3209* ⊕ *www.royalparks.org.uk* ⊗ *Mar.–late Dec., daily 7–dusk; late Dec.–Feb., daily 7:30–dusk* Ⓜ *Richmond, then Bus 371 or 65.*

White Lodge Museum. Though the school isn't open to the public, it does contain the small White Lodge Museum dedicated to the history of the school and ballet in general. Entry is available during the school year only (though it sometimes opens on a handful of dates during the summer holidays—call or check the website for details. Prebooking is essential. ✉ *Richmond Park* ☎ *020/8392–8440* ⊕ *www.royal-ballet-school.org.uk* ✉ *Free* ⊗ *School term, Tues.–Thurs. 1:30–3:30; occasional days in school holidays (call to check)* Ⓜ *National Rail: Mortlake, then walk to Sheen Gate (15 min) for park-and-ride bus.*

QUICK BITES

White Cross. Overlooking the Thames so closely that the waters almost lap at the door in high tide, the White Cross is a popular spot that serves traditional pub grub. ✉ *Water La., Richmond* ☎ *020/8940–6844* ⊕ *www.youngs.co.uk.*

Strawberry Hill. From the outside, this Rococo mishmash of towers, crenellations, and dazzling white stucco is almost fairytale-ish in its faux-medieval splendor. Its architect, Sir Horace Walpole (1717–97), knew a thing or two about imaginative flights of fancy—the flamboyant son of the first British prime minister, Robert Walpole, he all but single-handedly invented the Gothic Revival style with his novel *The Castle of Otranto* (1764). Once inside, the forbidding exterior gives way to a veritable explosion of color and light, for Walpole boldly decided to take elements from the exteriors of Gothic cathedrals and move them inside. The detail is extraordinary, from the cavernous entrance hall with its vast Gothic trompe l'oeil, to the Great Parlour with its Renaissance stained glass, to the Gallery, where extraordinary fan vaulting is a replica of the vaults found in Henry VIII's chapel at Westminster Abbey. Neglected for years, Strawberry Hill re-opened in 2011 after a stunningly successful £9 million restoration. The gardens have also been meticulously returned to their original 18th-century design, right down to a white marble loveseat sculpted into the shape of a shell. ▥ TIP➡ You can book a tour of the house at twilight for £20, including a glass of Prosecco. ✉ *268 Waldegrave Rd., Twickenham* ☎ *020/8744–3124* ⊕ *www.strawberryhillhouse.org.uk* ✉ *£8* ⊗ *Timed entry, every 20 min; Mar.–early Nov., Mon.–Wed. 2–5:30, Sat. and Sun. noon–5:30; 1 wk in early Dec., Mon.–Wed., Sat. and Sun. noon–5:30. Last admission*

Continued on page 237

Tower Bridge

A TOUR OF THE THAMES

*"I have seen the Mississippi. That is muddy water.
I have seen the St. Lawrence. That is crystal water.
But the Thames is liquid history."*
—*John Burns*

The twists and turns of the Thames River through the heart of the capital make it London's best thoroughfare and most compelling viewing point. Once famous for sludge, silt, and sewage, the Thames is now the cleanest city river in the world. Whether you take a river cruise or a leisurely stroll along its banks and bridges, traveling on or alongside the river is an unforgettable way to soak up views of the city.

MILLENNIUM BRIDGE TO THAMES FLOOD BARRIER

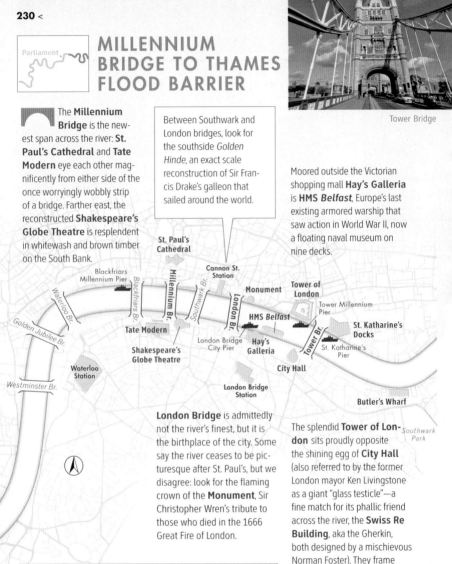

Tower Bridge

The **Millennium Bridge** is the newest span across the river: **St. Paul's Cathedral** and **Tate Modern** eye each other magnificently from either side of the once worryingly wobbly strip of a bridge. Farther east, the reconstructed **Shakespeare's Globe Theatre** is resplendent in whitewash and brown timber on the South Bank.

Between Southwark and London bridges, look for the southside *Golden Hinde*, an exact scale reconstruction of Sir Francis Drake's galleon that sailed around the world.

Moored outside the Victorian shopping mall **Hay's Galleria** is **HMS** *Belfast*, Europe's last existing armored warship that saw action in World War II, now a floating naval museum on nine decks.

London Bridge is admittedly not the river's finest, but it is the birthplace of the city. Some say the river ceases to be picturesque after St. Paul's, but we disagree: look for the flaming crown of the **Monument**, Sir Christopher Wren's tribute to those who died in the 1666 Great Fire of London.

The splendid **Tower of London** sits proudly opposite the shining egg of **City Hall** (also referred to by the former London mayor Ken Livingstone as a giant "glass testicle"—a fine match for its phallic friend across the river, the **Swiss Re Building**, aka the Gherkin, both designed by a mischievous Norman Foster). They frame the 1894 **Tower Bridge**, a magnificent feat of engineering and style, which leads past the elegant confines of **St. Katharine's Docks**, the trendy restaurants of **Butler's Wharf**, and the **Design Museum**.

LONDON BRIDGE

Viking invaders destroyed London Bridge in 1014, hence the nursery rhyme "London Bridge is falling down." By 1962, London Bridge really was falling down again, its 1831 incarnation unable to take the strain of traffic. It was saved by American tycoon Robert McCulloch, who—possibly confusing the bridge with its much more splendid neighbor, Tower Bridge—bought it in 1968 for $2.46 million and had it shipped, stone by stone, to Lake Havasu in Arizona.

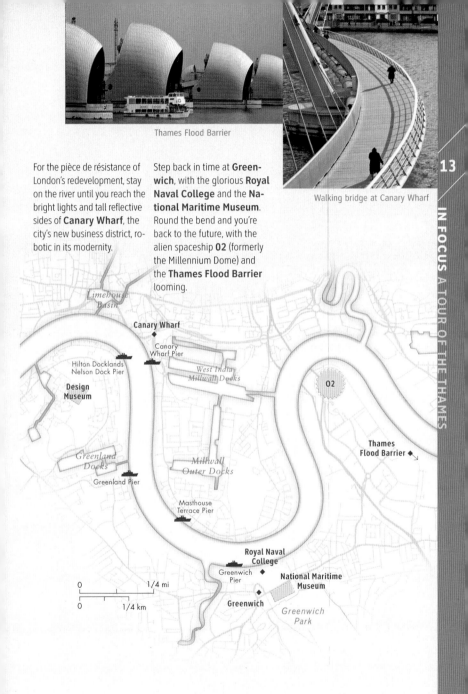

Thames Flood Barrier

For the pièce de résistance of London's redevelopment, stay on the river until you reach the bright lights and tall reflective sides of **Canary Wharf**, the city's new business district, robotic in its modernity.

Step back in time at **Greenwich**, with the glorious **Royal Naval College** and the **National Maritime Museum**. Round the bend and you're back to the future, with the alien spaceship **O2** (formerly the Millennium Dome) and the **Thames Flood Barrier** looming.

Walking bridge at Canary Wharf

Limehouse Basin

Canary Wharf

Canary Wharf Pier

Hilton Docklands Nelson Dock Pier

West India Millwall Docks

O2

Design Museum

Greenland Docks

Greenland Pier

Millwall Outer Docks

Thames Flood Barrier

Masthouse Terrace Pier

Royal Naval College

Greenwich Pier

National Maritime Museum

Greenwich

Greenwich Park

0   1/4 mi

0   1/4 km

Blackfriars Bridge at night.

0   1/2 mi

0   1/2 km

South Park

Wandsworth Br.

Battersea Br.

Albert Br.

Chelsea Harbour Pier

Chelsea Br.

Grosvenor Br.

Battersea Park

Battersea Power Station

WALKING THE THAMES

Even if you lack sea legs, you can still enjoy the river: not much beats a wander beside London's waterway. The Thames Path (www.nationaltrail.co.uk) follows the river 184 miles, from its source to the flood barriers in Greenwich. Some of the best riverside strolls:

- Hammersmith Bridge to Chiswick Mall
- Golden Jubilee Bridges to the South Bank's Queen's Walk
- Cleopatra's Needle to Parliament along Victoria Embankment
- Tate Modern to St. Paul's over Millennium Bridge

Beyond **Wandsworth Bridge**, the early part of this stretch by Battersea Bridge, rebuilt in 1890, was London's real industrial heartland, the southern side chock full of cottage housing for laborers, artisans at work, and factories.

The real treat of this stretch is the view of the **Houses of Parliament** and, beyond that, **Westminster Abbey**. **Victoria Embankment**, stretching all the way from Westminster to Blackfriars, was once all grim mudflats. In 1878 it became the country's first electrically illuminated street, and today its fine architecture, trees, and gardens are perfect strolling territory.

View from London Eye (left); House's of Parliament (right)

You can't miss the **London Eye**, whose parts were brought down the Thames one by one before being assembled on-location. Look out too for the London Aquarium and the Dalí museum, housed in the baroque-style County Hall.

Cleopatra's Needle, overlooking the Thames by Embankment, dates back to Heliopolis in 1450 BC. Look for World War I shrapnel holes and gouges at the base.

Further on is the **Oxo Tower**, whose red-glass letters were designed in 1928 to spell out the brand name while circumventing tight laws on exterior advertising.

By **Blackfriars Bridge**, named after the monks who wore black robes and lived on the north bank during the Middle Ages, the river used to run red by the riverside tanneries and slaughterhouses.

After **Albert Bridge**—glorious at night, with lights like luminescent pearls sweeping down on strings—the Thames is a metropolitan glory of a river, charging through fashionable **Chelsea** and past the now derelict **Battersea Power Station**, under Chelsea, Vauxhall and Lambeth Bridges, with **Lambeth Palace** to the south.

The **Golden Jubilee Bridges** by **Embankment**, two beautifully lit steel-cabled pedestrian walkways, are perfect for reaching the **South Bank**.

Look out for the golden eagle, a monument to World War I RAF fighters, and **Cleopatra's Needle**. For the ultimate double decker bus-viewing moment, look at **Waterloo Bridge**, once known as Ladies Bridge because it was built by female labor during World War II. The bridge has great views of the South Bank.

Blackfriars Bridge

HAMPTON COURT PALACE TO PUTNEY

The Great Conservatory at Syon Park

Waterlily House at Kew Gardens

Hampton Court Palace is a suitably lavish start or end to any trip on the Thames. The river skirts the grounds, giving magnificent views over the Tudor palace that Henry VIII and his daughter Elizabeth I made home, and continues north to **Kingston Bridge**, starting point for the river voyage of Jerome K. Jerome's *Three Men in a Boat* and home to hectic summer regattas. At **Teddington**, where the poet Alexander Pope and writer Horace Walpole entertained their female admirers in the 18th century, the river turns tidal but remains quiet and unspoiled all the way to **Kew**, passing herons and fine stately homes standing proud on the banks. From **Twickenham Bridge** you round the old deer park (to the south) and **Syon Park** (north), which has belonged to the Duke of

Northumberland's family for centuries. Beyond that is an even greater treat—the UNESCO World Heritage Site of **Kew Botanical Gardens**. All manner of rowboats set up for one, two, four, or eight people pull hard under **Chiswick Bridge** and **Barnes (railway) Bridge**, past the expensive riverside frontage of Chiswick Mall and under **Hammersmith Bridge**, to **Putney** and **Fulham**—smart urban villages facing each other across the banks.

Syon Park

Kew Botanical Gardens

Twickenham Br.

Richmond Landing Stage

Richmond Br.

Marble Hill Park

Eel Pie Island

Teddington

Kingston Br.

Bushy Park

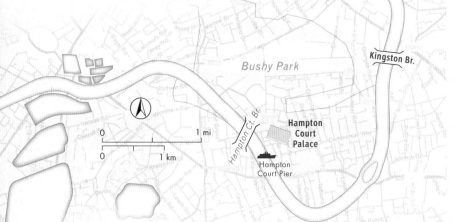

Hampton Ct. Br.

Hampton Court Palace

Hampton Court Pier

0   1 mi

0   1 km

Map Labels

Gunnersbury
Park

Kew Br.

Kew Pier

Furnival
Gardens

Hammersmith Br.

Chiswick
Mall

Barn Elms
Water Works

Temperate
House

Fulham

Chiswick Br.

Barnes Br.

Bishops
Park

Barnes
Common

Putney Br.

Hurlingham
Park

Wandsworth
Park

The stretch between Kew and Hammersmith is real rowing and riverside-pub territory, with a picturesque parade past Strand-on-the-Green by Kew Bridge.

ROWERS' ROW Every spring Britain's oldest universities, Oxford and Cambridge, compete not with their brains but with their brawn, in the **Boat Race**, which began in 1829. The race is 4¼ miles upstream from Putney Bridge to Chiswick Bridge: expect clashing oars, clenched teeth, and the occasional sinking (there have been six). The best views are from Hammersmith at the Surrey bend, which is also where most of the pubs are clustered. ⊕ www.theboatrace.org

---

A BRIEF HISTORY

An engraving by Claes Van Visscher showing Old London Bridge in 1616, with Southwark Cathedral in the foreground

The Thames has come a long way—and not just from its 344-km (214-mi) journey from a remote Gloucestershire

meadow to the sea. In the mid-19th century, the river was dying, poisoned by sewers that flushed into the river. The "Big Stink" was so awful that cholera and typhoid killed more than 10,000 in 1853, and Parliament abandoned sitting in 1858. "The odour is hardly that of frankincense," said one contemporary of the 1884 drought that forced down water levels, leaving elegant Victorian nostrils exposed to slimy ooze on the banks.

Joseph Bazalgette, star civil engineer of his time, was commissioned to design a new sewage system, and by the 1900s nearly all was forgiven. (His efforts did not go unappreciated: Bazalgette was later knighted.) Today 7.2 million people get their drinking water from the Thames River.

PLANNING A THAMES BOAT TOUR

"On the smallest pretext of holiday or fine weather the mighty population takes to the boats," wrote Henry James in 1877. You can follow in the footsteps of James, who took a boat trip from Westminster to Greenwich, or make up your own itinerary.

■ Frequent daily tourist-boat services are at their height between April and October.

■ In most cases you can turn up at a pier, and the next departure won't be far away. However, it never hurts to book ahead if you can.

■ Westminster and Tower piers are the busiest starting points, usually with boats heading east.

■ TIP➔ For a rundown of all the options, along with prices and timetables, contact **London River Services** (☎ 020/7222–1234 ⊕ www.tfl.gov.uk/river), which gives details of all the operators sailing various sections of the river.

■ The trip between Westminster Pier and the Tower of London takes about 30 minutes, as does the trip between the Tower and Greenwich.

■ A full round-trip can take several hours. Ask about flexible fares and hop on/off options at the various piers.

THE BEST WAYS TO EXPERIENCE THE THAMES WHILE...

GOING OFF THE BEATEN PATH (LITERALLY)	020/7928–3132 www.londonducktours.co.uk £21
	London Ducktours offers sightseeing with a twist—amphibious patrol vehicles used in World War II have been painted like rubber duckies and traverse land and sea. / Departs from the London Eye (on land): Daily, according to demand, 9:30 am–dusk. Approximately 1½ hrs.
SAVING TIME AND MONEY	020/7887–8888 www.tate.org.uk/tatetotate £5.50 one-way
	The playfully polka-dotted *Tate Boat* sails across the river from the Tate Britain to the Tate Modern with a London Eye stop in between. / Departs from the pier at either museum: Daily every 40 mins. Approximately 13 mins. one-way.
IMPRESSING A DATE OR CLIENT	0870/429–2451 www.bateauxlondon.com £32–£43 (lunch), £76–£144 (dinner)
	For ultimate glamour (and expense), look into lunch and dinner cruises with **Bateaux London**, often formal affairs with surprisingly good two- to five-course meals. Variations include jazz brunch cruises on Sundays. / Departs from Embankment Pier for lunch at 12: Apr.–Dec., Wed.–Sat. (also Tues. in Jul. and Aug.) and Jan.–Mar., Thur.–Sat.; for dinner at 7:15: Apr.–Dec., daily, and Jan.–Mar., Tue.–Sat.
ENJOYING ON-BOARD ENTERTAINMENT	020/7740–0400 www.citycruises.com £78
	The *London Showboat* lives up to its name, with four-course meals, snazzy cabaret acts from West End musicals, and after-dinner dancing. / Departs from Westminster Pier at 7:30: Apr.–Sept., Wed.–Sun.; Oct., March., Thurs.–Sun.; Nov., Dec. Thurs.–Sat.; Jan.–Feb., Fri.–Sat. (boarding starts 30 mins. prior to departure). Approximately 3½ hours. Book 48 hours in advance.

4:20. Garden daily 10–6:30 Ⓜ *Richmond, then Bus 33; National Rail: Strawberry Hill Station.*

FAMILY

Fodor's Choice

★

Syon House and Park. The residence of the duke and duchess of Northumberland, this is one of England's most lavish stately homes. Set in a 55-acre park landscaped by "Capability" Brown, the core of the house is Tudor—Henry VIII's fifth wife, Catherine Howard, and the extremely short-lived monarch, lady Jane Grey ("Queen for thirteen days"), made pit stops here before they were sent to the Tower. It was remodeled in the Georgian style in 1761 by famed decorator Robert Adam. He had just returned from studying the sights of classical antiquity in Italy and created two rooms sumptuous enough to wow any Grand Tourist: the entryway is an amazing study in black and white, pairing neoclassical marbles with antique bronzes, and the Ante-Room contains 12 enormous verd-antique columns surmounted by statues of gold—and this was just a waiting room for the duke's servants and retainers. The Red Drawing Room is covered with crimson Spitalfields silk, and the Long Gallery is one of Adam's noblest creations. ▮ **TIP➜ On certain Sundays and bank holidays in the summer you can take a miniature steam-train ride in the grounds.** ✉ *Syon Park, Brentford* ☎ *020/8560–0882* ⊕ *www.syonpark.co.uk* 🎫 *£11 for house, gardens, conservatory, and rose garden; £5 for gardens and conservatory* ⊙ *House mid-Mar.–Oct., Wed., Thurs., Sun., and bank holidays 11–5; gardens mid-Mar.–Oct., daily 10:30–5; Nov.–mid-Mar., weekends 10:30–4. Last admission 1 hr before closing* Ⓜ *Gunnersbury, then Bus 237 or 267 to Brentlea.*

13

WHERE TO EAT

Updated by Alex Wijeratna

As anyone knows who reads the papers, London's had a restaurant boom, or rather, a restaurant atomic-bomb explosion. More than ever, Londoners love their restaurants—all 6,700 of them—from its be-here-right-now, wow-factor West End gastro-emporiums to its tiny neighborhood joints. You, too, will be smitten, because you'll be spending, on average, 25% of your travel budget on eating out.

Today, nearly everything on the culinary front has dramatically changed from the days of steamed suet puddings and over-boiled Brussels sprouts. Everyone's mad about food, while a wall of City and hot global money has souped up standards remarkably. Celebrity chefs abound. One week it's Wolfgang Puck at CUT at 45 Park Lane that's the flavor of the month, the next it's Jason Atherton at the Pollen Street Social in Mayfair. Thankfully, pride in the best of authentic British food— local, seasonal, regional, wild, and foraged—has made a resurgence and appears on more menus by the day. The new wave of waste-not, want-not "nose-to-tail" eating—where every scrap of meat is deemed fair game for the plate—made its first spectacular comeback at St. John in Clerkenwell, and chimes perfectly with the new age of austerity.

Needless to say, it's the top of the food chain that hogs much of the news. Throughout London you'll find an ambitious bunch of haute-cuisine heroes kicking butt to world-class standards. Heston Blumenthal protégé Ashley Palmer-Watts single-handedly revives olde-English gastronomy with ultramodern methods at Dinner by Heston Blumenthal; Aussie Brett Graham is cooking on turbocharged gas at The Ledbury in Notting Hill; inventive Portuguese chef Nuno Mendes creates an inimitable modernist escapade at Viajante in Bethnal Green; and young gastro-warrior Ollie Dabbous sets the cat amongst the pigeons in his industrial-chic, knappery-free, haute haven at Dabbous.

To appreciate how far London has risen in the global culinary firmament, just look back at the days of famed author Somerset Maugham, who was once justified in warning "To eat well in England, you should

Continued on page 244

BEST BETS FOR LONDON DINING

With thousands of restaurants to choose from, how will you decide where to eat? Fodor's writers and editors have selected their favorite restaurants by price, cuisine, and experience in the Best Bets lists below. In the first column, Fodor's Choice properties represent the "best of the best" in every price category. You can also search by neighborhood for excellent eats—just peruse the following pages. Or find specific details about a restaurant in the full reviews, listed later in the chapter by neighborhood.

Fodor's Choice★

Brasserie Zédel, p. 255
Bubbledogs, p. 264
Chez Bruce, p. 271
CUT at 45 Park Lane, p. 248
Dabbous, p. 264
The Delaunay, p. 260
Dinner by Heston Blumenthal, p. 277
Giaconda Dining Rooms, p. 256
Harwood Arms, p. 274
The Ledbury, p. 280
Mari Vanna, p. 277
Petrus, p. 278
Pollen Street Social, p. 251
Roti Chai, p. 264
Rules, p. 262
Scott's, p. 251
Spuntino, p. 259
St. John, p. 268

10 Greek Street, p. 259
Tom Aikens, p. 273
Viajante, p, 270
Zucca, p. 272

Best by Price

$

Brasserie Zédel, p. 255
Bubbledogs, p. 264
Busaba Eathai, p. 255
Côte, p. 256
Roti Chai, p. 264

$$

Giaconda Dining Rooms, p. 256
Harwood Arms, p. 274
The Riding House Café, p. 251
10 Greek Street, p. 259
Zucca, p. 272

$$$

Dabbous, p. 264
The Delaunay, p. 260
Lima, p. 257
St. John, p. 268
Yashin, p. 273

$$$$

CUT 45 Park Lane, p. 248
Dinner by Heston Blumenthal, p. 277
The Ledbury, p. 280
Petrus, p. 278
Tom Aikens, p. 273

Best by Cuisine

BRITISH

Great Queen Street, p. 260
Harwood Arms, p. 274
Rochelle Canteen, p. 269

St. John, p. 268

CHINESE

Baozi Inn, p. 254
Hunan, p. 274
Yauatcha, p. 259

FRENCH

Hélène Darroze at the Connaught, p. 249
Koffmann's, p. 277
La Petite Maison, p. 250
The Ledbury, p. 280
Petrus, p. 278

ITALIAN

Bocca di Lupo, p. 255
Cecconi's, p. 247
L'Anima, p. 267
Pizza East, p. 269
Zucca, p. 272

JAPANESE

Koya, p. 257
Yashin, p. 273
Zuma, p. 278

SEAFOOD

Golden Hind, p. 252
J Sheekey, p. 261
Scott's, p. 251
Sweetings, p. 268

STEAK

Bar Boulud, p. 276
CUT at 45 Park Lane, p. 248
Goodman, p. 248
The Savoy Grill, p. 263

Best by Experience

BRASSERIE

Brasserie Zèdel, p. 255
Côte, p. 256
The Delaunay, p. 260
The Riding House Café, p. 251
The Wolseley, p. 247

BRUNCH

Dean Street Townhouse, p. 256
The Delaunay, p. 260
The Riding House Café, p. 251
The Wolseley, p. 247

BUSINESS DINING

The Delaunay, p. 260
Le Gavroche, p. 250
The Savoy Grill, p. 263
Scott's, p. 251

CELEB SPOTTING

J Sheekey, p. 261
Le Caprice, p. 246
Nobu Berkeley Street, p. 250
Scott's, p. 251
The Wolseley, p. 247

GASTROPUBS

Anchor & Hope, p. 270
Great Queen Street, p. 260
Harwood Arms, p. 274
The Mall Tavern, p. 281
The Orange, p. 275

GOOD FOR GROUPS

Bistrotheque, p. 269
Boundary, p. 266
Brasserie Zédel, p. 255
Pizza East, p. 269
The Riding House Café, p. 251

HISTORIC

Maison Bertaux, p. 258
Rules, p. 262
Simpson's Tavern, p. 268
Sweetings, p. 268
Wiltons, p. 246

HOTEL DINING

Bistro Bruno Loubet at The Zetter, p. 266
CUT at 45 Park Lane, p. 248
Dinner by Heston Blumenthal at the Mandarin Oriental, p. 277
Hélène Darroze at the Connaught, p. 249
Koffmann's at the Berkeley, p. 277

HOT SPOTS

Bubbledogs, p. 264
CUT at 45 Park Lane, p. 248
Dabbous, p. 264
Lima, p. 257
Mari Vanna, p. 277

LATE-NIGHT DINING

Dean Street Townhouse, p. 256
J Sheekey, p. 261
The Wolseley, p. 247

LOCAL FAVORITES

Alounak, p. 281
Chez Bruce, p. 271
The Henry Root, p. 274
Lemonia, p. 282
Pizza East, p. 269

LUNCH PRIX FIXE

Galvin Bistrot de Luxe, p. 252
Hereford Road, p. 281
Le Gavroche, p. 250
The Mall Tavern, p. 281
Racine, p. 275

PRETHEATER

Brasserie Zédel, p. 255
Côte, p. 256
Dean Street Townhouse, p. 256
The Opera Tavern, p. 262
The Savoy Grill, p. 263

QUIET MEAL

Angelus, p. 281
Hibiscus, p. 249
The Greenhouse, p. 249
Koffmann's, p. 277

ROMANTIC

The Delaunay, p. 260
J Sheekey, p. 261
Le Gavroche, p. 250
Mari Vanna, p. 277
Scott's, p. 251

SPECIAL OCCASION

Dabbous, p. 264
Dinner by Heston Blumental, p. 277
The Ledbury, p. 280
Petrus, p. 278
Zucca, p. 272

WINE LISTS

Bocca di Lupo, p. 255
The Greenhouse, p. 249
Hibiscus, p. 249
The Ledbury, p. 280

EXPERIMENTAL

Dabbous, p. 264
Hedone, p. 284
Hibiscus, p. 249
Tom Aikens, p. 273
Viajante, p. 270

14

have a breakfast three times a day." Change was slow in coming after World War II, for then it was still understood the British ate to live, while the French lived to eat. When people thought of British cuisine, fish-and-chips—a greasy grab-and-gulp dish that tasted best wrapped in old newspaper—first came to mind. Then there was always Shepherd's pie, ubiquitously available in smoke-filled pubs—though not made, according to the song from *Sweeney Todd,* "with real shepherd in it."

These days, standards are higher and poor-quality Shepherd's pie has been largely replaced by the city's unofficial dish, the ubiquitous spiced Indian curry. London's food quake is built on its incredible ethnic diversity, and you'll find the quality of other international cuisines has also grown immeasurably in recent years, with London becoming known for its Chinese, Japanese, Indian, Thai, Spanish, Italian, French, Persian, and North African restaurants. With all of the choices, traditional British food, when you track it down, appears as just one more exotic cuisine in the pantheon.

PLANNING

EATING OUT STRATEGY

Where should you eat? With thousands of London eateries competing for your attention, it may seem like a daunting question. But fret not—our expert writers and editors have done most of the legwork. The selections here represent the best this city has to offer—from kitschy desserts to to haute cuisine. *Search "Best Bets" for top recommendations by price, cuisine, and experience. Or find a review quickly in the neighborhood listings. Whichever way you look at it, you're sure to get a taste of London.*

RESERVATIONS

Plan ahead if you're determined to snag a sought-after reservation. Some renowned restaurants are booked weeks or even months in advance. It's always a good idea to book as far ahead as you can and reconfirm when you arrive in London. Note that some top restaurants also now take credit card details and charge a penalty fee if you're a no-show. *In the reviews, we mention reservations only when they're essential or not accepted.*

WHAT TO WEAR

When in England's style capital, do as the natives do: dress up to eat out. Whatever your style, dial it up a notch. Have some fun while you're at it. Pull out the clothes you've been saving for a special occasion and get a little glamorous. As unfair as it seems, the way you look can influence how you're treated—and where you're seated. Generally speaking, jeans and a button-down shirt will suffice at most table-service restaurants in the budget to moderate range. Moving up from there, many pricier restaurants require jackets, and some insist on ties. Shorts, sweatpants, and sports jerseys are rarely appropriate. *Note that in reviews we mention dress only when men are required to wear a jacket, or a jacket and tie.*

TIPPING AND TAXES

Do not tip bar staff in pubs and bars—though you can always offer to buy them a drink. In restaurants, tip 12.5% of the check for full meals if service is not already included; tip a small token if you're just having coffee or tea. If paying by credit card, double-check that a tip has not already been included in the bill.

CHILDREN

Unless your children behave impeccably, it's best to avoid the high-class establishments; you're unlikely to find a children's menu there, anyway. London's many Italian restaurants and pizzerias are popular with kids. Other family-friendly establishments include chains like Byron, Côte, Pizza Express, Busaba Eathai, Wagamama, Giraffe, and Carluccio's.

14

HOURS

In London you can find breakfast all day, but it's generally served between 7 am and noon. Lunch is between noon and 3 pm, and brunch between 11 am and 3 pm. Tea, often a meal in itself, is taken between 3 pm and 6 pm, and dinner or supper is typically eaten between 7 pm and 11 pm, though it can be taken earlier. Many ethnic restaurants, especially Indian, serve food until midnight. Sunday is proper lunch day, and some restaurants are open for lunch only. Over the Christmas period, London virtually shuts down and it seems only hotels are prepared to feed travelers.

PRICES

London is a very pricey city by global standards. A modest meal for two can easily cost £40, and the £110-a-head meal is not unknown. Damage-control strategies include making lunch your main meal—the top places have bargain midday menus—going for early- or late-evening deals, or sharing an à la carte entrée and ordering a second appetizer instead. Seek out fixed-price menus, and watch for hidden extras on the check, that is, bread or vegetables charged separately.

RESTAURANT REVIEWS

Listed alphabetically within neighborhoods. Use the coordinate (✛ 1:B2) at the end of each listing to locate a property on the Where to Eat and Stay in London atlas at the end of this chapter. Prices in the reviews are the average cost of a main course at dinner or, if dinner is not served, at lunch.

WESTMINSTER, ST. JAMES'S, AND ROYAL LONDON

ST. JAMES'S

St. James's—home to Buckingham Palace and Clarence House, where Prince Charles and Camilla live—has a decidedly olde-world, royal feel. Appropriately, most of the restaurants here are fit for a future monarch. This is where you'll find London's top-end restaurants—dining experiences that are geared toward a well-heeled, deep-pocketed clientele. Mere mortals should make reservations well in advance to dine at any of these restaurants for dinner (and reserve for the earlier or later shanks of the evening, when demand is less). Keep in mind that no-shows mean last-minute tables often crop up, and lunching here can be a great money-saving strategy.

$$$
MODERN
EUROPEAN
Fodor's Choice
★

✕ **Le Caprice.** Celeb-*ville* grande dame Le Caprice commands the deepest loyalty of any restaurant in London. *Why?* Because of the *memories*...and because it gets practically everything right—*every* time. It's the 30-year celebrity history—think Liz Taylor, Joan Collins, and Lady Di—the haunting David Bailey black-and-white portraits, designer Martin Brudnizki's updated decor, charming Bolivian-born Jesus Adorno the veteran maître d', the perfect service, and the appealing and long-standing menu that sits somewhere between Euro peasant and trendy fashion plate. Sit at the raised counter or at a corner table and enjoy calves' liver with crispy bacon, roast pheasant with caramelized quince, and signature Scandinavian iced berries with a theatrical swirl of white chocolate sauce—all served with an ample dollop of "*SHHush! Don't-Look-Now-Dear!*" star spotting. $ *Average main: £23* ⊠ *Arlington House, Arlington St., St. James's* ☎ *020/7629–2239* ⊕ *www.capriceholdings.co.uk* ⚠ *Reservations essential* Ⓜ *Green Park* ✦ *5:A1*.

$$$$
BRITISH

✕ **Wiltons.** Aristos, blue bloods, and the *extremely* well-to-do blow the family bank at this old-fashioned bastion of English fine dining on pedigreed Jermyn Street (the place first opened on the Haymarket as a shellfish stall in 1742). Invariably fresh from a little snooze in their nearby St. James's gentlemen's clubs, male diners are required to wear jackets at all times at this clubby time capsule and *frightfully* snooty ode to all things English. Signet ring-wearing posh patrons like to take half-a-dozen finest Colchester oysters, followed by grilled Dover sole on the bone, or fabulous native game in season, such as grouse, woodcock, partridge or teal. There are long-forgotten savories like anchovies or mushrooms on toast, plus nursery desserts like sherry trifle and bread and butter pudding. Service, naturally, would put Jeeves to shame. $ *Average main: £32* ⊠ *55 Jermyn St., St. James's* ☎ *020/7629–9955* ⊕ *www.wiltons. co.uk* ⌕ *Reservations essential* 🎩 *Jacket required* ☉ *Closed weekends* Ⓜ *Green Park* ✛ *5:A1.*

$$
AUSTRIAN
FAMILY
Fodor's Choice
★

✕ **The Wolseley.** The whole of beau London comes for the always-on-show spectacle and soaring elegance at this Viennese-style *Mitteleuropa* grand café on Piccadilly. Framed with black laquerware, silver service, and a few doors down from the Ritz, this all-day brasserie begins its long decadent days with breakfast at 7 am and serves until midnight. Don't be shy to pop in on spec (they hold seats back for walk-ins) to enjoy such highlights as Hungarian goulash, Austrian pork belly, chicken soup with salt beef sandwich, eggs Benedict, kedgeree, or the breaded Wiener schnitzel. For dessert, plump for the luscious *Kaiser-schmarrn*—caramelized pancake with stewed fruit and raisins—and don't forget to book a return table to savor the Viennoiserie pastries at one of their classy £9.75 to £32.50 afternoon teas. $ *Average main: £18* ⊠ *160 Piccadilly, St. James's* ☎ *020/7499–6996* ⊕ *www.thewolseley. com* ⌕ *Reservations essential* Ⓜ *Green Park* ✛ *5:A1.*

MAYFAIR AND MARYLEBONE

If you're looking for something more wallet-friendly, head north to Marylebone, formerly dowdy but now prized for its chic, village-like feel. Here are an array of low-key little cafés, boîtes and tapas bars, hot-dog joints, and the odd world-class sizzler (*see Dabbous*), offering everything from Moroccan and Spanish to Thai and Japanese.

MAYFAIR

$$$
MODERN ITALIAN

✕ **Cecconi's.** Spot the odd A-list celeb and revel in all-day buzz at this ever-fashionable up-scale Italian brasserie wedged handsomely between Old Bond St., Cork St., and Savile Row, and across from the Royal Academy of Arts. The *vaguely* familiar and important-looking Miu Miu, off-shore tax exile, and private jet set spill out onto the street for breakfast, brunch, and *cicchetti* (Italian tapas), and return later in the day for something more substantial. À la mode designer Ilse Crawford's luxe green-and-brown interior is a stylish backdrop for classics like stuffed baby squid, Umbrian sausages, lobster spaghetti, and a flavorful pick-me-up tiramisu. It's just the spot for a high-end pit stop during an ill-advised kamikaze West End shopping spree. $ *Average main: £23* ⊠ *5A Burlington Gardens, Mayfair* ☎ *020/7434–1500* ⊕ *www. cecconis.co.uk* ⌕ *Reservations essential* Ⓜ *Green Park, Piccadilly Circus* ✛ *3:A6.*

$$$$
BRITISH

✕ **Corrigan's Mayfair.** The nearby Mayfair streets may be a bit quiet, but there's a genuinely warm welcome and a lively glowing scene at burly Irish chef Richard Corrigan's flagship British haute cuisine haven off Park Lane. Corrigan's is self-assured and purring along on top of its game, and the dark blue banquettes, crisp Irish linen, and huntin', shootin', and fishin' motifs provide a seductively handsome setting for

14

a high-powered clientele who return repeatedly for wild, gamey, and foraged dishes like red-leg partridge ravioli, steamed pollack with clams, wild boar with crab apple, and even heartier offerings like haunch of venison, saddle of rabbit, game pie, or pork with pear and dandelion. There's a classy wine list, and you're likely to see Corrigan knocking around the place, too. ⑤ *Average main: £28* ⊠ *28 Upper Grosvenor St., Mayfair* ☎ *020/7499–9943* ⊕ *www.corrigansmayfair.co.uk* ♺ *Reservations essential* ☾ *No lunch Sat.* Ⓜ *Marble Arch* ✛ *1:G5.*

$$$$
STEAKHOUSE
Fodor's Choice
★

✕ **CUT at 45 Park Lane.** 87 quid for an 8 oz steak?! NOW we're talkin'! U.S.-based Austrian *übernoober* star-chef Wolfgang Puck amps up the steak stakes at this counterintuitive and strangely *smokin'* high-end steak extravaganza on Park Lane. Against a neo-'90s hotel-lobby luxe backdrop of polished marble, Damien Hirsts, and glitzy globe lights, and an '80s soundtrack of Elton John and Lynyrd Skynyrd, an army of private equity, petro-dollar, and hedge fund knuckleheads go gangbusters for perfectly seared prime cuts from the U.S., Chile, England, and Australia. Grilled over charcoal and hardwood, and finished under a 650°C broiler, there's awesome Arkansas Creekstone filet mignon for £34, incredible 35-day USDA Black Angus New York sirloins for £38 or £50, or outstandingly tender-is-the-night rib-eye of wagyu beef from Araucanía in Chile for a top ranked £87! Add bone marrow, french fries, Béarnaise, and creamed spinach with a fried egg on top for the whole nine yards. ⑤ *Average main: £35* ⊠ *45 Park La., Mayfair* ☎ *020/7493–4545* ⊕ *www.45parklane.com* ♺ *Reservations essential* Ⓜ *Marble Arch, Green Park* ✛ *1:G5.*

$$$$
STEAKHOUSE

✕ **Goodman.** This Russian-owned, Manhattan-themed, Mayfair-based steak house, named after Chicago jazz legend Benny Goodman, has everyone in agreement—here you'll find some of the best steaks in town. USDA-certified, 150-day corn-fed and dry-aged Black Angus T-bones, rib-eye, porterhouse, and New York sirloin steaks compete for taste and tenderness with heavily marbled grass-fed prime cuts from Scotland and Ireland. There's token Russian sweet herring, lobster bisque, and Caesar salad, but everyone here's got only one thing on their mind: the sizzling 250g–400g charcoal Josper oven grilled steaks, which can come with lobster tails or pan-fried foie gras, plus truffle chips, creamed spinach, and Béarnaise, pepper, or Stilton sauce. $ *Average main: £31* ⊠ *24–26 Maddox St., Mayfair* ☎ *020/7499–3776* ⊕ *www.goodmanrestaurants. com* ⌔ *Reservations essential* ⊘ *Closed Sun.* Ⓜ *Oxford Circus* ✛ *3:A5.*

$$$$ ✕ **The Greenhouse.** Discretely tucked away amid imposing Mayfair man-
FRENCH sions and approached via a sumptuous spotlighted garden, this ultra-elegant ground-floor dining salon quietly screams "Stealth Wealth!" and attracts well-healed aficionados of top-class French haute cuisine at any price. Feast on intricately arranged foie gras with smoked eel, wild turbot with pak-choi cress, or Scottish venison with slithers of pear and gingerbread. A mainly private equity, hedge fund, and global off-shore plutocracy crowd come for the overweening but achingly smooth service, the glassed-off private dining room, and the famed 90-page wine list—the ultimate in wine-buff porn, over 2,000 bottles in all (and with many wines by-the-glass). $ *Average main: £33* ⊠ *27A Hay's Mews, Mayfair* ☎ *020/7499–3331* ⊕ *www.greenhouserestaurant. co.uk* ⌔ *Reservations essential* ⊘ *Closed Sun. No lunch Sat.* Ⓜ *Green Park* ✛ *1:H5.*

$$$$ ✕ **Hélène Darroze at the Connaught.** London's *crème de la crème* flock to
FRENCH French virtuoso Hélène Darroze at the exclusive Connaught hotel for her dazzling regional French haute cuisine, all served up in an impressive Edwardian wood-paneled dining salon sumptuously kitted out by Parisian *It*-designer India Mahdavi. Taking inspiration from Les Landes in southwest France, Darroze sallies forth with a procession of magical dishes. Caviar d'Acquitaine wows with oyster tartare in a sleek martini glass, topped with black caviar jelly and white haricot bean velouté. Spit-roasted and flambéed pigeon is served gloriously pink, with duck foie gras and mini–Brussels sprouts. To finish, choose pear jelly or apple compote with black Sarawak pepper cream. Darroze may be perfect for celebrations but beware the high prices: £35 for lunch, £55 for Saturday brunch, and £80 to £115 for dinner. $ *Average main: £35* ⊠ *The Connaught, Carlos Place, Mayfair* ☎ *020/7107–8880* ⊕ *www.the-connaught.co.uk* ⌔ *Reservations essential* 🏛 *Jacket required* ⊘ *Closed Sun. and Mon.* Ⓜ *Green Park* ✛ *1:H5.*

$$$$ ✕ **Hibiscus.** Is chunky chef Claude Bosi the *new* Heston Blumenthal?
MODERN FRENCH Such is the acclaim showered on this burly French chef that—*whisper it!*—Bosi's now talked about in the same breath as Blumenthal, Britain's supernova TV chef. Bosi, unsurprisingly, bosses the scene at this disarmingly neutral Mayfair spot with peerless, take-no-prisoners nouvelle dishes like carpaccio of hand-dived Isle of Skye scallops with blobs of truffle and pickled radish, or Cornish John Dory with specs of Morteau sausage and *girolle* mushrooms. The desserts are as *original* as his mains, with an unlikely but flavorsome cèpe tart standing

out. Celebrations, CEOs, and global gastro-tourists are well-served by a copious wine list, which features a hefty selection of top-rank "orange" biodynamic, organic, and unadulterated fine wines. $ *Average main: £35* ☒ *29 Maddox St., Mayfair* ☏ *020/7629–2999* ⊕ *www. hibiscusrestaurant.co.uk* ⟁ *Reservations essential* ☉ *Closed Sun. and Mon.* Ⓜ *Oxford Circus, Piccadilly* ✛ *3:A5.*

$$$ ✕ **La Petite Maison.** Movie star and blogger Gwyneth Paltrow rates
FRENCH see-and-be-seen La Petite Maison, off New Bond Street, as one of
FAMILY her favorite London restaurants, and no wonder—there's nothing on the impressively well-sourced carbo-lite French Mediterranean, Côte d'Azur, and Provençale menu that fails to entice. Try figure-friendly broad bean and pecorino salad, the soft white burrata cheese with datterini tomato and basil spread, or the wonderfully aromatic baked turbot with artichokes, chorizo, five-spice, and white wine sauce. Based on the style of the original La Petite Maison in Nice, France, dishes come to the table as and when they're ready, and the chirpy, *jolie,* and informal waitstaff makes for a convivial Gucci Gucci Gangnam-style party-*ish* vibe. Rosé, anyone? $ *Average main: £26* ☒ *53–54 Brook's Mews, Mayfair* ☏ *020/7495–4774* ⊕ *www.lpmlondon.co.uk* ⟁ *Reservations essential* Ⓜ *Bond St.* ✛ *1:H4*

$$$$ ✕ **Le Gavroche.** Enthusiastic "MasterChef" judge Michel Roux Jr. thrives
FRENCH and works the floor at this clubby basement national institution in Mayfair—established by his uncle and father in 1967—and which many still rate to this day as the best *formal* dining in London. With silver domes and old-fashioned unpriced ladies' menus, Roux's mastery of technically precise and classical French cuisine hypnotizes all comers with signature dishes like foie gras with cinnamon-scented crispy duck pancake, langoustine with snails and Hollandaise, pig's trotters, or saddle of rabbit with Parmesan cheese. Desserts like Roux's famous chocolate omelet soufflé or upside-down apple tart are scaringly accomplished. Weekday three-course set lunches (£52) are the best and sanest way to experience such unashamed overwrought flummery—with a half bottle of wine, water, coffee, and petits fours thrown in. The decor is '80s-traditional-luxe: some might find it dated, but the V.I.P.s here must adore it. $ *Average main: £40* ☒ *43 Upper Brook St., Mayfair* ☏ *020/7408–0881* ⊕ *www.le-gavroche.co.uk* ⟁ *Reservations essential* 🎩 *Jacket required* ☉ *Closed Sun. and 10 days at Christmas* Ⓜ *Marble Arch, Bond St.* ✛ *1:G5*

$$$$ ✕ **Nobu Berkeley Street.** Soccer stars, supermodels, the F1 crowd, and
JAPANESE global fashion-bods pay *silly money* for new-style sashimi (with a Peruvian touch) at this so-hip-it-hurts Nobu spin-off near Piccadilly. Louder, more thumping, and more fashion-forward than nearby flagship Nobu on Park Lane, this younger sibling triples up successfully with a combined ground-floor scene bar, a first-floor cat-walk of a restaurant, and a wraparound late '90s West End nightclub vibe. Once safely past security and firmly seated, the oh-so-beautiful people go bananas for miso black cod, California sushi rolls, tuna teriyaki, yellowtail sashimi, dinky Bento boxes, mighty grilled peppers, and extortionate wagyu beef. Prices are midtown-Tokyo-extreme, but the white-hot people-watching is just *soooo* good. $ *Average main: £28* ☒ *15 Berkeley St.,*

Mayfair ☎ *020/7290–9222* ⊕ *www.noburestaurants.com* Ⓜ *Green Park* ✛ *1:H5.*

$$$
MODERN
EUROPEAN
Fodor's Choice
★

✕ **Pollen Street Social.** El Bulli–trained and stratospheric star chef Jason Atherton knocks the London dining scene for a loop at this smash-hit set in a quaint side alleyway off Regent Street. Gobsmacked fans mix-and-max on edgy, witty, and refined small-or-larger dishes ranging from a "full English" starter—a cute deconstructed miniature of poached egg, bacon, morels, tomato purée, and croutons—to sublime Dingley Dell pork belly, or tender Atlantic hake with cod cheeks and seaweed. Glamorous diners often move from their tables to perch at counter seats at London's first dessert bar, and watch the dessert staff chop, slice, fiddle about, and prepare immaculate creamy goat-milk rice pudding with hay ice cream or sensational sashimi-like pressed watermelon with an unlikely basil sorbet. Look out for Atherton, who's often around, and note the £27.50 three-course lunches. Ⓢ *Average main: £26* ⊠ *8–10 Pollen St., Mayfair* ☎ *020/7290–7600* ⊕ *www.pollenstreetsocial.com* ⋘ *Reservations essential* Ⓜ *Oxford Circus, Piccadilly Circus* ✛ *3:A5.*

$$
BURGER
FAMILY

✕ **The Riding House Café.** Stuffed squirrel lamp holders peer down on trendy London diners at this groovy New York–style small-plates-and-luxe-burgers all-day brasserie just north of Oxford Circus. Everything's appropriately salvaged or bespoke here, so you'll find stuffed birds and other taxidermy dotted around, reclaimed theater seats at the long counter bar, bright orange leather banquettes, or old snooker table legs holding up your dining table. Opt for the £5 small plates of sea bass ceviche with lime and chili or veal and pork meatballs with pomarola sauce, and then head for the poached egg chorizo hash browns, pearl-barley salt marsh lamb broth, a decadent cheeseburger, with gherkin and chips—a bargain at £12.50—or their famed tummy-filling lobster lasagna (£18.80). Service is NYC-standard friendly, and you'll find all-day breakfasts, hard shakes, and cocktails, plus sundaes on the kids' menu. Ⓢ *Average main: £14* ⊠ *43–51 Great Titchfield St., Noho* ☎ *020/7927–0840* ⊕ *www.ridinghousecafe.co.uk* ⋘ *Reservations essential* Ⓜ *Oxford Circus* ✛ *3:A2.*

$$$$
SEAFOOD
Fodor's Choice
★

✕ **Scott's.** Liveried doormen greet the A-list with a discreet nod at this glamorlicious seafood haven and crustacea bar on fashion-central Mount Street, the new heart of Mayfair. Orginally founded in 1851, and a former haunt of James Bond author Ian Fleming (he adored the potted shrimps), these days you're more likely to see Bill Clinton in one corner, Kate Winslet in another, and former hell-raiser Brit-pack artists, Damien Hirst or Tracy Emin, playing up on a banquette nearby. Scott's draws London's *real* movers-and-shakers and the attendant beautiful ones, who enjoy day-boat fresh Lindisfarne oysters, baked crab, cod cheeks, shrimp burgers, and lobster Americaine. Magnificent standouts like sautéed razor clams with wild boar sausages or sole Colbert with maître d'hôtel butter are to die for. Prices would make a Saudi sheik blanch, but fear not: this really is the *hottest* joint in town. Ⓢ *Average main: £32* ⊠ *20 Mount St., Mayfair* ☎ *020/7495–7309* ⊕ *www. scotts-restaurant.com* ⋘ *Reservations essential* Ⓜ *Bond St., Green Park* ✛ *1:H5.*

14

MARYLEBONE

$$$ ✕ **Galvin Bistrot de Luxe.** The accomplished Chris and Jeff Galvin brothers
BRASSERIE blaze a trail for the French *bistrot de luxe* approach on a fast-moving
stretch of Baker Street. Seasoned fans and a more discerning crowd go
for the impeccable food and service in a handsome slate-floor, bent-
wood chair, and mahogany-paneled Parisian-style salon. There's no
finer Dorset crab lasagna in town, and mains consistently punch above
their weight: Cornish brill, calves liver with Alsace bacon, stuffed pig's
trotter, and sumptuous daube of venison with quince and chestnuts are
all devilishly tasty, each one a superbly executed gastro triumph. The
£19.50 three-course set lunches or £21.50 early-evening dinners (6–7
pm) are top value, and look out for occasional live Sunday afternoon
jazz. ⑤ *Average main: £19* ✉ *66 Baker St., Marylebone* ☎ *020/7935–
4007* ⊕ *www.galvinrestaurants.com* ⌂ *Reservations essential* Ⓜ *Baker
St.* ✛ *1:G3*

$ ✕ **The Golden Hind.** You'll catch some of the best fish and chips in London
SEAFOOD at this great British "chippy" (or traditional fish and chip shop), run by
a long-standing Greek family in a retro 1914 art deco café. Gaggles of
tourists and hungry Marylebone village locals alike hunker down for the
homemade cod fishcakes, skate wings, feta fritters, and breaded scampi
tails, but it's the neatly prepared and non-greasy deep-fried or steamed
battered cod, plaice, and haddock from Grimsby (£4–£6.50), the classic
hand-cut Maris Piper chips, and the traditional mushy peas that are the
big draws. It's BYO and take away, but note it's only open noon–3 pm
weekdays, and 6–10 pm Monday–Saturday. ⑤ *Average main: £6* ✉ *73
Marylebone La., Marylebone* ☎ *020/7486–3644* ⌂ *Reservations not
accepted* ⊘ *No lunch Sat. Closed Sun.* Ⓜ *Bond St.* ✛ *1:G3*

$$ ✕ **Trishna.** Trishna's little-known £20 four-course early evening tast-
SEAFOOD ing menus are a smart way to savor this Mumbai-inspired seafood
ace in upmarket Marylebone village. Tiger prawn seafood salad with
Goan sausages, crispy squid, fish tikka, and spiced brown crab all
come with basmati rice, Hydrabadi *dhal*, naan bread, and a choice of
Indian desserts. Average price for dinner for two: £64. ⑤ *Average main:
£18* ✉ *15–17 Blandford St., Marylebone* ☎ *020/7935–5624* ⊕ *www.
trishnalondon.com* ⌂ *Reservations essential* Ⓜ *Bond St., Baker St.*
✛ *1:G3*

SOHO AND COVENT GARDEN

Soho and Covent Garden are the city's playground, an all-day, all-night
jostling neon wonderland of glitz, glamour, grit, and greasepaint. This
area is London's cultural heart, with old and new media companies,
late-night dive bars, West End musicals, and highbrow theater, ballet,
and opera houses. In the last decade, high rents have forced out many
of Soho's seedier businesses and ushered in top-notch restaurants. Just
follow your nose in Covent Garden, hard by Theatreland, to find many
options for pretheater dining.

LONDON'S HOTTEST TABLES

These hotties are more than just see-and-be-seen food 'n' flesh pots—truly exceptional cuisine is their raison d'être. To save, book lunch, when set menus can be half the dinner price.

Dabbous: Supernova wonder-chef Ollie Dabbous (pronounced Da-boo) rocks the crowds, blogosphere, and the critics with his stripped-back, pure, flavor-focused, modernist, Nordic-style dishes in an industrial-chic setting. ⊠ 39 Whitfield St., Fitzrovia ⊕ www.dabbous.co.uk ☎ 020/7323–1544 ✛ 3:C2.

The Delaunay: Enjoy 19th-century fin-de-siècle Viennese-style elegance and supreme dishes like Viennese hot dogs, Hungarian sausage stew, or Wiener schnitzel at this grand café on the Aldwych. ⊠ 55 Aldwych, Covent Garden ☎ 020/8499–8558 ⊕ www.thedelaunay.com ✛ 3:G4.

Dinner by Heston Blumenthal: Book ahead for Heston Blumenthal protégé Ashley Palmer-Watts's ultramodern olde-English gastronomy in Knightsbridge. Overlook Hyde Park, and marvel at 1730s-inspired hay-smoked mackerel or 1810 spit-roast pineapple "Tipsy" cake. ⊠ 66 Knightsbridge, Knightsbridge ⊕ www.dinnerbyheston.com ☎ 020/7201–3833 ✛ 4:F1.

The Ledbury: Aussie chef Brett Graham burnishes his world-class reputation with complex, game-focused, modern French haute cuisine in this handsome, high-ceilinged Notting Hill gourmand's paradise. ⊠ 127 Ledbury Rd., Notting Hill ☎ 020/7792–9090 ⊕ www.theledbury.com ✛ 1:A4.

Pollen Street Social: Whizz through a small- or large-dish tasting extravaganza at Jason Atherton's Mayfair gastro-playpen. Dive into scallop ceviche and ox cheeks with capers, and try chocolate pavé while perched at London's first dessert bar. ⊠ 8–10 Pollen St., Mayfair ⊕ www.pollenstreetsocial.com ☎ 020/7290–7600 ✛ 3:A5.

Viajante: El Bulli–trained Portuguese star Nuno Mendes bedazzles with urban-foraged and art-on-a-plate contemporary cuisine in far-off but happening Bethnal Green. ⊠ Patriot Sq., Bethnal Green ☎ 020/7871–0461 ⊕ www.viajante.co.uk ✛ 2:H1.

Zucca: Tuck into glorious all-homemade Italian breads, pasta, and ice cream, and a zippy wine list at this brilliant and always-packed modern Italian on white-hot Bermondsey Street. ⊠ 184 Bermondsey St., South Bank ☎ 020/7378–6809 ⊕ www.zuccalondon.com ✛ 5:H2.

14

SOHO

$$

MEDITERRANEAN

✕ **Andrew Edmunds.** Well-worn, candle-lighted, and with an overwhelming Dickensian vibe to it, Andrew Edmunds is a permanently packed, deeply romantic old-world Soho institution—though it could be larger, less creaky underfoot, and the reclaimed church-pew wooden bench seats more forgiving. Tucked away behind Carnaby Street, it's a cozy favorite with the insider Soho media mafia that come for daily changing, hand-written, fixed-price lunch menus and the overall quirky/historic vibe. Satisfyingly rustic and keenly priced starters and mains draw on the tastes of Ireland, the Med, and the Middle East. Harissa-spiced mackerel, woodcock on toast, goose rillettes, seafood paella, and pork belly with apple purée are all hale and hearty. $ *Average main: £16* ✉ *46 Lexington St., Soho* ☎ *020/7437–5708* ◇ *Reservations essential* Ⓜ *Oxford Circus, Piccadilly Circus* ✛ *3:C5.*

$ ✕ **Baozi Inn.** Vintage Communist Party paraphernalia and Chairman
SICHUAN Mao posters decorate the walls of this handy hole-in-the-wall Sichuan café on a busy side street in Chinatown. Baozi steamed buns—shrimp and radish, or pork and onion—are house specials, and there's dragon wonton broth, Dan Dan noodles with mustard greens and sesame paste, plus Chengdu pork dumplings with chili oil. Other warm and filling top choices include ginger juice spinach and "Peace and Happiness" noodle soup, topped with duck and Chinese toon tree shoots. Tables are cramped, prices are low, turnover is fast, and customer service is *bang! bang! bang!* $ *Average main: £8* ✉ *25 Newport Ct., Soho* ☎ *020/7287–6877* ⊕ *www.baoziinnlondon.com* ◇ *Reservations not accepted* Ⓜ *Leicester Sq.* ✛ *3:E5*

$ ✕ **Bar Italia.** This legendary Frith Street Italian coffee bar is Soho's unof-
CAFÉ ficial beating heart and a 22-hour-a-day institution. Still family-run and established in 1949 during the post-war coffee-bar craze, it is now positively football crazy and a honey-pot for a rum assortment of roués and weird and wonderful Soho-ites. Most regulars grab a frothy cappuccino, espresso, or sobering *macchiato* made from the old Gaggia coffee machine and wolf down a slice of pizza, panettone, a sausage bap, or chocolate cake at one of the mirrored counters (or at pavement seats out *da* front). The walls are plastered with Italian flags and old pics of lusty Italian singers, world boxing champs, and black-and-white movie legends, and it's the *primo* spot in London to watch Italy play in the soccer

World Cup. $ *Average main: £6* ✉ *22 Frith St., Soho* ☎ *020/7437–4520* ⊕ *www.baritaliasoho.co.uk* ▭ *No credit cards* Ⓜ *Leicester Sq.* ✛ *3:D5*

$$$ ✗ **Barrafina.** Soho's top tapas bar is modeled on Cal Pep, the famed tapas
SPANISH   joint in Barcelona, and similarly has only a few—23 in total—raised
counter seats. It's no-reservations but you might strike up with smart
fellow queuers, all eventually discover the tapas is supreme and well
worth the wait. Get ready to happily nosh on small plates of garlic
prawns, chorizo, tuna tartare, quail, salt cod fritters, sardines, and octo-
pus with capers, plus classics like cured Maldonado ham and Spanish
tortilla. There's an excellent selection of Spanish reds, whites, sherrys,
and sparkling Cavas (many by the glass), and leave room for desserts
like *crèma* Catalana or almond-based Santiago tart. Daily specials are
usually posted on Twitter, too. $ *Average main: £14* ✉ *54 Frith St.,
Soho* ☎ *020/7813–8016* ⊕ *www.barrafina.co.uk* ✍ *Reservations not
accepted* Ⓜ *Tottenham Court Rd.* ✛ *3:D4*

$$$ ✗ **Bocca di Lupo.** The place's always packed, the tables are too close
ITALIAN   together, and the acoustics suck, but everyone tips up for the buzz and
chef Jacob Kenedy's punchy and unusual regional Italian rustic fare.
Redbrick fronted and set in an unlikely street off Soho's red-light district, this popular family-run place offers a procession of small plates
and peasant-based dishes from Piedmont to Emilia, Lombardy to
Campania. Try drop-dead offerings like buffalo mozzarella, suckling
pig, teal, polenta with anchovies, Sicilian lobster spaghetti, or *baccala*
home-salted pollack. Limber up with a colorful Aperol spritz before
plunging into the regional Italian-focused wine list, which weaves from
Gavi di Gavi to rare Barolo's. There are intriguing marsala and aged-
Grappa digestifs, plus cute desserts like chocolate *semifreddo* or milk-
free espresso ice-cream. $ *Average main: £15* ✉ *12 Archer St., Soho*
☎ *020/7734–2223* ⊕ *www.boccadilupo.com* ✍ *Reservations essential*
Ⓜ *Piccadilly Circus* ✛ *3:C5.*

$ ✗ **Brasserie Zédel.** Vichyssoise *soupe du jour* with sliced baguette, butter,
BRASSERIE   and a jug of water for £2.25? A prix fixe with steak haché and frites
FAMILY   in a silver cup for £8.75? Or a three-course daily set meal with salade
Fodor's Choice   Mâche, confit duck, a glass of red, water, and coffee for £19.75? *And*
★   just off Piccadilly, in a glam and gilded art deco/Beaux Arts gastro and
jazz-bar basement emporium? *Surely* some mistake? But no, these are a
few indecently priced steals on offer at restaurateurs Corbin and King's
magnifique take on an all-day Parisian-style brasserie ("Chartier by
way of La Coupole," says King), just north of Piccadilly Circus. Save
centimes on a classic *céleri rémoulade* for £2.95 or *soupe de poisson* for
£4.95 in a soaring salon of leather banquettes, marbled columns, mirrors, and stained birch tops. You'll also find decent onglet steak, seafood
vol-au-vent, or *choucroute Alsacienne* with pork belly and frankfurters,
plus nifty profiteroles or nougat glacé. Afterwards, imbibe at the swank
Bar Américain, or enjoy live jazz or cabaret at the in-house The Crazy
Coqs. $ *Average main: £8* ✉ *20 Sherwood St., Soho* ☎ *020/7734 4888*
⊕ *www.brasseriezedel.com* Ⓜ *Piccadilly Circus* ✛ *3:C6.*

$ ✗ **Busaba Eathai.** It's top Thai nosh for little *moolah* at this sleek and
THAI   sultry modern Thai canteen in the heart of Soho. Fitted with dark-
FAMILY   wood bench seats and hardwood tables, this flagship restaurant has

14

communal dining, rapid service, low-lighting, and often fast-moving queues out front. Pour yourself a lemongrass tea, then try ginger beef with Thai pepper, classic crunchy green papaya salad, chicken with shiitake mushrooms, jungle curry, vermicelli with prawns, squid, and scallops, or other tasty winners. You'll escape for about £15 a head, and all in all, this makes for a top-value tummy-filler and a fine pit-stop during a West End shopping safari. $ *Average main: £11* ✉ *106–110 Wardour St., Soho* ☎ *020/7255–8686* ⊕ *www.busaba.com* ✍ *Reservations not accepted* Ⓜ *Tottenham Court Rd.* ✛ *3:C4*

$ ✕ **Côte.** Where else can you get a great two-course French meal in Cov-
BISTRO ent Garden for £9.95? The Côte brasserie chain—softly lit and smoothly
FAMILY decked out with natty gray-and-white striped awnings, banquettes, and Parisian-style round café tables—does just the trick, and offers these meal deals weekdays from noon until 7 pm, weekends from noon until 6 pm. With four choices per course, you'll find all your French brasserie favorites: tuna Niçoise salad, bœuf bourguignon, chargrilled Breton chicken, *moules marinières* (mussels with white wine), steak haché, and crème caramel for afters. If you're so lucky to be attending the nearby Royal Opera House, this is perfect for pre-theater . . . *or* post-theater, come to that. $ *Average main: £10* ✉ *17-21 Tavistock St., Covent Garden* ☎ *020/7379–9991* ⊕ *www.cote-restaurants.co.uk* ✍ *Reservations essential* Ⓜ *Covent Garden.* ✛ *3:G5*

$$$ ✕ **Dean Street Townhouse.** Everyone feels 10 times more glamorous once
BRITISH they step into this buzzy Soho mustering point, attached to the stylish 39-room Georgian hotel of the same name. Soft lighting, dark-wood floors, red leather banquettes, raised bar seats, and walls crammed with Brit-pack drawings and daubings create a hip hang-out for London's good-looking media elite. No-frills, no-fuss retro-British favorites include pea and ham soup, plain mince and potatoes, twice-baked smoked haddock soufflé, chicken, bacon and mushroom pie, or toad-in-the-hole, plus *yummilicious* sherry trifle, Trinity burnt cream, or sticky toffee pudding. You'll find fruit scones and buttered crumpets for afternoon tea, Welsh rarebit for "high tea," and a decent smattering of vaguely-familiar-looking celebs fiddling around on their iPhones. $ *Average main: £15* ✉ *69–71 Dean St., Soho* ☎ *020/7434–1775* ⊕ *www.deanstreettownhouse.com* ✍ *Reservations essential* Ⓜ *Tottenham Court Rd.* ✛ *3:D5*

$$ ✕ **The Giaconda Dining Rooms.** A gastro-landmark with an indie spirit
MODERN on Denmark Street's Tin Pan Alley—think Bowie, Marley, and The
EUROPEAN Clash—off Tottenham Court Rd., this super friendly Australian-run
Fodor'sChoice dining room has an eclectic menu that is both distinctive and inspired.
★ Chef Paul Merrony describes his food as "French-ish, with a couple of day trips to Italy thrown in," and this relaxed approach is reflected as he nonchalantly sends out mighty starters—creamed shallots with horseradish, crispy pig's trotters, or baked eggs with cream and tomatoes—and a full range of luscious entrées at decent prices. Try the ox tongue, rack of lamb with gnocchi "alla Romana," guinea fowl with prunes, or heartier dishes like veal kidneys, black pudding with potatoes, or ham hock hash with a fried egg on top. Puddings, like Eton Mess or iced nougat, are a snip at £5 to £6.50 a pop. $ *Average main:*

£16 ⊠ 9 Denmark St., Soho ☎ 020/7240–3334 ⊕ www.giacondadining. com ⌂ Reservations essential ⊘ Closed Sun. No lunch Sat. Ⓜ Tottenham Court Rd. ✦ 3:D4

$$$ ✕ **Hix.** Restaurateur, *bon viveur,* and gad-about-town Mark Hix's
BRITISH spunky Soho spot oozes class and panache, and remains a magnet for
FAMILY the slick-back Soho smart set. It serves simple but brilliant British fare:
think hanger steak with a chunk of bone marrow, red-leg partridge with
curly kale, or Shetland coley with cockles and sea purslane. You'll also
find epic feasts for tables of eight: chop and oysters, whole goose, or
suckling pig, plus riffs on classic dishes, like rabbit and crayfish Stargazy
pie. Check out Sarah Lucas's and Damian Hirst's mobiles, the base-
ment bar billiards, and famed mixologist Nick Strangeway's heritage
cocktails in the winning basement apothecary bar, known appropriately
enough as...Mark's Bar. Note the £17.50 lunch and pre- and post-
theatre deals, plus the £6.50 kids' menu. Ⓢ *Average main: £22* ⊠ 66–70
Brewer St., Soho ☎ 020/7292–3518 ⊕ *www.hixsoho.co.uk* ⌂ *Reserva-
tions essential* Ⓜ *Piccadilly Circus* ✦ 3:C5.

$ ✕ **Koya.** Is it the hours of foot kneading—albeit under canvas, to allay
JAPANESE hygiene concerns—that makes the hand-pulled Sanuki udon wheat-
flour noodles here so springy, spongy, slurpy, and *so* addictive? Lines of
Japanese diners and hip and heritage-clad Soho-ites are a testament to
the allure of the tasty dishes served at this tiny Zen-like cult *udon-ya,*
or noodle house, on Frith Street. Once inside, start with cold udon on
a bamboo basket with pungent miso and pickled pork, and then—*if*
you're up for it—slurp hot udon with smoked mackerel and Japanese
green leaves, or fried tofu and green onions. There are also pickled
plums, prawn tempura, duck-and-rice-in-a-bowl all-in-ones, seaweed
salad, slow-cooked *onsen tamago* poached eggs, and braised pork
belly dishes, but it's the mighty udon noodle that prevails. Ⓢ *Average
main: £12* ⊠ 49 *Frith St., Soho* ☎ 020/7434–4463 ⊕ *www.koya.co.uk*
⌂ *Reservations not accepted* Ⓜ *Tottenham Court Rd.* ✦ 3:D5

$$$ ✕ **Lima.** Wicked pisco sours and out-of-this-world biodiversity-driven
PERUVIAN modern Peruvian cuisine by chef Virgilio Martinez have blasted Lima
to the top rank of London's new-wave Peruvians. Kick back in an
informal sky-lighted dining room scattered with cushions and Inca-style
stitched banquettes, and put yourselves in the hands of the famously
bubbly staff, who'll guide you first to frisky pisco sours, made with
clear grape brandy, sugar syrup, bitters, and foamy egg white. Next
has to be a killer raw-fish sea bream ceviche, doused in lime-y white
tiger's milk ("leche de tigre"), with a tangle of sweet onion and Inca
corn. Charred chunks of braised octopus on white quinoa with purple
botija olive blobs is as vibrant a dish as any, and mains like suckling pig
with Amazonian cashews and lentils, or crab with purple corn, native
huayro potato, and red *kiwicha* (an Andean supergrain) will blow you
sky high. Hit the stunning 75% cacao Porcelana dessert with mango
and wafer-thin blue potato chips to finish, before lolloping your way
through the 12-strong pisco-based cocktail list downstairs. Ⓢ *Average
main: £18* ⊠ 31 *Rathbone Pl.* ⊕ *www.limalondon.com* Ⓜ *Tottenham
Court Road* ✦ 3:C3.

14

Many of Soho and Covent Garden's restaurants cater to the pre- and post-theatre crowds.

$ **✕ Maison Bertaux.** Romantics and Francophiles cherish this quirky, two-
CAFÉ story 1871 French pâtisserie, tea parlour, and occasional pop-up art
space, where nothing seems to have changed since the 1940s. Framed
with vintage blue-and-white awnings, the *choux* pastry, tarts, gateaux,
and gooey cakes at this time-warp Soho institution are renowned and
baked on-site. The chocolate or cream and fruit éclairs, Saint-Honoré,
and Black Forest gâteaux, marzipan figs, apricot tarts, and almond
croissants won't fail to delight. Run by glamorous Soho legend Michelle
Wade, Bertaux also hosts a retro and cheery tea service, which comes
with tasty savories, like broccoli quiche or a Dijon slice, with cheese,
peppers, and Dijon mustard. ⑤ *Average main: £6* ⊠ *28 Greek St., Soho*
☎ *020/7437–6007* ⊕ *www.maisonbertaux.com* ⊟ *No credit cards*
Ⓜ *Leicester Sq.* ✛ *3:D5*

$ **✕ Pitt Cue Co.** Everyone's gone bonkers for the super-smokey and cheap-
BARBECUE as-chips Midwest American BBQ-ed ribs and pulled pork-in-a-bun meal
Fodor's Choice combos here. A tiny, no-reservations hipster hangout, Pitt Cue has only
★ 18 basement seats, plus a few pavement berths and eight counter stools
in the ground-level bourbon-and-rye crush bar—little wonder queues
often snake down the street. Many order the £9.50 to £12.50 finger-
lickin' spreads, which come replete with authentic slaw and house pickles (and are even served up in regulation-white enamel and blue-rimmed
Shawshank Redemption baker-wear dishes). Charred rib-tips, sausages,
baked beans, and bone marrow mash sides are other temptation, but the
devout devour the sliders and sticky ribs (with their mucky paws). The
secret to Pitt Cue's famous barbequed pork and beef ribs? A stonkin'
coal-and-woodchip smoker, 28-day free-range cuts from North Devon,
and dry rubs and marinades which include smoked paprika, Sriracha

chili sauce, blackstrap molasses, and apricot preserve. $ *Average main: £12* ✉ *1 Newburgh St., Soho* ⊕ *www.pittcue.co.uk* ⌖ *Reservations not accepted* ☉ *Closed Sun.* Ⓜ *Oxford Circus* ✛ *3:B5.*

$$
DINER
Fodor's Choice
★
✕ **Spuntino.** Moody tin-tile ceilings, dangly low-wattage filament light bulbs, tattooed waitstaff, bluegrass tunes, and only 26 raised counter stools at this pewter-topped rectangular bar and Lower East Side/Italian-inspired Soho diner makes this the absolute, undisputed, most unimaginably cool gig in town. Naturally, there's no phone, no reservations, and minimal signage, but that only adds to the speakeasy vibe. Once seated after a wait, try truffled egg toast, grits, softshell crab, or Yankee sliders—like ground beef and bone marrow, or spiced mackerel—but don't forget there's mac and cheese or steak and eggs. How could you leave without trying the famed peanut butter and jelly sandwich or the Nutella pizzetta? And wash it all down with a shot or two of Elijah Craig or Knob Creek bourbon. $ *Average main: £12* ✉ *61 Rupert St., Soho* ⊕ *www.spuntino.co.uk* ⌖ *Reservations not accepted* Ⓜ *Piccadilly Circus* ✛ *3:C5.*

$$
MODERN
EUROPEAN
Fodor's Choice
★
✕ **10 Greek Street.** There may only be 28 seats and 9 counter stools overlooking the open kitchen at this stripped-back, Formica-topped, indy-spirited, and upstart Modern European humdinger, but talented Aussie chef Cameron Emirali and former wine merchant Luke Wilson dish up the gourmet goods and have seriously got their shtick together. Great food? *Tick.* Cheap wine? *Tick.* Cute service? *Tick.* Decent prices? *Tick.* Buzz? *Tick.* The only negative is the no reservations policy in the evenings, but most happily saunter off for a quick shifty in the pub, three doors down, and wait to be called back on their cell phones. Once seated, expect simple interchangeable starter/mains like grilled sardines with salsify and salsa verde, or octopus carpaccio with caperberries, chili, and lemon. Gutsy meats like Welsh Black rib-eye with horseradish, hare and polenta, or venison with parsnips and cranberry are big and bold, and swing with the seaons, as are the top-value £4–£6 puds, like lemon delicious, rum pannacotta, or quince and apple pie. $ *Average main: £16* ✉ *10 Greek Street, Soho* ☎ *020/7734–4677* ⊕ *www.10greekstreet.com* ☉ *Closed Sun.* ✛ *3:D4*

$$$
CHINESE
✕ **Yauatcha.** Four cheers for the all-day dim sum at this Cantonese Soho classic. Slinkily designed by the chic Christian Liaigre—with black granite floors, purple-lit aquarium, candles, exposed brick light wall, and a starry ceiling—the James Bond setting is the perfect stage for the exquisite dim sum. Try king crab, cuttlefish and zuccini, or prawn and Chinese chives, or the other lively dishes like crispy duck rolls, hot and sour soup, *congee* rice porridge, venison puffs, and seabass with lotus root. Look out for the fancy cocktails, plus aromatic Oriental loose-leaf teas and the dainty Chinese cakes and fancies in the first floor tearoom. Note the two-hour table turnover, and be sure to dine in the more happening and romantic basement at night. $ *Average main: £18* ✉ *15–17 Broadwick St., Soho* ☎ *020/7494–8888* ⊕ *www.yauatcha.com* ⌖ *Reservations essential* Ⓜ *Oxford Circus* ✛ *3:C4.*

14

COVENT GARDEN

$$$
AUSTRIAN
Fodor'sChoice
★

✕ **The Delaunay.** It's all fin-de-siècle Vienna and the "Radetsky March" at this magnificent low-lit and elegant Art Deco-style take on an all-day grand Central European café and Viennese coffeehouse located on the Aldwych. Want to feel Emperor Franz Joseph I fabulous? Here's a majestic 60-item menu that would do the dual-monarchy and Austro-Hungarian Empire proud. Dishes are von Trapp delicious: impressive Wiener schnitzel, goulash, and Viennese hot dogs, served with sauerkraut and onions. Plus other goodies like borscht and beef Stroganoff, kedgeree, and *choucroute*. Desserts delight, too, including *apfelstrudel* and an evocative three-peaked Salzburg soufflé, while the innocuous "Kinder" ice cream coupe is a blow-out knickerbocker glory bursting with meringue, marshmallows, and whipped cream. Classy breakfasts, brunch, Viennoiserie pastries and afternoon teas are served, and be sure to sniff out the hidden café within the café to while away a long lost afternoon. ⑤ *Average main: £21* ⊠ *55 Aldwych, Covent Garden* ☎ *020/7499-8558* ⊕ *www.thedelaunay.com* Ⓜ *Covent Garden, Charring Cross, Aldwych* ✣ *3:G4.*

$
INDIAN

✕ **Dishoom.** The humble curry is England's surrogate national dish and in London you'll find some of the best around. Sepia-colored, memorabilia-adorned, and *raj*-y Dishoom near Leicester Square is modeled on the Persian-run all-day Irani cafés of Victorian Bombay and it expertly churns out marvelous street food, from naan bread and hankerchief-thin *roomali* roti wraps, to masala prawns, lamb biryani, and yogurt-and-milk-based *lassi* drinks. ⑤ *Average main: £10* ⊠ *12 Upper St. Martin's La., Covent Garden* ☎ *020/7420–9320* ⊕ *www.dishoom.com* Ⓜ *Leicester Sq.* ✣ *3:E5*

$
VEGETARIAN
FAMILY

✕ **Food for Thought.** Covent Garden's hippy-vibey '70s-style subterranean BYO vegetarian café has a cult veggie and vegan following, so be prepared to queue onto Neal Street with the best of them. You'll find cramped wooden communal tables and a daily changing menu of wholesome soups, salads, pulses, stews, quiches, stir-fries, bakes, and casseroles—from mushroom Stroganoff to Rajistani red lentil curry. Wheat-free, gluten-free, GM–free, free-range, Fair Trade, vegan, and organic options are available throughout, and leave room for such puddings as their famous oat-based strawberry and banana "Scrunch." There's take-away, but note that it's only open from noon until 8:30 pm Monday through Saturday, and from noon until 5:30 pm on Sundays. ⑤ *Average main: £8* ⊠ *31 Neal St., Covent Garden* ☎ *020/7836–9072* ⊕ *www.foodforthought-london.co.uk* ✑ *Reservations not accepted* ⊟ *No credit cards* Ⓜ *Covent Garden* ✣ *3:F4.*

$$$
MODERN BRITISH
Fodor'sChoice
★

✕ **Great Queen Street.** Expect a wraparound din and a noisy British foodie crowd at Covent Garden's top gastropub, one that showcases the kind of retro-British classics that Londoners now devour with gusto. Not far from the Royal Opera House, the stripped-back eaterie is done up in a burgundy-walls, bare-oak-floor-and-table setting. Overexcited pear-and-prosecco and wine-fueled diners dive into old-fashioned offerings like pressed tongue, pickled herrings, chicken pie, partridge, or smoked mackerel with rhubarb. You'll find dishes from a bygone era, like brown crab on toast, or faggots with apple mash, plus roasts for the whole table—think 7-hour shoulder of lamb with dauphinoise potatoes (£64 for four)—although green veggies are few and far between. $ *Average main: £18* ✉ *32 Great Queen St., Covent Garden* ☎ *020/7242–0622* ✍ *Reservations essential* ☾ *No dinner Sun.* Ⓜ *Covent Garden, Holborn* ✛ *3:G4.*

$$$ ✕ **The Ivy.** The triple-A list spurn The Ivy for its upstairs private mem-
BRITISH bers' club (and other luxe spots like Scott's and J Sheekey) but, none-theless, this luvvies landmark still receives a thousand calls a day! A bewitching mix of daytime-and-satellite TV stars, gawkers, and out-of-towners dine on salt beef hash, squash risotto, Thai-baked sea bass, salmon fish cakes, pork meatballs, eggs Benedict, and English classics like Shepherd's pie or kedgeree (curried rice with smoked haddock, egg, and parsley) in a handsome mullioned stained-glass and oak-paneled dining salon. Service is flawless, and for low- to mid-wattage West End star-spotting this is a prime spot. ▦ TIP➔ Tip: If you can't snag a table by phone, try walking in on spec—it's been known to work. $ *Average main: £21* ✉ *1–5 West St., Covent Garden* ☎ *020/7836–4751* ⊕ *www.the-ivy.co.uk* ✍ *Reservations essential* Ⓜ *Covent Garden* ✛ *3:E5.*

$$$ ✕ **J Sheekey.** West End and Hollywood superduper stars slide into this
SEAFOOD classy 1896 alley-walk seafood haven, a top alternative to Scott's,
Fodor's Choice Nobu, or 34. Umbilically linked with the surrounding Theaterland
★ district, J Sheekey is one of Londoners' all-time favorite West End haunts. Magnificently orchestrated by incorrigibly amusing maître d' John Andrews, the place charms with warm wood paneling, vintage showbiz black-and-white portraits, a warren of alcove tables, and lava-rock bar tops. Opt for snappingly fresh Atlantic prawns, pickled Arctic herrings, crab bisque, slip soles, scallop, shrimp and salmon burgers, or famous Sheekey fish pie. Better still, sip Gaston Chiquet Champagne and polish off half a dozen Lindisfarne rock oysters at the old mirrored raised-counter oyster bar for the ultimate in true romance, or alterna-tively take advantage of the £26.50 weekend three-course set lunch deals. $ *Average main: £24* ✉ *28–32 St. Martin's Ct., Covent Garden* ☎ *020/7240–2565* ⊕ *www.j-sheekey.co.uk* ✍ *Reservations essential* Ⓜ *Leicester Sq.* ✛ *3:E6*

$$$$ ✕ **L'Atelier de Joël Robuchon.** A few doors down from The Ivy and argu-
FRENCH ably one of London's least publicized best restaurants, L'Atelier attracts both glitterati and food cognoscenti to sit side-by-side at the ground-floor open-kitchen. This is the seductive staging post of French non-plus-ultra superchef Joël Robuchon and the lure is being able to graze tapas-style on his famous creations. Framed with a green-leafy wall, James Bond lighting, and signature red glasses and raised counter seats, this space is custom-made for those who want to splurge on an unparal-leled orgy of exquisite French tapas—from frogs' legs and egg cocotte to foie gras, pig's trotters, scallops, langoustines, and roast quail with buttery truffle mash. The £129 eight-course "*decouverte*" menu is a wanton way to blow the bank, but the £28 and £33 lunch and pre-theater deals are an altogether more sensible way to go. There's a for-mal restaurant, La Cuisine, on the first floor, and a cozy, open-fire snug bar, too. $ *Average main: £27* ✉ *13–15 West St., Covent Garden*

14

☎ *020/7010–8600* ⊕ *www.joel-robuchon.net* ✍ *Reservations essential*
Ⓜ *Leicester Sq.* ✛ *3:E5*

$$$ ✕ **Les Deux Salons.** You're bound to spot a late-night theaterland celeb
BRASSERIE like Sienna Miller in one of those dark green leather bays at this clas-
sic 1930s-style French brasserie off St. Martin's Lane. The two-floor
mezzanine dining salons are an elegant profusion of brass rails, mosaic
floors, white linen, and flattering globe lights, where you'll find mas-
terful classics, from Marseille *bouillabaisse* fish soup to Bavette steak.
Some mains are truly outstanding—grilled sea bass with seashore veg-
etables, perhaps, or roast cod with pea and bacon—but it's the great
people-watching that makes it sparkle. ■ **TIP→ Tip: try the excellent pre-
and post-theater meals for £15.95.** Ⓢ *Average main: £18* ✉ *42–44 Wil-
liam IV St., Covent Garden* ☎ *020/7420–2050* ⊕ *www.lesdeuxsalons.
co.uk* ✍ *Reservations essential* Ⓜ *Leicester Sq.* ✛ *3:E6*

$$$ ✕ **Opera Tavern.** Mouthwatering acorn-rich Ibérico pig's-head terrine?
TAPAS Chargrilled salt-marsh lamb with broad beans? Mini Ibérico pork and
foie gras burgers? These are three of the outstanding Spanish and Italian
tapas dishes presented at the handily situated Opera Tavern, opposite
the historic Drury Lane theater, and not far from Covent Garden piazza
and the Royal Opera House. Clamber in at the overcrowded ground-
floor tapas bar (avoiding the accoustically challenged second-floor dining salon if you can) and, after enjoying an amuse-bouche of crispy
pig's ears, opt for the rich empanadas of venison, the Italian Scotch
eggs, braised cuttlefish, or Venetian-style sardines. Authentic? The menu
warns that all game here may have "shot" in it. ■ **TIP→ Watch out, too,
for the £40–£45 set tapas meals for groups of seven and up.** Ⓢ *Average main: £15* ✉ *23 Catherine St., Covent Garden* ☎ *020/7836–3680*
⊕ *www.operatavern.co.uk* ✍ *Reservations essential* Ⓜ *Covent Garden,
Holborn* ✛ *3:G5.*

$$$$ ✕ **Rules.** Come, escape the 21st century. Opened by Thomas Rule in
BRITISH 1798, London's oldest restaurant is, according to some, still London's
Fodor's Choice most *beautiful.* The main dining salons are, indeed, an all-round old-
★ world wonderland, what Maxim's is to Paris. The decor begins with the
plush red banquettes, lacquered yellow walls, and spectacular etched-
glass skylights. Then, in High Victorian fashion, every nook and cranny
is covered with vintage needlepoints, Regency oil paintings, antique
clocks, stuffed pheasants, antlers, bronze figurines, and hundreds of
framed prints. Little wonder Rules has been a stage across which everyone from Charles Dickens to Laurence Olivier has pranced. For your
shining day—be sure to ask for a table in one of the "glass house" skylight rooms, the bar area, or the cute Maggie Thatcher corner—dig into
the menu's pricey and historic British dishes, such as steak-and-kidney
pie, jugged hare, or roast beef and Yorkshire pudding. For a real taste
of the 18th century, you can choose, in season, daily specials of fabulous
game from the restaurant's High Pennines estate, including grouse, partridge, snipe, and woodcock. Ⓢ *Average main: £29* ✉ *35 Maiden La.,
Covent Garden* ☎ *020/7836–5314* ⊕ *www.rules.co.uk* ✍ *Reservations
essential* 🏠 *Jacket required* Ⓜ *Covent Garden* ✛ *3:F6.*

$$$$
BRITISH
FAMILY

✕**The Savoy Grill.** You can *feel* the history in the room at this glamorous 1889 Art Deco power dining salon, which has hosted all the greats from Oscar Wilde and Frank Sinatra to Elizabeth Taylor and Marilyn Monroe. Nowadays—buffed up with Swarovski chandeliers, velvet coverings, gold leaf–backed tortoiseshell walls, and period photos and mirrors—it caters for business barons and dreamy top-end tourists who come for the Grill's famous tableside trolley, which might trundle up with roasts like saddle of lamb, crown of pork, or traditional beef Wellington. Savoy dishes like omelet Arnold Bennett (with smoked haddock, Parmesan, and cream) or old-favorite egg cocotte with smoked bacon, wild mushrooms, and red wine sauce are to the fore, and there's impressive classics like T-bone, chateaubriand, and porterhouse steaks, plus oysters, Dover sole, and lobster thermidor. All delights from a bygone age—as is this dining room, which is very heavy on the Art Deco style (so, if you don't like that look . . .). $ *Average main: £30* ⊠ *The Savoy, 100 Strand, Covent Garden* ☎ *020/7592–1600* ⊕ *www.gordonramsay.com/thesavoygrill* ⚹ *Reservations essential* Ⓜ *Charing Cross, Covent Garden* ✛ *3:G5.*

$
MEXICAN
FAMILY

✕**Wahaca.** Brace for queues for the fab-value Mexican street market food at chef Thomasina Miers's brightly colored Covent Garden favorite. Concrete walls, bench seats, and green ceiling slats make for brisk and buzzy basement surrounds, but it's the cheap-as-chips, ethically and sustainably sourced £3.95–£7.95 Mexican tacos, enchiladas, quesadillas, taquitos, and burritos that pull in the cost-consious, studenty, and touristy crowds. A £19.95 spread for two hungry honchos will produce a feast of broad bean quesadillas, pork pibil tacos, slaw, chicken taquitas with green rice, tostadas, black beans, and guacamole, but note that it is often heaving by 6:30 pm. $ *Average main: £7* ⊠ *66 Chandos Place, Covent Garden* ☎ *020/7240–1883* ⊕ *www.wahaca.co.uk* ⚹ *Reservations not accepted* Ⓜ *Covent Garden* ✛ *3:F6.*

BLOOMSBURY AND HOLBORN

BLOOMSBURY

$
AMERICAN

✕**Bea's of Bloomsbury.** We don't know how it happened, but London's turned into cupcake central, and Bea's of Bloomsbury is one of the best American cupcake and tea shops in town. With its on-site bakery, Bea's churns out freshly baked sugary delights like blackberry cupcake with vanilla sponge, butter cream, and a fresh blackberry on top, or heavenly chocolate fudge cupcake with fudge icing. Don't miss the brightly colored peanut butter, praline, or carrot cake cupcakes, and try not to drool over the cornucopia of three-layered chocolate truffle cakes, New York cheese cakes, lemon drizzle Bundts, fruit cakes, and pecan pies. Afternoon tea (2 pm–7 pm weekdays, noon–7 pm on weekends) with cupcakes, scones, mini-meringues, flavored marshmallows, and Valrhona brownies is £19. $ *Average main: £6* ⊠ *44 Theobald's Rd., Bloomsbury* ☎ *020/7242–8330* ⊕ *www.beasofbloomsbury.com* Ⓜ *Mansion House* ✛ *3:H1.*

14

FITZROVIA

$ ✕**Bubbledogs.** Hot dogs and *Champagne?* Why didn't *we* think of that!

AMERICAN

FAMILY

Fodor's Choice

★

Bubbledogs has come up with one of the most unlikely food combinations this side of milk shakes and fries—and has miraculously hit the jackpot. Husband-and-wife team Sandia Chang and chef James Knappett have combined their respective loves of New York hot dogs and small-production-house Champagne, and gone back to basics with a bar menu that pays due homage to both. Classic 7-by-1 inch, all-British pork, beef, or vegetarian hot dogs cost a mere £6–£7.50, while the handcrafted Champagnes are some of the cheapest in town—including £6.50 for a glass of Gaston Chiquet or £7.50 for Christophe Mignon. Sit at raised counters with dog cartoons, brick walls, and cozy log-cabin paneling, and choose *scrumbilicious* hot dogs in baskets ranging from a superior BLT (bacon wrapped, with caramelized lettuce and truffle mayo), to a Sloppy Joe (with chili and cheese), or a K-DAWG (with kimchi and red bean paste). There's £2.50 coleslaw and sweet-potato fries, but expect to wait; they only take reservations for groups of six or more. ⑤ *Average main: £7* ✉ *70 Charlotte St., Fitzrovia* ☎ *020/7637–7770* ⊕ *www.bubbledogs.co.uk* ✍ *Reservations not accepted* ☉ *Closed Sun. and Mon.* Ⓜ *Goodge St.* ✛ *3:B2*

$$$ ✕**Dabbous.** It's a triumph of taste over technology at wunderkind Ollie

MODERN

EUROPEAN

Fodor's Choice

★

Dabbous's extraordinary game-changer off Charlotte Street. Startlingly stripped-back, pure, inventive, and seasonally based new-wave dishes elicit *Oohs!, Aahhs!, Wows!,* and *Oh-my-goshes!!* in a flummery-free NYC–industrial chic setting of exposed concrete, overhead ducting, and heavy metal screens and cages. Phenomenal flavors abound. Dishes like peas and mint ping your taste buds with frozen mint tea, edible violets, and broad-bean flowers, and a coddled hen's egg with woodland mushrooms and smoked butter sits handsomely in a cute bowl of hay. Palette-popping barbecued Ibèrico pork with acorn praline, turnip tops, and apple vinegar; halibut with coastal herbs (sea aster and oyster leaf); and brittle and crumbly chocolate ganache with green basil moss are *instant* classics, and set Dabbous apart as one of London's most dazzling young talents. Sorry: you have to book months ahead. ⑤ *Average main: £18* ✉ *39 Whitfield St., Fitzrovia* ☎ *020/7323–7323* ⊕ *www.dabbous.co.uk* ✍ *Reservations essential* ☉ *Closed Sun. and Mon.* Ⓜ *Goodge St.* ✛ *3:C2*

$ ✕**Roti Chai.** Incredible Indian street food hits the spot at this bright,

MODERN INDIAN

Fodor's Choice

★

yellow-ceilinged, superior curry canteen found behind Selfridges. The kitchen specializes in grub inspired by Indian street-cart vendors, roadside "dhaba" cafés, and bustling Victorian railway stations found across the subcontinent. You'll find a good sprinkling of smart Indians tucking in—often heartily with their fingers—into glass bowls of spicy street snacks like nibbly *bhel puri* (puffed rice with onion, cumin, and tamarind), fiery white cubes of "Hakka" chili paneer cheese, or flayed Keralan chicken "lollipops," which come with an irresistible coriander dip. There's Punjabi aloo (potato) *bun tikki* mini-burgers, and a tender tomato-based "Railway" lamb curry with chapatis (straight out of Bombay's Victoria Terminus station). You can imagine you're on the road with the authentic hot curried chickpea spreads, pea samosas, or Indian mango ice cream on a stick. This is a trip to India for which you

BRITISH TO A "T": TOP TEAS IN TOWN

It was a peckish Anna, 7th Duchess of Bedford, who began the tradition of British afternoon tea in the 1840s, and taking tea is now once more the height of fashion. Here are the best around, plus some places that are gently priced.

Tea at the Palm Court at the **Ritz** (✉ The Ritz, 150 Piccadilly ☎ 020/7300–2345 ⊕ www.theritzlondon.com) would moisten the eye of Marie Antoinette and is still an ultimate afternoon tea experience, with a rococo starburst of gilt work, crystal chandeliers, and floral displays. Expect egg and cress-and-cucumber sandwiches on three-tiered silver cake stands, plus fruit scones, cakes, and dainty British pastries (£45–£64).

In the northern reaches of Mayfair, a Hungarian quartet plays at hallowed **Claridge's** (✉ Brook St. ⊕ www.claridges.co.uk ☎ 020/7107–8872), where the green-and-white-striped porcelain tea service is straight out of the Mad Hatter's Tea Party. You'll find 40 loose-leaf teas to choose from, including rare Darjeeling First Flush tea (prices from £39, or £63 for a rosé Champagne tea). Nearby, off Mount Street in Mayfair, fashionistas splurge on flourless caramel sponge cake at the soigné **Connaught** (✉ Carlos Pl. ⊕ www.the-connaught.co.uk ☎ 020/7107–8861). Loyalists enjoy the open fires, Laurent-Perrier bubbles, smoked-salmon finger

sandwiches, Christine Ferber jams, and loose-leaf Ceylon tea.

If you can't afford to stay at London's best hotel, why not take tea for an hour or two and indulge in the fantasy of Noël Coward's favorite city spot for a fraction of the cost? Just a few blocks over from Mayfair on the Strand, the **Savoy** (✉ Strand ⊕ www.fairmont.com/savoy-london ☎ 020/7420–2111) offers the prettiest settings in London. In the heavenly glass-cupola-covered Upper Thames Foyer—all pink orchids and a black-and-white chinoiserie fabric—you can savor the Savoy's Afternoon, Champagne, and High Teas (£40–£60).

For cheaper tea options, there's a £10.50 Cream Tea, or an exquisite £34 Afternoon Tea with quail-egg-and-caviar sandwiches, in a quirky *Alice in Wonderland* meets *The Enchanted Wood* setting at the Glade at **Sketch** (✉ 9 Conduit St. ☎ 020/7659–4500 ⊕ www.sketch.uk.com). Similarly, the Soho crowd sinks into comfy velvet chairs with frilly cushions for Afternoon Tea at the Parlour anteroom at **Dean Street Townhouse** (✉ 69–71 Dean St. ⊕ www.deanstreettownhouse.com ☎ 020/7434–1775) restaurant for eminently affordable £16.75 teas, with buttered crumpets, Battenberg cake, or cheesy buck rarebit with an egg on top.

14

need no passport. ⑤ *Average main: £12* ✉ *3 Portman Mews S, Fitzrovia* ☎ *020/7408–0101* ⊕ *www.rotichai.com* Ⓜ *Marble Arch* ✢ *1:G4.*

THE CITY

Historic, and just beyond The City limits, chef-centric Clerkenwell is one of the most cutting-edge, radical, and trendy quarters for London gastro-dining, which sets it in marked contrast to the adjacent City,

Clerkenwell is a trendy playground of top chefs and inventive cuisines.

which caters overwhelmingly to business-focused conservative dining. In Clerkenwell, the starchiness of The City fades into relaxed artiness: a fertile ground for avant-garde chefs and restaurants.

$$$
FRENCH
✗ **Bistrot Bruno Loubet.** Seasoned French chef Bruno Loubet rules the roost at this ever-buzzy hotel dining room and bistrot at the Zetter hotel in historic-yet-cutting-edge Clerkenwell. Loubet tinkers away and creates so many must-try dishes it's genuinely hard to pick: deliciously pink quail comes with prune, Roquefort, and sautéed wild mushrooms, while guinea fowl *boudin blanc* sausages sit perfectly with leeks and chervil sauce, just to name two winners. You'll find wonderful sea bream with Pernod *beurre blanc*, yummy Mauricette snails and meatballs, and rabbit *royale*, followed by tarragon poached pear, or crêpes suzette (served with a touch of cardamom in a shiny copper pan). The ground-floor bistro is kitted out with appealing retro lamps and artifacts and overlooks St. John's Square. ⑤ *Average main: £19* ⊠ *The Zetter, 86–88 Clerkenwell Rd., Clerkenwell, Clerkenwell* ☎ *020/7324-4455* ⊕ *www.bistrotbrunoloubet.com* ⌘ *Reservations essential* Ⓜ *Farringdon St., Barbican* ✛ *2:F3.*

$$$
BRASSERIE
Fodor's Choice
★
✗ **Boundary.** Restaurateur and design-guru Sir Terence Conran scores a bull's-eye at Boundary at this eponymous boutique hotel and foodie complex in über-trendy Hoxton/Shoreditch. A theatrically glass-fronted open kitchen, sparkly lighting, smart acoustics, and plush red-and-blue upholstered throne-like seats, make this swanky, chic, and gayly carpeted modern French basement brasserie the glamorati's East End dining destination of choice. The menu's a wish list of crowd-pleasers designed to impress: classics like twice-baked soufflé Suisse, lobster

thermidor, cod cassoulet, pigeon pot-au-feu, and red wine-heavy bœuf Bordelaise are all big and brassy, and are well served by timeless sides like Dauphinois potatoes or cauliflower gratin. Desserts like lemon *tarte au citron* or cherry *clafoutis* bake are impossiby tasty and fairly priced, and look out, too, for the £19.50 or £24.50 prix-fixe deals. $ *Average main: £20* ✉ *2–4 Boundary St. (entrance at 9 Redchurch St.), The City* ☎ *020/7729–1051* ⊕ *www.theboundary.co.uk* ◬ *Reservations essential* ⊙ *No lunch Mon.* Ⓜ *Liverpool St.* ✛ *2:G1*

$ ✗ **E Pellicci.** It's all non-stop Cockney *gor blimey!* banter and all-day Eng-
CAFÉ   lish breakfasts at this tiny 1900 Italian family-run chrome-and-Vitrolite
FAMILY   landmark café near the East End's great Brick Lane and Columbia Road street markets. With colorful stained glass, Formica tables, art deco marquetry, and signed pics of *East Enders* TV soap stars, it's the rowdy hole-in-the-wall for the greasy "fry-ups" that Londoners adore: eggs, bacon, toast, baked beans, sausages, tomatoes, mushrooms, black pudding, tea, and "bubble 'n' squeak" (cabbage and mash). Matri-arch "Mama" Maria also rustles up "Toscana" spaghetti, plus steamed sponge or bread pudding. Your arteries most certainly will clog up, but at least the wallet is spared. Everything's less than £8.50, but remember this is the East End, and hence it's "*Cash only, Mate!*" $ *Average main: £7* ✉ *332 Bethnal Green Rd., East End* ☎ *020/7739–4873* ◬ *Reserva-tions not accepted* ▬ *No credit cards* ⊙ *Closed Sun.* Ⓜ *Bethnal Green* ✛ *2:H1.*

$$$$ ✗ **L'Anima.** Top-notch southern Italian cuisine in a love-it-or-loathe-it
ITALIAN   modern glass-sided shoe-box of a restaurant characterizes the breezy business-based scene here near Liverpool Street in the City. Italian chef Francesco Mazzei draws inspiration from Sicily, Puglia, Sardinia, and Calabria, and prowls the high-ceilinged bar, floor, and clear-fronted kitchen like the proud owner he is. Simple, fresh, modern, and restrained dishes like wild mushroom and black truffle *tagliolini* and Sardinian fish stew are near perfection, as is the wood-roasted turbot with artichoke and Calabrian sausage—as succulent as you could wish. Desserts, like liquorice zabayon wine custard, are *bellissimo*, and the winning wine list, naturally, is practically all Italian. $ *Average main: £26* ✉ *1 Snowden St., The City* ☎ *020/7422–7000* ⊕ *www.lanima.co.uk* ⊙ *Closed Sun.* Ⓜ *Liverpool St.* ✛ *2:G1*

$$$ ✗ **Moro.** Up from the City, near Clerkenwell and Sadler's Wells dance
MEDITERRANEAN   theater, is Exmouth Market, a cluster of cute indie shops, artisan baker-ies, bookstores, an Italian church, and more fine restaurants like Moro. Lovingly led for more than a decade by husband-and-wife chefs Sam and Sam Clark, the menu includes a mélange of Spanish and Moorish North African flavors. Rustic tapas—like baba ganouj and Syrian len-tils, baby squid with harissa, or grilled chorizo—compete with spiced meats, Serrano ham, salt cod, and char-grilled offerings. Wood-fired seabass with hispi cabbage or grilled sea bream with chickpea salad are among the stand-out mains. Sidle up to the zinc bar, or squeeze into a tiny table and lean in—it's *really* noisy here, but fun. $ *Average main: £19* ✉ *34–36 Exmouth Market, The City* ☎ *020/7833–8336* ⊕ *www. moro.co.uk* ◬ *Reservations essential* ⊙ *Closed Sun.* Ⓜ *Farringdon, Angel* ✛ *2:E3.*

14

$$ ╳ **Simpson's Tavern.** This old-world Dickensian chop house and tavern
BRITISH was founded by Thomas Simpson in 1757 and it's as raucous now as
FAMILY the day it opened. Approached via a tiny back alley near the Bank of
England, it draws tubby, ruddy-faced pinstriped City folk, who revel
in the old boarding school surrounds and guzzle down shedloads of
claret and old school grub: pork belly crackling, oxtail stew, steak and
kidney pie, potted shrimps, chump chops, and "stewed cheese" (the
house special of cheese on toast with béchamel sauce). Desserts, natu-
rally, are boarding school favorites, like bread and butter pudding or
spotted dick and custard. Shared oak bench stalls and grumpy service
only seem to add to the charm. Note it's only open weekdays for break-
fast and lunch from 8:30 am until 3 pm last orders. $ *Average main:*
£10 ⊠ *38½ Cornhill, at Ball Ct., The City* ☏ *020/7626–9985* ⊕ *www.*
simpsonstavern.co.uk ⌂ *Reservations essential* ⊙ *Closed weekends. No*
dinner Ⓜ *Bank* ✛ *2:G2.*

$$$ ╳ **St. John.** Foodies travel the globe for pioneering chef Fergus Hen-
MODERN BRITISH derson's ultra-British nose-to-tail cooking at this no-frills, stark-white
Fodor's Choice converted ham-and-bacon smokehouse near famed Smithfield Market
★ in Clerkenwell. Henderson famously uses *all* parts of a carcass, and his
waste-not, want-not chutzpah is laudable and chimes perfectly with the
new age of austerity: one appetizer is pig's skin, and others, like ox heart
or pig's ear and calves' brain and chicory, are marginally less extreme.
St. John signatures like bone marrow and parsley salad, chitterlings with
dandelion, or pheasant and pig's trotter pie appear stark on the plate,
but arrive with aplomb. Expect a cracking all-French wine list and finish with apple pie with custard, Eccles cakes and Lancashire cheese, or
half a dozen golden Madeleines. $ *Average main: £23* ⊠ *26 St. John St.,*
Clerkenwell ☏ *020/3301–8069* ⊕ *www.stjohnrestaurant.com* ⌂ *Reser-*
vations essential ⊙ *No dinner Sun.* Ⓜ *Farringdon, Barbican* ✛ *2:F4.*

$$$ ╳ **Sweetings.** A time-warp City seafood institution, Sweetings was estab-
SEAFOOD lished in 1889 and it powers serenely on as if the sun never set on the
British Empire. There are some things Sweetings really *doesn't* do: din-
ner, reservations, coffee, or weekends. It does, mercifully, do seafood—
and rather well. Not far from St. Paul's Cathedral, it's patronized by
self-assured old school City gents who down pewter tankards of Black
Velvet (Guinness and Champagne) and like to eat lobster salad, roe
on toast, Dover sole, Cornish brill, and succulent skate wings with
black butter sauce, all this at linen-covered raised counters or tables.
The snooty long-serving waitstaff wear whites, the oysters are plump
and fresh, and desserts, like fruit crumble and baked jam roll, are old
boarding school favorites. $ *Average main: £19* ⊠ *39 Queen Victoria*
St., The City ☏ *020/7248–3062* ⌂ *Reservations not accepted* ⊙ *Closed*
weekends. No dinner Ⓜ *Mansion House* ✛ *2:H6.*

$ ╳ **Tayyabs.** Unloved City bankers and doctors from the nearby Royal
PAKISTANI London Hospital swamp this neon-lit, high-turnover Pakistani curry
specialist (set in the eastern part of Whitechapel part of The City).
Expect queues after dark, and bear in mind it's BYO, jam-packed, noisy,
and often maddeningly chaotic. Nonetheless, prices are keen and you
can OD and gorge handsomely for under £20 on a mixed char-grill
extravaganza, which might include fiery Tandoori chicken and fish

tikka. Other best bets include karahi okra, slow-cooked "dry meat," minced meat *seekh* kebabs, karahi prawns, hot steaming naan breads, and Tayyab's famous spicy char-grilled karahi lamb chops (cooked to a secret receipe). $ *Average main: £12* ✉ *83 Fieldgate St., The City* ☎ *020/7247–9543* ⊕ *www.tayyabs.co.uk* ♨ *Reservations not accepted* M *Aldgate East* ✢ *2:H2.*

THE EAST END

$$$ ✕ **Bistrotheque.** You'll need a GPS or Google Maps to find this East London fashionista hub and all-round cool-hunters HQ, down a side alley in jam-hot Bethnal Green. Once inside, the striking first-floor loft dining space and Manchichi Bar is a bubbly post-industrial chic setting of all-white tiled walls and white concrete floor, factory pipes and beams, Crittal windows, dangly lights, marble-top tables, and black bentwood chairs. All the men seem to wear caps, spatz, Trilbys, skinny Acne jeans, or '30s tweed three-piece deer-stalker suits, while the Alexa Chung lookalike women are in capes, *Emmanuelle 2* organza get-ups, and oversize Scooby-Doo specs. Acomplished French and English-based dishes range from steak tartar, Croque Madame, and towering cheeseburgers, to cod and clams, or lamb rump with chestnuts and sage. Fashion-favorite puds like melba toast or brioche and butter pudding stand out, and be sure to catch Xavior, the resident pianist, at weekend brunch, camping up everything fom Girls Aloud to Katy Perry on the baby grand. $ *Average main: £15* ✉ *23-27 Wadeson St., East End* ☎ *020/8983–7900* ⊕ *www.bistrotheque.com* M *Bethnal Green* ✢ *2:H1.*

MODERN
EUROPEAN
Fodor's Choice
★

$ ✕ **Pizza East.** The whole *Wham!*-glam East End demimonde seems to have taken up residence at this knockabout gourmet pizza parlor, which serves up chewy, 10-inch, wood-fired, thin-crust, crispy pizzas in a former tea warehouse—actually, an achingly au courant setting of exposed concrete walls, raw brickwork, pillars, pipes, and industrial ducting. Amid a soundscape of Stone Roses, Baby Shambles, and vintage Bowie, mix things up at the long refractory-style shared tables with a starter of sea bass carpaccio with fennel and chili, or broad beans with pecorino, before tearing into the one of the eleven £8–£14, semolina-crust, rich pizzas, which might be topped with San Daniele ham, ricotta and pesto, or pancetta, eggplant, and scamorza (an Italian cow's-milk cheese). There's wine by the tap, cocktails by the jug (if you ask *nicely*), plus karaoke, slam poetry, hip-hop, or old-school tune sessions in the downstairs Concrete basement bar. $ *Average main: £12* ✉ *56 Shoreditch High St., East End* ☎ *020/729–1888* ⊕ *www.pizzaeast.com* M *Rail: Shoreditch High Street* ✢ *2:G1.*

PIZZA
FAMILY

$$ ✕ **Rochelle Canteen.** You feel quite the foodie insider once you've finally found the quirky Rochelle Canteen—it is set in the renovated bicycle shed of the old restored Victorian-era Rochelle School (off Arnold Circus in Shoreditch, not far from the boutiques of Redchurch Street and Liverpool Street station). Ring a buzzer next to a pale blue door, go in through the "Boys" entrance (passing a former playground) and enter chef Margot Henderson's long white, austere "canteen," which has an open kitchen and two long Formica tables, Ercol school chairs, and Shaker pegs on the wall. Gloriously understated British fare arrives at

BRITISH

14

a convivial pace, from simple deviled kidneys on toast to a retro plate of Yorkshire ham, carrots, and parsley sauce. Bump along with the art/architecture/designer crowd, and enjoy seasonal guinea fowl with bacon, or skate and capers, and finish with quince jelly or lemon posset. Note it is no-liquor-license BYO (£5 corkage), and only open Monday to Friday, for breakfast, elevenses, lunch, and tea. ⑤ *Average main: £16* ⊠ *Rochelle School, Arnold Circus, Shoreditch* ☎ *020/7729–5677* ⊕ *www.arnoldandhenderson.com* ⊗ *Closed weekends* Ⓜ *Liverpool St.* ✛ *2:G1*

$$$
MODERN
EUROPEAN
Fodor's Choice
★

✕ **Viajante.** It's quite a *schlep* from the West End to Viajante in Bethnal Green but Portuguese chef/patron/cultural leader Nuno Mendes's ultra-contemporary, avant-garde cuisine is some of the hottest, most exciting in town. Armed with tweezers in a fascinating open-kitchen, El Bulli-trained Mendes doubles down with 3- to 12-course tasting extravaganzas (£35–£95) in the à la modishly converted former Bethnal Green Town Hall. Unusual tastes, textures, and flavors abound—like skate with roasted yeast, set crab milk with beach herbs, or Thai basil panna cotta—but every dish tastes incredible, and *looks* like high art. Expect rare micro-herbs and Hackney's finest local urban foraged goodies, such as wood sorrel, sweet violets, and honeysuckle, and don't be surprised to be served at your table by the great man Mendes himself. Our advice is simple: *Go.* ⑤ *Average main: £25* ⊠ *Town Hall Hotel, Patriot Sq., Bethnal Green, East End* ☎ *020/7871–0461* ⊕ *www.viajante.co.uk* ☏ *Reservations essential* ⊗ *No lunch Sun.* Ⓜ *Bethnal Green tube/rail, Cambridge Heath rail* ✛ *2:H1*.

SOUTH OF THE THAMES

First mentioned in 1276 and believed to have existed in Roman times, Borough Market on the South Bank is a firm favorite with tourists, chefs, and foodies alike. Open for lunch Monday through Wednesday from 10 am to 3 pm, and for longer on Thursday (11 am–5 pm) and Friday (noon to 6 pm) and all-day to Saturday (8 am–5 pm), the unassuming location under Victorian wrought-iron railway arches at London Bridge is packed with foodie trekkers eager to pick up the finest and freshest fruit, veg, and grub in the capital. There are more than 130 stalls, plus a bunch of pubs, bars, and restaurants, and specialty shops, like Neal's Yard Diary (⊠ *6 Park St.*), where you'll be bowled over by the great mountains of stinky blue Stilton cheese stacked floor to ceiling. There are other noted eateries in south London, as the following reviews reveal.

$$
MODERN BRITISH

✕ **Anchor & Hope.** Hearty meaty dishes at wallet-friendly prices emerge from the open kitchen at this permanently packed, no-reservations leading gastropub on The Cut (between Waterloo and Southwark Tube), a few doors down from the excellent Young Vic contemporary theater. Pot roast duck, Herefordshire beef, deep-fried pig's head, pumpkin gratin, and cuttlefish with bacon stand out. Bear in mind that it's noisy, cramped, informal, and always overflowing. That said, the kitchen is highly original, and there are great dishes for groups—like the famous slow-roasted shoulder of lamb. Eager diners wait for a table over a drink in the pub's convivial saloon bar, and be prepared to share a wooden dining table with others once seated, too. $ *Average main: £17* ✉ *36 The Cut, South Bank* ☎ *020/7928–9898* ✍ *Reservations not accepted* ⊗ *No dinner Sun. No lunch Mon.* Ⓜ *Waterloo, Southwark* ✛ *5:F2.*

$$$$ ✕**Chez Bruce.** Deeply flavorsome French and Mediterrean cuisine, faultMODERN FRENCH less service, a winning wine list, and a glossy neighborhood vibe make Fodor'sChoice for one of London's all-time favorite destination restaurants. Take a ★ train or cab south of the Thames to lauded chef Bruce Poole's cozy, gimmick-free haunt overlooking Wandsworth Common and then get ready for an endless procession of wonders, ranging from delicious home-made charcuterie or offal to lighter, simply grilled fish dishes. Pot roast pig's cheek with polenta, pollack with wild mushrooms, and roast monkfish with scallops, ham hock, and Jerusalem artichokes are all immaculately conceived. The wine and desserts are stunning, the sommelier's superb and, pound-for-pound, Chez Bruce is nigh impossible to beat. Weekday lunches are £27.50; three-course dinners are £45. $ *Average main: £26* ✉ *2 Bellevue Rd., Wandsworth* ☎ *020/8672–0114* ⊕ *www.chezbruce.co.uk* ✍ *Reservations essential* Ⓜ *Tube: Wandsworth Common rail* ✛ *4:E6.*

$ ✕**Hot Stuff.** Hot Stuff in Vauxhall (south of the Thames) offers some of NORTH INDIAN the best-loved and best-priced curries in London. Run by Raj Dawood, it's a cult BYO café with its own Facebook appreciation society. Home-cooked specials include king prawn *biryani*, thick lamb bhuna curry, and cubed chili paneer white cheese. There's also wonderful pilau rice, onion *bhaji* snacks, Peshwari naan bread, and earthy *dhal* (curried lentils). Average price of dinner for two: £24. $ *Average main: £14* ✉ *19–23 Wilcox Rd., South Bank* ☎ *020/7720–1480* ⊕ *www.welovehotstuff. com* ✍ *Reservations essential* Ⓜ *Vauxhall* ✛ *5:C6.*

$$ ✕**José.** Rising Spanish chef José Pizarro packs 'em in like so many slices TAPAS of *jamón jamón* at this tapas-and-sherry treasure trove on happening Bermondsey Street, south of the river near Guy's Hospital and London Bridge. With only 30 seats and no reservations, you'll be hard-pressed to find a spot at the tapas bar or a perch at an upturned barrel after 6 pm, but stick with it, *hombre*, the tapas is astounding. Quaff a glass of Amontillado or Orloroso sherry, and keep those expertly crafted small white plates a comin': patatas bravas...croquetas...pisto and crispy duck eggs...hake and aioli...razor clams with chorizo...paprika-specked Ibérico pork fillets. You'll either love or hate the crush. $ *Average main: £7* ✉ *104 Bermondsey St., South Bank* ☎ *020/7403–4902* ⊕ *josepizzaro.com* ✍ *Reservations not accepted* Ⓜ *London Bridge* ✛ *5:H2.*

$$$ ✕**Magdalen.** South of the river between London and Tower bridges, MODERN BRITISH Magdalen is a self-assured beacon of class in a markedly up-and-coming part of town. It specializes in inventive but unpretentious modern British cuisine at keen prices; poached hake with fennel (£9), calves' sweetbreads with salsify (£18), wild turbot and clams (£19), and treacle tart for £7 will hardly break the bank. With dark-wood and bent-wood chairs, chandeliers, tea candles, the pleasing ox-blood-colored surrounds invite you to sit back with the clever wine list and ponder

14

whether to have a feast of whole hare or the stuffed suckling pig instead. $ *Average main: £17* ✉ *152 Tooley St., South Bank* ☎ *020/7403–1342* ⊕ *www.magdalenrestaurant.co.uk* ✍ *Reservations essential* ⊗ *No lunch Sat. Closed Sun.* Ⓜ *London Bridge* ✛ *5:H2.*

$$ ✕ **Tom Ilic.** Serbian-born chef Tom Ilic cooks with technical brilliance
EUROPEAN but thankfully charges only neighborhood prices at this thriving local hero in Battersea. Gob-smacked locals adore the big-on-meat menu (especially pork), and lap up intricate dishes like pig's cheek with chorizo, mash and pork crackling, or Irish Kettyle beef with ravioli and root vegetables. Set lunches offer plenty of value at £16.95, or £19.50 on Sunday. It's south of the Thames, the decor's a bit naff (uncool) and '90s, and it is best approached by cab or overland train (not the tube). $ *Average main: £15* ✉ *123 Queenstown Rd., Battersea* ☎ *020/7622–0555* ⊕ *www.tomilic.co.uk* ✍ *Reservations essential* Ⓜ *National Rail: Queenstown Rd. or Battersea Park* ✛ *4:G6.*

$$ ✕ **Zucca.** River Café alumnus Sam Harris has nailed the elusive winning
ITALIAN formula for London's *ultimate*—and commendably inexpensive—mod-
Fodor's Choice ern Italian on buzz-hot Bermondsey Street, doors down from the fab
★ White Cube gallery (and other happening eateries like tapas joints José and Pizzaro). Anywhere that notes on its menu that "The use of mobile phones is both unsociable and unnecessary" has got its head screwed on right, and this sure touch is in evidence throughout, from the white melamine tables and open kitchen, to the passionately prepared, all-homemade Italian breads, pasta, and ice cream. Start off sharing a punchy £5.50 antipasto like salt cod with chickpeas, then swoon over the Piedmontese egg-yoke-colored pappardelle pasta with veal ragu, or the incredible Le Marche white truffle *vincisgrassi* pasta bake. You'll only find three fish or meat mains to chose from, but anything like the ink-black squid with white polenta, or a perfect blush-pink veal chop with spinach and lemon will be *molto bellissimo*. The desserts and all-Italian wine list rock, too. $ *Average main: £16* ✉ *184 Bermondsey St., South Bank* ☎ *020/7378–6809* ⊕ *www.zuccalondon.com* ⊗ *Closed Mon. No dinner Sun.* Ⓜ *London Bridge* ✛ *5:H2.*

KENSINGTON, CHELSEA, AND KNIGHTSBRIDGE

If you you're fab, famous, wealthy, or perhaps all three, chances are you'll be living—and dining—in one of these neighborhoods among the world-class museums, parks, shops, hotels, monuments, fashion stores, and top restaurants (do the names of super-chefs Heston Blumenthal and Harvey Nichols ring a bell?). Chelsea, made famous in the swinging '60s, is where today's Prada velour–clad yummy mummies bomb around in V8 supercharged Range Rover 4x4s, which locals have dubbed "Chelsea tractors." Known for its top-drawer shopping, Chelsea's restaurants range from bijou boîtes to exclusive little frou-frou places ideal for a girly gossip and a bite on the go. Over in upscale Knightsbridge, you'll find Harrods and the high-end fashion boutiques of Sloane Street, plus a heap of platinum-class hotel-based restaurants. Come here for an amazing dining experience, but don't expect bargains (except at lunch). Nearby, Kensington is a residential neighbor-

Harwood Arms's modern take on the classic British dish, Scotch eggs.

hood with a wider range of restaurants, from French bistros to funky Vietnamese hideaways.

KENSINGTON

$$$$
FRENCH
Fodor's Choice
★

✕ **Tom Aikens.** Is so-called wonderchef Tom Aikens the real thing? Indeed. The flame-haired, former kitchen bad boy was always popping up in the gossip columns for having bust-ups with his staff, winning awards, hobnobbing with the gentry, or flirting with bankrupcy. Nonetheless, he's stripped all the *ancien régime* flummery away and it's now all freed up, colorful, joyous technique-*and*-ingredient-driven fireworks on the plate at his starkly revamped Nordic-style gastro-lair in tony Chelsea, and everyone's impressed. You'll bliss out over his marinated hand-dived scallops with apple vinegar, his new-found vegetable numbers—like baked celeriac, a jumbled-up raw turnip salad, or braised leeks with whey and marjoram—and his mains kick are even better: try the braised beef short rib with bone marrow and melting tendons, or herb-coated sea bass with clams and brown shrimps to encounter a grandmaster at work. ⓢ *Average main: £32* ✉ *43 Elystan St., Kensington* ☎ *020/7584–2003* ⊕ *www.tomaikens.co.uk* ⌂ *Reservations essential* ⊘ *Closed Sun. No lunch Sat.* Ⓜ *South Kensington* ✛ *4:E3.*

$$$
JAPANESE

✕ **Yashin.** *Without Soy Sauce . . . but if you want to* proclaims the neon sign on the glazed green-tiled wall behind the open chefs' counter at London's *best* sushi bar (right off Ken High Street). Take their advice, bag a ringside counter seat, and watch head chef and co-founder Yashuhiro Mineo and company tease, slice, tweak, and blowtorch their way through dish after dish of the most awesome/fresh/funky/spunky/colorful and exquisite "omakase" sushi, sashimi, salads, and carpaccios that you're likely to find this side of the East China Sea. Tofu-topped miso cappucino comes in a Victoriana cup-and-saucer, and softshell blue crab salad is a tangle of zingy mizuna leaves. Delectable 8-, 11-, or 15-piece omakase sushi spreads (£30–£60) might mesmerize with ponzu-spiked salmon, Japanese sea bream with rice cracker dust, salted wagyu, or Japanese botan prawns with foie gras. Alternatively, the bargain £12.50 5-piece salmon nigiri set-lunch, with hot miso and bracing salad, is a smashing way to sample Yashin's below-the-radar brilliance. ⑤ *Average main: £22* ⊠ *1A Argyll Rd., Kensington* ☎ *020/7938–1536* ⊕ *www.yashinsushi.com* Ⓜ *High Street Kensington* ✛ *4:B1.*

CHELSEA

$$
MODERN BRITISH
Fodor'sChoice
★

✕ **The Harwood Arms.** Modern British game doesn't get any better—or more inventive—than at this exceptional gastropub and game-lovers' paradise off Fulham Broadway. Enthusiast and co-owner Mike Robinson shoots and bags all the wild venison on the menu here in season (the two-star Aussie chef Brett Graham is another co-owner), and you'll find a catalogue of awesome game-based dishes like haunch of Berkshire roe deer with tarragon mustard or North Yorkshire grouse with Earl Grey–soaked prunes. Tuck into game pie with Somerset cider jelly or Herdwick lamb with rosemary curd in a relaxed comfy-sofas-and-newspapers Sloaney-pub type setting. A number of fine dishes are served on a slab of wood, and there are popular carve-your-own whole-roast beef, lamb, or pork joints for the table—and, *yes,* you can ask for doggy bags on the way out! ⑤ *Average main: £19* ⊠ *27 Walham Grove, Chelsea* ☎ *020/7386–1847* ⊕ *www.harwoodarms.com* ⌖ *Reservations essential* ☽ *No lunch Mon. Last dinners served 9 to 9:30 pm* Ⓜ *Fulham Broadway* ✛ *4:A5.*

$$$
WINE BAR

✕ **The Henry Root.** Named after the amusing, upper-class spoof letter writer, Henry Root, you'll find there's nothing fake about this winsome neighborhood joint-cum-wine-bar off the Fulham Road, which serves up a quirky menu in a friendly non-stop party salon. Well-spoken and casually attired local Chelsea denizens think nothing about using their fingers to pick their way through a whole globe artichoke with Dijon vinaigrette, and they rave about the hearty jellied ham hock or cured meat and piccalilli charcuterie platters. Besides small plates like Cornish mussels and bacon, and deep salad bowls, there are satisfying mains like lemon chicken, roast pheasant, or smoked haddock with poached egg and Champagne sauce. ⑤ *Average main: £18* ⊠ *9 Park Walk, Chelsea* ☎ *020/7352–7040* ⊕ *www.thehenryroot.com* ⌖ *Reservations essential* Ⓜ *Fulham Broadway, South Kensington* ✛ *4:D4.*

$$$
HUNAN

✕ **Hunan.** There's no menu at this quirky, top-rated family-run Chinese stalwart (est. 1982), south of Sloane Square in Pimlico. Instead, diners state their likes and dislikes to owner/chef Peng, or his son Michael, and sit back, relax, and chop-stix their way through a succession of highly tasty, tapas-size dishes to share. Using a profusion of garlic, ginger, Szechuan chili, and peppercorns, a loyal crowd might enjoy 12 to 14 unfailingly delicious dishes like Hunan water-fried dumplings, sliced duck, signature pork broth with Chinese mushrooms, crispy frogs' legs, pig's ears and tongues, or crab noodle soup. There's no rhyhm or reason to what you might receive, but portions are generous, the wine list is extensive, and the ongoing surprise is all part of the fun. $ *Average main: £22 ✉ 51 Pimlico Rd., Pimlico, Chelsea ☎ 020/7730–5712 ⊕ www.hunanlondon.com ✍ Reservations essential ⊘ Closed Sun.* Ⓜ *Sloane Sq.* ✛ *4:G3*

$$$ ✕ **Indian Zing.** Indian Zing's chef/owner Manoj Vasaikar woos the west
INDIAN London curry mafia with updated eclectic regional Indian cuisine on King's Street emergent "Curry Mile." Start with tamarind-spiced Rasam mussels and move onto Khyber Pass shank of lamb or Barbary duck with Chettinad spices. Average price of dinner for two: £66. $ *Average main: £17 ✉ 236 King St., Hammersmith ☎ 020/8748–5959 ⊕ www. indianzing.co.uk ✍ Reservations essential* Ⓜ *Ravenscourt Park* ✛ *1:A2.*

$$$ ✕ **Medlar.** What's *not* to like about Medlar? Sensationally assured Mod-
MODERN ern European cuisine, effortless service, a glossy crowd, elegant oak-
EUROPEAN wood floors, mirrored walls, and a luxe gray and lime-green stenciled color scheme make for a complete neighborhood package at the slightly quieter World's End stretch of the King's Road. Weekday set lunch is a steal at £26, where you'll find winners such as crab ravioli with fondant leeks and samphire, roast mallard with pear and star anise, or juicy fil- let steak with snails and triple-cooked chips. Wonderous desserts—like plum beignets with custard and ginger ice cream—couldn't be more delicious. $ *Average main: £21 ✉ 438 King's Rd., Chelsea ☎ 020/7349– 1900 ⊕ www.medlarrestaurant.co.uk ✍ Reservations essential* Ⓜ *Ful- ham Broadway, Sloane Sq.* ✛ *4:D4*

$$ ✕ **The Orange.** Four-square and handsome, this debs-delight Pimlico
MODERN BRITISH gastropub (with upstairs guest rooms) seems to get everything right,
FAMILY which is why it's packed with braying locals most nights and seemingly all weekend. The stage is set—light and airy, with stripped wood, a tony ochra color-scheme, and mini-potted orange trees—for service that is noticeably smiley, polite, and (dare we say it?) well-mannered. You can't go wrong with the chicken liver parfait, Trealy Farm cured meat platters, and the wood-fired spelt-based pizzas, or alternatively enjoy a leisurely Sunday roast like 28-day Castle of Mey beef rib, Kilravock pork rack, or Suffolk chicken with sage and bacon stuffing, all served with crispy duck-fat roast potatoes, seasonal vegetables, and traditional Yorkshire puddings. $ *Average main: £16 ✉ 37 Pimlico Rd., Chelsea ☎ 020/7881–9844 ⊕ www.theorange.co.uk ✍ Reservations essential* Ⓜ *Sloane Sq.* ✛ *4:G3*

$$$ ✕ **Racine.** There's always an upscale buzz at this star of the Brompton
BRASSERIE Road dining scene, not far from the V&A, Harrods, and the packed-
to-the-rafters Holy Trinity Brompton Church. This smooth-running chic-and-cheerful classic French *brasserie de luxe* excels in doing the simple things well—and not costing the earth. Veteran chef Henry Har- ris's signatures like roast partridge and juniper, foie gras with Calvados, soft roe on toast, skate wing, rack of lamb, or adventurous deep fried calf's brains and not-for-the-faint-hearted *tête de veau*—poached calf's head—all hit the high notes. Many of the satisfied-looking patrons are stealth-wealth local regulars, but even they seem to be tempted by the legendary three-course £15.50–£17.75 prix-fixe lunch or dinner deals (until 7:30 pm). $ *Average main: £18 ✉ 239 Brompton Rd., Chel- sea ☎ 020/7584–4477 ⊕ www.racine-restaurant.com ✍ Reservations essential* Ⓜ *South Kensington, Knightsbridge* ✛ *4:E2.*

14

The Orange serves a delicious prosciutto-topped wood-fired pizza.

$ **✕ Troubadour.** It's hard to hear yourself speak, and the food's a bit pricey
BRITISH for what it is, but everyone enjoys the 1950s bohemian scene, folksy
live music, and poetry readings at the Troubadour, a restaurant, coffee
shop, and music venue. The site of Bob Dylan's first London gig and
host to Led Zeplin, Joni Mitchell, Jimmy Hendrix, Joni Mitchell, and
Nick Drake, this place is where latter-day bohemians lounge around and
dine on breakfasts, burgers, pastas, omelets, and strong coffee. ⑤ *Average main: £14* ⊠ *263 Old Brompton Rd., Chelsea* ☎ *020/7370–1434*
⊕ *www.troubadour.co.uk* ✛ *4:B3.*

KNIGHTSBRIDGE

$$$ **✕ Bar Boulud.** U.S.-based star French superchef Daniel Boulud combines
BRASSERIE the best of French high-end brasserie fare with a dash of superior Yan-
kee gourmet burgers and fries, at this popular street-level all-day hang-
out in the luxe Mandarin Oriental hotel. Lilliputian-size platters of the
most delicate Gilles Verot charcuterie, heartier *coq au vin*, or positively
chunky truffled Boudin blanc sausages with Lyonnaise mashed potatoes
compete with palm-size Yankee, Frenchie, Piggie, or signature "BB"
foie-gras beef burgers and fries in sesame seed or black onion seed buns.
The knock-out grazing menu has something for everyone, and pro but
informal waitstaff make for a convivial vibe in this handy spot oppo-
site Harvey Nichols department store. ▮TIP→ **Note the £23 3-course
lunch or 5–7 pm prix-fixe deals.** ⑤ *Average main: £22* ⊠ *Mandarin Oriental Hyde Park, 66 Knightsbridge, Knightsbridge* ☎ *020/7201–3899*
⊕ *www.danielnyc.com/barbouludlondon.html* ✎ *Reservations essential*
Ⓜ *Knightsbridge* ✛ *4:F1.*

$$$$ ✕ **Dinner by Heston Blumenthal.** Exceptional Olde English–inspired dishes
BRITISH executed with ultramodern precision in an open kitchen is the shtick at
Fodor'sChoice Ashley Palmer-Watts' acclaimed award-winner at the Mandarin Orien-
★ tal in Knightsbridge (Palmer-Watts was the protégée of superstar chef
Heston Blumenthal, who is still closely involved in the restaurant). As
you take in the view of Hyde Park, you simply must slice into a Meat
Fruit starter (c. 1500), deceptively shaped like a mandarin, but encasing
the smoothest, most creamy chicken liver parfait on the *planet*. A plate
of Rice and Flesh (c. 1390) is a picture of yellow saffron rice with calf's
tails and red wine, and fans will recognise the snail-and-girolle Savoury
Porridge (c. 1660) from Blumenthal's Berkshire flagship, The Fat Duck.
There's juicy Beef Royale (c. 1720) cooked *sous vide* at 56°C for 72
hours, plus tender cod in cider with mussels and chard (c. 1940). Head
off with the marvelous spit roasted pineapple Tipsy cake (c. 1810)—a
triumphant homage to traditional English spit-roasting from centuries
past. For conversation-piece dishes, you can do no better. ⑤ *Average
main: £32* ✉ *Mandarin Oriental Hyde Park, 66 Knightsbridge, Knightsbridge* ☎ *020/7201–3833* ⊕ *www.dinnerbyheston.com* ⌕ *Reservations
essential* Ⓜ *Knightsbridge* ✚ *4:F1.*

$$$$ ✕ **Koffmann's.** Set in the Berkeley hotel, this is the "last hurrah" of
FRENCH noted French chef Pierre Koffmann, now in his mid-sixties, and the
very antithesis of a celebrity chef. Never paying heed to trends, the clientele here enjoys such classic signatures as delicately seared hand-dived
scallops with black squid ink and famed stuffed pig's trotters "Tante
Claire" with sweetbreads and morels. The Gascon-born Koffmann
showcases 35-odd years of experience and the best of unreconstructed
regional Gascony cuisine in a *jolie*, carpeted, and well-appointed informal basement setting. Alongside a steady stream of celebs and minor
British royalty, be sure to experience other renowned gastro goodies
like snails with garlic and parsley, wild duck à l'orange, Gascon apple
tart, or signature pistachio soufflé with pistachio ice cream—before it is
too late! Two neat ways in are the £25.50 to £28 three-course lunches
or the £28 pre-theater specials. ⑤ *Average main: £27* ✉ *The Berkeley,
Wilton Place, Knightsbridge* ☎ *020/7107–8844* ⌕ *Reservations essential* Ⓜ *Knightsbridge* ✚ *4:G1.*

$$$$ ✕ **Mari Vanna.** All of London's Russian molls, dolls, and porcelain-
RUSSIAN skinned *babushkas* squeeze into this kitsch White Russian fantasy
Fodor'sChoice dining salon in Knightsbridge, which overflows with a fay-gray and
★ maximalist decor of antique chandeliers, Tiffany lamps, knick-knacks,
pickles, tchotchkes, vintage books, pics, mirrors, Cheburashkas, and a
Russian *pechka* stove. Note the crochet and linen-covered tables tended
by chirpy Russian staff (some in dirndls) and dishes proffered with
what feels like great aunt Vanna's old family silver and jumbled crock-
ery. Then snap into character with a horseradish vodka shot or two,
then carb-up on Pirogi sea bass savories, clear Siberian Pelmeni dumpling soup, classic Russian "Olivier" ox-tongue salad, or feather-light
smoked salmon blinis. There's highly pleasing borsch, dill and potaotes,
and creamy beef Stroganoff with mash and wild mushrooms, and let's
not forget the sweet crepes with condensed milk. But it's the nostalgic
dacha-like antebellum home-from-home setting that makes you feel like

14

you're in some kind of *Anna Karenina*–esque episode. $ *Average main:* *£26* ✉ *116 Knightsbridge, Knightsbridge* ☎ *020/7225–3122* ⊕ *www.* *marivanna.co.uk* Ⓜ *Knightsbridge* ⊹ *4:F1.*

$$$$ ✕**Petrus.** Gordon Ramsay protégé Sean Burbidge presides over an abso-
MODERN FRENCH lutely flawless, world-class, modern French experience at Tripadvisor's
Fodor's Choice top-ranked London restaurant in very posh Belgravia. The softly car-
★ peted dining salon may be a bit beige and circa G. Ramsay-late-'90s, and
a central circular glass wine cellar a touch passé, but add in the warm
welcome, bonhomie, impeccable nibbles, *bonne bouches*, petit fours,
assured sommelier, stonking cheese board, and charming, fleet-footed
service, and you've got an unparalleled all-around gastro-embrace. Burbidge's go-forward cuisine is all *technique, technique, technique*, and
it's impossible not to swoon at starters like exemplary Les Landes duck
foie gras with grape jelly, or perfect lobster ravioli swimming in creamed
leaks and Champagne velouté. Bliss out on pink 25-day Casterbridge
beef fillet with braised shin and sticky Barolo sauce, and watch out
for surprises towards the end, like the honeycomb-and-dark-chocolate
sphere that theatrically melts in front of your eyes, cute cones with
syllabub, or white choc-ices on sticks that emerge from a bowl of dry
ice. $ *Average main: £28* ✉ *1 Kinnerton St., Belgravia, Knightsbridge*
☎ *020/7592–1609* ⊕ *www.gordonramsay.com/petrus* Ⓜ *Knightsbridge*
⊹ *4:G1.*

$$$$ ✕**Rasoi.** Star Indian chef Vineet Bhatia showcases the best new-wave
INDIAN Indian cuisine in London at this tony Victorian town house off the
King's Road. Ring the front door bell on arrival at this romantic celebration venue, which is decked out with colorful Indian prints, silks,
masks, bells, and ornaments. Bhatia pushes the boundaries with creative
signatures like popcorn prawns, crab lollies with lime and coconut soup,
wild mushroom rice with tomato ice cream, Bordeaux rogan-josh lamb
shanks, or Darjeeling tea grilled chicken. Naturally the prices are pretty
fiery for such inventive cuisine, but be sure not to leave without sam-
pling Madras coffee cheesecake or the famous warm chocolate samosas,
dubbed "Chocamosas." Two-course lunches are £22, while dinners
range from £49 to £89. $ *Average main: £32* ✉ *10 Lincoln St., Knights-*
bridge ☎ *020/7225–1881* ⊕ *www.rasoirestaurant.co.uk* ⌂ *Reservations*
essential ⊗ *No lunch Sat.* Ⓜ *Sloane Sq.* ⊹ *4:F3*

$$$ ✕**Zuma.** Hip, hip, hurrah! for this ever-fashionable, *celeb-tastic*, Tokyo-
JAPANESE style modern sushi restaurant and hipster hang-out near Harrods and
FAMILY Harvey Nichols. Well-lit and designed, with polished granite, blond
cedar wood, exposed pipes, and open timberwork, Zuma takes in a sake
bar, robata grill, and sushi counter—and *all* of the beautiful people from
SW7. You can't go wrong with the California maki rolls, eel sushi, sea
bass sashimi, pork with yuzo, or robata-grilled wagyu beef on a hoba
leaf. Sip a sake, kick back, and marvel at the amusing all-spray-tanned
Made In Chelsea *Mwah! Mwah!* clientele, and be sure to grab the
sake sommelier to guide you through the 40 varieties of sake rice wine
and other rare and obscure Japanese spirits. $ *Average main: £20* ✉ *5*
Raphael St., Knightsbridge ☎ *020/7584–1010* ⊕ *www.zumarestaurant.*
com ⌂ *Reservations essential* Ⓜ *Knightsbridge* ⊹ *4:F1.*

BURGER MANIA

The 'umble hamburger has come in from the cold and is now a viable gourmet option at a gaggle of recession-busting burger specialists. Here's where to go: **MeatLiquor** (✉ *74 Welbeck St., Marylebone* ☎ *020/7224–4239*), off Bond Street, attracts queues for its juicy cooked-to-order bacon cheeseburgers and double-patty Dead Hippie burgers at this grungy and graffiti-strewn Southern burger mosh pit. Famed all-British butchers The Ginger

Pig supplies the meat at **Honest Burgers** (✉ *4A Meard, Fitzrovia* ☎ *020/3609–9524*) in Soho, where you can bug-out on chunky, £8–£9 cheese- or Honest burgers, with skin-on fries with rosemary salt. A £20 hamburger, grilled lobster, or lobster rolls, with chips-and-salad combos are the only things on the menu at the cult **Burger & Lobster** (✉ *40 St. John's St., Farringdon* ☎ *020/7490–9230*), near Smithfield Market in Farringdon (closed Sun.).

14

NOTTING HILL AND BAYSWATER

Ever since Hugh Grant and Julia Roberts put the neighborhood on the global map, Notting Hill's had a reputation as one of London's most fashionable neighborhoods, with numerous boutiques, chic cafés, pâtisseries and restaurants, buzzy bars, and the famous Portobello Road market's collection of antiques shops, bric-a-brac, vintage-clothing stands, and delicious food stalls. The gentrification of Notting Hill has led to a battalion of merchant bankers and club-class high flyers moving into the area, and hence prices are stratospheric. Portobello Road Market is one of London's most popular outdoor street markets. Get there early on Saturday morning (the market is open 8 am–6 pm) to beat the crowds. Peruse the antiques and vintage clothes, and when you want to snack, head to the north end of the market. Get ready for fresh-fruit-and-veggie stands, bakeries, Spanish olive and French cheese purveyors, and numerous hot-food stalls peddling savory crepes, hamburgers, German chicken, wraps, paella, kebabs, and Malaysian noodles.

NOTTING HILL

$$$
MODERN BRITISH

✕ **The Cow.** Top supermodel Kate Moss and her rockstar hubby Jamie Hince are known to crash this archetypal boho-chic Notting Hill gastropub, which packs 'em in cheek-by-jowl in a faux-Dublin '50s backroom saloon bar that serves Fines de Claire oysters, bowls of whelks and winkles, Cherrystone clams, and whole Dorset crab with aioli. Upstairs the amiable chef whips up Brit specialties in a spartan dining salon, like deviled lamb's kidneys on toast, Stilton, chicory and hazelnut salad, or smoked eel with bacon and horseradish. Hard-up post triple-dip recession ex-millionaire Notting Hill locals seem quite happy to live off the house special in the saloon bar: a pint of draft Guinness with a pint of prawns and mayonnaise (£9.95). ⑤ *Average main: £19* ✉ *89 Westbourne Park Rd., Notting Hill* ☎ *020/7221–0021* ⊕ *www.thecowlondon.co.uk* ⌖ *Reservations essential* Ⓜ *Westbourne Park* ⌖ *1:B3.*

Ditch the fancy sit-down lunch and pick up fresh snacks from the Portobello Road market.

$$$ ✕**E&O.** Gywneth, Madonna, Stella, and a gazillion *flashionistas* and
MODERN ASIAN the Learjet set, give a well-manicured thumbs up to this long-standing
Asian tapas supremo off Portobello Road market. E&O's figure-friendly
medley of Japanese, Chinese, Vietnamese, and Thai all-star favorite
dishes includes dim sum, sushi, tempura, and sashimi, with a slew of
low-carb options. Don't skip lychee martinis in the see-and-be-seen
bar, before moseying over to the moody monochrome dining room for
miso black cod, snow crab maki, papaya salad, Thai rare beef, or lamb
rendang; the sea bass sashimi is achingly fresh. There are pavement
tables and curbside bench seats to people-watch on Blenheim Cres-
cent, and it's good for a girly girls' night get-together. $ *Average main:*
£15 ⊠ *14 Blenheim Crescent, Notting Hill* ☎ *020/7229–5454* ⊕ *www.*
rickerrestaurants.com/e-and-o ⌂ *Reservations essential* Ⓜ *Ladbroke*
Grove ✛ *1:B1.*

$$$$ ✕**The Ledbury.** Sensational Aussie chef Brett Graham wins hearts,
MODERN FRENCH minds—and global accolades—at this high-ceilinged destination din-
Fodor's Choice ing landmark on the crumbier edges of Notting Hill. In a handsome
★ four-square room full of drapes, mirrored walls, and plush seats, you
won't find a more inventive vegetable dish than Graham's ash-baked
celeriac with hazelnut and wood sorrel, and it's impossible to best his
roast quail with walnut cream, roe deer with bone marrow, or Cor-
nish turbot with fennel and elderflower. Besides an *obsessive* interest in
game, Graham's also famous for incredible desserts, so why not finish
with thinly sliced figs with ewes' milk yogurt and fig-leaf ice cream? Pro
service and a top sommelier round out this winning proposition, now
considered one of London's very best eateries by many foodies. $ *Av-*
erage main: £31 ⊠ *127 Ledbury Rd., Notting Hill* ☎ *0207/7792–9090*

⊕ *www.theledbury.com* ⚑ *Reservations essential* ⊗ *No lunch Mon.*
Ⓜ *Westbourne Park, Ladbroke Grove* ✛ *1:A4.*

$$ ✕ **The Mall Tavern.** It's all things unapologetically British at this embrac-
MODERN BRITISH   ing 1856 Notting Hill gastropub, which overflows with relaxed but
discerning locals. Check out the Coronation mugs, royal wedding, and
Prince Charles and Lady Diana crockery and memorabilia after sam-
pling some great British bar snacks, like pork scratchings, brawn (head
cheese), or lop-eared sausage rolls. Move through to dine on chef Jess
Dunford Wood's hearty cow pie with bone marrow poking through the
crust, or wallow in '70s nostalgia with chicken Kiev, macaroni cheese,
or high-quality fish fingers, mushy peas, and tartare sauce. There's old-
school Arctic Roll ice cream, "Hello to the Queen!" glacé bananas
with hot chocolate sauce, and some strong farmhouse cheeses, like Mrs
Kirkham's Lancashire, and Shorrock's Bomb. ▥ TIP➜ Note the bargain
£10 lunches from Tuesday to Friday. ⑤ *Average main: £13* ✉ *71 Palace
Gardens Terr., Notting Hill* ☎ *020/7229–3374* ⊕ *www.themalltavern.
com* ⚑ *Reservations essential* Ⓜ *Notting Hill Gate* ✛ *1:B5.*

BAYSWATER

$ ✕ **Alounak.** Wonderous Persian dips, unleavened breads, small tasty
MIDDLE EASTERN   plates, and steaming stews and grilled kebabs are found at this lantern-
filled Aladdin's Cave, a warm and inspired Iranian canteen beloved by
hoards of Middle Easterners. Lines form on Westbourne Grove for the
hot breads straight from the clay oven by the door. Try grilled aubergine
purée with walnuts, special lamb, and chicken Alounak kebabs, minced
lamb skewers with grilled tomato and rice, or the "Zereshk polo"—
saffron chicken with sweet and sour Iranian forest berries. Enjoy the
Persian black cardamon teas and sweets, and lime juice-and-pistachio
faloodeh sorbet, but know that the sour yogurt drinks are not to every-
one's taste. ⑤ *Average main: £13* ✉ *44 Westbourne Grove, Bayswater*
☎ *020/7229–4158* ⚑ *Reservations essential* Ⓜ *Queensway* ✛ *1:B4.*

$$$ ✕ **Angelus.** Owner, sommelier, and former pro rugby union player Thi-
FRENCH   erry Tomasin scores a brilliant individual try with his distinctive French
brasserie tucked away behind Lancaster Gate. Styled with Art Nouveau
mirrors and button-back banquettes in a 200-year-old converted former
pub, Angelus has a rep for intricate and unrivaled Paris-style *brasserie
de luxe* dishes. The duck liver crème brûlée, egg cocotte, frogs' legs,
loin of venison, and Grand Marnier soufflé are as good as can be.
Classy £16 breakfasts, all-day brunch, and light bites like omelets, steak
sandwichs, or *pichounette* short-eats are well conceived, and service
is notoriously—how should we say it?—... *Gallic!* Ex-Le Gavroche
sommelier Tomasin is sure to select a kinky bottle from the off-beat
French-focused wine list. ⑤ *Average main: £25* ✉ *4 Bathurst St., Bayswater* ☎ *020/402–0083* ⊕ *www.angelusrestaurant.co.uk* ⚑ *Reservations essential* Ⓜ *Lancaster Gate* ✛ *1:D4.*

$$$ ✕ **Hereford Road.** Bespeckled chef and co-owner Tom Pemberton mans
MODERN BRITISH   the front-of-house grill station at this must-visit Bayswater favorite,
renowed for its pomp-free, pared-down, and ingredient-driven sea-
sonal British fare. With an accent on well-sourced honest-to-goodness
regional and seasonal British produce, many dishes are as unfussy
as you'll find. Work your way though uncluttered combinations like

British Food Decoder

In London, local could mean any global flavor, but for pure Britishness, roast beef and Yorkshire puddings top the list. If you want a good-value traditional Sunday lunch, go to a traditional pub. Spruced up, stripped-back, and updated gastropubs, where Sunday roasts are generally made on-site with top-quality ingredients, are an even better bet. The meat is usually served with crisp roast potatoes, carrots, peas, and root vegetables, plus Yorkshire pudding, a savory batter baked in the oven until crisp. A rich, dark, meaty gravy is poured on top, and you'll get horseradish sauce on the side.

Other tummy liners include Shepherd's pie, made with stewed minced lamb and a mashed-potato topping and baked until lightly browned on top; cottage pie is a similar dish, but made with minced beef instead of lamb. Steak-and-kidney pie is a delight when done properly: with chunks of lean beef and ox kidneys, braised with onions and mushrooms in a thick meaty gravy, and topped with a light puff or short-crust pastry.

Fish-and-chips, usually battered deep-fried cod, haddock, or plaice, comes with thick chips, or french fries, as we call them in the States. A ploughman's lunch in a pub is crusty white bread, a strong-flavored English cheese with bite (cheddar, blue Stilton, crumbly white Cheshire, or smooth red Leicester), and tangy pickles with a side-salad garnish. For a hot, comforting dessert, seek out a sweet bread-and-butter pudding, made from layers of bread and dried currants baked in egg, cream, and nutmeg until crisp. And one can't forgo English cream tea, which consists of fruit scones served with jam and clotted cream, and finger sandwiches made with wafer-thin slices of egg, cress, or cucumber—served as an accompaniment to properly brewed loose-leaf tea.

steamed mussels with cider and thyme, lemon sole with sea dulse, duck breast with pickled walnuts, and English rice pudding and jam. Expect to brush past the entire well-heeled Tory party senior leadership and Notting Hill set on the way out, and ■TIP➔ NB: the express £9.50 or set £13 or £15.50 lunches are arguably the best high-quality lunches deals in town. $ *Average main: £16* ⊠ *3 Hereford Rd., Bayswater* ☎ *020/7727–1144* ⊕ *www.herefordroad.org* ⌕ *Reservations essential* Ⓜ *Bayswater, Queensway* ✛ *1:B4.*

REGENT'S PARK AND HAMPSTEAD

REGENT'S PARK

$$ ✕**Lemonia.** Hollywood-*ville* Primrose Hill's favorite Greek Cypriot res-
GREEK   taurant, vine-decked and '80s taverna–style Lemonia is large and light, and always packed with hordes of hungry locals. Besides an endless supply of small-dish *mezédes* dips and starters, there are rustic mains like slow-baked *kleftiko* lamb in lemon, aubergine and potato moussaka, and beef stewed in red wine. Expect generous Greek hospitality, tons of noise, and the odd fly-by from the ritzy boho-chic Primrose Hill/super-megastar set. Top-value weekday luncheons are a bargain £12.50. $ *Average main: £14* ⊠ *89 Regent's Park Rd., Regent's Park*

LOCAL CHAINS WORTH A TASTE

When you're on the go or don't have time for a leisurely meal, you might want to try a local chain restaurant or sandwich bar. *The ones listed below are well priced and are the best in their category.*

Byron: Bright and child-friendly, this 19-strong line of superior hamburger joints storms the burger market with its delicious Scotch beef hamburgers, onion rings, Cobb salads, and french fries. ⊕ *www.byronhamburgers.com.*

Busaba Eathai: It's always jam-packed at these eight Thai canteen supremos where you'll find Thai noodles, rice dishes, and spicy all-in-one meals in a bowl in sultry dark-wood surrounds. ⊕ *www.busaba.com.*

Café Rouge: A classic 35-strong French bistro chain that's been around for eons and churns out great £9.95–£14.50 *plats rapides* and prix-fixe deals—so enduringly uncool that it's now almost fashionable. ⊕ *www.caferouge.co.uk.*

Carluccio's Caffè: The Carluccio's chain of 14 all-day Italian café–bar–food shops are freshly sourced, family-friendly, and make for brilliant pasta and salad stops on a shopping spree. ⊕ *www.carluccios.com.*

Côte: High quality and very reliable £11.70–£13.65 classic French brasserie meal deals are order of the day at this upmarket and smartly decked

out 21-strong chain. ⊕ *www.cote-restaurants.co.uk.*

Ed's Easy Diner: Overdose on milk shakes, ice-cream floats, chili dogs, blues burgers, and other made-to-order hamburgers at this five-strong chain of shiny, retro-'50s-theme, American-style diners. ⊕ *www.edseasydiner.com.*

Gail's Artisan Bakery: *Chunky artisanal-bread sandwiches, fine breakfasts, and lunches like chorizo, butternut squash, and quinoa salad are found at this spanking-clean chain of 12 brilliant bakeries.* ⊕ *www.gailsbread.co.uk.*

Le Pain Quotidien: Try Belgian tartine open sandwiches, soups, salads, and cakes at the communal wooden tables. There are 15 branches, including ones at the soaring St. Pancras station and Eurostar terminus. ⊕ *www.lepainquotidien.co.uk.*

Pret a Manger: London's high street take-out supremo isn't just for wholesome store-made sandwiches: there are great-tasting wraps, toasties, noodles, sushi, salads, fruit, porridge, and tea cakes, too. ⊕ *www.pret.com.*

Wagamama: Londoners love to drain endless bowls of Asian ramen and noodle soups at this high-tech, child-friendly chain of canteens. ⊕ *www.wagamama.com.*

14

☎ *020/7586–7454* ☏ *Reservations essential* ☉ *No lunch Sat. No dinner Sun.* Ⓜ *Chalk Farm* ✛ *1:F1.*

ISLINGTON

$ ✗ **Ottolenghi.** Mesmerizing meringue-rich foodie window displays and
CAFÉ a funky modern all-white interior characterize this flagship North Afri-
FAMILY can and Mediterranean deli/bakery/café set in Islington's main Upper Street drag. Sit at shared tables and dig into exceptionally tasty—and healthy—dishes like roast sweet potato with burnt aubergine and pomegranate, lamb cutlets with okra, Tunisian harissa-spiced chicken, and

golden beetroot, red cabbage and sour cream, along with cult Otto-lenghi salads, savories, soups, pastries, and artisanal cakes. Go home with a take-out chocolate meringue, roasted plum and quince tart with yogurt, cream, and pistachios, and maybe pick up Ottolenghi's amazing cookbook, *Plenty*, on the way out, too. ⑤ *Average main: £13* ✉ *287 Upper St., Islington* ☎ *020/7288–1454* ⊕ *www.ottolenghi.co.uk* Ⓜ *Angel* ✛ *1:H1.*

THE THAMES UPSTREAM

CHISWICK

$$$

MODERN BRITISH

✕ **Hedone.** Only a loony or genius would serve an appetizer of half a plain white Cévennes onion with a few pear shavings and beurre blanc, but, luckily, maverick—and untrained—Swedish chef Mikael Jonsson falls in the latter camp at his spectacular debut in the wilds of Chiswick. A prolific food blogger and frustrated former lawyer, Jonsson's *extreme* approach to the provenance of his ingredients—often wild, rare, or foraged—means his dishes are some of the most intense, fresh, and unusual around. Watch him in an open kitchen prepare ingredient-driven wonders like wild Dorset sea bass with pickled black radishes and hyssop oil, hand-caught Devon scallops with a vividly stuffed courgette flower, or gloriously marbled 55-day-aged Darragh O'Shea Black Angus beef on the bone. Such is Hedone's global acclaim that tables are snaffled up weeks in advance. ⑤ *Average main: £25* ✉ *301–303 Chiswick High Rd., Chiswick* ☎ *020/8747–0377* ⊕ *www.hedonerestaurant. com* ⌕ *Reservations essential* ⊙ *Closed Sun. and Mon. No lunch Tues.–Thurs.* Ⓜ *Chiswick Park* ✛ *1:A2.*

LONDON
DINING AND
LODGING ATLAS

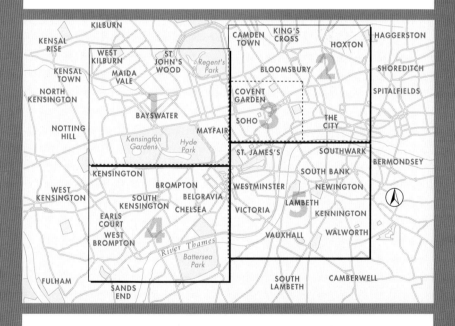

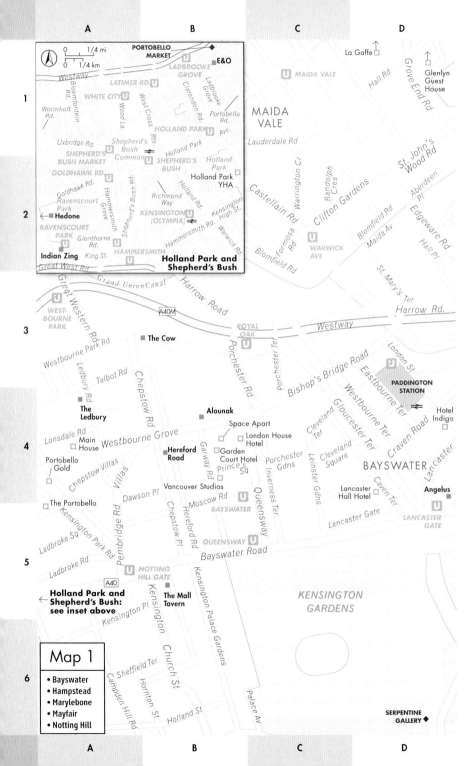

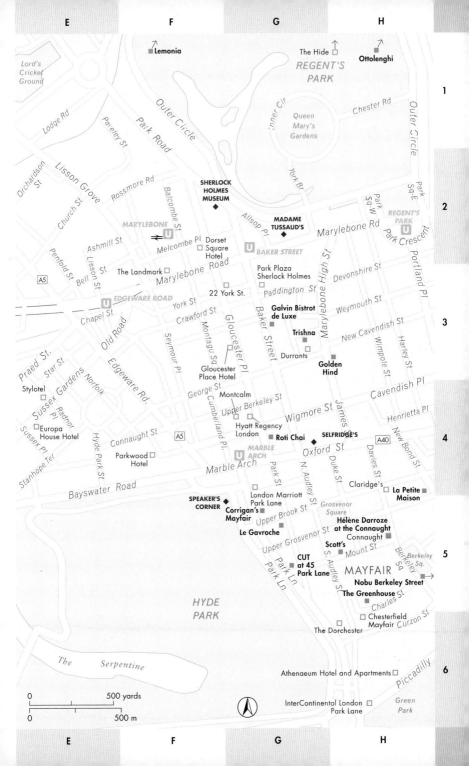

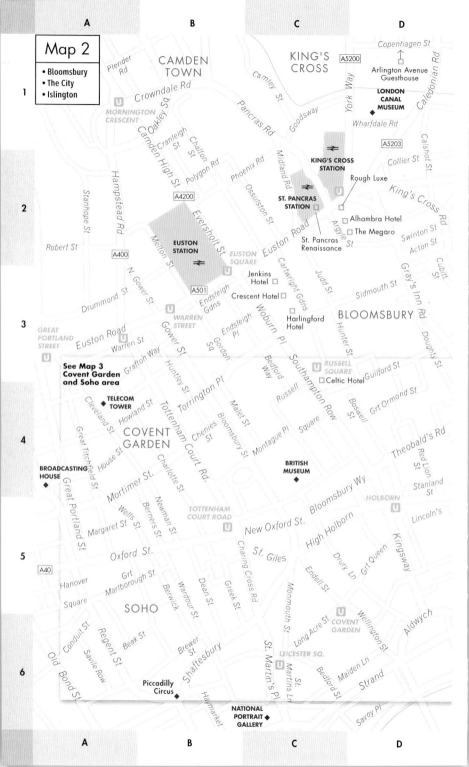

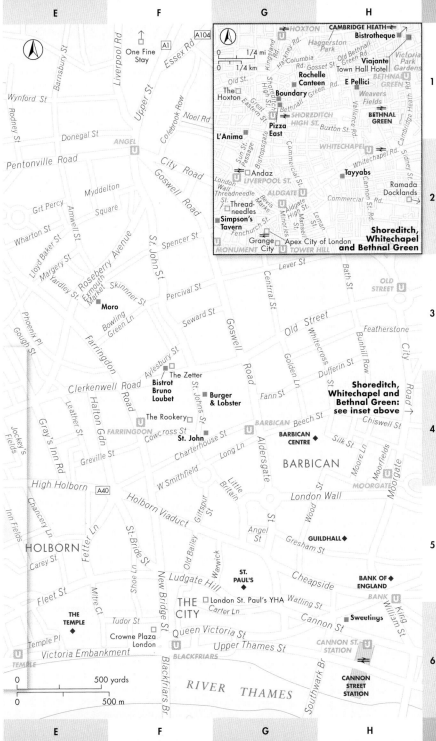

E   **F**   **G**   **H**

One Fine Stay

Wynford St
Rodney St
Bansbury St
Liverpool Rd
Upper St
Essex Rd
A104
A1

Donegal St
Noel Rd
Colebrook Row

ANGEL U

Pentonville Road
City Road
Goswell Road

Grt Percy
Myddelton Square
Amwell St
St. John St
Spencer St

Wharton St
Lloyd Baker St
Margery St
Yardley St
Roseberry Avenue
Exmouth Market
Skinner St
Percival St
Central St
Bath St

OLD STREET U

Moro
Bowling Green Ln
Seward St
Old Street
Whitecross St
Bunhill Row
City Road
Featherstone

Phoenix Pl
Gough St
Farringdon Road
Goswell Road
Golden Ln
Dufferin St

Clerkenwell Road
Aylesbury St
The Zetter
Bistrot Bruno Loubet
Burger & Lobster
Fann St

Shoreditch, Whitechapel and Bethnal Green: see inset above →

Leather St
Halton Gdn
The Rookery
St. Johns St
Chiswell St

Gray's Inn Rd
Jockey's Fields
FARRINGDON U
Cowcross St
St. John
Charterhouse St
Long Ln
BARBICAN CENTRE ◆
Silk St
Moore St
Moorfields

Greville St
Aldersgate St
BARBICAN
MOORGATE U
Moorgate

High Holborn
A40
W Smithfield
Giltspur St
Little Britain
London Wall

HOLBORN
Holborn Viaduct
Angel St
GUILDHALL ◆
Gresham St

Carey St
Old Bailey
Warwick
ST. PAUL'S ◆
Cheapside
BANK OF ENGLAND ◆

Fleet St
Fetter Ln
Ludgate Hill
Watling St
BANK U
King William St

Mitre Ct
St Bride St
New Bridge St
THE CITY
□ London St. Paul's YHA
Carter Ln
Cannon St
Sweetings

THE TEMPLE ◆
Tudor St
Crowne Plaza London
Queen Victoria St
CANNON ST. STATION

Temple Pl
TEMPLE U
Victoria Embankment
Upper Thames St
BLACKFRIARS U

0   500 yards
0   500 m
Blackfriars Br
RIVER THAMES
Southwark Br
CANNON STREET STATION

E   **F**   **G**   **H**

Inset:
HOXTON
CAMBRIDGE HEATH
Bistrotheque
Kingsland Rd
Hackney Rd
Haggerston Park
Columbia Rd
Gosset St
Old Bethnal Green Rd
Viajante
Town Hall Hotel
Victoria Park Gardens
Old St.
Rochelle Canteen
E Pellici
BETHNAL GREEN
The Hoxton
Boundary
Bethnal Green
Weavers Fields
Vallance Rd
Cambridge Heath Rd
BETHNAL GREEN U
Pizza East
SHOREDITCH HIGH ST.
Buxton St
L'Anima
Sun St Passage
Commercial St
WHITECHAPEL
Whitechapel Rd
Sidney St
Andaz
London Wall
Threadneedle St
LIVERPOOL ST. U
Tayyabs
Thread-needles
Bevis Marks
ALDGATE U
Ramada Docklands
Simpson's Tavern
Fenchurch St
Aldgate High St
Leman St
Cannon St Rd
Commercial Rd
Grange City
Minories
Mansell St
Apex City of London
TOWER HILL U
MONUMENT U
Lever St

Shoreditch, Whitechapel and Bethnal Green

1/4 mi
1/4 km

1

2

3

4

5

6

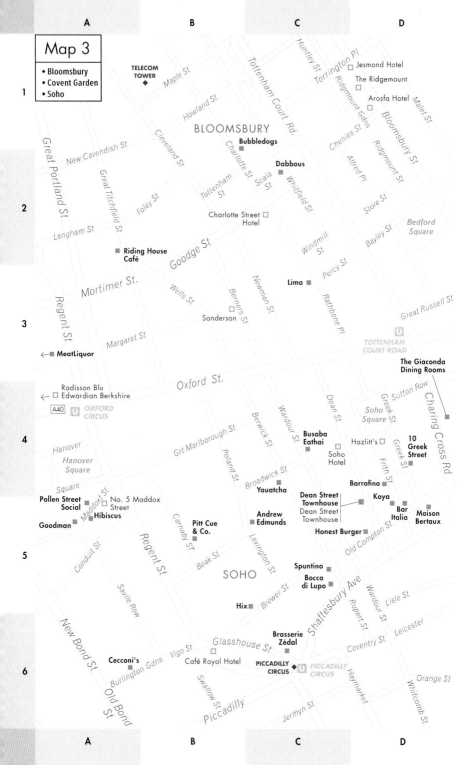

Map 3

- Bloomsbury
- Covent Garden
- Soho

TELECOM TOWER

Maple St
Howland St
Cleveland St
New Cavendish St
Great Portland St
Great Titchfield St
Foley St
Langham St

BLOOMSBURY

Tottenham Court Rd.
Huntley St
Torrington Pl
Jesmond Hotel
The Ridgemount
Arosfa Hotel
Ridgmount Gdns
Chenies St
Alfred Pl
Ridgmount St
Bloomsbury St
Malet St
Store St

Bubbledogs
Dabbous
Charlotte St
Scala St
Whitfield St
Tottenham St

Charlotte Street Hotel

Windmill St
Bayley St
Bedford Square

Riding House Café

Goodge St

Mortimer St.
Wells St
Newman St
Berners St
Lima
Percy St
Rathbone Pl
Great Russell St

Sanderson

Regent St
Margaret St

TOTTENHAM COURT ROAD

←■ MeatLiquor

The Giaconda Dining Rooms

Oxford St.

Radisson Blu
←□ Edwardian Berkshire
A40 **OXFORD CIRCUS**

Dean St
Sutton Row
Charing Cross Rd
Greek St
Soho Square

Hanover
Hanover Square
Square
Grt Marlborough St
Berwick St
Wardour St
Busaba Eathai
Hazlitt's □
10 Greek Street
Frith St
Greek St

Soho Hotel

Poland St
Broadwick St
Yauatcha
Barrafina
Koya

Pollen Street Social
Maddox St
No. 5 Maddox Street
Dean Street Townhouse
Dean Street Townhouse
Bar Italia
Maison Bertaux

Goodman ■
Hibiscus

Carnaby St
Pitt Cue & Co.
Andrew Edmunds
Honest Burger
Old Compton St

SOHO
Conduit St
Regent St
Savile Row
Beak St
Lexington St
Spuntino
Bocca di Lupo
Shaftesbury Ave
Wardour St
Lisle St
Leicester

Hix ■
Brewer St
Rupert St
Coventry St

Brasserie Zédal

Glasshouse St
Café Royal Hotel
Vigo St
Swallow St
PICCADILLY CIRCUS
PICCADILLY CIRCUS
Haymarket
Orange St
Whitcomb St

Cecconi's
New Bond St
Burlington Gdns
Old Bond St
Piccadilly
Jermyn St

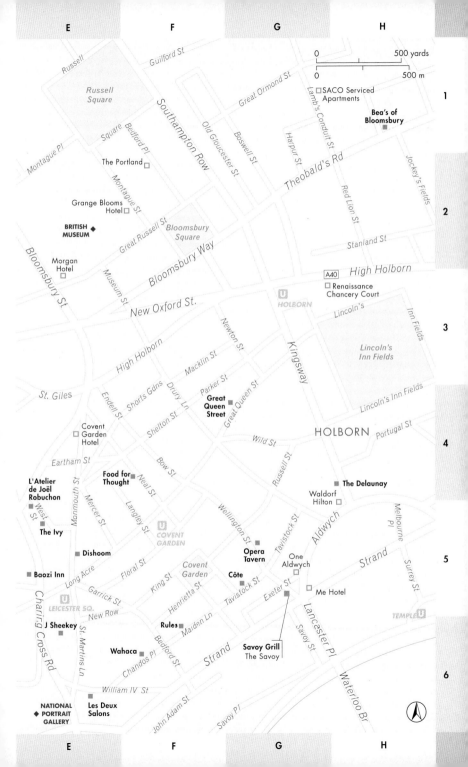

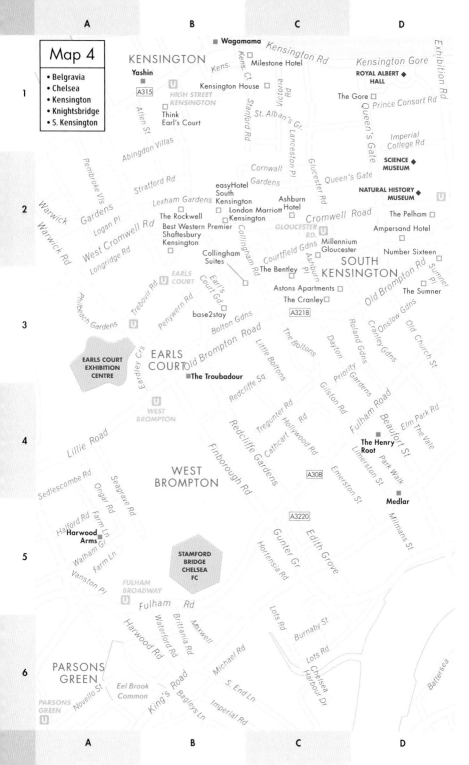

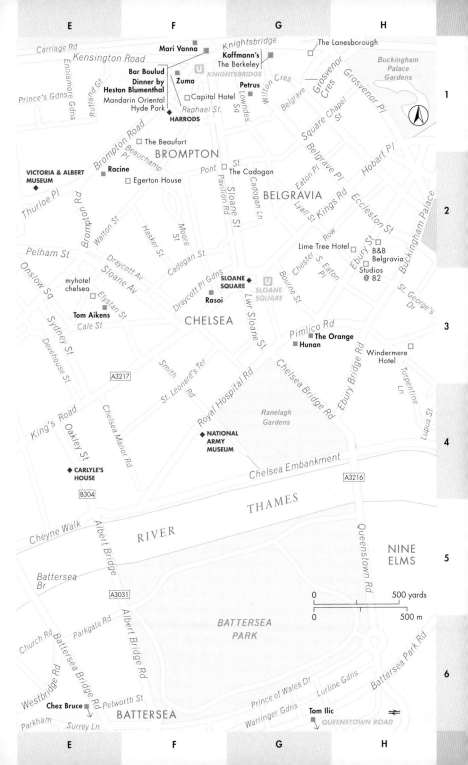

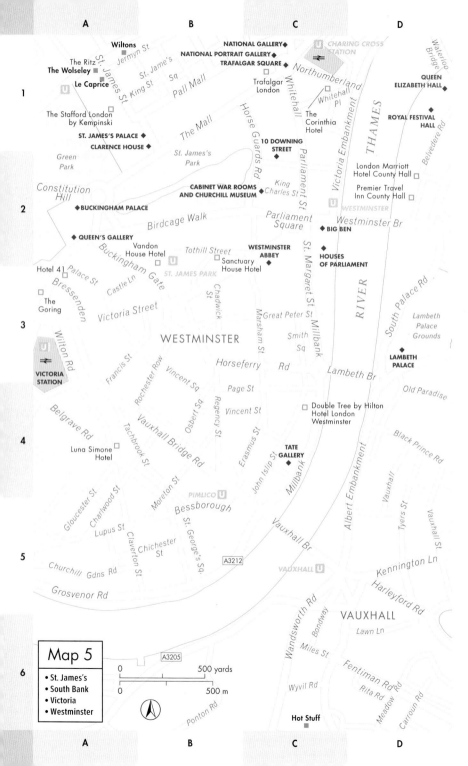

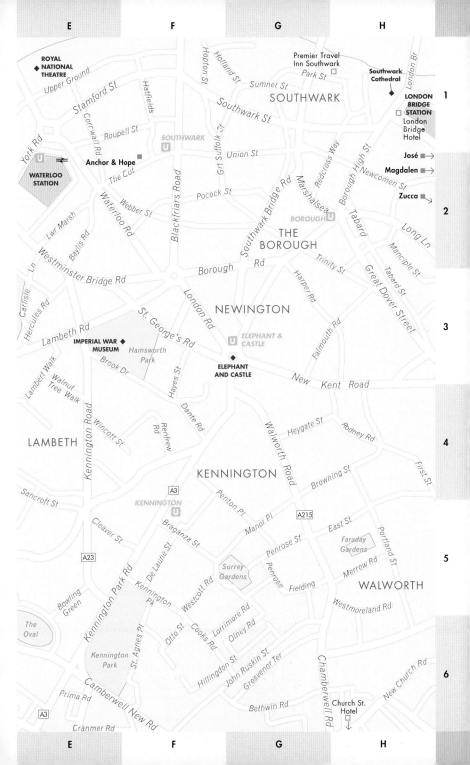

WHERE TO STAY

Updated by
Jack Jewers

Queen Elizabeth hasn't invited you this time? No matter. Staying at one of London's grande-dame hotels is the next-best thing to being a guest at the palace—and some say it's even better. Happily, however, there is no dearth of options where friendliness outdistances luxe—London, thank goodness, has plenty of atmospheric places that won't cost a king's ransom.

That noted, until fairly recently it was extremely difficult to find a decent hotel in the center for less than £150 per night. Things have improved, thanks in part to the global recession, but also to a flurry of new midprice hotels that have sprung up in the last few years.

It's all so different if money is no object. London has some of the very best and most luxurious hotels in the world. On the other hand, freshly minted billionaires favor the rash of new hot spots, like the Corinthia, while fashion plates always book Kit Kemp's super-stylish hotels (such as the Covent Garden). But even these places have sales, and you can sometimes snag a bargain within the reach of ordinary mortals—particularly in the off-season—or just be a spectator to all the glamour by visiting for that most traditional of high-society treats, afternoon tea. The top end has also seen a spectacular new arrival, with the rebirth of the gorgeous Victorian-meets-modern St. Pancras Hotel, which lay closed and virtually untouched for nearly 80 years.

Meanwhile, several midrange hotels have dropped their average prices in response to the choppy waters of the global economy, which has pulled some fantastic places, such as Hazlitt's and Town Hall, back into the affordable category. And there's a clutch of new, stylish, and super-cheap hotels that are a real step forward for the city. The downside is that these places tend to be a little out of the way, but that's often a price worth paying. Another attractive alternative includes hotels in the Premier and Millennium chains, which offer sleek, modern rooms, lots of up-to-date conveniences, and sales that frequently bring room prices well below £100 a night.

At the budget level, small and interesting bed-and-breakfasts such as Arlington Avenue and the Church Street Hotel stand out in a sea of battered and old-fashioned B&Bs. The once-drab Cromwell Road—where snazzy Kensington segues into the backpacker's favorite, Earl's Court—has been transformed by a mixture of interesting midprice boutiques, such as the Ashburn and the Rockwell, and better-than-average megachains, such as the Kensington Marriott. A true bargain-basement alternative is the easyHotel chain, with its tiny, bright-orange "pod" rooms. And if you're willing to fend for yourself, the city has some great rental options.

But if you are interested in Luxury, London is just the place. Although the image we love to harbor about Olde London Towne may be fast fading in the light of today's glittering city, when it comes time to rest your head, the old-fashioned clichés remain enticing. Choose one of London's heritage-rich hotels—Claridge's supplies perfect parlors; the Savoy has that river view—and these fantasies can, and always will, be fulfilled.

15

PLANNING

LODGING STRATEGY

Where should you stay? With hundreds of London hotels, it may seem like a daunting question. But it doesn't have to be. The 130-plus selections here represent the best this city has to offer—from the most-for-your-money budget B&Bs to the sleekest designer hotels. Scan "Best Bets" on the following pages for top recommendations by price and experience. Or look through the reviews. To find one quickly, search by neighborhood, then alphabetically. Happy hunting!

NEED A RESERVATION?

Yes. Hotel reservations are an absolute necessity when planning your trip to London, so book your room as far in advance as possible. The further in advance you can book, the better the deal you're likely to get. Just watch out if you change your mind—cancellation fees can be hefty. On the other hand, it is possible to find some amazing last-minute deals at mid- to high-range places, but this is a real gamble, as you could just as easily end up paying full rate. Fierce competition means properties undergo frequent improvements, so when booking inquire about any ongoing renovations that may interrupt your stay.

CHECKING IN

Typical check-in and checkout times are 2 pm and 11 am, respectively. Many flights from North America arrive early in the morning, but having to wait six hours for a room after arriving jet-lagged at 8 am isn't the ideal way to start a vacation. Alert the hotel of your early arrival; large hotels can often make special early check-in arrangements, but almost all will look after your luggage in the meantime. Be prepared to drop your bags and strike out for a few hours. On the plus side, this can effectively give you a whole extra day for sightseeing.

HOTEL QUALITY

Note that rooms can vary considerably in a single hotel. If you don't like the room you're given, ask to see another. Be prepared for the fact that, while smoking is now banned in public areas, this doesn't apply to hotel rooms—so be firm and ask to change if you're given a smoking room and didn't request one. Hotels often renovate room by room—you might find yourself allocated a dark, unrenovated room, whereas a bright, newly decorated room awaits just down the hall.

BREAKFAST

Some hotels include breakfast in the price of the room. It ranges from a gourmet spread to what is known as the "full English" (one fried egg, two "bangers"—that's English-style sausage links—two thick slices of bacon, a grilled tomato, sautéed mushrooms or baked beans, and toast). In most budget hotels and B&Bs, this is the only hot breakfast available. Most expensive hotels (and the most imaginative small ones) may also offer pancakes, French toast, waffles, and omelets. Luckily, virtually all accommodations also offer packaged cereals, muffins, yogurt, and fresh fruit, so when the sausage-and-bacon brigade begins to get you down, go continental.

FACILITIES

Keep in mind that some facilities come with the room rate while others cost extra. So, when pricing accommodations, always ask what's included. Modern hotels usually have air-conditioning, but B&Bs and hotels in older buildings often do not, and it is generally not the norm in London. Wi-Fi is increasingly common, but don't assume it's free (large hotels in particular can charge outrageous fees). If you want a double room, specify whether you want a double bed or a twin (two single beds next to each other). *All hotels listed here have private bathrooms unless otherwise noted.*

PRICES

If you're planning to visit in the fall, winter, or early spring, start monitoring bargain online prices a few months before your trip and book whenever you see a good rate. Chains such as Hilton, Premier, and Millennium are known for their low-season sales in which prices can be as little as half the normal rate. And business-oriented hotels frequently have lower rates on weekends.

The exchange rate between the pound and the dollar is also unpredictable, so if it's looking good when you book, an advance-payment deal could end up saving you a decent amount of money. ■TIP→ The Visit London Accommodation Booking Service (☎ 020/7932–2020 ⊕ www.visitlondon.com) offers a best-price guarantee. Also try the clearing websites Late Rooms (⊕ www.laterooms.com), Booking (⊕ www.booking.com), and Last Minute (⊕ www.lastminute.com).

Prices in the reviews are the lowest cost of a standard double room in high season, including 20% V.A.T.

WHERE SHOULD I STAY?

	Neighborhood Vibe	Pros	Cons
Westminster, St. James's, and Royal London	This historic section is home to major tourist attractions like Buckingham Palace.	Central area near tourist sites; easy Tube access; considered a safe area to stay.	Mostly expensive lodging options; few good restaurants and entertainment venues nearby.
Mayfair and Marylebone	Traditional, old money; a mixture of the business and financial set with fashionable shops.	In the heart of the action; some of London's best hotels are found here.	Pricey part of town; the city-that-never-sleeps buzz makes peace and quiet hard to come by.
Soho and Covent Garden	A tourist hub with endless entertainment—this is party central for young adults.	Buzzing area with plenty to see and do; late-night entertainment abounds; wonderful shopping district.	Perhaps London's busiest (and noisiest) district after dark; few budget hotels.
Bloomsbury and Holborn	Diverse area that is part bustling business center and part tranquil respite with tree-lined streets and parks.	Easy access to Tube, and 15 minutes to city center; major sights, like British Museum in Bloomsbury.	Holborn has busy and noisy streets; the area around King's Cross can be sketchy—particularly at night.
The City	The City is London's financial district, where most of the city's banks and businesses are headquartered.	The City is extremely central with easy transportation access and great hotel deals.	The City can be as quiet as a tomb at weekends—even the pubs close.
The East End	Increasingly trendy area east of the city center, with a great arts scene.	Great for art lovers, shoppers, and business execs with meetings in Canary Wharf.	Still a transitional area; parts of Hoxton can be a bit dodgy at night; 20-minute Tube ride from central London.
South of the Thames	South of the River is a vibrant cultural hub, centered around the South Bank, the Globe, and the Royal National Theatre.	South of the River is London's unofficial cultural quarter, and walking distance from the West End theaters.	You don't have to go very far from the South Bank before you hit some of London's dodgiest neighborhoods.
Kensington, Chelsea, Knightsbridge, and Belgravia	These are some of London's most upscale neighborhoods and a hub of London's tourist universe.	Diverse hotel selection; great area for meandering urban walks; London's capital of high-end shopping.	Depending on where you are, the nearest Tube might be a hike; residential area might be too quiet for some.
Notting Hill and Bayswater	This is an upscale, trendy area favored by locals, with plenty of good hotels.	Hotel deals abound if you know where to look; gorgeous greenery in Hyde Park.	Choose the wrong place and you may end up in a flea pit; residential area may be quiet.
Regent's Park and Hampstead	A mix of arty, fashionable districts with a village-like feel in other places.	Some of London's most fashionable neighborhoods, and easy to fall in love with.	Some distance from center; lack of hotel options.

15

HOTEL REVIEWS

Listed alphabetically by neighborhood. Use the coordinate (✚ 1:B2)
at the end of each listing to locate a site on the corresponding map. To
locate the property on a map, turn to the London Dining and Lodging
Atlas at the end of the Where to Eat chapter. The first number after the
✚ symbol indicates the map number. Following that is the property's
coordinate on the map grid.

For expanded hotel reviews, visit Fodors.com.

WESTMINSTER, ST. JAMES'S, AND ROYAL LONDON

WESTMINSTER

$$$$ 📷 **The Corinthia.** A star in the firmament of new hotels that have opened
HOTEL in London in this decade, the Corinthia is design heaven-on-earth, with
Fodor'sChoice levels of service that make anyone feel like a VIP. **Pros:** so much luxury
★ and elegance you'll feel like royalty. **Cons:** prices jump to the strato-
sphere once the cheapest rooms sell out. ⑤ *Rooms from: £420* ⊠ *Whitehall Pl., Westminster* ☎ *020/7930–8181* ⊕ *www.corinthia.com* ⤴ *294
rooms* ❤️ *Breakfast* Ⓜ *Embankment* ✚ *5:C1.*

$$$ 📷 **DoubleTree by Hilton Hotel London Westminster.** Spectacular views of the
HOTEL river, Big Ben, and the London Eye fill the floor-to-ceiling windows in
FAMILY this rather stark, steel-and-glass building steps from the Tate Britain,
and a plethora of techy perks await inside. **Pros:** amazing views; flat
screens and other high-tech gadgetry. **Cons:** small bedrooms; tiny bath-
rooms; TV has to be operated through a computer (confusing if you're
not used to it). ⑤ *Rooms from: £230* ⊠ *30 John Islip St., Westminster*
☎ *020/7630–1000* ⊕ *doubletree3.hilton.com* ⤴ *444 rooms, 16 suites*
❤️ *Some meals* Ⓜ *Westminster, Pimlico* ✚ *5:C4.*

$$$$ 📷 **The Goring.** With Buckingham Palace just around the corner, this
HOTEL hotel, built in 1910 and now run by third-generation Gorings, has
always been a favorite among discreet VIPs—including Kate Middle-
ton's family on the night before the royal wedding. **Pros:** elegant, spa-
cious rooms; prices have come down recently. **Cons:** price is still too
high for what you get; interiors a bit fussy. ⑤ *Rooms from: £315* ⊠ *15
Beeston Pl., Grosvenor Gardens, Victoria* ☎ *020/7396–9000* ⊕ *www.
thegoring.com* ⤴ *68 rooms, 6 suites* ❤️ *Some meals* Ⓜ *Victoria* ✚ *5:A3.*

$$$$ 📷 **Hotel 41.** Designer credentials and high-tech gadgets are everywhere
HOTEL in the impeccably coordinated black-and-white rooms, some split-level
Fodor'sChoice and all gorgeously furnished with extraordinary pieces drawn from
★ every corner of the globe. **Pros:** unique place opposite Buckingham
Palace; great service; unlimited free Wi-Fi. **Cons:** unusual design is not
for everyone. ⑤ *Rooms from: £323* ⊠ *41 Buckingham Palace Rd., Vic-
toria* ☎ *020/7300–0041* ⊕ *www.41hotel.com* ⤴ *26 rooms, 4 suites, 2
apartments* ❤️ *Breakfast* Ⓜ *Victoria* ✚ *5:A3.*

$$ 📷 **Lime Tree Hotel.** In a central neighborhood where hotels veer from
HOTEL grimy boltholes at one extreme to wildly overpriced at the other, the
homey Lime Tree stands out for its gracious proprietors, the Davies
family, who offer comfortable, contemporary rooms and hearty cooked
breakfasts that set you up nicely for the day. **Pros:** lovely and helpful

BEST BETS FOR LONDON LODGING

Fodor's offers a selective listing of high-quality lodging experiences at every price range, from the city's best budget motel to its most sophisticated luxury hotel. Here, we've compiled our top recommendations by price and experience. The very best properties—in other words, those that provide a particularly remarkable experience in their price range—are designated in the listings with the Fodor's Choice logo.

15

Fodor's Choice ★

Best by Price

Best by Experience

hosts; great location; rooms are decent size (though the cheaper rooms are small). **Cons:** some rooms are up several flights of stairs, and there's no elevator; family rooms don't allow kids under five. $ *Rooms from: £155* ✉ *135–137 Ebury St., Victoria* ☎ *020/7730–8191* ⊕ *www. limetreehotel.co.uk* ↗ *25 rooms* ❘○❘ *Breakfast* Ⓜ *Victoria, Sloane Sq.* ✛ *4:H2*

$$ 🖬 **Sanctuary House Hotel.** This is a classic example of what the British

B&B/INN   mean when they refer to an "inn"—a pub with bedrooms, albeit one of exceptionally good quality for London. **Pros:** cozy, authentically London feel; price can drop below £100 on weekends; wow-location right in the heart of Westminster. **Cons:** pub can be noisy (light sleepers should ask for a room as far from the ground floor as possible). $ *Rooms from: £115* ✉ *33 Tothill St., Westminster* ☎ *020/7799–4044* ⊕ *www.sanctuaryhousehotel.co.uk* ↗ *34 rooms* ❘○❘ *Breakfast* Ⓜ *St. James's Park* ✛ *5:B2.*

$$ 🖬 **Windermere Hotel.** This sweet and rather elegant old hotel, on the

HOTEL   premises of London's first B&B (in 1881), is a decent, well-located option—but only if you can't get a discount rate at a plusher hotel for the same price. **Pros:** good location; free Wi-Fi. **Cons:** price is a bit high for what you get; rooms and bathrooms are tiny; no elevator. $ *Rooms from: £160* ✉ *142–144 Warwick Way, Victoria* ☎ *020/7834–5163* ⊕ *www.windermere-hotel.co.uk* ↗ *19 rooms* ❘○❘ *Breakfast* Ⓜ *Victoria* ✛ *4:H3.*

ST. JAMES'S

$$$ 🖬 **The Stafford London by Kempinski.** This is a rare find: a posh hotel that's

HOTEL   equal parts elegance and friendliness, and it's in one of the few peace-

Fodor'sChoice   ful spots in the area, down a small lane behind Piccadilly. **Pros:** great

★   staff; big, luxurious rooms; quiet location. **Cons:** traditional style is not to all tastes; men must wear jackets in the bar. $ *Rooms from: £260* ✉ *St. James's Pl., St. James's* ☎ *020/7493–0111* ⊕ *www.kempinski.com/ london* ↗ *81 rooms* ❘○❘ *Breakfast* Ⓜ *Green Park* ✛ *5:A1.*

MAYFAIR AND MARYLEBONE

MAYFAIR

$$$ 🖬 **Athenaeum Hotel and Apartments.** This grand hotel overlooking Green

B&B/INN   Park offers plenty for the money: rooms are both comfortable and lavishly decorated, with deeply comfortable Hypnos beds, plasma-screen TVs, luxurious fabrics, and original contemporary artworks, and breakfasts are luxurious and varied, with endless Continental and cooked options. **Pros:** peaceful park views; handy for Buckingham Palace and Piccadilly; great value for elegant setting. **Cons:** bathrooms are almost all small. $ *Rooms from: £276* ✉ *116 Piccadilly, Mayfair* ☎ *020/7640– 3557* ⊕ *www.athenaeumhotel.com* ↗ *111 rooms, 46 suites and apartments* ❘○❘ *Breakfast* Ⓜ *Green Park* ✛ *1:H6.*

$$$$ 🖬 **Claridge's.** The original art deco public spaces of this super-glamor-

HOTEL   ous London institution are gloriously unspoiled (down to the grand

FAMILY   staircase and elevator, complete with upholstered sofa). **Pros:** seri-

Fodor'sChoice   ous luxury everywhere—this is an old-money hotel; comics, books,

★   and DVDs to help keep kids amused. **Cons:** better pack your designer wardrobe—guests in the hotel bar can be almost cartoonishly snobbish. $ *Rooms from: £390* ✉ *Brook St., St. James's* ☎ *020/7629–8860, 866/599–6991 in U.S.* ⊕ *www.claridges.co.uk* ⇆ *203 rooms* ⦿ *Breakfast* Ⓜ *Bond St.* ✛ *1:H4*

WORD OF MOUTH

"I LOVE the Dorchester, it's traditional but beautiful with wonderful service. The bar for pre dinner cocktails is fab."

—Smeagol

$$$$
HOTEL
Fodor's Choice
★

⬚ **The Connaught.** A huge favorite of the "we wouldn't dream of staying anywhere else" monied set since its opening in 1917, the Connaught has many dazzlingly modern compliments to its famously historic delights. **Pros:** legendary hotel; great for star-spotting. **Cons:** history comes at a price; bathrooms are small. $ *Rooms from: £400* ✉ *Carlos Pl., Mayfair* ☎ *020/7499–7070, 866/599–6991 in U.S.* ⊕ *www.the-connaught.co.uk* ⇆ *92 rooms* ⦿ *Breakfast* Ⓜ *Bond St.* ✛ *1:H5*

$$$$
HOTEL
Fodor's Choice
★

⬚ **The Dorchester.** The glamour level is off the scale here, with gold leaf and marble public rooms and guest quarters awash in English country-house-style furnishings, with more than a hint of art deco—yet few hotels this opulent manage to be as personable as the Dorchester. **Pros:** historic luxury in 1930s building; lovely views of Hyde Park; top-notch star-spotting; lots of modern technology, including web TVs. **Cons:** traditional look is not to all tastes; prices are high; some rooms are rather small. $ *Rooms from: £365* ✉ *Park Lane, Mayfair* ☎ *020/7629–8888* ⊕ *www.thedorchester.com* ⇆ *195 rooms, 55 suites* ⦿ *Breakfast* Ⓜ *Marble Arch, Hyde Park Corner* ✛ *1:H6.*

$$
HOTEL

⬚ **Gloucester Place Hotel.** Just a couple of blocks from Marble Arch and Hyde Park, this small, friendly hotel won't win any style awards—its guest rooms are far from fancy—but, almost better, they are clean and comfortable. **Pros:** great location; huge discounts for stays of four nights or more; free Wi-Fi. **Cons:** could use a face-lift; stairs to climb and no elevator; some rooms have shared bathrooms. $ *Rooms from: £149* ✉ *55 Gloucester Pl., Mayfair* ☎ *020/7486–6166* ⊕ *www.gloucesterplacehotel.com* ⇆ *19 rooms* ⦿ *Breakfast* Ⓜ *Marble Arch, Bond St.* ✛ *1:G3*

$$$
HOTEL

⬚ **InterContinental London Park Lane.** Overlooking busy Hyde Park Corner and the Queen's back garden (much to her chagrin, allegedly), this hotel's luxurious rooms are aimed at high-end business travelers. **Pros:** central location; business facilities. **Cons:** no park views with standard rooms; prices can shoot up in mid-summer; £15 a day charge for Internet access is a bit rich given the room rates. $ *Rooms from: £288* ✉ *1 Hamilton Pl., Park Lane, Mayfair* ☎ *020/7409–3131, 871/422–9200* ⊕ *www.intercontinental.com* ⇆ *447 rooms, 60 suites* ⦿ *Some meals* Ⓜ *Hyde Park Corner* ✛ *1:H6.*

$$$$
RENTAL
FAMILY

⬚ **No. 5 Maddox Street.** Just five minutes' walk from Oxford Street, this is a great option for those who tire of traditional hotels: 12 luxury suites—some with balconies and working fireplaces—filled with everything you could ever need, including a handy kitchen. **Pros:** cozy and surprisingly quiet, considering the location; extremely attentive room service. **Cons:** WiiFi costs £10 per day; you can feel isolated, as there's

15

no communal lobby. $ *Rooms from: £319* ⊠ *5 Maddox St., Mayfair* ☎ *020/7647–0200* ⊕ *www.living-rooms.co.uk* ⤶ *12 suites* ⦿ *No meals* Ⓜ *Oxford Circus* ⊕ *3:A5.*

$$ ⊞ **22 York Street.** This Georgian town house has a cozy, family feel,
B&B/INN with polished pine floors and plenty of quilts and French antiques in the homey, individually furnished bedrooms. **Pros:** outstanding location for shoppers; friendly hosts; very flexible check-in times; entirely non-smoking. **Cons:** if you take away the great location, you're paying a lot for a B&B; not everyone enjoys socializing with strangers over breakfast. $ *Rooms from: £130* ⊠ *22 York St., Mayfair* ☎ *020/7224–2990* ⊕ *www.22yorkstreet.co.uk* ⤶ *10 rooms* ⦿ *Breakfast* Ⓜ *Baker St.* ⊕ *1:G3*

MARYLEBONE

$$$ ⊞ **Dorset Square Hotel.** Reopened in June 2012 after extensive updates
HOTEL and refurbishment, this boutique hotel, in one of London's most fash-
Fodor'sChoice ionable neighborhoods, occupies a charming town house. **Pros:** ideal
★ location; lovely design; welcoming vibe. **Cons:** some rooms are small; no bathtub in some rooms; fee for Wi-Fi. $ *Rooms from: £260* ⊠ *39 Dorset Sq., Marylebone* ☎ *020/7723–7874* ⊕ *www.firmdalehotels.com* ⤶ *35 rooms, 3 suites* ⦿ *Breakfast* Ⓜ *Baker St.* ⊕ *1:F2*

$$$ ⊞ **Hyatt Regency London—The Churchill.** Even though it's one of London's
HOTEL largest hotels, the Churchill is always abuzz with guests smiling at the
Fodor'sChoice purring perfection they find here, including warmly personalized service
★ and calmly alluring guest rooms. **Pros:** comfortable and stylish; efficient service; up to three can stay in one room. **Cons:** feels more geared to business than leisure travelers. $ *Rooms from: £260* ⊠ *30 Portman Sq., Marylebone* ☎ *020/7486–5800* ⊕ *www.london.churchill.hyatt.com* ⤶ *389 rooms, 45 suites* ⦿ *Breakfast* Ⓜ *Marble Arch* ⊕ *1:G4.*

$$$ ⊞ **The Landmark London Hotel.** A glass-covered, eight-story atrium sets
HOTEL the scene at this truly grand hotel, where the huge bedrooms are richly furnished and have marble bathrooms (odd-numbered rooms overlook the Winter Garden beneath the glass roof). **Pros:** amazingly luxurious; one of the few really posh London hotels that doesn't make you dress up; good discounts are available. **Cons:** two-night minimum stay at certain times. $ *Rooms from: £285* ⊠ *222 Marylebone Rd., Marylebone* ☎ *020/7631–8000* ⊕ *www.landmarklondon.co.uk* ⤶ *299 rooms, 47 suites* ⦿ *Breakfast* Ⓜ *Marylebone* ⊕ *1:F3.*

$$ ⊞ **Park Plaza Sherlock Holmes Hotel.** In honor of the fictional detective
HOTEL who had his home on Baker Street, rooms here have a masculine edge with lots of earth tones and pinstripe sheets (along with hyper-modern bathrooms stocked with fluffy bathrobes). **Pros:** nicely decorated; near Marylebone High Street; international electrical outlets, including those that work with American equipment. **Cons:** have to walk through the bar to get to reception; not well soundproofed from the noisy street. $ *Rooms from: £180* ⊠ *108 Baker St., Marylebone* ☎ *020/7486–6161* ⊕ *www.sherlockholmeshotel.com* ⤶ *99 rooms, 20 suites* ⦿ *Breakfast* Ⓜ *Baker St.* ⊕ *1:G3*

$$ ⊞ **Radisson Blu Edwardian Berkshire Hotel.** In a dangerously good location
HOTEL for shopaholics, central to Oxford Street, this pleasant and well-run outpost of the Radisson chain offers a similar level of service to some of

The Corinthia

The Connaught

The Dorchester

Covent Garden Hotel

BED-AND-BREAKFASTS

You can stay in small, homey B&Bs for an up-close-and-personal brush with city life (Parkwood Hotel; Arlington Avenue), or find yourself in what is really a modern guest-house, where you never meet the owners (B&B Belgravia; The Main House). The main benefit of staying in a B&B is that the price is usually cheaper than a hotel room of comparable quality, and you receive more personal service. However, the limitations may be off-putting for some: although you can sometimes arrange for daily maid service, there's usually no restaurant, bar, or room service. Prices start at around £60 a night, and in that bracket the grimmer places are legion, so make your choice carefully. Prices usually (though not always) go up for more central neighborhoods and larger and more luxurious homes. It's a nice option, both for seasoned travelers who want a more authentic taste of London, and for those trying to travel well without busting their budgets.

Host & Guest Service. Host & Guest Service can find you a room in London as well as in the rest of the United Kingdom. This great source for bargains, and you know that all properties have been vetted by the agency, but the website functionality is a bit creaky. ⌧ *103 Dawes Rd., Fulham* ☎ *020/7385–9922* ⊕ *www. host-guest.co.uk* ☞ *Full payment in advance.*

the more established hotels in the neighborhood, at a less eye-watering rate. **Pros:** great location; good restaurant; free Wi-Fi; worthwhile deals and promotions. **Cons:** walk-in rate is still quite expensive; small bedrooms. ⑤ *Rooms from: £198* ⌧ *350 Oxford St., Mayfair* ☎ *020/7629-7474, 0800/374–411 toll-free in U.K., 1800/333–3333 toll-free in U.S.* ⊕ *www.radissonblu-edwardian.com* ☞ *145 rooms, 2 suites* ⑩ *Some meals* Ⓜ *Bond St., Oxford Circus* ✚ *3:A4.*

SOHO AND COVENT GARDEN

SOHO

$$
HOTEL
Fodor's Choice
★

🛏 **Dean Street Townhouse.** Discreet and unpretentious, but oh-so-stylish—and right in the heart of Soho—this place has a bohemian vibe and an excellent modern British restaurant, hung with art by, among others, Peter Blake and Tracy Emin. **Pros:** über-cool; resembles an upper-class pied-à-terre. **Cons:** full rate reflects location rather than what you get; some rooms are small; rooms at the front can be noisy, especially on weekends; occasional two-night minimum stay. ⑤ *Rooms from: £188* ⌧ *69–71 Dean St., Soho* ☎ *020/7434–1775* ⊕ *www. deanstreettownhouse.com* ☞ *39 rooms* ⑩ *Breakfast* Ⓜ *Leicester Sq., Tottenham Court Rd.* ✚ *3:D5.*

$$$
HOTEL

🛏 **Hazlitt's.** This disarmingly friendly place, full of personality, robust antiques, and claw-foot tubs, occupies three connected early-18th-century houses, one of which was the last home of essayist William Hazlitt (1778–1830). **Pros:** great for lovers of art and antiques; historic atmosphere with lots of small sitting rooms and wooden staircases; truly beautiful and relaxed. **Cons:** no in-house restaurant; breakfast is £12 extra; no elevators. $ *Rooms from: £216* ⊠ *6 Frith St., Soho* ☎ *020/7434–1771* ⊕ *www.hazlittshotel.com* ⇨ *20 rooms, 3 suites* ✗○✗ *No meals* Ⓜ *Tottenham Court Rd.* ✛ *3:D4*

COVENT GARDEN

$$$$
HOTEL
Fodor'sChoice
★
⊞ **Covent Garden Hotel.** It's little wonder this is now the London home-away-from-home for off-duty celebrities, actors, and style mavens, with its Covent Garden location and guest rooms that are *World of Interiors*–stylish. **Pros:** great for star-spotting, super-trendy. **Cons:** you can feel you don't matter if you're not famous; setting in Covent Garden can be a bit boisterous. $ *Rooms from: £315* ⊠ *10 Monmouth St., Covent Garden* ☎ *020/7806–1000, 800/553–6674 in U.S.* ⊕ *www.firmdale.com* ⇨ *55 rooms, 3 suites* ✗○✗ *Some meals* Ⓜ *Covent Garden* ✛ *3:E4.*

$$$
HOTEL
Fodor'sChoice
★
⊞ **Me London.** One can only imagine the endless concept meetings that went into this shiny new luxury hotel at the end of the Strand, but the result—a happy mix of high fashion and futuristic hipsterism—is achingly on-trend. **Pros:** very fashionable; beautifully designed; full of high-tech comforts; excellent service. **Cons:** you may find it hard to relax if you don't feel super-stylish yourself; design can sometimes verge on form over function. $ *Rooms from: £306* ⊠ *336 The Strand, Covent Garden* ☎ *0845/601–8980* ⊕ *www.melia.com* ⇨ *159 rooms, 16 suites* ✗○✗ *Breakfast* Ⓜ *Temple* ✛ *3:G5.*

$$$
HOTEL
⊞ **One Aldwych.** An Edwardian building, with an artsy lobby and understated blend of contemporary and classic, provides pure, modern luxury in a great location for theaters and shopping. **Pros:** understated luxury; ultracool atmosphere; kids stay free with certain packages. **Cons:** all this luxury doesn't come cheap; fashionable ambience is not always relaxing; design sometimes verges on form over function. $ *Rooms from: £300* ⊠ *1 Aldwych, Covent Garden* ☎ *020/7300–1000* ⊕ *www.onealdwych.co.uk* ⇨ *93 rooms, 12 suites* ✗○✗ *Breakfast* Ⓜ *Charing Cross, Covent Garden* ✛ *3:G5.*

$$$$
HOTEL
Fodor'sChoice
★
⊞ **The Savoy.** One of London's most famous hotels has emerged from a £220 million renovation, and the old girl is looking like a superstar again. **Pros:** the best hotel in London, period; Thames-side location; less snooty than many others of its pedigree. **Cons:** everything comes with a price tag; bedrooms can be surprisingly noisy, particularly on lower floors; right off the super-busy Strand. $ *Rooms from: £375* ⊠ *Strand, Covent Garden* ☎ *020/7836–4343, 800/257–7544 in U.S.* ⊕ *www.fairmont.com/savoy-london* ⇨ *268 rooms, 62 suites* ✗○✗ *Breakfast* Ⓜ *Covent Garden, Charing Cross* ✛ *3:G5.*

$$
HOTEL
⊞ **The Trafalgar London.** This former 19th-century office building, retaining many original features, is in a superb location, and some guest rooms have floor-to-ceiling windows with extraordinary views of Trafalgar Square and The City. **Pros:** amazing location and views; spacious rooms; a fresh, contemporary hotel that defies the Hilton norm; good reductions on weekends. **Cons:** interior is somewhat austere; rates rise sharply from Monday to Friday. $ *Rooms from: £157* ⊠ *2 Spring Gardens, Trafalgar Sq., Westminster* ☎ *020/7870–2900* ⊕ *www.hilton.co.uk* ⇨ *127 rooms, 2 suites* ✗○✗ *Breakfast* Ⓜ *Charing Cross* ✛ *5:C1.*

$$
HOTEL
⊞ **Waldorf Hilton.** The location of this branch of the Hilton chain is grand enough from the outside that many passersby mistake it for just

15

another of the West End theaters by which it is surrounded. **Pros:** superb choice for theaters; well-equipped modern rooms. **Cons:** few discounts or deals; feels more chain-hotel than the grand exterior would suggest. $ *Rooms from: £167* ✉ *Aldwych, Covent Garden* ☎ *020/7836–2400* ⊕ *www.hilton.co.uk* ↘ *303 rooms* ⦿| *Breakfast* Ⓜ *Charing Cross* ✛ *3:G4.*

BLOOMSBURY AND HOLBORN

BLOOMSBURY

$ ⛄ **Alhambra Hotel.** One of the best bargains in Bloomsbury is a stone's
B&B/INN throw from King's Cross and the Eurostar terminal, and though rooms are very small and the neighborhood is still "edgy," few places are this cheery and clean for the price. **Pros:** low price, with breakfast included; friendly service; central location. **Cons:** zero frills; stairs to climb; some rooms have shared bathrooms. $ *Rooms from: £75* ✉ *17–19 Argyle St., Bloomsbury* ☎ *020/7837–9575* ⊕ *www.alhambrahotel.com* ↘ *52 rooms* ⦿| *Breakfast* Ⓜ *King's Cross* ✛ *2:C2.*

$$ ⛄ **Arosfa Hotel.** Simple, friendly, and pleasantly quirky, this little B&B,
B&B/INN once the home of pre-Raphaelite painter Sir John Everett Millais, is on an elegant Georgian street within walking distance of the West End and the British Museum. **Pros:** friendly staff; check-in from 7 am; good location for museums and theaters; free Wi-Fi. **Cons:** some rooms are very small; bathrooms have showers only; few services. $ *Rooms from: £110* ✉ *83 Gower St., Bloomsbury* ☎ *020/7636–2115* ⊕ *www.arosfalondon. com* ↘ *15 rooms* ⦿| *Breakfast* Ⓜ *Goodge St., Euston Sq.* ✛ *3:D1*

$ ⛄ **Celtic Hotel.** This is a solid, dependable budget choice in a pricey
HOTEL district (close to the West End and British Museum)—clean and comfortable, but with basic ameneties. **Pros:** friendly staff; free Wi-Fi; good location close to the British Museum and the West End. **Cons:** no-frills approach means few extras; cheaper rooms don't have private bathrooms. $ *Rooms from: £80* ✉ *62 Guilford St., Bloomsbury* ☎ *020/7837–6737* ⊕ *www.stmargaretshotel.co.uk* ↘ *35 rooms* ⦿| *Breakfast* Ⓜ *Russell Sq.* ✛ *2:C4*

$$$ ⛄ **Charlotte Street Hotel.** Modern flair and the traditional are fused
HOTEL together in this super-stylish Soho retreat, beautifully decorated with unique printed fabrics from designer Kit Kemp. **Pros:** elegant, luxurious; great attention to detail. **Cons:** the popular bar can be noisy; reservations are necessary for the restaurant. $ *Rooms from: £300* ✉ *15 Charlotte St., Bloomsbury* ☎ *020/7806–2000, 800/553–6674 in U.S.* ⊕ *www.charlottestreethotel.com* ↘ *46 rooms, 6 suites* ⦿| *Breakfast* Ⓜ *Goodge St.* ✛ *3:C2*

$$ ⛄ **Crescent Hotel London.** On one of Bloomsbury's grand old squares and
B&B/INN wihin walking distance of many top attractions, this friendly, attractive B&B includes use the tennis courts and private gardens in the square—a great spot for picnics on a sunny day. **Pros:** lovely, convenient location; friendly staff. **Cons:** price too high for what you get; needs a facelift; no elevator; bathrooms are tiny and some have only a tub, so if you want a shower, ask when you book. $ *Rooms from: £116* ✉ *49–50 Cartright Gardens, Bloomsbury* ☎ *020/7387–1515* ⊕ *www.*

crescenthoteloflondon.com ↘ *27 rooms, 10 with bath* ⦿ *Breakfast* Ⓜ *Russell Sq.* ✛ *2:C3*

$$ 🏨 **Grange Blooms Hotel.** In this white Georgian town-house hotel, just
HOTEL around the corner from the British Museum, rooms are not too tiny by
London standards, and those in the back look out onto a leafy green
garden. **Pros:** great location; overall good value; good prices if you
book early through the website. **Cons:** bathrooms could use an upgrade;
guests can be bumped to sister hotel if fully booked; no air-conditioning;
street noise in some rooms. $ *Rooms from: £114* ✉ *7 Montague St.,
Bloomsbury* ☎ *020/7323–1717, 800/2247–2643* ⊕ *www.grangehotels.
com* ↘ *26 rooms, 1 suite* ⦿ *Some meals* Ⓜ *Russell Sq.* ✛ *3:F2*

$$ 🏨 **Harlingford Hotel.** The most contemporary of the Cartwright Gar-
HOTEL dens hotels offers sleek, quiet, and comfortable bedrooms and per-
fectly appointed public rooms. **Pros:** good location; friendly staff; use
of private garden; wider breakfast choice than many small London
hotels. **Cons:** rooms are quite small; no elevator. $ *Rooms from: £120*
✉ *61–63 Cartwright Gardens, Bloomsbury* ☎ *020/7387–1551* ⊕ *www.
harlingfordhotel.com* ↘ *43 rooms* ⦿ *Breakfast* Ⓜ *Russell Sq.* ✛ *2:C3*

$ 🏨 **Jesmond Hotel.** This friendly little hotel is great value given the loca-
B&B/INN tion: a short walk from the British Museum in one direction, and
Soho and Covent Garden in the other. **Pros:** great location; friendly
staff; free Wi-Fi. **Cons:** some rooms are very small; nearly half have
shared bathrooms. $ *Rooms from: £85* ✉ *63 Gower St., Bloomsbury*
☎ *020/7636–3199* ⊕ *www.jesmondhotel.org.uk* ↘ *15 rooms* ⦿ *Breakfast* Ⓜ *Goodge St., Euston Sq., Warren St., Russell Sq.* ✛ *3:C1*

$$ 🏨 **The Megaro.** Directly across the street from St. Pancras International
HOTEL station (for Eurostar), the snazzy, well-designed, modern bedrooms here
surround guests with startlingly contemporary style and amenities that
include powerful showers and espresso machines. **Pros:** comfortable
beds; great location for Eurostar; short hop on Tube to city center. **Cons:**
neighborhood isn't great; standard rooms are small; interiors may be a
bit stark for some. $ *Rooms from: £160* ✉ *Belgrove St., King's Cross*
☎ *020/7843–2222* ⊕ *www.hotelmegaro.co.uk* ↘ *49 rooms* ⦿ *Break-
fast* ✛ *2:C2.*

$$ 🏨 **Morgan Hotel.** Don't expect many bells or whistles in this former
B&B/INN Georgian house, but the rooms are sunny and attractive and it overlooks
the British Museum and is close to West End theaters. **Pros:** friendly
staff; double and triple rooms are large by London standards; good
location. **Cons:** mattresses are quite thin, as are walls; no elevator.
$ *Rooms from: £135* ✉ *24 Bloomsbury St., Bloomsbury* ☎ *020/7636–
3735* ⊕ *www.morganhotel.co.uk* ↘ *15 rooms, 5 apartments* ⦿ *Breakfast* Ⓜ *Tottenham Court Rd., Russell Sq.* ✛ *3:E3*

$ 🏨 **The Portland Hotel.** Around the corner from leafy Russell Square and
HOTEL an easy walk to the British Museum and Covent Garden, the Portland
offers spacious and comfortable bedrooms, with large bathrooms, seating areas, and kitchenettes. **Pros:** great location; large rooms; kitchenettes offer alternative to restaurants; staff is friendly. **Cons:** restaurant
is in neighboring hotel, requiring a walk down the street to breakfast;
prices rise hugely after cheap rooms are sold. $ *Rooms from: £91* ✉ *31–*

15

32 Bedford Pl., Bloomsbury ☎ *020/7580–7088* ⊕ *www.grangehotels. com* ⤵ *18 rooms* ⦿| *Breakfast* Ⓜ *Holborn Rd.* ✛ *3:F2*

$
B&B/INN
⚏ **The Ridgemount Hotel.** Mere blocks away from the British Museum and London's West End theaters, this handsomely fronted guesthouse has clean, neat, and plainly decorated rooms at a bargain. **Pros:** good location for theaters and museum; helpful staff; family rooms (accommodating up to five) are excellent value. **Cons:** decoration is basic; no elevator; cheapest rooms have shared bathrooms. ⑤ *Rooms from: £78* ⊠ *65–67 Gower St., Bloomsbury* ☎ *020/7636–1141* ⊕ *www.ridgemounthotel. co.uk* ⤵ *32 rooms, 15 with bath* ⦿| *Breakfast* Ⓜ *Goodge St.* ✛ *3:D1*

$$
B&B/INN
⚏ **Rough Luxe.** Undoubtedly Bloomsbury's most avant-garde hotel, this 19th-century building has been renovated with an appealing mix of shabby chic and modern comfort. **Pros:** art and design lovers will be dazzled; free Wi-Fi. **Cons:** no restaurant or bar; cheapest rooms are booked up fast; in a neighborhood locals would describe as "dodgy"; some rooms share bathrooms. ⑤ *Rooms from: £159* ⊠ *1 Birkenhead St., Bloomsbury* ☎ *020/7837–5338* ⊕ *www.roughluxe.co.uk* ⤵ *10 rooms* ⦿| *Breakfast* Ⓜ *King's Cross* ✛ *2:C2.*

$$$
HOTEL
Fodor's Choice
★
⚏ **St. Pancras Renaissance.** Reopened in 2011 after nearly a century of dereliction, this stunningly restored Victorian landmark—replete with gingerbread turrets and castle-like ornaments—started as a love letter to the golden age of railways; now it's one of London's most sophisticated places to stay (bait-and-switch department: note that the guest rooms are modern and sleek). **Pros:** Victorian heaven (in parts); unique and beautiful; faultless service; just an elevator ride to the Eurostar. **Cons:** very popular bar and restaurant; streets outside are always busy. ⑤ *Rooms from: £230* ⊠ *Euston Rd., King's Cross* ☎ *020/7841–3540* ⊕ *www.marriott.com* ⤵ *207 rooms, 38 suites* ⦿| *Breakfast* Ⓜ *King's Cross St. Pancras. National Rail: King's Cross St. Pancras* ✛ *2:C2.*

HOLBORN

$$$
HOTEL
⚏ **Chancery Court Hotel.** So striking it was featured in the movie *Howards End*, this landmark structure (built by the Pearl Assurance Company in 1914) now houses a beautiful hotel with a clubby feel and extraspacious guest rooms. **Pros:** gorgeous space; great spa; your every need catered to. **Cons:** area is deserted at night and on weekends. ⑤ *Rooms from: £212* ⊠ *252 High Holborn, Holborn* ☎ *020/7829–9888* ⊕ *www. chancerycourthotel.com* ⤵ *342 rooms, 14 suites* ⦿| *Some meals* Ⓜ *Holborn* ✛ *3:G3.*

$$$
RENTAL
⚏ **SACO Serviced Apartments, Holborn.** Down a quiet backstreet, a 10-minute walk from the British Museum, these apartments are spacious, modern, and extremely well equipped, including a kitchen with dishwasher and washing machine. **Pros:** more independence than hotels; pleasant and spacious accommodations; on-site parking. **Cons:** exterior is dated; you must provide own bedding for baby cots. ⑤ *Rooms from: £256* ⊠ *82 Lamb's Conduit St., Holborn* ☎ *020/7269–9930* ⊕ *www. sacoapartments.co.uk* ⤵ *30 apartments (mixture of studios, and 1-, 2-, and 3-bedroom)* ⦿| *No meals* Ⓜ *Russell Sq.* ✛ *3:G1*

Claridge's

The Stafford London by Kempinski

LONDON CHAIN HOTEL PRIMER

England has a number of hotel chains worth considering. Some are moderately priced, others are luxurious. Here's a quick rundown of our favorites:

easyHotel: One of the first chains to bring so-called "pod hotels" to London, the easyHotel chain specializes in very cheap (less than £50 a night for a double) rooms that are clean, secure and offer all the basics, but are teeny-tiny, and have no extras at all. ⊕ *www.easyhotel.com.*

Grange Hotels: This chain includes a good mix of large and small hotels, with reliable (if somewhat dull) neutral interior design, good service, and plenty of gadgets for business travelers. Prices vary, although most are moderately priced. ⊕ *www. grangehotels.com.*

Malmaison: With lavish, elegant small hotels around the country, this upscale chain offers luxurious designer style, good restaurants, and trendy bars. ⊕ *www.malmaison.com.*

Millennium: Similar in style to Premier Inns, Millennium (and its other brand, Copthorne) hotels are targeted at both business and leisure travelers. They offer well-designed rooms with plenty of gadgets and have frequent sales. ⊕ *www. millenniumhotels.co.uk.*

myhotel: A small chain of pricey boutique hotels, with a designer style, trendy bars, and a modern approach, myhotels offer reliable comfort and service, if you don't mind the price tag. ⊕ *www.myhotels.com.*

Premier Inns: This widespread chain features medium-size, moderately priced hotels. They're known for their attractive if bland look, and for frequent sales, which keep prices low. ⊕ *www.premierinn.com.*

THE CITY

$$ ⊡ **Apex City of London.** At this sleek, modern branch of the small Apex
HOTEL chain near the Tower of London, bedrooms are reasonably spacious, with contemporary color schemes and little sofas and desks that make life easier for the traveler. **Pros:** great location; helpful staff; full of modern comforts; free Wi-Fi. **Cons:** geared more to business than leisure travelers; price can rise sharply during busy times. $ *Rooms from: £129* ✉ *1 Seething La., The City* ☎ *020/7702–2020* ⊕ *www.apexhotels.co.uk* ⤵ *130 rooms, 49 suites* ❏❏ *Breakfast* Ⓜ *Tower Hill* ✛ *2:G2.*

$$ ⊡ **Crowne Plaza London—The City.** Don't let the hotel's all-business
HOTEL appearance and financial-district location put you off—it's a polished operation, with stylish minimalist rooms and a Michelin-starred restaurant, and it's just steps from a Tube station. **Pros:** good prices available with advance booking; kids stay free; lots of amenities. **Cons:** neighborhood is super-busy during the day and graveyard-quiet at night—you'll have to go elsewhere for a party scene. $ *Rooms from: £195* ✉ *19 New Bridge St., The City* ☎ *0871/423–4828* ⊕ *www.cplondoncityhotel. co.uk* ⤵ *203 rooms, 3 suites* ❏❏ *Breakfast* Ⓜ *Blackfriars* ✛ *2:F6.*

$$ ⊡ **Grange City Hotel.** With an eye on business, this sleek City hotel has
HOTEL everything the workaholic needs to feel right at home—chic bedrooms subtly decorated, modern furnishings, plenty of space (by London

standards), and more. **Pros:** good-size rooms; prices can drop considerably on weekends; women-only rooms are great for lone female travelers. **Cons:** a bit off the tourist track; some rooms overlook train platform; prices can soar midweek; online discounts tend to not allow changes or cancellation. ⑤ *Rooms from: £142* ✉ *8–14 Cooper's Row, The City* ☏ *020/7863–3700* ⊕ *www.grangehotels.com* ⤳ *307 rooms, 11 suites* ⓘⓞⓘ *Some meals* Ⓜ *Tower Hill, Aldgate, Monument* ✛ *2:G2.*

$$$
HOTEL
🛏 **The London Mal.** This chic spot, on the edge of The City and handy for The Barbican, has stylish rooms that come with huge comfortable beds, bathrooms with tub and power shower, and plenty of amenities. **Pros:** luxurious rooms; excellent service; good weekend discounts and package deals. **Cons:** neighborhood is off the tourist track; area can be quiet at night. ⑤ *Rooms from: £240* ✉ *18–21 Charterhouse Sq., The City* ☏ *0845/365–4247, 020/7012–3700* ⊕ *www.malmaison.com* ⤳ *95 rooms, 2 suites* ⓘⓞⓘ *Multiple meal plans* Ⓜ *Barbican, Farringdon* ✛ *2:F4.*

$$
HOTEL
Fodor'sChoice
★
🛏 **The Rookery.** An absolutely unique and beautiful 1725 town house, the Rookery is the kind of place where you want to allow quality time to enjoy and soak up the atmosphere. **Pros:** helpful staff; free Wi-Fi; good deals in the off-season. **Cons:** breakfast costs extra; short Tube ride to tourist sites. ⑤ *Rooms from: £144* ✉ *12 Peter's La., at Cowcross St., The City* ☏ *020/7336–0931* ⊕ *www.rookeryhotel.com* ⤳ *30 rooms, 3 suites* ⓘⓞⓘ *No meals* Ⓜ *Farringdon* ✛ *2:F4.*

$$$
HOTEL
🛏 **Threadneedles Hotel.** The elaborate building housing this grand hotel in the financial district is a former bank, and the vast old banking hall—beautifully adapted as the lobby, with luxurious marble and mahogany panels—really sets the scene. **Pros:** lap of luxury; excellent service. **Cons:** a bit stuffy for some tastes; neighborhood is quiet at night. ⑤ *Rooms from: £210* ✉ *5 Threadneedle St., The City* ☏ *020/7657–8080* ⊕ *www.theetoncollection.com* ⤳ *63 rooms, 6 suites* ⓘⓞⓘ *Breakfast* Ⓜ *Bank* ✛ *2:G2.*

$$$
HOTEL
Fodor'sChoice
★
🛏 **The Zetter.** The dizzying five-story atrium, art deco staircase, and slick European restaurant hint at the delights to come in this converted warehouse—a breath of fresh air with its playful color schemes, elegant wallpapers, and wonderful views of The City from the higher floors. **Pros:** huge amounts of character; big rooms; free Wi-Fi; gorgeous "Rainforest" showers. **Cons:** rooms with good views cost more. ⑤ *Rooms from: £234* ✉ *86–88 Clerkenwell Rd., Holborn* ☏ *020/7324–4444* ⊕ *www.thezetter.com* ⤳ *59 rooms* ⓘⓞⓘ *Breakfast* Ⓜ *Farringdon* ✛ *2:F3.*

15

THE EAST END

$$
HOTEL
🛏 **Andaz.** Swanky and upscale, this hotel sports a modern, masculine design, and novel check-in procedure—instead of standing at a desk, guests sit in a lounge while a staff member with a handheld computer takes their information. **Pros:** nice attention to detail; guests can borrow an iPod from the front desk; no standing in line to check in; "healthy minibars" are stocked with nuts, fruit, and yogurt. **Cons:** sparse interior design is not for all; rates rise significantly for midweek stays. ⑤ *Rooms from: £154* ✉ *40 Liverpool St., East End* ☏ *020/7961–1234, 800/492–8804 in U.S.* ⊕ *www.andaz.hyatt.com* ⤳ *267 rooms* ⓘⓞⓘ *Breakfast* Ⓜ *Liverpool St.* ✛ *2:G2*

$ 🛏 **The Hoxton Hotel.** The design throughout this trendy East London
HOTEL   lodging is contemporary—but not so modern as to be absurd—and
Fodor's Choice   in keeping with a claim to combine a country-lodge lifestyle with true
★   urban living, a fire crackles in the lobby. **Pros:** cool vibe; neighborhood
known for funky galleries and boutiques; huge weekend discounts;
way-cool restaurant; one hour of free international calls. **Cons:** price
rockets during the week; away from tourist sights; £1 rooms sell out
months ahead. $ *Rooms from: £90* ✉ *81 Great Eastern St., East End*
☎ *020/7550–1000* ⊕ *www.hoxtonhotels.com* ↳ *205 rooms* ¶⦶ *Break-*
fast ✛ *2:G1.*

$$ 🛏 **Ramada Hotel and Suites Docklands.** Many of the sleek and modern
HOTEL   rooms at this hotel, dramatically set at the edge of the river in the reju-
venated Docklands area of East London, have water views, while others
have views of the city. **Pros:** waterfront views. **Cons:** lacks character;
area is tumbleweed quiet on weekends; about a 20-minute Tube ride to
central London. $ *Rooms from: £129* ✉ *ExCel, 2 Festoon Way, Royal*
Victoria Dock, East End ☎ *020/7540–4820* ⊕ *www.ramadadocklands.*
co.uk ↳ *224 rooms* ¶⦶ *Breakfast* Ⓜ *Old St.* ✛ *2:H2*

$$ 🛏 **Town Hall Hotel and Apartments.** An art deco town hall, abandoned in
HOTEL   the early 1980s and turned into a chic hotel in 2010, is now a lively
and stylish place, with the best of the building's elegant original features intact. **Pros:** beautifully designed; lovely staff; big discounts on
weekends. **Cons:** though touted as "cool" and "cutting edge," this is
not a good part of town; a 15-minute Tube ride from Central London. $ *Rooms from: £174* ✉ *Patriot Sq., Bethnal Green, East End*
☎ *020/7657–8080* ⊕ *www.townhallhotel.com* ↳ *98 rooms* ¶⦶ *Break-*
fast Ⓜ *Bethnal Green* ✛ *2:H1.*

SOUTH OF THE THAMES

$ 🛏 **Church Street Hotel.** Like rays of sunshine in gritty South London, these
HOTEL   rooms above a popular tapas restaurant are individually decorated in
Fodor's Choice   rich, bold tones and authentic Central American touches—elaborately
★   painted crucifixes; tiles handmade in Guadalajara; homemade iron bed
frames. **Pros:** unique and arty; great breakfasts; lovely staff; closer to
central London than it might appear. **Cons:** a trendy but not great part
of town (stay out of neighboring Elephant and Castle); would suit
adventurous young things more than families; a mile from a Tube station (though bus connections are handier); some rooms have shared
bathrooms. $ *Rooms from: £90* ✉ *29–33 Camberwell Church St.,*
Camberwell, South East ☎ *020/7703–5984* ⊕ *www.churchstreethotel.*
com ↳ *28 rooms* ¶⦶ *Breakfast* Ⓜ *Oval St.* ✛ *5:H6*

$$ 🛏 **London Bridge Hotel.** Steps away from the London Bridge rail and
HOTEL   Tube stations, and handy for the South Bank, this thoroughly modern,
stylish hotel is popular with business travelers, but leisure travelers
find it just as handy and appealing. **Pros:** good location for visiting
South Bank attractions; free Wi-Fi; good deals available online in the
off-season. **Cons:** small bedrooms; prices rise by £100 or more mid-
week. $ *Rooms from: £132* ✉ *8–18 London Bridge St., Southwark*
☎ *020/7855–2200* ⊕ *www.london-bridge-hotel.co.uk* ↳ *138 rooms,*
3 apartments ¶⦶ *Breakfast* Ⓜ *London Bridge* ✛ *5:H1.*

$$$
HOTEL
London Marriott Hotel County Hall. This grand hotel on the Thames enjoys perhaps the most iconic view in the city—right next door is the London Eye, and directly across the River Thames are the Houses of Parliament and Big Ben. **Pros:** handy for South Bank arts scene, London Eye, and Westminster; great gym; good weekend discounts. **Cons:** interior design is overdone; breakfasts are pricey; rooms facing the river inevitably cost extra. $ *Rooms from: £266* ⊠ *County Hall, Westminster Bridge Rd., South Bank* ☎ *020/7928–5200, 888/236–2427 in U.S.* ⊕ *www.marriott.com* ⤳ *200 rooms* ❍ *Breakfast* Ⓜ *Westminster, Waterloo. National Rail: Waterloo* ✛ *5:D2.*

$$
HOTEL
FAMILY
Premier Travel Inn County Hall. The small but nicely decorated rooms at this budget choice share the County Hall complex with the grander London Marriott Hotel County Hall, and though they have none of the spectacular river views they share the convenient location—at a decidedly lower price. **Pros:** good location for the South Bank; bargains to be had if you book in advance, including very cheap breakfast and dinner rates; kids stay free. **Cons:** no river views; limited services. $ *Rooms from: £132* ⊠ *Belvedere Rd., South Bank* ☎ *0871/527–8648* ⊕ *www.premiertravelinn.com* ⤳ *313 rooms* ❍ *Breakfast* Ⓜ *Westminster, Waterloo. National Rail: Waterloo* ✛ *5:D2.*

$$
HOTEL
Premier Travel Inn Southwark (Borough Market). This excellent branch of the huge Premier Travel Inn chain is a bit out of the way on the South Bank, but is convenient for visits to the Tate Modern, Shakespeare's Globe Theatre, and Borough Market. **Pros:** ideally placed for visiting the Tate Modern or the Globe Theatre. **Cons:** small rooms; uninspiring building; limited extras or services; rooms near elevators can be a little noisy (ask for one farther down the hall). $ *Rooms from: £132* ⊠ *34 Park St., Southwark* ☎ *0871/527–8676* ⊕ *www.premiertravelinn.com* ⤳ *56 rooms* ❍ *Breakfast* Ⓜ *London Bridge* ✛ *5:H1.*

KENSINGTON, CHELSEA, KNIGHTSBRIDGE, AND BELGRAVIA

KENSINGTON

$$$
HOTEL
Ampersand. A sense of style rises like spritzed perfume from every surface of this sumptuous new hotel in the heart of Kensington—but the playful vibe stands in contrast to the cooler-than-thou atmosphere you'd often expect in this part of town. **Pros:** flawless design; great service; good restaurant. **Cons:** ground floor rooms can be noisy. $ *Rooms from: £300* ⊠ *10 Harrington Rd., Kensington* ☎ *020/7589–5895* ⊕ *www.ampersandhotel.com* ⤳ *111 rooms* ❍ *No meals* Ⓜ *South Kensington.* ✛ *4:D2*

$$
HOTEL
Ashburn Hotel. A short walk from Gloucester Road Tube station and within walking distance of Harrods and the Kensington museums, the Ashburn is one of the better "boutique" hotels in this part of town. **Pros:** friendly atmosphere; free Wi-Fi; turndown gift (different every night). **Cons:** summer prices sometimes hike the cost. $ *Rooms from: £159* ⊠ *111 Cromwell Rd., Kensington* ☎ *020/7938–8970 reservations, 020/7244–1999* ⊕ *www.ashburn-hotel.co.uk* ⤳ *38 rooms, 3 suites* ❍ *Breakfast* Ⓜ *Gloucester Rd.* ✛ *4:C2*

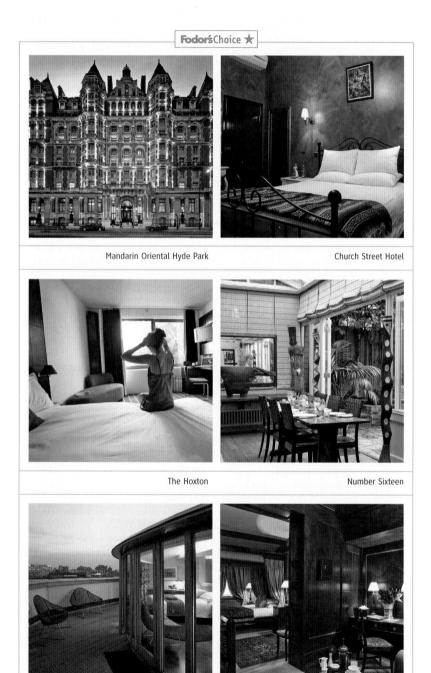

Fodor's Choice ★

Mandarin Oriental Hyde Park

Church Street Hotel

The Hoxton

Number Sixteen

The Zetter

The Rookery

$$$ ⊞ **Astons Apartments.** Three redbrick Victorian town houses on a quiet
RENTAL residential street are the setting for Astons's comfortable studios and
apartments. **Pros:** decent alternative to full-service hotel rooms; kitch-
enettes help save money on long stays. **Cons:** modern (if rather func-
tional) blond-wood furnishings advertised as "designer" but look a
bit cheap; few customer services; weekly discounts are hardly gener-
ous. ⑤ *Rooms from: £250* ⊠ *31 Rosary Gardens, South Kensington*
☎ *020/7590–6000, 800/525–2810 in U.S.* ⊕ *www.astons-apartments.*
com ⟿ *43 rooms, 12 suites* ⍾○⍾ *No meals* Ⓜ *Gloucester Rd.* ✛ *4:C3*

$$ ⊞ **base2stay Kensington.** This near-budget option in a creamy white
RENTAL Georgian town house offers comfortable double rooms that have a
stylish, modern look and tiny kitchenettes—and some even have bunk
beds for traveling friends or children. **Pros:** great value alternative to
hotel; attractive rooms; handy mini-kitchens; free Wi-Fi. **Cons:** bathrooms are small but well-designed; 15-minute Tube ride to central London. ⑤ *Rooms from: £135* ⊠ *25 Courtfield Gardens, South Kensington*
☎ *020/7244–2255, 800/511–9821 in U.S.* ⊕ *www.base2stay.com* ⟿ *67*
rooms ⍾○⍾ *No meals* Ⓜ *Earls Court* ✛ *4:B3.*

$$$ ⊞ **The Bentley London.** Close to, but just far enough to be shielded from
HOTEL the bustle of Kensington, this opulent hotel, owned by Hilton, is an
elegant escape within a creamy-white Victorian building. **Pros:** luxuri-
ous rooms; gorgeous spa; great location. **Cons:** can be a bit stuffy; old-
fashioned style won't please everyone. ⑤ *Rooms from: £240* ⊠ *27–33*
Harrington Gardens, South Kensington ☎ *020/7244–5555* ⊕ *www.*
thebentley-hotel.com ⟿ *52 rooms, 12 suites* ⍾○⍾ *Breakfast* Ⓜ *Glouces-*
ter Rd. ✛ *4:C3*

$$ ⊞ **Best Western Premier Shaftesbury Kensington.** These fresh and relaxing
HOTEL guest rooms, done in cool grays and earth tones and with firm queen-
size beds, are just steps from Earl's Court Tube station and offer a
lot for your money. **Pros:** good neighborhood; two-minute walk from
the Tube; frequent online sales. **Cons:** small rooms; temperamental
booking system, so make sure you bring your confirmation details;
at the far edge of Kensington, farther from the museums than you
might expect. ⑤ *Rooms from: £137* ⊠ *33–37 Hogarth Rd., Kensing-*
ton ☎ *020/7370–6831* ⊕ *www.bw-shaftesburykensingtonhotel.co.uk*
⟿ *144 rooms* ⍾○⍾ *Breakfast* Ⓜ *Earl's Court* ✛ *4:B2.*

$$ ⊞ **The Cranley Hotel.** Old-fashioned British propriety is the overall feel-
HOTEL ing at this small, Victorian town-house hotel, where high ceilings, huge
windows, and a pale, creamy color scheme flood the bedrooms with
light. **Pros:** good-size rooms; attractively decorated; friendly staff; free
evening nibbles are a nice touch. **Cons:** steep stairs into lobby; no res-
taurant; prices rise in mid-summer. ⑤ *Rooms from: £140* ⊠ *10–12 Bina*
Gardens, South Kensington ☎ *020/7373–0123* ⊕ *www.thecranley.com*
⟿ *29 rooms, 5 suites, 4 apartments* ⍾○⍾ *Breakfast* Ⓜ *Gloucester Rd.*
✛ *4:C3*

$ ⊞ **easyHotel South Kensington.** London's first "pod hotel" has tiny rooms
HOTEL with a double bed, private shower room, and little else, each brightly
decorated in the easyGroup's trademark orange and white (to match
their budget airline easyJet). **Pros:** amazing price; safe and pleasant
space. **Cons:** not for the claustrophobic; most rooms have no windows;

15

six floors and no elevator. $ *Rooms from: £44* ✉ *14 Lexham Gardens, Kensington* ☎ *020/7216–1717* ⊕ *www.easyhotel.com* ➦ *34 rooms* ⦿ *No meals* Ⓜ *Gloucester Rd.* ✛ *4:B2*

$$$ 🏨 **The Gore Hotel.** Just down the road from the Albert Hall, this gorHOTEL geous, friendly hotel has a luxurious mixture of the comfortable and the extraordinary. **Pros:** gorgeously designed spacious rooms; outstanding and attentive service. **Cons:** prices rather high; Wi-Fi is not free; bar can be noisy. $ *Rooms from: £228* ✉ *190 Queen's Gate, Kensington* ☎ *020/7584–6601, 888/757–5587 in U.S* ⊕ *www.gorehotel.com* ➦ *50 rooms* ⦿ *Breakfast* Ⓜ *Gloucester Rd.* ✛ *4:D1*

$$ 🏨 **Kensington House Hotel.** A short stroll from High Street Kensington HOTEL and Kensington Gardens, this refurbished 19th-century town house has streamlined, contemporary rooms with large windows letting in plenty of light, comfortable beds with luxurious fabrics and soft comforters. **Pros:** attractive design; relaxing setting; free Wi-Fi. **Cons:** rooms are small; bathrooms are minuscule; the elevator is Lilliputian. $ *Rooms from: £144* ✉ *15–16 Prince of Wales Terr., Kensington* ☎ *020/7937–2345* ⊕ *www.kenhouse.com* ➦ *39 rooms, 2 suites* ⦿ *Breakfast* Ⓜ *High Street Kensington* ✛ *4:C1.*

$$ 🏨 **Millennium Gloucester.** With a Tube station opposite and Kensington's HOTEL many attractions nearby, this hotel is both convenient and alluring, its sleek and opulent lobby, with polished wood columns, a warming fireplace, and glittering chandeliers giving way to guest rooms with a traditionally masculine look. **Pros:** good deals available if you book in advance. **Cons:** lighting in some bedrooms is a bit too subtle; bathrooms are relatively small but have all you need; public areas and restaurant can get crowded. $ *Rooms from: £150* ✉ *4–18 Harrington Gardens, Kensington* ☎ *020/7373–6030* ⊕ *www.millenniumhotels. co.uk/millenniumgloucester* ➦ *143 rooms* ⦿ *Breakfast* Ⓜ *Gloucester Rd.* ✛ *4:C2*

$$$ 🏨 **Number Sixteen.** Guest rooms at this lovely luxury guesthouse, just HOTEL around the corner from the Victoria & Albert Museum, look like they come from the pages of *Architectural Digest*, and the delightful garden is an added bonus. **Pros:** just the right level of helpful service; interiors are gorgeous. **Cons:** no restaurant; small elevator. $ *Rooms from: £285* ✉ *16 Sumner Pl., South Kensington* ☎ *020/7589–5232, 888/559–5508 in U.S.* ⊕ *www.firmdale.com* ➦ *42 rooms* ⦿ *Breakfast* Ⓜ *South Kensington* ✛ *4:D2.*

$$$ 🏨 **The Pelham Hotel.** One of the first and most stylish of London's famed HOTEL "boutique" hotels, this still-chic choice is but a short stroll away from Fodor's Choice the Natural History, Science, and V&A museums. **Pros:** great loca★ tion for museum-hopping; gorgeous marble bathrooms; soigné interior design; lovely staff; good package deals for online booking. **Cons:** taller guests will find themselves cursing the top-floor rooms with sloping ceilings. $ *Rooms from: £252* ✉ *15 Cromwell Pl., South Kensington* ☎ *020/7589–8288, 888/757–5587 in U.S.* ⊕ *www.pelhamhotel.co.uk* ➦ *47 rooms, 4 suites* ⦿ *Breakfast* Ⓜ *South Kensington* ✛ *4:D2.*

$$ 🏨 **The Rockwell.** Despite being on the notoriously traffic-clogged CromHOTEL well Road, this excellent little place is one of the best boutique hotels in this part of London—and windows have good soundproofing. **Pros:**

large bedroooms; stylish surroundings; helpful staff. **Cons:** on a busy, unattractive road; 20-minute Tube ride to central London. $ *Rooms from: £180 ⊠ 181 Cromwell Rd., South Kensington ☎ 020/7244–2000 ⊕ www.therockwell.com ⇗ 38 rooms, 2 suites ⧓ Breakfast ✛ 4:B2.*

$$ ⌗ **The Sumner.** You can feel yourself relaxing the minute you enter this
HOTEL elegant Georgian town house. **Pros:** excellent location for shopping; small enough that the staff knows your name; attractive conservatory and garden. **Cons:** services are limited but prices high. $ *Rooms from: £180 ⊠ 54 Upper Berkley St., Marble Arch, Marylebone ☎ 020/7723– 2244 ⊕ www.thesumner.com ⇗ 20 rooms ⧓ Breakfast Ⓜ Marble Arch ✛ 4:D3.*

$$ ⌗ **Think Earl's Court.** These serviced apartments are a stone's throw from
RENTAL Kensington High Street and a short walk from both Earl's Court and Olympia. **Pros:** brand new building; self-catering offers greater independence. **Cons:** payment is made when you book; bland, officelike exterior. $ *Rooms from: £168 ⊠ 26A Adam and Eve Mews, Kensington ☎ 020/3465–9100 ⊕ www.think-apartments.com ⇗ 133 rooms ⧓ No meals Ⓜ High Street Kensington ✛ 4:B1.*

CHELSEA

$$$ ⌗ **The Cadogan Hotel.** This elegant and luxurious hotel is one of Lon-
HOTEL don's most historically naughty hotels—once the home of scandalous actress Lillie Langtry (King Edward's mistress in the 1890s), and where Oscar Wilde was staying (in Room 118) when he was arrested for "indecency" with a young man on April 6, 1895. **Pros:** luxurious but not stuffy; friendly staff; great location for shopping; good advance discounts online. **Cons:** rooms are quite small. $ *Rooms from: £234 ⊠ 75 Sloane St., Chelsea ☎ 020/7235–7141 ⊕ www.cadogan.com ⇗ 65 rooms ⧓ Breakfast Ⓜ Sloane Sq. ✛ 4:G2*

$$ ⌗ **myhotel chelsea.** Rooms at this small, chic charmer—tucked away
HOTEL down a side street in an upscale neighborhood—are bijou tiny but sophisticated, with mauve satin throws atop crisp white down comforters. **Pros:** stylish rooms made for relaxation; good neighborhood. **Cons:** price a bit high for what you get; tiny rooms; no restaurant. $ *Rooms from: £200 ⊠ 35 Ixworth Pl., Chelsea ☎ 020/7225–7500 ⊕ www.myhotels.com ⇗ 45 rooms, 9 suites ⧓ Breakfast Ⓜ South Kensington ✛ 4:E3.*

KNIGHTSBRIDGE

$$$ ⌗ **The Beaufort.** The high-ceilinged, contemporary rooms at this gracious
HOTEL boutique hotel have muted, sophisticated colors and a plenthora of thoughtful extras—such as flowers, chocolates, free afternoon tea, and even free drinks in the evening. **Pros:** gorgeous interiors; friendly staff. **Cons:** two-night minimum on some dates; standard doubles are much smaller than the price might indicate. $ *Rooms from: £281 ⊠ 33 Beaufort Gardens, Knightsbridge ☎ 020/7584–5252 ⊕ www.thebeaufort. co.uk ⇗ 20 rooms, 7 suites ⧓ Breakfast Ⓜ Knightsbridge ✛ 4:F1.*

$$$$ ⌗ **The Berkeley.** Convenient for Knightsbridge shopping, the very ele-
HOTEL gant Berkeley is known for its renowned restaurants and luxuries that culminate—literally—in a splendid penthouse swimming pool. **Pros:** lavish and elegant; attentive service; prices aren't quite as stratospheric as some

15

APARTMENT RENTALS & HOME EXCHANGES

APARTMENT RENTALS

For a home base that's roomy enough for a family and that comes with cooking facilities, consider renting furnished "flats" (the British word for apartments). These can save you money, especially if you're traveling as a family or with a group.

INTERNATIONAL AGENTS

Hideaways International. This company offers boutique hotels, tours, and cruises. ☎ 603/430–4433, 800/843–4433 ⊕ www.hideaways.com.

Interhome. Dozens of flats (apartments) all over London, starting at about £750 per week per person, are on Interhome's books. ☎ 800/882–6864 ⊕ www.interhome.us .

Villas International. Exclusively priced flats all over London are available starting at around £1,800 per week—although as some sleep up to 10 people it can work out as a viable option for large groups. ☎ 415/499–9490, 800/221–2260 ⊕ www.villasintl.com.

LOCAL AGENTS

Acorn Apartments. Check out this agency for attractive small flats in Clerkenwell and Bloomsbury, starting at around £150. ☎ 020/7636–8325 ⊕ www.acorn-apartments.co.uk.

The Apartment Service. This agency specializes in executive apartments for business travelers, so prices are high, but so is the quality. ☎ 020/8944–1444 ⊕ www.apartmentservice.com.

At Home in London. Rooms in private homes in Knightsbridge, Kensington, Mayfair, Chelsea, and West London are handled by this agency. ☎ 020/8748–1943 ⊕ www.athomeinlondon.co.uk.

The Bed and Breakfast Club. Contact this company for delightful little London apartments, in Kensington, Chelsea, and Knightsbridge, costing from around £50–£125 per night with full English breakfasts. ☎ 01243/370–692 ⊕ www.thebedandbreakfastclub.co.uk.

Coach House London Vacation Rentals. This company arranges stays in the properties of Londoners who are temporarily away. ☎ 020/8133–8332 ⊕ www.rentals.chslondon.com .

Landmark Trust. Specializing in unusual and historic buildings, this agency has London apartments starting at around £100 a night, but many properties require a minimum stay of seven days. ☎ 01628/825–925 ⊕ www.landmarktrust.org.uk.

One Fine Stay. What sets this agency apart is the quality of the properties on offer and the outstanding support you get during your stay, from iPhones loaded with maps to local tips from the owners. ☎ 020/7097–8948.

HOME EXCHANGES

If you would like to exchange your home for someone else's, join a home-exchange organization, which will send you its updated listings of available exchanges for a year and will include your own listing in at least one of them. It's up to you to make specific arrangements.

Exchange Clubs Intervac U.S. It costs from $8.50 per month for a listing and online access with this company. ☎ 800/756–4663 ⊕ www.intervacus.com.

high-end places. **Cons:** You'll need your best designer clothes to fit in. $ *Rooms from: £390* ✉ *Wilton Pl., Knightsbridge* ☏ *020/7235–6000, 800/637–2869 in U.S.* ⊕ *www.the-berkeley.co.uk* ⤳ *103 rooms, 55 suites* ⦿ *Breakfast* Ⓜ *Knightsbridge* ✛ *4:G1.*

$$$$ ⛬ **The Capital Hotel.** Nothing is ever too much at this elegant hotel that
HOTEL was formerly a private house—mattresses are handmade, sheets are 450-thread count, bathrooms are marble, and everything is done in impeccable taste. **Pros:** beautiful space; handy for shopping at Harrods. **Cons:** breakfast is expensive. $ *Rooms from: £315* ✉ *22–24 Basil St., Knightsbridge* ☏ *020/7589–5171, 800/926–3199 in U.S.* ⊕ *www.capitalhotel.co.uk* ⤳ *40 rooms, 10 suites* ⦿ *Breakfast* Ⓜ *Knightsbridge* ✛ *4:F1.*

$$$ ⛬ **Egerton House.** Sensationally soigné, chicly decorated, and feeling
HOTEL like your own private London home, this option has some gorgeous pluses, including guest rooms lavishly decorated with luxurious fabrics in rich colors, a knockout white-on-gold dining room. **Pros:** lovely staff; great location; magnificent interiors; striking art. **Cons:** some style touches a little too frou-frou—but Toulouse-Lautrec would have approved. $ *Rooms from: £281* ✉ *17–19 Egerton Terr., Knightsbridge* ☏ *020/7589–2412, 877/955–1515 in U.S.* ⊕ *www.egertonhousehotel.co.uk* ⤳ *23 rooms, 6 suites* ⦿ *Breakfast* Ⓜ *Knightsbridge, South Kensington* ✛ *4:F2.*

$$$$ ⛬ **The Lanesborough.** A gilded cocoon for the seriously wealthy, this
HOTEL hotel exudes a spectacular richness and, when built by a Texan heiress, was the talk of the town, thanks to the magnificent 19th-century antiques, the personal butler service, and that 1770 cognac on the menu. **Pros:** lap of luxury; your wish is their command. **Cons:** prices are extraordinary; not everybody likes the constantly hovering service. $ *Rooms from: £495* ✉ *Hyde Park Corner, Belgravia* ☏ *020/7259–5599, 800/999–1828 in U.S.* ⊕ *www.lanesborough.com* ⤳ *52 rooms, 43 suites* ⦿ *Breakfast* Ⓜ *Hyde Park Corner* ✛ *4:G1.*

$$$$ ⛬ **Mandarin Oriental Hyde Park.** Built in 1880, the Mandarin Oriental
HOTEL welcomes you with one of the most exuberantly Victorian facades in
Fodor'sChoice town, then fast-forwards you to high-trend modern London, thanks to
★ striking and luxurious guest rooms filled with high-tech gadgets. **Pros:** great shopping at your doorstep; amazing views of Hyde Park; excellent service. **Cons:** nothing comes cheap; you must dress for dinner (and lunch and breakfast). $ *Rooms from: £570* ✉ *66 Knightsbridge, Knightsbridge* ☏ *020/7235–2000* ⊕ *www.mandarinoriental.com/london* ⤳ *177 rooms, 23 suites* ⦿ *Breakfast* Ⓜ *Knightsbridge* ✛ *4:F1.*

BELGRAVIA

$$ ⛬ **B&B Belgravia.** At this modern guesthouse near Victoria Station, a
B&B/INN clean, chic white color scheme, simple modern furniture, and a lounge where a fire crackles away in the winter are all geared to stylish comfort. **Pros:** nice extras like free use of a laptop in the hotel lounge; coffee and tea always available. **Cons:** rooms and bathrooms are small; unimaginative breakfasts; can be noisy, especially on lower floors. $ *Rooms from: £135* ✉ *64–66 Ebury St., Victoria* ☏ *020/7259–8570* ⊕ *www.bb-belgravia.com* ⤳ *17 rooms* ⦿ *Breakfast* Ⓜ *Sloane Square, Victoria* ✛ *4:H2.*

15

$$ ⊞ **The Luna Simone Hotel.** This delightful and friendly little family-run
HOTEL   hotel, a short stroll from Buckingham Palace, is a real find for the price
in central London. **Pros:** friendly and well-run; family rooms are out-
standing value; superb location. **Cons:** dated style; tiny bathrooms; no
elevator or air conditioning. ⑤ *Rooms from: £120* ✉ *47–49 Belgrave
Rd., Pimlico* ☎ *020/7834–5897* ⊕ *www.lunasimonehotel.com* ⤴ *36
rooms* |○| *Breakfast* Ⓜ *Pimlico, Victoria* ⊕ *5:A4.*

$ ⊞ **Studios@82.** A great little side operation from B&B Belgravia, these
RENTAL   self-catering apartments represent fantastic value for money; they're
pleasant, contemporary spaces that have everything you need, plus a
few useful extras such as free Wi-Fi. **Pros:** great price; lovely location;
all the independence of self-catering. **Cons:** lots of stairs and no eleva-
tor. ⑤ *Rooms from: £99* ✉ *64–66 Ebury St., Victoria* ☎ *020/7259–8570*
⊕ *www.bb-belgravia.com* ⤴ *9 apartments* |○| *Breakfast* Ⓜ *Knights-
bridge* ⊕ *4:H2.*

NOTTING HILL AND BAYSWATER

NOTTING HILL

$ ⊞ **Lancaster Hall Hotel.** This cheap and cheerful choice just north of Hyde
HOTEL   Park offers clean, simple rooms at a decent price, along with a good
buffet breakfast. **Pros:** decent, inexpensive, no-frills accommodations;
excellent central location 5-minute walk from Hyde Park; short Tube or
bus ride away from many sights. **Cons:** just the basics; only the Youth
Wing has nonsmoking rooms; beds could be better; all double rooms
have twin beds. ⑤ *Rooms from: £90* ✉ *35 Craven Terr., Marylebone*
☎ *020/7723–9276* ⊕ *www.lancaster-hall-hotel.co.uk* ⤴ *180 rooms*
|○| *Breakfast* Ⓜ *Lancaster Gate, Paddington. National Rail: Padding-
ton* ⊕ *1:D4.*

$$ ⊞ **The Main House.** A stay in this delightfully welcoming B&B feels more
B&B/INN   like sleeping over at a friend's house than in a hotel—albeit a par-
Fodor's Choice   ticularly wealthy and well-connected friend. **Pros:** unique and unusual
★   place; charming and helpful owners. **Cons:** few services; two-night
minimum stay. ⑤ *Rooms from: £110* ✉ *6 Colvile Rd., Notting Hill*
☎ *020/7221–9691* ⊕ *www.themainhouse.com* ⤴ *4 rooms* |○| *Breakfast*
Ⓜ *Notting Hill Gate* ⊕ *1:A4.*

$$ ⊞ **The Portobello Hotel.** One of London's quirkiest hotels, the little Por-
HOTEL   tobello (formed from two adjoining Victorian houses) is seriously hip,
attracting scores of celebrities to its small but stylish rooms that are
decorated with joyous abandon. **Pros:** stylish; celebrity vibe; guests have
use of nearby gym and pool. **Cons:** most rooms are quite small; may be
too eccentric for some. ⑤ *Rooms from: £174* ✉ *22 Stanley Gardens,
Notting Hill* ☎ *020/7727–2777* ⊕ *www.portobello-hotel.co.uk* ⤴ *24
rooms* ☽ *Closed 10 days at Christmas* |○| *Breakfast* Ⓜ *Notting Hill
Gate* ⊕ *1:A5.*

BAYSWATER

$$ ⊞ **London House Hotel.** Set in a row of white Georgian town houses,
HOTEL   this excellent new budget option in hit-or-miss Bayswater is friendly,
Fodor's Choice   well run, and spotlessly clean. **Pros:** friendly and efficient; emphasis on
★   value for money; good location. **Cons:** some public areas feel a bit too

clinical; smallest rooms are tiny. $) *Rooms from: £105* ⊠ *81 Kensington Garden Sq., Bayswater* ☏ *020/7243–1810* ⊕ *www.londonhousehotels. com* ⊲ *100 rooms* ❡*Breakfast* Ⓜ *Queensway, Bayswater* ✛ *1:B4.*

$ ⛣ **Parkwood Hotel.** Just seconds from Hyde Park in one of London's
B&B/INN   swankiest enclaves (the Blairs live a few doors away), this sweet little guesthouse is an oasis of value-for-money, with warm and helpful hosts and bright bedrooms. **Pros:** lovely hosts; free Wi-Fi; hotel guarantees to match or beat price of any other hotel of its class in the area. **Cons:** often booked up in advance; no elevator; front-facing rooms can be noisy. $) *Rooms from: £85* ⊠ *4 Stanhope Pl., Bayswater* ☏ *020/7402–2241* ⊕ *www.parkwoodhotel.com* ⊲ *18 rooms* ❡*Breakfast* Ⓜ *Marble Arch* ✛ *1:F4.*

$$ ⛣ **Space Apart Hotel.** These studio apartments near Hyde Park are done
RENTAL   in soothing tones of white and gray, with polished wood floors and attractive modern kitchenettes equipped with all you need to make small meals. **Pros:** especially good value for the money; the larger suites have space for four people; handy location. **Cons:** no in-house restaurant or bar; minimum two-night stay required. $) *Rooms from: £140* ⊠ *32–37 Kensington Gardens Sq., Bayswater* ☏ *020/7908–1340* ⊕ *www.aparthotel-london.co.uk* ⊲ *30 rooms* ❡*No meals* Ⓜ *Bayswater* ✛ *1:B4.*

$ ⛣ **Stylotel.** Just around the corner from Paddington station, this funky-
HOTEL   looking little place has small, functional rooms—done to death in contemporary style—and even tinier bathrooms, but it's clean, cheerful, and perfectly comfortable. **Pros:** bargain price; helpful staff; unique style. **Cons:** style will be *too* unique for some; small bedrooms and bathrooms. $) *Rooms from: £95* ⊠ *160–162 Sussex Gardens Sq., Bayswater* ☏ *0207/223–1026* ⊕ *www.stylotel.com* ⊲ *40 rooms* ❡*Breakfast* Ⓜ *Paddington, Edgware Rd. National Rail: Paddington* ✛ *1:E4.*

$$ ⛣ **Vancouver Studios.** All rooms in this Victorian town house are similar
RENTAL   to efficiency apartments, with mini-kitchens and microwaves, and you can even preorder groceries, which are stocked in your mini-refrigerator on arrival. **Pros:** more space than a hotel room; unique little apartments. **Cons:** a bit out of the way; a bargain only if several people share the space. $) *Rooms from: £140* ⊠ *30 Prince's Sq., Bayswater* ☏ *020/7243–1270* ⊕ *www.vancouverstudios.co.uk* ⊲ *45 studios* ❡*No meals* Ⓜ *Bayswater, Queensway* ✛ *1:B4.*

REGENT'S PARK AND HAMPSTEAD

HAMPSTEAD

$ ⛣ **Glenlyn Guest House.** An excellent option for travelers who don't mind
B&B/INN   being a long Tube ride away from the action, this converted Victorian town house offers a high standard of accommodation a few miles north of Hampstead. **Pros:** comfortable and friendly; you get more for your money than you would in central London; adjoining rooms can be converted to family suites; 5-minute walk from Tube station. **Cons:** you have to factor in the cost and inconvenience of a half-hour Tube ride to central London; no restaurant. $) *Rooms from: £85* ⊠ *6 Woodside*

Park Rd., North Finchley ☎ *020/8445–0440* 🌐 *www.glenlynhotel.com* *27* 🍽 *Breakfast* Ⓜ *Woodside Park* ✥ *1:D1.*

$ HOTEL Fodor's Choice ★ **The Hide.** This cozy, chic, little bolt-hole is exceptional value for money and exceeds virtually anything you could hope to find in central London for the price; the great downside is that the half-hour Tube ride into town can start to feel like penance at the end of a long day's sightseeing. **Pros:** excellent value for money; great service; free Wi-Fi; close to Tube station. **Cons:** far from the center; dull neighborhood. $ *Rooms from: £100* ✉ *230 Hendon Way, Hendon, Hampstead* ☎ *020/8203–1670* 🌐 *www.thehidelondon.com* *22 rooms* 🍽 *Breakfast* Ⓜ *Hendon Central* ✥ *1:H1.*

$ B&B/INN **La Gaffe.** The name of this simple B&B (located above an Italian restaurant) means "the mistake" in Italian but is also the punchline to the unlikely tale of how the original husband-and-wife proprietors met in the 1950s—but it also rather neatly chimes with the cockney term "gaff," meaning a simple, cozy residence. **Pros:** unusual place with a cheerful atmosphere; no shared bathrooms. **Cons:** few services; no elevator; outside city center. $ *Rooms from: £90* ✉ *107–111 Heath St., Hampstead* ☎ *020/7435–8965* 🌐 *www.lagaffe.co.uk* *18 rooms, 3 suites* 🍽 *Breakfast* Ⓜ *Hampstead* ✥ *1:D1.*

ISLINGTON

$ B&B/INN **Arlington Avenue.** A find like this in London is as rare as hen's teeth: an immaculate, friendly, Georgian town house B&B, full of character, just a bit far from the city center, *and* at a rock-bottom price. **Pros:** stylish and comfortable; quiet street; as cheap as you'll find for a place like this. **Cons:** feels very much like a private house; shared guest bathroom; neighborhood is trendy but verging on not-so-nice. $ *Rooms from: £50* ✉ *Arlington Ave., Islington* ☎ *07711/265–183* 🌐 *www.arlingtonavenue.co.uk* *2 rooms* 🍽 *Breakfast* Ⓜ *Angel, Essex Rd.* ✥ *2:D1*

PUBS AND
NIGHTLIFE

Updated by
Julius Honnor

There isn't a London nightlife scene—there are lots of them. As long as there are crowds for obscure teenage rock bands, Dickensian-style pubs, comedy cabarets, and "bodysonic" dance nights, someone will create clubs and venues for them in London. The result? London has become a veritable utopia for excitement junkies, culture fiends, and those who—simply put—like to party.

Nearly everyone who visits London these days will be mesmerized by the city's energy, which reveals itself in layers. Whether you prefer rhythm and blues with fine French food, the gritty guitar-riff music of Camden Town, the boutique beers of East London, a pint and gourmet pizza at a local gastropub, or swanky cocktails and sushi at London's sexiest lair, London is sure to feed your fancy.

PLANNING

GETTING AROUND

If you're out past 12:30 am, the best way to get home is by taxi (the Tube stops running around 12:30 am Monday–Saturday and midnight on Sunday), though the city's night buses are largely safe and reliable. The best place to hail a taxi is at the front door of one of the major hotels; you can also have the staff at your last stop of the evening call one for you. Avoid unlicensed taxis that tout for business around closing time.

LIQUOR AND SMOKING LAWS

Laws now allow London drinking establishments to extend their opening hours beyond the traditional 11 pm closing, and smoking is banned. Most pubs and bars still close by midnight or a few short hours later, and, in general, you'll find yourself drinking in environs that are healthier and more pleasant than was the case in the past.

CAN I TAKE MY KIDS TO THE PUB?

As pubs increasingly emphasize what's coming out of the kitchen alongside what's flowing from the tap, bringing the kids is more of an option. The law dictates that children 14 to 17 may enter a pub but are not permitted to purchase or drink alcohol, and children under 14 are not permitted in the bar area of a pub unless the pub has a "Children's Certificate" and they are accompanied by an adult. Some pubs have a section set aside for families, especially during the day, but many don't allow children in the evening.

WHAT TO WEAR

As a general rule, you won't see too many people in the upscale London nightspots wearing jeans and sneakers. People are more likely to dress down than up for an evening in the pub.

FIND OUT WHAT'S PLAYING WHERE

Because today's cool spot is often tomorrow's forgotten or closed venue, check out the weekly listings in of the *Evening Standard* (⊕ *www. thisislondon.co.uk*), and, especially, *Time Out* (⊕ *www.timeout.com/ london*). Other websites to consult are ⊕ www.londontown.com, ⊕ www.allinlondon.co.uk, and ⊕ *www.viewlondon.co.uk*. Although many clubs are for under-thirties, there are plenty of others that are popular with patrons of all ages and types.

PUBS

Pubs are where Londoners go to hang out, to see and be seen, act out the drama of life, and, for some, occasionally drink themselves into varying degrees of oblivion. The pub is still a vital part of London life, though many of the traditions of the pub experience are evolving. There are few better places to meet Londoners in their local habitat. There are somewhere around 4,000 pubs in London—some are dark and woody, others plain and functional, a few still have original Victorian etched glass, Edwardian panels, and art nouveau carvings.

Not long ago, pre-smoking ban, pubs tended to be smoky, male-dominated places with a couple of ubiquitous beers on tap and the only available food a packet of salt-and-vinegar-flavor crisps (chips). All that has changed. Gastropub fever swept through London around the turn of the 21st century and at many places, char-grills are installed in the kitchen and inventive pub grub is on the menu. A new wave of enthusiasm for craft beers is now having a similar effect on pubs' liquid sustenance.

The big decision is what to drink. The beers of choice among Britons are **"bitters,"** lightly fermented with an amber color that get their bitterness from hops. They are usually served at cellar temperature (that is, cooler than room temperature but neither chilled, nor, as common misconception would have it, warm). **Real ales,** served from wooden kegs and made without chilling, filtering, or pasteurization, are flatter than other bitters and are enjoying a renaissance. Many small London breweries have sprung up in recent years, and bottled designer and American beers can be found in most bars across London. **Stouts,** like Guinness, are a meal in themselves and something of an acquired taste—they have a dark, caramel-infused flavor and look like thickened flat Coke with a frothy top. Chilled **lagers,** most familiar to American drinkers, are light color and carbonated. ■**TIP**➔ What Americans call beer, the British call lager, the most commonly served of which are from continental Europe.

Many English pubs are owned by chains such as Mitchells and Butlers, Punch Taverns, or Samuel Smith, and are tenanted. Most are not obviously branded and retain at least some independence. Independently owned pubs, sometimes called "free houses," tend to offer a more extensive selection of beer. Other potations available include apple-based **ciders,** ranging from sweet to dry and from alcoholic to very alcoholic (Irish cider, served over ice, is now also ubiquitous), and **shandies,** a mix of beer and lemonade. Friendly pubs will usually be happy to give you a taste of the brew of your choice before you order.

The list below offers a few pubs selected for interesting beer, historical interest, a pleasant garden, music, or good food, but you might just as happily adopt your own temporary "local."

16

MAYFAIR

Audley. Big, smart, old-school, and a little on the brash side, the Audley makes up in friendly atmosphere what it lacks in charm. There's a good selection of beer on tap, and it's far enough away from the tourist hot spots that, on the right day, it can feel like a village pub. ⊠ *41–43 Mount St., Mayfair* ☎ *020/7499–1843* ⊕ *www.taylor-walker.co.uk* Ⓜ *Bond St., Green Park.*

Fodor'sChoice
★
Punch Bowl. In a quiet corner of Mayfair, the cozy little Punch Bowl has a worn wood floor and well-spoken staff dressed in pale checked shirts. The pub dates from 1750 and the interior remains steadfastly old-fashioned, with a painting of Churchill, candles, polished dark wood, and engraved windows. Try the place's eponymous ale, made specially in Scotland by Caledonian. A special dining area at the rear buzzes at lunchtime with locals who come for the upscale English pub grub. ⊠ *41 Farm St., Mayfair* ☎ *020/7493–6841* ⊕ *www.punchbowllondon.com* Ⓜ *Green Park, Bond St.*

SOHO AND COVENT GARDEN

SOHO

French House. In the pub where the French Resistance convened during World War II, Soho hipsters and eccentrics rub shoulders now with theater people and the literati—more than shoulders, actually, because this tiny, tricolor-waving, photograph-lined pub is almost always packed. Note that in French style, beer is served in half-pints only. If you're around on July 14, come and join in the rapturous Bastille Day celebrations. ⊠ *49 Dean St., Soho* ☎ *020/7437–2799* ⊕ *www.frenchhousesoho. com* Ⓜ *Tottenham Court Rd.*

Market Porter pub is directly across from foodie favorite Borough Market.

COVENT GARDEN

Harp. This is the sort of friendly little local you might find on some out-of-the-way backstreet, except that it's right in the middle of town, between Trafalgar Square and Covent Garden. As a result, the Harp can get crowded, especially since it was named British pub of the year by the Campaign for Real Ale, but the squeeze is worth it for the excellent beer (there are usually eight carefully chosen ales, often including a London micro-brewery) and a no-frills menu of high-quality British sausages, cooked behind the bar. ✉ *47 Chandos Pl., Covent Garden* 🕾 *020/7836–0291* ⊕ *www.harpcoventgarden.com* Ⓜ *Charing Cross.*

Lamb & Flag. This refreshingly un-gentrified 17th-century pub was once known as the Bucket of Blood because the upstairs room was used as a ring for bare-knuckle boxing. Now it's a friendly—and bloodless—place, serving food (lunch only) and real ale. It's on the edge of Covent Garden, up a hidden alley off Garrick Street. ✉ *33 Rose St., Covent Garden* 🕾 *020/7497–9504* ⊕ *www.lambandflagcoventgarden.co.uk* Ⓜ *Covent Garden.*

White Hart. Claiming to be the oldest licensed pub in London, this elegant, family-owned place on Drury Lane had already been here for more than 500 years when it served highwayman Dick Turpin in 1739, just before he was hanged. Nowadays it is one of the best places to mix with cast and crew of the stage. A female-friendly environment, a cheery skylight above the lounge area, and above-average pub fare make the White Hart a particularly sociable spot for a drink. ✉ *191 Drury La., Covent Garden* 🕾 *020/7242–2317* Ⓜ *Holborn, Covent Garden, Tottenham Court Rd.*

BLOOMSBURY AND HOLBORN

BLOOMSBURY

The Lamb. Charles Dickens and his contemporaries drank here, but today's enthusiastic clientele make sure this intimate and eternally popular pub avoids the pitfalls of feeling too old-fashioned. For private chats at the bar, you can close a delicate etched-glass "snob screen" to the bar staff, opening it only when you fancy another pint. ✉ 94 *Lamb's Conduit St., Bloomsbury* ☎ *020/7405–0713* ⊕ *www.youngs. co.uk* Ⓜ *Russell Sq.*

Museum Tavern. Across the street from the British Museum, this friendly and classy Victorian pub makes an ideal resting place after the rigors of the culture trail. Karl Marx unwound here after a hard day in the Library. He could have spent his *Kapital* on any of seven well-kept beers available on tap. ✉ *49 Great Russell St., Bloomsbury* ☎ *020/7242–8987* Ⓜ *Tottenham Court Rd.*

16

The Queen's Larder. The royal associated with this tiny pub is Queen Charlotte, who is said to have stored food here for her "mad" husband, George III, when he was being treated nearby. The interior preserves its antique feel, with dark wood and old posters, and in the evenings fills up quickly with office workers and students. In good weather, you might prefer to grab one of the seats outdoors. ✉ *1 Queen's Sq., Bloomsbury* ☎ *020/7837–5627* ⊕ *www.queenslarder.co.uk* Ⓜ *Russell Sq.*

HOLBORN

Holborn Whippet. An impressive number of craft beers are served from unmarked taps set into a brick column behind the bar in this new-breed London pub. Names of the brews are all chalked onto boards, while empty barrels outside testify to the popularity of the best; lunch and supper are served every day. It's popular, especially when nearby offices empty out in early evening, but you can sit outside under umbrellas (with heaters in winter) on small, ornate, pedestrian-only Sicilian Avenue. Inside, it's a deliberately plain affair, with little to detract from the liquid experience. ✉ *Sicilian Ave., Holborn* ☎ *020/3137–9937* ⊕ *holbornwhippet.com* Ⓜ *Holborn.*

Princess Louise. This fine, popular pub is an exquisite museum piece of a Victorian interior, with glazed tiles and intricately engraved glass screens that divide the bar area into cozy little annexes. It's not all show, either: There's a good selection of excellent-value Yorkshire real ales from the Samuel Smith's brewery. ✉ *208 High Holborn, Holborn* ☎ *020/7405–8816* Ⓜ *Holborn.*

FITZROVIA

Crown And Two Chairmen. Fine English beer from the likes of Purity and Sharps and a friendly, relaxed atmosphere make this an excellent option in the heart of Soho. The traditional pub grub is also good. The window

Order a pint at the 17th-century Lamb & Flag pub in Covent Garden.

seats are great spots from which to watch the world go by. ⊠ *31–32 Dean St., Fitzrovia* ☎ *020/7437–8192* ⊕ *www.thecrownandtwochairmenw1. co.uk* Ⓜ *Tottenham Court Rd.*

Fodor's Choice
★
Draft House Charlotte. The tiniest of a new microchain of craft-beer pubs, Draft House Charlotte is well placed for a quick pint of delicious beer en route between the retail juggernaut of Oxford Street and the high culture of Bloomsbury. The food is good, too, with such nouveau-pub-grub offerings as fish finger bap (or turkey in pale ale). There's not much space here, though, so you may have to perch on a blue wooden stool between the young, fashionable people who hang out here. ⊠ *43 Goode St., Fitzrovia* ☎ *020/7323–9361* ⊕ *www.drafthouse. co.uk* Ⓜ *Goode St.*

THE CITY

Fodor's Choice
★
Black Friar. A step from Blackfriars Tube station, this spectacular pub has an Arts and Crafts interior that is entertainingly, satirically ecclesiastical, with inlaid mother-of-pearl, wood carvings, stained glass, and marble pillars all over the place. In spite of the finely lettered temperance tracts on view just below the reliefs of monks, fairies, and friars, there is a nice group of ales on tap from independent brewers. The 20th-century poet Sir John Betjeman once led a successful campaign to save the pub from demolition. ⊠ *174 Queen Victoria St., The City* ☎ *020/7236–5474* ⊕ *www.nicholsonspubs.co.uk/theblackfriarblackfriarslondon* Ⓜ *Blackfriars.*

Fodor's Choice
★ **Craft Beer Company.** With 37 beers on tap and 300 more in bottles (some brewed exclusively for the Craft Beer Company), the main problem here is knowing where to start. Luckily, friendly and knowledgeable staff are happy to advise or give tasters—or why not sign up for a guided tasting session? A huge chandelier and a mirrored ceiling lend antique charm to the interior, and a smattering of tourists and beer pilgrims break up the crowds of Leather Lane workers and locals. ⊠ *82 Leather La., Clerkenwell* ⊕ *thecraftbeerco.com* Ⓜ *Chancery Lane.*

Fodor's Choice
★ **Jerusalem Tavern.** Owned by the well-respected St. Peter's Brewery from Suffolk, the Jerusalem Tavern is one-of-a-kind: small, and endearingly eccentric. Ancient Delft-style tiles meld with wood and concrete in a converted watchmaker and jeweler's shop dating back to the 18th century. The beer, both bottled and on tap, is some of the best available anywhere in London. It's loved by Londoners and often busy, especially after work. ⊠ *55 Britton St., Clerkenwell* ☎ *020/7490–4281* ⊕ *www. stpetersbrewery.co.uk/london-pub* Ⓜ *Farringdon.*

Viaduct Tavern. Queen Victoria opened the nearby Holborn Viaduct in 1869, and this eponymous pub honored the waterway by serving its first pint the same year. Much of the Victorian decoration is still extant, with gilded mirrors, carved wood, and engraved glass. The tavern's haunted reputation stems from its proximity to the former Newgate Prison, site of London's gallows in the 19th century, which once stood on the site. Ex-prison cells in the basement can be seen with a free tour before or after the lunchtime rush and before 5 pm. There are usually three or four ales on tap; lunch is also served. ⊠ *126 Newgate St., The City* ☎ *020/7600–1863* ⊕ *viaducttavern.co.uk* ☾ *Closed weekends* Ⓜ *St. Paul's.*

Ye Olde Cheshire Cheese. Yes, this extremely historic pub (it dates from 1667, the year after the Great Fire of London) is full of tourists, but it deserves a visit for its sawdust-covered floors, low wood-beam ceilings, and the 14th-century crypt of Whitefriars' monastery under the cellar bar. This was the most regular of Dr. Johnson's and Dickens's many locals. Food is served, except on Sunday (when it's only open from noon to 3). ⊠ *145 Fleet St., The City* ☎ *020/7353–6170* Ⓜ *Blackfriars.*

Ye Olde Mitre. Hidden off the side of 8 Hatton Gardens, this cozy pub's roots go back to 1547, though it was rebuilt around 1772. Originally built for the staff of the Bishop of Ely, whose London residence was next door, it remained officially part of Cambridgeshire until the 20th century. It's a friendly little place, with a fireplace, well-kept ales, wooden beams, and traditional bar snacks. ⊠ *1 Ely Ct., The City* ☎ *020/7405–4751* ⊕ *www.yeoldemitreholburn.co.uk* ☾ *Closed weekends* Ⓜ *Chancery La.*

Ye Olde Watling. This busy corner pub has been rebuilt at least three times since 1666. One of its incarnations was as the drawing office for Christopher Wren while nearby St. Paul's was being built. The ground floor is a laid-back pub, while upstairs houses an atmospheric restaurant, complete with wooden beams and trestle tables, with a basic English pub menu. ⊠ *29 Watling St., The City* ☎ *020/7248–8935*

16

⊕ *www.nicholsonspubs.co.uk/yeoldewatlingwatlingstreetlondon*
Ⓜ *Mansion House.*

THE EAST END

Prospect of Whitby. Named after a ship, this is London's oldest riverside pub, dating from around 1520. Once upon a time it was called the Devil's Tavern because of the lowlife criminals—thieves and smugglers—who congregated here. Ornamented with pewter ware and nautical objects, this much-loved "boozer" has a terrace with views of the Thames, from where boat trips often point it out. ⊠ *57 Wapping Wall, East End* ☎ *020/7481–1095* ⊕ *www.taylor-walker.co.uk* Ⓜ *Wapping; DLR: Shadwell.*

SOUTH OF THE THAMES

Fodor'sChoice
★

Anchor & Hope. One of London's most popular gastropubs, the Anchor & Hope doesn't take reservations (except for Sunday lunch). Would-be diners snake around the red-walled, wooden-floored pub, kept happy by some good real ales and a fine wine list as they wait for hours for a table. The excellent, meaty English food is old-fashioned English—think salt cod, tripe, and chips (fries)—with a few modern twists. ⊠ *36 The Cut, South Bank* ☎ *020/7928–9898* Ⓜ *Southwark.*

The George Inn. Shakespeare drank in this Southwark pub, Dickens featured the place in his writing, and it's the last galleried inn in London. Now owned by the National Trust, the George has a cobblestone courtyard, which can be a great place for a drink when the weather's good. Inside, several small, low-ceilinged rooms lead to a middling restaurant; the best way to soak up the atmosphere is with a pint at the bar. ⊠ *77 Borough High St., South Bank* ☎ *020/7407–2056* Ⓜ *London Bridge.*

Market Porter. Opposite the foodie treasures of Borough Market, this atmospheric pub opens at 6 am for the stallholders, and always seems busy. Remarkably, the place manages to remain relaxed, with helpful staff and happy customers spilling out onto the road right through the year. The wide selection of real ales is lovingly tended. The pub was used as a set for one of the Harry Potter movies. ⊠ *9 Stoney St., Borough* ☎ *020/7407–2495* ⊕ *www.markettaverns.co.uk* Ⓜ *London Bridge.*

Mayflower. An atmospheric 17th-century riverside inn (rebuilt in the following century) with exposed beams and a terrace near the onetime berth of the famous ship on which the Pilgrims sailed to what became the American colonies. The pub has a heated jetty where customers can sit outside; alternatively, opt to enjoy the wood-beamed interiors, although this can get quite packed with sightseers. ⊠ *117 Rotherhithe St., South Bank* ☎ *020/7237–4088* ⊕ *themayflowerrotherhithe.com* Ⓜ *Rotherhithe.*

PUB NAMES

Pictorial signs traditionally helped illiterate customers identify establishments; these popular names have an interesting historical element behind them.

The many terms related to the coat of arms reflects the fundamental role of heraldry in England's past. Other pub names highlight the importance of specific events (the Trafalgar), and others still reflect myths and legends (Robin Hood). Royal names are ubiquitous, such as the Crown—supposedly the most common pub name in the country, with more than 700 establishments—which became popular after the Restoration of the Monarchy in 1660.

CHELSEA AND KNIGHTSBRIDGE

CHELSEA

Admiral Codrington. Named after a hero of the Napoleonic Wars, this smart pub is a popular meeting place for the upwardly mobile of Sloane Square (Lady Diana Spencer is said to have been a regular in her teaching days). The "Admiral Cod," as it's known, houses a modern restaurant where excellent English fare is served at lunch and dinnertime (treat yourself to the flourless chocolate tart to finish). Activity at the island bar centers on the wine list; well-off Chelsea residents pack the bare wood interior on weekend evenings. ⊠ *17 Mossop St., Chelsea* ☎ *020/7581–0005* ⊕ *www.theadmiralcodrington.co.uk* Ⓜ *South Kensington.*

KNIGHTSBRIDGE

The Nag's Head. The landlord of this idiosyncratic little mews pub in Belgravia runs a tight ship, and no cell phones are allowed. If that sounds like misery, the lovingly collected artifacts (including antique penny arcade games) that decorate every inch of the place, high-quality beer, and old-fashioned pub grub should make up for it. ⊠ *53 Kinnerton St., Belgravia* ☎ *020/7235–1135* Ⓜ *Knightsbridge, Hyde Park Corner.*

NOTTING HILL

The Cow. Crowds head to this chic mix of fun, haute food, and friendly, quaint style for Guinness and oysters, either enjoying them in the unpretentious downstairs bar or the upstairs more formal restaurant. The food is excellent, if pricey for pub grub, with lots of seafood and steaks (and sometimes a mix, as in the smoked eel with mash and bacon). The atmosphere? Always warm, welcoming, and buzzing. ⊠ *89 Westbourne Park Rd., Notting Hill* ☎ *020/7221–0021* ⊕ *www.thecowlondon.co.uk* Ⓜ *Royal Oak, Westbourne Park.*

16

REGENT'S PARK AND HAMPSTEAD

REGENT'S PARK

Camden Arms. On the site of the last fatal duel in Britain, this funky-yet-chill place is off the High Street and is quieter than most of Camden's drinking holes. It has plenty of interesting features—check out the ornate spiral staircase after a good pint of beer. House tunes spun by DJs pervade this pub–lounge every Friday night, and often on Saturday. Modern cocktails are served alongside Thai cuisine. ⊠ *1 Randolph St., Camden* ☎ *020/7267–9829* ⊕ *www.thecamdenarms.com* Ⓜ *Camden.*

HAMPSTEAD

The Holly Bush. A short walk up the hill from Hampstead Tube station, the friendly Holly Bush was a country pub before London spread this far north. It retains something of a rural feel, with stripped wooden floors and an open fire, and is an intimate place to enjoy great ales and organic and free-range pub food. Try the homemade pork scratchings and pickled eggs. ⊠ *22 Holly Mount, Hampstead* ☎ *020/7435–2892* ⊕ *www.hollybushhampstead.co.uk* Ⓜ *Hampstead.*

Spaniards Inn. Ideal as a refueling point when you're on a Hampstead Heath hike, this historic, country-style, oak-beam pub has a gorgeous garden, scene of the tea party in Dickens's *Pickwick Papers*. Dick Turpin, the highwayman, frequented the inn before Dickens's time, and Shelley, Keats, and Byron hung out here as well. The place is extremely popular, especially on Sunday, when Londoners roll in. There's an exhibition space upstairs and it's very dog friendly—there's even a dog wash in the garden. ⊠ *Spaniards Rd., Hampstead* ☎ *020/8731–8406* ⊕ *www. thespaniardshampstead.co.uk* Ⓜ *Hampstead.*

THE THAMES UPSTREAM

RICHMOND

Roebuck. Perched on top of Richmond Hill, the Roebuck has perhaps the best view of any pub in London. The most sought-after seats are the benches, found directly across the road, which look out over the Thames as it winds its way into the countryside below. Friendly and surprisingly unpretentious, given its lofty surrounds, it is well worth the long climb up the hill from the center of Richmond. ⊠ *130 Richmond Hill, Richmond* ☎ *020/8948–2329* Ⓜ *Richmond. National Rail: Richmond.*

HAMMERSMITH

Blue Anchor. This unaltered Georgian pub has been seen in the movie *Sliding Doors* and was the site where *The Planets* composer Gustav Holst wrote his *Hammersmith Suite*. Sit out by the river, or shelter inside with a good ale. ⊠ *13 Lower Mall, Hammersmith* ☎ *020/8748–5774* ⊕ *www.blueanchorlondon.com* Ⓜ *Hammersmith.*

Dove Inn. Read the list of famous ex-regulars, from Charles II and Nell Gwyn to Ernest Hemingway, as you wait for a beer at this smart, comely, and popular 16th-century riverside pub by Hammersmith Bridge. After a few pints you can practice your singing skills to the English patriotic song that was composed here, "Rule, Britannia!" If (as is often the case) the Dove is too full, stroll upstream along the bank to the Old Ship or the Blue Anchor. ⊠ *19 Upper Mall, Hammersmith* ☎ *020/8748–9474* ⊕ *www.dovehammersmith.co.uk* Ⓜ *Hammersmith.*

NIGHTLIFE

As is true of nearly all cosmopolitan centers, the pace with which bars and clubs go in and out of fashion in London is mind-boggling. New trends, likewise, emerge all time. In one recent development, the dreaded velvet rope has been usurped by the doorbell-ringing mystique of members-only drinking clubs. Some of the city's most talked-about nightlife spots these days are those attached to some of the best restaurants and hotels—no wonder, when you consider the increased popularity of London cuisine in international circles. Moreover, the gay scene in London continues to flourish. One constant on the nightlife scene is variety. The understated glamour of North London's Primrose Hill, which makes movie stars feel so at ease, might be considered dull by the über-trendy club goers of London's East End. Likewise, the price of a pint in Chelsea would be dubbed blasphemous by the musicians and poets of multicultural Brixton.

Whatever your pleasure, however your whim turns come evening, chances are you'll find what you're looking for in London's ever-changing arena of activity and invention.

WESTMINSTER, ST. JAMES'S, AND ROYAL LONDON

WESTMINSTER

BARS

Bedford and Strand. The wine bar enjoyed something of a renaissance in the first decade of the 21st century in London, and this is one of the best of a new generation. It's sunk atmospherically down below the streets of Covent Garden, with dark wood and hanging shades; the wine list is short but well chosen, the service is faultless, and the bistro food is created with plenty of care. ⊠ *1A Bedford St., Charing Cross* ☎ *020/7836–3033* ⊕ *www.bedford-strand.com* ⊗ *Mon.–Fri. noon–midnight; Sat. 5 pm–midnight* Ⓜ *Charing Cross.*

Cinnamon Club. In the basement of what was once Old Westminster Library, the Club Bar of this contemporary Indian restaurant (treat yourself to a superb curry) has Bollywood scenes projected onto the glass back wall, Asian-theme cocktails (mango mojitos, Delhi mules), delicious bar snacks, and a clientele that includes fashionable young politicos. Upstairs, the Library Bar also serves cocktails through the day. ⊠ *The Old Westminster Library, Great Smith St., Westminster* ☎ *020/7222–2555* ⊕ *www.cinnamonclub.com* ⊗ *Mon.–Sat. 6–11:45 pm* Ⓜ *Westminster.*

The Mint Leaf Bar. The renowned long bar is stocked with more than 500 spirits and serves more than 1,000 well-prepared cocktails. Nibbles and light snacks with an Indian twist are available, and if you're up for some more substantial spicy food, treat yourself to a meal at the sophisticated restaurant. DJs play nightly from Wednesday to Saturday.

16

THE GAY SCENE

The U.K. capital's gay and lesbian culture is as thriving as it is in New York or Los Angeles, with Soho serving as the traditional hub, though "Voho," previously unfashionable Vauxhall, south of the river, is the new upstart area of gay London.

Clubs in London cater to almost every desire, whether that be the suited-up Tommy Hilfiger–look-alike scene, cruisers taking on dingy dives, flamboyant drag shows, lesbian tea dances, or themed fetish nights.

There's also a cornucopia of queer theater and performance art that runs throughout the year. Whatever your tastes, you'll be able to satisfy them with a night on the town in London.

Choices are admittedly much better for males than females here; although many of the gay clubs are female-friendly, those catering strictly to lesbians are in the minority.

The British Film Institute puts on the BFI London Lesbian and Gay Film Festival (⊕ www.bfi.org.uk/llgff) in late March and early April every year.

Pride London in June (an annual event that was originally largely political but these days encompasses a parade, sports, art, comedy, theater, music, cabaret, and dance) welcomes anyone and everyone, and claimed a million participants in 2010. This extravagant pageant spirals its way through London's streets, with major events taking place in Trafalgar Square and Leicester Square, then culminates in Victoria Embankment with ticketed parties continuing on afterward (⊕ www.pridelondon.org for details).

For up-to-date listings, consult *Time Out* (⊕ www.timeout.com/london/lgbt), *Boyz* (⊕ www.boyz.co.uk), *Gay Times* (⊕ www.gaytimes.co.uk), *Attitude* (⊕ www.attitude.co.uk), or the lesbian monthly *Diva* (⊕ www.divamag.co.uk).

Online resources include Rainbow Network (⊕ www.rainbownetwork.com).

BARS, CAFÉS, AND PUBS

Most bars in London are gay-friendly, though there are a number of cafés and pubs that are known as gay hangouts after hours. The latest serve drinks until 3 am (11 pm on Sunday).

CLUBS

Many of London's best gay dance clubs are in mixed clubs like Fabric on theme nights designated for gays.

Almost all dance clubs in London are gay-friendly, but if you want to cruise or mingle only with other gays, it's best to call ahead or check website listings.

There is a sister bar and restaurant in Angel Court in The City. ⊠ *Suffolk Pl., Haymarket* ☎ *020/7930–9020* ⊕ *www.mintleafrestaurant.com* ☉ *Mon.–Wed. noon–midnight, Thurs. and Fri. noon–1 am, Sat. 5 pm–1 am, Sun. 5 pm–midnight* Ⓜ *Piccadilly Circus.*

DANCE CLUBS

Pacha. London's version of the Ibizan superclub is in a restored 1920s dance hall next to Victoria Coach Station. The hedonistic surroundings include a (smoking) roof terrace for alfresco clubbing and a state-of-the-art VIP room. The stylish crowd is slightly older than average, but not necessarily as moneyed as you might expect. ⊠ *Terminus Pl., Victoria* ☎ *0845/371–4489* ⊕ *www.pachalondon.com* 💷 *£5–£20* 🕙 *Fri. and Sat. 10 pm–5 am* Ⓜ *Victoria.*

ST. JAMES'S

BARS

American Bar. Festooned with a chin-dropping array of club ties, signed celebrity photographs, sporting mementos, and baseball caps, this sensational hotel cocktail bar has superb martinis. The name dates from the 1930s, when hotel bars in London started to cater to growing numbers of Americans crossing the Atlantic in ocean liners, but it wasn't until the 1970s, when a customer left a small carved wooden eagle, that the collection of paraphernalia was started. ⊠ *Stafford Hotel, 16–18 St. James's Pl., St. James's* ☎ *020/7493–0111* ⊕ *www.thestaffordhotel.co.uk* 🕙 *Daily 11:30 am–1 am* Ⓜ *Green Park.*

MAYFAIR

BARS

Fodor'sChoice
★
Claridge's Bar. This elegant Mayfair meeting place remains unpretentious even when it brims with beautiful people. The bar has an art deco heritage made hip by the sophisticated touch of designer David Collins. A library of rare champagnes and brandies as well as a delicious choice of traditional and exotic cocktails—try the Flapper or the Black Pearl—will occupy your taste buds. Request a glass of vintage Cristal in the darkly moody Fumoir. ⊠ *55 Brook St., Mayfair* ☎ *020/7629–8860* ⊕ *www.claridges.co.uk* 🕙 *Mon.–Sat. noon–1 am, Sun. noon–midnight* Ⓜ *Bond St.*

JAZZ AND BLUES

Dover Street Restaurant & Jazz Bar. Dance the night away after you've feasted from the French Mediterranean menu. Fun for dates as well as groups, Dover Street Restaurant has three bars, a DJ, and a stage with the latest live bands performing everything from jazz to soul to R&B, all this encircling linen-covered tables with a friendly staff catering to your every whim. ⊠ *8–10 Dover St., Mayfair* ☎ *020/7491–7509* ⊕ *www. doverst.co.uk* 💷 *£7–£15* 🕙 *Mon.–Thurs. 5:30 pm–3 am, Fri.–Sat. 7 pm–3 am* Ⓜ *Green Park.*

SOHO AND COVENT GARDEN

SOHO

BARS

Le Beaujolais. Around 60 lovingly selected French wines are available, and you can snack on olives, charcuterie, and homemade *croque monsieur* (grilled ham and cheese) sandwiches while snug and warm under the bottle-laden ceiling as a funky blues sound track plays. The romantically shabby-around-the-edges feel and authentically French insouciance may come as a surprise in the heart of tourist-centric London. ⊠ *25 Litchfield St., Soho* ☎ *020/7836–2955* 🕙 *Mon.–Sat. noon–11* Ⓜ *Leicester Sq.*

16

Le Salon Bar. Renowned chef Joël Robuchon's intimate, relaxed, and elegant bar with red undertones is in the same premises as his L'Atelier and La Cuisine restaurants. New cocktails await you, as the drink menu changes every six months, with new flavors and textures sure to entice your taste buds. ⊠ *13–15 West St., Soho* ☎ *020/7010–8600* ⊕ *www.joel-robuchon.com* ⊗ *Mon.–Sat. noon–2 am, Sun. noon–10:30 pm* Ⓜ *Leicester Sq.*

Nordic. With shooters called "Husky Poo" and "Danish Bacon Surprise" and crayfish tails and meatballs on the smorgasbord menu, Nordic takes its Scandinavian feel the whole way. This secluded, shabby-chic bar serves many couples cozied up among travel brochures promoting the Viking lands. If you can't decide what to drink, the cocktail roulette wheel on the wall may help. ⊠ *25 Newman St., Soho* ☎ *020/7631–3174* ⊕ *www.nordicbar.com* ⊗ *Mon.–Wed. 5 pm–midnight, Thurs. noon–midnight, Fri. noon–2 am, Sat. 5 pm–midnight* Ⓜ *Tottenham Court Rd.*

Sketch. One seat never looks like the next at this collection of esoteric living-room bars. The exclusive Parlour, a patisserie during the day, exudes plenty of rarefied charm; the intimate East Bar at the back is reminiscent of a sci-fi film set; and in the Glade it's permanently sunset in a forest. ⊠ *9 Conduit St., Soho* ☎ *020/7659–4500* ⊕ *www.sketch. uk.com* ⊗ *Parlour Mon.–Fri. 8 am–2 am, Sat. 10 am–2 am; The Glade 6:30 pm–2 am* Ⓜ *Oxford Circus.*

COMEDY AND CABARET

Amused Moose. This Soho basement/retro nightclub is often considered the best place to see breaking talent as well as household names doing "secret" shows. Ricky Gervais, Eddie Izzard, and Russell Brand are among those who have graced the stage, and every summer a handful of the Edinburgh Fringe comedians preview here. The bar is open late (and serves food), and there's a DJ and dancing after the show. Tickets are often discounted with a printout from their website, and shows are mainly on Saturday. ⊠ *Moonlighting, 17 Greek St., Soho* ☎ *020/7287–3727* ⊕ *www.amusedmoose.com* ▨ *£9 and up* ⊗ *Doors open at 7:30 pm* Ⓜ *Tottenham Court Rd.*

Comedy Store. Known as the birthplace of alternative comedy, this is where the United Kingdom's funniest stand-ups have cut their teeth before being launched onto prime-time TV. Comedy Store Players, a team with six comedians doing improvisation with audience suggestions, entertain on Wednesday and Sunday; the Cutting Edge steps in every Tuesday. Thursday, Friday, and Saturday have the best stand-up acts. There's also a bar with food. Note that children under 18 are not admitted to this venue. ⊠ *1A Oxendon St., Soho* ☎ *0844/847–1728* ⊕ *www.thecomedystore.co.uk* ▨ *£14–£28* ⊗ *Shows daily 7:30 or 8 pm, with extra shows Fri. and Sat. at 11 pm* Ⓜ *Piccadilly Circus, Leicester Sq.*

100 Club. Since this small club opened in 1942, many of the greats have played here, from Glenn Miller and Louis Armstrong to The Who and the Sex Pistols. Saved from closure in 2010 by a campaign led by Sir Paul McCartney, the space now reverberates to jazz, '60s R&B, and northern soul. ⊠ *100 Oxford St., Soho* ☎ *020/7636–0933* ⊕ *www.the100club.*

co.uk £7–£15 ⊘ *Fri.–Sun. 7:30 pm–late; weekdays vary, depending on gigs* Ⓜ *Oxford Circus, Tottenham Court Rd.*

Fodor's Choice

★ **Soho Theatre.** This innovative theater's programs include comedy shows by established acts and up-and-coming comedians and new writers. The relaxed Soho Theatre Bar has food, free Wi-Fi, simple tables, and a late license until 1 am for members and ticket holders. Check local listings or the website for what's on, and book tickets in advance. ✉ *21 Dean St., Soho* ☎ *020/7478–0100* ⊕ *www.sohotheatre.com* £10–£30 ⊘ *Mon.–Sat. usually 7–11 although show times vary* Ⓜ *Tottenham Court Rd.*

ECLECTIC MUSIC

12 Bar Club. This small and rough-and-ready acoustic club hosts notable singer-songwriters. Four different acts of new folk, contemporary country, blues, and even ska and punk perform each night in the intimate venue. There's a good selection of bottled beer and gastropub food here. ✉ *22–23 Denmark Pl., Soho* ☎ *020/7240–2622 tickets, 020/7240–2120* ⊕ *www.12barclub. com* £5–£10 ⊘ *Fri. and Sat. 7 pm–3 am, Sun. 6 pm–12:30 am. Café serves food 9–9* Ⓜ *Tottenham Court Rd.*

JAZZ AND BLUES

Ain't Nothin' but . . . The Blues Bar. The name sums up this bar that whips up a sweaty environment. Local musicians, as well as some notable names, squeeze onto the tiny stage. There's good bar food of the chili-and-gumbo variety. Most weekday nights there's no cover. ✉ *20 Kingly St., Soho* ☎ *020/7287–0514* ⊕ *www.aintnothinbut.co.uk* £5 *Fri. and Sat. after 8:30 pm, otherwise free* ⊘ *Mon.–Thurs. 5 pm–1 am, Fri. 5 pm–2:30 am, Sat. 3 pm–2:30 am, Sun. 3 pm–midnight* Ⓜ *Oxford Circus.*

Fodor's Choice

★ **Pizza Express Jazz Club Soho.** One of the capital's most ubiquitous pizza chains also runs a great Soho jazz venue. The dimly lighted restaurant hosts top-quality international jazz acts every night. The Italian-style thin-crust pizzas are good, too, though on the small side. ✉ *10 Dean St., Soho* ☎ *0845/602–7017* ⊕ *www.pizzaexpresslive.com* £10–£25 ⊘ *Daily 11:30 am–midnight for food; music after 7:30 pm (timings vary)* Ⓜ *Tottenham Court Rd.*

Ronnie Scott's. This legendary jazz club has attracted big names since the 1960s. It's usually crowded and hot, the food isn't great, and service is slow—but the mood can't be beat, even since the sad departure of the eponymous founder and saxophonist. Reservations are recommended. ✉ *47 Frith St., Soho* ☎ *020/7439–0747* ⊕ *www.ronniescotts.*

JAZZ AND BLUES

Jazz in London is highly eclectic. You can expect anything from danceable, smooth tunes played at a supper club to groovy New Orleans–style blues to exotic world-beat rhythms, which can be heard at some of the less central venues throughout the capital. London hosts the **London Jazz Festival** (⊕ *www. londonjazzfestival.org.uk*) in November, which showcases top and emerging artists in experimental jazz. The **Ealing Jazz Festival** (⊕ *www.ealing.gov.uk*), at the end of July, claims to be the biggest free jazz event in Europe.

16

co.uk ✉ *£20–£36 nonmembers, 20% off for members (members plus up to three guests free after 11 pm Mon.–Fri.). Annual membership £195.* ⊗ *Mon.–Sat. 6 pm–3 am, Sun. 6:30 pm–11 pm* Ⓜ *Leicester Sq.*

THE GAY SCENE

Candy Bar. London's top girls' bar is intimate, chilled, and cruisey, with DJs mixing the latest sounds. Live music, DJs, speed dating, and comedy are also featured on some nights. Men are welcome only as guests of female patrons. ✉ *4 Carlisle St., Soho* ☎ *020/7287–5041* ⊕ *www.candybarsoho.com* ✉ *Free–£5* ⊗ *Mon.–Sat. 1 pm–3 am, Sun. 1 pm–12:30 am* Ⓜ *Tottenham Court Rd.*

Fodor's Choice   **Friendly Society.** This haute moderne hot spot hops with activity almost
★   any night of the week; the basement feels a bit like something out of *Star Trek* with its white-leather pod seats. The place is known for being gay yet female-friendly. ✉ *79 Wardour St., Soho* ☎ *020/7434–3805* ⊗ *Weekdays 4–11, Sat. 2–11, Sun. 2–10:30* Ⓜ *Leicester Sq.*

Rupert Street. For smart boyz, this gay chic island among the sleaze has a lounge feel with brown-leather sofas and floor-to-ceiling windows. It's crowded and cruisey at night with preclubbers; bright, civilized, and cafélike by day; and a good spot for brunch. Traditional British food is served until 10 pm. ✉ *50 Rupert St., Soho* ☎ *020/7494–3059* ⊕ *www. rupert-street.com* ⊗ *Mon.–Wed. noon–11, Thurs.–Sat. noon–11:30, Sun. noon–10:30* Ⓜ *Leicester Sq., Piccadilly Circus.*

The Shadow Lounge. This fabulous little lounge and dance club glitters with faux jewels and twinkling fiber-optic lights over its sunken dance floor, which comes complete with pole for those inclined to do their thing around it. It has a serious A-list celebrity factor, with the glamorous London glitterati camping out in the VIP booth. Members are given entrance priority when the place gets full, especially on weekends, so show up early, book onto the guestlist online, or prepare to wait in line. ✉ *5–7 Brewer St., Soho* ☎ *020/7317–9270* ⊕ *www.theshadowlounge. co.uk* ✉ *Mon. free, Tues.–Thurs. £5, Fri.–Sat. £10* ⊗ *Mon.–Sat. 10 pm–3 am* Ⓜ *Leicester Sq.*

COVENT GARDEN

BARS

Café des Amis. This relaxed basement wine bar near the Royal Opera House is the perfect pre- or post-theater spot, popular among musicians and other performers. More than 30 wines are served by the glass, along with a good selection of cheeses and plates of charcuterie as well as more substantial dishes for those with more of an appetite (there's also a French restaurant with a Mediterranean twist on the ground floor serving everything from moules marinieres to risotto). ✉ *11–14 Hanover Pl., Covent Garden* ☎ *020/7379–3444* ⊕ *www.cafedesamis.co.uk* ⊗ *Mon.–Sat. noon–11:30 pm, Sun. noon–8 pm* Ⓜ *Covent Garden.*

Terroirs. Specializing in "natural wines" (organic and sustainably produced with minimal added ingredients), Terroirs has an unusually careful selection of 200 wines from artisan French and Italian winemakers. These are served, along with delicious, relatively simple dishes: charcuterie, tapas, and more substantial French-inspired dishes, at a bar and tables in whitewashed, wooden-floored environs. ✉ *5 William*

St., Covent Garden ☎ *020/7036–0660* ⊕ *www.terroirswinebar.com* ⊗ *Mon.–Sat. noon–11 pm (bar menu only 3 pm–5:30 pm)* Ⓜ *Charing Cross.*

THE GAY SCENE

Fodor's Choice **Heaven.** With the best light show on any London dance floor, Heaven is
★ unpretentious, loud, and huge, with a labyrinth of rooms, bars, and live-music parlors. Friday and Saturday there's a gay comedy night (£10 in advance, 7–10 pm). Tuesday, Wednesday, and Thursday often have live performances. If you go to just one gay club in London, Heaven should be it. ⊠ *The Arches, Villiers St., Covent Garden* ☎ *020/7930–2020* ⊕ *www.heavennightclub-london.com* 💳 *£4–£12* ⊗ *Mon. 11 pm–5:30 am, Tues.–Fri. 11 pm–5 am, Sat. 10:30 pm–5 am* Ⓜ *Charing Cross, Embankment.*

BLOOMSBURY AND FITZROVIA

BLOOMSBURY

BARS

All Star Lanes. One of London's most chic bars is an unlikely combination—it's in a sleek, underground, retro bowling alley in the heart of literary Bloomsbury. Here, surrounded by 1950s Americana, you can sit on the red leather seats and choose from the largest selection of bourbons in London. DJs play on Friday and Saturday nights; there are also locations in Bayswater, Brick Lane, and Stratford. ⊠ *Victoria House, Bloomsbury Pl., Bloomsbury* ☎ *020/7025–2676* ⊕ *www.allstarlanes.co.uk* ⊗ *Mon.–Wed. 4–11:30, Thurs. 4–midnight, Fri. noon–2 am, Sat. 11 am–2 am, Sun. 11–11* Ⓜ *Holborn.*

Booking Office. Taking full advantage of the soaring Victorian redbrick vaults and arches of the newly restored St. Pancras hotel, Booking Office is closer in feel to a cathedral than a traditional station bar. Seasonal cocktails using traditional English ingredients are high on flavor and low on mixers, and there's also a restaurant and live music Thursday through Saturday evenings. ⊠ *St. Pancras Renaissance Hotel, Euston Rd., King's Cross* ☎ *020/7841–3566* ⊕ *www.bookingofficerestaurant.com* Ⓜ *King's Cross St. Pancras.*

ROCK

Water Rats. This high-spirited pub hosted Bob Dylan on his 1963 tour, as well as the first Oasis gig. Alt-country, hip-hop, and indie guitar bands thrash it out most nights of the week. ⊠ *328 Gray's Inn Rd., Bloomsbury* ☎ *020/7837–7269* ⊕ *www.themonto.com* 💳 *£8 and up* ⊗ *Mon.–Sat. noon–11:30* Ⓜ *King's Cross.*

FITZROVIA

BARS

Fodor's Choice **Crazy Bear.** This sexy basement bar with cowhide stools and croc-skin
★ tables feels like Casablanca in Fitzrovia. As you enter Crazy Bear, a spiral staircase leads to a mirrored parlor over which presides a 1947 Murano chandelier. But don't let the opulence fool you: Waitstaff here are warm and welcoming to an all-ages international crowd abuzz with chatter. The menu advertises high-quality Thai, Chinese, and Japanese

16

food alongside the drinks. There's another Crazy Bear in nearby Covent Garden. ⊠ 26–28 Whitfield St., Fitzrovia ☎ 020/7631–0088 ⊕ www.crazybeargroup.co.uk ⊗ Mon.–Wed. noon–midnight, Thurs.–Fri. noon–1 am, Sat. 6–10:45 Ⓜ Goodge St.

Long Bar at Sanderson Hotel. The 80-foot-long shimmering white onyx bar in the Philippe Starck–designed Sanderson Hotel attracts a trendy crowd, while the large but welcoming outdoor area exudes a relaxing, Zen-like feel, with soothing running water, dim lighting, and decorative vegetation. The hotel's **Purple Bar** provides a more intimate and romantic setting and serves excellent chocolate martinis. ⊠ 50 Berners St., Fitzrovia ☎ 020/7300–5588 ⊕ www.sandersonlondon.com ⊗ Mon.–Sat. 11 am–late, Sun. noon–late Ⓜ Oxford Circus.

THE EAST END

BARS

Book Club. Light and friendly, the Book Club tops off a dose of Shoreditch's fashionable industrial chic with a dollop of culture. White tiles, bricks, and big black-and-white photos set the tone and there's a separate room for table-tennis. Breakfast is served morning weekdays, a full lunch menu is offered through the week, and a modern menu of cocktails accompanies music, book launches, and workshops in the evenings. ⊠ 100 Leonard St., Shoreditch ☎ 020/7684–8618 ⊕ www.wearetbc.com ⊗ Mon.–Wed. 8 am–midnight, Thurs.–Fri. 8 am–2 am, Sat. 10 am–2 am, Sun. 10 am–midnight. Ⓜ Shoreditch High St., Old St.

DANCE CLUBS

Cargo. Housed under a series of old railroad arches, this vast brick-wall bar, restaurant, dance floor, and live-music venue pulls a young, international crowd with its hip vibe and diverse selection of music. Long tables bring people together, as does the food, which draws on global influences and is served tapas-style. Drinks, though, are expensive. ⊠ *83 Rivington St., Shoreditch* ☎ *020/7739–3440* ⊕ *www.cargo-london.com* ☑ *Free–£20* ⊙ *Mon.–Thurs. 6 pm–1 am, Fri. 6 pm–3 am, Sat. 6 pm–3 am, Sun. 6 pm–midnight (restaurant opens at noon)* Ⓜ *Old St.*

Fabric. This sprawling subterranean club opposite Smithfield Meat Market is now a firm fixture on the London scene and is regularly voted as one of the top clubs in the world. "FabricLive" hosts drum 'n' bass, dubstep, and hip-hop crews and live acts on Friday; international big-name DJs play slow, sexy bass lines and cutting-edge music on Saturday. The devastating sound system and vibrating "bodysonic" dance floor ensure that bass riffs vibrate through your entire body. ▉ **TIP** Get there early to avoid a lengthy queue, and don't wear a suit. ⊠ *77A Charterhouse St., The City* ☎ *020/7336–8898* ⊕ *www.fabriclondon.com* ☑ *£15–£20; discounts after 3 or 4 am* ⊙ *Fri. 10 pm–6 am, Sat. 11 pm–8 am, Sun. 11 pm–6 am* Ⓜ *Farringdon.*

333. Fashionable bright young Shoreditch things dance to indie rave, dubstep, twisted disco, and underground dance genres. There are three floors, each with its own theme. You can chill on leather sofas at the relaxed Mother Bar upstairs, which is open from 8 pm daily and always has DJs. ⊠ *333 Old St., Shoreditch* ☎ *020/7739–5949* ⊕ *www.333mother.com* ☑ *Free–£10* ⊙ *Fri. and Sat. 10 pm–3 am, bar Mon.–Sun., 8 pm–3 am* Ⓜ *Old St.*

SOUTH OF THE THAMES

BARS

The Dogstar. This popular South London hangout is frequented by local hipsters and counterculture types. It was the first DJ bar in the world and has since enjoyed a fabulous reputation. The vibe at this "surrealist boudoir" is unpretentious, with top-name DJs playing cutting-edge sounds every night (free Tuesday–Thursday) and pizza available until midnight. ⊠ *389 Coldharbour La., Brixton* ☎ *020/7733–7515* ⊕ *www.antic-ltd.com/dogstar* ☑ *Free–£8* ⊙ *Tues. and Wed. 4 pm–11 pm, Thurs. 4 pm–2 am, Fri. 4 pm–4 am, Sat. noon–4 am, Sun. noon–10:30 pm* Ⓜ *Brixton.*

DANCE CLUBS

Ministry of Sound. It's more of an industry than a club, with its own record label, online radio station, and international DJs. Though it's too much a part of the establishment these days to be at the forefront of cool, the stripped-down warehouse-style club has a super sound system and still pulls in the world's most legendary names in dance. There are chill-out rooms, two bars, and three dance floors. ⊠ *103 Gaunt St., Borough* ☎ *020/740–8600* ⊕ *www.ministryofsound.com* ☑ *£15–£23* ⊙ *Fri. 10 pm–5 am, Sat. 11 pm–7 am* Ⓜ *Elephant & Castle.*

16

ECLECTIC MUSIC

Fodor's Choice
★
O2 Academy Brixton. This legendary Brixton venue has seen it all—mods and rockers, hippies and punks—and it remains one of the city's top indie and rock venues. Despite a capacity for almost 5,000, this refurbished Victorian hall with original art deco fixtures retains a clublike charm; it has plenty of bars and upstairs seating. ✉ *211 Stockwell Rd., Brixton* ☎ *020/7771–3000* ⊕ *www.o2academybrixton.co.uk* 🎫 *£10–£50* ⊘ *Opening hrs vary* Ⓜ *Brixton.*

CHELSEA AND KNIGHTSBRIDGE

CHELSEA

JAZZ AND BLUES

606 Club. This civilized Chelsea club showcases mainstream and contemporary jazz by well-known British-based musicians. ▮▮TIP➔ You must eat a meal in order to consume alcohol, so allow for an extra £20. Reservations are advisable. Sunday lunchtime jazz takes place once or twice a month; call ahead. ✉ *90 Lots Rd., Chelsea* ☎ *020/7352–5953* ⊕ *www.606club.co.uk* 🎫 *£8–£12 music charge added to bill* ⊘ *Mon.– Wed. 7–12:30, Thurs. 7–11:30, Fri. and Sat. 8–1:30, Sun. 12:30–4 and 7–11:15* Ⓜ *Earl's Court, Fulham Broadway.*

KNIGHTSBRIDGE

BARS

Fodor's Choice
★
The Blue Bar at the Berkeley Hotel. With low-slung dusty-blue walls, this hotel bar is ever so slightly sexy. Immaculate service, an excellent cocktail list—try the Sex in the City—and a trendy David Collins design make this an ideal spot for a romantic tête-à-tête, complete with jazzy music in the background. ✉ *Wilton Pl., Knightsbridge* ☎ *020/7235– 6000* ⊕ *the-berkeley.co.uk* ⊘ *Mon.–Sat. 9 am–1 am, Sun. 9 am–11 pm* Ⓜ *Knightsbridge.*

NOTTING HILL

BARS

Beach Blanket Babylon. In a Georgian house in Notting Hill, close to Portobello Market, this always-packed bar is distinguishable by its eclectic indoor-outdoor spaces with Gaudí-esque curves and snuggly corners— like a fairy-tale grotto or a medieval dungeon. A sister restaurant-bargallery offers a slightly more modern take on similar themes in an ex-warehouse in Shoreditch (✉ *19–23 Bethnal Green Rd.* ☎ *020/7749– 3540*). ✉ *45 Ledbury Rd., Notting Hill* ☎ *020/7229–2907* ⊕ *www. beachblanket.co.uk* ⊘ *Daily noon–midnight* Ⓜ *Notting Hill Gate.*

DANCE CLUBS

Notting Hill Arts Club. Rock stars like Liam Gallagher and Courtney Love have been seen at this small basement club-bar. What the place lacks in looks it makes up for in mood, and an alternative crowd swills beer to eclectic music that spans Asian underground, hip-hop, Latin-inspired funk, deep house, and jazzy grooves. ✉ *21 Notting Hill Gate, Notting Hill* ☎ *020/7460–4459* ⊕ *www.nottinghillartsclub.com* 🎫 *Free–£8*

The Thameside Bulls Head has live jazz every night.

🕐 *Tues. noon–2 am, Wed. and Thurs. 7 pm–2 am, Fri. and Sat. 7 pm–midnight* Ⓜ *Notting Hill Gate.*

REGENT'S PARK AND HAMPSTEAD

REGENT'S PARK
COMEDY AND CABARET
Canal Café Theatre. Famous comics and cabaret stars perform every night of the week in this intimate, canal-side venue. The long-running News-Revue is a topical song-and-sketch show performed Thursday–Sunday evenings. ✉ *Bridge House, Delamere Terr., Little Venice* ☎ *020/7289–6054* ⊕ *www.canalcafetheatre.com* 🎫 *£5–£11* 🕐 *Mon.–Sat. 7:30–11, Sun. 7–10:30* Ⓜ *Warwick Ave., Royal Oak, Paddington.*

DANCE CLUBS
KOKO. This Victorian theater, formerly known as Camden Palace, has seen acts from Charlie Chaplin to Madonna, and genres from punk to rave. Updated with lush reds not unlike a cockney Moulin Rouge, this is still one of London's most stunning venues. Sounds of live indie rock, cabaret, funky house, and club classics keep the big dance floor moving, even when it's not heaving. ✉ *1A Camden High St., Camden Town* ☎ *0870/432–5527* ⊕ *www.koko.uk.com* 🎫 *£6–£25* 🕐 *Opening hrs vary, depending on shows* Ⓜ *Mornington Crescent.*

JAZZ AND BLUES
Jazz Café. A palace of high-tech cool in bohemian Camden, this remains an essential hangout for fans of both the mainstream end of the jazz repertoire and hip-hop, funk, world music, and Latin fusion. It's also

the unlikely venue for Saturday "I Love the '80s" nights. Book ahead if you want a prime table in the balcony restaurant overlooking the stage. ✉ *5 Parkway, Camden Town* ☎ *020/7688–8899 restaurant reservations, 020/7485–6834 venue info, 0844/847–2514 Tickets (Ticketmaster)* ⊕ *venues.meanfiddler.com/jazz-cafe/home* 💷 *£6–£35* ⊙ *Daily 7 pm–2 am* Ⓜ *Camden Town.*

ROCK

Barfly Club. At one of the finest small clubs in the capital, punk, indie guitar bands, and new metal rock attract a nonmainstream crowd. Weekend club nights upstairs host DJs (and live bands) who rock the decks. ✉ *49 Chalk Farm Rd., Camden Town* ☎ *020/7424–0800 Venue, 0844/847–2424 Tickets* ⊕ *www.mamacolive.com/thebarfly/* 💷 *£5–£11* ⊙ *Mon. and Tues. 7–midnight, Wed. and Thurs. 7 pm–2 am, Fri. and Sat. 7 pm–3 am* Ⓜ *Camden Town, Chalk Farm.*

The HMV Forum. The best up-coming and medium-to-big-name rock performers consistently play at this 2,000-capacity club. It's a converted 1920 art deco movie theater, with a balcony overlooking the grungy dance floor. ✉ *9–17 Highgate Rd., Kentish Town* ☎ *020/7428–4099 Venue, 0843/221–0100 Tickets* ⊕ *theforumlondon.com* 💷 *£12–£60* ⊙ *Opening hrs vary, depending on concert schedule* Ⓜ *Kentish Town.*

ISLINGTON
ECLECTIC

Union Chapel. The beauty of this sublime old chapel and its impressive multicultural programming make this spot one of London's best musical venues, especially for acoustic shows. Performers have included Björk, Beck, and Goldfrapp, though now you're more likely to hear lower-key alternative country, world music, and jazz, alongside poetry and literary events. ✉ *Compton Terr., Islington* ☎ *020/7226–1686 Venue (no box office; ticket sales numbers vary with each event)* ⊕ *www.unionchapel. org.uk* 💷 *Free–£25* ⊙ *Opening hrs vary* Ⓜ *Highbury & Islington.*

ARTS AND ENTERTAINMENT

Updated by
Julius Honnor

"All the world's a stage," said Shakespeare, immortal words heard for the first time right here in London. And whether you prefer your theater, music, and art classical or modern, or as contemporary twists on time-honored classics, you'll find that London's vibrant cultural scene holds its own on the world stage.

Divas sing original-language librettos at the Royal Opera House, Shakespeare's plays are brought to life at the reconstructed Globe Theatre, and challenging new writing is produced at the Royal Court. Whether you feel like basking in the lighthearted extravagance of a West End musical or taking in the next shark-in-formaldehyde at the White Cube gallery, the choice is yours.

There are international theater festivals, innovative music festivals, and critically acclaimed seasons of postmodern dance. Short trip or long, you'll find the cultural scene in London is ever-changing, ever-expanding, and ever-exciting.

No matter where you head, you'll find that London's art and performing arts scenes have been setting global trends for decades—and when you include Shakespearean theater and Handel oratorios, for centuries. Fringe theater, classical ballet, participatory chorales, you name it, London probably did it first and often does it best.

PLANNING

TOP THEATER TIPS

Behind the pillars. Many theaters and concert halls sell discounted seats with restricted views.

Matinees. Afternoon performances are almost always a better value than evening ones.

Previews. Tickets to shows are usually less expensive in the first few weeks of their run, before the critics have had their say.

Monday. Most cinemas and some theaters, including the Royal Court, have a reduced-price ticketing policy on Monday.

Standing. The Globe Theatre and the Proms are the two most prominent places where remaining upright saves you money.

FIND OUT WHAT'S PLAYING WHERE

To find out what's showing now, the weekly magazine *Time Out* (now free, issued every Tuesday outside major stations and around the city; also online at ⊕ *www.timeout.com*) is invaluable.

The free *Evening Standard* carries listings, many of which are also available online at ⊕ *www.thisislondon.co.uk*. *Metro*, London's other widely available free newspaper, is also worth checking out, as are many Sunday papers, and the Saturday *Independent, Guardian,* and *Times*.

You can pick up the free fortnightly *London Theatre Guide* from hotels and tourist-information centers.

There are hundreds of small private galleries all over London with interesting work by famous and not-yet-famous artists. The bimonthly free pamphlet "new exhibitions of contemporary art" (⊕ *www. newexhibitions.com*), available at most galleries, lists and maps nearly 200 art spaces in London.

ARTS AND ENTERTAINMENT REVIEWS

17

ST. JAMES'S

ART GALLERY

Institute of Contemporary Arts. Housed in an elegant John Nash–designed Regency terrace, the ICA's two galleries have changing exhibitions of contemporary visual art. The ICA also programs performances, underground and vintage movies, talks, and photography, and there's an arts bookstore, cafeteria, and bar. ⊠ *Nash House, The Mall, St. James's* ☏ *020/7930–3647* ⊕ *www.ica.org.uk* ▤ *Free* ☯ *Tues.–Sun. 11–11; galleries Tues., Wed., Fri.–Sun. 11–6, Thurs. 11–9* Ⓜ *Charing Cross, Piccadilly Circus.*

CLASSICAL MUSIC

St. James's Church. The organ was brought here in 1691 after fire destroyed its former home, the Palace of Whitehall. St. James's holds regular classical-music concerts and free lunchtime recitals Monday, Wednesday, and Friday at 1:10 pm (free but donation of £3.50 suggested). ⊠ *197 Piccadilly, St. James's* ☏ *020/7381–0441 concert program and tickets* ⊕ *www.st-james-piccadilly.org* Ⓜ *Piccadilly Circus, Green Park.*

MAYFAIR AND MARYLEBONE

MAYFAIR

ART GALLERY

Royal Academy of Arts. Housed in an aristocratic mansion and home to Britain's first art school (founded in 1768), the academy is best known for its blockbuster special exhibitions—like a controversial Sensation show drawn from the Saatchi collection and a record-breaking Monet show—though it also has a permanent collection that includes Michelangelo's marble *Taddei Tondo*. The annual Summer Exhibition has been a popular London tradition since 1769. ⊠ *Burlington House, Piccadilly, Mayfair* ☏ *020/7300–8000* ⊕ *www.royalacademy.org.uk* ✉ *From £8, prices vary with exhibition* ⊙ *Daily 10–6, except Fri. 10–10* Ⓜ *Piccadilly Circus.*

MARYLEBONE

ART GALLERY

Lisson. Owner Nicholas Logsdail represents about 40 blue-chip artists, including minimalist Sol Lewitt and Dan Graham, at one of the most respected galleries in London. The gallery is most associated with New Object sculptors like Anish Kapoor and Richard Deacon, many of whom have won the Turner Prize. A branch down the road at 29 Bell Street features work by younger, up-and-coming artists, and the gallery has another branch in Milan. ⊠ *52–54 Bell St., Marylebone* ☏ *020/7724–2739* ⊕ *www.lissongallery.com* ✉ *Free* ⊙ *Weekdays 10–6, Sat. 11–5* Ⓜ *Edgware Rd., Marylebone.*

THE ARTS FOR FREE

CLASSICAL MUSIC AND JAZZ

The Barbican, the Royal National Theatre, and the Royal Opera House often have free music in their foyers or in dedicated spaces, usually of high standard. On the South Bank, free festivals and special performances often take place alongside the river.

Many of London's world-class music colleges give free concerts several times a week. The Royal Academy of Music and the Royal College of Music often have free recitals. St. Martin-in-the-Fields has free lunchtime concerts, as does Christchurch Spitalfields. Other churches, including Westminster Abbey, St. James's Piccadilly, and St. Paul's in Covent Garden, also have frequent free music. For the Proms, which run from July to September at the Royal Albert Hall, good seats are expensive, but hundreds of standing tickets are available at £5: not quite free, but a good value.

CONTEMPORARY MUSIC

Brixton's Dogstar pub has a great selection of DJs, often playing for free on weekday evenings. Ain't Nothing But the...Blues Bar in Soho has live music most nights, often without a cover charge, and pubs such as the Monarch and the Hawley Arms near Camden Market offer the chance to see tomorrow's indie stars today. The largest of the music superstores, such as HMV Oxford Street, have occasional live performances of pop and rock bands, often to accompany album or single launches.

DRAMA AND PERFORMANCE ARTS

Look out for occasional festivals where innovative performances take place on the South Bank. Check the newspapers and *Time Out* for upcoming performances.

MUSEUMS AND GALLERIES

Few if any other cities in the world offer the number of free art venues available in London. Most of the city's museums and galleries do not charge entrance fees. The monthly *Galleries* magazine, available from galleries themselves or online at ⊕ www.galleries.co.uk, has listings for all private galleries in the capital.

PARK LIFE

London's parks come to life in summer with a wide-ranging program of music, dance, and visual arts (⊕ www.royalparks.gov.uk for details, or ☎ 020/7298–2000). There are several summer festivals in London parks, some with lots of big-name pop stars, like the Wireless festival in Hyde Park and the somewhat more indie Lovebox in Victoria Park. Notable contemporary art fairs are October's Frieze in Regent's Park (⊕ www.friezeartfair.com) and the Affordable Art Fair in Battersea Park in spring (⊕ www.affordableartfair.com).

RADIO AND TELEVISION

With so much broadcast material made in London, much of it recorded in front of live audiences, there are often opportunities to watch a free quiz show, current-affairs debate, comedy, or even drama. Check the BBC website for forthcoming recordings (⊕ www.bbc.co.uk/tickets).

17

CLASSICAL MUSIC

Fodor's Choice
★

Wigmore Hall. Hear chamber music and song recitals in this charming hall with near-perfect acoustics. Don't miss the Sunday morning concerts (11:30 am). ⊠ *36 Wigmore St., Marylebone* ☎ *020/7935–2141* ⊕ *www.wigmore-hall.org.uk* Ⓜ *Bond St.*

SOHO AND COVENT GARDEN

SOHO

ART GALLERY

Photographer's Gallery. Reopened in 2012 following a major refurbishment and extension, Britain's first and foremost photography gallery continues to program cutting-edge and provocative photography exhibitions. The prestigious Deutsche Börse Photography Prize is exhibited and awarded here annually. The gallery also has a print sales room, a bookstore, and a café. ⊠ *16–18 Ramillies St., off Oxford St., Soho* ☎ *0845/262–1618* ⊕ *www.thephotographersgallery.org.uk* 🖅 *Free* ⊙ *Mon.–Wed., Fri., and Sat. 10–6, Thurs. 10–8, Sun. 11:30–6* Ⓜ *Oxford Circus.*

Riflemaker. In the oldest public building in the West End, and taking its name from a former Georgian riflemaker's workshop here, this hip gallery exhibits ambitious works by emerging artists. It hosted debuts by Francesca Lowe, Chosil Kil, Jaime Gili, and Jamie Shovin. ⊠ *79 Beak St., Soho* ☎ *020/7439–0000* ⊕ *www.riflemaker.org* 🖅 *Free* ⊙ *Weekdays 10 am–6 pm, Sat. noon–6 pm* Ⓜ *Piccadilly Circus, Oxford Circus.*

TOP FIVE FOR THE ARTS

Stand with the "plebs" in Shakespeare's Globe Theatre. There are seats, but to really experience theater Shakespearean-style you should stand in the yard, with the stage at eye level (plus, it's a bargain at £5).

Visit the latest grand art installation in the Turbine Hall at the Tate Modern. The enormity of the Tate's central space either intimidates or inspires artists challenged to fill it.

Catch a world-class performance at the Proms. There's a surprisingly down-to-earth atmosphere among the elated company at these great concerts.

Enjoy a night at the National Film Theatre. Mingle with the real aficionados at screenings of foreign, classic, and experimental films.

Watch a Hollywood star in a West End production. Film stars often come to London to boost their artistic credibility in small-scale theaters.

FILM

Curzon Soho. This popular, comfortable movie theater runs a vibrant and artsy program of mixed repertoire and mainstream films, with a good calendar of director talks and other events, too. There are branches in Mayfair, Bloomsbury, Chelsea, and Richmond. ✉ *99 Shaftesbury Ave., Soho* ☎ *0330/500–1331* ⊕ *www.curzoncinemas.com* Ⓜ *Piccadilly Circus, Leicester Sq.* ✉ *38 Curzon St., Mayfair* ☎ *0330/500–1331* Ⓜ *Green Park.*

FAMILY **Prince Charles Cinema.** This repertory cinema right off Leicester Square offers a chance to catch up with independent features, documentaries, and even blockbusters you may have missed, and tickets start at £6, or £4 if you purchase a £10 annual membership. A second screen upstairs shows newer movies at more usual West End prices. This is where the "sing-along" screening took off—come in character and warble along to *The Sound of Music, Grease,* or *The Rocky Horror Picture Show.* ✉ *7 Leicester Pl., Soho* ☎ *0207/494–3654* ⊕ *www.princecharlescinema. com* Ⓜ *Leicester Sq., Piccadilly Circus.*

THEATER

Soho Theatre. This sleek theater in the heart of Soho is devoted to fostering new work and is a prolific presenter of plays by emerging writers, comedy performances, cabaret shows, and other entertainment. ✉ *21 Dean St., Soho* ☎ *020/7478–0100* ⊕ *www.sohotheatre.com* Ⓜ *Tottenham Court Rd.*

COVENT GARDEN

CLASSICAL MUSIC

St. Martin-in-the-Fields. Popular lunchtime concerts (free but £3.50 donation suggested) are held in this lovely 1726 church, as are regular evening concerts. ▮▮▮TIP→ Stop for a snack at the Café in the Crypt. ✉ *Trafalgar Sq., Westminster* ☎ *020/7766–1100* ⊕ *www.stmartin-in-the-fields.org* Ⓜ *Charing Cross.*

17

THEATER: LONDON TODAY

In London the play really *is* the thing, ranging from a long-running popular musical like *Mamma Mia!*, a groundbreaking reworking of Pinter, imaginative physical theater from an experimental company like Complicite, a lavish Disney spectacle, or a small fringe production above a pub. West End glitz and glamour continue to pull in the audiences, and so do the more innovative productions. Only in London will a Tuesday matinee of the Royal Shakespeare Company's *Henry IV* sell out a 1,200-seat theater.

In London the words "radical" and "quality," or "classical" and "experimental" are not mutually exclusive. The Royal Shakespeare Company (⊕ *www.rsc.org.uk*) and the National Theatre (⊕ *www.nationaltheatre.org. uk*) often stage contemporary versions of the classics. The Almeida, Battersea Arts Centre (BAC), Donmar Warehouse, Royal Court Theatre, Soho Theatre, and Old Vic attract famous actors and have excellent reputations for new writing and innovative theatrical approaches. These are the venues where you'll see an original production before it becomes a hit in the West End or on Broadway (and for a fraction of the cost).

The London theater scene remains vibrant throughout the summer months. Open-air productions of Shakespeare are particularly well served, whether in the faithful reconstruction of the Elizabethan Globe Theatre or under the stars in Regent's Park's Open Air Theatre. Theater festivals such as **LIFT** (the London International Festival of Theatre ⊕ *www.liftfestival.com*) and **BITE** (Barbican International Theater Events ⊕ *www.barbican.org.uk*) provide the chance to see international and cutting-edge companies throughout the year.

Theatergoing isn't cheap. Tickets less than £10 are a rarity, although designated productions at the National Theatre have seats at this price. At the commercial theaters you should expect to pay from £15 for a seat in the upper balcony to at least £25 for a good one in the stalls (orchestra) or dress circle (mezzanine). However, last-minute returns available on the night may provide some good deals. Tickets may be booked through ticket agents, at individual theater box offices, or over the phone by credit card. Be sure to inquire about any extra fees—prices can vary enormously, but agents are legally obliged to reveal the face value of the ticket if you ask. All the larger hotels offer theater bookings, but they tack on a hefty service charge. ■TIP➔ Be very wary of ticket touts (scalpers) and unscrupulous ticket agents outside theaters and working the line at "tkts" (a half-price ticket booth, www.tkts. co.uk).

Ticketmaster (☎ *0844/277-4321* ⊕ *www.ticketmaster.co.uk*) sells tickets to a number of different theaters, although they charge a booking fee. For discount tickets, **Society of London Theatre** (☎ *020/7557-6700* ⊕ *www.tkts.co.uk*) operates "tkts," a half-price ticket booth on the southwest corner of Leicester Square, and sells the best available seats to performances at about 25 theaters. It's open Monday–Saturday 9–7, Sunday 10:30–4:30; there's a £3 service charge (included in the price). Major credit cards are accepted.

DANCE

The London Coliseum. Ballet troupes are often booked into the spectacular Coliseum during the summer and the Christmas season, and generally any time when the resident English National Opera is not holding down the fort here. The restored Edwardian baroque theater (1904) is known for its magnificent auditorium and a rooftop glass dome. The top dance company to perform here is the English National Ballet (⊕ *www.ballet.org.uk*). Guided tours (every Saturday at 11:30 am) cost £10. ⊠ *St. Martin's La., Covent Garden* ☎ *020/7632–8300* ⊕ *www. eno.org* Ⓜ *Leicester Sq.*

Fodor'sChoice ★ **Royal Opera House.** As well as the Royal Opera, the renowned Royal Ballet performs classical and contemporary repertoire in this spectacular theater, where the interior may be Victorian but the stagecraft behind the red velvet curtain is state-of-the-art. Backstage tours are £12. ⊠ *Bow St., Covent Garden* ☎ *020/7304–4000* ⊕ *www.roh.org.uk* ☉ *Backstage tours (1 hr 15 min) Mon.–Fri. 10:30, 12:30, and 2:30, Sat. 10:30, 11:30, 12:30* Ⓜ *Covent Garden.*

THEATER

Fodor'sChoice ★ **Donmar Warehouse.** Hollywood stars often perform in this not-for-profit theatre in diverse and daring new works, bold interpretations of the classics, and small-scale musicals. Nicole Kidman, Gwyneth Paltrow, and Ewan McGregor have all been featured. ⊠ *41 Earlham St., Seven Dials, Covent Garden* ☎ *0844/871–7624* ⊕ *www.donmarwarehouse. com* Ⓜ *Covent Garden.*

OPERA

The London Coliseum. A veritable architectural extravaganza of Edwardian exoticism, the restored baroque-style theater (1904) has a magnificent auditorium and a rooftop glass dome with a bar and great views. As one of the city's largest and most venerable theaters, the Coliseum functions mainly as the home of the English National Opera. Seemingly in better financial shape than it has been for some time, ENO continues to produce innovative opera, sung in English, for lower prices than the Royal Opera House. During opera's off-season, the house hosts a number of dance troupes, including the English National Ballet (⊕ *www.ballet.org.uk*). Guided tours (every Saturday at 11:30am) cost £10. ⊠ *St. Martin's La., Covent Garden* ☎ *0871/911–0200 box office, 020/7836–0111 enquiries* ⊕ *www.eno.org* Ⓜ *Leicester Sq.*

Fodor'sChoice ★ **Royal Opera House.** Along with Milan's La Scala, New York's Metropolitan, and the Palais Garnier in Paris, this is one of the world's greatest opera houses. The resident troupe has mounted famously spectacular productions in the past, though recent productions have tended toward starker, more contemporary operas. Whatever the style of the performance, the extravagant theater itself—also home to the famed Royal Ballet—delivers a full dose of opulence. Tickets range in price from £8 to £800. The box office opens at 10 am, but lines for popular productions can start as early as 7 am; unsold tickets are offered at half price four hours before a performance. If you wish to see the hall but are not able to procure a ticket, you can join one of the daily tours of the auditorium (£9.50) or backstage (£12). There are free lunchtime recitals most Mondays in the Crush Room (arrive early to get a ticket—between

17

11 am and noon; some tickets are available online from nine days before the event). ROH2, the Opera House's contemporary arm, stages more experimental dance and voice performances in locations including the Linbury Studio Theatre, a 400-seater space below the Opera House. ⊠ *Bow St., Covent Garden* ☎ *020/7304–4000* ⊕ *www.roh.org. uk* ⊙ *Public areas generally 10–3:30; Auditorium tours daily at 4; Backstage tours Mon.–Fri. 10:30, 12:30, and 2:30, Sat. 10:30, 11:30, 12:30, and 1:30* Ⓜ *Covent Garden.*

BLOOMSBURY

CLASSICAL MUSIC

Kings Place. This airy concert venue opened in 2008: the cultural jewel in the huge new developments near the Eurostar terminal in King's Cross. It is the permanent home of the London Sinfonietta and the Orchestra of the Age of Enlightenment. It offers weeklong programs by musicians in a range of genres, and there are weekly chamber music masterclasses on Sundays. There's also a hugely varied cultural calendar of jazz, comedy, folk, and political and literary lectures. ⊠ *90 York Way, King's Cross* ☎ *020/7520–1490 box office, 020/7520–1440 enquiries* ⊕ *www.kingsplace.co.uk* Ⓜ *King's Cross.*

DANCE

Peacock Theatre. Sadler's Wells's West End annex, the modernist theater near the London School of Economics (which uses it as a lecture hall during the day), focuses on younger companies and shows in popular dance genres like flamenco, tango, and hip-hop. ⊠ *Portugal*

CONTEMPORARY ART: LONDON TODAY

In the 21st century, the focus of the city's art scene has shifted from the past to the future. Helped by the prominence of the Tate Modern, London's contemporary art scene has never been so high profile. In publicly funded exhibition spaces like the Barbican Gallery, the Hayward Gallery, the Institute of Contemporary Arts, and the Serpentine Gallery, London now has a modern-art environment on par with Bilbao and New York. Young British Artists (YBAs, though no longer as young as they once were) Damien Hirst, Tracey Emin, and others are firmly planted in the public imagination. The celebrity status of British artists is in part thanks to the annual Turner Prize, which always stirs up controversy in the media during a month-long display of the work, usually at Tate Britain.

Depending on whom you talk to, the Saatchi Gallery is considered to be either the savior of contemporary art or the wardrobe of the emperor's new clothes. After a couple of moves it is now ensconced in the former Duke of York's barracks off Chelsea's King's Road.

The South Bank's Tate Modern may house the giants of modern art, but East London is where the innovative action is. There are dozens of galleries in the fashionable spaces around Old Street, and the truly hip have already moved even farther east, to areas such as Bethnal Green. The Whitechapel Art Gallery and Jay Jopling's influential White Cube, now in a new venue in Bermondsey as well as in Soho, remain at the epicenter of the new art establishment and continue to show exciting work by emerging British artists.

On the first Thursday of every month, more than 100 museums and galleries of East London stay open until late (more information at ⊕ www.firstthursdays.co.uk).

17

St., Holborn ☎ 020/7863–8065, 0844/412–4300 box office ⊕ www.sadlerswells.com/page/peacock-theatre Ⓜ Holborn.

The Place. The Robin Howard Dance Theatre at The Place is London's only theater dedicated to contemporary dance, and with tickets often under £15 it's good value, too. "Resolution!" is the United Kingdom's biggest platform event for new choreographers. ⊠ 17 Duke's Rd., Bloomsbury ☎ 020/7121–1100 ⊕ www.theplace.org.uk Ⓜ Euston.

THE CITY

PERFORMANCE CENTERS

FAMILY **Barbican Centre.** Opened in 1982, the Brutalist-style Barbican is the largest performing arts center in Europe. The main concrete theater is most famous as the home of the London Symphony Orchestra. As well as the LSO (⊕ www.lso.co.uk), the Barbican is also the frequent host of the English Chamber Orchestra and the BBC Symphony Orchestra, and has an excellent concert season of big-name virtuosos. Performances by British and international theater companies make up part of its year-round **BITE** (Barbican International Theatre Events), which also features groundbreaking performance, dance, drama, and musical theater.

Innovative exhibitions of 20th-century and current art and design are shown in the Barbican Gallery and the Curve (usually free). In addition to Hollywood films, obscure classics and film festivals with Screen Talks are programmed in the three movie theaters here. Saturday Family Film Club has adventure and animation to please all ages. You could listen to Elgar or watch some Russian theater, see some 1960's photography or an exhibition on art and science, and catch some German animation with live musical accompaniment, possibly all in one evening. ⊠ *Silk St., The City* ☎ *020/7638–8891 box office* ⊕ *www.barbican.org.uk* ⊗ *Mon.–Sat. 9 am–11 pm, Sun. noon–11 pm* Ⓜ *Barbican.*

THE EAST END

ART GALLERIES

Whitechapel Art Gallery. Established in 1897 and recently expanded, this large, independent East End gallery is one of London's most innovative and consistently interesting. Jeff Wall, Bill Viola, Gary Hume, and Mark Rothko have exhibited here and there is an interesting program of events as well as an excellent restaurant. ⊠ *80–82 Whitechapel High St., Shoreditch* ☎ *020/7522–7888* ⊕ *www.whitechapel.org* 🎫 *Free* ⊗ *Tues., Wed., and Fri.–Sun. 11–6, Thurs. 11–9* Ⓜ *Aldgate East.*

White Cube. The English role in the exploding contemporary art scene has been major, thanks in good portion to Jay Joplin's influential gallery, which has regularly moved around London over the past 15 years. The striking modern concrete structure was the first free-standing building to be built in the area for 30 years when it opened in 2006. It is homebase for an array of British artists who have won the Turner Prize—Hirst, Emin, Hume, et al. A larger space, in an ex-warehouse south of the river in Bermondsey, opened in 2011 and is Europe's largest commercial gallery. ⊠ *25–26 Mason's Yard, St. James's* ☎ *020/7930–5373* ⊕ *www.whitecube.com* 🎫 *Free* ⊗ *Tues.–Sat. 10–6* Ⓜ *Green Park, Piccadilly Circus.*

THEATER

Hackney Empire. The history of this treasure of a theater is drama in its own right. Charlie Chaplin is said to have appeared here during its days as a thriving variety theater and music hall in the early 1900s. It now hosts traditional family entertainment and variety shows, opera, music, musical theater, dance, and drama, often with a multicultural slant. ⊠ *291 Mare St., Hackney* ☎ *020/8985–2424* ⊕ *www.hackneyempire. co.uk* Ⓜ *National Rail: Hackney Central.*

FILM: LONDON TODAY

There are many wonderful movie theaters in London and several that are committed to non-mainstream and repertory cinema, in particular the excellent Curzon cinemas and the National Film Theatre. Now nearly 60 years old, the **Times BFI London Film Festival** (⊕ *www.bfi. org.uk/lff*) brings hundreds of films made by masters of world cinema to London for 16 days each October, accompanied by often-sold-out talks and other events. The smaller, avant-garde **Raindance Film Festival** (⊕ *www.raindance.co.uk*) highlights independent filmmaking, September into October.

West End movie theaters continue to do good business. Most of the major houses, such as the Odeon Leicester Square and the Empire, are in the Leicester Square–Piccadilly Circus area, where tickets average £15. Monday and matinees are often cheaper, at around £6–£10, and there are also smaller crowds.

Check out *Time Out*, one of the London papers, or ⊕ *www.viewlondon. co.uk* for listings.

SOUTH OF THE THAMES

ART GALLERY

Fodor'sChoice ★ **Tate Modern.** This converted power station is one of the largest modern-art galleries in the world, so give yourself ample time to take it all in. The permanent collection includes work by all the major 20th-century artists, though only a fraction is shown at any one time. There are also blockbuster touring shows and solo exhibitions of international artists. The huge onetime oil tanks of the old power station were opened up in 2012 for a season of performance art. These new spaces are the first stage in a new extension of the gallery that is scheduled for completion in 2016. ▓ TIP➔ The bar on the top floor has gorgeous views overlooking the Thames and St. Paul's Cathedral. ⊠ *Bankside, South Bank* ☏ *020/7887–8888* ⊕ *www.tate.org.uk* ◨ *Free–£14* ☾ *Sun.–Thurs. 10–6, Fri. and Sat. 10–10* Ⓜ *Southwark, St. Paul's, London Bridge.*

FILM

BFI London IMAX Cinema. The British Film Institute's glazed drum-shaped IMAX theater has the largest screen in the United Kingdom (approximately 75 feet wide and the height of five double-decker buses), showing state-of-the-art 2-D and 3-D films. ⊠ *1 Charlie Chaplin Walk, South Bank* ☏ *0870/7199–6000* ⊕ *www.bfi.org.uk/imax* Ⓜ *Waterloo.*

FAMILY **BFI Southbank.** With the best repertory programming in London, the three movie theaters and studio at what was previously known as the National Film Theatre are effectively a national film center run by the British Film Institute. They show more than 1,000 titles each year, favoring art-house, foreign, silent, overlooked, classic, noir, and short films over Hollywood blockbusters. The center also has a gallery, bookshop, and "mediatheque," where visitors can watch film and television from the National Archive for free (closed Mon). This is one of the venues for the Times BFI London Film Festival; throughout the year there are minifestivals, seminars, and guest speakers. ▓ TIP➔ Members

17

(£40) get priority bookings (useful for special events) and £1.50 off each screening. ⊠ *Belvedere Rd., South Bank* ☎ *020/7928–3535 information, 020/7928–3232 box office* ⊕ *www.bfi.org.uk* Ⓜ *Waterloo.*

PERFORMANCE CENTERS

Southbank Centre. The Royal Festival Hall is one of London's best spaces for large-scale choral and orchestral works and is home to the Philharmonia and London Philharmonic orchestras. Other venues in the Southbank Centre host smaller-scale music performances: The Queen Elizabeth Hall is a popular venue for chamber orchestras and top-tier soloists, and the intimate Purcell Room is known for chamber music and solo recitals. Southbank also hosts everything from the London International Mime festival to large-scale dance performances, including a diverse and exciting season of international and British-based contemporary dance companies. Also part of the complex is the **Hayward Gallery** (10–6 daily), a landmark Brutalist-style 1960s building and one of London's major venues for contemporary art exhibitions. ⊠ *Belvedere Rd., South Bank* ☎ *020/7960–4200, 0844/875–0073 box office* ⊕ *www.southbankcentre.co.uk* Ⓜ *Waterloo, Embankment.*

THEATER

BAC. Battersea Arts Centre has a reputation for producing innovative new work. Check out Scratch events, low-tech cabaret theater by emerging artists where the audience provides feedback on works-in-progress. Tuesday shows often have pay-what-you-can entry. ⊠ *176 Lavender Hill, Battersea* ☎ *020/7223–2223* ⊕ *www.bac.org.uk* Ⓜ *National Rail: Clapham Junction.*

National Theatre. When this theater, designed by Sir Denys Lasdun, opened in 1976 Londoners weren't all so keen on the low-slung, multilayered Brutalist block. Prince Charles described the building as "a clever way of building a nuclear power station in the middle of London without anyone objecting." But whatever its merits or demerits as a feature on the landscape, the National Theatre's interior spaces are definitely worth a tour. Interspersed with the three theaters—the 1,120-seat Olivier, the 890-seat Lyttelton, and the 300-seat Cottesloe—is a multilayered foyer with exhibitions, bars, and restaurants, and free entertainment. Musicals, classics, and new plays are all performed by top-flight professionals. Some shows offer £12 ticket deals. ⊠ *Belvedere Rd., South Bank* ☎ *020/7452–3000 box office, 020/7452–3400 information* ⊕ *www.nationaltheatre.org.uk* ☜ *Tour £8.50* ☽ *Foyer Mon.–Sat. 9:30 am–11 pm; 75-min tour backstage up to 6 times daily weekdays, twice on Sat., often on Sun.* Ⓜ *Waterloo.*

The Old Vic. This grand old theater, former haunting grounds of such stage legends as John Gielgud, Vivien Leigh, Peter O'Toole, Richard Burton, and Judi Dench, is now masterminded by American actor Kevin Spacey. The theater had suffered decades of financial duress before being brought under the ownership of a dedicated trust headed by Spacey. His production record has had a few hiccups but his tenure is these days regarded by most as a success. As well as being artistic director, Spacey often appears on stage. ⊠ *The Cut, Southwark*

CLASSICAL MUSIC: LONDON TODAY

Whether it's a concert by pianist Lang Lang or a Mozart requiem by candlelight, it's possible to hear first-rate musicians in world-class venues almost every day of the year. The London Symphony Orchestra is in residence at the Barbican Centre, although other top orchestras—including the Philharmonia and the Royal Philharmonic—also perform here. The Barbican also hosts chamber-music concerts, with celebrated orchestras such as the City of London Sinfonia. Kings Place, the new kid on London's concert block, has a great, and greatly varied calendar of musical events. The Southbank Centre has an impressive international music season, held in the Queen Elizabeth Hall and the small Purcell Room as well as in the Royal Festival Hall, now completely refurbished. Full houses are rare, so even at the biggest concert halls you should be able to get a ticket for £12. If you can't book in advance, arrive at the hall an hour before the performance for a chance at returns.

■ TIP→ Lunchtime concerts take place all over the city in smaller concert halls, the big arts-center foyers, and churches; they usually cost less than £5 or are free, and feature string quartets, singers, jazz ensembles, or gospel choirs. St. John's, Smith Square, and St. Martin-in-the-Fields are popular locations. Performances usually begin about 1 pm and last one hour.

Classical-music festivals range from the stimulating avant-garde **Meltdown** (⊕ meltdown.southbankcentre. co.uk), curated each year by a prominent musician—Yoko Ono in 2013—at the Southbank Centre in June, to church hall recitals including the **Spitalfields Festival** (⊕ www. spitalfieldsfestival.org.uk), a program of recitals held in beautiful, historic East End churches in June, December, and January, and the month-long **City of London Festival** (⊕ www.colf.org) in the Square Mile in summer. A great British tradition since 1895, the **Henry Wood Promenade Concerts** (more commonly known as the "Proms" ⊕ www.bbc. co.uk/proms) run eight weeks, from July to September, at the Royal Albert Hall. Despite an extraordinary quantity of high-quality concerts, it's renowned for its (atypical) last night: a madly jingoistic display of singing "Land of Hope and Glory," Union Jack–waving, and general madness. For regular Proms, tickets run £5–£90, with hundreds of standing tickets for £5 available at the hall on the night of the concert. ■ TIP→ The last night is broadcast in Hyde Park on a jumbo screen, but even here a seat on the grass requires a paid ticket that can set you back around £25.

17

☎ 0844/871–7628 box office, 020/7928–2651 ⊕ www.oldvictheatre. com Ⓜ Waterloo, Southwark.

Fodor's Choice ★ **Shakespeare's Globe Theatre.** This faithful reconstruction of the open-air playhouse where Shakespeare worked and wrote many of his greatest plays marvelously re-creates the 16th-century theatergoing experience. Standing room in the yard or "pit" right in front of the stage costs £5. The season runs April through October. A replica Jacobean (early-17th-century) indoor theater is being constructed next to the Globe, and should open in winter 2013/2014. ⇨ *For more on the Globe Theatre,*

OPERA: LONDON TODAY

The two key players in London's opera scene are the Royal Opera House (which ranks with the Metropolitan Opera House in New York) and the more innovative English National Opera (ENO), which presents English-language productions at the London Coliseum. Only the Theatre Royal, Drury Lane, has a longer theatrical history than the Royal Opera House—the third theater to be built on the site since 1858.

Despite occasional performances by the likes of Björk, the Royal Opera House struggles to shrug off its reputation for elitism and ticket prices that can rise to £800. It is, however, more accessible than it used to be—the cheapest tickets are less than £10. Conditions of purchase vary; call for information. Prices for the ENO are generally lower, ranging from around £20 to £95.

In summer, the increasingly adventurous Opera Holland Park presents the usual chestnuts alongside some obscure works under a canopy in leafy Holland Park.

International touring companies often perform at Sadler's Wells, the Barbican, the Southbank Centre, and Wigmore Hall, so check the weekly listings for details.

see our special photo-feature, "Shakespeare and the Globe Theater" in Chapter 8. ✉ *21 New Globe Walk, Bankside, South Bank* ☎ *020/7401–9919 box office, 020/7902–1400 enquiries* ⊕ *www.shakespearesglobe. com* Ⓜ *London Bridge, Mansion House (then cross Southwark Bridge), Blackfriars (then cross Blackfriars Bridge), St. Paul's (then cross Millenium Bridge).*

Young Vic. In a home near Waterloo, big names perform alongside young talent, often in daring, innovative productions of classic plays that appeal to a more diverse audience than is traditionally found in London theaters. ✉ *66 The Cut, Waterloo, South Bank* ☎ *020/7922–2800, 020/7922–2922 box office* ⊕ *www.youngvic.org* Ⓜ *Southwark, Waterloo.*

KENSINGTON AND CHELSEA

KENSINGTON

ART GALLERY

Serpentine Gallery. Built in 1934 as a tea pavilion in Kensington Gardens, the Serpentine has an international reputation for exhibitions of modern and contemporary art. Man Ray, Henry Moore, Andy Warhol, Bridget Riley, Damien Hirst, and Rachel Whiteread are a few of the artists who have had exhibits here. An extension to the gallery is scheduled to open in the fall of 2013. The annual Summer Pavilion, a striking temporary structure designed by a different leading architect every year, is always worth catching. ✉ *Kensington Gardens, Kensington* ☎ *020/7402–6075* ⊕ *www.serpentinegallery.org* 🎟 *Free* ☉ *Daily 10–6* Ⓜ *Lancaster Gate, Knightsbridge, South Kensington.*

London's Royal Opera House is also home to the Royal Ballet and an in-house orchestra.

CLASSICAL MUSIC

Cadogan Hall. Formerly a church, Cadogan Hall has been turned into a spacious concert venue. It's home to the Royal Philharmonic Orchestra, and the English Chamber Orchestra performs here regularly. ✉ *5 Sloane Terr., Kensington* ☎ *020/7730–4500* ⊕ *www.cadoganhall.com* Ⓜ *Sloane Sq.*

Royal Albert Hall. Built in 1871, this splendid iron-and-glass–dome auditorium hosts music programs in a wide range of genres. Its terra-cotta exterior surmounted by a mosaic frieze depicting figures engaged in artistic, scientific, and cultural pursuits, this domed, circular 5,223-seat auditorium was made possible by the Victorian public, who donated the money to build it. After funds were diverted toward the Albert Memorial (opposite), more money was raised by selling 999-year leases for 1,276 "Members'" seats at £100 apiece—today a box with five Members' Seats goes for half a million pounds. The notoriously poor acoustics were fixed after a 2004 renovation and the sightlines are excellent. The RAH hosts everything from pop and classical headliners to Cirque du Soleil, ballet on ice, awards ceremonies, and Sumo wrestling championships, but is best-known as the venue for the annual July–September BBC Promenade Concerts—the "Proms"—with bargain-price standing (or promenading, or sitting-on-the-floor) tickets sold on the night of the concert. The hall is also open daily for daytime guided tours (£11.50) and occasional afternoon tea (£30–£38) and Victorian experience tours (£11). ✉ *Kensington Gore, Kensington* ☎ *020/7589–8212, 0845/401–5034 box office* ⊕ *www.royalalberthall.com* Ⓜ *South Kensington.*

OPERA

Opera Holland Park. In summer, well-loved operas and imaginative productions of relatively unknown works are presented under a spectacular new canopy against the remains of Holland House, one of the first great houses built in Kensington. Ticket prices range from £12 to £67.50, with 1,100 tickets offered free to young people ages 9–18 every season. Tickets go on sale in April. ⊠ *Holland Park, Kensington High St., Kensington* ☎ *0300/999–1000 box office (opens late Apr.), 020/7361–3570 enquiries* ⊕ *www.operahollandpark.com* Ⓜ *High Street Kensington, Holland Park.*

CHELSEA

ART GALLERY

Saatchi Gallery. Charles Saatchi lit the fuse to the contemporary art explosion in Britain and though he and his art investments may not be quite as ubiquitous as they once were, he remains a key figure. After migrating to several museums and being shown around the world, Saatchi's collection now resides in this modern gallery that sprawls through 70,000 square feet of the Duke of York's HQ building in Chelsea, complete with a bookshop and café-bar. ⊠ *Duke of York's HQ, King's Rd., Chelsea* ☎ *020/7823–2332* ⊕ *www.saatchi-gallery.co.uk* ▣ *Free* ◯ *Daily 10–6* Ⓜ *Sloane Sq.*

THEATER

Royal Court Theatre. Britain's undisputed epicenter of new theatrical works, the RCT is now 50 years old and continues to produce gritty British and international drama. ■**TIP**➔ Don't miss the best deal in town—four 10-pence standing tickets go on sale one hour before each performance, and £10 tickets are available on Monday. ⊠ *Sloane Sq., Chelsea* ☎ *020/7565–5000* ⊕ *www.royalcourttheatre.com* Ⓜ *Sloane Sq.*

NOTTING HILL

FILM

FAMILY   **The Electric Cinema.** This refurbished Portobello Road art house screens mainstream and international movies. The emphasis is on comfort, with leather sofas for two, armchairs, footstools, and mini–coffee tables for your tapas-style food and wine. Saturday matinees for kids are popular. Edible Cinema combines experimental food and cocktails with the cinema experience. The Electric also has another sumptuous movie theater in east London—the Aubin, on Redchurch Street, with sofas and wine-coolers. ⊠ *191 Portobello Rd., Notting Hill* ☎ *020/7908–9696* ⊕ *www.electriccinema.co.uk* ▣ *£12.50–£22.50* Ⓜ *Ladbroke Grove, Notting Hill Gate.*

REGENT'S PARK AND HAMPSTEAD

REGENT'S PARK

THEATER

Fodor'sChoice   **Open Air Theatre.** On a warm summer evening, open-air classical theater
★   in the pastoral and royal Regent's Park is hard to beat for a magical adventure. Enjoy a supper before the performance, a bite during the

DANCE: LONDON TODAY

Dance fans in London can enjoy the classicism of the world-renowned Royal Ballet, as well as innovative works by several contemporary dance companies—including Rambert Dance Company, Matthew Bourne's New Adventures, and the Wheeldon Company—and scores of independent choreographers. The English National Ballet and visiting international companies perform at the Coliseum and at Sadler's Wells, which also hosts various other ballet companies and dance troupes. Encompassing the refurbished Royal Festival Hall, the Southbank Centre has a seriously good contemporary dance program that hosts top international companies and important U.K. choreographers, as well as multicultural offerings ranging from Japanese Butoh and Indian Kathak to hip-hop. The Place and the Lilian Bayliss Theatre at Sadler's Wells are where you'll find the most daring, cutting-edge performances.

The following theaters are the key dance venues. Also check ⊕ www. londondance.com for current performances and fringe venues.

Dance Umbrella. The biggest annual event is Dance Umbrella, 10 days in October that host international and British-based artists at various venues across the city. ☎ 020/7407–1200 ⊕ www. danceumbrella.co.uk.

17

intermission on the picnic lawn, or drinks in the spacious bar. The only downside is that warm summer nights in London are not always entirely reliable. ✉ *Inner Circle, Regent's Park* ☎ *0844/826–4242* ⊕ *www. openairtheatre.com* Ⓜ *Baker St., Regent's Park.*

HAMPSTEAD
THEATER
Tricycle Theatre. Committed to representing the cultural diversity of its community, the Tricycle shows the best in black, Irish, Jewish, Asian, and South African drama, and also promotes new work. There is a movie theater too: Expect the best of new European and international cinema, including films from the United States, occasionally screened at film festivals the theater organizes. A year-round program of film-related activities is geared to children, and discounted movie tickets are available on Monday. ✉ *269 Kilburn High Rd., Kilburn* ☎ *020/7372 6611 information, 020/7328–1000 box office* ⊕ *www.tricycle.co.uk* Ⓜ *Kilburn.*

ISLINGTON
ART GALLERY
Victoria Miro Gallery. This large, important commercial gallery, in a former furniture factory, has exhibited some of the biggest names on the British contemporary art scene—Grayson Perry, the Chapman brothers, and Peter Doig, to name a few. Some exhibitions spill out into the gallery's own garden. It also brings in exciting talent from abroad. ✉ *16 Wharf Rd., Islington* ☎ *020/7336–8109* ⊕ *www.victoria-miro. com* 🎟 *Free* 🕓 *Tues.–Sat. 10–6* Ⓜ *Old St., Angel.*

DANCE

Sadler's Wells. This gleaming building opened in 1998, the seventh on the site in its 300-year history, and is devoted to presenting leading classical and contemporary dance companies. The Random Dance Company is in residence, and the little Lilian Bayliss Theatre hosts avant-garde work. ✉ *Rosebery Ave., Islington* ☎ *0844/412–4300 tickets, 020/7863–8198 general enquiries* ⊕ *www.sadlerswells.com* Ⓜ *Angel.*

THEATER

Almeida Theatre. This Off–West End venue premieres excellent new plays and exciting twists on the classics, often featuring high-profile actors. There's a good café and a licensed bar that serves "sharing dishes" as well as tasty main courses. ✉ *Almeida St., Islington* ☎ *020/7359–4404* ⊕ *www.almeida.co.uk* Ⓜ *Angel, Highbury & Islington.*

SHOPPING

Updated by
Ellin Stein

As befits one of the great trading capitals of the world, London has a shop for almost everything. From the quiet and rarified (the private fitting rooms at Vivienne Westwood's couture salon) to the busy and bustling (the Brick Lane street market), no matter where you go, you'll find plenty to tempt you.

You can try on underwear fit for a Queen at Her Majesty's lingerie supplier, track down a leather-bound Brontë classic at an antiquarian bookseller, or find a bargain antique on Portobello Road. Whether you're just browsing—there's nothing like the size, variety, and sheer theater of London's street markets to stimulate the acquisition instinct—or on a fashion-seeking mission, London shopping offers something for all tastes and budgets.

Although it's impossible to pin down one particular look that defines the city, London style tends to fall into two camps: one is the quirky, individualistic, somewhat romantic look exemplified by homegrown designers like Matthew Williamson, Westwood, and Lulu Guinness. The other reflects Britain's celebrated tradition of classic knitwear and suiting, with labels like Jaeger, Pringle, and Brora, while Oswald Boateng, Paul Smith, and Richard James take tradition and give it a very modern twist. Traditional bespoke men's tailoring can be found in the menswear stores of Jermyn Street and Savile Row—there's no better place in the city to buy custom-made shirts and suits, while the handbags at Mulberry, Asprey, and Anya Hindmarch are pure classic quality. If your budget can't stretch this far, no problem; the city's chain stores like Topshop, Zara, and H&M, aimed at the younger end of the market, are excellent places to pick up designs copied straight from the catwalk at a fraction of the price, while mid-market chains like Reiss, Jigsaw, and L.K. Bennett offer smart design and better quality for the more sophisticated shopper.

If there's anything that unites London's designers, it's a commitment to creativity and originality, underpinned by a strong sense of heritage. This combination of posh and rock-n-roll sensibilities turns up

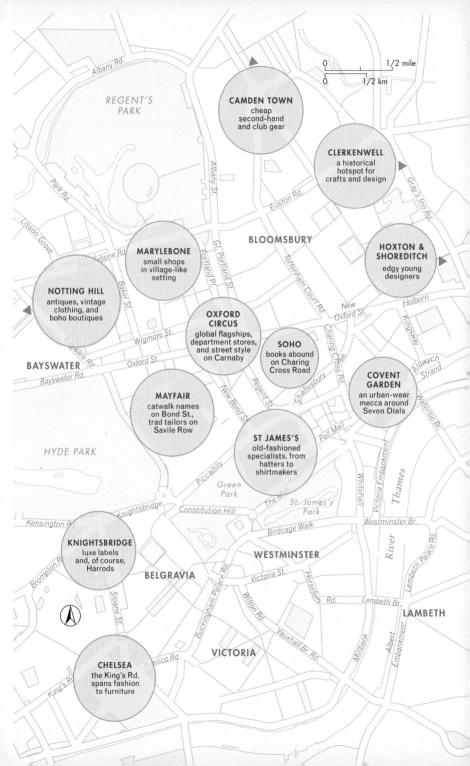

in everyone from Terence Conran, who revolutionized product and housewares design in the '60s (and is still going strong), to Alexander McQueen, who combined the Punk aesthetic with the rigor of couture. You'll see it in fanciful millinery creations by Philip Treacy and Stephen Jones, and in the work of imaginative shoemakers Nicholas Kirkwood, United Nude, and Terry de Havilland; and it keeps going, right through to current hot designers Erdem, Christopher Kane, and Christopher Bailey, the latter responsible for making traditional label Burberry relevant again.

One reason for London's design supremacy is the strength of local fashion college Central St. Martin's, whose graduates include Conran, Kane, McQueen, his successor at his eponymous label—and designer of the Duchess of Cambridge's wedding dress—Sarah Burton, and Stella McCartney's equally acclaimed successor at Céline, Phoebe Philo.

To find the McQueens, McCartneys, and Baileys of tomorrow, head for the independent boutiques of Shoreditch and Spitalfields and the "Newburgh Quarter" off Carnaby Street. If anything, London is even better known for its vibrant street fashion than for its high-end designers. Stock up from the stalls at Portobello, Camden, and Spitalfields markets.

Aside from bankrupting yourself, the only problem you may encounter is exhaustion. London's shopping districts are spread out all over the city, so do as savvy locals do: plan your excursion with military precision, taking in only one or two areas in a day, and stop for a lunch with a glass of wine or a pint at a pub.

PLANNING

OPENING HOURS

Most shops are open from about 9:30 or 10 am to 6 or 6:30 pm. Some may open at 11 and stay open until 7. Because shop hours, particularly for the smaller shops, are varied, it's a good idea to phone or check websites ahead. Stores that have late shopping—and not all do—are usually open until 7 or 8 pm on Wednesday or Thursday only. Most department stores stay open late one day a week. On Sunday, many shops open between 11 am and noon and close at 5 or 6 pm. Most stores are open on Sunday in December for the Christmas season.

WATCH YOUR LANGUAGE

Locals like to say that Brits and Americans are separated by a common language. Here are a few confusing terms to watch for when out and about in the shops:

Pants means underwear. Every other type of long-legged bottoms (except jeans) are called **trousers.** Also in the underwear category is the **vest** (undershirt in the United States); if you are looking for a vest, ask for a waistcoat.

Knickers are ladies' underwear. If you want pantyhose, ask for **tights.**

Jumper means sweater—unless it's a cardigan, in which case it may be shortened to **cardie**. If you ask for a **sweater**, you may be offered a sweatshirt.

Men use **braces** to hold up their trousers; in England **suspenders** is another word for garters.

If you want some Adidas- or Nike-type athletic shoes, ask for **trainers**, not sneakers.

Don't ask for a **pocketbook** or a **purse** if you mean a handbag—the former will be incomprehensible, and the latter will produce a coin purse. Ask for a **fanny pack** and it will produce a laugh—"fanny" means something altogether different in the United Kingdom, so ask for a "bum-bag."

Nightgowns are usually abbreviated to **nighties** and bathrobes may be **dressing gowns.**

A WORD ABOUT SERVICE

American standards of customer service are rare in London—you may find attentive customer service at old-school, traditional names and some independent stores, but salespeople elsewhere can seem abrupt or indifferent.

SHOPPING REVIEWS

ST. JAMES'S

ACCESSORIES: HATS

James Lock & Co. Ltd. Need a silk top hat, a flat-weave Panama, or a traditional tweed flat cap? Or, for ladies, an occasion hat? James Lock of St. James's has been providing hats from this cozy shop since 1676 for customers ranging from Admiral Lord Nelson, Oscar Wilde, and Frank Sinatra to, more recently, Robert Downey Jr. and Guy Ritchie, as well as trend-setting musicians and models. ⊠ *6 St. James's St., St. James's* ☎ *020/7930–8884* ⊕ *www.lockhatters.co.uk* ☯ *Closed Sun.* Ⓜ *Green Park.*

Fodor's Choice ★ **Swaine Adeney Brigg.** Providing practical supplies for country pursuits since 1750, Swaine Adeney Brigg, now in new Mayfair premises, carries beautifully crafted umbrellas, walking sticks, or hip flasks, or ingenious combinations of same, such as the umbrella with a slim tipple-holding flask secreted inside the stem. The same level of quality and craftsmanship applies to the store's leather goods, which include attaché cases and wallets. You'll find scarves, caps, and the Herbert Johnson "Poet Hat," the iconic headgear (stocked since 1890) worn by Harrison Ford in every Indiana Jones film. Satellite branches are in the Piccadilly Arcade and the City. ⊠ *41 S. Audley St., Mayfair* ☎ *020/7409–7277* ⊕ *www.swaineadeney.co.uk* ☯ *Closed Sun.* Ⓜ *Green Park.*

BEAUTY

Fodor's Choice ★ **Floris.** What do Queen Victoria and Marilyn Monroe have in common? They both used fragrances from Floris, one of the most beautiful shops in London, with gleaming glass-and-Spanish-mahogany showcases salvaged from the Great Exhibition of 1851. In addition to scents for both

18

CLOSE UP

Know Your Shopping Personality

"Where is the best place to shop in London?" There are thousands of shops in the city, and dozens of neighborhoods worth shopping in. Start by identifying your shopping personality to narrow your choices for a successful outing.

Easygoing. If you want to pop in and out of a variety of shops, as well as avoid the crowds around Oxford Street, head to the King's Road in Chelsea. You'll find department store Peter Jones, plus Marks & Spencer and plenty of chains and trendy boutiques. Another safe bet is High Street Kensington for the usual big chains, in addition to some smaller ones less oriented toward disposable fashion, such as Cos, Karen Millen, and Oliver Bonas.

Eclectic. If you are looking for well-crafted, original items, start at Liberty on Regent Street, then head to Marylebone to the north, or the "Newburgh Quarter" off Carnaby Street, immediately to the south—a warren of cobblestone streets lined with independent shops.

Fashionista. When only the top designers will do, start at the designer boutiques along Sloane Street in Knightsbridge before hopping on bus No. 19 to Green Park. From there you can cover Bond Street (both Old and New) finishing at Fenwick, or veer off onto Conduit Street, designer-heavy Bruton Street, or, at the northwest end of Berkeley Square, ultrachic Mount Street. If you still have time and energy, check out South Molton Street opposite Bond Street Tube or St. Christopher's Place across Oxford Street.

Funky and Avant-Garde. For cutting-edge fashion and housewares, head east to the city's trendy East End neighborhoods. Start at Columbia Road in Hoxton, with its charming specialty shops (and the Sunday flower market), then wander through Shoreditch, Spitalfields, and Bethnal Green, where you'll find shops filled with one-of-a-kind designs. There's also lots here to appeal to vintage hunters.

Whirlwind. If you're after a one-stop-shopping experience, head to one of the big department stores. Selfridges and Fenwick are near the Bond Street Tube station, Liberty is near Oxford Circus Tube station, while Harvey Nichols and Harrods share the Knightsbridge Tube station.

---

men and women, Floris makes its own shaving products, reflecting its origins as a barbershop. Other gift possibilities include goose-down powder puffs, a famous rose-scented mouthwash, and beautifully packaged soaps and bath essences. There's another branch in Belgravia. ⊠ *89 Jermyn St., St. James's* ☎ *020/7930–2885* ⊕ *www.florislondon. com* ☼ *Closed Sun.* Ⓜ *Piccadilly Circus, Green Park.*

BOOKS

Fodor'sChoice   **Hatchards.** This is London's oldest bookshop, open since 1797 and
★   beloved by writers themselves (customers have included Oscar Wilde, Rudyard Kipling, and Lord Byron). Despite its wood-paneled, "gentleman's library" atmosphere, and eclectic selection of books, Hatchards is owned by the large Waterstone's chain. Nevertheless, the shop still retains

its period charm, aided by the staff's old-fashioned helpfulness and expertise. Look for the substantial number of books signed by notable contemporary authors on the well-stocked shelves. ⊠ *187 Piccadilly, St. James's* ☎ *020/7439–9921* ⊕ *www. hatchards.co.uk* Ⓜ *Piccadilly Circus.*

CLOTHING: MEN

Thomas Pink. This specialist chain is best known for its colorful and stylish formal shirts for both men and women, many in such fine fabrics as Sea Island or Egyptian cotton. More casual shirts are for sale as well, along with ties, boxers, pajamas, belts, and other accessories, as are dresses, skirts, jackets, and knitwear for women. Bespoke shirts for men can be ordered at the Jermyn Street branch. There are other branches in The City, Chelsea, Canary Wharf, St. Pancras Int'l, and the Westfield shopping center. ⊠ *85 Jermyn St., St. James's* ☎ *020/7930–6364* ⊕ *www.thomaspink.co.uk* Ⓜ *Green Park, Piccadilly Circus.*

Fodor'sChoice ★ **Turnbull & Asser.** This is *the* custom shirtmaker, dripping exclusivity from every fiber—after all, Prince Charles is a client and every filmic James Bond has worn shirts from here. At least 15 separate measurements are taken, and the cloth, woven to the company's specifications, comes in 1,000 different patterns—the cottons feel as good as silk. The first order must be for a minimum of six shirts, which start from £195 each. As well as jackets, cashmeres, suits, ties, pajamas, and accessories perfect for the billionaire who has everything, the store also carries less expensive, though still exquisite, ready-to-wear shirts. There's another branch in the City. ⊠ *71–72 Jermyn St., St. James's* ☎ *020/7808–3000* ⊕ *www. turnbullandasser.com* ☾ *Closed Sun.* Ⓜ *Green Park.*

FOOD

Fodor'sChoice ★ **Berry Bros. & Rudd.** Nothing matches Berry Bros. & Rudd for rare offerings and a unique shopping experience. A family-run wine business since 1698, "BBR" stores its vintage bottles and casks in vaulted cellars that are more than 300 years old. The shop has a quirky charm and the staff is extremely knowledgeable—and not snooty if you're on a budget. ⊠ *3 St. James's St., St. James's* ☎ *020/396–9600* ⊕ *www.bbr. com* ☾ *Closed Sun.* Ⓜ *Green Park.*

Fodor'sChoice ★ **Fortnum & Mason.** Although F&M is popularly known as the Queen's grocer and the impeccably mannered staff wear traditional tailcoats, its celebrated food hall stocks gifts for all budgets, such as loads of irresistibly packaged luxury foods stamped with the gold "By Appointment" crest for less than £5. Try the teas, preserves (unusual products include rose-petal jelly), condiments, or Gentleman's Relish (anchovy paste). The store's famous hampers are always a welcome gift. The gleaming food hall spans two floors and includes a sleek wine bar designed by David Collins, with the rest of the store devoted to upscale homewares, men's and women's clothing and accessories, toiletries,

ROYAL WARRANT

Many stores carry items with the Royal Warrant seal (even some sugar brands). Though not personally endorsed by the royals, it does mean that the palace has used the item for five consecutive years—and it could enliven a gift for royal-watchers.

18

women's jewelry and cosmetics, and clothing and toys for children. If you start to flag, break for afternoon tea at one of the four other restaurants (one's an indulgent ice-cream parlor)—or a treatment in the Beauty Rooms. ⊠ *181 Piccadilly, St. James's* ☎ *020/7734–8040* ⊕ *www. fortnumandmason.com* Ⓜ *Green Park.*

SHOES

Loake Shoemakers. Long established in England's Midlands and a provider of boots to the British armed forces in both world wars, this family-run firm specializes in classic handcrafted men's shoes at reasonable prices. Whether you're after brogues, loafers, or deck shoes, the staff will take the time to ensure you have the right fit. In terms of quality and service, Loake represents real value for money. ⊠ *8–10 Princes Arcade, off Jermyn St., St. James's* ☎ *020/7734–8643* ⊕ *www. loake.co.uk* ⊙ *Closed Sun.* Ⓜ *Piccadilly.*

SPECIALTY STORES

Geo F. Trumper. If you don't have the time for an old-fashioned hot-towel shave, pick up some accessories to take home for yourself or as a gift. The Extract of West Indian Lime is a popular, zingy aftershave, and the Coconut Oil Hard Shaving Soap, which comes in a hand-turned wooden bowl, is a classic. There is also a store at 9 Curzon Street in Mayfair. ⊠ *1 Duke of York St., St. James's* ☎ *020/7734–1370* ⊕ *www. trumpers.com* ⊙ *Closed Sun.* Ⓜ *Piccadilly Circus.*

TOYS

The Armoury of St. James's. The fine toy soldiers and military models in stock here are collectors' items. Painted and mounted knights only 6 inches high can cost up to £1,200 (though figures start at a mere £7.50 for a toy soldier). Besides lead and tin soldiers, the shop has regimental brooches, porcelain figures, military memorabilia, and military antiques. ⊠ *17 Piccadilly Arcade, St. James's* ☎ *020/7493–5082* ⊕ *www.armoury.co.uk* ⊙ *Closed Sun.* Ⓜ *Piccadilly Circus.*

MAYFAIR AND MARYLEBONE

MAYFAIR
ACCESSORIES

Mulberry. Staying true to its roots in rural Somerset, this luxury goods company epitomizes *le style Anglais*, a sophisticated take on the earth-tones and practicality of English country style. Best-known for highly desirable luxury handbags such as the Alexa and the Bayswater, the company also produces gorgeous leather accessories, from wallets to luggage, as well as shoes and clothing. Aside from the New Bond Street flagship, there are branches in Knightsbridge and Covent Garden, and Mulberry concessions in most of the major department stores. The small store on St. Christopher's Place in Marylebone stocks accessories only. ⊠ *50 New Bond St., Mayfair* ☎ *020/7491–3900* ⊕ *www.mulberry. com* Ⓜ *Bond St.*

William & Son. William Asprey, scion of the jewelry dynasty, has opened his own store with a more friendly, less formal approach to selling carefully chosen, British-made luxury goods. Here's where you'll find all sorts of items you didn't know you needed, like silver-tipped retractable

Continued on page 385

TO MARKET, TO MARKET

Londoners love a good market. With their cluttered stalls and crowds of people, they are a visible reminder that, in this world of global chain stores and supermarkets, London is still, in many respects, an Old World European city.

Every neighborhood has its cluster of fruit, vegetable, and flower stalls, or its weekend car-boot sales—gigantic garage sales where ordinary people pay a fiver for the privilege of selling their castoffs. Some, like Broadway Market near London Fields, source locally whenever possible. Others, like Brixton Market, Europe's biggest Caribbean-food market, featuring more than 300 stalls, specialize in ethnic ingredients and products. Still others crop up in the most unexpected places: on Berwick Street in the heart of Soho, for example, media moguls, design-ers, ad execs, actors, and dancers, mingle over the punnets of strawberries, wedges of cheddar, and slabs of wet fish.

The big neighborhood markets, tradi-tionally open on weekends, are not only great for the occasional bargain but also for people-watching, photo ops, and all around great days out. And though the markets are popular with visitors, they aren't tourist traps. In fact, browsing the London markets is one of the few activities in London where natives and tourists mix and enjoy themselves as equals.

PORTOBELLO ROAD MARKET

⊙ **Mon.–Wed., Fri., and Sat. 8 am–6:30 pm, Thurs. 8 am–1 pm**

✉ Portobello Rd., Notting Hill W11

Ⓤ Ladbroke Grove (Hammersmith & City Line), Notting Hill (District, Circle, or Central Line)

☞ Antiques, fruits and vegetables, vintage and designer clothing, household goods

★ **Fodor's**Choice **London's most famous market** still wins the prize (according to some) for the all-around best. It sits in a lively multicultural part of town; the 1,500-odd antiques dealers don't rip you off (although you should haggle where you can); and it stretches over a mile, changing character completely as it goes.

The southern end, starting at Chepstow Villas, is lined with shops and stalls selling antiques and bric-a-brac; the middle, above Elgin Crescent, is where locals buy fruits and vegetables (weekends only). On Friday and Saturday the section near the elevated highway (called the Westway) has the best flea market in town, with vintage-clothing stores along the edges. Here, young designers sell their wares in and around the Portobello Green arcade. After that, the market trails off into a giant rummage sale of the kinds of cheap household goods the British call tat.

Some say Portobello Road has become a bit of a tourist trap, but if you acknowledge that it's a circus and get into the spirit, it's a lot of fun. Perhaps you won't find many bargains, but this is such a cool part of town that just hanging out is a good enough excuse to come. There are some food and flower stalls throughout the week, but to see the market in full swing, Saturday is the only day to come, although fashion designers prefer Friday mornings.

A PORTOBELLO DAY

In good weather the market gets very crowded by midday, especially during the Saturday antiques market.

For a Londoner's day at Portobello, come as early as you can (7 am) and enjoy the market when the traders have time for a chat and you can actually get near the stalls.

By 10:30 you'll have seen plenty of the market and can stop for a late breakfast or brunch at the **Electric Brasserie** (✉ 191 Portobello Rd. ☎ 020/7908–9696), next to the area's famous Electric Cinema.

If you still have the will to shop, move on to the less crowded boutiques along Westbourne Grove, Blenheim Crescent, or Ledbury Road.

BOROUGH MARKET

🕐 **Thurs. 8–5, Fri. noon–4:30, Sat. 9–4**

✉ E Borough High St., Borough SE1 1TL

Ⓤ London Bridge (Jubilee or Northern Line),

☞ Cheese, olives, coffee, baked goods, meats, fish, fruits, vegetables

★ **There's been a market** in Borough since Roman times. This one, spread under the arches and railway tracks leading to London Bridge Station, is the descendant of a medieval market once held on London Bridge.

Post-millennium, it has been transformed from a noisy collection of local stalls to a trendy foodie center.

With a reputation as the best food market in London, the Farmers Market held on Thursdays, Fridays and Saturdays has attracted some of London's best merchants of comestibles.

Fresh coffees, gorgeous cheeses, olives, jams, terrines, and baked goods complement the organically farmed meats, fresh fish, fruit, and veggies.

Don't make any other lunch plans for the day; celebrity chef Jamie Oliver's scallop man cooks them up fresh from the Dorset coast at Shell Seekers; wild boar sausages sizzle on a grill, and there is much more that's tempting to gobble on the spot.

There are chocolates, preserves, and Burnt Sugar's fudge, but the best souvenirs are the memories.

If you'd rather eat sitting down, pop into the sleek restaurant Roast, which specializes in local seasonal food—much of it purchased at the market.

A BARGAIN DAY ON THE SOUTH BANK

Combine a visit to the Tate Modern (free) and a walk across the Millennium Bridge from the Tate to St. Paul's with a Thames-side picnic of goodies foraged at Borough Market. There are gourmet breads and farmhouse cheeses from France and Italy.

Or how about a wedge of Stinking Bishop cheese (Wallace and Gromit's favorite) from Neal's Yard Dairy? Fishmonger Applebee's serves up freshly sautéed garlic prawns in a wrap with chili and crème fraîche.

A PUB RIGHT OUT OF DICKENS

On the way back to Borough Tube station, stop for a pint at the **George Inn** (✉ 77 Borough High St., Southwark SE1 ☎ 020/7407–2056 Ⓤ London Bridge), mentioned by Dickens in *Little Dorrit*. This 17th-century coaching inn was a famous terminus in its day, and is the last galleried inn in London. Now owned by the National Trust, it is leased to a private company and still operates as a pub.

THE EAST END MARKETS

Brick Lane. The noisy center of the Bengali community is a hubbub of buying and selling. Sunday stalls have food, hardware, household goods, electrical goods, books, bikes, shoes, clothes, spices, and saris. The salt beef at Beigel Bake, a survivor of the neighborhood's Jewish past, may be kosher, but the DVDs may not be entirely legitimate, and the bargain iron may not have a plug—so be careful. But people come more to enjoy the ethnic buzz by eating curries or Bengali sweets. Brick Lane's activity spills over into nearby Petticoat Lane Market with similar goods but with less atmosphere.

From Brick Lane it's a stone's throw to the **Columbia Road Flower Market**. Markets don't get much more photogenic than this street lined with some 60 quirky shops plus, on Sundays, 52 stalls selling flowers, shrubs, bulbs, and trees. About half a mile north is Broadway Market, which on Saturdays becomes north London's answer to Borough Market.

Stop to smell the roses and have Sunday brunch on Columbia Road before plunging into **Spitalfields Market**. This restored Victorian market hall is at the center of this area's gentrified revival. The original building is now largely occupied by boutiques, with traders' stalls relegated to the courtyard and an adjoining, glass-canopied modern shopping precinct. Wares include crafts, retro clothing, handmade rugs, soap, cakes. And, from Spanish tapas to Thai satays, it's possible to eat your way around the world.

BRICK LANE
🕑 Sun. 9 am–5 pm

✉ Brick La., Spitalfields

Ⓤ Shoreditch High Street (London Overground), Aldage East (Hammersmith & City, Circle or Central Line)

☞ Food, hardware, household goods, electric goods, books, bikes, shoes, clothes, spices, saris

COLUMBIA ROAD FLOWER MARKET
🕑 Sun. 8 am–3 pm

✉ Columbia Rd., Shoreditch E2 7RG

Ⓤ Old Street (Northern Line), Hoxton (London Overground)

☞ Flowers, shrubs, bulbs, trees, garden tools, accessories

SPITALFIELDS
🕑 Stalls weekdays 10–5, Sun. 9–5.
Restaurants weekdays 8 am–11 pm, weekends 9–11.
Retail shops daily 10–7.

✉ Brushfield St., Spitalfields

Ⓤ Liverpool St. (Central, Hammersmith & City, District, Circle, Metropolitan, or Central Line), Shoreditch High Street (London Overground)

☞ Crafts, foods, retro and modern clothing, rugs, vintage vinyl

BERMONDSEY ANTIQUES MARKET

Come before dawn and bring a flashlight to bag a bargain antique at this famous market. Dealers arrive as early as 4 AM to snap up the best bric-a-brac and silverware, paintings, objets d'art, China, and furniture. The early start grew out of a wrinkle in the law under which thieves could sell stolen goods with impunity in the hours of darkness when provenance could not be ascertained. That law was changed, and the market has been shrinking ever since.

The disappearance of nearby antiques warehouses and the rise of online auctions have contributed to the market's declining fortunes. However, its new (since 2009) location in Bermondsey Square (⊕ www.bermondseysquare.co.uk), a modern development that includes a hotel, an arthouse cinema, and restaurants, along with the general regeneration of the area, have improved its prospects.

🕐 Fri. 4 am–about 1 pm

✉ Long La. and Bermondsey Sq., Bermondsey SE1 4QB

Ⓤ London Bridge (Jubilee or Northern Line), Borough (Nothern Line)

☞ Antiques (silverware, paintings, furniture, China)

THE CAMDEN MARKETS

The U.K.'s largest street market is actually several markets gathered around a pair of locks in the Regent's Canal. Camden Lock Market proper began in 1973 on the site of a former timber yard. The lock studios attracted artists with reasonable rents and gave customers the chance to see goods being made. Today, the stalls at Camden Market still offer individually-crafted items along with a spectacular array of merchandise: vintage and new clothes, antiques and junk, accessories, and toys.

The markets on Camden High Street (both outdoors and within the Electric Ballroom) mainly sell cheap T-shirts, secondhand clothes, and tacky pop-culture paraphernalia with an emphasis on punk and goth; it's best to head to Camden Lock Market and Stable Markets. Though much of the merchandise is youth oriented, the markets have a lively appeal to aging hippies, fashion designers, and anyone with a taste for the bohemian who doesn't mind crowds and a bit of a madhouse scene. Don't miss the Horse Hospital (weekends only) for quirky antiques dealers.

CAMDEN MARKET
🕐 **Daily 9:30 am–6 pm**

CAMDEN CANAL MARKET (CAMDEN LOCK VILLAGE)
🕐 **Weekends 10–6**

ELECTRIC BALLROOM
🕐 **Sun. 10–5**

✉ Camden Town, Camden NW1

Ⓤ Camden Town, Chalk Farm (Northern Line)

☞ Vintage clothing, antiques, jewelry, shoes, mirrors, toys

IN FOCUS TO MARKET, TO MARKET

18

THE GREENWICH MARKET

On Wednesday and weekends, the focus is on crafts and food, while on Tuesday, Thursday, and Friday it's on antiques: china, old books, cameras, vintage clothing, marine memorabilia, and other curiosities. On weekends, the Village Market down the road offers yet more flea-market miscellany and cheap goods. Less crowded than Camden, less touristy than Covent Garden, this part-indoor, part-outdoor market is surrounded by interesting shops and close to historic sites. If you make a day of it, you can see the Greenwich Observatory, stand on Longitude 0 (marked in brass and stone in front of the observatory), and visit the restored Cutty Sark, the last surviving 19th Century tea clipper.

🕐 **Tues.–Sun. 10 am–5:30 pm**

✉ Greenwich Market (off Greenwich Church St.), Greenwich SE10 9HZ

Ⓤ DLR: Cutty Sark for Maritime Greenwich

☞ Antiques, arts, crafts, food, jewelry, clothing, leather goods, books, toys paraphernalia

Know-How

■ **TWO MARKET TIPS TO REMEMBER →** In the end, if you like something and you can afford it, it's worth buying; you're the best judge of that. But it's annoying to buy an "English antique" only to find the Made in China label when you get home. To avoid disappointment:

Look for hallmarks. A lot of what passes for English silver is plate or outright fake. English gold and silver must, by law, be marked with hallmarks that indicate their material and the year in which they were made. Books of hallmarks are inexpensive to buy in London bookshops.

Buy crafts items directly from the makers. Ceramicists, jewelers, clothing designers and other artisans often sell their own work at markets. Besides buying the item, you may have a conversation worth remembering.

■ **MARKET ETIQUETTE →** You've probably heard that you're expected to bargain with the market traders to get the best price. That's true to a degree, but London markets

are not Middle Eastern souks, and most bargaining is modest. Unless you are an expert in the item you want to buy and really know how low you can go, don't offer a ridiculously low price. Instead ask the dealer, "Is that the best you can do?" If the dealer is willing to bargain, he or she will suggest a slightly lower price, maybe 10% less. You might try to get another 10% off and end up meeting in the middle.

LONDON SHOPPING STEALS AND DEALS

Even at the best of times London has never been known as a budget-shopping destination, and when the pound is strong prices can seem stratospheric. However, whatever the exchange rate, there are still bargains to be had as long as you know where, and when, to look. To get the maximum mileage out of your cash, visit during the widespread biannual sales, which kick off in late June and just after Christmas, and last about a month.

Fashion insiders attend the many sales held throughout the year, from big warehouse clearances, such as the Designer Warehouse Sales (⊕ www.designerwarehousesales. com) and Designer Sales UK (⊕ www. designersales.co.uk), to individual designers' sample sales—check out ⊕ www.fashionconfidential.co.uk

or *Time Out* (⊕ www.timeout.com) for information, and to register for updates. London outlets, such as Browns Labels for Less, Paul Smith Sale Shop, and the Joseph Sale Shop on King's Road offer year-round designer bargains. If time permits, travel outside London to Bicester Village (⊕ www.bicestervillage.com), a luxury outlet mall in Oxfordshire. It's completely worth the nearly one-hour train journey, if only for the opportunity to score an item from such highly coveted British brands as Alexander McQueen, Temperley, Mulberry, Burberry, and Aquascutum, as well as top international labels.

If you're not fussy about labels, there are even more choices, including Pokit and Primark (⇨ *see Soho listings*).

18

pencils, lizard-skin passport holders, crocodile backgammon sets, or a silver piggy bank. The jewelry is tasteful rather than knock-your-eyes-out, and the store encourages requests for custom-made pieces. ⊠ *10 Mount St., Mayfair* ☎ *020/7493–8385* ⊕ *www.williamandson. com* ⏱ *Closed weekends* Ⓜ *Bond St.*

ANTIQUES

Grays Antique Market. Open weekdays from 10 to 6 and from 11 to 5 on Saturday (when not all stalls are open), Grays has approximately 200 dealers specializing in everything from Bakelite homeware to Mughal art. The majority focus on jewelry, ranging from contemporary to antique. Bargains are not out of the question, and proper pedigrees are guaranteed. Also try Grays in the Mews around the corner—stalls there sell less expensive merchandise, including antique dolls at Glenda's and excellent vintage clothing at Vintage Modes. ⊠ *58 Davies St., Mayfair* ☎ *020/7629–7034* ⊕ *www.graysantiques.com* ⏱ *Closed Sun.* Ⓜ *Bond St.*

BOOKS AND STATIONERY

Fodor's Choice **Heywood Hill.** Established for more than 70 years on Curzon Street, ★ and considered by some to be the best small bookstore in the English-speaking world (John Le Carré and Larry McMurtry are longstanding customers), Heywood Hill stocks both new and antiquarian books. Here's where you can pick up a leather-bound volume on architecture, gardening, natural history, and topography—in which the antiquarian collection specializes. The contemporary selection emphasizes literature, history, biography, travel, architecture, and children's books. During World War I, author Nancy Mitford helped keep the bookstore going. Today, the descendant of her brother-in-law, the Duke of Devonshire, remains the major stockholder. ✉ *10 Curzon St., Mayfair* ☎ *020/7629–0627* ⊕ *www.heywoodhill.com* ✆ *Closed Sun.* Ⓜ *Green Park.*

> ## BESPOKE LONDON
>
> Having anything made to order used to be restricted to the upper class. One had one's tailor, one's milliner, one's dressmaker, and so forth. Things are more egalitarian these days, but whether you want a custom-made Savile Row suit or handmade leather shoes, the price is steep.

Maggs Brothers Ltd. How could any book lover resist a shop with such a deliciously Dickensian name? Located in a Georgian town house in one of Mayfair's most elegant squares, Maggs, established 1853, is one of the world's oldest and largest rare-book dealers. Shop staff is expert enough to advise important collectors, but is nonetheless friendly and helpful to all interested visitors. ✉ *50 Berkeley Sq., Mayfair* ☎ *020/7493–7160* ⊕ *www.maggs.com* ✆ *Closed weekends* Ⓜ *Green Park.*

Smythson of Bond Street. Hands down, this is the most elegant stationer in Britain. No hostess of any standing would consider having a leather-bound guest book made by anyone else, and the shop's distinctive pale-blue–page diaries and social stationery are thoroughly British. Diaries, stationery, and small leather goods can be personalized. Smythson also produces a small range of leather handbags and purses. You'll find other branches in Chelsea, Notting Hill, and the City. ✉ *40 New Bond St., Mayfair* ☎ *020/7629–8558* ⊕ *www.smythson.com* Ⓜ *Bond St., Oxford Circus.*

Waterstone's. At this mega-bookshop (Europe's largest) located in a former art deco department store near Piccadilly Circus, browse through your latest purchase or admire the view while sipping a glass of bubbly or getting a bite to eat at the sixth-floor Champagne and Seafood Bar, which is open until 9. Waterstone's is the country's leading book chain, and they've pulled out all the stops to make their flagship as comfortable and welcoming as a bookstore can be. There are several smaller branches located throughout the city. ✉ *203–206 Piccadilly, Mayfair* ☎ *0843/290–8549* ⊕ *www.waterstones.com* Ⓜ *Piccadilly Circus.*

CLOTHING

Burberry. Known for its trademark tartan, this company has cultivated an edgy, high-fashion image in recent years, with designs like fetish-y boots and sexy leather jackets perfect for any catwalk. The raincoats are still a classic buy, along with plaid scarves in every color imaginable and handbags. If you're up for a trek, there's a huge factory outlet in Hackney on Chatham Place that has clothes and accessories for men, women, and children at half price or less. There are also branches in Mayfair, Knightsbridge, and Covent Garden, in addition to this spectacular new flagship store. ✉ *121 Regent St., Mayfair* ☎ *020/7806–8904* ⊕ *uk.burberry.com* Ⓜ *Piccadilly Circus.*

If you want to keep up with the Windsors' latest fashions, head to the designers in St. James's and Mayfair.

18

Dover Street Market. Visiting this six-floor emporium isn't just about buying; with its creative displays and eclectic, well-chosen mix of merchandise, it's as much art installation as store. The creation of Comme des Garçons' Rei Kawakubo, it showcases all of the label's collections for men and women alongside a changing roster of other designers including Erdem, Alaia, and YSL—all of whom have their own customized mini-boutiques—plus avant-garde art books, vintage couture, and curiosities such as antique plaster anatomy models. With merchandise and configuration changing every six months, you never know what you will find, which is half the fun. ▥TIP➔ An outpost of the Rose Bakery on the top floor makes for a yummy break. ✉ *17–18 Dover St., Mayfair* ☎ *020/7518–0680* ⊕ *www.doverstreetmarket.com* ☽ *Closed Sun.* Ⓜ *Green Park.*

Mackintosh. Think of Victorian and you think of corsets, bodices, and frock coats—but did you know that the era also created the modern rubberized raincoat? Back in 1823, a Glasgow chemist named Mackintosh successfully came up with the way to interweave rubber with cloth and, in so doing, finally designed rainproof clothes (then used for horseback riding), to the extent that the brand name became synonymous with the item. This byword for tradition has now been revitalized with designs that infuse the label's classic outerwear with contemporary zing. ✉ *104 Mount St., Mayfair* ☎ *020/7493–4678* ⊕ *www.mackintosh-uk.net* ☽ *Closed Sun.* Ⓜ *Bond St.*

CLOTHING: MENSWEAR

Gieves and Hawkes. One of the grand men's tailoring houses of Savile Row, this company made its name outfitting British Royals who served as officers in the armed forces and still supplies custom-made military uniforms, as well as beautifully tailored civilian wear. Prices for a bespoke suit start around £3,800 but there are also off-the-peg designs starting at around £600. ⊠ *1 Savile Row, Mayfair* ☎ *020/7434–2001* ⊕ *www.gievesandhawkes.com* Ⓜ *Piccadilly Circus.*

Fodor's Choice ★ **Ozwald Boateng.** The dapper menswear by Ozwald Boateng (pronouned Bwa-teng) combines contemporary funky style with traditional Savile Row quality. His made-to-measure suits have been worn by trend-setters such as Jamie Foxx, Mick Jagger, and Laurence Fishburne, who appreciate the sharp cuts, luxurious fabrics, and occasionally vibrant colors (even the more conservative choices sport jacket linings in bright silk). ⊠ *30 Savile Row, Mayfair* ☎ *020/7437–2030* ⊕ *www.ozwaldboateng. co.uk* ⊘ *Closed Sun.* Ⓜ *Piccadilly Circus.*

CLOTHING: WOMEN'S WEAR

Fodor's Choice ★ **Alexander McQueen.** Since McQueen's untimely death in 2010, his right-hand woman Sarah Burton has been at the helm, receiving raves for continuing his tradition of theatrical, darkly romantic, and beautifully cut clothes incorporating corsetry, lace, embroidery, and hourglass silhouettes, all of which were exemplified in Burton's celebrated wedding dress for Kate Middleton. Can't afford a gala gown? Go home with a skull-printed scarf. ⊠ *4–5 Old Bond St., Mayfair* ☎ *020/7355–0088* ⊕ *www.alexandermcqueen.com* Ⓜ *Bond St.*

Fodor's Choice ★ **Browns.** This shop—actually a collection of small shops—was a pioneer designer boutique in the 1970s and continues to talent-spot the newest and best around. You may find the windows showcasing the work of top graduates from this year's student shows or displaying well-established designers such as Marni, Chloé, Dries Van Noten, or Temperley. The men's store at No. 23 has a similar designer selection, while Browns Focus, across the street at Nos. 38–39, showcases youthful, hip designs and denim. There is a bargain outlet in Marylebone and a smaller boutique on Sloane Street. If you're about to go down the aisle, check out the two bridal boutiques; one at 12 Hinde Street, which stocks various designers, and another at 59 Brook Street devoted to Vera Wang gowns exclusive to Browns in the U.K. ⊠ *24–27 South Molton St., Mayfair* ☎ *020/7514–0000* ⊕ *www.brownsfashion.com* ⊘ *Closed Sun.* Ⓜ *Bond St.*

Fenwick. A manageably sized department store, Fenwick is a welcome haven of affordability in a shopping area where stratopheric prices are the norm. The store is particularly strong on accessories (notably lingerie, wraps, and hats), cosmetics, perfumes and chic, wearable fashion by both established and emerging designers such as Issa and Richard Nicholl. There are also three small spas (Chantecaille, Clarins, and Pure Massage), a nail bar, a brow bar, and a restaurant, plus a men's department in the basement. ⊠ *163 New Bond St., Mayfair* ☎ *020/7629–9161* ⊕ *www.fenwick.co.uk* Ⓜ *Bond St.*

Matthew Williamson. Sinuous, feminine, and floaty, Williamson's designs, often incorporating bright prints and embellishment, are the epitome of rich-hippie chic, and are favorites with such well-heeled free spirits as Kate Moss and Sienna Miller. Even if you can't manage to get to a beach party on Ibiza, a Williamson dress will put you in the spirit. ✉ *28 Bruton St., Mayfair* ☎ *020/7629–6200* ⊕ *www.matthewwilliamson. com* ☼ *Closed Sun.* Ⓜ *Bond St.*

Nicole Farhi. Busy working women who value unfussy quality invest in Farhi's softly tailored yet functional dresses and separates, and her contemporary yet timeless styles are wardrobe staples. This flagship Conduit Street store sells clothes for both men and women as well as shoes and homeware. There are also branches in Covent Garden, Fulham, and Hampstead. ✉ *25 Conduit St., Mayfair* ☎ *020/7499–8368* ⊕ *www.nicolefarhi.com* Ⓜ *Bond St.*

Fodor's Choice ★ **Stella McCartney.** It's not easy emerging from the shadow of a Beatle father, but Stella McCartney has become a major force in fashion in her own right. Her signature jumpsuits and tuxedo pantsuits embody her design philosophy, combining minimalist tailoring with femininity and sophistication with ease of wear. Her love of functionality and clean lines has led to her branching off into sportswear, designing a line for Adidas and dressing Team GB for the London Olympics. A vegetarian like her mother Linda, she refuses to use fur or leather, making her a favorite with ethical fashionistas. There's another boutique on the Brompton Road. ✉ *30 Bruton St., Mayfair* ☎ *020/7518–3100* ⊕ *www. stellamccartney.com.uk* Ⓜ *Bond St.*

Vivienne Westwood. From beginnings as the most shocking and outré designer around, Westwood has become a standard bearer for high-style British couture. The Chelsea boutique is where it all started: the lavish corseted ball gowns, the dandyfied nipped-waist jackets, and the tartan with a punk edge that formed the core of her signature look. Here you can still buy ready-to-wear, mainly the more casual Anglomania diffusion line and the exclusive Worlds End label based on the archives. The small Davies Street boutique sells only the more exclusive, expensive Gold Label and Couture collections (plus bridal), while the flagship Conduit Street store carries all of the above. ✉ *44 Conduit St., Mayfair* ☎ *020/7439–1109* ⊕ *www.viviennewestwood.co.uk* ☼ *Closed Sun.* Ⓜ *Oxford Circus* ✉ *World's End Shop, 430 King's Rd., Chelsea* ☎ *020/7352–6551* ⊕ *www.worldsendshop.co.uk* ☼ *Closed Sun.* Ⓜ *West Brompton.*

18

DEPARTMENT STORES

Fodor's Choice ★ **Liberty.** The wonderful black-and-white mock-Tudor facade, created from the timbers of two Royal Navy ships, reflects this store's origins in the late-19th-century's Arts and Crafts movement. Leading designers were recruited from this and the Aesthetic movement to create the classic art nouveau Liberty prints that are still a centerpiece of the brand, gracing everything from cushions and silk kimonos to embossed leather bags and photo albums. Inside, Liberty's is a labyrinth of nooks and crannies stuffed with thoughfully chosen merchandise. The carpets and furniture departments are worth a look even if you're not buying.

Clothes for both men and women focus on high quality and high fashion. The store regularly commissions new prints from contemporary designers, and sells both these and its archival patterns by the yard. If you're not so handy with a needle, an interior design service will create soft furnishings for you. ⊠ *Regent St., Soho* ☎ *020/7734–1234* ⊕ *www. liberty.co.uk* Ⓜ *Oxford Circus.*

Thomas Goode. This spacious luxury homeware shop has been at the same smart Mayfair address since 1845. The china, silver, crystal, and linens are either of the store's own design and manufacture or are simply the best that money can buy, a legacy of its original customer base of international royals and heads of state. The store still holds two royal warrants, but anyone who can afford it can commission their own bespoke set of china. ■TIP➔ If such luxury is beyond you, visit anyway for the shop's small museum of plates, either antique or designed for royalty, including some created for Princess Diana's wedding. ⊠ *19 South Audley St., Mayfair* ☎ *020/7499–2823* ⊕ *www.thomasgoode. co.uk* Ⓜ *Green Park.*

FOOD

Charbonnel et Walker. Established in 1875, this master chocolatier's Mayfair shop specializes in traditional handmade chocolates (violet and rose-petal creams, for example) and has been creating these beautifully packaged, high-quality sweets from long before most of today's fashionable brands appeared. ■TIP➔ Their drinking chocolate—coarsely grated fine chocolate in a tin—is worth carrying home in a suitcase. ⊠ *The Royal Arcade, 28 Old Bond St., Mayfair* ☎ *020/7491–0939* ⊕ *www.charbonnel.co.uk* ⊘ *Closed Sun.* Ⓜ *Green Park.*

JEWELRY

Asprey. Created by architect Norman Foster and interior designer David Mlinaric, this "global flagship" store displays exquisite jewelry—as well as silver and leather goods, watches, china, and crystal—in a discreet, very British setting that oozes quality, expensive good taste, and hushed comfort. If you're in the market for an immaculate 1930s cigarette case, a crystal vase, or a pair of pavé diamond and sapphire earrings, you won't be disappointed. And, for the really well-heeled, there's a custom-made jewelry service available as well. ⊠ *167 New Bond St., Mayfair* ☎ *020/7493–6767* ⊕ *www.asprey.com* Ⓜ *Green Park.*

Garrard. Formally known as "Garrard, the Crown Jeweler," this company has been creating royal crowns since Queen Victoria's reign (you can see several on display in the Tower of London). Today the focus is on precious gems in simple, classic settings, along with silver accessories. Although some collections, such as Entanglement and Wings (minimalist hoop earrings and pendants with a wing motif), are definitely contemporary, many of the designs are traditional and impressive, should you be in the market for an old-school diamond tiara. ⊠ *24 Albemarle St., Mayfair* ☎ *020/7518–1070* ⊕ *www.garrard.com* Ⓜ *Green Park.*

SHOES

Fodor's Choice ★ **Nicholas Kirkwood.** You won't be able to hike in Kirkwood's imaginative, elegant, sky-high stilettos, but you will be able to make quite an entrance. Pick up something from the creative shoemaker's own line, his collaborations with designers Rodarte and Peter Pilotto, or even one of the 12 designs inspired by artist Keith Haring at Kirkwood's first retail boutique. ⊠ *5 Mount St., Mayfair* ☎ *020/7290–1404* ⊕ *www. nicholaskirkwood.com* ☉ *Closed Sun.* Ⓜ *Green Park.*

Fodor's Choice ★ **Rupert Sanderson.** Designed in London and made in Italy, Sanderson's elegant shoes have been a huge hit in fashion circles. Ladylike styles, bright colors, smart details, and a penchant for peep toes are signature elements. Prices reflect the impeccable craftsmanship. There's now a tiny outpost next to Harrods at 2A Hans Road. ⊠ *19 Bruton Pl., Mayfair* ☎ *0207/491–2260* ⊕ *www.rupertsanderson.com* ☉ *Closed Sun.* Ⓜ *Bond St., Green Park.*

MARYLEBONE

ANTIQUES

Fodor's Choice ★ **Alfie's Antique Market.** This four-story, bohemian-chic labyrinth is London's largest indoor antiques market, housing dealers specializing in art, lighting, glassware, textiles, jewelry, furniture, and collectibles, with a particular strength in vintage clothing and 20th-century design. Come here to pick up Victorian and Edwardian clothes and textiles at Melinda Colthurst, 19th- and 20th-century furniture and decorative objects from Christopher, or a spectacular mid-20th-century Italian lighting fixture at Vincenzo Caffarrella. There's also a rooftop restaurant if you need a coffee break. In addition to the market, this end of Church Street is lined with excellent antiques shops. ⊠ *13–25 Church St., Marylebone* ☎ *020/7723–6066* ⊕ *www.alfiesantiques.com* ☉ *Closed Sun. and Mon.* Ⓜ *Marylebone.*

BOOKS

Daunt Books. An independent bookstore chain (there are additional branches in Belsize Park, Chelsea, Hampstead, Holland Park, and Cheapside), Daunt favors a thoughtful selection of contemporary and classic fiction and nonfiction over self-help books and ghost-written celebrity "autobiographies." It is especially noted for its travel selection, which includes not only guidebooks but also relevant poetry and literature organized by country, and childrens' books. The striking Marylebone branch is an original Edwardian bookstore where a dramatic room lined with oak galleries under lofty skylights houses the travel section. Meanwhile, biographies and fiction are piled on tables at the entrance for eclectic browsing. ⊠ *83 Marylebone High St., Marylebone* ☎ *020/7224–2295* ⊕ *www.dauntbooks.co.uk* Ⓜ *Baker St.*

CERAMICS

Emma Bridgewater. Here's where you'll find fun and funky casual plates, mugs, jugs, and breakfast tableware embellished with polka dots, hens, hearts and flowers, amusing mottoes, or matter-of-fact labels (sugar or coffee). There's another branch in Fulham. ⊠ *81a Marylebone High St., Marylebone* ☎ *020/7486–6897* ⊕ *www.emmabridgewater.co.uk* Ⓜ *Regent's Park.*

18

CLOTHING

Matches. The rising British designers featured in this carefully curated boutique include Christopher Kane, Jonathan Saunders, Issa, and Goat, as well as more-established figures like McCartney and McQueen and international labels such as J Brand, Acne, Vanessa Bruno, Lanvin, and Chloe. There's also an equally stylish menswear department, plus jewelry, lingerie, and accessories. Other branches are in Notting Hill and southwest London. ⊠ *87 Marylebone High St., Marylebone* ☎ *020/7487–5400* ⊕ *www.matchesfashion.com* Ⓜ *Regent's Park, Baker St.*

DEPARTMENT STORES

Marks & Spencer. You'd be hard-pressed to find a Brit who doesn't have something in the closet from Marks & Spencer (or "M&S," as it's affectionately known). This major chain is known for its classic, dependable clothing for men, women, and children—affordable cashmere and lambswool sweaters are particularly good buys—and occasionally scores a fashion hit with its Per Una and Autograph lines. The food department at M&S is consistently superb, especially for frozen food, and a great place to pick up a sandwich or premade salad on the go (look for M&S Simply Food stores all over town). The flagship branch at Marble Arch and the Pantheon location at 173 Oxford Street have extensive fashion departments. ⊠ *458 Oxford St., Marylebone* ☎ *020/7935–7954* ⊕ *www.marksandspencer.com* Ⓜ *Marble Arch.*

Fodor's Choice ★ **Selfridges.** This giant, bustling store (the second-largest in the U.K. after Harrods) gives Harvey Nichols a run for its money as London's most fashionable department store. Packed to the rafters with clothes ranging from midprice lines to the latest catwalk names, the store continues to break ground with its innovative retail schemes, especially the high-fashion Superbrands section, the ground-floor Wonder Room showcasing extravagant jewelry and luxury gifts, and the Concept Store, which features a rotating series of themed displays. There are so many zones that merge into one another—from youth-oriented Miss Selfridge to audio equipment to the large, comprehensive cosmetics department—that you practically need a map. Don't miss the Shoe Galleries, the world's largest shoe department filled with more than 5,000 pairs from 120 brands, displayed like works of art under spotlights. ▓TIP➔ Take a break with a glass of wine from the Wonder Bar, or pick up some rare tea in the Food Hall as a gift. ⊠ *400 Oxford St., Marylebone* ☎ *0800/123–400* ⊕ *www.selfridges.com* Ⓜ *Bond St.*

JEWELRY

Fodor's Choice ★ **Kabiri.** A dazzling array of exciting contemporary jewelry by emerging and established designers from around the world is packed into this small shop. There is something to suit most budgets and tastes, from flamboyant statement pieces to subtle, delicate adornment. Look out for British talent Johanne Mills, among many others. There's another branch in Chelsea. ⊠ *37 Marylebone High St., Marylebone* ☎ *020/7317–2150* ⊕ *www.kabiri.co.uk* Ⓜ *Baker St.*

HOUSEHOLD

Fodor's Choice ★ **Decoratum.** One of those chic little shops that is making Marylebone chicer by the hour, this extraordinary place has been in the secret "little black books" of the world's design glitterati for years. It is deliberately set up like an art gallery—you're encouraged to come to look and admire, although everything is for sale (the price tags are hefty and can hit six figures). The shop specializes in high-end 20th-century art, furniture, and design, although they also showcase work by hot new talents. ✉ *31–33 Church St., Marylebone* ☎ *020/7724–6969* ⊕ *www.decoratum.com* ◷ *Tues.–Sat. 10–6.*

SOHO AND COVENT GARDEN

SOHO

ACCESSORIES

Fodor's Choice ★ **Peckham Rye.** The epicenter of "Swinging London" in the mid-'60s has recently undergone a renaissance, particularly in the "Newburgh Quarter," the small cobblestone streets leading off Carnaby Street. Here's where you'll find small specialist boutiques such as Peckham Rye, a tiny bolt-hole showcasing heritage-style men's accessories—handmade silk and twill ties (the name is Cockney rhyming slang for same), bow ties, and scarves, all using traditional patterns from the archives of this family-run business that go back to 1799. More Ralph Lauren than Ralph Lauren, the socks, striped shirts, and handkerchiefs attract modern-day Beau Brummels such as Mark Ronson and David Beckham. ✉ *11 Newburgh St., Soho* ☎ *0207/734–5181* ⊕ *www.peckhamrye.com* Ⓜ *Oxford Street.*

BOOKS

Fodor's Choice ★ **Foyles.** Founded in 1903 by the Foyle brothers after they failed the Civil Service exam, this family-owned store, recently relocated into this historic 1930s Art Deco building, carries almost every title imaginable. One of London's best sources for textbooks, Foyles also stocks everything from popular fiction to military history, sheet music, medical tomes, graphic novels, and handsome illustrated fine arts books. It also offers the store-within-a-store Ray's Jazz (one of London's better outlets for music) and a cool café. Foyles has branches in the Southbank Centre, St. Pancras International train station (the Eurostar's U.K. terminus), and the Westfield shopping centers in Shepherd's Bush and Stratford. In 2014, they are planning a move right next door. ✉ *107–109 Charing Cross Rd., Soho* ☎ *020/7437–5660* ⊕ *www.foyles.co.uk* Ⓜ *Tottenham Court Rd.*

CLOTHING

Other. Aimed at men and women in search of stylish cool, this independent boutique stocks its own brand of entirely made-in-England clothing, as well as accessories, housewares, books, and clothing from other carefully selected brands such as b store, Opening Ceremony, Sophie Hulme, and Peter Jensen. The look is understated, slightly geeky, and totally contemporary. ✉ *21 Kingly St., Soho* ☎ *020/7734–6846* ⊕ *www.other-shop.com* Ⓜ *Oxford Circus.*

18

Pokit. Sharp but comfortable made-to-measure suits for men and women start from just £800 (jackets £500) at this contemporary tailor shop. It also has a wide range of leather goods. ⊠ *132 Wardour St., Soho* ☎ *020/7434–2875* ⊕ *www.pokit.co.uk.*

Primark. Fantastic for low-cost, trendy clothing, this is Primark's huge, two-story flagship (there are other branches in Hammersmith and Kilburn). But keep in mind, you get what you pay for: some of the fabrics and finishes reflect the store's budget prices. This is the home of fast, youthful, disposable fashion, so don't expect attentive service or classic styling and you won't be disappointed. ⊠ *499 Oxford St., Soho* ☎ *020/7495–0420* ⊕ *www.primark.co.uk* Ⓜ *Marble Arch.*

Reiss. With an in-house design team whose experience includes stints at Gucci and Calvin Klein and customers like Beyoncé and the Duchess of Cambridge (formerly Kate Middleton), who wore a Reiss dress for her official engagement picture, this hot chain brings luxury standards of tailoring and details to mass-market women's and menswear. The sleek and contemporary style is not cheap, but does offer value for money. There are branches in Knightsbridge, The City, Covent Garden, Chelsea, Hampstead, Notting Hill, Soho, and basically all over London. ⊠ *10 Barrett St., Fitzrovia* ☎ *020/7486–6557* ⊕ *www.reiss. com* Ⓜ *Oxford Street.*

Fodors Choice
★

Topshop. A hotspot for straight-from-the-runway affordable fashion, Topshop is destination shopping for teenagers and fashion editors alike. Clothes and accessories are geared to the youthful end of the market, although women who are young at heart and girlish of figure can find plenty of wearable items here. However, you will need a high tolerance for loud music and busy dressing rooms. The store also features collections designed by a rotating roster of high-end designers as well as offering its own premium designer line called Topshop Unique. Topman brings the same fast-fashion approach to clothing for men. ■ TIP➔ If the crowds become too much, head to one of the smaller Topshops in Kensington High Street, Knightsbridge, Victoria, Marble Arch, or Holborn. ⊠ *36–38 Great Castle Street, Fitzrovia* ☎ *0844/848–7487* ⊕ *www. topshop.com* Ⓜ *Oxford Circus*

MUSIC

BM Soho. House, drum 'n' bass, electro, dubstep—this shop (formerly Black Market Records) is London's longest-established dance music store and stocks the hottest club music around. They carry some CDs, but this is really a shop for vinyl lovers. ⊠ *25 D'Arblay St., Soho* ☎ *020/7437–0478* ⊕ *www.bm-soho.com* Ⓜ *Oxford Circus, Tottenham Court Rd.*

SHOES

Irregular Choice. If you want to blend in with the crowd, these shoes are not for you. But if you like footwear that is fun, quirky, and flattering (not to mention reasonably priced), head for Irregular Choice. Styles tend towards Louis XIV-like court shoes ornamented with ribbon ties or silk flowers, or pumps in interesting patterns ranging from polka dots to houndstooth to florals, as well as bejeweled flats, leopard-print boots, and red patent leather stilettoes. Best of all, many have round

Soho and Covent Garden have a mix of trendy boutiques and stylish chains.

toes and supportive heels, proving that comfortable doesn't have to be dull. There's another branch in Shoreditch. ⊠ *35 Carnaby St., Soho* ☎ *020/7494–4811* ⊕ *www.irregularchoice.com* Ⓜ *Oxford Circus.*

TOYS

FAMILY **Hamleys.** Besieged by pester power? Don't worry, help is at hand—this London institution has six floors of the latest dolls, soft toys, video games, and technological devices (plus such old-fashioned pleasures as train sets, drum kits, and magic tricks), with every must-have on the pre-teen shopping list. Some may find the offerings to be overly commercialized (it's heavy on movie and TV tie-ins), and the store only got rid of its separate pink and blue floors for girls and boys in 2011 after a protest campaign. Nevertheless, when British children visit London, Hamleys is at the top of their agenda. It's a madhouse at Christmastime, but Santa's grotto is one of the best in town. There's a smaller branch in St. Pancras International train station. ⊠ *188–196 Regent St., Soho* ☎ *0800/280–2444* ⊕ *www.hamleys.com* Ⓜ *Oxford Circus, Piccadilly Circus.*

COVENT GARDEN

BOOKS AND PRINTS

Fodor's Choice
★
Grosvenor Prints. London's largest collection of 17th- to early-20th-century prints emphasizes views of the city and architecture as well as sporting and decorative motifs. The selection is eclectic, with prices ranging from £5 into the thousands. ⊠ *19 Shelton St., Covent Garden* ☎ *020/7836–1979* ⊕ *www.grosvenorprints.com* ☉ *Closed Sun.* Ⓜ *Covent Garden, Leicester Sq.*

Fodor's Choice
★
Stanfords. When it comes to encyclopedic coverage, there is simply no better travel shop on the planet. Stanfords is packed with a comprehensive selection of maps, travel books, travel gadgets, globes, notebooks, replicas of antique maps, and more. Even the floor is decorated with giant maps. Whether you're planning a day trip to Surrey or an adventure to the South Pole, this should be your first stop. ⊠ *12–14 Long Acre, Covent Garden* ☎ *020/7836–1321* ⊕ *www.stanfords.co.uk* Ⓜ *Covent Garden.*

CLOTHING

Fodor's Choice
★
Paul Smith. British classics with an irreverent twist define Paul Smith's collections for women, men, and children. Beautifully tailored suits for men and women take hallmarks of traditional British style and turn them on their heads with humor and color, combining exceptional fabrics with flamboyant linings or unusual detailing. Gift ideas abound—wallets, scarves, diaries, spectacles, even a soccer ball—all in Smith's signature rainbow stripes. There are several branches throughout London, in Notting Hill, South Kensington, Chelsea, and Borough Market, plus a vintage furniture shop at 9 Albemarle Street in Mayfair and a shoes and accessories shop on Marylebone High Street. ⊠ *40–44 Floral St., Covent Garden* ☎ *020/7379–7133* ⊕ *www.paulsmith.co.uk* Ⓜ *Covent Garden.*

Poste Mistress. The Office chain's more glamorous sibling, this boudoir-styled boutique features fashion-forward but wearable styles from some 40 brands including Stella McCartney, Acne, and Miu Miu. Casual alternatives such as Vivienne Westwood rubber booties and Converse sneakers are also available, and prices are not eye-watering. There's a branch devoted to men's designer shoes at 10 South Moulton Street in Mayfair. ⊠ *61–63 Monmouth St., Covent Garden* ☎ *020/7379–4040* ⊕ *www.office.co.uk* Ⓜ *Covent Garden.*

Fodor's Choice
★
United Nude. Co-created by noted architect Rem D. Koolhaas (who also designed this Covent Garden flagship store) and Galahad Clark (of the Clark's shoes dynasty), these distinctive, futuristic designs that use up-to-the-minute techniques such as carbon fiber heels and injection-molded soles are flattering and surprisingly comfortable. There's another branch in Knightsbridge. ⊠ *13 Floral St., Covent Garden* ☎ *0207/240–7106* ⊕ *www.unitednude.com* Ⓜ *Covent Garden.*

HOUSEHOLD

Cath Kidston. If you love chintz and colorful patterns, then stop by Cath Kidston. Her signature look is bright, feminine textiles—ginghams, polka dots, and lots of big, blooming roses—pasted over everything in sight, from ceramics and bed linens to fine china, stationery, and doggie beds. There are several clothing and nightwear lines for women and children, along with handbags, totes, and cosmetic bags. Everything in this shop is basically a canvas for Kidston's ladylike prints. There are branches throughout the city, including ones in Chelsea, Marylebone, and Notting Hill. ⊠ *28–32 Shelton St., Covent Garden* ☎ *020/7240–8324* ⊕ *www.cathkidston.co.uk* Ⓜ *Covent Garden.*

BRING A BIT OF ENGLAND HOME

To avoid panic-buying a bulk pack of Cadbury chocolate at Heathrow, it's wise to plan your gift purchasing with care.

For a well-chosen, eclectic selection, unique department store Liberty is hard to beat—here you'll find everything from exquisite Miller Harris fragrances by British perfumer Lyn Harris to small leather goods embossed with the famous Liberty prints.

Fortnum & Mason has equally carefully curated, though perhaps more sedate, offerings, such as leather-covered hip flasks and model boats with Union Jack sails. The big attraction here is the world-famous food hall with its beautifully packaged cookies, teas, and unusual condiments. A. Gold is another source of British-made treats.

Looking for a gift for the hard-to-shop-for man in your life? Consider some traditional shaving cream from Geo. F. Trumper.

The museum shops are also bursting with original gift ideas, from Brit Art books and posters at Tate Modern to double-decker bus models and Tube-map mouse pads at the London Transport Museum in Covent Garden.

TOYS

FAMILY

Fodor's Choice
★

Benjamin Pollock's Toyshop. This landmark shop still carries on the tradition of its eponymous founder, who sold minature theater stages made from richly detailed paper from the late-19th century until his death in 1937. Among his admirers was Robert Louis Stevenson, who wrote, "If you love art, folly, or the bright eyes of children, speed to Pollock's." Today the antique model theaters tend to be expensive, but there are plenty of magical reproductions for under 10 pounds. There's also an extensive selection of new but nostalgic puppets, marionettes, teddy bears, spinning tops, jack-in-the-boxes, and similar traditional children's toys from the days before batteries were required. ✉ *44 Clare Market, The Piazza, Covent Garden* ☎ *020/7379–7866* ⊕ *www. pollocks-coventgarden.co.uk* Ⓜ *Covent Garden.*

18

BLOOMSBURY AND HOLBORN

BLOOMSBURY
ACCESSORIES
James Smith & Sons Ltd. This has to be the world's ultimate umbrella shop, and a must for anyone interested in real Victorian London. The family-owned shop has been in this location on a corner of New Oxford Street since 1857, and sells every kind of umbrella, cane, and walking stick imaginable. The interior is unchanged since the 19th century; you will feel as if you have stepped back in time. If the umbrellas are out of your price range, James Smith also sells smaller accessories and handmade wooden bowls. ✉ *Hazelwood House, 53 New Oxford St., Bloomsbury* ☎ *020/7836–4731* ⊕ *www.james-smith.co.uk* ☉ *Closed Sun.* Ⓜ *Tottenham Court Rd., Holborn.*

BOOKS

Gay's the Word. Open since 1979, this is London's leading gay and lesbian bookshop. Thousands of titles, from literature and thoughtful nonfiction, erotica to pro-diversity children's books, fill the shelves. The shop is a well-loved fixture on the scene, and often hosts discussion groups, readings, and other events. ⊠ *66 Marchmont St., Bloomsbury* ☎ *020/7278–7654* ⊕ *www.gaystheword.co.uk* ۞ *Closed Sun. morning* Ⓜ *Russell Sq.*

Persephone Books. A must for all lovers of women's fiction and nonfiction, Persephone is a gem of a bookshop specializing in reprints of mostly neglected 20th-century works from predominately female writers. Exquisitely decorated endpapers make these books perfect gifts for your bibliophile friends. ⊠ *59 Lamb's Conduit St., Bloomsbury* ☎ *020/7242–9292* ⊕ *www.persephonebooks.co.uk* ۞ *Closed Sun.* Ⓜ *Russell Sq., Holborn.*

SPECIALTY STORES

Blade Rubber. This unique shop near the British Museum specializes in rubber stamps, with everything from businesslike "Paid" stamps to Alice in Wonderland characters, Egyptian gods, VW Beetles, flying saucers, and more. Get a custom-made personal stamp—a great gift for a young person—or bring back an iconic double-decker bus stamp as a souvenir. It also carries scrapbooking materials. ⊠ *12 Bury Pl., Bloomsbury* ☎ *020/7831–4123* ⊕ *www.bladerubber.co.uk* Ⓜ *Holborn.*

HOLBORN

ANTIQUES

Fodor's Choice ★ **London Silver Vaults.** Housed in a basement vault, this extraordinary space holds stalls from more than 30 silver dealers. Products range from the spectacularly over-the-top costing thousands to smaller items—like teaspoons, candlesticks, or a set of Victorian cake forks—starting at £25. ▥**TIP➔** Most of the silver merchants actually trade out of room-size, underground vaults, which were originally rented out to London's upper crust to store their valuables. ⊠ *53–64 Chancery La., Holborn* ☎ *020/7242–3844* ⊕ *www.thesilvervaults.com* ۞ *Closed Sat. after 1 and Sun.* Ⓜ *Chancery La.*

ISLINGTON

HOUSEHOLD

TwentyTwentyOne. The best in modern and vintage furniture is showcased here. There are design classics like a chaise longue from Le Corbusier, as well as curvy daybeds from designer Jacob Pringiers. The kids' range is particularly cool, with items like the classic elephant sculpture/toy from husband-and-wife design team Charles and Ray Eames. Small accessories like tote bags and cushions will easily fit into your luggage. There's another branch in the City. ⊠ *274–275 Upper St., Islington* ☎ *020/7288–1996* ⊕ *www.twentytwentyone.com* Ⓜ *Highbury & Islington.*

THE CITY

JEWELRY

Fodor's Choice ★ **Lesley Craze Gallery.** This serene gallery displays unique jewelry by some 100 innovative designers from around the world (with a strong British bias). A textiles room showcases colorful handmade scarves. Prices start at £45. ☒ *33–35A Clerkenwell Green, Clerkenwell* ☎ *020/7608–0393* ⊕ *www.lesleycrazegallery.co.uk* ☉ *Closed Sun.; open Mon. in Nov. and Dec. only* Ⓜ *Farringdon.*

THE EAST END

ACCESSORIES: HATS

Fodor's Choice ★ **Bernstock Speirs.** Here since 1982, Paul Bernstock and Thelma Speirs turn traditional hats on their head with street-smart trilbies and knitted hats that feature unusual colors and quirky details. ☒ *234 Brick La., Spitalfields* ☎ *020/7739–7385* ⊕ *www.bernstockspiers.com* ☉ *Closed Mon.* Ⓜ *London Overground: Shoreditch High St.*

CLOTHING

Absolute Vintage. This is a warehouse of handpicked items from the 1930s through the 1980s, but the specialty here is shoes and bags. The shop has the largest collection of vintage shoes in the United Kingdom— more than 1,000 pairs—and, best of all, prices are reasonable. There's another branch on Berwick Street in Soho. ☒ *15 Hanbury St., Spitalfields* ☎ *020/7274–3883* ⊕ *www.absolutevintage.co.uk* Ⓜ *London Overground: Shoreditch High St.*

Beyond Retro. More than 10,000 vintage items for men and women, from cowboy boots to bowling shirts to prom dresses—it's got the largest collection of American retro in the United Kingdom. There's another outpost in Hoxton and one in Soho. ☒ *110–112 Cheshire St., Spitalfields* ☎ *020/7729–9001* ⊕ *www.beyondretro.com* Ⓜ *Whitechapel. London Overground: Shoreditch High St.*

Blitz. This vast former furniture factory, the world's first (self-proclaimed) "vintage department store," now has separate floors devoted to antiques and vintage clothing as well as period goods ranging from bikes to luggage. Look for racks filled with denim jackets, '80s Ralph Lauren, chunky ski sweaters, and Liberty shirts. ☒ *55 Hanbury St., Spitalfields* ☎ *020/7377–0730* ⊕ *www.blitzlondon.co.uk* Ⓜ *London Overground: Shoreditch High St.*

Hostem. Here's a place for the man who wants to be well dressed without looking like he's trying too hard. The interior here—a cross between the lounge of a private members' club and a basement rec room— mirrors Hostem's retail philosophy, which mixes luxury, casual street wear with future-forward fashion. Clothing from established names, including Rick Owens and Ann Demeulemeester, mixes with beautiful cashmere sweaters from newcomers like The Elder Statesmen. ☒ *41– 43 Redchurch St., Shoreditch* ☎ *020/7739–9733* ⊕ *www.hostem.co.uk* Ⓜ *London Overground: Shoreditch High St.*

Fodor's Choice ★ **Junky Styling.** This brand was launched by designers Annika Sanders and Kerry Seager, who used to "deconstruct" old clothing when they wanted

18

something unique to wear clubbing. They recycled traditional suits and shirts into wild outfits, and the business grew from there. Each piece is unique, and the highly original (and eco-friendly) garments, for both men and women, are funky but retain the sophistication of their tailored origins. ⊠ *21 Hackney Rd., Shoreditch* ☎ *020/7247–1883* ⊕ *www.junkystyling.co.uk* Ⓜ *Old St. London Overground: Hoxton, Shoreditch High St.*

Fodor's Choice ★ **The Laden Showroom.** Sienna Miller and Victoria Beckham are among the celebs who regularly check out emerging talent at this East End showroom for young designers. The store retails the work of more than 50 new designers, some selling one-off items—so the look you find is likely to be original. ⊠ *103 Brick La., Spitalfields* ☎ *020/7247–2431* ⊕ *www.laden.co.uk* Ⓜ *London Overground: Shoreditch High St.*

Rokit. Magazine and rock stylists love this place. It consists of two shops along Brick Lane that carry everything from handbags and ball gowns to jeans, military garb, and Western wear. The ever-changing stock spans the 1920s to the '90s. There are also branches in Camden and Covent Garden. ⊠ *101 and 107 Brick La., Spitalfields* ☎ *020/7375–3864* ⊕ *www.rokit.co.uk* Ⓜ *London Overground: Shoreditch High St.*

Start London. An ever-changing roster of cutting-edge designers like Rick Owens, Helmut Lang, and Alexander Wang is on offer here, and, for men (down the street at No. 59), everything from Comme des Garçons to Nudie Jeans. Although the emphasis is on chic directional fashion, co-owner and American expat Brix Smith-Start is more mother hen than formidable fashionista and is happy to gently guide customers into trying something new. ⊠ *42–44 Rivington St., Shoreditch* ☎ *020/7033–3951* ⊕ *www.start-london.com* Ⓜ *Old St. London Overground: Shoreditch High St.*

Sunspel. This British firm has been making fine men's underwear since the mid-19th century and it's still their specialty, along with luxury basics. Prince Charles is an actual customer and James Bond a fictional one (he wore their shorts in "Thunderball" and polo shirt in "Quantum of Solace"). They also carry elegant, minimalist T-shirts, sweaters, and sweats for women. There are also branches in Marylebone and Soho. ⊠ *7 Redchurch St., Shoreditch* ☎ *020/7739–9729* ⊕ *www.sunspel.com* Ⓜ *London Overground: Shoreditch High St.*

FOOD

A. Gold. All of the traditional or retro foodstuffs—such as bottles of mead, jars of London-produced honey, or handmade fudge—sold in this re-creation of a village shop, in an old milliner's premises, are British-made and make excellent portable presents. Stylish gift baskets and old-fashioned picnic hampers are available. ⊠ *42 Brushfield St., Spitalfields* ☎ *020/7247–2487* ⊕ *www.agoldshop.com* Ⓜ *London Overground: Shoreditch High St.*

HOUSEHOLD

Fodor'sChoice **Labour & Wait.** Although such household items as colanders and clothes-
★ pins may not sound like ideal souvenirs, this shop may make you reconsider. The owners are on a mission to revive functional, old-fashioned British goods, such as enamel kitchenware, "Brown Betty" glazed teapots, Guernsey sweaters, and vintage Welsh blankets. ⊠ *85 Redchurch St., Shoreditch* ☎ *020/7729–6253* ⊕ *www.labourandwait.co.uk* Ⓜ *London Overground: Shoreditch High St.*

Maison Trois Garçons. If your motto is too much ain't enough, you'll love this shrine to all things over the top. A mixture of antique, vintage, and contemporary pieces sourced in England, France, Sweden, and elsewhere, this eclectic interiors shop does not shy away from the roccoco, the opulent, and even the kitsch. But there's also plenty of lovely porcelain, glassware, mirrors, furniture, and light fixtures. And if you're looking for something more portable, you can pick up a unique candleholder, cushion, or photo frame. ⊠ *45 Redchurch St., Shoreditch* ☎ *07879/640858* ⊕ *www.lestroisgarcons.com/shop* Ⓜ *London Overground: Shoreditch High St.*

MUSIC

Fodor'sChoice **Rough Trade East.** While many London record stores are struggling, this
★ veteran indie-music specialist seems to have gotten the formula right. The spacious surroundings are as much a hangout as a shop, complete with a stage for live gigs, a café, and Internet access. There's another branch on Portobello Road in Notting Hill. ⊠ *Dray Walk, Old Truman Brewery, 91 Brick La., Spitalfields* ☎ *020/7392–7788* Ⓜ *Liverpool St. London Overground: Shoreditch High St.*

18

KENSINGTON, CHELSEA, KNIGHTSBRIDGE, AND BELGRAVIA

KENSINGTON
CLOTHING

Fodor'sChoice **Jigsaw.** Jigsaw specializes in clothes that are classic yet trendy, ladylike
★ without being dull. The style is epitomized by the former Kate Middleton, who was a buyer for the company before her marriage. The quality of fabrics and detailing bely the reasonable prices and cuts are kind to the womanly figure. Although there are numerous branches across London, no two stores are the same. The pre-teen set have their own line, Jigsaw Junior. ⊠ *The Chapel, Duke of York Sq., King's Rd., Chelsea* ☎ *020/730–4404* ⊕ *www.jigsawonline.com* Ⓜ *Sloane Sq.*

FAMILY **Marie-Chantal.** If you love beautiful, tasteful clothing for babies and children, head to this boutique created by Princess Marie-Chantal of Greece. As you'd imagine, the look is elegant and the prices are high. Materials used include silk, linen, and Liberty prints. There are other branches in Chelsea and Notting Hill. ⊠ *148 Walton St., South Kensington* ☎ *020/7838–1111* ⊕ *www.mariechantal.com* Ⓜ *South Kensington.*

Orsini. Designer fashion from the 1930s to '80s is the trademark at this tiny but desirable boutique, with big names like Pucci, Biba, and Alaïa at bargain prices. Victoria Beckham is a fan. ⊠ *76 Earl's Court Rd., Kensington* ☎ *020/7937–2903* ⊕ *www.orsinivintage.co.uk* Ⓜ *Earl's Court.*

HOUSEHOLD

Fodor's Choice ★ **Mint.** Owner Lina Kanafani has scoured the globe to curate an eclectic mix of conceptual statement furniture, art, ceramics, and home accessories. Mint also showcases works by up-and-coming designers and sells plenty of limited edition and one-off pieces. If you don't want to ship a couch home, consider a miniature flower vase or a handmade ceramic pitcher. ⊠ *2 North Terr., South Kensington* ☎ *020/7225–2228* ⊕ *www. mintshop.co.uk* Ⓜ *South Kensington.*

Skandium. Largely thanks to its thrillers and chefs, Scandanavia is having a moment in Britain. Skandium brings together many of the region's top designers of furniture, lighting, rugs, and homewares under one roof. Designers include Knoll, Fritz Hansen, Artek, and Design House Stockholm. Clean lines and stripped-back, unfussy elegance abounds (although the Moomins make an appearance on ceramics). ⊠ *245–249 Brompton Rd., South Kensington* ☎ *020/7584–2066* ⊕ *www.skandium. com* Ⓜ *South Kensington.*

CHELSEA
ACCESSORIES

The Shop at Bluebird. The brainchild of the couple behind popular womenswear brand Jigsaw, this 10,000-square-foot space in the old Bluebird garage brings together fashion, furniture, books, and music—all chosen for style and originality. It's worth visiting for the displays alone, which change regularly, although the funky ceiling-light installation of more than 1,000 bulbs seems to be a constant feature. After browsing, unwind with a treatment at the on-site spa or join the ladies who lunch at the restaurant in the same complex. ▮▮TIP➔ It's a good 20-minute walk from the nearest Tube station at Sloane Square, so catch a No. 11 or No. 22 bus along the King's Road. ⊠ *350 King's Rd., Chelsea* ☎ *020/7351–3873* ⊕ *www.theshopatbluebird.com* Ⓜ *Sloane Sq.*

ANTIQUES

Fodor's Choice ★ **Rupert Cavendish.** This most elevated of Chelsea dealers had the Biedermeier market cornered so has now expanded to Empire and art deco antiques. The shop is a museum experience. ⊠ *610 King's Rd., Fulham* ☎ *020/7731–7041* ⊕ *www.rupertcavendish.co.uk* Ⓜ *Fulham Broadway.*

BOOKS

Green & Stone. This fabulous cave of artists' materials, papers, art books, easels, and mannequins is one of the longest-established shops on the King's Road. It began life in 1927 as part of the Chenil Gallery, run by a distinguished group that included artist Augustus John and playwright George Bernard Shaw. At the current location since 1934, the shop also has a framing service, antique paint boxes, and artists' tools. ⊠ *259 King's Rd., Chelsea* ☎ *020/7352–0837* ⊕ *www.greenandstone. com* Ⓜ *Sloane Sq.*

Dream of British ultraluxury and you'll think of Chelsea, Kensington, and Knightsbridge, one of the most exclusive shopping areas in London.

CLOTHING

Austique. Fans of such trendy brands as Shoshanna, Alice + Olivia, or Goat need look no farther than Austique. This sophisticated boutique, created by sisters Lindy Lopes and Katie Canvin, is home to a gorgeous array of dresses, lingerie, jewelry, and accessories for the ultimate fashionista. It's almost impossible to leave empty-handed. There's another branch in Marylebone. ⊠ *330 King's Rd., Chelsea* ☎ *020/7376–4555* ⊕ *www.austique.co.uk* Ⓜ *Sloane Sq.*

FAMILY **Brora.** The knitwear is cozy, but the style is cool in this contemporary Scottish cashmere emporium for men, women, and kids. There are dressed-up camisoles, sweaters and cardigans, and adorable baby ensembles, as well as noncashmere items such as picnic blankets and scarves. Other branches can be found in Notting Hill, Marylebone, Islington, Wimbledon, Richmond, Covent Garden, and Sloane Square. ⊠ *344 King's Rd., Chelsea* ☎ *020/7352–3697* ⊕ *www.brora.co.uk* Ⓜ *Sloane Sq.*

Jack Wills. The British preppie's answer to Abercrombie & Fitch, Jack Wills specializes in heritage and country sports–inspired styles for men and women but gives them a youthful, sexy edge. This means music-pumping stores crammed with slim-line Fair Isle sweaters, fitted plaid shirts, and short floral sundresses for the girls, plus sweatshirts, blazers, skinny cords, hoodies, and rugby shirts for the boys. Add in a delightful array of shocking pink gypsy pillows, Union Jack carry-on bags, bobble hats galore, knitted jackets for hot-water bottles, and other ironically traditional items and the result are crowds of plugged-in buyers. Branches are in Notting Hill, Covent Garden, Islington, and

Soho. ⊠ *72 Kings Rd., Chelsea* ☎ *020/7581–0347* ⊕ *www.jackwills. com* Ⓜ *Sloane Sq.*

Rigby & Peller. Lovers of luxury lingerie shop here for brands like Prima Donna and Aubade, as well as R&P's own line. If the right fit eludes you and you fancy being fitted by the Queen's *corsetiére*, the made-to-measure service starts at around £300. Many of London's most affluent women shop here, not only because of the royal appointment but also because the quality is excellent and the service impeccably knowledge-able while being much friendlier than you might expect. There are also branches in Mayfair, Chelsea, and the City. ⊠ *2 Hans Rd., Knights-bridge* ☎ *020/7225–4760* ⊕ *www.rigbyandpeller.com* Ⓜ *Knightsbridge.*

FOOD

L'Artisan du Chocolat. Praised by top chefs Gordon Ramsay and Heston Blumenthal, L'Artisan raises chocolate to an art form. "Couture" choc-olates are infused with fruits, nuts, and spices (including such exotic flavorings as Szechuan pepper and tobacco). This is one of the few chocolate shops in the world that makes liquid salted caramels. Leave the kids at home, though; this shop is total wish fulfillment for grown-up chocolate lovers. There's also a branch in Notting Hill. ⊠ *89 Lower Sloane St., Chelsea* ☎ *0845/270–6996* ⊕ *www.artisanduchocolat.co.uk* Ⓜ *Sloane Sq.*

HOUSEHOLD

Fodor's Choice
★
The Conran Shop. This is the brainchild of Sir Terence Conran, who has been informing British taste since he opened Habitat in the 1960s. Although he is no longer associated with Habitat, his eponymous stores are still bastions of similarly clean, unfussy modernist design. Home enhancers from furniture to stemware and textiles—both handmade and mass-produced, by famous names and emerging designers—are displayed in a suitably gorgeous building that is a modernist design landmark in its own right. Both the flagship store and the branch on Marylebone High Street are bursting with great gift ideas. ⊠ *Michelin House, 81 Fulham Rd., South Kensington* ☎ *020/7589–7401* ⊕ *www. conranshop.co.uk* Ⓜ *South Kensington.*

JEWELRY

Fodor's Choice
★
Butler & Wilson. Long before anybody ever heard the word "bling," this shop was marketing the look—in diamanté, colored rhinestones, and crystal—to movie stars and secretaries alike. Specialists in bold costume jewelry, they've added semiprecious stones to the collections and the look is anything but subtle, so it may not suit all tastes unless you're in the market for a rhinestone Union Jack pin. Even if you're not a fan, the shop is worth a visit for its vintage (and vintage-influenced) clothes, once used only to display the jewelry. There's also another shop at 20 South Molton Street. ⊠ *189 Fulham Rd., South Kensington* ☎ *020/7352–3045* ⊕ *www.butlerandwilson.co.uk* Ⓜ *South Kensington.*

SHOES

Fodor's Choice
★
Manolo Blahnik. Blink and you'll miss the discreet sign that marks fash-ionista footwear central. Blahnik, the man who single-handedly man-aged to revive the sexy stiletto and make it classier than ever, has been trading out of this small shop on a Chelsea side street since 1973. It's

a must for shoe lovers with a generous budget. If you decide to wear your new Manolos, hop on the No. 11 or No. 22 bus or grab a cab—the nearest Tube station is about a 20-minute totter away. ⊠ *49–51 Old Church St., Chelsea* ☎ *020/7352–3863* ⊕ *www.manoloblahnik. com* ☾ *Closed Sun.* Ⓜ *Sloane Sq., South Kensington.*

KNIGHTSBRIDGE

ACCESSORIES

Fodor's Choice ★ **Anya Hindmarch.** Exquisite leather bags and personalized, printed canvas totes are what made Hindmarch famous, along with her "I'm Not A Plastic Bag" eco-creation. Her designs are sold at Harrods, Liberty, and Harvey Nichols, but in her stores you can see her complete collection of bags and shoes, or order a bespoke piece such as the "Be A Bag," a tote bag imprinted with your chosen photo. There are also branches around the corner on Pont Street, in Mayfair, and in Notting Hill. ⊠ *157–158 Sloane St., Knightsbridge* ☎ *020/7730–0961* ⊕ *www.anyahindmarch. com* Ⓜ *Sloane Sq., Knightsbridge.*

CLOTHING

Agent Provocateur. Created by Vivienne Westwood's son, this line of sexy, saucy lingerie in gorgeous fabrics and lace tends toward the kind of underwear that men buy for women—more provocative than practical. The original boudoir-like shop is in what was Soho's red light district, but the brand has gone thoroughly mainstream and now sells bathing suits, bedlinen, and luggage in Knightsbridge, Mayfair, Notting Hill, and the City, as well as in Harrods, Harvey Nichols, and Selfridges. ⊠ *6 Broadwick St., Soho* ☎ *020/7439–0229* ⊕ *www.agentprovocateur.com* ☾ *Closed Sun.* Ⓜ *Oxford Circus.*

Egg. Tucked away in a residential mews a short walk from Harvey Nichols, this shop is the brainchild of Maureen Doherty, once Issey Miyake's right-hand person. More than half the minimalist, unstructured styles for men and women in natural fabrics such as silk, cashmere, and antique cotton are handmade. The shop is a former Victorian dairy, and garments are casually hung on hooks or folded on wooden tables in the simple, white space. The price tags, however, are anything but humble and the clientele includes the likes of Donna Karan and photographer Bruce Weber. Unusual ceramics and jewelry are also on display. ⊠ *36 Kinnerton St., Knightsbridge* ☎ *020/7235–9315* ☾ *Closed Sun.* Ⓜ *Knightsbridge.*

Hackett. If J. Crew isn't preppy enough for you, try Hackett, with branches in Covent Garden, Spitalfields, St. James's, Soho, and The City. Originally a posh thrift shop recycling cricket flannels, hunting pinks, Oxford brogues, and other staples of a British gentleman's wardrobe, Hackett now creates its own line and has become a genuine—and very good—men's outfitter. The look is traditional and classic, with best buys including polo shirts, corduroys, and striped scarves. There's also a boys' line for the junior man-about-town. ⊠ *137–138 Sloane St., Chelsea* ☎ *020/7730–3331* ⊕ *www.hackett.com* Ⓜ *Sloane Sq.*

FAMILY **Rachel Riley.** Looking for traditional English style for the younger ones? Riley's expensive, vintage-inspired collection includes classics like duffle coats, cashmere booties, and floral dresses for girls and teens. Mothers

18

who love the Riley look can pick even up coordinating outfits for themselves at the Knightsbridge or Marylebone High Street locations. ⊠ *14 Pont St., Knightsbridge* ☎ *020/7259–5969* ⊕ *www.rachelriley.com* Ⓜ *Knightsbridge.*

Virginia. With perhaps the best collection of vintage clothing in London, Virginia Bates's shop offers dresses, hats, and accessories from the late Victorian era (circa 1880) to the early 1930s. These are wearable collector's items and are priced accordingly. ⊠ *98 Portland Rd., Holland Park, Knightsbridge* ☎ *020/7727–9908* ⊙ *Closed Sun.; open Sat. by appointment only* Ⓜ *Holland Park, Ladbroke Grove.*

DEPARTMENT STORES

Harrods. With an encyclopedic assortment of luxury brands, this Knightsbridge institution has more than 300 departments and 20 restaurants, all spread over 1 million square feet on a 5-acre site. If you approach Harrods as a tourist attraction rather than as a fashion hunting ground, you won't be disappointed. Focus on the spectacular food halls, the huge ground-floor perfumery, the revamped toy and technology departments, the excellent Urban Retreat spa, and the Vegas-like Egyptian Room. At the bottom of the nearby Egyptian escalator, there's a bronze statue depicting the late Princess Diana and Dodi Fayed, son of the former owner, dancing beneath the wings of an albatross. Nevertheless, standards of taste are enforced with a customer dress code (no shorts, ripped jeans, or flip-flops). ▣TIP➔ Be prepared to brave the crowds (avoid visiting on a Saturday if you can), and be prepared to pay if you want to use the bathroom on some floors(!). ⊠ *87–135 Brompton Rd., Knightsbridge* ☎ *020/7730–1234* ⊕ *www.harrods.com* Ⓜ *Knightsbridge.*

Harvey Nichols. While visiting tourists flock to Harrods, true London fashionistas shop at Harvey Nichols, aka "Harvey Nicks." The womenswear and accessories departments are outstanding, featuring of-the-moment designers like Roland Mouret, Peter Pilotto, and 3.1 Phillip Lim. The furniture and housewares are equally gorgeous (and pricey), though they become somewhat more affordable during the twice-annual sales in January and July. The Fifth Floor restaurant is the place to see and be seen, but if you're just after a quick bite, there's also a more informal café on the same floor or sushi-to-go from Yo! Sushi. ⊠ *109–125 Knightsbridge, Knightsbridge* ☎ *020/7235–5000* ⊕ *www. harveynichols.com* Ⓜ *Knightsbridge.*

BELGRAVIA
ACCESSORIES

Fodor's Choice ★ **Lulu Guinness.** Famous for her flamboyantly themed bags (think the satin "bucket" topped with roses or the elaborately beaded red snakeskin "lips" clutch), Guinness also showcases vintage-inspired luggage and beauty accessories in this frilly little shop, which is just as whimsical as her designs. There are other branches in Mayfair and the City. ⊠ *3 Ellis St., Belgravia* ☎ *020/7823–4828* ⊕ *www.luluguinness.com* ⊙ *Closed Sun.* Ⓜ *Sloane Sq.*

Fodor's Choice ★ **Philip Treacy.** Magnificent hats by Treacy are annual showstoppers on Ladies' Day at the Royal Ascot races and regularly grace the glossy magazines' society pages. Part Mad Hatter, part Cecil Beaton, Treacy's creations always guarantee a grand entrance (remember the eye-popping chapeaux that adorned many famous heads at the Westminster Abbey marriage of Prince William and his queen-to-be Kate?). In addition to the extravagant, haute couture hats handmade in the atelier, ready-to wear hats and bags are also for sale. ⊠ *69 Elizabeth St., Belgravia* ☎ *020/7730–3992* ⊕ *www.philiptreacy.co.uk* ⊙ *Closed Sun.* Ⓜ *Sloane Sq.*

SPECIALTY STORES

Mungo & Maud. If you don't want to leave London without buying something for your best friend, head to the city's chicest pet emporium. Elegant, comfortable beds, coats, collars, leashes, blankets, bowls, toys, and treats will make your dog the snazziest pooch in town. Cats are also catered to with baskets, suede collars, and catnip toys. Even owners get a nod with luxurious merino throws (soon to be covered in pet hair) and a leather poop pouch. There's also a branch in Notting Hill. ⊠ *79 Elizabeth St., Belgravia* ☎ *020/022–1207* ⊕ *www.mungoandmaud.com* Ⓜ *Sloane Sq.*

NOTTING HILL

BOOKS

Books for Cooks. It may seem odd to describe a bookshop as delicious-smelling, but the aromas wafting out of Books for Cooks' test kitchen will whet your appetite even before you've opened one of the 8,000 cookbooks. Just about every world cuisine is represented along with a complete lineup of books by celebrity chefs. A tiny café at the back offers lunch dishes drawn from recipes on the shelves, as well as desserts and coffee. Menus change daily. ■ TIP➜ Before you come to London, visit the shop's website to sign up for a cooking class. ⊠ *4 Blenheim Crescent, Notting Hill* ☎ *020/7221–1992* ⊕ *www.booksforcooks.com* ⊙ *Closed Sun. and Mon.* Ⓜ *Notting Hill Gate, Ladbroke Grove.*

CLOTHING

Aimé. French-Cambodian sisters Val and Vanda Heng-Vong launched this shop to showcase the best of French clothing and designer housewares. Expect to find fashion by Isabel Marant, Forte Forte, and A.P.C. You can also pick up A.P.C. candles, Rice homewares, and a well-edited collection of ceramics. Just next door, Petit Aimé sells children's clothing. ⊠ *32 Ledbury Rd., Notting Hill* ☎ *020/7221–7070* ⊕ *www. aimelondon.com* Ⓜ *Notting Hill Gate.*

FAMILY **Caramel Baby & Child.** Here you'll find adorable yet unfussy clothes for children six months and up: hand-crafted Peruvian alpaca cardigans in sherbet colors, twill skirts, and floral cotton blouses and dresses for girls; check shirts and earth-tone tees for boys; comfortable pants in twill, corduroy, and cotton for both; and Merino/cashmere sweaters for extremely fashionable toddlers and babies. Caramel also sells a small selection of decorative/functional items like mobiles, child-friendly chairs and stools, teddy bears, and sheep-shaped pillows. There are also branches in South Kensington and Chelsea. ⊠ *77 Ledbury Rd., Not-*

18

ting Hill ☎ *020/7727–0906* ⊕ *www.caramel-shop.co.uk* Ⓜ *Westbourne Park, Notting Hill Gate.*

Rellik. Now in the modernist landmark known as the Trellick Tower and favored by the likes of Kate Moss, Rellik began as a stall in the Portobello Market. Vintage hunters looking to splurge can find a selection of YLS, Dior, and Ossie Clark as well as items from lesser-known designers. ✉ *Trellick Tower, 8 Golborne Rd., Notting Hill* ☎ *020/8962–0089* ⊕ *www.relliklondon.co.uk* Ⓜ *Westbourne Park.*

MUSIC

Music & Video Exchange. This store is a music collector's treasure trove, with a constantly changing stock refreshed by customers selling and exchanging as well as buying. The main store focuses on rock pop, soul, and dance, both mainstream and obscure, in a variety of formats ranging from vinyl to CD, cassette, and even mini-disk. Don't miss the discounts in the basement and the rarities upstairs. Classical music is at No. 40 and there are branches in Soho and Greenwich. ✉ *38 Notting Hill Gate, Notting Hill* ☎ *020/7243–8574* ⊕ *www.mgeshops.com* Ⓜ *Notting Hill Gate.*

SHOES

Emma Hope. The signature look of the footwear here is elegant and ladylike, with pointed toes and kitten heels, often ornamented with bows, lace, crystal, or exquisite embroidery. Ballet flats and sneakers in velvet or animal prints provide glamour without sacrificing comfort. Small-but-perfectly-formed handbags, as well as shoes and accessories for men, are stocked both here and in the Sloane Square branch. ✉ *207 Westbourne Grove, Notting Hill* ☎ *020/7313–7490* ⊕ *www.emmahope.com* Ⓜ *Notting Hill Gate.*

SPECIALTY STORES

The Village Bicycle. With a style that might best be described as punk *luxe*, this "lifestyle concept store" offers witty, *haute* Goth homewares like a phone disguised as Damien Hirst's notorious artwork *For The Love of God* (a diamond-encrusted skull, except in this case the diamonds are glass). There are also toys, coffee-table books, trinkets, shoes, hi-tops, and art, as well as clothes—most involving leather, black, or fur from ultra-hip labels like House of Holland, Opening Ceremony, and the Olsens' Elizabeth & James that are designed for girls with small frames and big credit limits. ✉ *79–81 Ledbury Rd., Notting Hill* ☎ *020/7313–9031* ⊕ *www.imavillagebicycle.com* Ⓜ *Notting Hill Gate, Westbourne Park.*

SIDE TRIPS FROM LONDON

Updated by Kate Hughes and Jack Jewers

Londoners are undeniably lucky. Few urban populations enjoy such glorious—and easily accessible—options for day-tripping. Even if you have only one day to spare, head out of the city. A train ride past hills dotted with sheep, a stroll through a medieval town, or a visit to one of England's great castles could make you feel as though you've added another week to your vacation.

Not only is England extremely compact, the train and bus networks, although somewhat inefficient and expensive compared with their European counterparts, are extensive and easily booked (though pricing structures can be confusing), making "a brilliant day out" an easy thing to accomplish.

Although you can do the Warner Bros. Harry Potter Studio Tour in a day, visiting many of the towns near London will be a frenzied day trip. Heavy summer crowds make it difficult to cover the sights in a relaxed manner, so consider staying for a day or two. You'd then have time to explore a different England—one with quiet country pubs, tree-lined lanes, and neat fields. No matter where you go, lodging reservations are a good idea from June through September, when foreign visitors saturate the English countryside.

PLANNING

GETTING AROUND
Normally the towns near London are best reached by train. Bus travel costs less, but can take twice as long. Wherever you're going, plan ahead: check the latest timetables before you set off, and try to get an early start. ⇨ *Also see Travel Smart London.*

STATION TIPS
You can reach any of London's main-line train stations by Tube. London's bus stations can be confusing for the uninitiated, so here's a quick breakdown:

Green Line Coach Station is on Bulleid Way (in front of the Colonnades Shopping Centre on Buckingham Palace Road) and is the departure point for most Green Line and Megabus services.

Victoria Bus Station is where many of the local London bus services arrive and depart, and is directly outside the main exits of the train and Tube stations.

Victoria Coach Station is on Buckingham Palace Road: it's a five-minute walk from Victoria Tube station. This is where to go for coach departures; arrivals are at a different location, a short walk from here.

TO GET TO...	TAKE THE TRAIN FROM ...	TAKE THE BUS FROM ...
Cambridge	King's Cross (47–90 minutes; every 10 or 20 minutes); Liverpool St. (80 minutes; every 30 minutes)	Victoria Coach (about 2½ hours; every hour–90 minutes)
Oxford	Paddington (55–110 minutes; every 3–20 minutes)	Victoria Coach (100 minutes; every half hour; Oxford Tube, Buckingham Palace Rd. (100 minutes; every 12–20 minutes)
Stratford-upon-Avon	Marylebone (2 hours, 2 minutes to 3 hours, 14 minutes; every 2 hours); or Euston (2 hours, 40 minutes to 3 hours; every 20 or 40 minutes or hourly)	Victoria Coach (3 hours, 25 minutes; about 3 times daily)
Warner Bros. Harry Potter Studio Tour	Euston Station (20 minutes) to Watford; then shuttle bus to attraction	Watford (15 minutes; every 20 minutes; after taking London train from Euston).
Windsor	Paddington (25–50 minutes; every 5–30 minutes) or Waterloo (1 hour, 5 minutes; every half hour)	Green Line Bus Station, Victoria (1 hour, 5 minutes; hourly)

19

CAMBRIDGE

60 miles (97 km) northeast of London.

With the spires of its university buildings framed by towering trees and expansive meadows, and its medieval streets and passages enhanced by gardens and riverbanks, the city of Cambridge is among the loveliest in England. The city predates the Roman occupation of Britain, but there's confusion over exactly how the university was founded. The most widely accepted story is that it was established in 1209 by a pair of scholars from Oxford, who left their university in protest over the wrongful execution of a colleague for murder.

This university town may be beautiful, but it's no museum. Even when the students are on vacation, there's a cultural and intellectual buzz here. Well-preserved medieval buildings sit cheek-by-jowl next to the latest in modern architecture (for example the William Gates building,

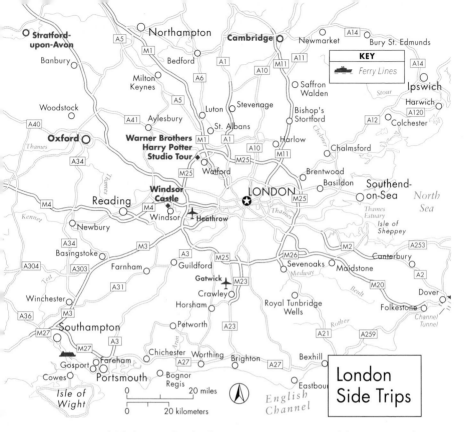

KEY

Ferry Lines

London
Side Trips

which houses Cambridge University's computer laboratory) in this growing city dominated culturally and architecturally by its famous university (whose students make up around one-fifth of the city's 109,000 inhabitants), and beautified by parks, gardens, and the quietly flowing River Cam. A quintessential Cambridge pursuit is punting on the Cam (one occupant propels the narrow, square-end, flat-bottom boat with a long pole), followed by a stroll along the Backs, the left bank of the river fringed by St. John's, Trinity, Clare, King's, and Queens' colleges, and by Trinity Hall.

VISITING THE COLLEGES

College visits are certainly a highlight of a Cambridge tour, but remember that the colleges are private residences and workplaces, even when school isn't in session. Each is an independent entity within the university; some are closed to the public, but at others you can see the chapels, dining rooms (called halls), and sometimes the libraries, too. Some colleges charge a fee for the privilege of nosing around. All are closed during exams, usually from mid-April to late June, and the opening hours often vary. Additionally, all are subject to closures at short notice, especially King's; check the websites in advance. For details about visiting specific colleges not listed here, contact Cambridge University.

TOURS

Visit Cambridge has good walking tours led by an official Blue Badge guide, as well as other tours. The two-hour tours (£18.50) leave from the tourist information center at Peas Hill. Hours vary according to the tour, with the earliest leaving at 11 am and the latest at 1 pm in winter, 2 in summer. City Sightseeing operates open-top bus tours of Cambridge—the Backs, the colleges, the Imperial War Museum in Duxford, and the Grafton shopping center. Tours can be joined at marked bus stops in the city. Tickets are £13.

ESSENTIALS

Visitor and Tour Information Cambridge University ☎ *01223/337733* ⊕ *www.cam.ac.uk.* **City Sightseeing** ✉ *Cambridge Train Station, Station Rd.* ☎ *01223/423578* ⊕ *www.city-sightseeing.com.* **Visit Cambridge** ✉ *Peas Hill* ☎ *0871/226–8006* ⊕ *www.visitcambridge.org.*

EXPLORING

TOP ATTRACTIONS

Fodor's Choice
★
Fitzwilliam Museum. In a Classical Revival building renowned for its grand Corinthian portico, the Fitzwilliam, founded by the seventh viscount Fitzwilliam of Merrion in 1816, has one of Britain's most outstanding collections of art and antiquities. Highlights include two large Titians, an extensive collection of French impressionist painting, and many paintings by Matisse and Picasso. The opulent interior displays its treasures to marvelous effect, from Egyptian pieces such as inch-high figurines and painted coffins, to sculptures from the Chinese Han dynasty of the 3rd century BC. Other collections of note here are a fine assortment of medieval illuminated manuscripts and a fascinating room full of armor and muskets. ✉ *Trumpington St.* ☎ *01223/332–900* ⊕ *www.fitzmuseum.cam.ac.uk* ✇ *Free* ⊙ *Tues.–Sat. 10–5, Sun. noon–5.*

King's College. Founded in 1441 by Henry VI, King's College has a magnificent late-15th-century chapel that is its most famous landmark. Other notable architecture is the neo-Gothic Porters' Lodge, facing King's Parade, which was a relatively recent addition in the 1830s, and the classical Gibbs building. ▮ TIP➔ **Head down to the river, from where the panorama of college and chapel is one of the university's most photographed views.** Past students of King's College include the novelist E.M. Forster, the economist John Maynard Keynes, and the World War I poet Rupert Brooke. ✉ *King's Parade* ☎ *01223/331100* ⊕ *www.kings. cam.ac.uk* ✇ *£7.50, includes chapel* ⊙ *Term time, weekdays 9:30–3:30, Sat. 9:30–3:15, Sun. 1:15–2:30; out of term, daily 9:30–4:30.*

Fodor's Choice
★
King's College Chapel. Based on Sainte-Chapelle, the 13th-century royal chapel in Paris, this house of worship is perhaps the most glorious flowering of Perpendicular Gothic in Britain. Henry VI, the king after whom the college is named, oversaw the work. From the outside, the most prominent features are the massive flying buttresses and the fingerlike spires that line the length of the building. Inside, the most obvious impression is of great space—the chapel was once described as "the noblest barn in Europe"—and of light flooding in from its huge windows. Behind the altar is *The Adoration of the Magi*, an enormous

19

painting by Peter Paul Rubens. ■TIP➔ The chapel, unlike the rest of King's College, stays open during exam periods. Every Christmas Eve, a festival of carols is sung by the chapel's famous choir. To compete for the small number of tickets available, join the line at the college's main entrance early—doors open at 7 am. ⊠ *King's Parade* ☎ *01223/331212* ⊕ *www.kings.cam.ac.uk* ✉ *£7.50, includes college and grounds* ⊙ *Term time, weekdays 9:30–3:30, Sat. 9:30–3:15, Sun. 1:15–2:30; out of term, daily 9:30–4:30. Chapel occasionally closed for services and private events; call or check online.*

Fodor's Choice ★ **Polar Museum.** Beautifully designed, this museum at the university's Scott Polar Research Institute chronicles the history of polar exploration. There's a particular emphasis on the British expeditions of the 20th century, including the ill-fated attempt by Robert Falcon Scott to be the first to reach the South Pole in 1912. Norwegian explorer Roald Amundsen reached the pole first; Scott and his men perished on the return journey, but his story became legendary. There are also collections devoted to the indigenous people of northern Canada, Greenland, and Alaska. ⊠ *Scott Polar Research Institute, Lensfield Rd.* ☎ *01223/336540* ⊕ *www.spri. cam.ac.uk/museum* ✉ *Free* ⊙ *Tues.–Sat. 10–4.*

WORTH NOTING

Emmanuel College. The master hand of architect Christopher Wren (1632–1723) is evident throughout much of Cambridge, particularly at Emmanuel, built on the site of a Dominican friary, where he designed the chapel and colonnade. A stained-glass window in the chapel has a likeness of John Harvard, founder of Harvard University, who studied here. The college, founded in 1584, was an early center of Puritan learning; a number of the Pilgrims were Emmanuel alumni, and they remembered their alma mater in naming Cambridge, Massachusetts. ⊠ *St. Andrew's St.* ☎ *01223/334200* ⊕ *www.emma.cam.ac.uk* ✉ *Free* ⊙ *Daily 9–6, except exam period.*

Queens' College. One of the most eye-catching colleges, Queens' is named after Margaret, queen of Henry VI, and Elizabeth, queen of Edward IV. Founded in 1448, the college is tucked away on Queens' Lane, next to the wide lawns that lead down from King's College to the Backs. The secluded "cloister court" looks untouched since its completion in the 1540s. Queens' masterpiece is the **Mathematical Bridge,** the original version of which is said to have been built without any fastenings. The current bridge (1902) is securely bolted. The college is closed to visitors late May to late June. ⊠ *Queens' La.* ☎ *01223/335511* ⊕ *www. quns.cam.ac.uk* ✉ *£2.50* ⊙ *Mid-Mar.–mid-May and late June–Sept., daily 10–4:30; Oct., weekdays 2–4, weekends 10–4:30; Nov.–mid-Mar., daily 2–4.*

Trinity College. Founded in 1546 by Henry VIII, Trinity replaced a 14th-century educational foundation and is the largest college in either Cambridge or Oxford, with nearly 700 undergraduates. In the 17th-century great court, with its massive gatehouse, is **Great Tom,** a giant clock that strikes each hour with high and low notes. The college's greatest masterpiece is Christopher Wren's **library,** colonnaded and seemingly constructed with as much light as stone. Among the things you can see here is A. A. Milne's handwritten manuscript of *The House at Pooh Corner.* Trinity alumni include Isaac Newton, William Thackeray, Lord Byron, Alfred Tennyson, and 31 Nobel prize winners. ✉ *St. John's St.* ☎ *01223/338400* ⊕ *www.trin.cam.ac.uk* 🎫 *£1* ◷ *College and chapel daily 10–4, except exam period and event days; great court and library weekdays noon–2, Sat. in term time 10:30 12:30.*

WHERE TO EAT

$$ ✕ **Loch Fyne.** Part of a Scottish chain that harvests its own oysters, this
SEAFOOD airy, casual place across from the Fitzwilliam Museum is deservedly popular. The mussels and salmon are fresh and well prepared, and line-caught tuna is served with a mint-and-caper salsa. Try the smoky, sweet Bradan Rost smoked salmon flavored with Scotch whisky if it's on the menu. The place is open for breakfast, lunch, and dinner. ⑤ *Average main: £15* ✉ *37 Trumpington St.* ☎ *01223/362433* ⊕ *www.lochfyne-restaurants.com.*

$$ ✕ **River Bar & Kitchen.** Across the river from Magdalene College, this
MODERN BRITISH popular waterfront bar and grill serves delicious steak and burgers, plus specialties such as lobster macaroni and cheese and blackened salmon with soy and ginger greens. Light lunches are served in the afternoon, and the evening cocktail list is small but elegant. Try the French 75, which is gin with lemon juice, sugar, and sparkling wine. ⑤ *Average main: £17* ✉ *Quayside, Thompsons La., off Bridge St.* ☎ *01223/307030* ⊕ *www.riverbarsteakhouse.com* 🍴 *Reservations essential.*

OXFORD

55 miles (90 km) northwest of London.

With arguably the most famous university in the world, Oxford has been a center of learning since 1167, with only the Sorbonne preceding it. It doesn't take more than a day or two to explore its winding medieval streets, photograph its ivy-covered stone buildings and ancient churches and libraries, and even take a punt down one of its placid waterways. The town center is compact and walkable, and at its heart is Oxford University. Alumni of this prestigious institution include 48 Nobel prize winners, 26 British prime ministers (including David Cameron), and 28 foreign presidents (including Bill Clinton), along with poets, authors, and artists such as Percy Bysshe Shelley, Oscar Wilde, and W. H. Auden.

Oxford is northwest of London, at the junction of the rivers Thames and Cherwell. The city is more interesting and more cosmopolitan than Cambridge, and although it's also bigger, its suburbs aren't remotely interesting to visitors. The interest is all at the center, where the old town curls around the grand stone buildings, good restaurants, and historic pubs. Victorian writer Matthew Arnold described Oxford's "dreaming spires," a phrase that has become famous. Students rush past you on the sidewalks on the way to their exams, clad with marvelous antiquarian style in their requisite mortar caps, flowing dark gowns, stiff collars, and

19

crisp white bow ties. ■TIP➔ Watch your back when crossing roads, as bikes are everywhere.

VISITING THE COLLEGES

You can explore major sights in town in a day or so, but it takes more than a day to spend an hour in each of the key museums and absorb the scene at the colleges. Some colleges are open only in the afternoons during university terms. When the undergraduates are in residence, access is often restricted to the chapels, dining rooms, and libraries, too, and you're requested to refrain from picnicking in the quadrangles. All are closed certain days during exams, usually from mid-April to late June.

TOURS

The Oxford Tourist Information Centre has information on the many guided walking tours of the city. The best way of gaining access to the collegiate buildings is to take the two-hour university and city tour, which leaves the Tourist Information Centre daily at 11 and 1. City Sightseeing offers hop-on, hop-off bus tours (£13.50) with 19 stops around Oxford; your ticket, purchased from the driver, is good for 24 hours. City Sightseeing offers hop-on, hop-off bus tours (£13.50) with 19 stops around Oxford; your ticket, purchased from the driver, is good for 24 hours.

ESSENTIALS

Visitor and Tour Information City Sightseeing ☎ *01865/790522* ⊕ *www.citysightseeingoxford.com.* **Oxford Tourist Information Centre** ⊠ *15/16 Broad St.* ☎ *01865/252200* ⊕ *www.visitoxfordandoxfordshire.com.*

EXPLORING

TOP ATTRACTIONS

Fodor's Choice ★ **Ashmolean Museum.** Britain's oldest public museum displays its rich and varied collections from the Neolithic to the present day over five floors. Innovative and spacious galleries on the theme of "Crossing Cultures, Crossing Time" explore connections between the priceless Egyptian, Greek, Roman, Chinese, and Indian artifacts, and also display a superb art collection. Among the highlights are drawings by Raphael, the shell-encrusted mantle of Powhatan (father of Pocahontas), the lantern belonging to Guy Fawkes, and the Alfred Jewel. This ancient piece features a large semiprecious stone set in gold carved with the words "*Aelfred mec heht gewyrcan,*" which translates from old English as "Alfred ordered me to be made." It piece dates from the reign of King Alfred the Great (ruled 871–899). ■TIP➔ There's too much to see in one visit, but the free admission makes return trips easy. The Ashmolean Dining Room, Oxford's first rooftop restaurant, is a good spot

Radcliffe Camera, an unmissable circular library at Oxford University

for refreshments. ⊠ *Beaumont St.* ☎ *01865/278002* ⊕ *www.ashmolean. org* 🎟 *Free* ⊘ *Tues.–Sun. and national holidays 10–6.*

Fodor'sChoice **Magdalen College.** Founded in 1458, with a handsome main quadrangle
★ and a supremely monastic air, Magdalen (pronounced *maud*-lin) is one
of the most impressive of Oxford's colleges and attracts its most artistic
students. Alumni include such diverse people as P.G. Wodehouse, Oscar
Wilde, and John Betjeman. The school's large, square tower is a famous
local landmark. ■TIP➔ To enhance your visit, take a stroll around the
Deer Park and along Addison's Walk; then have tea in the Old Kitchen,
which overlooks the river. ⊠ *High St.* ☎ *01865/276000* ⊕ *www.magd.
ox.ac.uk* 🎟 *£5* ⊘ *July–Sept., daily noon–7 or dusk; Oct.–June, daily
1–6 or dusk.*

FAMILY **Pitt Rivers Museum.** More than half a million intriguing archaeological
Fodor'sChoice and anthropological items from around the globe, based on the col-
★ lection bequeathed by Lieutenant-General Augustus Henry Lane Fox
Pitt Rivers in 1884, are crammed into a multitude of glass cases and
drawers. Items are organized thematically rather than geographically,
an eccentric approach that's surprisingly thought-provoking. Labels are
handwritten, and children are given flashlights to explore the farthest
corners and spot the world's smallest dolly. Give yourself plenty of time
to wander through the displays of shrunken heads, Hawaiian feather
cloaks, and fearsome masks. Children will have a field day. ⊠ *S. Parks
Rd.* ☎ *01865/270927* ⊕ *www.prm.ox.ac.uk* 🎟 *Free, suggested donation £3* ⊘ *Mon. 10–4:30, Tues.–Sun. and national holidays noon–4:30.*

WORTH NOTING

Christ Church. Built in 1546, the college of Christ Church is referred to by its members as "The House." This is the site of Oxford's largest quadrangle, Tom Quad, named after the huge bell (6¼ tons) that hangs in the Christopher Wren–designed gate tower and rings 101 times at five past nine every evening in honor of the original number of Christ Church scholars. The vaulted, 800-year-old chapel in one corner has been Oxford's cathedral since the time of Henry VIII. The college's medieval dining hall, re-created for the Harry Potter films, contains portraits of many famous alumni, including 13 of Britain's prime ministers. ■ TIP➡ **Plan carefully, as the dining hall is only open weekdays 10:30–11:40 and 2:30–4:30 and weekends 2:30–4:30.** Lewis Carroll, author of *Alice in Wonderland*, was a teacher of mathematics here for many years; a shop opposite the meadows on St. Aldate's sells Alice paraphernalia. ✉ *St. Aldate's* ☎ *01865/276492* ⊕ *www.chch.ox.ac.uk* 🎫 *£8; £8.50 in July and Aug.* ⊙ *Mon.–Sat. 10–5, Sun. 2–5; last admission 30 mins before closing.*

Radcliffe Camera and Bodleian Library. A vast library, the domed Radcliffe Camera is Oxford's most spectacular building, built in 1737–49 by James Gibbs in Italian baroque style. It's usually surrounded by tourists with cameras trained at its golden-stone walls. The Camera contains part of the Bodleian Library's enormous collection, begun in 1602. Much like the Library of Congress in the United States, the Bodleian contains a copy of every book printed in Great Britain and grows by 5,000 items a week. Tours reveal the magnificent Duke Humfrey's Library, which was the original chained library and completed in 1488. (The ancient tomes are dusted once a decade.) Guides will show you the spots used for Hogwarts School in the Harry Potter films. ■ TIP➡ **Arrive early to secure tickets for the three to six daily tours. These are sold on a first-come, first-served basis (except for the extended tour on Wednesday and Saturday, which can be prebooked).** Audio tours, the only tours open to kids under 11, don't require reservations. Call ahead to confirm tour times. ✉ *Broad St.* ☎ *01865/277216* ⊕ *www.bodleian.ox.ac.uk* 🎫 *Audio tour £2.50, minitour £5, standard tour £7, extended tour £13* ⊙ *Bodleian and Divinity School weekdays 9–5, Sat. 9–4:30, Sun. 11–5.*

St. John's College. One of Oxford's most attractive campuses, St. John's has seven quiet quadrangles surrounded by elaborately carved buildings. You enter the first through a low wooden door. This college dates to 1555, when Sir Thomas White, a merchant, founded it. His heart is buried in the chapel (by tradition, students curse as they walk over it). The Canterbury Quad represented the first example of Italian Renaissance architecture in Oxford, and the Front Quad includes the buildings of the old St. Bernard's Monastery. ✉ *St. Giles* ☎ *01865/277300* ⊕ *www.sjc.ox.ac.uk* 🎫 *Free* ⊙ *Daily 1–5.*

University Church of St. Mary the Virgin. Seven hundred years' worth of funeral monuments crowd this church, including the tombstone of Amy Robsart, the wife of Robert Dudley, Elizabeth I's favorite. One pillar marks the site of Thomas Cranmer's trial under Queen Mary for his marital machinations on behalf of Henry VIII. ■ TIP➡ **The top of the**

14th-century tower has a panoramic view of the city's skyline. It's worth the 127 steps. The Vaults and Garden Café, a part of the church accessible from Radcliffe Square, serves breakfasts and cream teas as well as good lunches. ⊠ *High St.* ☎ *01865/279111* ⊕ *www.university-church. ox.ac.uk* ⊐ *Church free, tower £3* ⊙ *Mon.–Sat. 9–5, Sun. noon–5; last admission 30 mins before closing.*

WHERE TO EAT

$$ ✕ **Brasserie Blanc.** Raymond Blanc's sophisticated brasserie in the Jericho neighborhood, a hipper cousin of Le Manoir aux Quat' Saisons in Great Milton, is one of the best places to eat in Oxford. Wood floors, pale walls, and large windows keep the restaurant open and airy. The changing menu always lists innovative, visually stunning adaptations of bourgeois French fare, sometimes with Mediterranean or Asian influences. Try the pasta with Jervaulx blue cheese, chestnut, and apple or the chicken stuffed with Armagnac-soaked prunes. There's a good selection of steaks as well. The £11.50 fixed-price lunch is a good value, and kids have their own menu. ⑤ *Average main: £15* ⊠ *71–72 Walton St.* ☎ *01865/510999* ⊕ *www.brasserieblanc.com.*

FRENCH

$ ✕ **Grand Café.** Golden-hue tiles, towering columns, and antique marble tables make this café both architecturally impressive and an excellent spot for sandwiches, salads, or other light fare. It's packed with tourists and the service can be slow, but this is still a pretty spot for afternoon tea. On Thursday and Friday nights, it transforms into a popular cocktail bar. ⑤ *Average main: £8* ⊠ *84 High St.* ☎ *01865/204463* ⊕ *www. thegrandcafe.co.uk.*

CAFÉ

$$ ✕ **Jamie's Italian.** Gazing through the window at the shelves of freshly made pasta, the multicolor gourds, and the abundant hams hanging from the ceiling is enough to entice you into this buzzing eatery. Chef Jamie Oliver's mission is to re-create the best rustic Italian fare, as shown in a diverting range of antipasti and mains such as tuna fusilli slow-cooked with tomatoes and cinnamon, and steak tagliata with crunchy fennel and garlic. The various dishes served on a wood plank are a steal, desserts are light and refreshing—tutti frutti lemon meringue pie and fruit sorbets, for example—and the lively crowd appreciates it all. ⑤ *Average main: £15* ⊠ *24–26 George St.* ☎ *01865/838383* ⊕ *www. jamieoliver.com.*

ITALIAN

19

STRATFORD-UPON-AVON

104 miles (167 km) north of London.

Stratford-upon-Avon has become adept at accommodating the hordes of people who stream in for a glimpse of William Shakespeare's world. Filled with all the distinctive, Tudor half-timber buildings your heart could desire, this is certainly a handsome town, and the Royal Shakespeare Theatre is a don't-miss for those who want to see Shakespeare performed in England. But the town can feel, at times, like a literary amusement park, so if you're not a fan of the Bard, you may want to explore elsewhere.

Stratford-upon-Avon honors Shakespeare's birthday with an annual procession.

TOURS AND TICKETS

City Sightseeing runs hop-on, hop-off guided tours of Stratford (£12.50), and you can combine the tour (about an hour with no stops) with entry to either three (£25.50) or four (£29) Shakespeare houses.

The Shakespeare Birthplace Trust runs the main places of Shakespearean interest: Anne Hathaway's Cottage, Hall's Croft, Mary Arden's House, Nash's House and New Place, and Shakespeare's Birthplace and Shakespeare's Grave. ■■■TIP➜ Buy a money-saving combination ticket to all six properties for £22.50, or pay separate entry fees if you're visiting one or two. Family tickets are an option, too. Advance booking online gives you a 10% saving. Tickets for Hall's Croft and Nash's House and New Place are available as a pricey (£14.95) joint ticket that includes the birthplace and grave.

ESSENTIALS

Visitor and Tour Information City Sightseeing ☎ 01789/412680 ⊕ www.city-sightseeing.com. **Shakespeare Birthplace Trust** ☎ 01789/204016 ⊕ www.shakespeare.org.uk. **Stratford Town Walk** ☎ 01789/292–478, 0785/576–0377 ⊕ www.stratfordtownwalk.co.uk. **Stratford-upon-Avon Tourist Information Centre** ✉ Bridgefoot ☎ 01789/264293 ⊕ www.shakespeare-country.co.uk.

EXPLORING

Hall's Croft. One of the finest surviving Jacobean (early-17th-century) town houses, this impressive residence has a delightful walled garden. Hall's Croft was the home of Shakespeare's elder daughter, Susanna, and her husband, Dr. John Hall, a physician who, by prescribing an herbal cure for scurvy, was well ahead of his time. His consulting room and medical dispensary are on view along with the other rooms, all containing Jacobean furniture of heavy oak and some 17th-century portraits. The café serves light lunches and afternoon teas. ⊠ *Old Town* ☎ *01789/292107* ⊕ *www.shakespeare.org.uk* ⌧ *£14.95, includes admission to Shakespeare's Birthplace, New Place, and Shakespeare's Grave* ⊙ *Apr.–Oct., daily 10–5; Nov.–Mar., daily 11–4.*

Holy Trinity Church. The burial place of William Shakespeare, this 13th-century church sits on the banks of the Avon, with a graceful avenue of lime trees framing its entrance. Shakespeare's final resting place is in the chancel, rebuilt in 1465–91 in the late Perpendicular style. He was buried here not because he was a famed poet but because he was a lay rector of Stratford, owning a portion of the township tithes. On the north wall of the sanctuary, over the altar steps, is the famous marble bust created by Gerard Jansen in 1623 and thought to be a true likeness of Shakespeare. The bust offers a more human, even humorous, perspective when viewed from the side. Also in the chancel are the graves of Shakespeare's wife, Anne; his daughter Susanna; his son-in-law John Hall; and his granddaughter's husband, Thomas Nash. Nearby, the Parish Register is displayed, containing Shakespeare's baptismal entry (1564) and his burial notice (1616). ⊠ *Trinity St.* ☎ *01789/266316* ⊕ *www.stratford-upon-avon.org* ⌧ *£2 for chancel* ⊙ *Mar. and Oct., Mon.–Sat. 9–5, Sun. 12:30–5; Apr.–Sept., Mon.–Sat. 8:30–6, Sun. 12:30–5; Nov.–Feb., Mon.–Sat. 9–4, Sun. 12:30–5; last admission 20 mins before closing.*

Nash's House. This heavily restored house was the residence of Thomas Nash, who married Shakespeare's last direct descendant, his grand-daughter Elizabeth Hall. It has been furnished in 17th-century style and contains a museum containing finds from the excavations of **New Place,** the house in which Shakespeare died in 1616. Built in 1483 "of brike and tymber" for a lord mayor of London, New Place was Stratford's grandest piece of real estate when Shakespeare bought it in 1597 for £60. It was torn down in 1759 by the Reverend Francis Gastrell, who was angry at the hordes of Shakespeare-related sightse-ers. You can see an Elizabethan knot garden in the gardens. ⊠ *Chapel St.* ☎ *01789/292325* ⊕ *www.shakespeare.org.uk* ⌧ *£14.95, includes admission to Shakespeare's Birthplace, Hall's Croft, and Shakespeare's Grave* ⊙ *Apr.–Oct., daily 10–5; Nov.–Mar., daily 11–4.*

Fodor'sChoice ★ **Royal Shakespeare Company.** One of the finest repertory troupes in the world and long the backbone of the country's theatrical life, the company performs plays year-round in Stratford and at venues around Brit-ain. The stunning Royal Shakespeare Theatre, home of the RSC, has a thrust stage based on the original Globe Theater in London. The Swan Theatre, part of the theater complex and also built in the style of Shake-speare's Globe, stages plays by Shakespeare and contemporaries such as Christopher Marlowe and Ben Jonson, as well as works by contem-porary playwrights. Prices usually are £14 to £60. ▥TIP➔ Seats book up fast, but day-of-performance and returned tickets are often avail-able. ⊠ *Waterside* ☎ *0844/800–1110 ticket hotline* ⊕ *www.rsc.org.uk.*

19

Fodor'sChoice   **Shakespeare's Birthplace.** A half-timber house typical of its time, the
★   playwright's birthplace is a much-visited shrine that has been altered
and restored since he lived here. Entering through the modern visitor center, you are immersed in an entertaining but basic introduction
to Shakespeare through a "Life, Love, and Legacy" visual and audio
exhibition; this can be crowded. The house itself is across the garden
from this large modern center. Colorful wall decorations and the furnishings in the actual house reflect comfortable, middle-class Elizabethan domestic life. Shakespeare's father, John, a glove maker and wool
dealer, purchased the house; a reconstructed workshop shows the tools
of the glover's trade. There's also a café and bookshop on the grounds.
⊠ *Henley St.* ☎ *01789/201822* ⊕ *www.shakespeare.org.uk* ⊒ *£14.95,
includes entry to Hall's Croft, Nash's House, and Shakespeare's Grave*
⊙ *Apr.–June and Sept.–Oct., daily 9–5; July and Aug., daily 9–6; Nov.–
Mar., daily 10–4.*

STRATFORD ENVIRONS

Two additional stops on the Shakespeare trail are just outside Stratford;
also nearby is spectacular Warwick Castle.

Fodor'sChoice   **Anne Hathaway's Cottage.** The most picturesque of the Shakespeare Trust
★   properties, on the western outskirts of Stratford, was the family home
of the woman Shakespeare married in 1582. The "cottage," actually a
substantial Tudor farmhouse, has latticed windows and a grand thatch
roof. Inside is period furniture, including the settle where Shakespeare
reputedly conducted his courtship, and a rare carved Elizabethan bed;
outside is a garden planted in lush Victorian style with herbs and flowers. A stoll through the adjacent orchard takes you to willow cabins
where you can listen to sonnets, view sculptures with Shakespearean
themes, and try a yew and a heart-shaped lavender maze. ■TIP➔ The
best way to get here is on foot, especially in late spring when the apple
trees are in blossom. The signed path runs from Evesham Place (an
extension of Grove Road) opposite Chestnut Walk. Pick up a leaflet
with a map from the tourist office; the walk takes a good half hour.
⊠ *Cottage La., Shottery* ☎ *01789/295517* ⊕ *www.shakespeare.org.uk*
⊒ *£9* ⊙ *Apr.–Oct., daily 9–5; Nov.–Mar., daily 10–4; last admission
30 mins before closing.*

FAMILY   **Mary Arden's Farm.** A working farm, where food is grown using methods
common in the 16th century, is the main attraction at Mary Arden's
House (the childhood home of Shakespeare's mother) and Palmer's
Farm. This bucolic stop is great for kids, who can try their hand at
basket weaving and gardening, listen as the farmers explain their work
in the fields, and watch the cooks prepare food in the Tudor farmhouse
kitchen. It all brings the past to life. There are crafts exhibits, a café,
and a garden. The site is 3 miles northwest of Stratford; you need to
walk or drive here, or else go with a tour. ⊠ *Off A3400, Wilmcote*
☎ *01789/293455* ⊕ *www.shakespeare.org.uk* ⊒ *£9.95* ⊙ *Apr.–Oct.,
daily 10–5.*

FAMILY

Fodor's Choice

★

Warwick Castle. The vast bulk of this medieval castle rests on a cliff overlooking the Avon—"the fairest monument of ancient and chival-rous splendor which yet remains uninjured by time," to use the words of Sir Walter Scott. Today the company that runs the Madame Tus-sauds wax museums owns the castle, and the exhibits and diversions can occupy a full day. Warwick is a great castle experience for kids, though it's pricey (there are family rates). Warwick's two soaring tow-ers, bristling with battlements, can be seen for miles: the 147-foot-high Caesar's Tower, built in 1356, and the 128-foot-high Guy's Tower, built in 1380. The castle's most powerful commander was Richard Neville, earl of Warwick, known during the 15th-century Wars of the Roses as the Kingmaker. Warwick Castle's monumental walls enclose an impres-sive armory of medieval weapons, as well as state rooms with historic furnishings and paintings by Peter Paul Rubens, Anthony Van Dyck, and other old masters. Twelve rooms are devoted to an imaginative wax exhibition, "A Royal Weekend Party—1898." Other exhibits dis-play the sights and sounds of a great medieval household as it prepares for an important battle, and of a princess's fairy-tale wedding; in the Dragon Tower, Merlin and a talking dragon breathe life into the Arthu-rian legend. ■ TIP➔ **Arrive early to beat the crowds. If you book online, you save on ticket prices.** Lavish medieval banquets (extra charge) and special events, including festivals, jousting tournaments, and a Christ-mas market, take place throughout the year, and plenty of food stalls serve lunches. ☒ *Castle La., off Mill St., Warwick* ☎ *01926/495421, 0871/265–2000 24-hr information line* ⊕ *www.warwick-castle.com* ☜ *Castle, Dragon Tower, and Dungeon £30.60, Castle and Dungeon £28.20, Castle £22.80; parking £6* ☉ *Late July and Aug., daily 10–6; mid-Sept.–mid-July, daily 10–5; last admission 30 mins before closing.*

WHERE TO EAT

19

$

BRITISH

Fodor's Choice

★

✕ **The Black Swan/The Dirty Duck.** The only pub in Britain to be licensed under two names (the more informal one came courtesy of American GIs who were stationed here during World War II), this is one of Strat-ford's most celebrated pubs—it's attracted actors since the 18th-century thespian David Garrick's days. A little veranda overlooks the theaters and the river here. Along with your pint of bitter, you can choose from the extensive menu of daily specials, wraps, ciabattas, steaks, burgers, and grills. Few people come here for the food, though you will need to book ahead for dinner: the real attraction is the ambience and your fellow customers. ⑤ *Average main: £10* ☒ *Waterside* ☎ *01789/297312* ⊕ *www.dirtyduck-pub-stratford-upon-avon.co.uk.*

$

MODERN BRITISH

✕ **Opposition.** Hearty, warming meals are offered at this informal, family-style restaurant in a 16th-century building on the main dining street near the theaters. The English and international dishes—chicken roasted with banana and served with curry sauce and basmati rice, for instance—win praise from the locals. There's a good range of lighter and vegetarian options and fixed-price menus as well. Make reserva-tions a month ahead in summer. ⑤ *Average main: $14* ☒ *13 Sheep St.* ☎ *01789/269980* ⊕ *www.theoppo.co.uk* ☉ *Closed Sun.*

WARNER BROS. HARRY POTTER STUDIO TOUR

20 miles (32 km) northwest of London.

Popular and family friendly, the Warner Bros. Harry Potter Studio Tour has sets and props from the successful films, and plenty of engaging interactive diversions for all ages. The train and a special shuttle bus from Watford get you here.

EXPLORING

FAMILY

Fodor'sChoice

★

Warner Bros. Harry Potter Studio Tour. Muggles, take note: this spectacular attraction opened for wizarding business just outside Watford in 2012. From the Great Hall of Hogwarts to magical props, each section of this attraction showcases the real sets, props, and special effects used in the eight movies. Visitors enter the Great Hall, a fitting stage for costumes from each Hogwarts house. The spooky charm of the Defense Against the Dark Arts Classroom will tempt some to start experimenting, but others will hurry on to the comforting confines of Dumbledore's office. Tickets, pegged to a 30-minute arrival time slot, must be prebooked online. The studio tour is a 20-minute drive from St. Albans. You can also get here by taking a 20-minute train ride from London's Euston Station (then a 15-minute bus ride). Via car from London, use M1 and M25 and enjoy the free parking. ✉ *Studio Tour Dr., Leavesden* ☎ *0845/084–0900* ⊕ *www.wbstudiotour.co.uk* ▭ *£29* ⊘ *Daily 10–4 (until 6:30 at some times of year).*

WINDSOR CASTLE

21 miles (34 km) west of London.

The tall turrets of Windsor Castle, one of the homes of the Royal Family, can be seen for miles around. The grand stone building is the star attraction in this quiet town with some remaining medieval elements—though Eton College, England's most famous public school, is also just a lovely walk away across the Thames.

ESSENTIALS

Visitor Information Royal Windsor Information Centre ✉ *Old Booking Hall, Windsor Royal Station, Thames St.* ☎ *01753/743900, 01753/743907 for accommodations* ⊕ *www.windsor.gov.uk.*

EXPLORING

Fodor'sChoice

★

Windsor Castle. From William the Conqueror to Queen Victoria, the kings and queens of England added towers and wings to this brooding, imposing castle, visible for miles and now the largest inhabited castle in the world. Despite the multiplicity of hands involved in its design, the palace manages to have a unity of style and character. The most impressive view of Windsor Castle is from the A332 road, coming into town from the south. Admission includes an audio guide and, if you wish, a guided tour of the castle precincts. Entrance lines can be long in season and you're likely to spend at least half a day here, so come early.

William the Conqueror began work on the castle in the 11th century, and Edward III modified and extended it in the mid-1300s. One of Edward's largest contributions was the enormous and distinctive **Round Tower**. Later, between 1824 and 1837, George IV transformed the still essentially medieval castle into the fortified royal palace you see today. Most of England's kings and queens have demonstrated their undying attachment to the

DID YOU KNOW?

The Queen uses Windsor often—it's said she likes it much more than Buckingham Palace—spending most weekends here, often joined by family and friends. You know she's in when the Royal Standard is flown above the Round Tower but not in when you see the Union Jack.

castle, the only royal residence in continuous use by the Royal Family since the Middle Ages.

As you enter the castle, **Henry VIII's gateway** leads uphill into the wide castle precincts, where you're free to wander. Across from the entrance is the exquisite **St. George's Chapel** (closed Sunday). Here lie 10 of the kings of England, including Henry VI, Charles I, and Henry VIII (Jane Seymour is the only one of his six wives buried here). One of the noblest buildings in England, the chapel was built in the Perpendicular style popular in the 15th and 16th centuries, with elegant stained-glass windows; a high, vaulted ceiling; and intricately carved choir stalls. The colorful heraldic banners of the Knights of the Garter—the oldest British Order of Chivalry, founded by Edward III in 1348—hang in the choir. The ceremony in which the knights are installed as members of the order has been held here with much pageantry for more than five centuries.

The **North Terrace** provides especially good views across the Thames to Eton College, perhaps the most famous of Britain's exclusive "public" boys' schools. From the terrace, you enter the **State Apartments,** which are open to the public most days. On display to the left of the entrance to the State Apartments in Windsor Castle, **Queen Mary's Dolls' House** is a perfect miniature Georgian palace-within-a-palace, created in 1923. Electric lights glow, the doors all have tiny keys, and a miniature library holds Lilliputian-size books written especially for the young queen by famous authors of the 1920s. Five cars, including a Daimler and Rolls-Royce, stand at the ready.

Although a fire in 1992 gutted some of the State Apartments, hardly any works of art were lost. Phenomenal repair work brought to new life the **Grand Reception Room,** the **Green and Crimson Drawing Rooms,** and the **State and Octagonal Dining Rooms.** A green oak hammer-beam (a short horizontal roof beam that projects from the tops of walls for support) roof looms magnificently over the 600-year-old **St. George's Hall,** where the Queen gives state banquets. The State Apartments contain priceless furniture, including a magnificent Louis XVI bed and Gobelin tapestries; and paintings by Canaletto, Rubens, Van Dyck, Holbein, Dürer, and Bruegel. The tour's high points are the **Throne Room** and the **Waterloo Chamber,** where Sir Thomas Lawrence's portraits of Napoléon's victorious foes line the walls. You can also see arms and

19

armor—look out for Henry VIII's ample suit. A visit between October and March also includes the Semi-State rooms, the private apartments of George IV, resplendent with gilded ceilings.

■ TIP➜ To see the castle come magnificently alive, check out the Changing the Guard, which takes place daily at 11 am from April through July and on alternate days at 11 am from August through March. Confirm the exact schedule before traveling to Windsor. When the Queen is in town, the guard and a regimental band parade through town to the castle gate; when she's away, a drum-and-fife band takes over. ⊠ *Castle Hill* ☎ *020/7766–7304 tickets, 01753/831118 recorded information* ⊕ *www.royalcollection.org.uk* ⊠ *£17.75 for Precincts, State Apartments, Gallery, St. George's Chapel, and Queen Mary's Dolls' House; £9.70 when State Apartments are closed* ⊘ *Mar.–Oct., daily 9:45–5:15, last admission at 4; Nov.–Feb., daily 9:45–4:15, last admission at 3.*

Fodor'sChoice **Eton College.** Signs warn drivers of "Boys Crossing" as you approach
★ the splendid Tudor-style buildings of Eton College, the distinguished boarding school for boys ages 13 through 18 that was founded in 1440 by King Henry VI. It's all terrifically photogenic, because during the college semester students still dress in pin-striped trousers, swallow-tailed coats, and stiff collars. Rivaling St. George's at Windsor in terms of size, the Gothic **Chapel** contains superb fifteenth-century grisaille wall paintings juxtaposed against modern stained glass by John Piper. Beyond the cloisters are the school's playing fields where, according to the duke of Wellington, the Battle of Waterloo was really won, since so many of his officers had learned discipline and strategy during their school days. Among the country's prime ministers to be educated here is David Cameron. The **Museum of Eton Life** has displays on the school's history and vignettes of school life. ⊠ *Brewhouse Yard, Eton, Berkshire* ☎ *01753/671177* ⊕ *www.etoncollege.com* ⊠ *£7.50* ⊘ *Guided tours at 2 and 3:15: mid-Mar.–mid-Apr. and July–early Sept., daily; mid-Apr.–June and mid-Sept.–early Oct., Wed. and Fri.–Sun.*

WHERE TO EAT

$ ✕ **Two Brewers.** Locals congregate in a pair of low-ceiling rooms at this
BRITISH 17th-century establishment by the gates of Windsor Great Park. Those under 18 aren't allowed inside the pub (though they can be served at a few outdoor tables), but adults will find a suitable collection of wine, espresso, and local beer, plus an excellent menu with such dishes as sausages with mash and pea gravy, fish cakes, and a good selection of sandwiches. On Sundays the pub serves a traditional, hearty lunchtime roast. ⑤ *Average main: £15* ⊠ *34 Park St.* ☎ *01753/855426* ⊕ *www.twobrewerswindsor.co.uk* ⌕ *Reservations essential* ⊘ *No dinner Fri.–Sun.*

UNDERSTANDING LONDON

London at-a-Glance

English Vocabulary

Books and Movies

LONDON AT-A-GLANCE

FAST FACTS

Type of government: Representative democracy. In 1999 the Greater London Authority Act reestablished a single local governing body for the Greater London area, consisting of an elected mayor and the 25-member London Assembly. Elections, first held in 2000, take place every four years.

Population: Inner city 3 million, Greater London 7.7 million

Population density: 12,331 people per square mile

Median age: 38.4

Infant mortality rate: 5 per 1,000 births

Language: English. More than 300 languages are spoken in London. All city government documents are translated into Arabic, Bengali, Chinese, Greek, Gujurati, Hindi, Punjabi, Turkish, Urdu, and Vietnamese.

Ethnic and racial groups: White British 70%, White Irish 3%, Other White 9%, Indian 6%, Bangladeshi 2%, Pakistani 2%, other Asian 2%, Black African 6%, Black Caribbean 5%, Chinese 1%, Other 3%.

Religion: Christian 58%, nonaffiliated 15%, Muslim 8%, Hindu 4%, Jewish 2%, Sikh 1%, other religion 1%, Buddhist 0.8%.

When a man is tired of London, he is tired of life; for there is in London all that life can afford.

—Samuel Johnson

GEOGRAPHY AND ENVIRONMENT

Latitude: 51° N (same as Calgary, Canada; Kiev, Ukraine; Prague, Czech Republic)

Longitude: 0° (same as Accra, Ghana). A brass line in the ground in Greenwich marks the prime meridian (0° longitude).

Elevation: 49 feet

Land area: City, 67 square miles; metro area, 625 square miles

Terrain: River plain, rolling hills, and parkland

Natural hazards: Drought in warmer summers, minor localized flooding of the Thames caused by surge tides from the North Atlantic

Environmental issues: The city has been improving its air quality, but up to 1,600 people die each year from health problems related to London's polluted air. Only half of London's rivers and canals received passing grades for water quality from 1999 through 2001. More than £12 million ($22 million) is spent annually to ensure the city's food safety.

I'm leaving because the weather is too good. I hate London when it's not raining.

—Groucho Marx

ECONOMY

Workforce: 3.8 million; financial/real estate 28%, health care 10%, manufacturing 4%, education 7%, construction 5%, public administration 5%

Unemployment: 7.2%

Major industries: The arts, banking, government, insurance, tourism

London: a nation, not a city.

—Benjamin Disraeli, Lothair

ENGLISH VOCABULARY

You and a Londoner may speak the same language, but some phrases
definitely get lost in translation once they cross the Atlantic.

British English	American English

BASIC TERMS AND EVERYDAY ITEMS

British English	American English
bill	check
flat	apartment
lift	elevator
nappy	diaper
holiday	vacation
note	bill (currency)
plaster	Band-Aid
queue	line
row	argument
rubbish	trash
tin	can
toilet/loo/WC	bathroom

CLOTHING

British English	American English
braces	suspenders
bum bag	fanny pack
dressing gown	robe
jumper	sweater
pants/knickers	underpants/briefs
rucksack	backpack
suspender	garter
tights	pantyhose
trainers	sneakers
trousers	pants
vest	undershirt
waistcoat	vest

TRANSPORTATION

British English	American English
bonnet	hood
boot	trunk

coach	long-distance bus
pavement	sidewalk
petrol	gas
pram	baby carriage
puncture	flat
windscreen	windshield

FOOD

aubergine	eggplant
banger	sausage
biscuit	cookie
chips	fries
courgette	zucchini
crisps	potato chips
jam	jelly
main course (or main)	entrée
pudding	dessert
rocket	arugula
starter	appetizer
sweet	candy
tea	early dinner

SLANG

all right	hi there
cheers	thank you
chuffed	pleased
fit	attractive
geezer	dude
guv'nor, gaffer	boss
hard	tough
mate	buddy
sound	good
ta	thank you

BOOKS AND MOVIES

London has been the focus of countless books and essays. For sonorous eloquence, you still must reach back more than half a century to Henry James's *English Hours* and Virginia Woolf's *The London Scene*. Today most suggested reading lists begin with V. S. Pritchett's *London Perceived* and H. V. Morton's *In Search of London*, both decades old. Four more-up-to-date books with a general compass are Peter Ackroyd's *Thames* and anecdotal *London: The Biography*, which traces the city's growth from the Druids to the 21st century; John Russell's *London*, a sumptuously illustrated art book; and Christopher Hibbert's *In London: The Biography of a City*. Stephen Inwood's *A History of London* explores the city from its Roman roots to its swinging '60s heyday. Piet Schreuders's *The Beatles' London* follows the footsteps of the Fab Four.

That noted, there are books galore on the various facets of the city. *The Art and Architecture of London*, by Ann Saunders, is fairly comprehensive. *Inside London: Discovering the Classic Interiors of London*, by Joe Friedman and Peter Aprahamian, has magnificent color photographs of hidden and overlooked shops, clubs, and town houses. For a wonderful take on the golden age of the city's regal mansions, see Christopher Simon Sykes's *Private Palaces: Life in the Great London Houses*. For various other aspects of the city, consult Mervyn Blatch's helpful *A Guide to London's Churches*, Andrew Crowe's *The Parks and Woodlands of London*, Sheila Fairfield's *The Streets of London*, Ann Saunders's *Regent's Park*, Ian Norrie's *Hampstead, Highgate Village, and Kenwood*, and Suzanne Ebel's *A Guide to London's Riverside: Hampton Court to Greenwich*. For keen walkers, there are two books by Andrew Duncan: *Secret London* and *Walking Village London*. *City Secrets: London*, edited by Robert Kahn, is a handsome book of anecdotes from London writers, artists, and historians about their favorite places in the city. For the last word on just about every subject, see *The London Encyclopaedia*, edited by Ben Weinreb and Christopher Hibbert. HarperCollins's *London Photographic Atlas* has a plethora of bird's-eye images of the capital. For an alternative view of the city, it would be hard to better Iain Sinclair's witty and intelligent *London Orbital: A Walk Around the M25* in which he scrutinizes the history, mythology, and politics of London from the viewpoint of its ugly ring road. Sinclair is also the editor of *London: City of Disappearances*, an anthology exploring what has vanished.

Of course, the history and spirit of the city are also to be found in celebrations of great authors, British heroes, and architects. Peter Ackroyd's massive *Dickens* elucidates how the great author shaped today's view of the city; Martin Gilbert's magisterial, multivolume *Churchill* traces the city through some of its greatest trials; J. Mansbridge's *John Nash* details the London buildings of this great architect. Liza Picard evokes mid-18th-century London in *Dr. Johnson's London*. For musical theater buffs, Mike Leigh's *Gilbert and Sullivan's London* takes a romantic look at the two artists' lives and times in the capital's grand theaters and wild nightspots. *Rodinsky's Room*, by Rachel Lichtenstein and Iain Sinclair, is a fascinating exploration of East End Jewish London and the mysterious disappearance of one of its occupants.

Maureen Waller's *1700: Scenes from London Life* is a fascinating look at the daily life of Londoners in the 18th century. Nineteenth-century London—the city of Queen Victoria, Tennyson, and Dickens—comes alive through *Mayhew's London*, a massive study of the London poor by Henry Mayhew, and Gustave Doré's *London*, an unforgettable series of engravings of the city (often reprinted in modern editions) that detail its horrifying slums and grand avenues. When it comes to fiction, of course, Dickens's immortal works top the list. Stay-at-home detectives have long walked the streets of London, thanks to great mysteries by Dorothy L. Sayers, Agatha Christie, Ngaio Marsh, and Antonia Fraser. Cops and bad guys wind their way around 1960s London in Jake Arnott's pulp fiction books, *The Long Firm* and *He Kills Coppers*. Martin Amis's *London Fields* tracks a murder mystery through West London. For so-called "tart noir," pick up any Stella Duffy book. Marie Belloc-Lowndes's *The Lodger* is a fictional account of London's most deadly villain, Jack the Ripper. Victorian London was never so salacious as in Sarah Waters's story of a young girl who travels the theaters as a singer, the Soho squares as a male prostitute, and the East End as a communist in *Tipping the Velvet*. Late-20th-century London, with its diverse ethnic makeup, is the star of Zadie Smith's famed novel *White Teeth*. The vibrancy and cultural diversity of London's East End come to life in Monica Ali's *Brick Lane*.

Many films—from *Waterloo Bridge* and *Georgy Girl* to *Secrets and Lies* and *Notting Hill*—have used London as their setting. The great musicals Walt Disney's *Mary Poppins*, George Cukor's *My Fair Lady*, and Sir Carol Reed's *Oliver!* evoke the Hollywood soundstage version of London.

Children of all ages enjoy Stephen Herek's *101 Dalmatians*, with Glenn Close as fashion-savvy Cruella de Vil. King's Cross Station in London was shot to cinematic fame by the movie version of J.K. Rowling's *Harry Potter and the Philosopher's Stone*. Look for cameos by the city in all other *Harry Potter* films.

The swinging '60s are loosely portrayed in M. Jay Roach's *Austin Powers: International Man of Mystery*, full of references to British slang and some great opening scenes in London. For a truer picture of the '60s in London, Michelangelo Antonioni weaves a mystery plot around the world of a London fashion photographer in *Blow-Up*. British

gangster films came into their own with Guy Ritchie's amusing tales of London thieves in *Lock, Stock, and Two Smoking Barrels*, filmed almost entirely in London, and the follow-up *Snatch*. More sobering portraits of London criminal life include Neil Jordan's *Mona Lisa*, Paul McGuigan's *Gangster No. 1*, and John Mackenzie's *The Long Good Friday*. Of course, the original tough guy is 007, and his best exploits in London are featured in the introductory chase scene in *The World Is Not Enough*.

Sir Arthur Conan Doyle knew the potential of London as a chilling setting, and John Landis's *An American Werewolf in London* and Hitchcock's *39 Steps* and *The Man Who Knew Too Much* exploit the Gothic and sinister qualities of the city. For a fascinating look at Renaissance London, watch John Madden's *Shakespeare in Love*. Dickens's London is indelibly depicted in David Lean's *Oliver Twist*.

Some modern-day romantic comedies that use London as a backdrop are Peter Howitt's *Sliding Doors* with Gwyneth Paltrow and the screen adaptations of Helen Fielding's *Bridget Jones's Diary* (and its sequel), starring Renée Zellweger, Hugh Grant, and Colin Firth. Glossy London is depicted in Woody Allen's *Match Point*, bohemian London in David Kane's *This Year's Love*, gritty London in Shane Meadow's *Somers Town*, and post-zombie London in Danny Boyle's *28 Days Later*, while Patrick Kellior's *London* offers a uniquely informed, idiosyncratic view of the city.

TRAVEL SMART LONDON

GETTING HERE AND AROUND

Central London and its surrounding districts are divided into 32 boroughs—33, counting the City of London. More useful for finding your way around, however, are the subdivisions of London into postal districts. Throughout the guide we've given the full postal code for most listings. The first one or two letters give the location: N means north, NW means northwest, and so on. Don't expect the numbering to be logical, however. You won't, for example, find W2 next to W3. The general rule is that the lower numbers, such as W1 or SW1, are closest to Buckingham Palace, but it is not consistent—SE17 is closer to the city center than E4, for example.

▌ AIR TRAVEL

Flying time to London is about 6½ hours from New York, 7½ hours from Chicago, 11 hours from San Francisco, and 21½ hours from Sydney.

For flights out of London, the general rule is that you arrive one hour before your scheduled departure time for domestic flights and two hours before international flights for off-peak travel.

Airline Security Issues Transportation Security Administration ☎ 866/289-9673 ⊕ www.tsa.gov.

AIRPORTS

International flights to London arrive at either Heathrow Airport (LHR), 15 miles west of London, or at Gatwick Airport (LGW), 27 miles south of the capital. Most flights from the United States go to Heathrow, which is the busiest and is divided into five terminals, with Terminals 3, 4, and 5 handling transatlantic flights. Gatwick is London's second gateway. It has grown from a European airport into an airport that also serves dozens of U.S. destinations. A smaller third airport, Stansted (STN), is 35 miles northeast of the city. It handles mainly European and domestic traffic, although there's also

scheduled service from New York. Two smaller airports, Luton (LTN), 30 miles north of town, and business-oriented London City (in East London E16) mainly handle flights to Europe.

Airport Information Gatwick Airport ☎ 0844/892-0322 ⊕ www.gatwickairport.com. **Heathrow Airport** ☎ 0844/335-1801 ⊕ www. heathrowairport.com. **London City Airport** ☎ 020/7646-0088 ⊕ www.londoncityairport. com. **Luton Airport** ☎ 01582/405-100 ⊕ www.london-luton.co.uk. **Stansted Airport** ☎ 0844/355-1803 ⊕ www.stanstedairport. com.

GROUND TRANSPORTATION

London has excellent if pricey bus and train connections between its airports and central London. If you're arriving at Heathrow, you can pick up a map and fare schedule at the Transport for London (TfL) Information Centre located in the Underground station serving Terminals 1, 2, and 3. Train service can be quick, but the downside (for trains from all airports) is that you must get yourself and your luggage to the train via a series of escalators and connecting trams. Airport link buses (generally National Express Airport buses) may ease the luggage factor and drop you closer to central hotels, but they're subject to London traffic, which can be horrendous and make the trip drag on for hours. Taxis can be more convenient than buses, but beware that prices can go through the roof. Airport Travel Line has additional transfer information and takes advance booking for transfers between airports and into London. The BAA (British Airport Authority) website is a useful resource, giving all transportation options from Gatwick, Heathrow, and Stansted.

FROM HEATHROW TO CENTRAL LONDON		
TRAVEL MODE	TIME	COST
Taxi	1 hour+	£55+
Heathrow Express Train	15 minutes	£19 (£34 round-trip) and £28 for first class
Underground	50 minutes	£5.50 one way (less with Oyster card)
National Express Bus	1 hour	£7 one way
Hotel by Bus	1 hour+	£22.50 one way

Heathrow by Bus: National Express buses take one hour to reach the city center (Victoria) and cost from £7 one way and £14 round-trip. A rival service, easyBus, offers buses from as little as £2 (book online for best prices). The National Express Hotel Hoppa service runs from all airports to around 20 hotels near the airport (from £4). Alternatively, nearly every hotel in London itself is served by the Hotel By Bus service. Fares to central London average around £22.50. SkyShuttle also offers a shared minibus service between Heathrow and any London hotel. The N9 night bus runs to Trafalgar Square every half hour from midnight to 5 am; it takes an hour and costs £2.30.

Heathrow by Train: The cheap, direct route into London is via the Piccadilly line of the Underground (London's extensive subway system, or "Tube"). Trains normally run every four to eight minutes from all terminals from early morning until just before midnight. The 50-minute trip into central London costs £5.50 one way and connects with other central Tube lines. The Heathrow Express train is comfortable and convenient, if costly, speeding into London's Paddington station in 15 minutes. Standard one-way tickets cost £19 (£34 round-trip) and £28 for first class. Book ahead (online is the cheapest option; at a

NAVIGATING LONDON

London is a confusing city to navigate, even for people who've visited it a few times. Its streets are arranged in medieval patterns that no longer make much sense, meaning that you can't always use logic to find your way around. A good map is essential, and public transportation can be a lifesaver: buses will take you magically from point A to point B, and the Tube is often the quickest way to reach your destination. Here are some basic tips to help you find your way around:

■ Although free tourist maps can be handy, they're usually quite basic and include only major streets. If you're going to be doing lots of wandering around, buy the pocket-size map book London A–Z sold in bookstores and Tube and train stations throughout the city. Its detailed maps are invaluable.

■ To find your way, look for tall landmarks near where you are headed: the London Eye, for example, or the cross atop St. Paul's Cathedral—or the most obvious of all, Big Ben.

■ If you get properly lost, the best people to ask are the Londoners hustling by you, who know the area like nobody else. The worst people to ask are the people working in souvenir kiosks, and street vendors handing out the local Evening Standard newspaper; they're famously rude and unhelpful to lost tourists.

■ The tourist hubs of Soho, Covent Garden, Leicester Square, and Trafalgar Square are separated from one another by only a few blocks. Taking the Tube from one to another actually takes longer than walking.

■ On the other hand, when you're lost, the Tube is often the shortest distance between two points. Don't hesitate to use it.

counter/kiosk less so), as tickets are more expensive to buy on board. There's daily service from 5:10 am (5:50 am on Sunday) to 11:25 pm (10:50 pm on Sunday), with departures every 15 minutes. The Heathrow Connect service leaves from Paddington station and makes five local stops before arriving at Terminals 1, 3, and 5. At 25 minutes, journey time is only slightly slower than the Express and one-way tickets are £9.10.

Gatwick by Bus: An hourly bus service runs from Gatwick's north and south terminals to London's Victoria station, with stops at Hooley, Coulsdon, Mitcham, Streatham, Stockwell, and Pimlico. The journey takes up to 90 minutes and costs from £8 one way. The easyBus service runs to west London (Fulham) from as little as £2; the later the ticket is booked online, the higher the price (up to £10 on board).

Gatwick by Train: The fast, nonstop Gatwick Express leaves for Victoria station every 15 minutes 4:35 am–1:35 am. The 30-minute trip costs £18.90 one way, £33.20 round-trip. Book in advance, as tickets cost more on board. The First Capital Connect rail company's nonexpress services are cheaper; Capital Connect train runs regularly throughout the day to St. Pancras International, London Bridge, and Blackfriars stations; departures are every 15 minutes (hourly during the night), and the journey takes 48 minutes. Tickets are from £9.90 one way. FlyBy service to Victoria (£8.50 single) is not express, takes almost an hour, and the fare applies only on trains operated by Southern Trains.

Stansted by Bus: Hourly service on National Express Airport bus A6 (24 hours a day) to Victoria Coach station costs from £10 one way, £17 round-trip, and takes about 1 hour and 40 minutes. Stops include Golders Green, Finchley Road, St. John's Wood, Baker Street, Marble Arch, and Hyde Park Corner. The easyBus service to Victoria via Baker Street costs from £2.

Stansted by Train: The Stansted Express to Liverpool Street station (with a stop at Tottenham Hale) runs every 15 minutes 6 am–12:30 am, Monday to Thursday; until 1:30 am, Friday to Sunday. The 45-minute trip costs £21.50 one way, £29.50 round-trip if booked online. Tickets cost more when purchased on board.

Luton by Bus and Train: A free airport shuttle runs from Luton Airport to the nearby Luton Airport Parkway station, from which you can take a train or bus into London. From there, the First Capital Connect train service runs to St. Pancras, Farringdon, Blackfriars, and London Bridge. The journey takes about 35 minutes. Trains leave every 10 minutes or so during the day, and hourly during the night. Single tickets cost £13.60. The Green Line 757 bus service from Luton to Victoria station runs three times an hour, takes about 90 minutes, and costs from £17 one way.

Heathrow, Gatwick, Stansted, and Luton by Taxi: This is an expensive and time-consuming option. The city's congestion charge (£10) may be added to the bill if your hotel is in the charging zone, you run the risk of getting stuck in traffic, and if you take a taxi from the stand, the price will be even more expensive (whereas a minicab booked ahead is a set price). The trip from Heathrow, for example, can take more than an hour and cost more than £55.

TRANSFERS BETWEEN AIRPORTS

Allow at least two to three hours for an interairport transfer. The cheapest option—but most complicated—is public transportation: from Gatwick to Stansted, for instance, you can catch the nonexpress commuter train from Gatwick to Victoria station, take the Tube to Liverpool Street station, then catch the train to Stansted from there. To get from Heathrow to Gatwick by public transport, take the Tube to King's Cross, then change to the Victoria line, get to Victoria station, and then take the commuter train to Gatwick.

The National Express Airport bus is the most direct option between Gatwick and Heathrow. Buses pick up passengers every 15 to 20 minutes from 5:20 am to midnight from both airports. The trip takes around 70 minutes, and the fare is £20 one way, but it's advisable to book tickets in advance. National Express buses between Stansted and Gatwick depart every 30 to 45 minutes and can take around 3 hours and 45 minutes. The adult one-way fare is from £25. Some airlines may offer shuttle services as well—check with your travel agent in advance of your journey.

Contacts BAA ☎ 020/8745–9800 ⊕ www.baa.com. **easyBus** ⊕ www.easybus.co.uk. **First Capital Connect** ☎ 0845/026–4700 ⊕ www.firstcapitalconnect.co.uk. **Gatwick Express** ☎ 0845/850–1530 ⊕ www.gatwickexpress.com. **Heathrow Express** ☎ 0845/600–1515 ⊕ www.heathrowexpress.com. **National Express** ☎ 08717/818–178 ⊕ www.nationalexpress.com. **SkyShuttle** ☎ 0845/481–0960 ⊕ www.skyshuttle.co.uk. **Stansted Express** ☎ 0845/600–7245 ⊕ www.stanstedexpress.com.

Transfer Information Airport Travel Line ☎ 0871/200–2223.

FLIGHTS

British Airways is the national flagship carrier and offers mostly nonstop flights from 16 U.S. cities to Heathrow and Gatwick airports, along with flights to Manchester, Birmingham, and Glasgow. It also offers flights to New York from London City Airport near Docklands.

Airline Contacts American Airlines ☎ 800/433–7300, 0844/499–7300 in London ⊕ www.aa.com. **British Airways** ☎ 800/247–9297, 0844/493–0787 in London ⊕ www.ba.com. **Delta Airlines** ☎ 800/241–4141 for international reservations, 0871/221–1222 in London ⊕ www.delta.com. **United Airlines** ☎ 800/864–8331 for international reservations, 0845/844–4777 in London ⊕ www.united.com. **US Airways** ☎ 800/622–1015 for international reservations, 0845/600–3300 in London ⊕ www.usairways.com. **Virgin Atlantic** ☎ 800/862–8621, 0844/209–7777 in London ⊕ www.virgin-atlantic.com.

▌ BIKE TRAVEL

London's mayor, Boris Johnson, is a real cycling enthusiast and keen to make the capital more bike-friendly. A 24-hour cycle-for-hire scheme, the Barclays Cycle Hire, introduced in 2010 to enable Londoners to pick up a bicycle at one of more than 570 docking stations and return it at another, has proved very popular. The first 30 minutes are free. After that, charges rise incrementally from £1 for one hour up to £50 for the entire 24 hours. There is also a £1 per-day access charge. Fees are payable online, by phone, or at docking stations, by credit or debit cards only—cash is not accepted. To sign up, a user goes to the TfL (Transport for London) website and then receives a bike key in the mail, so this scheme is really meant for locals, not tourists.

▌ BUS TRAVEL

ARRIVING AND DEPARTING

National Express is the biggest British long-distance bus operator and the nearest equivalent to Greyhound. It's not as fast as traveling by train, but it's comfortable (with washroom facilities on board). Services depart mainly from Victoria Coach station, a well-signposted short walk behind the Victoria mainline train station. The departures point is on the corner of Buckingham Palace Road; this is also the main information point. The arrivals point is opposite, at Elizabeth Bridge. National Express buses travel to all large and midsize cities in southern England and the midlands. Scotland and the north are not as well served. The station is extremely busy around holidays and weekends. Arrive at least 30 minutes before departure so you can find the correct exit gate. Smoking is not permitted on board.

Another bus company, Megabus, has been packing in the budget travelers in recent years, since it offers cross-country fares for as little as £1 per person. The company's single- and double-decker buses serve an extensive array of cities across Great Britain with a cheerful budget attitude. In London, buses for all destinations depart from the Green Line bus stand at Victoria station. Megabus does not accommodate wheelchairs, and the company strictly limits luggage to one piece per person checked, and one piece of hand luggage.

Green Line serves the counties surrounding London, as well as airports. Bus stops (there's no central bus station) are on Buckingham Palace Road, between the Victoria train station and Victoria Coach station.

Tickets on some long-distance routes are cheaper if purchased in advance, and traveling midweek costs less than over weekends and at holiday periods.

GETTING AROUND LONDON

Private, as opposed to municipal, buses are known as coaches. Although London is famous for its double-decker buses, the old beloved rattletrap Routemasters, with the jump-on/off back platforms, now only serve two "heritage" routes: the No. 9 travels through Piccadilly, Trafalgar Square, and Knightsbridge, and the No. 15 travels from Trafalgar Square down Fleet Street and on to St. Paul's Cathedral. That said, a modernized Routemaster has taken to the streets in recent times, replacing the failed experiment that was the so-called "bendy buses" (long, articulated vehicles that struggled to navigate London's narrow roads).

Bus stops are clearly indicated; signs at bus stops feature a red TfL symbol on a plain white background. You must flag the bus down at some stops. Each numbered route is listed on the main stop, and buses have a large number on the front with their end destination. Not all buses run the full route at all times; check with the driver to be sure. You can pick up a free bus guide at a TfL Travel Information Centre (at Euston, Liverpool Street, Piccadilly Circus, King's Cross, and Victoria Tube stations; and at Heathrow Airport).

Buses are a good way of seeing the town, particularly if you plan to hop on and off to cover many sights, but don't take a bus if you're in a hurry, as traffic can really slow them down. To get off, press the red "Stop" buttons mounted on poles near the doors. You will usually see a "Bus Stopping" sign light up. Expect to get sardined during rush hour, from 8 am to 9:30 am and 4:30 pm to 6:30 pm.

Night buses, denoted by an "N" before their route numbers, run from midnight to 5 am on a more restricted route than day buses. However, some night bus routes should be approached with caution and the top deck avoided. All night buses run by request stop, so flag them down if you're waiting or push the button if you want to alight.

All journeys cost £2.40, and there are no transfers. If you plan to make a number of journeys in one day, consider buying a Travelcard (⇨ *Underground Travel: The Tube*), good for both Tube and bus travel. Also consider getting a prepaid Oyster card, as single journeys are just over a pound using a prepaid card. Travelcards are also available in one-, three-, or seven-day combinations. Visitor Oyster cards cost £5 and can be topped up. They are available from ticket desks at Gatwick and Stansted airports or at any Tube station and are transferable if you have money left over. Traveling without a valid ticket makes you liable for a fine (£20). Buses are supposed to swing by most stops every five or six minutes, but in reality, you can often expect to wait a bit longer, although those in the city center are quite reliable.

In central London, if you don't have a prepaid Travel- or Oyster card, you must pay before you board the bus. Automated ticket machines are set up at these bus stops, which are clearly marked with a yellow sign "Buy Tickets Before Boarding." Otherwise, you can buy tickets at most central London Tube stations as well as at newsagents and shops that display the sign "Buy Your Travel Cards & Bus Passes Here." Outside the central zone, payment may be made to the driver as you board (exact change is best so as to avoid incurring the driver's wrath).

Bus Information easyBus ⊕ *www.easybus. co.uk.* **Green Line** ☎ *0844/801–7261* ⊕ *www. greenline.co.uk.* **Megabus** ☎ *0900/160–0900* ⊕ *www.megabus.com.* **National Express** ☎ *08717/818–178* ⊕ *www.nationalexpress. com.* **Transport for London** ☎ *0843/222– 1234* ⊕ *www.tfl.gov.uk.* **Victoria Coach Station** ☎ *08717/818–181.*

▍CAR TRAVEL

The best advice on driving in London is this: don't. London's streets are a winding mass of chaos, made worse by one-way roads. Parking is also restrictive and expensive, and traffic is tediously slow at most times of the day; during rush hours—from 8 am to 9:30 am and 4:30 pm to 6:30 pm—it often grinds to a standstill, particularly on Friday, when everyone wants to leave town. Avoid city-center shopping areas, including the roads feeding Oxford Street, Kensington, and Knightsbridge. Other main roads into the city center are also busy, such as King's Cross and Euston in the north. Watch out also for cyclists and motorcycle couriers, who weave between cars and pedestrians and seem to come out of nowhere, and you may be fined heavily for straying into a bus lane during its operating hours—check the signs.

If you are staying in London for the duration of your trip, there's virtually no reason to rent a car since the city and its suburbs are widely covered by public transportation. However, you might want a car for day trips to castles or stately homes out in the countryside. Consider renting your car in a medium-size town in the area where you'll be traveling, and

then journeying there by train and picking up the car once you arrive. Rental rates are generally reasonable, and insurance costs are lower than in comparable U.S. cities. Rates generally begin at £40 a day for a small economy car (such as a subcompact General Motors Vauxhall Corsa, or Renault Clio), usually with manual transmission. Air conditioning and unlimited mileage generally come with the larger-size automatic cars.

In London your U.S. driver's license is acceptable (as long as you are over 23 years old, with no driving convictions). If you have a driver's license from a country other than the United States, it may not be recognized in the United Kingdom. An International Driver's Permit is a good idea no matter what; it's available from the American (AAA) or Canadian (CAA) Automobile Association and, in the United Kingdom, from the Automobile Association (AA) or Royal Automobile Club (RAC). International permits are universally recognized, and having one may save you a problem with the local authorities.

Remember that Britain drives on the left, and the rest of Europe on the right. Therefore, you may want to leave your rented car in Britain and pick up a left-side drive if you cross the Channel.

CONGESTION CHARGE

Designed to reduce traffic through central London, a congestion charge has been instituted. Vehicles (with some exemptions) entering central London on weekdays from 7 am to 6 pm (excluding public holidays) have to pay a £10 daily fee; it can be paid up to 90 days in advance, on the day of travel, or on the following charging day, when the fee goes up to £12. Day-, month-, and yearlong passes are available on the Congestion Charging page of the Transport for London website, at gas stations, parking lots (car parks), by mail, by phone, and by SMS text message. One day's payment is good for all access into the charging zone on that day. Traffic signs designate the entrance to congestion areas, and cameras read car license plates and send the information to a database. Drivers who don't pay the congestion charge by midnight of the next charging day following the day of driving are penalized £120, which is reduced to £60 if paid within 14 days.

Information Congestion Charge Customer Service ☎ 0845/900–1234 ⊕ www.cclondon. com. **Transport for London** ☎ 0843/222– 1234 ⊕ www.tfl.gov.uk.

GASOLINE

Gasoline (petrol) is sold in liters and is expensive (at this writing about £1.40 per liter—around $8 per gallon). Unleaded petrol, denoted by green pump lines, is predominant. Premium and Super Premium are the two varieties, and most cars run on regular Premium. Supermarket pumps usually offer the best value. You won't find many service stations in the center of town; these are generally on main, multilane trunk roads out of the center. Service is self-serve, except in small villages, where gas stations are likely to be closed on Sunday and late evening. Most stations accept major credit cards.

PARKING

During the day—and probably at all times—it's safest to believe that you can park nowhere except at a meter, in a pay-and-display bay, or in a garage; otherwise, you run the risk of an expensive ticket, plus possibly even more expensive clamping and towing fees (some boroughs are clamp-free). Restrictions are indicated by the "No Waiting" parking signpost on the sidewalk (these restrictions vary from street to street), and restricted areas include single yellow lines or double yellow lines, and Residents' Parking bays. Parking at a bus stop is prohibited; parking in bus lanes, restricted. On Red Routes, indicated by red lines, you are not allowed to park or even stop. It's illegal to park on the sidewalk, across entrances, or on white zigzag lines approaching a pedestrian crossing.

Meters have an insatiable hunger in the inner city—a 20p coin may buy just three minutes—and some will permit only a maximum two-hour stay. Meters take 20p and £1 coins, pay-and-display machines 10p, 20p, 50p, £1, and £2 coins. Some take payment by credit card. In some parts of central London, meters have been almost entirely replaced by pay-and-display machines that require payment by cell phone. You will need to set up an account to do this (⊕ www.westminster. gov.uk). Meter parking is free after 6:30 or 8:30 in the evening, on Sunday, and on holidays. Always check the sign. In the evening, after restrictions end, meter bays are free. After meters are free, you can also park on single yellow lines—but not double yellow lines. In the daytime, take advantage of the many NCP parking lots in the center of town (about £4 per hour, up to eight hours).

INFORMATION
NCP ☎ 0845/050–7080 ⊕ www.ncp.co.uk.

ROADSIDE EMERGENCIES

If your car is stolen, you're in a car accident, or your car breaks down and there's nobody around to help you, contact the police by dialing ☎ 999.

The general procedure for a breakdown is the following: position the red hazard triangle (which should be in the trunk of the car) a few paces away from the rear of the car. Leave the hazard warning lights on. Along highways (motorways), emergency roadside telephone booths are positioned at intervals within walking distance. Contact the car-rental company or an auto club. The main auto clubs in the United Kingdom are the Automobile Association (AA) and the RAC. If you're a member of the American Automobile Association (AAA), check your membership details before you depart for Britain, as, under a reciprocal agreement, roadside assistance in the United Kingdom should cost you nothing. You can join and receive roadside assistance from the AA on the spot, but the charge is higher—around £85—than a simple membership fee.

Emergency Services American Automobile Association ☎ *800/564-6222* ⊕ *www.aaa. com.* **Automobile Association** ☎ *0800/085-2721, 161/333-0004 from outside the U.K., 0800/887-766 for emergency roadside assistance* ⊕ *www.theaa. com.* **RAC** ☎ *01922/437-000, 0800/828-282 for emergency roadside assistance* ⊕ *www. rac.co.uk.*

RULES OF THE ROAD

London is a mass of narrow, one-way roads, and narrow, two-way streets that are no bigger than the one-way roads. If you must risk life and limb and drive in London, note that the speed limit is either 20 or 30 mph—unless you see the large 40 mph signs found only in the suburbs. Speed bumps are sprinkled about with abandon in case you forget. Speed is strictly controlled and cameras, mounted on occasional lampposts, photograph speeders for ticketing.

Medium-size circular intersections are often designed as "roundabouts" (marked by signs in which three curved arrows form a circle). On these, cars travel left in a circle and incoming cars must yield to those already on their way around from the right. Signal when about to leave the roundabout.

Jaywalking is not illegal in London and everybody does it, despite the fact that striped crossings with blinking yellow lights mounted on poles at either end—called "zebra crossings"—give pedestrians the right-of-way to cross. Cars should treat zebra crossings like stop signs if a pedestrian is waiting to cross or already starting to cross. It's illegal to pass another vehicle at a zebra crossing. At other crossings (including intersections) pedestrians must yield to traffic, but they do have the right-of-way over traffic turning left at controlled crossings—if they have the nerve.

Traffic lights sometimes have arrows directing left or right turns; try to catch a glimpse of the road markings in time, and don't get into the turn lane if you mean to go straight ahead. Turning on a red light is not permitted. Signs at the beginning and end of designated bus lanes give the time restrictions for use (usually during peak hours); if you're caught driving on bus lanes during restricted hours, you will be fined. By law, seat belts must be worn in the front and back seats. Drunk-driving laws are strictly enforced, and it's safest to avoid alcohol altogether if you'll be driving. The legal limit is 80 milligrams of alcohol per 100 milliliters of blood, which roughly translated means two units of alcohol—two small glasses of wine, one pint of beer, or one glass of whiskey.

▌ DLR: DOCKLANDS LIGHT RAILWAY

For destinations in East London, the quiet, driverless Docklands Light Railway (DLR) is a good alternative, offering interesting views of the area.

The DLR connects with the Tube network at Bank and Tower Hill stations as well as at Canary Wharf. It goes to London City Airport, the Docklands financial district, and Greenwich, running 5:30 am–12:30 am Monday–Saturday, 7 am–11:30 pm Sunday. The DLR takes Oyster cards and Travelcards, and fares are the same as those on the Tube. A £14.50 River Rover ticket combines one-day DLR travel with hop-on, hop-off travel on City Cruises riverboats between Westminster, Waterloo, Tower, and Greenwich piers.

Information Transport for London ☎ *0843/222-1234* ⊕ *www.tfl.gov.uk.*

▌ RIVER BUS

One legacy of the 2012 Olympics has been a new push to develop river travel as part of London's overall public transportation system. The service now stops at 10 piers between the London Eye/Waterloo and Greenwich, with peak-time extensions to Putney in the west and Woolwich Arsenal in the east. The Waterloo-Woolwich commuter service runs every 20 minutes from 6 am to 1 am on weekdays, 8:30 am–midnight on weekends. Tickets are £6, with a one-third discount for Oyster card and Travelcard holders (full integration into the Oyster-card system is expected in 2013). When there are events at the O2 (North Greenwich Arena), a half-hourly express service runs to and from Waterloo starting three hours before the event. There is also the special Tate to Tate express, a 20-minute trip between Tate Modern and Tate Britain that costs £5.50. Boats run every 40 minutes from 10 to 5. A £13.60 per day River Roamer ticket offers unlimited river travel after 9 am.

Contacts Thames Clippers ☎ 020/7001–2200 ⊕ www.thamesclippers.com.

▌ TAXI

Universally known as "black cabs" (even though many of them now come in other colors), the traditional big black London taxicabs are as much a part of the city's streetscape as red double-decker buses, and for good reason: the unique, spacious taxis easily hold five people, plus luggage. To earn a taxi license, drivers must undergo intensive training on the history and geography of London. The course, and all that the drivers have learned in it, is known simply as "the Knowledge." There's almost nothing your taxi driver won't know about the city.

Hotels and main tourist areas have cabstands (just take the first in line), but you can also flag one down from the roadside. If the yellow "For Hire" sign on the top is lighted, the taxi is available. Cabdrivers often cruise at night with their signs unlighted so that they can choose their passengers and avoid those they think might cause trouble. If you see an unlighted, passengerless cab, hail it: you might be lucky.

Fares start at £2.40 and charge by the minute—a journey of a mile (which might take between 5 and 12 minutes) will cost anything from £4.90 to £8.60 (the fare goes up between 10 pm and 6 am—a system designed to persuade more taxi drivers to work at night). A surcharge of £2 is applied to a telephone booking. At Christmas and New Year, there is an additional surcharge of £4. You can, but do not have to, tip taxi drivers 10% of the tab. Usually passengers round up to the nearest pound.

Minicabs, which operate out of small, curbside offices throughout the city, are generally cheaper than black cabs, but are less reliable and trusted. These are usually unmarked passenger cars, and their drivers are often not native Londoners, and do not have to take or pass "the Knowledge" test. Still, Londoners use them in droves because they are plentiful and cheap. If you choose to use them, do not ever take an unlicensed cab: anyone who curb-crawls looking for customers is likely to be unlicensed. Unlicensed cabs have been associated with many crimes and can be dangerous. All cab companies with proper dispatch offices are likely to be licensed. Look for a small purple version of the Underground logo on the front or rear windscreen with "private hire" written across it.

There are plenty of trustworthy and licensed minicab firms. For London-wide service try Lady Mini Cabs, which employs only women drivers, or Addison Lee, which uses comfortable minivans but requires that you know the full postal code for both your pickup location and your destination. When using a minicab, always ask the price in advance when you phone for the car, then verify with the driver before the journey begins.

Black Cabs Dial-a-Cab ☎ 020/7253–5000 cash bookings, 020/7426–3420 credit/debit card bookings ⊕ www.dialacab.co.uk. **Radio Taxis** ☎ 020/7272–0272 ⊕ www.radiotaxis. co.uk.

Minicabs Addison Lee ☎ 0844/800–6677 ⊕ www.addisonlee.com. **Lady MiniCabs** ☎ 020/7272–3300 ⊕ www.ladyminicabs.co.uk.

▌ TRAIN TRAVEL

The National Rail Enquiries website is the clearinghouse for information on train times and fares as well as to book rail journeys around Britain—and the earlier the better. Tickets bought two to three weeks in advance can cost a quarter of the price of tickets bought on the day of travel. However, journeys within commuting distance of city centers are sold at unvarying set prices, and those can be purchased on the day you expect to make your journey without any financial penalty. You may also be able to purchase a PlusBus ticket, which adds unlimited bus travel at your destination. Note that, in busy city centers such as London, all travel costs more during morning rush hour. You can purchase tickets online, by phone, or at any train station in the United Kingdom. Check the website or call the National Rail Enquiries line to get details of the train company responsible for your journey and have them give you a breakdown of available ticket prices. Regardless of which train company is involved, many discount passes are available, such as the 16–25 Railcard (for which you must be under 26 and provide a passport-size photo), the Senior Railcard, and the Family & Friends Travelcard, which can be bought from most mainline stations. But if you intend to make several long-distance rail journeys, it can be a good idea to invest in a BritRail Pass (which you must buy in the United States).

You can get a BritRail Pass valid for London and the surrounding counties, for England, for Scotland, or for all of Britain. Discounts (usually 20%–25%) are offered if you're between 16 and 25, over 60, traveling as a family or a group, or accompanied by a British citizen. The pass includes discounts on the Heathrow Express and Eurostar. BritRail Passes come in two basic varieties. The Classic pass allows travel on consecutive days, and the FlexiPass allows a number of travel days within a set period of time. The cost (in U.S. dollars) of a BritRail Consecutive Pass adult ticket for eight days is $359 standard and $509 first class; for 15 days, $535 and $759; and for a month, $759 and $1,139. The cost of a BritRail FlexiPass adult ticket for four days' travel in two months is $315 standard and $445 first class; for eight days' travel in two months, $459 and $649; and for 15 days' travel in two months, $689 and $975. Prices drop by about 25% for off-peak travel passes between November and February.

Most long-distance trains have refreshment carriages, called buffet cars. Most trains these days also have "quiet cars" where use of cell phones and music devices is banned. Smoking is forbidden in all rail cars.

Generally speaking, rail travel in the United Kingdom is expensive and the ticketing system unnecessarily convoluted: for instance, a round-trip ticket to Bath from London can cost more than £150 per person at peak times but for an off-peak ticket purchased far enough in advance, that fee can drop to £20 or even less. It's best to avoid the frantic business commuter rush (before 9:30 am and after 4:30 pm). Credit cards are accepted for train fares paid both in person and by phone.

Delays are not uncommon, but they're rarely long. You almost always have to go to the station to find out if there's going to be one (because delays tend to happen at the last minute). Luckily, most stations have coffee shops, restaurants, and pubs where you can cool your heels while you wait for the train to get rolling. National Rail Enquiries provides an up-to-date state-of-the-railroads schedule.

Most of the time, first-class train travel in England isn't particularly first-class. Some train companies don't offer at-seat service, so you still have to get up and go to the buffet car for food or drinks. First class is generally booked by business travelers on expense accounts because crying babies and noisy families are quite rare in first class, and quite common in standard class.

Short of flying, taking the Eurostar train through the Channel Tunnel is the fastest way to reach the continent: 2 hours and 15 minutes from London's St. Pancras International station to Paris's Gare du Nord. The high-speed Eurostar trains use the same tunnels to connect St. Pancras International directly with Midi station in Brussels in around two hours. If purchased in advance, round-trip tickets from London to Belgium or France cost from as little as £69, especially if you travel in the very early or very late hours of the day. If you want to bring your car over to France (if it's a rental, ask the rental company if this is permitted), you can use the Eurotunnel Shuttle, which takes 35 minutes from Folkestone to Calais, plus at least 30 minutes to check in. The Belgian border is just a short drive northeast of Calais.

Information BritRail Travel ☎ 866/938–7245 in U.S. and Canada ⊕ www.britrail.com. **Eurostar** ☎ 08432/186–186, 1233/617–575 outside U.K. ⊕ www.eurostar.com. **National Rail Enquiries** ☎ 0845/748–4950, 020/7278–5240 outside U.K. ⊕ www.nationalrail.co.uk.

Channel Tunnel Car Transport Eurotunnel ☎ 0844/335–3535 in U.K., 3–21–00–20–61 from outside Europe—use country code 33 ⊕ www.eurotunnel.com.

∎ UNDERGROUND TRAVEL: THE TUBE

London's extensive Underground train (Tube) system has color-coded routes, clear signage, and many connections. Trains run out into the suburbs, and all stations are marked with the London Underground circular symbol. (Do not be confused by similar-looking signs reading "subway"—in Britain, the word subway means "pedestrian underpass.") Trains are all one class; smoking is *not* allowed on board or in the stations. There is also an Overground network serving the farther reaches of Inner London. These now accept Oyster cards.

Some lines have multiple branches (Central, District, Northern, Metropolitan, and Piccadilly), so be sure to note which branch is needed for your particular destination. Do this by noting the end destination on the lighted sign on the platform, which also tells you how long you'll have to wait until the train arrives. Compare that with the end destination of the branch you want. When the two match, that's your train.

London is divided into six concentric zones (ask at Underground ticket booths for a map and booklet, which give details of the ticket options), so be sure to buy a ticket for the correct zone or you may be liable for an on-the-spot fine of £20. Don't panic if you do forget to buy a ticket for the right zone: just tell a station attendant that you need to buy an "extension" to your ticket. Although you're meant to do that in advance, generally if you're an out-of-towner, they don't give you a hard time.

For one-way fares paid in cash, a flat £4.50 price per journey now applies across all six zones, whether you're traveling one stop or 12 stops. If you're planning several trips in one day, it's much cheaper to buy a tourist Oyster card or even a Travelcard, which is good for unrestricted travel on the Tube, buses, and some Overground railroads for the day. The off-peak Oyster-card fare for Zones 1–2, for example, is £2.10. Bear in mind that Travelcards cost more if purchased before the 9:30 am rush-hour threshold. A one-day Travelcard for Zones 1–2 costs £8.80 if purchased before 9:30 am, and £7.30 if bought after 9:30 am. The more zones included in your travel, the more the Travelcard will cost. For example, Kew is Zone 4, and Heathrow is Zone 6. If you're going to be in town for several days, buy a seven-day Travelcard (£30.40 for Zones 1–2, £55.60 for Zones 1–6). Children 11–15 can travel at discounted rates on the Tube and free on buses and trams with an Oyster photocard (order at least four weeks before date of travel), while children under 11 travel free on the Tube if accompanied by an adult or with an Oyster photocard and on buses at all times. Young people 16–18 and students over 18 get discounted Tube fares with an Oyster photocard.

Oyster cards are "smart cards" that can be charged with a cash value and then used for discounted travel throughout the city. Each time you take the Tube or bus, you swipe the blue card across the yellow readers at the entrance and the amount of your fare is deducted. The London mayor is so eager to promote the cards that he set up a system in which those using Oyster cards pay lower rates. Oyster-card Tube fares start at £1.60 and go up depending on the number of zones you're covering, time of day, and whether you're traveling into Zone 1. You can open an Oyster account online or pick up an Oyster card at any London Underground station, and then prepay any amount you wish for your expected travel while in the city. Using an Oyster card, bus fares are £1.40 instead of £2.40. If you make numerous journeys in a single day, your Oyster-card deductions will always be capped at the standard price of a one-day Travelcard.

Trains begin running just after 5 am Monday–Saturday; the last services leave central London between midnight and 12:30 am. On Sunday, trains start two hours later and finish about an hour earlier. The frequency of trains depends on the route and the time of day, but normally you should not have to wait more than 10 minutes in central areas.

There are TfL Travel Information Centres at the following Tube stations: Euston, Liverpool Street, Piccadilly Circus, King's Cross, and Victoria, open 7:15 am–9:15 pm; and at Heathrow Airport (in Terminals 1, 2, and 3), open 6:30 am–10 pm.

Important note: as with the Metro system in Paris—and unlike the subway system in New York City—you need to have your ticket (Oyster-card pass or regular ticket) handy in order to exit the turnstiles of the Tube system, not just to enter them.

Information Transport for London
☎ *0843/222–1234* ⊕ *www.tfl.gov.uk.*

ESSENTIALS

▌BUSINESS SERVICES AND FACILITIES

There are several FedEx Kinko's and Mail Boxes Etc. locations in London to handle your photocopying, next-day mail, and packaging needs. Check their websites for more locations.

Contacts The Color Company (*FedEx Kinko's*). ⊠ *1 Curzon St., Mayfair* ☎ *020/7717–4900* ⊕ *www.color.co.uk.* **Mail Boxes Etc.** ⊠ *19–21 Crawford St., Marylebone* ☎ *020/7224–2666* ⊕ *www.mailboxes-etc.co.uk.*

▌COMMUNICATIONS

INTERNET

If you're traveling with a laptop, carry a spare battery and adapter: new batteries and replacement adapters are expensive; if you do need to replace them, head to Tottenham Court Road (W1), which is lined with computer specialists. For Macintosh computers, Micro Anvika is a good chain for parts and batteries, and the Apple Stores on Regent Street off Oxford Street and in the Covent Garden Piazza do repairs. John Lewis department store and Selfridges, on Oxford Street (W1), also carry a limited range of computer supplies.

The United Kingdom is finally catching up to the United States in terms of the spread of high-speed and Wi-Fi. In London, free Wi-Fi is increasingly available in hotels, pubs, coffee shops—even certain branches of McDonald's—and broadband coverage is widespread; generally speaking, the pricier the hotel, the more likely you are to find Wi-Fi there.

Contacts Cybercafes. More than 4,000 Internet cafés worldwide are listed. ⊕ *www.cybercafes.com.* **My Hot Spots** ⊕ *www.myhotspots.co.uk.*

PHONES

The good news is that you can now make a direct-dial telephone call from virtually any point on Earth. The bad news? You can't always do so cheaply. Calling from a hotel is almost always the most expensive option; hotels usually add huge surcharges to all calls, particularly international ones. Calling cards usually keep costs to a minimum, but only if you purchase them locally. And then there are cell phones, which are sometimes more prevalent—particularly in the developing world—than landlines; as expensive as cell phone calls can be, they are still usually a much cheaper option than calling from your hotel.

The minimum charge from a public phone is 60p for a 110-second call. To make cheap calls it's a good idea to pick up an international phone card, available from newsstands, which can be used from residential, hotel, and public pay phones. With these, you can call the United States for as little as 5p per minute.

To dial from the United States or Canada, first dial 011, then Great Britain's country code, 44. Continue with the local area code, dropping the initial "0." The code for London is 020 (so from abroad you'd dial 20), followed by a 7 for numbers in central London, or an 8 for numbers in the Greater London area. Freephone (toll-free) numbers start with 0800, 0500 or 0808; low-cost national information numbers start with 0845 or 0844.

A word of warning: 0870 numbers are *not* toll-free numbers; in fact, numbers beginning with this, 0871, or the 0900 prefix are "premium rate" numbers, and it costs extra to call them. The amount varies and is usually relatively small when dialed from within the country but can be excessive when dialed from outside the United Kingdom.

CALLING WITHIN BRITAIN

There are three types of phones: those that accept (1) only coins, (2) only British Telecom (BT) phone cards, or (3) BT phone cards and credit cards, although with the advent of cells, it's increasingly difficult to find any type of public phone, especially in London.

The coin-operated phones are of the push-button variety; the workings of coin-operated telephones vary, but there are usually instructions on each unit. Most take 10p, 20p, 50p, and £1 coins. Insert the coins *before* dialing (the minimum charge is 10p). If you hear a repeated single tone after dialing, the line is busy; a continual tone means the number is unobtainable (or that you have dialed the wrong—or no—prefix). The indicator panel shows you how much money is left; add more whenever you like. If there is no answer, replace the receiver and your money will be returned.

There are several different directory-assistance providers. For information anywhere in Britain, try dialing 118–888 (49p per call, then 9p per minute) or 118–118 (49p per call, then 14p per minute); you'll need to know the town and the street (or at least the neighborhood) of the person or organization for which you're requesting information. For the operator, dial 100.

You don't have to dial London's central area code (020) if you are calling inside London itself—just the eight-digit telephone number. However, you do need to use it if you're dialing an 0207 (Inner London) number from an 0208 (Outer London) number, and vice versa.

For long-distance calls within Britain, dial the area code (which begins with 01), followed by the number. The area-code prefix is used only when you are dialing from outside the destination. In provincial areas, the dialing codes for nearby towns are often posted in the booth.

CALLING OUTSIDE BRITAIN

For assistance with international calls, dial 155.

To make an international call from London, dial 00, followed by the country code and the local number.

When calling from overseas to access a London telephone number, drop the first 0 from the prefix and dial only 20 (or any other British area code) and then the eight-digit phone number.

The United States country code is 1.

Access Codes AT&T Direct ☎ *0800/890–011 in U.K., 0500/890–011 in U.K.* **MCI** ☎ *0800/279–5088 in U.K., 800/888–8000 for U.S. and other areas.* **Sprint International Access** ☎ *0808/234–6616 in U.K.*

CALLING CARDS

Public card phones operate either with cash or with special cards that you can buy from post offices or newsstands. Ideal for longer calls, they are composed of units of 10p, and come in values of £5, £10, and more. To use a card phone, lift the receiver, insert your card, and dial the number. An indicator panel shows the number of units used. At the end of your call, the card will be returned. Where credit cards are taken, slide the card through, as indicated.

CELL PHONES

If you have a multiband phone (Britain uses different frequencies from those used in the United States) and your service provider uses the world-standard GSM network (as do T-Mobile, AT&T, and Verizon), you can probably use your phone abroad. Roaming fees can be steep, however: 99¢ a minute is considered reasonable. And overseas you normally pay the toll charges for incoming calls. It's almost always cheaper to send a text message than to make a call, since text messages have a very low set fee (often less than 5¢).

If you just want to make local calls, consider buying a new SIM card (note that your provider may have to unlock your phone for you to use a different SIM card) and a prepaid service plan in London. You'll then have a local number and can make local calls at local rates. If your trip is extensive, you could also simply buy a new cell phone in your destination, as the initial cost will be offset over time.

■ TIP➔ If you travel internationally frequently, save one of your old cell phones or buy a cheap one online; ask your cell phone company to unlock it for you, and take it with you as a travel phone, buying a new SIM card with pay-as-you-go service in each destination.

Any cell phone can be used in Britain if it's tri-band/GSM. Travelers should ask their cell phone company if their phone is tri-band and what network it uses, and make sure it is activated for international calling before leaving their home country.

You can rent a cell phone from most car-rental agencies in London. Some upscale hotels now provide loaner cell phones to their guests. Beware, however, of the per-minute rates charged, as these can be shockingly high.

Contacts Cellular Abroad. This company rents and sells GMS phones and sells SIM cards that work in many countries. ☎ 800/287–5072 in U.S., 310/862–7100 International, 800/3623–3333 in U.K. ⊕ www.cellularabroad.com. **Mobal.** Cell phone rentals and GSM phone purchases (starting at $49) that will operate in 150 countries are available here. Per-call rates vary throughout the world. ☎ 888/888–9162 in U.S., 01543/426–999 in U.K. ⊕ www.mobal.com. **Planet Fone.** Here, you can rent cell phones, but the per-minute rates are expensive. ☎ 888/988–4777 ⊕ www.planetfone.com. **Rent a Mobile Phone.** Phones with short contracts can be rented. ☎ 020/7353–7705 ⊕ www.rent-mobile-phone.com.

▌ CUSTOMS AND DUTIES

You're always allowed to bring goods of a certain value back home without having to pay any duty or import tax. But there's a limit on the amount of tobacco and liquor you can bring back duty-free, and some countries have separate limits for perfumes; for exact figures, check with your customs department. The values of so-called "duty-free" goods are included in these amounts. When you shop abroad, save all your receipts, as customs inspectors may ask to see them as well as the items you purchased. If the total value of your goods is more than the duty-free limit, you'll have to pay a tax (most often a flat percentage) on the value of everything beyond that limit.

There are two levels of duty-free allowance for entering Britain: one for goods bought outside the European Union (EU) and the other for goods bought within the EU.

Of goods bought outside the EU you may import the following duty-free: 200 cigarettes or 100 cigarillos or 50 cigars or 250 grams of tobacco; 4 liters of still wine and 16 liters of beer and, in addition, either 1 liter of alcohol over 22% by volume (most spirits), or 2 liters of alcohol under 22% by volume (fortified or sparkling wine or liqueurs).

Of goods bought within the EU, you should not exceed the following (unless you can prove they are for personal use): 800 cigarettes, 400 cigarillos, 200 cigars, or 1 kilo of tobacco, plus 10 liters of spirits, 20 liters of fortified wine such as port or sherry, 90 liters of wine, or 110 liters of beer.

Pets (dogs and cats) can be brought into the United Kingdom from the United States without six months' quarantine, provided that the animal meets all the PETS (Pet Travel Scheme) requirements, including microchipping and vaccination. Other pets have to undergo a lengthy quarantine, and penalties for breaking this law are severe and strictly enforced.

Fresh meats, vegetables, plants, and dairy products may be imported from within the EU. Controlled drugs, flick knives, obscene material, counterfeit or pirated goods, and self-defense sprays may not be brought into the United Kingdom; firearms (both real and imitation) and ammunition, as well as souvenirs made from endangered plants or animals, are barred except with relevant permits.

Information HM Revenue and Customs ⊠ *Crownhill Court, Tailyour Rd., Plymouth* ☎ *0845/010–9000* ⊕ *www.hmrc.gov.uk.* **U.S. Customs and Border Protection** ⊕ *www. cbp.gov.*

▌ ELECTRICITY

The electrical current in London is 220–240 volts (coming into line with the rest of Europe at 230 volts), 50 cycles alternating current (AC); wall outlets take three-pin plugs, and shaver sockets take two round, oversize prongs. For converters, adapters, and advice, stop in one of the many STA Travel shops around London or at Nomad Travel.

Consider making a small investment in a universal adapter, which has several types of plugs in one lightweight, compact unit. Most laptops and cell phone chargers are dual voltage (i.e., they operate equally well on 110 and 220 volts), and thus require only an adapter. These days the same is true of small appliances such as hair dryers. Always check labels and manufacturer instructions to be sure. Don't use 110-volt outlets marked "For Shavers Only" for high-wattage appliances such as hair dryers.

Contacts Nomad Travel ⊠ *43 Bernard St., Bloomsbury* ☎ *020/7833–4114* ⊕ *www. nomadtravel.co.uk* ⊠ *52 Grosvenor Gardens, Victoria* ☎ *020/7823–5823* ⊕ *www. nomadtravel.co.uk.* **STA Travel** ☎ *0333/321–0099* ⊕ *www.statravel.co.uk.* **Steve Kropla's Help for World Travelers.** Information is available here on electrical and telephone plugs around the world. ⊕ *www.kropla.com.* **Walkabout Travel Gear.** Offers some helpful advice on electricity; search for "Adapters." ⊕ *www.walkabouttravelgear.com.*

▌ EMERGENCIES

London is a relatively safe city, though crime does happen (even more so than in New York City), especially in areas of built-up public project housing or tourist meccas. If you need to report a theft or an attack, head to the nearest police station (listed in the Yellow Pages or the local directory) or dial 999 for police, fire, or ambulance (be prepared to give the telephone number you're calling from). National Health Service hospitals give free round-the-clock treatment in Accident and Emergency sections, where waits can be up to four hours, depending on the severity of your ailment or injury. As a non-EU foreign visitor, you will be expected to pay for any treatment you receive before you leave the country. Prescriptions are valid only if made out by doctors registered in the United Kingdom. All branches of Boots are dispensing pharmacies.

Doctors and Dentists Dental Emergency Care Service ☎ *020/8748–9365* ⊕ *www.24hour-emergencydentist.co.uk.* **Medical Express Clinic** ⊠ *117A Harley St., Marylebone* ☎ *020/7499–1991, 0800/980–0700* ⊕ *www.medicalexpressclinic.com.* **UCL Eastman Dental Hospital** ⊠ *256 Gray's Inn Rd., King's Cross* ☎ *020/3456–7899, 0845/155–5000* ⊕ *www.uclh.nhs.uk.*

Foreign Embassies U.S. Embassy ⊠ *24 Grosvenor Sq., Mayfair* ☎ *020/7499–9000* ✎ *londonpassport@state.gov* ⊕ *www. usembassy.org.uk.*

General Emergency Contacts Ambulance, fire, police ☎ *999 U.K. only, 112 pan-European.*

Hospitals and Clinics Charing Cross Hospital ⊠ *Fulham Palace Rd., Fulham* ☎ *020/3311–1234* ⊕ *www.imperial.nhs.uk/ charingcross.* **Royal Free Hospital** ⊠ *Pond St., Hampstead* ☎ *020/7794–0500* ⊕ *www. royalfree.nhs.uk.* **St. Thomas's Hospital** ⊠ *Westminster Bridge Rd., Lambeth* ☎ *020/7188–7188* ⊕ *www.guysandstthomas. nhs.uk.* **University College Hospital** ⊠ *235*

Euston Rd., Bloomsbury ☎ *0845/155–5000,*
020/3456–7890 ⊕ *www.uclh.nhs.uk.*

Hotlines Samaritans. Counseling service.
☎ *0845/790–9090* ⊕ *www.cls.org.uk.*

Pharmacies Boots ⊠ *44–46 Regent St., Pic-cadilly Circus* ☎ *020/7734–6126* ⊕ *www.boots.
com.*

▌ HOLIDAYS

Standard holidays are New Year's Day,
Good Friday, Easter Monday, May Day
(first Monday in May), spring and sum-mer bank holidays (last Monday in May
and August, respectively), Christmas, and
Boxing Day (December 26). On Christmas
Eve and New Year's Eve, some shops, res-taurants, and businesses close early. Some
museums and tourist attractions may
close for at least a week around Christ-mas, or operate on restricted hours—call
to verify.

▌ MAIL

Stamps can be bought from post offices
(generally open weekdays 9–5:30, Sat-urday 9–noon), from stamp machines
outside post offices, and from some
newsagents and newsstands. Mailboxes
are known as post or letter boxes and
are painted bright red; large tubular ones
are set on the edge of sidewalks, whereas
smaller boxes are set into post-office walls.
Allow seven days for a letter to reach the
United States. Check the Yellow Pages for
a complete list of branches, though you
cannot reach individual offices by phone.

Airmail letters up to 10 grams (0.35
ounce) to North America, Australia, and
New Zealand cost 87p. Letters under 9.4
inches by 6.4 inches within Britain are
from 60p for first class, 50p for second
class. Large letters (over 9.4 inches by 6.4
inches, under 13.8 inches by 9.8 inches)
cost from 90p first class, 69p second class
within the United Kingdom, depending
on weight. Airmail is assessed by weight
alone.

If you're uncertain where you'll be stay-ing, you can have mail sent to you at the
London Main Post Office, c/o poste res-tante. The post office will hold interna-tional mail for one month.

Contact Post Office ☎ *08457/223–344*
⊕ *www.postoffice.co.uk.*

Main Branches London Main Post Office
⊠ *24–28 William IV St., Charing Cross* ⊕ *www.
postoffice.co.uk* ⊠ *43–44 Albemarle St., May-fair* ⊠ *111 Baker St., Marylebone* ⊠ *54–56
Great Portland St., Fitzrovia* ⊠ *181 High Hol-born, Holborn.*

SHIPPING PACKAGES

Most department stores and retail outlets
can ship your goods home. You should
check your insurance for coverage of
possible damage. Private delivery com-panies such as DHL, FedEx, and Parcel-force offer two-day delivery service to the
United States, but you'll pay a consider-able amount for the privilege.

Express Services DHL ☎ *0844/248–0844*
⊕ *www.dhl.com.* **FedEx** ☎ *0845/607–0809*
⊕ *www.fedex.com.* **Parcelforce** ☎ *0844/800–
4466* ⊕ *www.parcelforce.com.*

▌ MONEY

No doubt about it, London is one of the
most expensive cities in the world: getting
around is expensive, eating can be expen-sive, travel is pricey, and hotels aren't
cheap. However, for every yin there's
a yang, and travelers do get a break in
other places: most museums are free, for
example, and Oyster cards help cut the
price of travel.

ATMS AND BANKS

Your own bank will probably charge a
fee for using ATMs abroad; the foreign
bank you use may also charge a fee. Nev-ertheless, you'll usually get a better rate
of exchange at an ATM than you will
at a currency-exchange office or even
when changing money in a bank. And
extracting funds as you need them is a

safer option than carrying around a large amount of cash.

TIP→ PIN numbers with more than four digits are not recognized at ATMs in many countries. If yours has five or more, remember to change it before you leave.

Credit cards or debit cards (also known as check cards) will get you cash advances at ATMs, which are widely available in London. To make sure that your Cirrus or Plus card (to cite just two of the leading names) works in European ATMs, have your bank reset it to use a four-digit PIN number before your departure.

CREDIT CARDS

TIP→ Remember to inform your credit-card company before you travel, especially if you're going abroad and don't travel internationally very often. Otherwise, the credit-card company might put a hold on your card owing to unusual activity—not a good thing halfway through your trip. Record all your credit-card numbers—as well as the phone numbers to call if your cards are lost or stolen—in a safe place, so you're prepared should something go wrong. Both MasterCard and Visa have general numbers you can call (collect if you're abroad) if your card is lost, but you're better off calling the number of your issuing bank, since MasterCard and Visa usually just transfer you to your bank; your bank's number is usually printed on your card.

If you plan to use your credit card for cash advances, you'll need to apply for a PIN at least two weeks before your trip. Although it's usually cheaper (and safer) to use a credit card abroad for large purchases (so you can cancel payments or be reimbursed if there's a problem), note that some credit-card companies *and* the banks that issue them add substantial percentages to all foreign transactions, whether they're in a foreign currency or not. Check on these fees before leaving home, so there won't be any surprises when you get the bill.

TIP→ Before you charge something, ask the merchant whether he or she plans to do a dynamic currency conversion (DCC). In such a transaction the credit-card processor (shop, restaurant, or hotel, not Visa or MasterCard) converts the currency and charges you in dollars. In most cases you'll pay the merchant a 3% fee for this service in addition to any credit-card company and issuing-bank foreign-transaction surcharges.

Dynamic currency conversion programs are becoming increasingly widespread. Merchants who participate in them are supposed to ask whether you want to be charged in dollars or the local currency, but they don't always do so. And even if they do offer you a choice, they may well avoid mentioning the additional surcharges. The good news is that you *do* have a choice. And if this practice really gets your goat, you can avoid it entirely thanks to American Express; with its cards, DCC simply isn't an option.

Credit cards are accepted virtually everywhere in London.

Reporting Lost Cards American Express ☎ *800/528–4800 in U.S., 01273/696–933 in U.K.* ⊕ *www.americanexpress.com.* **Diners Club** ☎ *800/234–6377 in U.S., 514/877–1577 collect from abroad* ⊕ *www.dinersclub. com.* **MasterCard** ☎ *800/627–8372 in U.S., 0800/964–767 in U.K.* ⊕ *www.mastercard.com.* **Visa** ☎ *800/847–2911 in U.S., 0800/891–725 in U.K.* ⊕ *www.visa.com.*

CURRENCY AND EXCHANGE

The units of currency in Great Britain are the pound sterling (£) and pence (p): £50, £20, £10, and £5 bills (called notes); £2, £1 (100p), 50p, 20p, 10p, 5p, 2p, and 1p coins. At this writing, the exchange rate was about Australian $1.55, Canadian $1.61, New Zealand $1.94, U.S. $1.63, and €1.23 to the pound (also known as quid).

Even if a currency-exchange booth has a sign promising no commission, rest assured that there's some kind of huge, hidden fee. (Oh . . . that's right. The sign didn't say no *fee*.) And as for rates, you're almost always better off getting foreign currency at an ATM or exchanging money at a bank or post office.

■ TIP➜ Banks never have every foreign currency on hand, and it may take as long as a week to order. If you're planning to exchange funds before leaving home, don't wait until the last minute.

▌PACKING

London's weather is unpredictable. It can be cool, damp, and overcast, even in summer, but the odd summer day can be uncomfortably hot, as not many public venues, theaters, or the Tube are air conditioned. In general, you'll need a heavy coat for winter and light clothes for summer, along with a lightweight coat or jacket. Always pack a small umbrella that you can easily carry around with you. Pack as you would for any American city: jackets and ties for expensive restaurants and nightspots, casual clothes elsewhere. Jeans are popular in London and are perfectly acceptable for sightseeing and informal dining. Sports jackets are popular with men. In five-star hotels men can expect to be asked to wear a jacket and tie in the restaurant and bar, and women might feel out of place unless they're in smart clothes. Otherwise, for women, ordinary dress is acceptable just about everywhere.

▌PASSPORTS AND VISAS

U.S. citizens need only a valid passport to enter Great Britain for stays of up to six months. If you're within six months of your passport's expiration date, renew it before you leave—nearly extinct passports are not strictly banned, but they make immigration officials anxious, and may cause you problems.

PASSPORTS

We're always surprised at how few Americans have passports—only 35% at this writing. This number is expected to grow now that it is impossible to reenter the United States from trips to neighboring Canada or Mexico without one. Remember this: a passport verifies both your identity and nationality—a great reason to have one.

U.S. passports are valid for 10 years. You must apply in person if you're getting a passport for the first time; if your previous passport was lost, stolen, or damaged; or if your previous passport has expired and was issued more than 15 years ago or when you were under 16. All children under 18 must appear in person to apply for or renew a passport. Both parents must accompany any child under 14 (or send a notarized statement with their permission) and provide proof of their relationship to the child.

There are 24 regional passport offices, as well as 7,000 passport acceptance facilities in post offices, public libraries, and other governmental offices. If you're renewing a passport, you can do so by mail. Forms are available at passport acceptance facilities and online.

The cost to apply for a new passport is $140 for adults, $95 for children under 16; renewals are $140. There is an additional "execution fee" of $25. Allow six weeks for processing, both for first-time passports and renewals. For an expediting fee of $60 you can reduce this time to about two weeks. If your trip is less than two weeks away, you can get a passport even more rapidly by going to a passport office with the necessary documentation. Private expediters can get things done in as little as 48 hours, but charge hefty fees for their services.

■ TIP➜ Before your trip, make two copies of your passport's data page (one for someone at home and another for you to carry separately). Or scan the page and email it to someone at home and/or yourself.

VISAS

A visa is essentially formal permission to enter a country. Visas allow countries to keep track of you and other visitors—and generate revenue (from application fees). You *always* need a visa to enter a foreign country; however, many countries routinely issue tourist visas on arrival, particularly to U.S. citizens. When your passport is stamped or scanned in the immigration line, you're actually being issued a visa. Sometimes you have to stand in a separate line and pay a small fee to get your stamp before going through immigration, but you can still do this at the airport on arrival. Getting a visa isn't always that easy. Some countries require that you arrange for one in advance of your trip. There's usually—but not always—a fee involved, and said fee may be nominal ($10 or less) or substantial ($100 or more).

If you must apply for a visa in advance, you can usually do it in person or by mail. When you apply by mail, you send your passport to a designated consulate, where your passport will be examined and the visa issued. Expediters—usually the same ones who handle expedited passport applications—can do all the work of obtaining your visa for you; however, there's always an additional cost (often more than $50 per visa).

Most visas limit you to a single trip—basically during the actual dates of your planned vacation. Other visas allow you to visit as many times as you wish for a specific period of time. Remember that requirements change, sometimes at the drop of a hat, and the burden is on you to make sure that you have the appropriate visas. Otherwise, you'll be turned away at the airport or, worse, deported after you arrive in the country. No company or travel insurer gives refunds if your travel plans are disrupted because you didn't have the correct visa.

U.S. Passport Information U.S. Department of State ☎ *877/487-2778* ⊕ *travel.state.gov/passport.*

U.S. Passport and Visa Expediters A. Briggs Passport & Visa Expediters ☎ *800/806-0581, 202/388-0111* ⊕ *www.abriggs.com.* **American Passport Express** ☎ *800/455-5166* ⊕ *www.americanpassport.com.* **Passport Express** ☎ *800/362-8196* ⊕ *www.passportexpress.com.* **Travel Document Systems** ☎ *800/874-5100, 202/638-3800* ⊕ *www.traveldocs.com.* **Travel the World Visas** ☎ *866/886-8472* ⊕ *www.world-visa.com.*

▌ SAFETY

The rules for safety in London are the same as in New York or any big city. If you're carrying a considerable amount of cash and do not have a safe in your hotel room, it's a good idea to keep it in something like a money belt, but don't get cash out of it in public. Keep a small amount of cash for immediate purchases in your pocket or handbag.

Beyond that, use common sense. In central London, nobody will raise an eyebrow at tourists studying maps on street corners, and don't hesitate to ask for directions. However, outside of the center, exercise general caution about the neighborhoods you walk in: if they don't look safe, take a cab. After midnight, outside of the center, take cabs rather than waiting for a night bus. Although London has plenty of so-called "minicabs"—normal cars driven by self-employed drivers in a cab service—don't ever get into an unmarked car that pulls up offering you "cab service." Take a licensed minicab only from a cab office, or, preferably, a normal London "black cab," which you flag down on the street. Unlicensed minicab drivers have been associated with a slate of violent crimes in recent years.

If you carry a purse, keep a firm grip on it (or even disguise it in a local shopping bag). Store only enough money in the purse to cover casual spending. Distribute the rest of your cash and any valuables among deep front pockets, inside jacket or vest pockets, and a concealed money pouch. Some pubs and bars have "Chelsea clips" under the tables where you can hang your handbag at your knee. Never leave your bag beside your chair or hanging from the back of your chair. Be careful with backpacks, as pickpockets can unzip them on the Tube, or even as you're traveling up an escalator.

Advisories U.S. Department of State ⊕ *travel.state.gov.*

▌ TAXES

Departure taxes are divided into four bands, depending on destination. The Band A tax on a per-person Economy fare is £13, Band B is £67, Band C is £83, and Band D is £94. The fee is subject to government tax increases.

The British sales tax (V.A.T., value-added tax) is 20%. The tax is almost always included in quoted prices in shops, hotels, and restaurants.

Most travelers can get a V.A.T. refund by either the Retail Export or the more cumbersome Direct Export method. Many, but not all, large stores provide these services, but only if you request them; they will handle the paperwork. For the Retail Export method, you must ask the store for Form VAT 407 when making a purchase (you must have identification—passports are best). Some retailers will refund the amount on the spot, but others will use a refund company or the refund booth at the point when you leave the country. For the latter, have the form stamped like any customs form by U.K. customs officials when you leave the country, or, if you're visiting several European Union countries, when you leave the EU. After you're through passport control, take the form to a refund-service counter for an on-the-spot refund (which is usually the quickest and easiest option), or mail it to the address on the form (or the envelope with it) after you arrive home. You receive the total refund stated on the form (the retailer or refund company may deduct a handling fee), but the processing time can

be long, especially if you request a credit-card adjustment. This may be preferable to a check, however, as U.S. banks will charge a fee for depositing a check in a foreign currency.

With the Direct Export method, the goods are shipped directly to your home. You must have a Form VAT 407 certified by customs, the police, or a notary public when you get home and then send it back to the store, which will refund your money. For inquiries, contact Her Majesty's Customs & Excise office.

Global Refund is a worldwide service with 240,000 affiliated stores and more than 200 Refund Offices. Its refund form, called a Tax Free Check, is the most common across the European continent. The service issues refunds in the form of cash, check, or credit-card adjustment. Again, the cost of cashing a foreign currency check may exceed the amount of the refund.

V.A.T. Refunds Global Refund ☎ 866/706–6090 in U.S., 800/3211–1111 in U.K. ⊕ *www.globalrefund.com.* Her Majesty's Revenue & Customs ☎ 0845/010–9000 within U.K., 292/050–1261 from outside U.K. ⊕ *www.hmrc.gov.uk/vat.*

▌ TIME

London is five hours ahead of New York City. In other words, when it's 3 pm in New York (or noon in Los Angeles), it's 8 pm in London. Note that Great Britain and most European countries also move their clocks ahead for the one-hour differential when daylight saving time goes into effect (although they make the changeover several weeks after the United States).

Time Zones Timeanddate.com. This site can help you figure out the correct time anywhere in the world. ⊕ *www.timeanddate.com/worldclock.*

▌ TIPPING

Tipping is done in Britain just as in the United States, but at a lower level. So, although it might make you uncomfortable, tipping less than you would back home in restaurants—and not tipping at all in pubs—is not only accepted, but standard. Tipping more can look like you're showing off. Do not tip movie or theater ushers, elevator operators, or bar staff in pubs—although you can always offer to buy the latter a drink.

TIPPING GUIDELINES FOR LONDON	
Bartender	In cocktail bars, on the other hand, if you see a tip plate, it's fine to leave £1 or £2. For table service, tip 10% of the cost of the bill. However, the gratuity is often included in the check at more expensive bars.
Bellhop	£1 per bag, depending on the level of the hotel.
Hotel Concierge	£5 or more, if a service is performed for you.
Hotel Doorman	£1 for hailing taxis or for carrying bags to check-in desk.
Hotel Maid	It's extremely rare for hotel maids to be tipped; £1 or £2 would be generous.
Porter at Airport or Train Station	£1 per bag
Skycap at Airport	£1–£3 per bag
Taxi Driver	Optional 10%–12%, perhaps a little more for a short ride.
Tour Guide	Tipping optional; £1 or £2 would be generous.
Waiter	10%–15%, with 15% being the norm at high-end restaurants; nothing additional if a service charge is added to the bill.
Other	Restroom attendants in expensive restaurants expect some small change (50p or so). Tip coat-check personnel £1 unless there is a fee (then nothing). Hairdresser and barbers get 10%–15%.

▌ TOURS

BIKE TOURS

Whether you join the Barclays Cycle Hire scheme or just, per usual, get one from a rental shop, remember that London is still a busy metropolis: unless you're familiar with riding in London traffic, the best way to see it on two wheels is probably to contact one of the excellent cycle-tour companies.

Tour Operators Barclays Cycle Hire ☎ *0845/026–3630 within U.K., 208/216–6666 from outside U.K.* ⊕ *www.tfl.gov.uk/roadusers.* **Cycle Tours of London** ☎ *0778/899–4430* ⊕ *www.biketoursoflondon.com.* **Fat Tire Bike Tours** ☎ *0788/233–8779* ⊕ *www. fattirebiketours.com.* **London Bicycle Tour Company** ☎ *020/3318–3088* ⊕ *www. londonbicycle.com.*

BOAT TOURS

Year-round, but more frequently from April to October, boats cruise the Thames, offering a different view of the London skyline. Most leave from Westminster Pier, Charing Cross Pier, and Tower Pier. Downstream routes go to the Tower of London, Greenwich, and the Thames Barrier via Canary Wharf. Upstream destinations include Kew, Richmond, and Hampton Court (mainly in summer). Most of the launches seat between 100 and 250 passengers, have a public-address system, and provide a running commentary on passing points of interest. Some include musical entertainment. Depending upon the destination, river trips may last from one to four hours.

Details on all other operators are available as a PDF from Transport for London's River Services page. ⊕ *www.tfl.gov.uk*

River Cruise Operators Bateaux London ☎ *020/7695 1800* ⊕ *www.bateauxlondon. com.* **London Duck Tours** ☎ *020/7928–3132* ⊕ *www.londonducktours.co.uk.* **Thames Cruises** ☎ *020/7928–9009* ⊕ *www. thamescruises.com.* **Thames River Boats** ☎ *020/7930–2062* ⊕ *www.wpsa.co.uk.* **Thames River Services** ☎ *020/7930–4097* ⊕ *www.thamesriverservices.co.uk.*

BUS, COACH, AND TAXI TOURS

Guided sightseeing tours from the top of double-decker buses, which are open-top in summer, are a good introduction to the city, as they cover all the main central sights. A number of companies run daily bus tours that depart (usually between 8:30 and 9 am) from central points. In hop-on, hop-off fashion, you may board or alight at any of the numerous stops to view the sights, and reboard on the next bus. Most companies offer this hop-on, hop-off feature but others, such as Best Value, remain guided tours in traditional coach buses. Tickets can be bought from the driver and are good all day. Prices vary according to the type of tour, although £25 is the benchmark. For that more personal touch, try out a tour in a guided taxi. Other guided bus tours, like those offered by Golden, are not open-top or hop-on, hop-off, but enclosed (and more expensive) coach bus versions.

Bus Tour Operators Best Value Tours ☎ *0870/803–1316* ⊕ *www.bestvaluetours. co.uk.* **Big Bus Tours** ☎ *020/7233–9533* ⊕ *www.bigbustours.com.* **Black Taxi Tour of London** ☎ *020/7935–9363* ⊕ *www. blacktaxitours.co.uk.* **Golden Tours** ☎ *0844/880–5050 in U.K., 800/509–2507 in U.S.* ⊕ *www.goldentours.co.uk.* **Original London Sightseeing Tour** ☎ *020/8877–1722* ⊕ *www.theoriginaltour.com.* **Premium Tours** ☎ *020/7713–1311, 888/990-1209 from the US* ⊕ *www.premiumtours.co.uk.*

CANAL TOURS

The tranquil side of London can be found on narrow boats that cruise the city's two canals, the Grand Union and Regent's Canal; most vessels operate on the latter, which runs between Little Venice in the west (nearest Tube: Warwick Avenue on the Bakerloo line) and Camden Lock (about 200 yards north of Camden Town Tube station). Fares start at about £9 for 1½-hour round-trip cruises.

Canal Tour Operators Canal Cruises ☎ *020/8440–8962* ⊕ *www.londoncanalcruises. com.* **Jason's Trip** ☎ *020/7286–3428* ⊕ *www. jasons.co.uk.* **London Waterbus Company** ☎ *020/7482–2550* ⊕ *www.londonwaterbus. co.uk.*

EXCURSIONS

Evan Evans, Green Line, and National Express all offer day excursions by bus to places within easy reach of London, such as Hampton Court, Oxford, Stratford-upon-Avon, and Bath.

Tour Operators Evan Evans ☎ *020/7950–1777, 800/422–9022 in U.S.* ⊕ *www. evanevanstours.co.uk.* **Green Line** ☎ *0844/801–7261* ⊕ *www.greenline.co.uk.* **National Express** ☎ *0871/781–8178* ⊕ *www. nationalexpress.com.*

WALKING TOURS

One of the best ways to get to know London is on foot, and there are many guided and themed walking tours from which to choose. Richard Jones's London Walking Tours includes the Jack the Ripper Walk, following in the footsteps of the titular killer, as does the Blood and Tears Walk. Other tours include Secret London, the West End with Dickens, and Hampstead—A Country Village. Context London's expert docents lead small groups on walks with art, architecture, and similar themes. The London Walks Company hosts more than 100 walks every week on a variety of themes, including a Thames pub walk, Literary Bloomsbury, and Spies and Spycatchers. For more options, pick up a copy of *Time Out* magazine and check the weekly listings for upcoming one-off tours.

Walking Tour Operators Blood and Tears Walk ☎ *07905/746–733* ⊕ *www. shockinglondon.com.* **Blue Badge** ☎ *020/7403–1115* ⊕ *www.blue-badge-guides. com.* **Context London** ☎ *020/3514–1780, 800/691–6036 in U.S.* ⊕ *www.contexttravel. com/london.* **London Walks** ☎ *020/7624–3978* ⊕ *www.walks.com.* **Richard Jones's London Walking Tours** ☎ *020/8530–8443* ⊕ *www.walksoflondon.co.uk.* **Shakespeare City Walk** ☎ *07905/746–733* ⊕ *www. shakespeareguide.com.*

▌ VISITOR INFORMATION

When you arrive in London, you can get good information at the Travel Information Centre near the Eurostar arrivals area at St. Pancras International train station and at Victoria and Liverpool Street stations. These are helpful if you're looking for brochures for London sights, or if something's gone horribly wrong with your hotel reservation—if, for example, you don't have one—as they have a useful reservations service. The Victoria station center, opposite Platform 8, is open Monday–Saturday 7:15 am–9:15 pm, Sunday 8:15 am–7 pm; the St. Pancras center Monday–Saturday 7:15 am–9:15 pm, Sunday 8:15 am–8:15 pm; while Liverpool Street and Euston station centers open Saturday–Thursday 8:15 am–7:15 pm, Friday 8:15 am–8:15 pm. The one at Piccadilly Circus Tube station is open daily 9:15 am–7 pm. The Travel Information Centre at Heathrow is open Monday–Saturday 7:15 am–8 pm and Sunday 8:15 am–8 pm. There are also London Tourist Information Centres in Greenwich and some other Outer London locations.

Official websites ⊕ *www.visitbritain.com*, ⊕ *www.visitlondon.com*.

Other websites ⊕ *www.londontown.com*, the *Evening Standard*'s online ⊕ *www.thisislondon. com*, No. 10 Downing Street ⊕ *www. number-10.gov.uk*, and the BBC ⊕ *www.bbc. co.uk*.

Entertainment Information ⊕ *www.timeout. com/london*, ⊕ *www.officiallondontheatre. co.uk*, and ⊕ *www.kidslovelondon.com*.

INDEX

PHOTO CREDITS